Contemporary Scottish Studies

The Scottish
Educational Journal

Organ of the Educational Institute of Scotland
WITH WHICH ARE INCORPORATED
" The Educational News," " The Secondary School Journal," and " The Scottish Class Teacher."

Vol. IX.
No. 8. [*Registered as a*]
[*Newspaper*]

February 19, 1926.

Price 2d.

THE WEEK.

Last Week's Committee Meetings.

The following Committees of the Institute met last week :—Glasgow, 10th February—Law and Tenure Committee ; Edinburgh, 12th February—Board of Examiners, Special Committee on the Relations of Primary and Secondary Teachers ; Edinburgh, 13th February—Finance and Publications Committee, Modern Languages Central Committee.

Educational Institute of Scotland:
Special General Meeting of Delegates.

A Requisition having been received, signed by 218 Graduates of the Institute, requesting me to convene a SPECIAL GENERAL MEETING to be held in Edinburgh on Saturday, 27th February, 1926, at 10.15 a.m., to consider :—

(1) The Report of the Salaries Committee, and
(2) The Report from the Special Meeting of Council on the Scheme of the Conciliation Committee dealing with the Relations of Primary and Secondary Teachers,

I hereby summon a SPECIAL GENERAL MEETING OF DELEGATES to be held, for the above objects in the United Free Church Assembly Hall, The Mound, Edinburgh, on Saturday, 27th February, 1926, at 10.15 a.m.

GEORGE C. PRINGLE, *General Secretary.*

47 Moray Place, Edinburgh,
2nd February, 1926.

Special General Meeting of Delegates.

In connection with the Special General Meeting of Delegates in the United Free Church Assembly Hall, Edinburgh, on Saturday, 27th February, at 10.15 a.m., delegates are requested to note that owing to the International Rugby Football Match on that day, those who require accommodation in Edinburgh for Friday night, 26th inst., should make early application for same. The Railway Companies have agreed to issue, as usual, reduced fare tickets (single fare and one-third) to passengers attending the Special Meeting on presentation of the customary voucher at the time of booking. These vouchers may be obtained on application to the General Secretary at 47 Moray Place, Edinburgh, a stamped addressed envelope being enclosed for a reply. Delegates will receive their vouchers direct along with their other papers. Non-delegates who wish to hear the discussion will be accommodated in the galleries.

An Interesting Experiment.

Clackmannan Education Authority recently arranged a special exhibition of the League of Nations Union film " Star of Hope " for the senior pupils in their schools. In all 3240 pupils saw the film, which had been discussed beforehand in class. Attendance at the cinemas was sanctioned by H.M. Inspector as counting as a school attendance. Several other films were exhibited :—" Lorna Doone," a nature film, and a geographical film. The results were, it is stated, of considerable educational value.

A Scottish Renaissance.

The Glasgow Centre of the English Association announces what should be a piquant evening's discussion for Friday, 19th inst., in the Humanity Classroom of Glasgow University. This meeting has been arranged to enable the members of the Centre to hear the views of enthusiasts on the question of a national artistic and literary revival. The following subjects will be introduced by gentlemen who have shown themselves experts in practice as well as in theory, and it is hoped the ensuing discussion will be of value :—" Braid Scots as a Literary Medium," Mr C. M. Grieve ; " The Scottish Renaissance and Scottish Schools," Mr Alexander M'Gill ; " A Native Scottish Drama," Mr R. F. Pollock ; " Scottish Music, Contemporary and Future," Mr F. G. Scott, Mus.Bac.

Hugh MacDiarmid

CONTEMPORARY SCOTTISH STUDIES

Edited with an introduction by
Alan Riach

CARCANET

Mid Northumberland Arts Group

This edition first published
in Great Britain in 1995 by
Carcanet Press Limited
402-406 Corn Exchange Buildings
Manchester M4 3BY
in association with the
Mid Northumberland Arts Group
Wansbeck Square, Ashington
Northumberland NE63 9XL

A CIP catalogue record for this book
is available from the British Library.
ISBN 1 85754 130 8 (Carcanet)
0 904790 88 6 (MidNAG)

The publisher acknowledges financial assistance
from the Arts Council of England & Northern Arts

Designed by Janet Allan
10 Dale Road, New Mills, Stockport SK12 4NW
Set in 10/12 pt New Caledonia by XL Publishing Services, Nairn
Printed and bound in England by SRP Ltd, Exeter

Contents

Acknowledgements

I am very grateful to the University of Waikato Research Grants Committee for their support of my work on the 'MacDiarmid 2000' project. I am also grateful to Michael Grieve, W.R. Aitken and Marshall Walker, for helpful suggestions and for gaining me access to obscure items. I am especially grateful to the present editor of *The Scottish Educational Journal*, Simon Macauley, for permission to present material here originally published in the pages of that *Journal*, and for helping me acquire copies of it. I should also like to thank the staff of the National Library of Scotland, and to acknowledge the support of the Institute for Advanced Studies in the Humanities at the University of Edinburgh.

A.R.

Demolition Man
An Introduction to *Contemporary Scottish Studies*

BY ALAN RIACH

1. Biographical and Historical Contexts

Contemporary Scottish Studies is a landmark in modern Scottish literature. The essays that form the book were first published between 1925
and 1927 in *The Scottish Educational Journal*, a weekly paper read principally by teachers. Thirty-eight of them were published as a book in
1926. They caused a furore.

After the First World War, Hugh MacDiarmid took hold of the pillars
of the Scottish literary and cultural establishment and did the job of
Samson. These essays proposed an almost total demolition of Scotland's
cultural identity as it had come to be accepted through the nineteenth
century. On 25 June 1926, MacDiarmid described Scotland as 'a country
that has been at a literary standstill for the best part of a century so far as
the production of work of European consequence is concerned'. And on
23 July, he quoted Lewis Spence: 'From the death of Burns to the end
of the late war may, perhaps, be regarded as the most jejune and uninspired period in Scottish letters.' A new, radical national reconstruction
was demanded. The storm followed.

The essays were signed with MacDiarmid's patronymic, C.M. Grieve.
At the time, the name 'MacDiarmid' (or 'M'Diarmid') was associated
with experimental poetry in Scots. Grieve was known as a journalist,
critic, and occasional poet writing in English. After demobilisation, he
had gone to work as a journalist in Montrose. He contributed syndicated
articles to local Scottish newspapers throughout the 1920s, while writing
more intellectually provocative essays for A.R. Orage's London-based
journal *The New Age*, one of the most influential cultural periodicals of
the decade. He was married in 1918 to his first wife, Margaret Skinner,
and they had a daughter, Christine, in 1924. He was an Independent
Socialist member of Montrose town and parish councils and a Justice of

the Peace. He was, in short, a family man in his thirties attempting a new life of domestic balance after the war years spent on the continent as a bachelor.

He was also fiercely busy, embroiled in social business, local politics, international intellectual ideas and literary movements, and discovering for himself the language and literature of his own country. The fact that so much of Scotland's cultural history was hidden from him reflects the disintegration of the national culture in the project of British imperialism. With the rise of the British Empire, two things happened to Scotland: it became invisible, and it became internationally recognisable in stereotypes and caricatures.

It became invisible in the sense that many of its major artists, composers and writers were exiled from their own national identity and became bulwarks of the British establishment, while an incalculable number of Scots became both the victims and the perpetrators of the Empire itself. They and their country became dissolved in the great imperial project. Thomas Carlyle in his lectures *On Heroes and Hero-Worship* (1841), refers to Samuel Johnson as his countryman – an Englishman. Further down the line, when Field Marshall Montgomery spoke in the Royal Albert Hall on 23 October 1946 to an enormous reunion of El Alamein veterans, he subsumed Irish, Welsh and Scots in the patriotic declaration: 'We are all Englishmen here!'

But at the same time, throughout the countries of the world, Scots were becoming recognised in stereotypical ways. Perhaps the best example is one of the most famous photographs ever taken: of John Brown, standing just to the left of Queen Victoria (who is on horseback), with the gamekeeper, John Grant, standing to the right. After the photograph was taken, John Grant was cut out of the picture and it was made into a postcard. In 1863 alone, its first year of issue, it sold over 13,000 copies and was sent all over the world. The image of John Brown presents the features that were to hold sway (and in some respects, still do): a dour, serious expression suggests the conscience and determination of the set of his character, staring straight at the camera: a direct man, without subtlety or humour. The seriousness, to us, seems at odds with and yet part of his self-important costume: the bonnet, the kilt and the outlandish sporran. Above all, he is standing before the mounted monarch – clearly, he is in her service, at her command, a man who, if called, can be counted on not to reason why, but to do as he's told, and die.

MacDiarmid considered the Great War to be the ultimate consequence of imperialism, and thought of Scotland as one of Europe's small nations especially fit for post-war regeneration. The list of 'Books to Read' which he compiled as an appendix to the 1926 edition of *Contemporary Scottish Studies* is a fascinating cross-section of late nineteenth and early twentieth century publications on various aspects of national identity. Attenuated as the list is, there is a kind of tenacity in it. If a similar list compiled in the late twentieth or early twenty-first century would offer a more full and varied selection of titles, that is at least partly due to MacDiarmid's effort, and the kind of deconstruction these essays began to encourage.

His earliest poetry and criticism is in English, and signed C.M. Grieve. The English-language poetry he published in the three anthologies he edited, entitled *Northern Numbers* (1920-22), was followed by MacDiarmid's early lyrics in Scots, in *Sangschaw* (1925) and *Penny Wheep* (1926) and the book-length 'lyric medley' or 'gallimaufry' *A Drunk Man Looks at the Thistle* (1926), which, in the words of David Daiches, 'broke on a startled and incredulous Scotland with all the shock of a childbirth in a church'. In other words, MacDiarmid's greatest Scots poems were being written at the same time as the essays which form *Contemporary Scottish Studies*. The poetry found a small but appreciative readership; but it was rather this series of essays which was widely read and caused a storm of protest, consolidating his reputation as a remorseless critic of the literary, educational and cultural establishment. As Kenneth Buthlay has said in his study of MacDiarmid (Edinburgh: Scottish Academic Press, 1982), 'it should be noted that opposition to MacDiarmid as a writer in Scotland was based more on these articles than upon his early experiments in Scots verse.' This was one reason why a distinction was maintained between the names MacDiarmid and Grieve, though their shared identity became an open secret before the series ended. Subsequently, it was MacDiarmid's name which came to signify the author of the body of writing we read today. MacDiarmid was the lyrical, meditative, philosophical and epic poet, and accepted the role of a tireless polemicist; while Grieve became known as a gentle and hospitable private man.

As Buthlay has said, MacDiarmid addressed his work in the first place to his fellow Scots, and since there were no good literary periodicals in Scotland in the early 1920s, he created his own. These were small-press, short-run, limited circulation journals and papers such as *The Scottish Chapbook*, *The Scottish Nation* and *The Northern Review*. When they folded, his cause was taken up and made known to a wider public by three men at that time on the staff of the *Glasgow Herald* (one of the two leading national daily newspapers): William Power, Alexander McGill and Robert Bain, who, in Buthlay's words, 'quickly recognised MacDiarmid's gifts'. As early as 16 May 1922, an article entitled 'Modern Scottish Verse' signalled the *Herald*'s support for MacDiarmid, and he would publish in that paper's columns from time to time thereafter. He was well able to make strategic use of whatever platforms became available, and to press-gang a crew he would subsequently jettison. Indeed, among the angriest reactions to *Contemporary Scottish Studies*, were those of Donald A. Mackenzie (1873–1936), whose poetry MacDiarmid had published in the *Northern Numbers* anthologies a few years earlier, while Neil Munro (1864–1930) and Charles Murray (1864–1941), also contributors to *Northern Numbers*, were summarily dismissed from the company of new poets of the Scottish Renaissance – John Ferguson, William Jeffrey, Muriel Stuart, Roderick Watson Kerr, for example – proposed in the essays. Many of these younger poets had also been represented in these anthologies, filing past their nodding elders.

The contrast between the old guard and the younger writers must have been striking to the first readers of the anthologies. For example, one of the poems by which Mackenzie was represented in the first series, 'Isle of My Heart', began in an unmistakably sentimental and nostalgic tone:

> I'm sighing here my lone-self
> In a foreign land and fair,
> Where the sun is ever gleaming
> And I can live at ease:
> For it's me that will be dreaming
> Of the dear days that were,
> On that jewel of an island
> In the sweet Hebrides.

By contrast, John Ferguson was writing sonnets about unemployed chorus-girls and music-hall comedians, bank accountants and the inmates of a sanatorium, and Roderick Watson Kerr (known at that time as 'the Scottish Siegfried Sassoon'), was writing bitterly of urban squalor in a Christian Mission hall for the poor:

> Around
> Comes tea – philanthropy must know no bound –
> And buns – weeks old, but oh, twopence the lot

How very cheap! Magnanimous, God wot!
Quite fit for gentle ladies' palates – God!
And monkeys in a cage get nuts; and, odd
Enough – oh, very odd! the tea and buns
Just cost the soul of any of these ones –
The female things, I mean. Two pence? Ah, yes,
That woman's body sells each night for less.

It was Alexander McGill, according to Buthlay, who saw a new way of reaching potential readers through *The Scottish Educational Journal*, and the article McGill published there on 16 January 1925, '"Towards a Scottish Renaissance" paved the way for MacDiarmid's highly provocative (and often critically acute) series, "Contemporary Scottish Studies", which began in June 1925 and led to violent controversies in the columns of the *Journal*.' By the time MacDiarmid published the first thirty-eight articles in book-form the following year, he had become notorious, and the 'Scottish Renaissance Movement' was fully under way. Indeed, in a crucial passage in the essay dated 4 December 1925, MacDiarmid suggests that the Renaissance had already occurred:

> A certain type of critic is apt to say that the movement so far has consisted only of propaganda – only 'of the posters' – that the actual work has still to be done. This is a mistake. The Scottish Renaissance has taken place. The fruits will appear in due course. Earlier or later – it does not alter the fact. For the Scottish Renaissance has been a propaganda of ideas and their enunciation has been all that was necessary.

On 5 February 1926, some of these ideas were spelled out:

> From the Renaissance point of view… it is utterly wrong to make the term 'Scottish' synonymous with any fixed literary forms or to attempt to confine it… The Scottish Renaissance movement… sets out to do all that it possibly can to increase the number of Scots who are vitally interested in literature and cultural issues; to counter the academic or merely professional tendencies which fossilise the intellectual interests of most well-educated people even; and, above all, to stimulate actual art-production to a maximum.

The best way to do this, the essay continued, is to attack and destroy existing preconceptions responsible for the status quo, in religious, political, and social terms and on every other front. As MacDiarmid's notoriety spread, the *Journal* began to be more widely read beyond its primary constituency of professional teachers. MacDiarmid's friend and contemporary, Helen Burness Cruikshank, recalled once being asked by a railway station bookshop manager why copies of *The Scottish Educational Journal* were selling out so quickly. 'People buy it to see who is being castigated by C.M. Grieve this week,' she told him. Her next-door neighbour at the time was Thomas Henderson, the *Journal's* editor, so she knew what she was talking about. The columns were followed from week to week as if they were a cliff-hanging cinema serial. MacDiarmid was shooting from the hip, finding his targets, never wasting a bullet.

Writing to his early teacher and mentor, George Ogilvie, on 9 December 1926, MacDiarmid mentions a 'very understanding' review in the *Glasgow Evening News* (25 November 1926), which described *Contemporary Scottish Studies* as 'a book very likely to take an important place in Scottish letters'. Anglocentric highbrow response was not so keen, however. On 6 January 1927, page 14 of *The Times Literary Supplement* carried a review of the book-version of *Contemporary Scottish Studies* which began: 'Mr Grieve's title arouses expectations, even though one finds that his imposing-looking volume confines itself almost wholly to Scottish literature. But a critic of literature needs knowledge, a sense of proportion, some power of writing lucidly his own language, and, for choice, a certain standard of good breeding...' Presumably this was the same reviewer who gave most of the space allocated to covering MacDiarmid's earlier poetry collections to complaints about what he or she considered philological inaccuracies – as useful a thing to do as attempting to regularise Shakespeare's spelling, and a pernicious way of denying MacDiarmid's work the recognition it demanded.

Despite the patrician tone, when *The Times Literary Supplement* reviewer came to *A Drunk Man Looks at the Thistle* (22 September 1927, pp. 650-51), he or she was accurate in essence: 'Its main theme, in so far as a main theme can be discerned, is simply the human adventure, the wonder (deepening in the light of science) of a being "begotten of mannës sperme uncleanne" who yet aspires beyond the stars. There is much idolatry of Dostoevski and Hermann [*sic*] Melville, in whom the author recognises kindred spirits...' A similar quest for fundamental and ultimate truths animates *Contemporary Scottish Studies*. By the end of the first paragraph of the 'Introductory' chapter written for the 1926 edition, MacDiarmid suggested that he hoped the book would allow him to 'make sure of being able to accommodate the Deity with a better grace than I can yet command'. The purpose of the book he described as being 'to examine the ethos of Scotland today; to enquire into the contemporary and, generally, post-Union contribution of Scotland to world culture; to institute comparisons between the stock-conceptions of things Scottish today and the qualities which manifested themselves in Scotland before the Union – even to consider anew what really *is* the Chief End of Man and, more particularly, the best possible destiny that Scotland can secure, or, at least, plan and purpose for itself.'

If the ultimate aim of MacDiarmid's essays was spiritual regeneration, their pragmatic effect in Scotland has been extensive and long-term. In an essay dated 19 February 1926, MacDiarmid was writing of Ruaraidh Erskine of Marr:

> He has been persistently derided and insulted and denounced by all the anonymous nonentities who staff the Anglo-Scottish Press. But despite them, and the overwhelming odds confronting his programme (the restoration of Scottish independence and of Gaelic culture in Scotland), he has maintained decade after decade a propaganda which the Press must keep subterranean, but to which they could not deny an ultimate ubiquity... His persistent propaganda has at last taken shape in what is the most promising nationalist organisation that has been formed in Scotland since the Union – the Scottish National League.

After the series came to an end in 1927, MacDiarmid joined Erskine and others in founding the National Party of Scotland (in 1928), bringing together various groups which had been campaigning for Scottish independence (including Erskine's Scottish National League, the Scottish National Movement, the Scottish Home Rule Association, and the Glasgow University Scottish Nationalist Association). The rise of the independence movement in Scotland followed the formation of the national party of Wales, Plaid Cymru, in 1925, and the Irish war of independence, 1919-21. Behind these was the example of the Russian Revolution of 1917. In different ways, the struggle against imperialism empowered all these movements. In Scotland, MacDiarmid's involvement remains difficult to over-estimate. As Kenneth Buthlay says, 'The inter-relationship between his work and the rise of Scottish Nationalism, an altogether deeper matter than the recorded rise of political parties, will always be beyond calculation.' In an address commemorating the centenary of MacDiarmid's birth, published in the magazine *Chapman*,

69-70, Autumn 1992 (pp. 185-88), Edwin Morgan referred to Moses Znaimer, a man from Tajikistan who, in the early 1990s, was a mighty force in the world of Canadian television, who allegedly declared, 'Any sissy can make programmes. I make channels.' MacDiarmid, Morgan commented, 'made channels, extraordinary channels which we are still sailing and exploring, and will do for a long time to come.'

2. Subjects and Themes

Edwin Morgan has a succinct appraisal of the achievement of *Contemporary Scottish Studies* in his booklet on MacDiarmid (Harlow: Longman, 1976, pp. 29-30):

> He never ceased to attack those persons and institutions (not without having made use of them where necessary) that he regarded as dead-weight establishments ripe for a well-placed kick into history, and in the same way he kept an eager eye for every new development in Britain or abroad that held out promise of forward-moving values. The series of sprightly articles he wrote for *The Scottish Educational Journal* between 1925 and 1927... offer the strongest proof we have of the confidence of the new broom, of the man who mounts the *Zeitgeist* at the right moment and points the fresh paths which are in fact the ones that are going to be taken. Whether savaging Mrs Kennedy-Fraser's sentimentally doctored *Songs of the Hebrides* of early this century in comparison with the enlightened and scientific use of folk-song by Bartók and Kodály in Hungary, or prophetically recommending young Scottish writers like Edwin Muir and Neil Gunn at the expense of established favourites such as Charles Murray and Neil Munro, or pleading for an end to the 'sabotage' of true cultural and intellectual values by an increasingly utilitarian education system, MacDiarmid impresses by his indefatigable concern to cause change, to undermine provincialism, sloth, and complacence, to expose the old guard and get them to condemn themselves through their own self-defence, as frequently happened in the correspondence columns. He was not right in everything, but a reader today is surprised to see how often he was, and how sharply at that time – the time also of his creative achievement in *Sangschaw* and *A Drunk Man Looks at the Thistle* – his critical faculties uncovered the significant roots of the matters he was discussing.

Morgan's description of the essays as 'sprightly' seems accurate in one sense – MacDiarmid never forgets he is writing journalism and the vigour and elasticity of the articles are unflagging – yet it seems a rather feeble word to apply to the enormous Wagnerian arias of prose which form each of MacDiarmid's perorations on his chosen subjects. In Wagnerian style, there are subjects, themes and leitmotifs to which MacDiarmid returns again and again. Perhaps it will be helpful to summarise these briefly here.

1. The predominant subject is Scotland's **literature**, considered comprehensively with reference not only to poetry and fiction but to drama as well. MacDiarmid emphasises the potential value of developing an experimental Scots theatre movement, and on 13 November 1925, he writes of an imagined repertory company of twenty-five people who might approach their task by abandoning conventional performance theatre altogether. Such a group might begin by 'educating its playwrights as it went along by imposing upon them a method of collaboration with the producers and players with mere suggestions instead of concrete plays to work from'. On 22 January 1926, he suggests that Chekhov is the dramatist who might be most profitably studied. 'His indirect method – his use of irrelevancies consist with the complex, curious Scots mind. The future of the Scots theatre lies in… the employment of expressionist technique…'

The predominant theme arising from the consideration of literature is that of the conflict between popularity and élitism, and this calls into question the relations between art and society, writing and publishing, traditional and experimental forms not only of literature, but also of music and art. MacDiarmid early and astutely recognised the significance of the greatest works of modern literature and he knew how far they were from being popular among the newly rising tide of the masses. Writing on 5 November 1926, he describes James Joyce's *Ulysses* and T.S. Eliot's *The Waste Land* as the works which, 'when all that most people know and esteem has vanished as it had never existed, will, almost certainly, survive as the representative expressions of early 20th century life and thought in the English language'.

Against this he had written, on 31 July 1925: 'The overwhelming taste (I do not blame the masses of the people – they are the victims of the system under which we live) is for crude films, trashy literature, silly songs, and so on. Conjoined to that is an utter incapacity for and impatience with dialects, a very wide-spread refusal to think, and a detestation for "highbrowism".' In the 'Introductory' chapter to the 1926 book-version, he regrets that he has not had space to deal with other important Scots of recent times, including 'J.L. Baird (with his invention of "television")'. This is a salient reminder of the technological context in which MacDiarmid was writing, and the degree to which popular taste was being manipulated by new technologies only just coming into general practice. Writing on 26 June 1925, MacDiarmid claims that it is a false premise to consider Sir J.M. Barrie a writer of any literary or intellectual consequence. 'His popularity, which is an entirely different matter, is not in dispute, and the causes and consequences of that would take us far afield into questions of human destiny, educational purpose and method, and the way in which public opinion is formed and directed.'

2. A corollary of MacDiarmid's discussion of literature is the second principal subject, **language**, and the relative merits of English, Scots and Gaelic. Introducing the book version, he regrets the substantial omission of any consideration of the Gaelic movement and contemporary Gaelic literature, and although these are mentioned, they did not fully occupy MacDiarmid until the late 1920s and 1930s. Of much greater concern to him here is the relation between English and the Scots vernacular, both as literary languages and in speech. Concurrent with these essays, he had developed a 'Theory of Scots Letters' and published it in his journal, *The Scottish Chapbook* (collected in the *Selected Prose* published by Carcanet in 1992). This presents the case of Scots as a literary medium. But in *Contemporary Scottish Studies*, he is also concerned with the way Scots is treated by Scottish teachers. His challenge has never been met.

The proposal to consider Scots as a language in its own right, worthy of recognition and study in its national context and its dialectal variations from Aberdeen to Ecclefechan, has generally received a response similar to that of John Cook, writing on 13 November 1925: 'Most of us have a struggle getting rid of the dialect from the speech and compositions of the pupils; the teaching of it could only heap up confusion. The recognised test of an educated child (or adult) is his ability to write and speak the English language... [which is] the medium of business, social intercourse, of the platform, pulpit and Press, even on this side of the Border...' This ignores the fact that teaching Scots as a language might lessen a confusion which has riddled more than one generation, and might make teaching English easier, and it dismisses the moral claim of Scots to be recognised as a language in its own right. Some headway has been made, of course. Dictionaries of Scots and understanding of the Scots language are more widely available now than in the 1920s, but the general and universal misconception that Scots is merely a dialect of English persists.

On 5 February 1926, MacDiarmid said that his sense of the value of Scots was based on 'the belief that Scotland still has something to say to the imagination of mankind, something that she alone among the nations can say, and can say only in her native tongue.' He opposed the 1920s vernacular revivalists as people who 'do not wish to say anything to the imagination of mankind.' He wrote with reference to Edwin Muir on 4 September 1925 that in some of his ballads he employed 'a full Braid Scots canon of his own devising based upon a *de novo* consideration of the entire resources of the language on the one hand, and its tractability to the most significant processes and purposes of ultra-modern literature on the other.' The comment would be more aptly applied to himself with regard to the language of the early lyrics and *A Drunk Man Looks at the Thistle*.

In a very different way from England, the matter of language has been the focus of literary and political debate in Scotland throughout the twentieth century. It came to a crisis in 1936, with the publication of Muir's *Scott and Scotland*. Muir advocated the use of English by Scottish writers and the surrender of Scottish literature to an Anglocentric tradition. MacDiarmid, who had been quick to recognise the value of a vernacular idiom as an antidote to English gentility, and foresaw the post-colonial nationalist movements which were to open Anglocentricism to a vast range of different cultures, opposed Muir's argument as a betrayal of the Scottish literary movement he had initiated in the 1920s.

3. A third subject was the whole body of **literary and cultural criticism**, both in terms of professional literary criticism and in terms of journalism. Arising from this came the conflict between the demands of Modernism and the conventions of the Kailyaird, and the conflict between artistic forms of naturalism or realism and a more disruptive aesthetic and, concomitantly, a different ethical imperative. Sir George Douglas, for example, is described on 7 August 1925 as holding a key position in Scottish letters as a representative critic, but his relationship to a real critic is described as that of an amateur to a professional. Employing an impudently Joycean vocabulary, MacDiarmid takes him to task: 'his work has a diathesis of progressive obsolescence rather than of

effective conservation of even the little that within the limits of his disposition it has obviously been his desire and aim to conserve.'

As for journalism, on 19 February 1926, we read: 'The same type of person as fought for the freedom of the Press is today recognising the need for its regulation in the interests of the integrity of thought and public opinion.' MacDiarmid was concerned not just with the informed opinion of literary experts but with the general public good as well. He was hypersensitive to the antagonisms between the ethos of small-town Scotland, the inward-turning, conciliatory aspects of the culture of rural and depopulated areas, and the international, European *Zeitgeist*: he wished to avoid, as he wrote on 17 July 1925, 'narrow chauvinism on the one hand and colourless internationalism on the other'.

4. Scotland's **music** forms a fourth subject, and MacDiarmid was remarkably proleptic in the light of recent rediscoveries and reappraisals by John Purser, recorded in his BBC radio series and book *Scotland's Music* (Edinburgh: Mainstream, 1992), and others, of neglected master-works and the suppressed history of one of the nation's most distinctive and internationally recognised arts. MacDiarmid is concerned not only with promoting such reconsideration and research but also with contemporary opportunities for composing, performing and teaching music as an essential part of one's education.

5. The **art** of Scotland, specifically painting and sculpture, receives considerable attention, and here one might suggest that MacDiarmid's prompts are in need of a response. Stewart Carmichael, for example, who seems to have been the only good thing to have come out of Dundee in MacDiarmid's opinion (on 25 December 1925, he refers to his studio as 'one of the very few spots in Dundee where there is any spiritual life'), receives no mention in Duncan MacMillan's monumental *Scottish Art 1460-1990* (Edinburgh: Mainstream, 1990). And a full study of modern Scottish art and its relation to MacDiarmid and the literary renaissance remains to be done; the work of William Johnstone, William McCance and J.D. Fergusson alone suggests how rich such a study might be.

6. Of course, the writing of Scotland's history, or the whole approach to the subject which MacDiarmid terms **'historiography'** is of major concern, and relates principally to the matter of national self-determination, and the conflict between Anglocentrism and Scottish self-definition. He was not unconcerned with the nation's history as such; he

indicated on 18 December 1925, 'There is, generally speaking, no coherent conception of the course of events in Scotland – as distinct from England – in the past century at least.' But he was more concerned with the way in which that history was presented, whether from an Anglocentric or independent Scottish perspective.

7. It is a crucial component of the general **education** MacDiarmid proposes, within which the larger themes of the differences between male and female psychology, the constructions of national and racial psychology, the legacies of imperialism and colonialism, all have their place. This takes us to the quintessential proposition at the heart of these essays: a balance between creativity (among artists, teachers and students) and education (as process and as product functioning in terms of a culture's prevalent attitude towards experience). It is this balance MacDiarmid wishes to affirm, in the context of a national identity on an international stage. In that desire, he is the peer of his better-known English contemporaries, I.A. Richards and F.R. Leavis.

Despite the comprehensiveness of MacDiarmid's subjects and themes, certain areas of enquiry remained conspicuous by their absence. He was not unaware of them, and in the 'Books to Read' section of the 1926 book-version, he included sections on 'Philosophy' and 'Theology'. However, there was only one book under the former heading and four under the latter; the section on 'Bibliography and Printing' had more than both 'Philosophy' and 'Theology' put together. A section on 'History, Politics and Economics' gathers twenty titles, but there is no extended treatment in the essays themselves of Scotland's political and economic history. Mac-Diarmid intended to redress this imbalance in the 1930s when he planned to write a radically reinterpretive history book entitled *Red Scotland: or, What Lenin Has Meant to Scotland*. This was never published.

Perhaps the single most conspicuous absence is any study of sexuality. The masculine bias of nationalism concomitant with the feminisation of the nation appears repeatedly, but there is little space given to studying the differences between writing by men and writing by women. Yet there is more than one might have expected. In the 'Introductory' chapter to the 1926 edition, MacDiarmid complains that his task in writing the book was made heavier by 'an occasional bit of moral censorship; my article on Muriel Stuart would have been rather longer but for the excision of a passage in which I examined a quotation from her poems alongside one of Milton's. Both dealt with Sex; and this volume ought certainly to have had an article on The Sexual History of Scotland. The Scottish atmosphere will not be effectively improved until our tacit Comstockery [prudery; the word derives from Anthony Comstock, 1844-1915, an American denunciator of the nude in art]... has been dragged out into the light and examined unflinchingly.'

What we do have, however, is worth noting. For example, writing of Violet Jacob (17 July 1925), MacDiarmid quotes a reviewer who had commented: 'There is always the note of restraint. It is generally very effective, but the reader may be pardoned if he wishes that sometimes Mrs Jacob would let herself go more freely.' MacDiarmid's judgement here is acute: 'the writer in his mind was italicising the word "go," whereas the real trouble with Mrs Jacob's work can only be indicated by stressing the word "herself" – not "would let herself *go*" but "would let *herself* go," which is a very different thing.'

MacDiarmid is far from being merely a misogynistic chauvinist; in such comments he is at least proto-feminist. It may well be rewarding to revisit some of his recommendations. He backed more horses than were ever in the races, and time has not agreed with all his judgements. But his accounts are not yet closed. Who were the women in the 'ladies' choir'? do we know enough about all of them and their work to dismiss them from consideration?

There are, then, seven principal subjects dealt with in the book, and several different themes develop from them in different ways. Each of these themes might warrant a commentary in itself, but they are so thoroughly composed into the body of *Contemporary Scottish Studies* as a whole that such a commentary might become larger than the book. Similarly, individual biographies of all the men and women named in the course of the book are less significant than the comprehensiveness of these themes and subjects. MacDiarmid is attempting nothing less than an overview and overhaul of a particular national identity and the people he foregrounds are always considered in the service of a larger purpose. It is not, therefore, the work of individuals (or even individual works) he is primarily concerned to present, but the components of the character and potential of a nation.

3. Premises and Programmes

If he was conscious of the magnitude of his assault in *Contemporary*

Scottish Studies, he was also sensitive to its shortcomings, both in pragmatic and in theoretical terms. He wrote to Neil Gunn on 14 December 1926:

> I am very conscious of its faults – and just as conscious of the necessity of most of those very faults to enable it to effect its purpose which it undoubtedly will, no matter what anybody says about it or doesn't say. It is bound to tell enormously. In the second series I propose not to go on with similar personal studies at all – but to deal with the whole subject of Nationality, Future of Literature, Essence of Languages, etc. To write for Europe apropos Scotland instead of for Scotland apropos Scotland. And I don't care what anybody says about my English style. The only test of any style is its effectiveness for the author's purpose – and there is no mistake about mine for that! So there. Other people can chew over niceties. I want to win through and do things – and will!

Reaction from some correspondents was extremely hostile. T. Robertson wrote on 16 October 1925: 'It is time to lodge a strong protest against the continuance in your columns of the articles entitled "Contemporary Scottish Studies"... [The author's] every paragraph is burdened with bombast and self-adulation, and his vague, involved and irrelevant prolixity renders his deliverances utterly worthless either as appreciations or as adverse criticisms.' In response, the educationalist A.S. Neill wrote on 6 November 1925 for the defence: 'I thoroughly enjoy reading his articles... he can make the unknown interesting... his attempt to valuate Scots literature as apart of *welt-literatur* is the most... valuable piece of journalism I have seen in a Scots paper.' As the series progressed, a more comprehensive understanding of the fundamental beliefs underlying the essays developed. A correspondent named H. Brown described the author on 11 December 1925 as 'a constructive idealist with a reasoned creed' and proceeded to summarise what he took to be that creed. Some of the points made are worth quoting, for they shed light not only on what MacDiarmid thought he was doing and wanted to do, but because they describe fundamental positions in a nationalist programme which are still deeply lodged in Scotland's understanding of itself.

1. Man's chief end is to develop a culture which shall extend his consciousness and guide his behaviour.
2. Culture is the concern of the human race as a whole, and should be pursued by the joint efforts of all nations.

3. Each nation must make its independent contribution to world culture along lines determined by its distinctive psychology.
4. Scotland is a single indivisible cultural unit independent of England.
5. The main characteristic of Scottish psychology is an intense consciousness of the great mysteries, combined with a matter of fact attitude to them.
14. What is possible and desirable is a creative modern development of the interrupted Scots-English culture of the fifteenth century.
15. The effective force in the Renaissance will be an intellectual aristocracy consisting of those in whom the distinctive characteristics of Scottish psychology are naturally powerful, and carefully cultivated by a thorough study of Scottish cultural history and contemporary international creativity.
16. The duty of the relatively uninstructed multitude is to recognise these finer spirits, and follow their lead.

In response, MacDiarmid agreed that these points 'admirably describe my position and programme.'

If phrases like 'an intellectual aristocracy' and 'the duty of the uninstructed multitude' are unsavoury reminders of MacDiarmid's interest in and support for a form of Scottish Fascism (in 1923), the nationalist programme he assents to here is saved from any more repugnant totalitarianism by its adamant insistence upon the role of human creativity in the struggle for history. As Douglas Dunn puts it in his introduction to *The Faber Book of Twentieth Century Scottish Poetry*, MacDiarmid believed that he 'was obliged to remake Scottish poetry on the basis of a pre-1707 mentality. That is, write *as if history had never happened*; or write in such a way that history would be rewritten, and unknitted, in the work.' Dunn judges the former to be 'a forlorn choice' and the latter, 'to say the least, a challenge'. He recognises that MacDiarmid was 'trying to make a nation, as well as poetry.' The point is that MacDiarmid was trying to find a creative way to work with the unresolved and perhaps unresolvable difficulties presented by aesthetic ideals and the desire for political autonomy.

For an artist to engage his work in the understanding of a nation's political history is one of the great commitments of modern literature: one thinks of Pablo Neruda and Wole Soyinka, and the risks involved. To write as if certain events in history had never happened is, in the work of such writers, not simply a forlorn choice; it is rather a temporary strategy in the struggle to rewrite that history, to unknit the fabric of constraint and suppression. The truly forlorn choice had been made by the late nineteenth-century Scottish writers of the Kailyaird and the versifiers of the Whistlebinkie anthologies, whose writings couthily submitted to the status quo: Anglocentric hegemony, explicitly in politics, implicitly in culture. Terry Eagleton, writing on 'Aesthetics and Politics in Edmund Burke' in a collection edited by Michael Kenneally entitled *Irish Literature and Culture* (Gerrards Cross: Colin Smythe, 1992, pp. 25-34), perfectly describes the situation:

> Within the alarmingly amorphous flux of our subjective lives, certain objects stand out in a kind of ideality akin to reason, objects which we can all judge alike, and these are the beautiful. Beauty is a crucial constituent of our sociality: it is the way social order is lived out on the body, the way such delightful symmetry strikes the eye and stirs the heart. No vulgar utilitarian rationale is needed for such an experience, any more than one is required for human fellowship. The social bonds of bourgeois society require no more theoretical validation than does our quick feeling for a magnificent seascape. The moral, social and aesthetic senses are deeply intertwined; and this means that submitting to authority is a source of delight for us, is indeed as natural as following out our own deepest spontaneous impulses and desires. The aesthetic is a name for this hegemonic project, which is why it looms so large in a form of society which, as Marx once commented, actually has exceedingly little time for art.

'Submitting to authority is a source of delight for us' – it might have been the motto of more than one generation of Scottish writers whose works became literary leafmould. Yet if the idea is essential to the Kailyaird writers it is also a fundamental tenet of the hero-worship elaborated by Carlyle upon a larger stage. Writing of Sir Walter Scott in an essay of 1838, Carlyle says: 'Veneration of great men is perennial in the nature of man; this, in all times, especially in these, is one of the blessedest facts predictable to him.' Here Calvinism's doctrine of the elect is made over into a secular doctrine of the hero whose leadership lesser mortals should be delighted to follow. The striking similarity with MacDiarmid's identification of 'an intellectual aristocracy' is not coincidental.

Like Carlyle, MacDiarmid is saved from fascist absolutism by his love for those whose lot is to recognise greatness, and who have difficulty taking delight in accepting its authority. It is not simply a pure love of greatness that drives him; it is also the troubled desire that others should become great in their own ways; for example, that Scots should recognise the full extent of their potential, and realise it. For MacDiarmid, therefore, Anglocentric authority required to be challenged.

In *Contemporary Scottish Studies*, MacDiarmid's procedure is to assert a European and international scale of quality, and to accord a location within it to the popular Scottish writers of the day; he also introduces new Scottish writers and assesses their potential significance in the same way. For example, on 3 July 1925, rejecting George Blake's assessment of Neil Munro as a writer who had achieved 'short story perfection', MacDiarmid asks us to think of Maupassant, Poe, Chekhov, Bunin and Katherine Mansfield. The first three names are familiar, but few would be so familiar with Ivan Alekseyevich Bunin (1870-1953), whose stories, charting the disintegration of traditional Russian country life at the turn of the century, had only begun to be translated, and it was astute to mention Katherine Mansfield in the same breath – her best stories had only just appeared, between 1918 and 1923. Scotland's art, music, education and historiography are given a similar treatment. MacDiarmid's deeper intention was to re-establish Scotland's national culture in an international context. Central to this was a complex and developing understanding of Scotland's linguistic situation. Writing on 17 July 1925, with reference to the novelist, short story writer and poet Violet Jacob, MacDiarmid said:

> She has failed just as, as Edwin Muir has pointed out, every other Scottish writer writing in English has failed to achieve greatness in even the second or third degree, for the simple reason that in attempting what she did attempt she was not going about her proper business. The proper business of any Scottish imaginative writer is to found or further a Scottish – not an English – tradition. There are exceptions, of course, such as Conrad, to the rule I am indicating, but no Scot has so far proved to be one of them.

This 'rule' – that only the native English qualify to write great English literature – betrays itself a little later in MacDiarmid's career, as he recognises the effects of colonialism in different parts of the world. Joseph Conrad proves to be the exception who, implicitly, is also the standard to aspire towards.

If there are reactionary and purist elements to MacDiarmid's insistence on a Scottish tradition, there are also a radical understanding of artistic quality and a profound commitment to the psychology that produces it. These are riveted to a love of his native land, and it is this latter quality that distinguishes MacDiarmid's career, as he tries to reconcile it with the former. Unlike Conrad, Joyce, Eliot or Pound, MacDiarmid was a resident, never committed to exile; or, perhaps more accurately, his only exile was internal. For him, loyalty to art was always wrestling with loyalty to a political ideal of national autonomy and social fulfilment.

It is this conflict which he recognises in R.B. Cunninghame Graham, whose friendship he shared with Conrad. On 24 July 1925, he praises Cunninghame Graham as one of Scotland's finest modern writers, yet regrets the fact that circumstances 'discentred' his writing, and wishes he might have continued to be inspired with 'what Ford Madox Ford calls his friend Conrad's "idea of career" – his "belief in the ship-shape"!' The value placed on thoroughness here is best expressed in MacDiarmid's four-line poem, 'Shipshape' (which dates from 1943, and looks as though it might have been transcribed from a passage of Conrad's prose):

> Every inch of canvas must catch and pull,
> Every line, brace, and clew hold,
> The running rigging render
> And the standing rigging stand.

The same value was affirmed in an essay dated 27 November 1925, on new poetry written in vernacular Scots:

Ford Madox Ford in his book on Conrad tells how they used to drive 'over a country of commonplace downlands and ask ourselves how we would render a field of ripe corn, a ten-acre patch of blue-purple cabbage. We would try the words in French: *silonné, bleu-foncé, bleu-du-roi*; we would try back into English; cast around in the back of our minds for French words to which to assimilate our English and thus continue for quiet hours.' It is only by like methods that Braid Scots can be resuscitated and lifted out of the deplorable pass to which it has been reduced.

But, he goes on to say, this is not the project proposed by vernacular Scots circles or Burns clubs.

The problem is most clearly stated in the essay of 25 June 1926, on Scottish fiction. MacDiarmid asserts that Scots would contribute to English literature 'nothing "central" but strange mosaic work, curious *pastiche, tours de force*, stylistic exercises in the absence of that essential (indefinable but yet very definite and always recognisable) substance which is the stuff of great literature in English. They have not fought out their problems in their proper field (Scotland), but have flown them, with the consequence that in the ends of the earth the Thistle clings all the

more grotesquely to others and is in no way to be shaken off.' The greatest
of such Scots, MacDiarmid claims, was Herman Melville. In an America
predominantly 'sane' Melville was an Ishmael, Hawthorne a recluse and
Irving an exile; only Cooper throve upon such sanity.

Writing in 1926, MacDiarmid was early to latch on to Melville's greatness, and he was prophetic; that Melville's work goes beyond the saner
formal boundaries of Cooper's novels is more easily understood in the
1990s than it was in the 1920s. MacDiarmid's claim on Melville as a Scot
may seem pretty wild (though Melville was extremely curious about his
Scottish ancestry and visited Glasgow and Edinburgh on his way to
Constantinople, Alexandria, Jerusalem and the Holy Land in 1856); nevertheless, MacDiarmid's general identification of Scots as wayward,
outsiders, others, a breed of *isolatos*, implies a theory of aesthetics and
politics specifically fashioned to deal with the post-colonial world.

Later in the same essay, he attempts to describe certain 'distinctively
Scottish qualities', referring, in a grammatically dense and clotted way, to:
'the old "antithesis between the real and the fantastic"... "intermingledons"... fine frenzies... the lust of ratiocination, that almost mystical devotion to detail, that delight in "playing with the pieces" they have, who,
"unable to comprehend an ordered and lovely system" (or rather unable to
belong to it or devise its likes to suit themselves in accordance with their
inmost needs) "find their compensation in an abnormal sensitiveness to its
momentous and detached manifestations, absorbed in the interest of
disparate phenomena, delighted with individual things".' These are peculiarly Scottish characteristics, MacDiarmid claims, and are evident in all
forms of Scottish life.

MacDiarmid concludes that in such conditions, 'great art is impossible'
– but, he says, it is at least possible to produce art that is alive: 'alive – and
obviously preliminary to a synthesis which will not be achieved within the
field of English literature, since its achievement, if it ever is achieved, will
automatically establish Scottish literature in a field of its own.'

4. Politics, Aesthetics and National Literatures

When Henry S. Salt, who had written a critical appraisal of Herman
Melville in the *Scottish Art Review* in 1889, began his 1892 obituary of
Melville in the *Gentleman's Magazine*, he asked 'Has America a litera-
ture?' When T.S. Eliot posed a similar question with regard to Scottish

literature in 1919, he employed a slightly different emphasis. 'Was there a Scottish literature?' he queried, in a review of G. Gregory Smith's *Scottish Literature: Character and Influence*. It is this book which stands behind MacDiarmid's characterisation of Scottish culture as, typically, one of wayward, paradoxical impulses in which the 'absolute propriety of the grinning gargoyle sitting by the elbow of a kneeling saint' could be clearly affirmed.

The uncertainty of both questions reflects the characterisation of both literatures: Salt sees American literature as a grand, chaotic empire with a brilliant but suppressed imagination; Scotland's literature is seen as religious and profane, ecclesiastical and earthly. Both are worlds of contradiction in themselves, and the judgement of them as such is made from an Anglocentric position of relative stability. The description of any colonial literature as contradictory or unstable is a paradigm of imperial certainty. There is no better way for the centre of power to characterise and stigmatise the colonial condition other than as one of contradictory energies.

Yet virtues are made from necessity. In reference to Caribbean literature, Derek Walcott has emphasised the empowering force of the colonial legacy in calling himself 'a mulatto of style', and the critic Michael Gilkes has described the Caribbean cultural challenge as one of 'creative schizophrenia' – emphasising again the creative potential in the colonial condition, rather than the disabling, disempowering condition which is described, for example, in the work of V.S. Naipaul. If these are now conventional ways of understanding West Indian literature, it is less frequently argued that the same or similar paradigms might apply (or might have applied at specific historical moments) to the literatures of America and Scotland. Edwin Morgan, in an essay entitled 'Scottish Poetry in English' (collected in *Crossing the Border: Essays on Scottish Literature*, Carcanet Press, 1990, pp. 14-15) relates these questions to Scotland's principal literary languages:

> It may be that an awareness of the continuously shifting potentialities and admixtures of a varied and unsettled language situation can stimulate the art of writing in individual cases, even while at the same time it makes steady development within any literary genre more difficult than it ought to be. A fair corollary of finding some virtue in the ramshackle tabernacle of our language systems would be that we should burnish the several treasures kept therein and exert ourselves to make sure they are in good order. If Gaelic is dying, people are still

writing very good poetry in it; therefore they must continue to write poetry in it, including poetry which will stretch and test the language. If Scots is a case of arrested development, yet still alive and kicking in its own (sometimes misunderstood) ways, in both speech and writing, then poets are not going to stop trying to find out what it can still be used to express. If English came last on the scene and was often poorly used in the past, there is absolutely no reason for poets now, in the twentieth century, not to employ and extend its resources with confidence and flair. From Edwin Muir to W.S. Graham, and including MacDiarmid himself, the evidence this century became clear that a Scottish poet could produce work of quality in English.

MacDiarmid's practice differs from Morgan's however, in that he insists upon placing the language question in the context not only of literary work, but *along with* literary and cultural work, in an ideological struggle.

The best recent examples of a similar practice have occurred with reference to Irish literature. The Field Day project, involving plays, cultural criticism and a vast three-volume anthology of Irish writing has effected the most thorough exploration of the colonial position and social legitimation of the status of Ireland as a 'home colony' or 'subject nation' under the Anglocentric yoke. Introducing an essay collection entitled *Nationalism, Colonialism and Literature* by Terry Eagleton, Frederic Jameson and Edward W. Said (Minneapolis: University of Minnesota Press, 1990, p. 17), Seamus Deane draws attention to the function of sectarian violence in a society whose procedures of legitimation are themselves held in question.

> A society needs a system of legitimation and, in seeking for it, always looks to a point of origin from which it can derive itself and its practices. That origin may be a document like the 1916 Proclamation of the Irish Republic, it may be the Magna Carta, the Scottish Covenant, the revolution of 1688, 1789, or 1917. The Irish Revival and its predecessors had the right idea in looking to some legendary past for the legitimating origin of Irish society as one distinct from the British, which had a different conception of origin. But the search for origin, like that for identity, is self-contradictory. Once the origin is understood to be an invention, however necessary, it can never again be thought of as something 'natural'. A culture brings itself into being by an act of cultural invention that itself depends on an anterior legitimating nature... Priority is a claim to power.

If, as Deane argues, 'priority is a claim to power', then Scotland's claim to priority among European nations deserves some attention as one of the fundamental empowering myths MacDiarmid inherited. As Roger Mason has written in a review of R. James Goldstein's *The Matter of Scotland*, Scottish national consciousness was forged ('in more senses than one') in the Middle Ages, 'by a deliberate elaboration of a mythical history which was designed to explain and legitimise Scotland's status as an autonomous kingdom of unrivalled antiquity.' This 'mythical history' was adumbrated in two masterpieces of medieval Scottish literature, John Barbour's *Bruce* and Blind Hary's *Wallace*, both developing an ideology of freedom generated in the Wars of Independence and validated by sources such as the *Declaration of Arbroath* and the *Chronicle* of John of Fordun. The 'mythistoire' of Scotland's national autonomy was extended from the feudal, conservative society depicted by Barbour to the racial mythology (an 'ideology of blood') in Hary's *Wallace*, and on into the writings of Hector Boece and John Mair in the sixteenth century. The 'Brucean' ideology was later extended to ensure the legitimacy of the Stewart succession. Its presence in the twentieth century is not invalidated by being ironised. When R.B. Cunninghame Graham was told by an admirer that he should have been the first president of a republican Scotland, he is said to have replied, with reference to his own ancestral link to Bruce, 'Madame, by rights I should be the King of this country – and what a glorious three weeks that would be!'

In *Contemporary Scottish Studies*, MacDiarmid links coherent aesthetic sensibility to a unified political state, and notes the vitality to be found in an art of resistance, an art which arises outside such political and aesthetic coherence. Such an art, MacDiarmid asserts, would resist political conformity, and this might be done explicitly and/or in terms of its own aesthetics. Explicitly or implicitly, such art would oppose the dominant political ideology. 'Great art', in these terms is only possible when 'an ordered and lovely system' is fully empowered, and the artist and his or her audience, readers, listeners, etc., are fully able to comprehend and participate in it, finding it 'in accordance with their inmost needs'. Since such a condition is impossible in Scotland because of its political condition, MacDiarmid asks, what might be possible? And he answers that the fragmentary, vital, resistant art might herald a 'synthesis' – a kind of reconciliation – which would establish a new, distinctive national literature in a field of its own.

As a literary theory, this could be tested. One might compare the historical shift from fragmented yet 'lively' art to synthesised 'great' art as exemplified by the hybrid forms of pre-independence post-colonial literatures in various parts of the world establishing their own distinct traditions. In Nigerian literature, one could point to the pioneering work of Amos Tutuola. When *The Palm-Wine Drinkard* was first published in 1952 it was greeted enthusiastically by Dylan Thomas and then by MacDiarmid himself, in the course of his long poem *In Memoriam James Joyce* (1955): 'Amos Tutuola, the Yoruba writer,/Who has begun the structure of new African literature'. In MacDiarmid's terms, the beginning made by Tutuola was 'preliminary to a synthesis' in which a new African literature could be established. This began to take firm shape with Chinua Achebe's *Things Fall Apart* (1960) and the subsequent establishment of a distinct tradition of West African literature in English. Paradoxically, while this synthesis established a Nigerian literary tradition 'in a field of its own', it is itself necessarily hybrid: written in English and engaged with the form of the novel, it is nevertheless concerned with the experience and consciousness of Africans, sometimes Africans who had no English themselves. (Similar examples could be given from the West Indies, India, and other post-colonial societies.)

Yet questions remain. If *The Palm-Wine Drinkard* is more aesthetically 'fragmented' than *Things Fall Apart*, does that necessarily mean it is not such 'great art'? The aesthetic standards seem inapplicable once the synthesis has brought about the new field of reference in its own right, because that new field includes Tutuola as well as Achebe. Similarly, the emphatic cultural identity Scotland enjoys in the 1990s has involved a massive reappraisal of composers, poets and other artists whose work has been neglected, misrepresented, caricatured or marginalised, often for long periods of time. In the 1990s, Scotland affords the paradox of national cultural fecundity coupled with total political ineffectuality.

MacDiarmid's aesthetics may be prophetic of the post-colonial literatures of the modern world. Yet MacDiarmid himself recognises the tension between the desire for formal closure and the vitality of openness in his depiction of literature as a dialectical process; he knows that there are still unanswered questions, and that no explanation is final. In his own later work, there is a greater commitment to variousness and a range of different forms. In the 1940s, he wrote:

> The effort of culture is towards greater differentiation
> Of perceptions and desires and values and ends,
> Holding them from moment to moment
> In a perpetually changing but stable equilibrium

And in his own poetry, he moves from perfectly formed, aesthetically accomplished lyrics, through long lyric sequences and discursive poems, to epic poetry largely composed of transcriptions from a disparate variety of sources (including scientific, biological and linguistic experts whose writing is boldly incorporated into MacDiarmid's vision). This accompanies his increasingly international scope, as he moves beyond what the American poet Charles Olson once called 'the European box'.

'Because English is the international language of modernisation, the mask is also the modern world.' Thus writes T.J. Cribb in an essay on the Nigerian novelist Ben Okri (in a collection entitled *From Commonwealth to Post-Colonial* edited by Anna Rutherford, Dangaroo Press, 1992, pp. 145-50). This is a subtle recognition of how the language functions in the post-colonial text:

> Hence, although the English used is perfectly standard, the way it is used is not; it is calqued on a quite different set of cultural and syntactic relations. In some situations Standard English itself is slightly altered. Usually it remains superficially standard, but is made to respond to unfamiliar lines of force, like a mask occupied by a different spirit.

A nation is another kind of mask. These words are a gentle warning as we approach one of modern Scotland's most essential foundational texts.

A Note on the Text

In the first instance, 'Contemporary Scottish Studies' was the title of a series of essays published from 1925 to 1927 in *The Scottish Educational Journal*, a weekly publication read mainly by teachers. Before the series ended, thirty-eight of the essays were collected and published as a book by Leonard Parsons, London, in 1926. An introductory chapter, a conclusion and a list of 'Books to Read' were added for the book publication. The by-line for the series of articles and the author of the book were both given as C.M. Grieve.

In 1976, to commemorate the centenary of weekly paper publishing by the Educational Institute of Scotland, *The Scottish Educational Journal* published the series in its entirety as a large-format, double-column book, including in the appropriate places the correspondence to which the essays gave rise. The author was named as Hugh MacDiarmid. This edition included a 'Foreword' by the then editor of the journal, Angus McIntyre, and a new 'Introduction' to the series by MacDiarmid himself, then in his 84th year. McIntyre wrote in his 'Foreword' that commemorating the centenary in this way, it was hoped, would be 'to do something of value for education and for Scotland today.' Moreover, the republication with the inclusion of the correspondence had been prompted by MacDiarmid himself, writing in an essay entitled 'Scottish Studies After 50 Years' contributed to the *Journal* in 1975. This forms part of the Appendix to the present edition.

The present edition begins with the essay which introduced the series in the *Journal*, 'Towards a Scottish Renaissance' by Alexander McGill. There follows the text of the full series of essays, with the correspondence. The text of the 1976 edition has been followed. This adopted the convention of printing the articles precisely as they first appeared in the *Journal* (with the dates above the essays and letters indicating their first appearance in the *Journal*), except that account was taken of amendments made by the author for the selection published in book form in 1926. One error that was allowed to stand occurs in the essay on Edwin Muir, where it is stated that Muir came from the Shetlands rather than the Orkneys. This gave rise to correspondence which was included, so the original error has been retained with a footnote. The present edition follows this procedure. Some divergencies between the 1926 and 1976 editions have been noted in the present edition and a number of typographical errors in the 1976 edition have been silently corrected. An appendix includes the 'Introductory' and 'Conclusion' chapters of the 1926 edition and the 'Books To Read' list compiled for that edition; the essay 'Scottish Studies after 50 Years' which was published in *The Scottish Educational Journal* on 3 October 1975, as a distant coda to the 1925-7 series, and also as an opening essay in a series in which other Scottish writers looked at Scottish education; and the 'Introduction' to the 1976 edition.

Towards a Scottish Renaissance
(from *The Scottish Educational Journal*, 16 January 1925)

BY ALEXANDER McGILL

It has been said that much of the European unrest and discontent of recent times has been due to the rampant nationalism which has resulted from the Peace Treaties. There is, however, a wide difference between the chauvinism which demands a mighty Poland stretching from the Black Sea to the Baltic and the nationalism which is groping for a living expression in Scotland. Scots nationalism has had a slow birth, so slow, in fact, that people occasionally ask if it really is alive. It is peculiar and distinct in the fact that the really aggressive nationalism in Scotland is almost purely and exclusively intellectual and cultural; it is hardly, in fact, interested in the political movement which aims at re-establishing the Estates in Parliament House.

The purpose of this article is to call attention to the work of a group which is committed to an intellectual revival, or revolt, in Scotland. This group, to which has been given the nickname of the Scottish Renaissance Group by Professor Denis Saurat, in an article which he wrote for the *Revue Anglo-Americaine*, has formed itself gradually in the last few years round the personality of a young Scots journalist, C.M. Grieve. Although some of the members of the group favour the Left in politics, some are inclined towards the other extreme, and others are entirely contemptuous of the political aspect of the revival. All, however, are at one in an endeavour to create a definitely Scottish literature. They do not mean thereby to fly the Blue-Blanket from a parish church spire and shut their eyes to the world beyond. By increasing the intensity of the Scottish note in the literature which they create, they believe they will thereby be more able to approach matters of a continental and world-wide interest. They wish to do more than strut about the High Street of Drumtochtie or Thrums. They would view the vanities of Princes Street with the eye of the good European. They consider that it is of infinitely more importance to have their work appreciated in Berlin,

Vienna, Salzburg, Paris, or even Reykjavik, than to be dismissed with a paragraph in a third-rate paper in Edinburgh or Dundee. *The Glasgow Herald* alone has taken a broader view of their work than is possible from a kirk-session. It has not yet formally constituted itself as a group, although Professor Saurat's description of its members has come to be accepted by them. Though it thus causes comparisons to be made with the aggressive and enthusiastic groups of young men who have given new life to the literature of the Continent, only as far as enthusiasm is concerned can the comparison hold good. They do not seek to enunciate a new literary theory, nor create new forms of expression, nor set up new standards of criticism, and in this respect they form an association of allies rather than a unified group. As C.M. Grieve says in one of his editorials in the *Northern Review*:

> It [the *Review*, and, at the same time the Group] is a battle-ground, and the more bitter the battle, the harder the blows, the more evident friend from foe, the more shall we believe that out of battle shall come achievement. In the meantime we fight each for his own hand, for there is no more unity on the editorial board than in these pages.

On certain issues, however, the Scottish Renaissance Group is one. The prime purpose of the members is to create a new Scottish literature and to experiment in every possible manner in order to express in essential truthfulness the racial genius of the Scots. To do this it may be necessary, as in Ireland, to go far back into the past in order to draw sustenance from the very roots of the race; it may be necessary to discard the past and evolve new forms of expression; some of the group may be content to use such forms as exist and exploit them to the utmost. The most revolutionary member of the group in this respect is C.M. Grieve, and the most moderate, though not thereby the least dangerous, is George Insh, and at first thought one may ask what bond of unity is there between the author of such intimately introspective work as *Annals of the Five Senses* and the historian of the Darien Scheme. The other members of the group are Edwin Muir, George Reston Malloch, and Hugh M'Diarmid.

Some of the work of the group will be critical, some will take the form of prose-fiction, or poetry or drama, but all will be actuated by the idea of being Scottish and of expressing their thoughts in a Scots mode. With the arrogance and enthusiasm of youth they tend to ignore organs already existing in Scotland because the latter represent a point of view quite alien to a distinct Scots racial genius. They have founded their own journals, which have had their bright day and died, but after their death they have attracted great notice by their absence. To begin with, C.M. Grieve founded *The Scottish Chapbook*, which published a fine body of new poetry in Scots and English. His next venture was a weekly paper, *The Scottish Nation*, which provided a platform for poets, prophets, and politicians who were interested in the Scottish nation. It lasted for eight months and improved with age, and finally died with a sneer upon its lips, we may say. Then, in May last, appeared the first number of the *Northern Review*, which died with its September issue and had its epitaph in a particularly fine article on the Renaissance which appeared in the *Glasgow Herald* – 'it bravely lived and bravely died.' And now, 'even defeated, yet undefeated,' the restless minds of the group are laying new plans with greater care for the publication of yet another magazine. Surely, if enthusiasm and persistence count for anything, the Renaissance, for which the young men of the Group are dreaming their dreams, will eventually come.

The question of the medium of expression will cause most discussion, for one of the group at least, Hugh M'Diarmid, is resolved to exploit the Lowland Scots' speech to its utmost. Scottish poetasters have been content to follow in the steps of Burns in idiom and form because they have shared in the idolatry which has almost destroyed Burns and certainly has very little relation to his poetry. Of all the articles, foolish or praiseworthy, which have had Burns as their subject, the sanest is one by Edwin Muir, which appears in his newly-published volume *Latitudes*, but, while he is able to appreciate Burns, his own poetry has its origin in the border ballads. Muir is the least parochial of the whole group, although he is less inclined to knock Burns from his pedestal than M'Diarmid is, and his Burns essay is likely to serve as a corrective to the iconoclastic enthusiasm of the others. Saurat, indeed, goes so far as to say that it is necessary for M'Diarmid to take the place of Burns. M'Diarmid is the fanatic of the group, and it is around his work that the most contrary criticisms will be bandied. It is not at all difficult to understand his position, for, briefly, it is that it is impossible to bring out all the possibilities of the Scots genius unless the Scots vernacular is restored again to its status as a national speech. He recognises the fact that Scots has been greatly degraded until it requires much labour to find beneath the corruption the pure stream of the Scots language. The decadence had already set in when Burns was writing, and, therefore, it is necessary to go farther back than Burns to find the source of that pure stream of Scots undefiled, back as far as Dunbar and the Makars, who wrote a Scots which was a fearful weapon in the hands of an angry debater. Much of the fine Scots of the Makars has gone under, but of that speech no two districts have lost the same idioms. It is, therefore, quite legitimate for M'Diarmid or any other Renaissance writer to incorporate into his own dialect whatever expressive word or noble idiom he may come across. These poets, however, are fortunate in that Scots was their childhood speech, so that the Scots of their poetry is as spontaneous as the conventional English of poets who write in a fine burst of ecstasy and then alter a phrase or word here and there in order to express their purpose better. That is all M'Diarmid has done, and he has already discarded many of the mannerisms and peculiarities which annoyed readers of the *Scottish Chapbook*.

The Renaissance Group is still in a state of experiment, out of which some order and discipline will certainly evolve, but though they may feel inclined to compromise in certain things they are prepared to do battle for the language. They are likely to be a little more moderate in their methods than the Gaelic enthusiasts in Ireland, though a great deal will depend on the general attitude of the educated or intellectual portion of the Scottish people. One thing is certain, however, and that is that a greater number of Scots than formerly is eager to help in the work which the Renaissance Group is striving to accomplish. The article 'Follow the Gleam', by William Power, published in the *Herald*, shows this to be true, and, while it appreciates all that has been done, lays down the lines along which the Group will progress sanely. Scotland, however, is badly off for a publishing organisation, though some means may be yet adopted to increase the scope of the Porpoise Press. A new spirit, however, is evident in the land, fresh and bright with the enthusiasm of youth. George Reston Malloch expresses that spirit in a poem:

> And all thy land shall stir and thrill,
> The fading legends glow and live,
> The Fiery Cross wake strath and hill,
> The gallant Lion banner give
> Its splendour to the winds of home,
> And ancient mastery of the foam.
> Awake, thou! Bless the eager faces,
> The hearts that hunger for thy sake,
> Come from thy dream in sleep's far places,
> Before the eager hearts shall break,
> And on the hill and down the glen
> Indifferent night shall fall again.

In another place he gives the Group its working philosophy:

> Let us be proud, knowing what last defeat
> This bannered host will meet,
> By towers beleaguered where Beauty sits alone,
> With Time and Death her dreadful garrison.
> Let us be haughty, seeing the gaping grave
> Importunate for the youth we have.
> Let us be swift upon the wild attack
> That brings no lovely prisoner back.
> Though one brief glance through rain of falling swords
> Makes Time and Death but words.

Contemporary Scottish Studies

BY HUGH MacDIARMID (C.M. Grieve)

1. John Buchan

The title of John Buchan, son of the manse, barrister-at-law, managing director of Messrs. Thos. Nelson & Sons, Ltd., fisher, deer-stalker, and mountaineer, to be regarded in his fiftieth year as Dean of the Faculty of Contemporary Scottish Letters cannot be contested – despite the fact that he is only incidentally a man of letters, a finding with which he would himself, I am sure, readily enough concur, although it may seem not unlike the *Athenaeum's* remark that 'upon the whole, we do not think the short story represents Mr Conrad's true *métier*,' which drew from Arnold Bennett the comment that

> it may be that Mr Conrad's true métier, was, after all, that of an auctioneer; but, after 'Youth,' 'To-morrow,' 'Typhoon,' 'Karain,' 'The End of the Tether,' and half-a-dozen other mere masterpieces, he may congratulate himself on having made a fairly successful hobby of the short story.

Mr Buchan has, during his short life, somehow found time to make fairly successful hobbies of almost every branch of literature. A bibliography of his work would range through practically every field of letters and into strange places inhabited by what Charles Lamb calls *biblia a biblia*. And yet (though the conceptions of Bohemia may belong to the past, and 'Jack of all trades' is certainly a phrase rendered utterly inapplicable by the excellence of his writing in every direction his pen has taken him, and one, moreover, that misses the point of the failure that lies at the heart of his work by a thousand miles) what real author could ever give as his clubs: Alpine, Union, Political Economy? Many good people in Scotland who do not know what poetry is (few do!) regard him as a distinguished poet: he is, of course, under no such illusion himself. He won the Newdigate at Oxford – Euterpe's chosen have always very other fish to fry at competition-times. That he is, all the same, one of the three or four most accomplished versifiers of contemporary Scotland proves nothing but our country's singular poverty of poets – and the fact that I personally prefer his work (when I am not speaking *ex cathedra*) to almost the whole body of 'Georgian Poetry' is irrelevant. Actually he is pretty much on the level of John Drinkwater – who will occupy an inconspicuous enough place in the literary history of England – but, in his vernacular verse, he reaches a somewhat higher plane. I agree, for example, with Professor A.M. Clark, that

> one of the most truthful of all the war poems is a poignantly sincere utterance in dialect of the love of home, no vague patriotism or imperialism, but the love of one's own folk and nook of the hills. It is Mr Buchan's 'Home Thoughts from Abroad'.

His 'Fisher Jamie' will live with 'The Whistle' and 'Tam i' the Kirk' as a little classic of Doric verse.

Professor Clark's reference is one of the few to Buchan in books on contemporary literature, and he has curiously enough been even more completely disregarded in Scots manuals than in English. W. M. Parker's *Modern Scots Writers* (1917) dealt with twelve men – Andrew Lang, R.L.S., William Sharp ('Fiona Macleod'), Sir James Barrie, Professor W.P. Ker, Sir W. Robertson Nicoll, Kenneth Grahame, Sir George Douglas, William Archer; R.B. Cunninghame Graham, John Davidson, George Douglas Brown – only four of whom survive. John Buchan, with Neil Munro, should certainly have been included in that gallery; their absence is unaccountable. The omission of neither is explained by the author's prefatorial remark that 'one or two writers are excluded for the reason that they are not modern in outlook; some have been left out of account, either because their reputations are not firmly established, or their works are not of sufficient importance to warrant consideration.' On the first count none of the twelve – except Archer and Cunninghame Graham – were 'modern' in any sense in 1917: Buchan is in every respect as 'modern' as any of them ever were except Davidson and Brown. His reputation is – and was then – as well established as that of any of them save R.L.S. and, perhaps, Barrie. And Robertson Nicoll never wrote anything of the slightest – other than commercial – importance. Barrie alone is just mentioned in Henderson's *Scottish Vernacular Literature* (1910), but, although Buchan had not then published his *Poems Scots and English,* he is one of some half-a-dozen who within the next few years called for no little modification of the concluding sentence of that excellent book which declares that 'as regards vernacular poetry, his (Burns's) death was really the setting of the sun; the twilight deepened very quickly; and such twinkling lights as from time to time appear only serve to disclose the darkness of the all-encompassing night.' When a new day is indisputably dawning we can afford to smile at the resignation of those who regarded the nightfall as the end of the world! It was, of course, impossible at that time to foresee that fourteen years later Buchan was to perform a very notable service by issuing *The Northern Muse*, which stands in relation to Scots poetry as Palgrave's *Golden Treasury* to English, and is in even respect worthy to sit cheek-by-jowl with the latter: a labour of love, equipped with a delightful apparatus of notes which shows what a fine, and so far as Scots letters are concerned hitherto quite unequalled, critic (conservative albeit rather than creative) other, and less necessitous, branches of literature have so largely denied us in this Admirable Crichton: a definitive book, supplying a long-felt want in a fashion that seems likely to give such an impetus to Scottish poetry that it will stand as a landmark in our literary history not far from the beginning of what seems destined to be known as the period of our National Renaissance. It was, indeed, compiled in the renaissance spirit – literary merit being the criterion of selection. It was not too rigorously applied, perhaps, but Buchan thus quietly, but decisively, aligned himself with the younger men who were clamouring for the erection of literary standards in Scotland comparable to those obtaining elsewhere. It will probably be unique among his works in its effect. His influence otherwise has been almost wholly social, only very obliquely, if at all, cultural, and never literary. Professor Gregory Smith's *Scottish Literature* (1919) does not mention him either – or any other living writer save Barrie and Neil Munro – but then his book is a brilliant bit of special pleading on behalf of certain theories of Scots letters capable of being applied and extended in ways of which he did not wot: and certainly in his concluding section, 'A Modern Epilogue,' he was driven from excellent premises to false conclusions by his failure to more than casually allude to John Davidson, Robert Buchanan, George Douglas Brown, and 'Fiona Macleod' (to name no more) and his total ignoring of Cunninghame Graham, Buchan, Charles Murray, Mrs Violet Jacob, and others. Much, however, can be forgiven to the man who declared that 'we rule out the whole company of "stickit ministers" and all the things done and said within reach of the "bonnie brier bush."'

Buchan bulks most largely in the public eye as a novelist, no doubt. It has been well said that, with the brilliant exception of Sir A.T. Quiller-Couch, he has inherited more of the Stevensonian spirit and tradition than any other modern writer, although with more classical restraint. I am not surprised, however, that he is not mentioned in Gerald Gould's *Contemporary English Novel*. The interpretation of that statement depends upon how one rates the Stevensonian spirit and tradition. If I had been going to write essays on the fifty principal English (or British) novelists, Quiller-Couch's name would not have occurred to me; nor Mr Buchan's. Living Scottish novelists would be another matter in which Buchan would deserve a very substantial chapter to himself. But this is only another way of saying that the novel in Scotland is on a plane where molehills are mountains. I can agree with all the grateful things that can be said about Buchan's novels: I owe them many happy hours: but it is essential despite one's private likes and dislikes to preserve a sense of proportion: some people apply such adjectives to Buchan that one wonders how their stock would last out if they had to deal with the literary world as a whole. (After all these *are* the days of relativity – but nothing that I am saying gainsays the fact that Buchan's books abound in loving and delightful studies of Scottish landscape and shrewd analyses and subtle aperçus of Scottish character, and are, of course, indispensable *en bloc* to every Scottish library and *seriatim* to every Scottish reader worthy of the name. Only——!) In our literary history, Buchan as a novelist will be of the respectable but unexciting company of James Grant, William Black, and George Macdonald – well above the Crocketts and Ian MacLarens. His fiction well deserves its vogue: would that many whose popularity is greater wrote half so well. But that is saying little! And very moderately-sized in the British scale, his work as a novelist disappears entirely in the light of European assessment. There are no doubt worthy folk who regard *Chambers's Journal* as an organ of culture; Reginald Bickley's remark in a *Bookman* essay that 'in his own peculiar manner Buchan is probably the best modern exponent of the short story' must have been designed for the consumption of such, if (for it is most ambiguously framed) it means what it appears to mean. Even if it only means that Buchan excels in the particular type of short story he writes it shows a remarkable ignorance of the modern short story of (for so this journalist correctly enough classifies Buchan's work) 'the classical-romantic school, with all its restraint and severity of style; its poise and balance; the coldness even of its romance; the clear-cut concise phrase.' If he meant that Buchan was the best contemporary British exponent of a demoded form he was right; as again he would have been had he termed him the best living Scottish short story writer (leaving out the 'new hands' who are just beginning to be noticed). In an intermediate and very interesting form the present writer must confess an abiding predilection for *A Lodge in the Wilderness;* dated, and in some ways badly, though the speculations are in that very dissimilar variant of *The New Republic.*

There remain, chief amongst the remainder, Buchan the biographer, the historian, the essayist, and – the man. His work as biographer stands between (but well to the good side!) Lytton Strachey's and the conventional biography he trounced. It lacks the verbal and stylistic brilliance – and also the malice – of the new mode; but it is high above the ruck, in an air of integrity and excellent commonsense, devoid of dullness, of its own. *The Marquis of Montrose* should certainly be read by every Scot. As a war historian, he accomplished a *tour de force:* his work is far better than most war histories – in its handling of the stupendous masses of fact, in its lucid exposition of the factors in play, in its general balance and tone; but in the nature of things it could only serve as a useful contemporary outline (a means of seeing the wood despite the trees), and have little, if any, permanent value. The way in which he carried through his tremendous task, however, illustrated his wonderful capacity of organisation and his resource in affairs. His essays are the most delightful written by any contemporary Scot.

The man himself, with this great tale of work to his credit, is utterly unspoiled: and his best is probably yet to come. Mr Bickley has said that 'he has but to weave some of the joy and laughter of his own sunny personality into his work to reach that wider public that demands that an author shall amuse as well as enthral.' I venture to hope that his aim shall be not to reach that wider public but the smaller one which matters infinitely more. It is true that 'we still wait for the great work, the more ambitious flight of his matured imagination' – he can well afford to shed some of his present popularity and bigger sales should certainly be his last objective – and, if I may suggest a clue to his comparative failure and the means whereby he may yet redeem it, it will be *via* the advice, opposite of that usually given which has betrayed many a splendid Scot, 'to haud *North*,' for, just as R.L.S. is indubitably best the 'Scotcher' he is, so John Buchan may well find that his sister, better known as 'O. Douglas,' gave him a true hint as to the direction along which he may yet realise his undoubted genius when, addressing the Vernacular Circle of the London Burns Club, she said that 'if we lose our old Scottish tongue we lose our biggest and best chance in literature.'

Books referred to: – *Modern Scottish Writers*, W.M. Parker (Messrs W. Hodge and Co.); *Scottish Literature*, G. Gregory Smith (Messrs Macmillan and Co.); *Scottish Vernacular Literature*, T.F. Henderson (Edinburgh: John Grant); *The Realistic Revolt in Modern*

Poetry, A.M. Clark (Oxford: Basil Blackwell).

John Buchan's books include: – Novels: *John Burnet of Barns*, *Prester John*, *Salute to Adventurers*, *The Thirty-nine Steps*, *Greenmantle*; Short Stories: *Grey Weather*, *The Watcher by the Threshold'*, *The Moon Endureth*; Essays: *Scholar Gipsies*, *Some Eighteenth Century Byways*; Politics and Travel: *The African Colony*, *A Lodge in the Wilderness*; History and Biography: *Sir Walter Raleigh*, *The Marquis of Montrose*, *A History of the War*; Poetry: *Poems Scots and English*, *The Northern Muse* (Anthology), etc., etc.

Mr Bickley's article referred to appeared in *The Bookman* Special Xmas Number, 1912.

[19.6.25]

2. Sir J.M. Barrie

In the essay on Charlie Chaplin in the Fourth Series of his *Contemporary Portraits*, Frank Harris reports Chaplin as saying, while talking of a visit to London, 'Oh! I saw Barrie – Sir James Barrie; he is getting old and takes himself very seriously. He criticised my "Kid," telling me that all the heavenly part was nonsensical, "absurd and worthless."' 'The author of "Peter Pan,"' added Chaplin, with dancing eyes again, 'the inventor of the crocodile with the clock in its stomach, seemed to think my scene in Heaven absurd and therefore worthless, as if the two adjectives were synonymous,' and Charlie grinned again. Chaplin has got a smile that not only lights up his eyes and mouth, but lights up the man he is talking about with irresistible kindly mockery. Of course, everybody knows perfectly well that the absurdities of *Peter Pan* have made Barrie a millionaire! – and certainly there are elements in Barrie, and these the elements which have won him his world-fame and his wealth, which cannot be adequately treated save with irresistible, if kindly, mockery! The 'bipsychic duality' Barrie has invented for himself, christening one-half M'Connochie, only serves to throw into clearer relief the incompatible elements so curiously associated in his life – but however psychologically amusing it may be such a juxtaposition establishes an internal dichotomy which is the antithesis of genius. That a house so divided against itself can really stand is against nature: literary history is, however, full of examples of the achievement of a temporary equilibrium which, for the time being, succeeded famously and gave all the appearance of permanent success. But once such a Humpty-Dumpty falls, as fall it must, not all the king's horses and all the king's men can set it up again – although, to be sure, clever press-agents may succeed for an indeterminate period in continuing to make the Great Public believe that it has not fallen, and cannot fall, but remains *in situ* and intact.

The literary world is an amusing place. A highly-diverting light shoots out obliquely and irradiates Barrie's shrinking little figure from such a sentence as this of Arnold Bennett's: 'I see that Dr Robertson Nicoll has just added to his list of patents by inventing Leonard Merrick, whom I used to admire in print long before Dr Nicoll had ever heard that Mr J.M. Barrie regarded Leonard Merrick as the foremost English novelist.' Critical ability is certainly the last quality that need be looked for in Barrie; and, above all, self-criticism. My own opinion would be frankly that it is unfortunate that he ever turned to drama – were it not that despite certain rare elements of psychologising subtlety in *Tommy and Grizel* (which I hold to be by far his most interesting, characteristic and promising work – albeit the promise has never been redeemed), I am by no means sure that even so he would have made sufficiently good in a literary sense to counterbalance the monetary and other sacrifices he would undoubtedly have made. On the whole, I am afraid that – since the choice must be made – in preferring mammon to God Barrie has not refused services of any very particular value to the latter: the regrettable thing is that he has contributed so powerfully to the former. In other words, there is little to choose between M'Connochie and Barrie. I have no difficulty, of course, in going so far as Miss Agnes Stewart who says that Barrie's 'characters have more individuality than those of the average "Kailyairder."' Quite: but that is to say – what? I cannot accord any very high place save in the restricted field of Scottish letters either to Neil Munro or to Barrie: but the fact that the former is more exclusively Scottish, and that in respect of certain portions of his mixed output the latter has secured world-fame, only need to be analysed by anyone who knows anything about contemporary circulations qualitatively to show why a certain meed of respect cannot be denied to the former, to which the latter is entirely unentitled. Even in times such as the present, I am sure that no writer worth his salt would not rather have 'failed' with Neil Munro than 'succeeded' with Barrie.

I must leave it to Mr W.M. Parker and his like – they have the satisfaction of knowing that an infinitely greater public than any I appeal to will endorse their views, and even admire their manner of expression – to write this sort of thing: 'They say, he came from Kirriemuir, N.B., and he himself even hints at it, but we know differently – don't we? Fifty-seven years ago, forsooth, why 'tis only twelve years since he fell to earth with his brother snowflakes. What a pure and delicately scooped-out snowflake he is too!' This is the sort of thing that is instantly accepted by the Big Public as exceedingly clever literary criticism. It is, of course, fudge! There are certain styles in which it is impossible to tell the truth –

to maintain any intellectual integrity – and the above quotation exemplifies one of the commonest of them infesting what presently passes for literary journalism. But it is precisely in that style that most of his admirers think of Barrie – that sort of sugary sentimentality is indispensable to thorough participation in the great Barrie legend. It cannot be overemphasised that a reputation dependent upon such assumptions as underlie the phrase 'brother snowflakes' is likely to disappear like them – and the sooner the better. It is destitute of reality. And criticism must be founded on reality. 'Like his brother snowflake, Peter,' continues the fanciful Mr Parker, 'he (Barrie) will never grow up.' I agree: that is why his work is already dating. I do not envy anyone who at some moment in his life fails to wax enthusiastic over Peter and Wendy, Sentimental Tommy, and so forth; but I envy still less anyone for whom these do not more or less speedily become intolerable. After the 'first fine, careless rapture,' Barrie is acceptable only in increasingly homoeopathic doses: no matter what happens to Peter, other people – if they are not born idiots – grow up; and it is therefore certain that Barrie's immortality will be of an exceedingly partial and intermittent kind. The quintessence of Barrie shares the unseizable attributes of quicksilver: but for that single scintillating fly-away element the work upon which his great reputation rests would be altogether negligible. No fame of equal dimensions – and profitability – ever depended on so exiguous a factor. This element is *sui generis* – it defies analysis – it exists in almost infinitesimal quantities – it is certainly priceless. Barrie takes his place with the inventors of the fairy-tales – but he is less than most of these unknowns; his achievements are derived, in part at least, from theirs, and he would be a daring individual who would affirm that Peter Pan will live as long and affect as many people as profoundly as Jack of the Beanstalk has done, or that Mary Rose can take her place alongside Cinderella. Barrie has deftly caught some of the qualities of mythic composition; but his work lacks the profound unsearchable power of the true myth. His triumphs are hollow; he misses the core of the matter. And as a master of absurdity, a manipulator of the irrational, he falls far short of Edward Lear and Lewis Carroll at their best. He seldom gets beyond mere sentiment. He nowhere reaches that purely poetic and phantasmagoric plane upon which his kind of work could conceivably be carried to the nth degree. And great art of whatever kind is great only in so far as it approaches that unachieved nth which, like an unseen star, can nevertheless be accurately enough located. His work is destitute of spiritual purpose; it is *réchauffé* Maeterlinck gaudily tricked out and spiced with insincerity.

When he first set his easel up on the banks of the Quharity, [says
Dixon Scott,] his intention was to paint the simple truth; if the reader
will glance back at his earliest canvases, the opening studies in *Auld
Licht Idylls*, he will see that their manner is the circumstantial one of
Galt, with perhaps a touch of Thoreau of 'The Winter's Walk,' and
just a trace of the truthful Stevenson of 'Pastoral.' They are not 'idylls'
at all; the word was used ironically: the artist's idea was to show us,
with a dogged Dutch fidelity, the dour reality of our sentimentalised
Arcadia. He would bring out the slowness of these weavers – their
ludicrous love-making; he would paint 'the dull vacant faces' of the
Tammas Haggarts and Pete Lunans as pitilessly as any Degas drawing
washerwomen. And then, suddenly, came a change. Tammas began
to grow eldritch. Pete became a quaint gnome. Gnarled idiosyncrasies
sprouted, the stolid features swelled or shrunk; Thrums grew into a
goblin market, all quirks and wynds and cobbles, its weavers were a
race of hobnailed elves.

All this is true enough. I have no objection to any artist doing what he
likes with the world ('intermingledons' as Burns called them of the realistic and the incredible are nothing new in Scottish literature), but – there
are ways and ways of dealing with it, and the consensus of competent critical opinion throughout the ages does not look for results of any particular
artistic moment from the particular process Barrie was constrained to
adopt: and in these post-Freudian days the matter is susceptible of ready
explanations which do not redound to the credit of Barrie's mentality.
Nor are Dixon Scott's subsequent reflections on Scottish psychology any
longer tenable by anyone competent to discuss the matter.

Barrie feared sentiment, [he says,] because, as a Scotchman, he loved
the seductive thing too well. Ours is a queer country. Caresses being
rare in it, we gloat furtively over the idea of them. Prettiness and
daintiness seldom appearing among our lean naked hills, we write
passionate poems about tiny daisies and gemmy-eyed fieldmice.
Endearments and graces which you think nothing of in the South,
making free with them, with wondrous hardihood, every day, are
always invested for us with a dark dreadful deliciousness; the
suppressed love of tenderness, felt by every human heart, is made
feverish by the fascination of the forbidden.

To go no further, Dixon Scott knew little of poems about mice and
daisies if he thought them a Scottish speciality – they are nothing of the

kind: Verlaine wrote wonderfully of mice – and his whole hypothesis (his erotic misconception of his country gives his measure as a critic) is built on equally false premises. The chief of these is that Barrie is a great writer – that he is of any particular literary or intellectual consequence. His popularity, which is an entirely different matter, is not in dispute, and the causes and consequences of that would take us far afield into questions of human destiny, educational purpose and method, and the way in which public opinion is formed and directed. But it has been well said that the opinions of a million incompetent persons are no better than the opinion of one incompetent person – Barrie's immense popularity is no evidence of his literary quality. So far as Scottish literature is concerned, Barrie has long severed any effective connection he ever had with Scottish life or thought: the great bulk of his work has been conditioned by the requirements of a vehicle – the commercial theatre – entirely non-Scottish in its evolution and present condition, so that, despite the fact that he is a Scot, he is the very antithesis of anything that can legitimately be called a Scottish dramatist: and so far as Scottish psychology is concerned he has only used those stock-conceptions of it – adroitly enough remanipulated to achieve effects of novelty – the general acceptance of which has so largely prevented the profitable (in other than a financial sense) – *i.e.*, the realistic – exploration of our racial genius in every branch of art.

G.J. Nathan has described Barrie's work as 'The triumph of sugar over diabetes,' and Ludwig Lewisohn has said of him:

> His plays are commended for their purity. He surrounds with the gentlest pathos and all the beauty he can comprehend a triviality of soul that is as shameful as one hopes it is rare. Spiritual triviality – we come very close to Barrie with that phrase. He makes harsh things sweetish and grave things frivolous and noble things to seem of small account. No wonder he is popular among all the shedders of easy comfortable tears. He dramatises the cloud in order to display its silver lining... Barrie's imagination is as uncontrolled as his ideas are feeble and conventional. Yet this is the dramatist whose position is seriously undebated. This purveyor of sentimental comedy to the unthinking crowd deceives the semi-judicious by moments of literary charm and deftness and mellow grace that recall the years when he wrote *Sentimental Tommy* and *Margaret Ogilvie*. But these years are gone. His noisy stage successes have left him increasingly bare of scruple, of seriousness, of artistic and intellectual coherence. They

have left him 'whimsical' and false and defeated in the midst of wealth and fame.

I agree, and have only one word to add to that. It is this – Courage!

See article on Barrie by Dixon Scott, *The Bookman*, Special Xmas Number, 1913; George Jean Nathan's *The Critic and The Drama*, New York, 1922; Ludwig Lewisohn's *The Drama and The Stage*, New York, 1922. See also Patrick Braybrooke's *J.M. Barrie* (Drane's) 1925, and Barrett H. Clark's *A Study of the Modern Drama* (Appleton) 1925, a comprehensive survey of its subject from the time of Ibsen to the present day. [26.6.25]

3. Neil Munro

There are quite a large number of competent well-read Scots even today – albeit fewer than there were ten years ago, and like to be progressively fewer as the years pass and post-war mentality asserts its complete difference from pre-war or wartime mentality – who swear by Neil Munro and regard him as a great writer. There is no need to be hard upon them for this misconception: rather let us seek to understand it – for it is perfectly, if a little subtly, understandable, and understanding of it is a key to many other things in contemporary Scottish literature. For the truth of the matter may be just as dogmatically – if regretfully! – stated as the untruth is: Neil Munro is not a great writer, he is not even a good writer – at best he is no more than a (somewhat painfully) respectable craftsman. The opposition of a mere denial to a mere assertion does not carry us far, however – although it is necessary, perhaps, (since a certain type of mind regards a dogmatic statement provided it be complimentary – and, more especially, if it accord with popular opinion – as almost a self-evident truth, whereas an adverse judgment is suspect in proportion to the force with which it is stated) to emphasise that any opinion is as good as any other so long as it remains a mere opinion. But the test of the matter is comparison. Let those who so esteem Neil Munro simply be asked to 'place' him – either in relation to British, or to European, literature. I venture to assert that few of his admirers will be found able to do so with any convincingness – which simply demonstrates that their admiration for him has causes rather than reasons, and that their predilection for him, however creditable it may be on other grounds, is destitute of literary judgment. The more intellectually honest and competent of them will speedily discover, confronted with such a demand, that Neil Munro has literally no place in British, let alone European, literature: he simply does not count: his existence – his popularity – is simply a commercial phenomenon, an element (of a comparatively very restricted nature) in contemporary entertainment, of no particular literary consequence at all. It is only when one narrows the field to – not British nor European but – contemporary Scottish literature that he acquires any appreciable stature as an artist.

It is inconceivable that any responsible literary critic to-day should endorse, as having been even plausibly true then, what Andrew Lang said of 'The Lost Pibroch' – that 'in "The Lost Pibroch" we meet genius as obvious and undeniable as that of Mr Kipling... Mr Munro's powers are directed to old Highland life, and he does what genius alone can do – he makes it alive again, and makes our imagination share its life – his knowledge being copious, original, at first hand.' Andrew Lang to-day has no tittle of reputation as a literary critic – less even than he has a poet, despite his four-volume collected poems which all due efforts of piety allied to publicity failed to make less than a complete failure. Typical enough of the sort of thing that is said by reviewers in every generation of all sorts of writers, the futility of his remarks quoted above should have been when they were made – and should be now – only too apparent on the slightest examination. What do they amount to? Nothing but words. Take the remark about genius. What is life? Is this an adequate definition of one of the powers of genius? Could it not be equally well – or ill – applied to all sorts of writers without telling us anything about their specific powers and distinctive qualities? Knowledge at first hand is immaterial: as Arnold Bennett and others have shown some of the most brilliantly realistic writing in the world has been done by writers who had never seen what they were writing about. So I could go on. These two or three sentences of Lang's contain all manner of critical *non sequiturs* and, in the last analysis, mean nothing but amiability! It is upon comments of this kind that Neil Munro's (all things considered) not inconsiderable reputation has been built: but it is destitute of critical foundation. His work has never really been subjected to criticism. I know of no competent essay – or, such is the state of British journalism, review – devoted to him. If a tithe of what Lang said were true he would be one of our most critic-neglected contemporaries.

George Blake, writing on him in *The Book Monthly* (June 1919), in a curious blend of useful fact and futile hyperbole, said, *inter alia,*

> Sensitive to the most minute degree, this artist shrinks from the merest suggestion of professed artistry. He has no mannerisms and

no arrogances; he conceals the author beneath the mask of the journalist – he is a bundle of inhibitions successfully decked out as a man of business... His first published story appeared in the *Speaker* in 1893. The collected tales were published in 1896 – *The Lost Pibroch, and other Sheiling Stories*, and lo! Britain had a new author. His style was exotically beautiful. (Mr Munro acknowledges a debt for rhythmic sense to Alexander Smith's *Dreamthorp*.) His romance was pure Celtic, fundamentally different from that of Scott and Stevenson. His plots had all the swiftness and fatality and economy of short story perfection. So the wise critics marked his name; Henley and Lang proclaimed it abroad. It remained for Neil Munro to carry on the good work. This he has done beautifully, if sparingly.

So far we can go with Mr Blake, with an indulgent smile for what could pass as exotic thirty years ago, the reservation that *wise* in its application to Henley and Lang as critics has an illuminating meaning of its own and is certainly not synonymous either with judicious or prudent, the feeling that the art of the short story is a subject that is more than a little beyond Mr Blake and that at least 'the half has not been told' here in relation thereto, and finally the caveat that what he says about 'a bundle of inhibitions' says a great deal more than he imagined, and reveals the truth of the matter in a fashion inconceivable to him.

'Short story perfection'? – That forces some impossible comparisons – with Maupassant, Poe, Chekhov, Bunin, Katherine Mansfield, and several scores of others: but Munro cannot be thought of in comparison with any of these: he must – to do justice to him – be compared (to his great advantage) with Ian Maclaren, Barrie, Galt (and still I think to his advantage but slightly) with Stevenson, Fiona Macleod, and even Cunninghame Graham, though he is an inferior stylist to either of the two last-named, and lacks entirely Macleod's amazing powers of word-painting and of spiritual insight, even if he *is* more faithful to the scenic facts and psychology of his chosen region and types. But I part company with Blake most decidedly when he goes on to say: 'He has done classic work; it is enough. If you would test that judgment, read first a short story called "War" in *The Lost Pibroch* anthology, then "Young Pennymore" in *Jaunty Jock and other Stories*. Finally, read *Gillian the Dreamer* and learn how a major artist reveals the artistic soul.' (A phrase that has a perilous affinity to sob-stuff!)

Now the fact of the matter is simply that Neil Munro is a minor artist and even so lacks the personality to make the most of the limited, yet

indubitable gifts, he possesses. He has consistently served two Gods –
and has not succeeded in avoiding the consequences of divided alle-
giance. His persistence in remaining a journalist instead of devoting
himself entirely to letters is illuminating. It argues, perhaps, self-criticism of an uncommon penetration. He was not a great journalist in any
sense of the term; it is difficult to imagine why any man of even such parts
as he had should continue to devote himself to work that in the last
analysis can only be regarded as useless – unless it were sheer economic
necessity, or an incurable hesitancy to 'burn his boats behind him.'
Inhibitions! That is the fault of all his writing – the inability to let himself
go; a defect of temperament, and, perhaps, an infirmity of will, at war with
his best instincts, and, on the whole, winning! His reticence, a certain
high, if narrow, integrity, an aversion to log rolling, to being classed with
any school, and so forth – qualities not without their value in contemporary letters, and which must certainly be acknowledged here – are, after
all, comparatively unessential matters, when a 'house is divided against
itself and cannot stand'. Neil Munro is the lost leader of Scottish
Nationalism. He has chosen to be without following and without influence. That he has carried off his spiritual unsuccess with a certain air, a
melancholy reserve, goes without saying in a Celt, touched as he has been,
however ineffectually, to the higher things. He is a promise that has not
been kept and while it is not permissible, and perhaps not possible, to
describe here just how and why it came to be broken, I may speak perhaps
of such a thing as a disabling fear of life, a soul-destroying tyranny of
respectability, and add that I never think of the essential problem of Neil
Munro – who went so far and yet could not encompass that 'little more
and how much it is' – without remembering what Frank Harris says:

> Or take John Davidson, a poor little Scotch lad who brought it (genius)
> to a schoolmastership and came to London. He, too, wrote magnifi-
> cent poetry and great prose, yet at the height of his achievement at
> fifty years of age, standing surely among the greatest Englishmen of
> his time, he blew his brains out because he could not endure the
> poverty and daily humiliations of his life. For all the great ones there is
> the crown of thorns, the dreadful valley of humiliation, and the
> despairing loneliness of Gethsemane, even if they do not fall beneath
> the Cross and suffer the agonies of Calvary... The great poet, the
> supreme artist, must have all the handicaps, in my opinion; must know
> the extremes of poverty and misery and humiliation, or he will never
> reach the cloud-capped heights.

So I think unworthy hesitations – whatever their nature, economic, moral, psychological – have made Neil Munro 'unequal to himself'. All men have spoken well of him. He has preferred the little wars of Lorn to the conflict of real life in which he ought to have engaged. His literature is a literature of escape – and, in so far as it has succeeded in escaping, in being a sort of antithesis of self-expression, a substitute for it, it is without life – for life cannot escape from its destiny! And it 'succeeds' in that way to an extraordinary degree. I do not think any of his prose work will live. It nowhere verges upon major art. As to style, certainly Munro conserved a creditable attitude towards the written word, even towards the concept of form, in a singularly undistinguished period, 'without form and void', in Scottish letters. So much may readily be accounted to him for grace. But it was a negative achievement at best, although even so not without a tiny but appreciable value. It was a style, rather than Style, that he conserved – a style that now seems at once limited, constrained and 'precious'. It was a literary style – rather than a style of life; and upon the latter and not upon the former depends the creation of literature.

Yet Neil Munro's novels and short stories, although even now they have begun to 'date' badly, are documents in our literary history. He will be remembered as having been in some ways the greatest of his contemporaries amongst our countrymen: and his books will retain a Scottish – even when they have lost all literary – interest. Nothing that I have said impugns their eminent readability: there are certain qualities of the Scottish spirit – certain elements of the Scottish tradition – nowhere else reproduced or nowhere else so well; for the true Scotsman, savouring his heritage, he is indispensable, and for the Scottish literary student at all events he will remain so. I have read and re-read almost all that he has written, and brooded long hours over it. I could write pages of keen appreciation about each of his books. What I have said here would be unconscionably mean and ingrate were my scale forgotten. Let me repeat I am here regarding him from the standpoint of world literature – from the standpoint of a Scot who is not content that in any department of art his countrymen should fail to produce work – specifically Scottish yet universal – comparable to the best of its kind produced anywhere else. Neil Munro remains, on the whole, one of the six best short story writers Scotland has yet produced, the others being R.L. Stevenson, 'Fiona Macleod,' John Buchan, R.B. Cunninghame Graham, and (to count them as one) the Misses Findlater.

Neil Munro has also written a certain amount of verse. Most of it is no more. It has not yet been collected into volume form. One little poem – a gem of its kind – is sure of life. This is 'John o' Lorn,' already appearing in many anthologies. It is like Violet Jacob's 'Tam i' the Kirk' and Charles Murray's 'The Whistle,' a little classic of our literature. It will serve better than anything else he has written, I think, to perpetuate its author's memory. His other poems are rhetorical, windy, empty for the most part and bear a curious vague impression of having been *translated.* Perhaps here we stumble upon a real clue. Had Neil Munro never learned English – and lived quietly in an entirely Gaelic-speaking community – he might have come to his true stature as an artist. Is the cardinal flaw that vitiates all his work, so easy to detect and so difficult to explain, really the product of a species of mental miscegenation?

See 'A Wizard of the North', by George Blake, *Book Monthly*, June 1919. Full list of Neil Munro 's books from Messrs Wm. Blackwood & Sons.   [3.7.25]

4. Charles Murray

There are a large number of people in Scotland, and Scots abroad – chiefly Aberdonians – who regard Charles Murray as a great poet, as,indeed, the greatest contemporary Scottish poet and one of the very few of his successors who have inherited aught of the 'magic of Burns.' I am not one of them. On the contrary, I say that Charles Murray has not only never written a line of poetry in his life, but that he is constitution-ally incapable of doing so – his style of mind, his attitude to life, make him so, just as it is the nature of Aberdeen granite to be non-diamondif-erous. To put it in other words 'you can't make a silk purse out of a sow's lug.' The majority of his compatriots – even Aberdonians – may have little or no use for silk-purses and, on the contrary, a robust interest in porcine ears – but it would be a more than usually courageous Philistine who would contend that what cannot be denied the name of poetry without being at variance with all competent opinion both to-day and in the past (I thus throw a sufficiently wide net to allow for the furthest variations of literary taste) inclines so much to the former and so little to the latter as to thrust the latter out of the sphere of the poetical alto-gether, or, at any rate, to allow no more than that, at its highest and best, it may be cognisable as having a place on the very lowest plane of poetry. On the other hand, to make even such a modest claim for its recognition as poetry at all, seems to me most misguided – for, after all, sow's lugs have functions of their own which those who are addicted to them should frankly recognise and honestly proclaim, instead of trying to justify their predilections on false or flimsy scores.

Strict literary criticism. at any rate, cannot equivocate on a matter of this kind. Whatever Charles Murray's work may be it is not poetry and incapable of consideration as such. But from a less narrowly literary point of view – remembering that books have to sell, and also remembering that, if the choice has to be made (and any Scottish anthologist compiling a selection – or, more often, collection – for commercial purposes is faced with precisely this choice) half-a-loaf is better than no bread – it must be conceded that what is popularly regarded and to some extent 'appreciated' as Poetry is a very much wider and less finical thing than what really is Poetry, and, as such, almost wholly *caviare* to the general. In the popular poetry of Scotland today Charles Murray holds a considerable place. To discuss how that was acquired for him (for it is by no means entirely due to the kind of his work and still less to its transcendent quality in that kind) would involve us in intricate considerations as to the cultural state of Scotland to-day, the ways in which public taste is manufactured, the art of publishing and the science of publicity, and so forth, into which I do not propose to enter. But, *qua* poet, who will contend that Charles Murray at his best can be mentioned in the same breath as (to keep to Scots) John Davidson or Robert Buchanan or, even, 'Fiona Macleod' at their worst, or (if to get a better parallel it is desirable to mention someone who could 'handle the Doric') at his not-disreputable average – his worst being very, very bad just as his scanty best was extremely good – 'J.B. Selkirk'? And yet he has had a commercial success and a popular esteem far beyond that accorded to any of these. *Hamewith*, his best-known book, is in its fifteenth edition. The book was issued by Messrs Constable in the Autumn of 1909 (a number of the poems in it having been previously published in a volume issued by Messrs Wylie, Aberdeen, in 1900) and by December 1912 had sold no fewer than 5000 copies at 5s – somewhat of a record sale among new poetry at that time, despite the fact that it was in dialect. And, of course, Mr Murray is an LL.D. of Aberdeen University. Imagine John Davidson as an LL.D.! I have mentioned 'J.B. Selkirk.' He is one of the very few of our modern poets who, via the Doric, rises above verse-making at its best and achieves poetry – not at its worst! When anyone talks of Mr Murray's *mastery* of Braid Scots – although I appreciate his *uses* of it in certain directions – I think of 'J.B. Selkirk's'

Miles and miles round Selkirk toun.
Where forest flow'rs are fairest
Ilka lassie's stricken doun
Wi' the fate that fa's the sairest.
A' the lads they used to meet
By Ettrick braes or Yarrow
Lyin' thrammelt head and feet
In Brankstone's deadly barrow!
                                       O Flodden Field!

That rises infinitely beyond Mr Murray's compass. Compare it with any
passage in *Hamewith* or *In the County Places*; the difference between it
and anything to be found there is a measure of the difference between
Scottish poetry and Scottish verse – between the power of the Doric and
the merely prosaic, if vigorous and diverting, uses to which Mr Murray
puts an inferior form of it. For his particular dialect is perhaps the
poorest of them all and certainly the least capable of being used to
genuine poetic purpose.

Andrew Lang was very guarded in his introduction to *Hamewith* –
and yet not guarded enough. as those who read that preface and
compare it with his 'Unposted Letter' to Burns will appreciate. In such
slight commendation of Murray as he contrives to imply – rather than
gives – he is at variance with his other far more authentic-sounding
utterance; he is feigning a love for the haggis – or, at least, some of the
constituents or accompaniments, of the haggis – which he certainly
would have been unable to substantiate if put to the test. Confessing
himself a Scot 'whose critics in England banter him on his patriotism,
while his critics in Scotland revile him as rather more unpatriotic than
the infamous Sir John Menteith, who "whummled the bannock"' he
proceeds to say that 'the Scots of Mr Murray is so pure and so rich that it
may puzzle some patriots whose sentiments are stronger than their
linguistic acquirements.' That can easily be believed – similar gentry
abound to-day and are seriously impeding the movement for the Revival
of the Doric by their ill-founded enthusiasm – but 'pure' and 'rich'?; his
Scottish critics certainly knew him best. Aberdeenshire Scots is certainly
the reverse of 'pure': anything further from the conceivable norm –
anything more corrupt – it would be difficult to find in any dialect of any
tongue. And as to 'rich' – yes, as the 'haggis' is, in the sense in which
Lang refers to the 'haggis' in that criticism of Burns: but the very reverse
of rich in beauty-creating powers, in intellectual resource, in technical

accomplishment. 'The imitations of Horace,' continues the preface, 'are among the best extant, and Mr Murray might take Professor Blackie's advice, trying how far the most rustic idylls of Theocritus, say the "Oaristus", can be converted into the Doric of the Lowlands.' What the phrase the 'Doric of the Lowlands' means in this connection I cannot imagine – certainly Mr Murray has no command of the Lallan tongue – but Professor Blackie's advice as to Theocritus has been taken by my friend, The Rev. Wallace Gardiner, of Greyfriars, Edinburgh, and his translations – similar in kind, in tone – are to my mind superior to Murray's of Horace as verse. With them as anything else – as mere translations – a literary critic is not concerned. But the significant thing about the preface is Lang's silence as to Mr Murray's literary merits as such. All he says is: 'Poetry more truly Scots than that of Mr Murray is no longer written – was not written even by Mr Stevenson, about "a' the bonny U.P. Kirks," for, in his verses there was a faint twinkle of the spirit of mockery.' And is the spirit of mockery – the ability to take ourselves with a grain of salt or put our tongues in our cheeks so very Un-Scottish? Mr Murray could certainly have done with a *soupçon* of it here and there. It would have lightened – and perhaps eliminated – many a stodgy stanza of tenth-rate moralising and laborious 'wut.'

'Poetry more truly Scots is no longer written' might mean anything. But we know what it means. In his introductory note to his anthology of *Scottish Minor Poets*, Sir George Douglas well says – adroitly, but very excusably, understating the case so as to do no unnecessary violence to his own selection – that 'this popular character of Scottish poetry is by no means without its correlative disadvantage. The range of subject treated is limited to the comparatively few and simple feelings, the comparatively few and ordinary incidents, of an humble and uneventful life… Thus, in reading a collection of Scottish poems identical situations, identical trains of feeling will be found to recur with an iteration which only poetic beauty of an uncommon order can save from becoming wearisome.' Charles Murray has certainly made no effort to take Scottish verse out of the narrow and dismal rut in which he found it – he has done nothing to repurify a dialect which he found in a corrupt state and to put it to nobler and higher uses – and, in lieu of any distinctive and significant intellection, he is almost always content to versify platitudes and commonplaces and be a sort of miniature Scottish Martin Tupper to whom pawkiness is, if anything, an added disfigurement.

And yet – occasionally, and, above all, if not quite only, in 'The Whistle' – where he deals objectively with pure reminiscence and contrives to forego either 'drawing the moral' or 'improving the occasion' – he certainly has written verses which would demand inclusion in any reissue of *Scottish Minor Poets* and which I do not even grudge inclusion in Mr Buchan's *Northern Muse* (albeit only purely literary criteria were supposed to be applied there – unless a way out be taken, as it certainly can be found, by the contention that 'purely literary' is not quite the same thing as 'purely poetical.') In 'The Whistle,' Murray certainly reaches the top of his form – it is immeasurably better than anything else he has written – so far better, indeed, that from the average of his work it could reasonably have been predicted that he could never write anything even half so good. It will live in Scottish literature. But one swallow does not make a summer, and, though there have been instances where one poem has revealed poetic genius of a high order which for one reason or other gave no other evidences of itself, this is not one of them. On the contrary!

Hamewith (with an introduction by Andrew Lang); *A Sough o' War* and *In the Country Places* – all published by Messrs Constable and Coy. Ltd. (London).   [10.7.25]

5. Violet Jacob

I remember Mrs Jacob saying to me, apropos something I was to be writing about her, to be sure and make it perfectly clear that she was *Mrs* Jacob (since Violet Jacob, *tout court*, would have denationalised her). She is so proud of being a Scotswoman. Markedly racial in character she is yet seldom, if ever, nationalistic in tone. Avoiding narrow chauvinism on the one hand and colourless internationalism on the other, she is an admirable example of that type, essentially and most distinctively Scottish, whom circumstances have led to accept without question the cultural consequences of the established political relationship between Scotland and England: by some psychological sleight her Scottish patriotism is constrained to express itself solely in non-controversial directions and to turn a blind eye to all else: and her attitude as a Scotswoman resembles that to which J.S. Machar as a Czech confesses in his 'Tractate of Patriotism': –

> I am a Czech, even as I might be
> A German, Turk, Gypsy, or negro, if
> I had been born elsewhere. My Czechdom is

> The portion of my life, which I do feel
> Not as delight and bliss, but as a solemn
> And inborn fealty. My native land
> Is within me alone…

From the fact that Scotland is thus personal to her – a quality of her being – she cannot descend to argument, even with herself. Her work is therefore conservative rather than creative. Her readers must come to her: she does not go out of her way to meet them. She appeals only to 'the converted,' as it were: she makes no appeal to the lapsed masses for whom Scotland has ceased to mean what it means to her – regardless of the fact that unless they can somehow be reclaimed the Scotland which means so much to her may soon disappear altogether. This is too apt to give her work the effect of pose – of merely striking an attitude – which, were it real, would be alert to the dangers threatening the existence of such a spirit to-day. Lacking that recognition, and the resource that would accompany it, the work too easily acquires the appearance of mere sentimentality. But Mrs Jacob's work is far from being merely sentimental, and although very often superficially she may seem through her choice of subject and angle of treatment to be merely a belated and somewhat etherealised Kailyairder her 'direction' is subtly but none the less completely different. The difference between her sentiment even at its worst and her humour even in its most hackneyed vein, and theirs, is never less than the difference between butter and margarine.

> What is love of one's land?…
>   I don't know very well.
> It is something that sleeps
> For a year – for a day –
> For a month – something that keeps
> Very hidden and quiet and still
> And then takes
> The quiet heart like a wave
>   The quiet brain like a spell
> The quiet will
> Like a tornado: and that shakes
> The whole of the soul.

So sings Ford Madox Hueffer and it is true of Mrs Jacob's experience, I am sure: but all her work is such emotion remembered in a most deceptive tranquility: if she reveals herself at the moment of the paroxysm it must be that in her case the vibrations are so swift in their succession as to induce an illusion of immobility. She never tears a passion to rags – she simply transforms it into an insubstantialised waif of itself. There is certainly more art in the latter feat: but, practically, it comes to much the same thing in the long run. 'Life is in the movement by which it is transmitted.' The art that conceals art can conceal it too completely. Mrs Jacob is one of the Kennedy-Erskines of Dun – a history of whom she is presently writing. (Her niece, Miss Marjory Kennedy-Erskine, has recently been writing verse of some merit.) It may seem a little strange that a lady in her position (living largely outwith Scotland, too) should have so good a grip of the vernacular and should find in it her medium of most intimate utterance – but there is nothing strange about it really. There are those to-day who are deploring that Braid Scots is falling into the hands of 'highbrows' – but the fact of the matter is, of course, that Braid Scots, like any other language has never been employed and never can be employed to good effect for literary purposes, except in very rare cases, save by those who comparatively to the great mass of the people are, indeed, 'highbrows.' Those who are deploring the intellectualisation of the vernacular are those who know nothing of our literary history. The desuetude of the Doric is largely due to the fact that it has been almost entirely relegated to those who simply haven't the brains to use it – local bards who have dragged it down to the level of their own intelligences and made it a fit vehicle for doggerel that no more resembles poetry than a brokendown cart-horse resembles a blood mare. Mrs Jacob's work is like the latter – only the difference is not always perfectly clear in the confused air of minor Scottish letters because it is often the same colour as the former, and few people have an eye for difference in form.

The truth of the matter is, of course, that by far the largest proportion of work of the slightest literary merit in the Doric has been done not by 'the common people,' with whom, according to that idea, its safety lies from the taint of 'highbrowism', but by aristocrats; it is an aspect of *noblesse oblige*. Mrs Jacob belongs by birth and breeding to the company which includes Lady Grisell Baillie, Lady Nairne, Lady Ann Lindsay, Lady Wardlaw, Jean Elliot, and, to come to our own time, Lady John Scott. Who from any lower walk of life has given us work comparable to theirs in the whole history of Scottish vernacular poetry? Only Isobel Pagan, perhaps, can be admitted of their company, Tibby, as Sir George Douglas has called her, 'the withered, smoke-dried, half-witch-woman, half-smuggler, of the hovel on the Ayrshire waste.' And if none of these have proved more than minor poets, that merely reveals the inadequacy of *noblesse oblige* as an agent of inspiration.

'Mrs Jacob has this rare distinction,' wrote John Buchan in his introduction to her *Songs of Angus.*

> She writes Scots because what she has to say could not be written otherwise and retain its peculiar quality. It is good Scots, quite free from misspelt English or that perverted slang which too often nowadays is vulgarising the old tongue. But above all it is a living speech, with the accent of the natural voice, and not a skilful mosaic of robust words, which, as in sundry poems of Stevenson, for all the wit and skill remains a mosaic. The dialect is Angus, and in every song there is the sound of the east wind and the rain. Its chief note is longing, like all the poetry of exiles, a chastened melancholy which finds comfort in the memory of old unhappy things as well as of the beatitudes of youth. The metres are cunningly chosen, and are most artful when they are simplest: and in every case they provide the exact musical counterpart to the thought. Mrs Jacob has an austere conscience. She eschews facile rhymes and worn epithets, and escapes the easy cadences of hymnology which are apt to be a snare to the writer of folksongs.

'Accent of the natural voice' is a phrase that needs to be treated with care: were to be like ordinary speech the criterion, practically all true and certainly all great poetry would be ruled out, of course, nor is normalcy in a wider sense any truer test – real poetry can be quite non-human; what should be said is that true poetic utterance always conveys the impression of being the natural, the inevitable, utterance of the poet in question. It is one of Mrs Jacob's distinctions that this is peculiarly true of her work at its best – exceedingly subdued though her utterance is. In what he says of her metres and the way in which they marry her thought, however, Mr Buchan reaches the heart of the matter. This is Mrs Jacob's distinctive contribution to vernacular verse – a new consciousness of technique. It is her form, and but seldom her content, that has significance. She may eschew facile rhymes and worn epithets and escape the cadences of hymnology: but she all too frequently accepts the stock-conception, the platitude, the 'line of least resistance,' the obvious joke – and yet by mere technical variations she can give this old stuff 'the little more and how much it is,' give that elusive *je ne sais quoi* which lifts it out of the ruck and makes it indubitably poetry, however minor. In content her work for the most part belongs to a vast mass which is so bad as to be beneath criticism altogether; yet her technique raises it, ever so unobtrusively, to a plane upon which it acquires a definite if almost indefinable value. This is no inconsiderable accomplishment. 'An austere conscience' is another phrase liable to be sadly misconstrued. One reviewer, indeed, wrote: 'That is manifest. There is always the note of restraint. It is generally very effective, but the reader may be pardoned if he wishes that sometimes Mrs Jacob would let herself go more freely. There might be some little loss of finish, but there would be a gain of abandon' – an utterance all too typical of contemporary Scottish 'criticism.' It derives from a fallacy: for the writer in his mind was italicising the word 'go,' whereas the real trouble with Mrs Jacob's work can only be indicated by stressing the word 'herself' – not 'would let herself *go*', but 'would let *herself* go', which is a very different thing. And her work is always best when it is at its most artful. She drops into banality all too easily as it is.

Small collection though it was, *Songs of Angus* made far from a homogeneous book – and in her two subsequent volumes of verse the inferior element predominates still more: she drops with increasing frequency beneath her own best standard, and further. A great deal of nonsense has been written about her work – as about everybody else's. 'There is no weak number in the book,' says one writer of *Songs of Angus*. Indiscrimination of this kind is a left-handed compliment and reacts badly on many writers. Buchan rightly expressed a predilection for 'Tam i' the Kirk' (Mrs Jacob's finest – but by no means most characteristic – poem) and 'The Gowk,' which is almost as good poetry and far more characteristic of her work as a whole. But a certain reviewer in an important daily thought that '"The Lang Road"' is even more appealing.' This is so typical of Scottish artistic imperceptiveness – the refusal of, or constitutional incapacity for, aesthetic experience – that it is well worth while quoting a stanza from the effort in question: –

> Below the brae o' heather, and far along the glen,
> The road rins southward, southward, that grips the souls o' men,
> That draws their fitsteps aye awa' frae hearth and frae fauld
> That pairts ilk freen frae ither, and the young frae the auld.

And so on. If it were not almost incredible that the same hand that gave us Mrs Jacob's work at its best could descend to such flat-footed stuff as that, this essay would not have been written. But Mrs Jacob's work would have been very much more popular than it is if it had never risen above that level – but not quite with the same people. As it is Mr Buchan justly represented her in *The Northern Muse*, with six pieces, as against three by Charles Murray, one by Neil Munro, three by himself, and three by James Logie Robertson ('Hugh Haliburton'). So judged – and rightly in my opinion – Mrs Jacob, slight though her output is and exceedingly attenuated the sheaf of her best, appears as by far the most considerable of contemporary vernacular poets. In this connection it must be remembered that these poets and a few others – always minor and for the most part very minor although their work is – have produced amongst them within the past quarter of a century or thereabouts a greater bulk of work of distinction in the Doric, assessed by purely literary standards, than (except for Burns) was produced during the preceding three to four centuries – i.e., since the time of the Old Makars. And Mrs Jacob is the latest comer of those mentioned, and has transcended the others simply because she is more of a conscious artist. These are facts of significance at the present juncture. Already a little stream of influence is proceeding from Mrs Jacob's vernacular verse. I trace an indebtedness in recent poems by 'Tamar Faed,' Winifred Duke, and Marion Angus amongst others – just as Charles Murray has his little following, as in the work of Mary Symon.

Securely of the choice company of ladies I have named who have, albeit each of them but in a single poem or two, given us so much of the finest of our Scots poetry, Mrs Jacob equally belongs to the small list of Scottish novelists of either sex whose work rises – however unobtrusively – into the category of literature. For want of a stronger creative urge, she is a good regional novelist *manqué*. In *The Interloper* and *Flemington*, both set in her beloved Angus, she adumbrates herself as a potential Sheila Kaye-Smith of that part of Scotland. That potentiality has not been realised, and it is now unlikely to be: in her prose work as in her verse her output has been restricted to a minimum by a certain dilettantism (not to be despised, however, since but for it in all likelihood we would have had far more of her inferior work and less of her highest quality). Yet she has shown powers that make the slightness of her work surprising. Both *The Interloper* and *Flemington*, although written in English with but a shading of dialect here and there, are Scottish novels in contradistinction to English novels as few of Buchan's but most of Neil Munro's are. This is not merely a matter of setting but of spirit. The characters are not only nominally Scottish; they are fundamentally Scottish. Neither is a great novel in any sense of the term: but both stand in the category of respectable work in the novel form – and this is true of a relatively extremely small number of novels which are at the same time distinctively Scottish (leaving out of question the Waverley Novels).

They have therefore a value for Scottish readers out of all proportion to their purely literary value. In other words, English novels of equally sound workmanship are very numerous – so numerous that work has to rise perceptibly above even that level to merit any particular critical attention – whereas such Scottish novels are comparatively few and therefore of more importance – to Scotland.

In an excellent study of 'The Prose of Violet Jacob' in *The Northern Review* (June-July, 1924), Miss Winifred Duke – herself a novelist whose work has in some ways been influenced by Mrs Jacob's – said of Mrs Jacob's 'English' novels:

> *The Sheep-Stealers*, Mrs Jacob's first novel, is good with that excellence which just escapes being greatness. It is puzzling to say why this should be so, as the book, although long, is uniformly fine throughout and never becomes involved or wearisome... The promise of *The Sheep-Stealers* becomes performance in *The Interloper*, and achievement in *The History of Aythan Waring*. This, Mrs Jacob's third novel, handicapped by a clumsy and unattractive title, is a notable piece of work which never obtained the full recognition it deserves.

The element of truth in both these judgments has a two-fold reason behind it. In the first place, both these novels are historical novels – and the historical novel, when all is said and done, is a bastard form and seldom rises superior to the bar sinister. And in the second place, they fall between two stools. They are miscegenate work in the sense that the inverted commas I have used are necessary in calling them 'English' novels. They are really Anglo-Scottish novels: and the subtle failure that infects them despite all the fine qualities brought to their writing is due to the fact of the writer's insufficient naturalisation in the tradition of the English novel. She has failed just as, as Edwin Muir has pointed out, every other Scottish writer writing in English has failed to achieve greatness in even the second or third degree, for the simple reason that in attempting what she did attempt she was not going about her proper business. The proper business of any Scottish imaginative writer is to found or to further a Scottish – not an English – tradition. There are exceptions, of course, such as Conrad, to the rule I am indicating, but no Scot has so far proved one of them. I do not share Miss Duke's high opinion of Mrs Jacob's short stories. None of them rise above a very indifferent magazine work level. It only remains to add that such verses as she has written in English have no distinction. Mrs Jacob thus typifies the whole position of Scottish letters in a period which happily seems likely to be seen in retrospect as having closed with her work and been succeeded by a far richer one of which it afforded scant grounds for hope – in the slight body of her vernacular verse at its best, by which her name will be long and lovingly remembered, in the greater body of her vernacular verse which appertains to that 'kailyaird' to which Scottish genius has for the most part so long and so lamentably been confined, and in the divided and, in the last analysis, ineffectual nature of her prose work – as in her apparent obliviousness to the vital problems confronting Scottish nationality to-day, which a better-oriented spirit with her raciality of character could not have refrained from addressing. In other words, the present position of Scotland as a nation has deprived us of all but a shadow of the Mrs Jacob whom in less over-Anglicised circumstances we might have had.

Mrs Jacob's books include, in addition to those already mentioned: Novel, *Irresolute Catherine*; Short Stories, *The Fortune-Hunters and Other Stories*, *Stories Told by the Miller*, and *Tales of My Own Country*; Poetry, *More Songs of Angus, Bonnie Joan and Other Poems*, and two poems in one of the Porpoise Press's Broadsheet Series. [17.7.25]

Letters

CONTEMPORARY SCOTTISH STUDIES

Sir, – I have read C.M. Grieve's interesting articles on Contemporary Scottish Studies. In the article this week on Charles Murray he states – 'Charles Murray is constitutionally incapable of writing a line of poetry.'

This brings up at once the vexed question – What is poetry?

Could C.M. Grieve give some indication of what he means by poetry and how The Whistle *fails to meet it? – I am, etc.,*

R.H.

Sir, – Mr C.M. Grieve, in his vigorous criticism of the verse of Mr Charles Murray, incidentally makes some remarks upon what he terms 'dialects' of Scottish speech.

With the work of Mr Murray I am not qualified to deal; his status as a Scots poet will be duly established by his country. But I consider him a descriptive realist with a fine command of the northern vernacular – the nucleus and mainspring of the reviving Scottish language.

The basis of Northern Scots is the primitive Norse (urnordisk) *of the*

Jutish and Anglian colonists of Northumbria, between the Forth and the Humber. Before, and for some time after, the Invasions, the oldest Runic inscriptions of Denmark and Norway constitute our only records of this tongue, but its development is easily marked. In later times, it was reinforced by the distinctive Norse of the Vikings, and gradually assimilated many Gaelic words and idioms. All these ingredients, with the well-known influences of environment, tended to differentiate it from literary English (a Saxon-Norman product) and from the Scots spoken nearer the Border. It is thus a blended tongue, nearly as divergent from standard English as the modern Scandinavian languages are from one another.

The nations of the North are patriotically endeavouring to accentuate the mutual variations of their idioms, once dialects of primitive Norse. With these brilliant examples before us, surely workers in the cause of Scottish national culture cannot allow the weapon of language to rust.

The North of Scotland leads, and it is for the South to accept leadership, or furbish up their own disused tools. The word 'dialect' is sadly overworked. I trust that the day will soon arrive when vernacular Scottish literature, whether in Southern or Northern form or spelling, will be read freely and lovingly throughout our mitherland.

Without discussing the poetic quality of the verse quoted by Mr Grieve from 'J.B. Selkirk,' I venture to affirm that it is not Scots. Linguistically, it is 'neither fish, flesh, nor guid reid herrin'.' Let me endeavour to render it in the Northern shade.

> *Miles an' miles roon Selkirk toon,*
> *Faur forest flooers are fairest*
> *Ilka lassie's stricken doon*
> *Wi' the fate 'at fa's the sairest.*
> *A' the lads they eest tae meet*
> *By Ettrick braes or Yarrow*
> *Lyin' thrammelt heid an' feet*
> *In Bankstone's deidly barrow.*

'Thrammelt' is the only strong Scots word used. The thought was evidently formulated in English. – I am, etc.,

R.L. Cassie.
[17.7.25]

6. R.B. Cunninghame Graham

'The eyes of the fool are in the ends of the earth' – but R.B. Cunninghame Graham is not a fool but a victim of folly. The folly is in that condition of Scotland which almost always disperses its genius as Cunninghame Graham's has been dispersed. This involves waste – to the country first of all, and then, almost always, to the men it affects themselves, and through them to the world at large. Unable to acquire in Scotland itself that natural orientation which is available for the artist in practically every other civilised country (and I by no means use civilised as a synonym for European) he is driven out to attempt to organise himself effectively in other lands to whose cultural atmospheres he can seldom, if ever, adapt himself as can the native-born handicapped as he is by instinct at variance with that special interplay of traditions, tastes, and tendencies which characterises each and any of them. He remains a foreigner there: he becomes exotic here. Scotland – despite its reputation for shrewdness and economy – deals centrifugally with its artists instead of centripetally. And in Cunninghame Graham it has lost, to a very large extent, one who was potentially the greatest Scotsman of his generation, and, at that, a type of Scotsman, thrown up from time to time but never numerous, an example of whom on the major scale would have been especially good for Scotland at a time desolated with a nimiety of small and sordidly decadent varieties of the opposite type – which, be it confessed, is not, when timeously and adequately moderated by the presence of its antithesis, to be despised and has also from time to time given us Men as well as Mobs. The one type is to-day exemplified in, say, such forms as those of Norman Douglas, the Hon. R. Erskine of Marr, John Henry Mackay, Pittendrigh Macgillivray, S.J. Peploe, J.D. Fergusson, F.G. Scott, F.W. Bain, Isadora Duncan, and Cunninghame Graham himself, and the other in such feeble and petty travesties of itself as Joseph Laing Waugh, Annie S. Swan, Gilbert Rae, Dr Stewart Black, and the like. Buchan, Neil Munro, Violet Jacob, and Charles Murray blend elements of both with varying success. Their work is best when the former prevails, and popular in proportion as the latter predominates. It is to the detriment of Scotland that either type should be absent at any given time: it is in the nature of things that the latter should always immensely outnumber the former – but it is, on that ground, and others, all the more urgent that the over-development of the latter type should not put it in a position to reduce the former qualitatively as well as quantitatively. Yet that is precisely what has happened

– mainly as one of the cultural consequences of the existing political relationship between Scotland and England, although prior causes operated to ensure that overdevelopment of the opposite type of Scot to Mr Cunninghame Graham which secured the acceptance of the *fait accompli* of the Union and the continuance since then of a like-minded majority, sufficiently overwhelming, despite obviously adverse results in certain directions, to prevent any effective criticism of the existing condition of affairs evolving as the inevitable sequelae of the Act of Union, let alone any redressing of the balance. So Scotland is influenced by her men of outstanding genius for the most part only at third hand. They can devote only a fraction of their genius to her – and then only obliquely and with vague and indeterminate results. Scottish life is deprived of its natural self-corrective. Driven out into alien cultures, deprived of the possibility of devoting themselves to a distinctive tradition equivalent to their distinctive natures as Scotsmen, their force is to some extent at least dissipated. They might, had there been a separate Scottish tradition, as there is, for example, a separate English and a separate French tradition, have risen in it to a first rank in comparative literature – but without that, forced to fit into a foreign tradition, they are handicapped by being unable to bring to it all the essential qualities and further handicapped by being unable to entirely rid themselves of qualities extraneous to that tradition, and the consequence is that they are restricted to second or third rank. It is a measure of Mr Cunninghame Graham's power that, despite this double disability – and other disabilities which it in turn has forced upon him – he is the only Scotsman of his generation to win to the second rank as an imaginative artist – the second rank, be it remarked, in the British, not in the European or the World, scale – and it is a measure of the pass to which Scotland has been brought culturally that he should be practically unknown and destitute of influence in his native country. Any energetic parson can command a larger following in inverse ratio to his intellectual integrity. He contributes from time to time to certain English periodicals whose aggregate circulation and influence in Scotland is negligible. No Scottish periodical exists to which he can contribute: this is one of the most significant features of modern Scotland – the entire absence of any such rallying-post. A contribution from Cunninghame Graham to any of the periodicals we have (and we have not one that is purely literary) would be like a blood-mare among donkeys, or an eagle in a hen-house.

A somewhat similar, if not identical, combination of qualities to that which constitutes Cunninghame-Graham and differentiates him so

completely from the great masses of Scottish people to-day, has been the
recurring agency in the production of almost all Scottish literature
worthy of the name. That explains the dichotomy between Scottish literature in its most distinctive forms (exemplified in, say, Hermann [sic]
Melville's *Moby Dick*) and the reading public in Scotland to-day, which
regards as exclusively Scottish all that is most completely destitute of
those peculiar qualities which any careful study of our literary history
will reveal as characteristically Scottish. In Cunninghame Graham these
are carried to an excess which, however, has by no means redeemed
them from their historical disparateness and ineffectuality – so far as
Scotland is concerned. Their incidence on Scottish consciousness as a
whole remains erratic and very partial. The truth about Scottish imaginative genius is admirably put by Professor Gregory Smith in the following
passage which might at the same time pass for an excellent description
of the salient features, and faults, of Cunninghame Graham. 'One characteristic or mood [of Scottish literature] stands out clearly, though it is
not easily described in a word,' he says.

> We stumble over 'actuality', 'grip of fact', 'sense of detail', 'realism',
> yet with the conviction that we are proceeding in the right direction.
> We desire to express not merely the talent of close observation, but
> the power of producing, by a cumulation of touches, a quick and
> perfect image to the reader. What we are really thinking of is 'inti-
> macy' of style. Scottish literature has no monopoly of this, which is to
> be found in the best work everywhere and is indeed a first axiom of
> artistic method, no matter what processes of selection and recollec-
> tion may follow; but in Scots the zest for handling a multitude of
> details rather than for seeking broad effects by suggestion is very
> persistent... An exhaustive survey would show that the completed
> effect of the piling up of details is one of movement, suggesting the
> action of a concerted dance or the canter of a squadron. We have
> gone astray if we call this art merely meticulous, a pedant's or cata-
> loguer's vanity in words. The whole is not always lost in the parts; it is
> not a compilation impressive only because it is greater than any of its
> contributing elements, but often single in result, and above all things
> lively... The Scottish Muse has, however, another mood. Though she
> has loved reality, sometimes to maudlin affection for the common-
> place, she has loved not less the airier pleasure to be found in the
> confusion of the senses, in the fun of things thrown topsy-turvy, in the
> horns of elfland and the voices of the mountains... The Scot is not a

quarrelsome man, but he has a fine sense of the value of provocation, and in the clash of things and words has often found a spiritual tonic. Does any other man combine so strangely the severe and tender in his character, or forgo the victory of the most relentless logic at the sudden bidding of sentiment or superstition? Does literature anywhere of this small compass, show such a mixture of contraries as his in outlook, subject, and method: real life and romance, everyday fact and the supernatural, things holy and things profane, gentle and simple, convention and 'cantrip', thistles and thistledown.

But while Professor Gregory Smith concedes that 'there is more in the Scottish antithesis of the real and fantastic than is to be explained by the familiar rules of rhetoric,' he opines that 'the Northerner may still, and to the end of time, show "an uncontented care to write better than he can," and may continue, with varying success, to obliterate the narrow differences between his and the Englishman's use of the common speech' but it must be left to Scotsmen themselves to determine whether they will continue to embalm in this preciosity or that, excellent as it may be in itself, the embryonic elements of entirely different and thus far wholly unrealised possibilities, or whether conditions cannot yet be so altered as to enable Scottish genius to achieve its own essential synthesis instead of decorating a borrowed one with idiosyncratic excrescences. For Professor Gregory Smith presupposes the continuance of the present relationship between Scotland and England, and he is unquestionably right in concluding that as long as that subsists Scottish genius must remain fragmentary and discrete – perhaps an intuitive realisation that he was thus doomed to be frustrated and unfulfilled made Cunninghame Graham the ardent Scottish nationalist that he was until he recognised that so far as his day was concerned no saltatory developments would be forthcoming. Alas, that at the present moment, he should not inspire and lead the Scottish Renaissance movement but be instead to those of us who would fain encompass it a living example of the unregarded pass of exoticism, spiritual exile, and *fronde* to which we may be reduced!

For a Scot so significantly and unmistakably aligned with those elements which throughout our history have always revealed themselves as the most peculiar and essential elements of our national genius – albeit, in their practical artistic purposes, at all events. so utterly at variance with the 'ethos' of our nation as a whole, so diametrically opposed in 'direction' – is thus transformed into an incredible figure, the antithesis of everything that is accepted as Scottish. 'Cunninghame Graham,' says Bernard Shaw, in acknowledging his indebtedness to *Mogreb-el-Acksa* for the basis of his play, *Captain Brassbound's Conversion,*

> is the hero of his own book, but I have not made him the hero of my play, because so incredible a personage must have destroyed its likelihood – such as it is. There are moments when I do not myself believe in his existence. And yet he must be real; for I have seen him with these eyes; and I am one of the few men living who can decipher the curious alphabet in which he writes his private letters. The man is on public record too. The battle of Trafalgar Square, in which he personally and bodily assailed civilisation as represented by the concentrated military and constabular forces of the capital of the world, can scarcely be forgotten by the more discreet spectators, of whom I was one... He is a fascinating mystery to a sedentary person like myself. The horse, a dangerous animal whom, when I cannot avoid, I propitiate with apples and sugar, he bestrides and dominates fearlessly, yet with a true republican sense of the rights of the four-legged fellow-creature of whose martyrdom, and man's shame therein, he has told most powerfully in his 'Calvary,' a tale with an edge that will cut the soft cruel hearts and strike fire from the hard kind ones. He handles the other lethal weapons as familiarly as the pen: medieval sword and modern Mauser are to him as umbrellas and kodaks are to me... He is, I understand, a Spanish hidalgo. He is, I know, a Scotch laird. How he contrives to be authentically the two things at the same time is no more intelligible to me than the fact that everything that has ever happened to him seems to have happened in Paraguay or Texas instead of in Spain or Scotland.

It only remains to add to that, that, despite the Trafalgar Square battle referred to and a few other nigh-forgotten episodes, and despite the fact that he was the other day Chairman of the W.H. Hudson Memorial Committee and vigorously defended Epstein's *Rima*, which for once in England made art almost as exciting as a new soap (a curious enough feat, in itself, for a member of a nation which to all appearances consists entirely to-day of Somerville Hagues), he combines with his incredible picturesqueness an equally incredible capacity for failing to be in the news. He began well: but for those of us who are connected with either the Scottish Nationalists or the Socialist movements he has become like a curious and unseizable dream by which we are tantalisingly haunted but which we can by no means effectively recall.

And yet is it altogether *his* fault? He has suffered by the alienation of his work from a great deal of the influence it might have had, which, in turn, would have benefited his work. But perhaps it is an effect upon the movements in question of the very things they are ostensibly contending against – complementary rather than truly antithetical – that has estranged him and us. He describes how his

> prince of palfreys trots the air and makes the earth sing when he touches it – the basest horn of his hoof is more musical than the pipe of Hermes… It is a beast for Perseus: he is pure air and fire… His neigh is like the bidding of a monarch and his countenance enforces homage… Nay, the man hath no wit that cannot, from the rising of the lark to the lodging of the lamb, vary deserved praise on the palfrey: it is a theme as fluent as the sea.

In this connection then Mr D.H. Lawrence would compel his admiration: and more, for I believe that he would be at one with Lawrence when he writes, in his last book *St Mawr*, that volume of just and magical praise of a horse,

> mankind no longer its own master. Ridden by this pseudo-handsome ghoul of outward loyalty, inward treachery, in a game of betrayal, betrayal, betrayal. The law of the gods of our era, Judas supreme! People performing outward acts of loyalty, piety, self-sacrifice. But inwardly bent on undermining, betraying. Directing all their subtle evil will against any positive living thing. Masquerading as the ideal, in order to poison the real. Creation destroys as it goes, throws down one tree for the rise of another. But ideal mankind would abolish death, multiply itself million upon million, rear up city upon city, save every parasite alive, until the accumulation of mere existence is swollen to a horror… The accumulation of life and things means rottenness. Life must destroy life, in the unfolding of creation.

I am reminded, too, here, of Robert Buchanan's magnificent thanksgiving for the need for the continuance of Death – which again is evidence of Cunninghame Graham's essential connection with the real, if invisible, continuity of our Scottish literary tradition. But in that passage from Lawrence (which might, written in a different style, have as easily been Cunninghame Graham's) there is a realisation which is perhaps the clue to the failure of the Socialist movement as it exists today to prevent the existing system so infecting it that it rids itself of such men as Cunninghame Graham – and wins, instead, its… Jack Joneses. Or – to stick to Scotland – let those of my readers who know the intellectual tone of the Clyde Group make their own comparisons. Had

Scotland been his prime concern, Cunninghame Graham's declarations would have largely had to paraphrase Miguel de Unamuno's of Spain: 'the poisonous wells of what Menéndez Pelayo called clerical democracy are reopened, the inquisitorial sense of demagogy, and now the terrible cancer of Spain is visible – envy, envy, hatred of intelligence.'

Cunninghame Graham possesses to a higher degree than any other Scot of his generation those vital qualities of the Scottish genius which have during the past hundred years – so far as Scotland is concerned (and that is what I am primarily concerned about!) – been suppressed by the over-development of their own counterparts, to the detriment (by way of fatty degeneration) of these too. One who knows Scotland well, knows how well-nigh hopelessly it is bogged in mediocrity and platitudes in the last stages of decomposition – knows it as well as does Edwin Muir who happily came in it to his intense realisation of the necessity to 'support new truths against old dogmas, simply because they are new, and in being new are a mark of life, of health, and of unconscious wisdom' – may have the true measure of indignant regret that circumstances have compelled one of Scotland's greatest sons to apply his genius otherwise than to his native country – and therefore less effectively, since that which is most truly nationalistic is also most universal in its appeal. It is lamentable to find Scotland still so largely preoccupied with what is conventionally regarded as Scottish literature, the mindless vulgarities of parochial poetasters and the cold-haggis-and-gingerbeer atrocities of prose Kailyairdism and presenting an inaccessibility, of which the general Puritan conspiracy of silence, the bourgeois blindness that won't see, and the incorrigible *suppressio veri* and *suggestio falsi* of commercial journalism, are only parts, to the genius of such a great contemporary as Cunninghame Graham – the essence of whose philosophy – calculated to open the windows of most of his countrymen's minds for the first time and let in pure air – is expressed more succinctly perhaps than anywhere in his own writings, all of which it bracingly informs, and in all of which it is magnificently if less quotably illustrated, in the following passage from George Santayana: –

> What a despicable creature must a man be, and how sunk below the level of the most barbaric virtue, if he cannot bear to live and die for his children, for his art, or for his country!... Nothing can be meaner than the anxiety to live on, to live on any how and in any shape: a spirit with any honour is not willing to live except in its own way, and a spirit with any wisdom is not over-eager to live at all.

Yes! Cunninghame Graham has written for the most part about distant countries, lost causes and side-issues: but if you would know something of what the bearing of his spirit on the conditions of industrial civilisation in such countries as Britain and the United States is you must read, not only all that he has written – for the pregnant, little asides scattered through his work – but, also, I think, Lawrence's St *Mawr* and the essays of Santayana. Would that circumstances had not so discentred his own output, that the central tie-beam had not been awanting! Or that he had continued as he began to kick against the pricks, inspired with something like what Ford Madox Ford calls his friend Conrad's 'idea of the Career' – his 'belief in the ship-shape'!

Cunninghame Graham's books include *Notes on the District of Menteith* (1895), *Thirteen Stories* (1900), *Success* (1902), *Progress* (1905), *The People* (1906), *Hope* (1910), *A Hatchment* (1913), *Scottish Stories* (1914), and *Doughty Deeds* (a biography of his ancestor, Robert Graham of Gartmore) (1925). Also *Self-Government for Scotland* (pamphlet).

See *Bibliography of Cunninghame Graham* (Dulac 1924).

See also excellent essay in W.M. Parker's *Modern Scottish Writers* – excellent factually but disfigured critically by, for example, an enthusiasm for the following phrase (italicised to draw attention to its great beauty), 'Again night yielded up its mysteries to the dawn, advancing, conquering, and flushed with power' – a sentence which might as easily have been, and probably has been scores of times written by Annie S. Swan. If there was no more 'to' Cunninghame Graham's prose than that, there would be little need to say anything about him. But there is. [24.7.25]

Letters

CONTEMPORARY SCOTTISH STUDIES

Sir, – I am delighted to hear from my friend, Mr Cassie (to whose varied and valued work I shall be referring later in my series) via your correspondence columns. My main difference with him and those associated with him in what may be termed the North-East Revival is easily seen. He says that he is not qualified to deal with Mr Murray's work (in a way that implies that I am not either – and that posterity alone will be competent to do so), but later on he uses the phrase 'workers in the cause of Scottish national culture.' What is this Scottish national culture? It seems to me that unless we have very clear ideas about that to begin with we cannot very well work in the cause of it. That is precisely what is the matter with the movement in the Nor'-East corner – that, and a mental parochialism, a constitutional incomprehension and hatred of culture. I

*certainly do not see how any reasonable person can make common cause
in the interests of Scottish national culture with those to whom* Johnny
Gibb o' Gushetneuk *is a classic, and the Bible and plenty of porridge the
only other requisites to a perfect life.*

I do not quite know what he means by saying that Mr Murray's status
as a Scottish poet 'will be duly decided by his country.' In a sense it has
been: Mr Murray has a certain vogue. That means nothing to me. All
sorts of writers have a certain vogue. Why? and amongst whom? are the
questions that matter. Perhaps Mr Cassie means that a fair judgment can
only be arrived at in the perspective of posterity. I would recommend
him to read Ernest Newman's A Musical Critic's Holiday *if he subscribes
to the popular fallacy that contemporary criticism is generally wrong,
and posterity right. Literary history, like musical, gives no warrant for
any such assumption.*

My bewilderment grows as I reach the phrase 'the northern vernacular – the nucleus and mainspring of the reviving Scottish language.' I
simply cannot imagine what Mr Cassie means by this. I know, of course,
that the initiative in the vernacular revival movement came from Mr
Will, Dr Bulloch, Mr Cassie, and others – most of them Aberdonians and
personally prepossessed by the Northern vernacular. But however large
the accession of Norse and Gaelic terms in Northern Scots, its interest so
far as a movement for the revival of the Scots vernacular is concerned,
must surely depend not upon its differences from – but upon its connections with – Scots in other districts. It was, indeed, the largeness of that
accession that led me to declare that Aberdeenshire Scots is furthest from
any conceivable norm of Scots. I agree that the word 'dialect' is out of
place if it is applied to Scots as a whole – which is a language, not a
dialect. But the Aberdeenshire or Ayrshire or Mearns variants of Scots
are properly called dialects of Scots. As John Buchan says:

> The Scots speech was in its beginnings the Northern dialect of
> English, which, as a spoken tongue, soon acquired minor local differ-
> ences... As the Midland dialect became the literary language of
> England, Scots preserved its Northern quality and drew farther apart,
> developing powers and beauties of its own, though much clogged by
> an imperfect assimilation of its borrowings. It called itself English, but
> it was a substantive national speech, and its literature was a national
> literature, close enough to the common people to be intelligible to
> them, and yet capable of treating of all themes from the homeliest to
> the highest. Had circumstances been different Scots might have devel-

oped into a true world-speech, 'perhaps', as Mr Henderson says, 'more than rivalling literary English in fertility of idioms, and in wealth, beauty and efficacy of diction,' or Southern and Northern might have united in one majestic stream.

It is with the former of these past potentialities of Scots that any Renaissance movement worthy of the name must concern itself – not, perhaps, with any hope now of making Scots – on a basis generalised without regard to the dialectical purists – 'a true world speech,' but of reviving its power of dealing (for the benefit of no matter how comparatively circumscribed an audience – for if two things are of equal literary merit it does not affect their quality if the one be written in a language known only to ten people and the other in a language used by ten million) with 'all things from the homeliest to the highest.'

Nor have I the slightest idea of what Mr Cassie means by saying: 'The North of Scotland leads, and it is for the South to accept leadership.' Personally I regard the selection of Scots vernacular poetry in The Northern Muse as just about as fine a one as it is possible to make, but neither there – nor in the entire corpus of Scottish work which by the widest stretching of the term can be regarded as having the very slightest literary quality – does the North of Scotland lead. Far from it. It scarcely appears at all. The dialect used by Mr Murray is thus proven from our literary history to be by far the poorest of them all from the point of view of creative art. Nor can I agree that Mr Murray has done much worth mentioning to redress the balance. And the 'translation' of Scottish poems written in other dialects into that used by Mr Murray would be a process in which – as in Sir James Wilson's Ayrshire phoneticisations of Burns's lyrics – they would be shockingly disfigured. My quotation from 'J.B. Selkirk' may not be Scots in Mr Cassie's opinion – but it cannot be translated into English, nor yet, as Mr Cassie himself has shown us, into Northern Scots, without loss of poetic force: and it is, in my opinion, Scottish in sound as in subject, sentiment and setting, consonant with the Scottish tradition as exemplified in The Northern Muse and at variance with the English tradition as represented in The Golden Treasury. Besides, if linguistically, as I quoted it, it is 'neither fish, flesh, nor guid reid herrin',' and if to phoneticise a few words in accordance with contemporary Scottish pronunciation – as if Scots more than English were obliged to adopt phonetic spelling – and to alter 'where' to 'faur,' 'that' to 'at,' and 'used' to 'eest' is sufficient to put it right in this respect, it seems to me that we are quibbling about exceedingly small potatoes.

Considerations of that sort will not detain for two seconds any but orthographers run to seed. There has been too much nonsense of this sort about Scots literature. It is high time we were less concerned with the letter and a great deal more with the spirit – and we have certainly nothing to gain from people who are content to leave over questions of mere poetic status, but exceedingly anxious to concentrate on philological punctilio. 'First things first' will be a good motto for the Scottish Renaissance: and there are a thousand and one ways in which any Scot anxious to share in such a movement can help, more likely to be productive of useful results than the serialised lexicography into which discussions of vernacular issues are generally subverted by the word-hunters, spelling faddists and the other 'old men of the sea' who haunt Scottish correspondence columns.

I do not quarrel with Mr Cassie's definition of Charles Murray as a 'descriptive realist' (leaving over the question of his quality as such): my main point was that there was no particular reason for our fidgin' particularly fain at this time of day in welt literatur *over even a master (and Mr Murray is by no means that) of mere* naturalismus.

I had meant to reply too to 'R.H.'s' far more interesting questions: but space is limited, and I have written enough for one issue. With your kind permission I will reply to 'R.H.' next week. – I am. etc.,

C.M. Grieve
[24.7.25]

7. James Pittendrigh Macgillivray

Raising the question as to who is the greatest contemporary Scottish poet, I have frequently found myself able to disconcert people who ought to have known better by asking, after they had named so-and-so, and so-and-so. 'And what about Macgillivray?' They had not thought of him in that connection. It is amazing how few of those who consider that they are competent to express opinions on contemporary Scottish literature have the slightest knowledge of Macgillivray's poetry. 'What? – the sculptor you mean?' they asked surprisedly. Few of them know that he writes. He has escaped even the anthologists. This is not surprising in most cases; the majority of our anthologists have brought Anglo-Scottish tastes to their task which ill fit them to recognise the quality of such work as Macgillivray's – even if they so much as know of it. (And, be it said in passing, that such anthologies as the *Edinburgh Book of Scottish Verse* and the *St Andrews Treasury of Scottish Verse* show that their makers had, apart from other defects, very far from an all-in purview of their field.) But the absence of even a single example of Macgillivray's work from *The Northern Muse* is amazing, for John Buchan was certainly not ignorant of it; it is, indeed, perhaps the most outstanding blemish upon that best by far of our vernacular anthologies – the more so in that it is precisely from Macgillivray's corpus that Buchan could and should have drawn for certain kinds of poetry the infrequent production of which in Scotland he repeatedly comments upon. Macgillivray, in fact, is by far our best complement to Burns as a vernacular poet: he essays many of the kinds of poetry which were outwith Burns's range, and, to an infinitely greater degree than most, eschews mere imitation of Burnsian models and the Burnsian spirit. I would roundly submit that any cultivated Scot who fails to appreciate Macgillivray's work can only do so because of over-Anglicisation – because Macgillivray stands so wholly outwith the English standards upon which his tastes have been formed and which insidiously determine his reactions no matter how enthusiastically he may imagine that he can view Scottish and English literatures as separate traditions, his Anglicised education being effectively counterbalanced by his sharpened exile's love for his native country. It is, indeed, this delusion which has caused so many Scottish-born critics even to do Scottish literature, albeit unconsciously, the injustice of bringing to its consideration alien prepossessions: and while this has largely deprived of what should have been their natural public our old and certain subsequent Makars too exclusively Scottish to answer easily to such mixed tests, it has borne upon no contemporary so hardly as upon Macgillivray; for the simple reason that none is so purely and uncompromisingly Scottish. So far from the appreciation of English literature, which is so assiduously drilled into our Scottish school children, facilitating an appreciative approach to his work, the reverse is the case; and a glib application of contemporary English criteria of taste (and it is excessively difficult for contemporary Scots to acquire any other) only serves to deprive Macgillivray's work of that appeal which it might have to the profounder and less articulate elements of their nature which remain predominantly Scottish, despite the bright veneer of current Anglo-Scottishry, and transforms it for them into a somewhat primitive and quite indecipherable phenomenon of which they can make little or nothing. The general ignorance of the very existence of Macgillivray's work is not altogether the public's blame, since the author published it privately at prices which only a mere handful of readers in Scotland would not consider exorbitant for work of supreme quality. But he was right in doing so. It is questionable whether the result would have been appreciably different had he published it in the ordinary way at the usual prices: both his books would have been practically still-born. There is a very small public for poetry of quality even in English – let alone Braid Scots – unless along with quality, happen to be combined, as very infrequently occurs, extra-literary causes of a popular vogue: and Macgillivray's work is for the most part – despite certain resemblances which would only further baffle naive readers going to it with popular predilections – at the furthest remove from what is commonly understood – especially by Scots themselves – as 'Scotch poetry.' Despite certain superficial similarities he has nothing whatever in common with any of the amazing array of mediocrities represented in the endless series of volumes of Mr D.H. Edwards' *Modern Scottish Poets* – all of whom were dreadful examples of the excesses of self-parody into which imitative post-Burnsianism has been forced under conditions of progressive Anglicisation. Macgillivray's work, constitutionally incapable of being affected by Anglicising influences, remains free from any such distortion and degradation. The consequence is that it does not appear Scottish at all to those accustomed to wallow in the obviousnesses of Kailyairdism: while, on the other hand, it is so far removed from stock-conceptions of what is Scottish, as to be for the most part inappreciable by any non-Scot. For foreign, and especially English, readers it can only be seen in its true aspect once the independent literary traditions of Scotland are re-established in general estimation as a distinctive department of *welt-literatur,* and effectively purged of the denationalised elements which have been progressively obscuring and corrupting them for the past hundred years and more. In other words, Macgillivray cannot be properly approached except *via* a thorough knowledge and genuine appreciation of the Old Makars, from whom he stands in the direct line of descent – and, in some important respects, stands entirely alone.

Commenting on his remark in his preface to *Bog Myrtle and Peat Reek* that 'the following *not unduly polished* verses have been written from time to time during the past twenty-five years,' I have elsewhere written: –

'Not unduly polished!' The strength of Dr Macgillivray's personality stands revealed in that and many another characteristic phrase. His verse has the traditional dourness and undemonstrativeness of the

Scot. A deliberate plainness, that subtle choice of the prosaic which in sum-effect can be so startling and distinctive, a Spartan aesthetic, lift these verses into a category of their own as undoubtedly the most authentic expressions of certain well-known but seldom-articulated aspects of the Scottish genius since the days of the Old Makars. Beauty lies deep in the heart of his work; but superficial graces and allurements are rigorously eschewed. He does not meet the Sasunnach half-way. The cleavage is complete between these poems and any Scottish verse that can be regarded as a contribution to 'English literature.' Not only in subject and in the tone and texture of the language and metres employed, but in psychological content, and (to use the term in its old Scots sense) *animosity*, Dr Macgillivray's poetry is utterly different from any that can be called English... Austere and uncompromising, his work resembles the mountains of Scotland: grey, gaunt, cold, fog-bound – it is only on intimate approach that their marvellous colouring may be appreciated or their wealth of unobtrusive flowers discovered. So with these poems. They do not yield up their treasures to Tom, Dick, and Harry. A casual reading will not discover their beauties. Facile critics may well find them barren and forbidding. Dr Macgillivray does not write for such. The mountain will not go to Mahomet. Mahomet can come to the mountain, but it depends entirely upon Mahomet himself what he finds there. 'Eyes or no eyes?' These poems will measure the perceptive powers of many a reader in the most ruthless way. Those who have eyes to see, let them see.

Dr J.M. Bulloch perhaps hit upon the cause of Macgillivray's difference from most contemporary Scottish poets – and of his comparative unpopularity – when he wrote: 'Dr Macgillivray is an artist to his fingertips, and unlike many of our native artists, he can not only explain what he is driving at, but he can express himself with ease in more than one medium.' He should have added that perhaps Macgillivray's main difference from most contemporary vernacular poets is that he actually is a poet and not a mere versifier. It is an effect of the present national and cultural subordination of Scotland to England that Macgillivray's work should be so little known and less appreciated by the great majority even of that small minority of his countrymen interested with any measure of aptitude in poetry, that his name would be perhaps the last to occur to them while, were they canvassing claims for the poet-laureateship of Scotland, they would be busy with such names as those of Charles

Murray and Violet Jacob, both of whom stand on an altogether lower plane although each of them has achieved by happy accident, as Dr Macgillivray has not, a single poem which deservedly ranks as one of the little classics of Scots letters. But I entirely mistrust the judgment – and the adequate nationalism – of any critic concerned with Murray or Mrs Jacob and indifferent to Macgillivray, just as I condemn the vast majority of self-styled lovers of Scottish poetry who are bogged in an over-whelming admiration for Burns and a few others such as Motherwell and Fergusson, who belong to the same school and indifferent to, and indeed for the most part entirely ignorant of, the Old Makars on the one hand and on the other of Scottish poets wholly outwith the kailyard tradition such as Robert Buchanan and John Davidson, not to mention some of our great Gaelic bards. Mr James A. Morris has well said that,

> as a sculptor Dr Macgillivray writes verse with a restraint that is not only natural but inevitable, and while he never riots as a colourist, he yet has and in abundance all the inherent Scots temperament of poetry, colour and romance. The initial classical severity imposed by sculpture maintains, however, its traditional control, and it is this reti-cence and refinement of form that gives much of his verse its unusual aesthetic value.

The Scottish Renaissance, so far as vernacular poetry is concerned, will not get properly underweigh until Dr Macgillivray's work is appreciated at its true value, and the technical lessons inherent in it studied and mastered by our coming poets. It offers many a useful lever to lift Scottish poetry out of the dreary and denationalised rut into which it has fallen. There is one point, however, upon which I am at thorough disagreement with Dr Macgillivray – his theory of Scots as a literary medium. He believes in the use of vernacular dialects in so far only as he has a living knowledge of their words, idioms, and accents, and says that

> to assemble obsolete words from periods remote and from dialects of districts apart and strange to each other in idiom and in the pronunci-ation of the same words, may produce a kind of literary language of Scots for the scholarly appreciation of those who have no intimacy with any of our dialects: but the result, although often witty enough, and obviously truly sympathetic in intention, can never, I think, touch the heart like a true native diction from any one of the quarters.

So far as Scotland is concerned that remains to be seen; the literary history of other countries drives me to a contrary conclusion. I see no reason why an artificially and quite arbitrarily contrived 'generalised' Scots should not yet become an effective medium just as the Norwegian *landsmaal* has done. Dr Macgillivray's view is the conventional one of our vernacular revivalists or conservators: but a new nationalistic spirit is abroad and is elsewhere achieving – as it may yet even in Scotland – miracles unimaginable to an older generation. Macgillivray has justified his own methods in his own work: they were the proper methods for him. But other artists may yet arise who will have more revolutionary aims and objects and yet be not less Scottish than he is, if very differently so. Certain it is that even the dialectical integrity Macgillivray advocates appeals increasingly but to scholarly appreciation and is but little literary. And it should be remembered that Burns himself was of the opposite opinion – or, at least, of the opposite practice. For he did precisely what Macgillivray contemns – established his own canon of the vernacular – with very other results than those Macgillivray declares must follow any such attempt. And Burns's canon was, on the whole, for purely literary, as distinct from popular ends a poor one and fell far short of the potentialities of Scots. Thinking along these lines, younger Scots to-day are at all events far less pessimistic as to the ultimate fate of the vernacular than Macgillivray has declared himself to be. The – if only potential – national status of the Doric must not be lost sight of, and mere regionalism is a poor substitute for it. Nor is it only from a nationalistic standpoint that a regard for dialectical demarcation is to be deplored: Scotland is not so rich in native genius, nor so large a country, that she can afford to have her poets expressing themselves in forms which require special local intimacies, which in the nature of things few can have, from their readers if their work is to be thoroughly appreciated. And Scottish poets are sufficiently handicapped if they write in the vernacular and have, as matters stand, a sufficiently circumscribed public, without further handicapping themselves in that way by subscribing to a formula the ultimate outcome of which is progressive parochialisation and then obsolescence. Braid Scots must not be thus stereotyped into dialects: any Renaissance can only be achieved by bringing it fully into relation again with the life of the country as a whole.

Not only is Macgillivray one of the most important vernacular poets since Burns – one, indeed, of the very few real poets in any normal use of the term – but in occasional passages in some of his published addresses (notably in his 1911 address to the '45 Club in Edinburgh, appended to *Pro Patria*) he displays prose gifts which have been singularly lacking in Scotland recently. How far he might have gone in that direction had he been able to develop these gifts fully it is impossible to gauge. Suffice it to say that Scotland, despite what he has given it in other directions, can very ill afford to lose the prose of which he has shown himself potentially capable. Macgillivray has suffered not only in lack of due literary recognition and the circumscription of his influence, as well as financially, by being too wholly and purely Scottish in a sadly denationalised period: the same cause has largely inhibited him in his prime capacity as sculptor and artist by denying him the outlets he ought to have had – at least in far more generous measure – in a supposedly civilised country. These are lean enough times for sculpture even in larger and wealthier countries than Scotland, and sculpture has in great measure failed to adapt itself to the changed conditions obtaining in our highly-industrialised civilisation. Dr Macgillivray is a classical sculptor: he writes somewhere of 'the inhumanities of this age of wheels.' But then all but a moiety of contemporary Scots share his attitude; it is certainly not because he has any ultramodern proclivities that he has been so largely denied the opportunities he ought to have had – but for the very much simpler reason that Scotland as a whole has not got beyond the stage of preferring 'monumental masonry' to genuine sculpture of any kind. The difference is simply not appreciated. All sorts of tombstone makers pass for sculptors *pari passu* with Macgillivray in the general estimation – the general estimation not of the masses of the people even, but of what passes in Scotland for an intelligentsia. But it is vaguely realised that Macgillivray's 'direction' is different somehow from that of the others: their fashionable conventionalisms are preferred to his artistic integrity. He suffers too from his known attitude to Scottish arts and affairs, for political considerations affect public contracts. Macgillivray was the only sculptor associated with what came to be known widely as 'The Glasgow School' in the eighteen-eighties. I have written elsewhere that

the Art of Sculpture can scarcely yet be said to have struck root in Scotland, notwithstanding a fair start in the first half of last century. But a writer discussing the Gladstone Memorial (Edinburgh – a composite work of nine figures) justly observed: 'Scotsmen all the world over, and especially those to whom their national art is dear, will welcome a monument that carries Scottish sculpture a stage further on its line to development. For, apart from a derivation from classic sources, inevitable at this date, it owes nothing to immediate foreign styles. In bearing, it is more tense, of higher potentiality, than current English: less flamboyant and picturesque, as distinguished from sculpturesque, than characteristically French and Flemish sculpture; and worlds away from the truculence and studied barbarousness of those graven images that Germanism has recently set up. By virtue of imagination and nervous execution the sculpture of the memorial is nearer to the High Renaissance of Italy than to any lesser and later neo-classic style!'

Owing, [I continued,] to the subordinate position of Scotland and the steady progress of Anglicisation Dr Macgillivray's genius has been denied the wider outlets it should have had. One writer points out that 'as is inevitable, perhaps, in a country in which sculpture is much less appreciated than painting, the opportunities offered to sculptors in Scotland are limited, and there is little encouragement to produce work of an idealistic character... He (Macgillivray) has had regrettably few commissions for ideal sculpture on a large scale!' Not only so: but time and again those important public commissions which should have helped to strengthen the foundation of the art of sculpture in Scotland have foolishly been drafted away to London. The Gladstone Memorial itself had a narrow escape from going that road – would, indeed, have done so but for the late Sir George Reid. In other directions English predominance works to the disadvantage of Scottish artists seeking to develop distinctively Scottish traditions.

The revival in his favour of the office of sculptor to His Majesty for Scotland in 1921 – after it had been in abeyance for 30 years – may be taken as an index of the extent to which Dr Macgillivray has reversed an ignominious and demoralising state of affairs: but he has not yet acquired the influence which he would immediately exercise were a thorough-going national renaissance to develop. This happily does not affect his personal achievement, which stands ready to make its due influence felt if and when the time comes that an effective group of young men – and women – are ready to create a national school of sculpture. There is no sign of that time coming so far: but, against it, one would fain that Dr Macgillivray would write a succinct account – if only for posthumous publication – of the lets and hindrances to Scottish Art as he has encountered them. His relations with the Royal Scottish Academy – such matters as his spirited protest against the denial of a separate section to Scottish Art in the Wembley Exhibition – his knowledge of the intrigues and sycophancies of divers figureheads who occupy too much of the public eye to the detriment of truer artists – of these and kindred topics he has much to say and he would that might be of great moment to the younger men when – I will not say if – that happy conjunction of circumstances comes which, by re-orienting the minds of Scotsmen everywhere in an intensively nationalistic direction, will overthrow those influences against which he has so long, valiantly and single-handedly, contended, and let him be seen as the founder and fountain-head of a truly national school of sculpture and as one of the most delightful, versatile, bracing and vital artists Scotland has ever-possessed and lamentably misprized, despite a certain amount of lip-service, and as a giant among pigmies so far as all his self-conceived rivals in the Art of Sculpture in Scotland to-day are concerned. Pittendrigh Macgillivray – the very name is a guarantee and a slogan! He will assuredly come into his own yet.

Dr Macgillivray's books are – *Bog Myrtle and Peat-Reek* (Printed privately, 1922. One guinea) and *Pro Patria* (Messrs Robert Grant and Son, Edinburgh, 1915).
See also the following articles by the present writer: – 'Pittendrigh Macgillivray I. – As Sculptor' (*Scottish Nation*, Oct. 9, 1923) and 'Pittendrigh Macgillivray II. – As Poet' (*Scottish Nation*, Oct. 16, 1923).
Dr Macgillivray's most important public works include Robert Burns (Irvine), 1893; the Dean Montgomery Memorial, St Mary's Cathedral, Edinburgh; the Dr Peter Cowe Memorial, Glasgow Cathedral; the Sir William Geddes Memorial, Aberdeen University; the John Knox Memorial, St Giles' Cathedral, Edinburgh; and the Gladstone Memorial, Edinburgh; and the Byron Statue, Aberdeen.   [31.7.25]

Letters

CONTEMPORARY SCOTTISH STUDIES

Sir, – In reply to 'R.H.,' I would not have attempted to answer the question 'What is Poetry?' in less than a complete issue of this Journal, *but fortunately he narrows it to asking only for some indication of what I mean by it, and how 'The Whistle' fails to meet it.*

Let me tackle the matter negatively first. As E. Phillips Oppenheim says in his last novel: 'There are drawbacks to democracy. Also a ridiculous side to it. The German confectioner in the next street has exactly as much voting weight on this or any other matter as a Harvard professor who has made a study of European politics and probably visited every capital.' To explain anything of any consequence to the average audience one has to simplify and falsify it out of all recognition. It may be necessary to explain things despite the fact that that is the inevitable process but however useful such explanations may be to the people who need them there can be no question as to their comparative valuelessness. The overwhelming taste (I do not blame the masses of the people – they are the victims of the system under which we live) is for crude films, trashy literature, silly songs, and so on. Conjoined to that is an utter incapacity for and impatience with dialects, a very wide-spread refusal to think, and a detestation of 'highbrowism.' Classics are either best-sellers or a mere pose. There are as a matter of fact exceedingly few classics in this sense at all. It is nonsense to imagine that Burns, Scott and so forth are widely read by the people of Scotland – Miss Agnes Mitchell commands a far larger and more sincere public than all the classics combined. But Burns's songs are popular, you say. Certainly – but among the very people who have no use for or knowledge of poetry of any other kind, and, therefore, I suggest, for purely extra-literary reasons. This is true of all the classics. The judgment of posterity (so far as the general public is concerned) simply condemns all that is not amenable to mob taste on some score or other to oblivion – and academic criticism is mainly a matter of justifying the process. The effect is to destroy superior literary art – at any rate, as such. Now – to get down to the case in hand – I find that 'The Whistle' is becoming nearly as popular as the favourite items of Burns or as 'Casabianca' or 'The Song of the Shirt' or the latest ragtime song with the general public – in Scotland. I find also that the people in my own acquaintance who most highly esteem and delight in Charles Murray are precisely the people who have the least knowledge of or appetency for the highest forms of poetry in English or Scots – people who could make nothing of 'The Hound of Heaven,' for example, or of Dunbar's 'Rorate Coeli Desuper.' And I therefore conclude that Murray's 'The Whistle,' to commend itself so quickly to vulgar taste, must be on an exceedingly low plane and have a like status to the opinions of the man in the street, the song of the hour, the latest best-seller, or Mary Pickford's new super-production. Poems, like people, can be judged by the company they keep – and I shall begin to be interested in Charles Murray from a literary point of view when I find him having a vogue amongst the same people as, say, Thomas Hardy (as poet), Edmund Blunden and 'AE', or better still, amongst those equally appreciative of Blok, Spitteler, and Valéry.

But, to turn to the positive side, Charles Murray writes in Scots – and as John Buchan says: 'Scots poetry is apt to be self-absorbed, to become the scrupulous chronicle of small beer, to lack the long perspective and the "high translunary things."' This is a tremendous understatement of the pass to which Scots poetry has been reduced. It is generally agreed –

and easily demonstrated – at any rate that 'it does not enter for the greater contests of the muses.' If this is true of the Scots which for practical purposes can be called the canon – the Scots which is, with slight variations, the same Scots throughout the whole body of our Corpus Poeticum Boreale *– how much further incapable of poetry of any considerable degree at all must be the Aberdeenshire Scots in which Mr Murray writes, a dialect 'pang-fu' of borrowings totally unassimilated by the canon such as it is, and a dialect, at that, in which Mr Murray had not the advantage of a single forerunner of the slightest consequence. Mr Murray's work, I submit, is what could only be expected – genius lacking – under such conditions. As Buchan has said, Burns Scots was 'a literary language subtly blended from the old "makars" and the refrains of folk-poetry, much tinctured with the special dialect of Ayrshire and with a solid foundation of English, more Boreali.' Murray's dialect stands in the main outwith the whole of this tradition. Much of Burns to-day would only find, were it being sent out to editors, gratis insertion in, say,* The Weekly Scotsman *and would deserve no more. That is of the same kind – and better of its kind (if only because it came first in time) – as most of Murray's work, while the latter has to contend with additional intractabilities of uncouthness on the one hand and the clipping devitalising pronunciation with its transmutations of 'wh' into 'f' and so on.*

'The Whistle' is his best work – but what does he add even there to the choses donnés *that makes it more than a bit of neat reporting? Versification is a mechanic exercise, not always sad, but poetry subsumes it into a further dimension, giving it a moving power which, whatever its 'direction,' has an effect of finality, of completeness, and, along with that, of having achieved it by miraculous means – as Christ fed the five thousand with five loaves and two small fishes. Can anyone say that the facts strung together in 'The Whistle' undergo this magical transmutation – that they are lifted into a dimension beyond that of the prosaic? Are a little sentiment and a little humour and the elementary 'tricks of the trade' sufficient to effect such a miracle? Surely not. Mrs Jacob's 'Tam i' the Kirk' goes just a little further than 'The Whistle' – an authentic passion inhabits and informs it. But in 'The Whistle' we only see what eyes see – and never a glint of anything that 'never was on land or sea.' It is versified prose and of a* passéist *order at that: Mr Murray is one of the descendants of Lot's Wife. But even if 'The Whistle' had undergone the furthest transmutation of which such material was capable, it would have remained poetry of so minor a quality and low a kind that it would have been not worth bothering about – as poetry!*

With reference to Clive Bell's term, 'significant form,' Edwin Muir has well said, 'The germ of this theory was in Pater's remark that all art aspires to the condition of music: but Mr Bell, in claiming audaciously that all that we acknowledge in literature as pure art is one or two lyrics in which the sense is dissolved and lost in form and sound, became for a moment, perhaps out of perversity, profound. He was right. All that men in their hearts finally call art is pure music, pure fantasy... what is called magic.'

It is by the inconceivable distance that separates 'The Whistle' – which is entirely dependent upon its sense, utterly undistinguished in form, and demonstrably poor in, if not entirely destitute of, music – from anything that can be called magic that I claim that I am right in refusing to regard it as poetry in any appreciable sense of the term. I am. etc.,

C.M. Grieve.

Sir, – Mr C.M. Grieve's articles seem to have caused a flutter in the parochial dovecotes, but his candour is just what we need to rouse us from our smugness in literary matters.

There is a point in which I have a special interest when comparing the colloquial speech of the North-East and that of the Borders. I mean the sense of music in the utterance of them. J.B. Selkirk's 'Flodden Field,' emended as Mr Cassie suggests, and recited by a master of the Aberdonian tongue, would lose all the haunting sadness and sense of tragedy which its utterance by a delicate-tongued Borderer from the Ettrick Forest would convey. I lately had the pleasure of hearing it spoken by a lassie from the Forest. It was like finest music. But you cannot set down the Border speech on paper.

On the contrary, I have listened to many varieties of North-Eastern speech, and have always been repelled by a suggestion of harshness. In a well-known magazine devoted to Scottish affairs there are published many examples, in prose and verse, of the attempt to fit in a rich vocabulary of words like 'faur,' 'eest,' etc., and the result, compared with pieces like 'Flodden Field,' is like the effect of sauerkraut upon one accustomed to clear soup, somewhat inclined to heaviness.

We must have music in utterance, and no amount of the vocabulary of Buchan will provide it.

For musical speech, give me the glens of Ettrick and Yarrow, or the main street of Kirkwall, but they cannot be set down in writing. – I am, etc.,

Harry Fraser (Je Suis Prêt)

Sir, – My friend, Mr Grieve, defines his attitude towards the Scottish vernacular movement in an interesting letter, from which I am very glad to gather that our differences are not necessarily fundamental. He views the Scottish Renaissance chiefly from a literary angle, while I consider that the regeneration of our auld tongue should be among the 'first things first.'

In disclaiming ability to criticise the writings of Mr Murray, I had not the slightest intention of implying that Mr Grieve was in the same position. He is a literary man, and I am not. As a humble worker in the vernacular field, I wrote mainly from a linguistic standpoint.

I do not undervalue the efforts of the band of earnest and talented workers who prefer to use English, or an attenuated form of semi-Scots in their appeals to the soul of the nation. I entirely agree with Mr Grieve as to the value of 'Scottish subject, setting and sentiment' in work written in the English medium. But I venture to think that such propaganda, whatever be its literary merit in the medium selected, is of less vital importance to Scotland, in this period of her life, than the preservation of our own tongue in the purest and most beautiful forms at our command.

Reformers in language and literature should try to capture the good-will and enthusiasm of the nation. Only a small minority in any land can rise to delighted appreciation of literary masterpieces. But, if the popular taste has lapsed from literature and from patriotism, surely the latter should be restored first, if possible.

I believe that Scotland is now suffering from a dry-rot of English imitation, and the substitution of extraneous ideals and aspirations for those that have guided us to greatness since the days of Wallace and Bruce. These imitative ideals find expression in the vague glorification of young and free nations at the ends of the earth, in preference to the auld land, with the eager cult of Kipling and other writers who – great in themselves – are not sympathetic towards the Scottish national idea.

As one of the first antidotes to this disease, I advocate the restoration of our old tongues of Scots and Gaelic. The multiplicity of 'dialects' does not, in my opinion, constitute any serious difficulty. Their over-rated variations do not interfere with mutual comprehension. With tolerance among counties, the free circulation of printed work of slightly varying shades of expression, and the placing of Scotland before Locality, the tongue would grow and purge itself of the less desirable elements. Backed by national enthusiasm. masters may yet mould the language into a delicate and responsible literary instrument.

With every respect for Mr Grieve, I must adhere to the contention that the North is now leading in the linguistic field. We have a rich mine of potential material, which has been worked with some diligence in recent years. I earnestly hope that other districts will rescue their treasures from oblivion while there is yet time. Our first task is the realistic recording of the medium. setting purity before 'literature' in semi-English or semi-Doric. The 'semi-Doric' habit has been the bane of our writers for centuries. I would appeal to Mr Grieve and his school to put the Pure Tongue in the forefront of their programme, as a fresh and vigorous Scottish ideal.

If the nation can be reawakened to the love of the language, the rivalry of 'dialects' would become less acute, because every pure form would be appreciated throughout the land. The fittest would probably survive, or the printed medium would generalise itself – as indicated by Mr Grieve – and the speech of our country would again grow hale and hearty.

I do not agree with Mr John Buchan as to Scots being a dialect of English. The latter tongue did not exist when the Jutes and Angles settled in Northumbria. They brought the speech of the early Runic monuments – the Golden Horn of Gallepus and others. The idiom was closely akin to the Gothic of Bishop Ulfilas, and older in some aspects. The first foundation – or parent – of English in Britain is the idiom of the Saxons from North Germany. The allied Mercian – later adopted as 'English' – differed materially from Northumbrian. This is evident (among other records) from the Lord's Prayer in Durham Northumbrian and Mercian, as quoted by Mr Sweet. I am aware that it is usual to call all the tongues O.E., but I take the liberty of disagreeing with this generalisation. As I read the records, English, as a national tongue, dates from about 1000 A.D.

I think that Mr Grieve is perhaps inclined to undervalue the importance of phonetic differences between closely related languages. These slight variations, in their totality, represent the differences in the national modes of thought. If Mr Grieve will compare Swedish with literary Danish or Norwegian, or Spanish with Portuguese, I think he will see that there is something in this contention. If, then, our mode of thought differs from that of England. should it not have expression in our pure speech?

I hope you will kindly allow me to deprecate the well-meant efforts to provincialise our language by registering phonetic 'dialects' for so many counties. It does not seem fitting, either, that the preparation of Scottish dictionaries should be in the hands of the English Association. – I am, etc.,

R.L. Cassie.
[31.7.25]

8. Sir George Douglas, Bt.

Sir George Douglas is bookish but not literary. His relationship to a real critic in any sense of the term is like that of an amateur to a professional. It is not so much that he does not take the business as seriously as that he does not (in more than one sense of the term) 'make a business of it.' One can have independent means of course, and be a professional in the sense in which I am using the term; one does not require to be in any way dependent upon the proceeds of one's work or upon public appreciation – professionalism which entails any form of sycophancy or opportunism is, in fact, necessarily 'unprofessional.' It is not because Sir George Douglas is a 'gentleman of letters' rather than a 'slave of the pen' that he remains in the amateur class, nor is there a *cachet* attaching to that status that is absent from the other (save with those foolish people who affect even in a literary matter to despise the 'merely literary,' and discount expertise and specialism in favour of qualities naturally favoured by those who delight in dabbling, but are perilously aware that at any moment they may get out of their depth and so compromise on the sufficiently shallow which yet contrives to give the sensation of the adequately deep), but on the contrary! An amateur of this kind remains so because of insufficient incentive mainly, and because all is not grist that comes to his mill. He chooses his own material – the material does not bear down inexorably and incessantly upon him and strain his powers to the uttermost to cope with it. It is by the latter process that the better critic is evolved. There were great tasks implicit in the matters which from time to time came under Sir George Douglas's view, but, his position being that of a dilettante, they did not force themselves upon him and compel him to deal with them in a fashion which has not infrequently discovered unsuspected powers to himself in a man, nor was Sir George Douglas ever moved to deal exhaustively with these matters, and as a consequence the majority of the unobtrusive opportunities lurking in them escaped his notice, or he was so *épris* by some idea of his own that he failed to recognise them for what they were. In any case the tasks went undone and the opportunities unseized. He picked and chose inconsequently, and, as those who are bookish but not literary necessarily must, was generally so preoccupied with superficial phenomena that he failed to detect the underlying movement, or, in other words, failed to see the wood for the trees. And the essence of a real critic is his conception of the wood. It matters little if he ignores this author or that and unduly magnifies another, so long as he conveys the *ethos* of a particular school or movement. He is not concerned with the interplay of lights or shadows over a particular reach of water so much as with the quality and force of the current. His facts may be inadequate or even erroneous: his feelings are what matter. It is the kind and direction of his mind that is important: literary history is *corpus vile* to him. But the 'amateur' lacks, as a rule, the essential egotism and the programmaticism: he interposes only here and there as the mood takes him or some occasion demands – his work is comparatively impurposive. His work is less the product of a vital reaction than of a casual if recurrent or indeed more or less continuous impulse. His material has what importance it has: but no particular significance attaches to his own attitude towards it. Sir George Douglas is an amateur critic in this sense – in so far as he is a critic at all.

For 'literary critic' means all sorts of things. Sir George Douglas's literary criticism is a blend of literary history, biographic detail, reminiscential matter and ordinary platitudinous padding, with a minimum of original evaluation or revaluation – of the genuine independent *de novo* and *du fond* work – a couple of paragraphs of which from a mind of any moment is worth a ton of the other stuff which any hack can put together passably enough in these days of wide-spread literacy – though, to be sure, any hack cannot put it together as neatly and engagingly as some folks can. There are tricks in all trades – but the most effective conceivable presentation of matter of this kind remains at best but the trick of a trade. Why then devote an article to Sir George Douglas at all – or, at any rate, to his literary criticism? Because his position is a key to the condition of Scottish letters to-day. He is our representative critic in the general esteem of our cultured class or classes – or those of them, at any rate, who retain from one cause or another a special interest in Scottish life and letters as such: and it is against the Pyrrhonism of the spirit he and they embody and disengage that young Scots must be encouraged to direct their energies if a Scottish Literary Renaissance is to be encompassed. This is the type that has not relapsed into mere Burnsianism or Kailyairdism, still less is it denationalised – it retains an interest, unshared by any other class, in the whole range of Scottish history and literature: it buys what books are written on these matters: it is educated, and for the most part 'well-educated'!: and is as a rule well-grounded in the classics and in those whom conservative British opinion (for conservative Scottish opinion in this matter is almost indistinguishably at one with its counterpart in England) regard as the most important modern European writers. The latter are for the most part known only in translations: French is, however, generally known, and a smaller number may combine with that German or Spanish or Italian or Russian – but the percentage who are trilingual or more and really *au fait* with the literatures of these countries as conservatively esteemed – eschewing the ultra-moderns – is exceedingly small. The number of contemporary Scots thoroughly abreast of *welt-literatur* cannot exceed a dozen at the outside – and of these how many are effectively so, either as creators or critics, how many have a point of view with regard to it of either national or international consequence? However that may be, it is a matter of prime importance to Scotland that this class to which I refer, and of which, and to a large extent to which, Sir George Douglas is the representative spokesman, should be maintained in its unfashionable regard for Scottish letters as a whole – rather than for Burns or Scott or Stevenson – and for the idea of a distinctive Scottish culture and literary tradition, and that this interest and idea should be quickened and whatever evolutionary momentum resides in it released and effectively related to the position and prospects of Scotland – or rather the business of being Scottish – to-day. And it is equally a matter of prime importance that the appetencies of this class for foreign literatures should be effectively catered for and developed and that they should be fecundated with international ideas in such a fashion as to evoke vital national reactions and developments in taste and tendency, corresponding to and qualifying those in other countries. And by the extent to which he has fulfilled these functions Sir George Douglas must be judged in his capacity as a guardian and interpreter of Scottish letters on the one hand, and as *proxenos* or liaison officer with foreign letters on the other. In so far as what he has done shows him as in any measure naturally designed to fulfil these functions at this juncture in the history of Scottish letters, if only for want of better, he cannot be absolved of responsibility for what he has left undone. I am afraid that if this line of argument were pursued it would have to be admitted that so far from realising what was required in either direction he has done little to relieve the moribundity of attitude of this class to Scottish letters, he has failed even to attempt to stimulate it to any progressive position – although he may be conceded the negative achievement of having prevented it from losing even that sterile or at least comparatively profitless interest in Scottish letters which distinguishes it – while his international liaison work has been of a very scanty and on the whole ill-gauged and unproductive character. There is little or no livelier interest in Scottish letters and no wider acquaintance with foreign literatures in our midst attributable to his activities: and it may be that the existence, and comparative prominence, of these activities have prevented the emergence of other activities that would have been better conceived and more effective. For there is only a limited amount of space available for articles on Scottish letters anywhere, or on foreign literatures in Scottish papers – only a limited number of opportunities in Scotland for lecturing on either: and Sir George Douglas has taken up for many years a considerable proportion of both.

To act in either capacity is not a task to be lightly undertaken, and whoever does so must justify himself in the issue. Is Sir George Douglas a critic capable of representing his country's viewpoint in *welt-literatur* and of being the interpreter of *welt-literatur* to his country? I have no hesitation in saying that no matter how impressive they were as lectures to the least literary body of students in any European country or to audiences with the *passéist* and sometimes pedantic and sometimes wholly provincial and generally all three, proclivities of the sort of audiences available in Scotland, or however effectively they lightened the monotony of the week-end page of the *Glasgow Herald* or transcended the tittle-tattle of the usual run of 'literary' articles in the *Weekly Scotsman*, nothing of literary criticism has been produced by Sir George that would have been found capable of acceptance by, say, *The Nation and Athenaeum*, the *Spectator*, the *New Statesman*, let alone the *Fortnightly*, or the *Contemporary*, or the *Edinburgh* – and the contributors to any of these are relatively very small fry, and few achieve any real standing as critics. It is a measure of our condition in Scotland to-day that the writings of our leading literary critic should be comparatively empty and worthless, destitute of distinction in either content or form, as compared with the general level of pure literary journalism as exemplified in a score of organs over the Border. But, I will be at once told, scores of Scots write for these periodicals. Of course they do – but who are they? I know them, of course, but the Scottish reading public doesn't – they seldom, if ever, take a text from Scottish literature, they are for the most part indistinguishable from their English confreres, and certainly not one of them is a Scottish man of letters in the sense that Sir George Douglas is, living in Scotland, writing for the most part for Scottish papers and predominantly on Scottish matters, and addressing Scottish audiences. Sir George's reputation, such as it is, is practically confined to Scotland: he cuts no figure on the British literary stage as a whole. I am not contending that Sir George, who is essentially a conservative critic, ought to have developed intransigent attitudes of which he is constitutionally incapable, but simply that his work has a diathesis of progressive obsolescence rather than of effective conservation of even the little that within the limits of his disposition it has obviously been his desire and aim to conserve. Scottish letters to-day, then, must present a hopeful appearance precisely in proportion to the impatience of those, whose concern is predominantly with them (who belong, that is to say, to this class of which I have spoken), with Sir George's work – to the extent to which it is becoming recognised as intolerably *vieux jeu.* But Professor Denis Saurat was right when he said that the aim of a Scottish Renaissance in any real sense of the term in this connection must be to bring the whole range of *welt-literatur* under distinctively Scottish tests, and, on the other hand, to create a condition of affairs under which those interested in literature will, when there is anything new afoot, be at least as apt to ask: 'What is Scotland thinking about it?' as 'What is England thinking about it?' No other state of affairs is compatible with Scottish pride: and an ambition that falls below that is a form of treason to our particular racial genius and, indirectly, to civilisation as a whole. Judged by these standards it cannot be denied that Sir George's work falls lamentably far short: and it is a negative consolation to reflect that even so, within the confines of Scotland to which he is one of the few even of his abilities, let alone higher abilities, to adhere, there is no other living man of his generation who has done better than he has done. Compare anything that he has written with the 'literary' journalism of Dr Lauchlan Maclean Watt, for example, or Mr Davidson Good or Mr D.H. Edwards or Mr W. Forbes Gray and the scores of others who periodically rediscuss the authorship of 'There's nae luck aboot the hoose' or give the 'Immortal Memory' in even the principal Burns Clubs every January or earn the F.S.A. (Scot.) in other ways: he is a welcome and wholesome and even distinguished figure in comparison with any of these – but then, on the other hand, just to get him into proper perspective, compare him with, say, Professor Gregory Smith, whose book on *Scottish Literature* is, with all its faults, the first text-book I would like to place in the hands of any young Scot likely to play a part in bringing about a National Renaissance, just as – not Hume Brown and certainly not Professor Rait, but the section on Scotland in Buckle's *History of Civilisation* is the text-book for history I would prefer to see in use. The main trouble with Sir George Douglas is that all his thinking has been severely limited to conventional lines: the only distinction of his critical work that it happened to be the convention of his class to have a piety for Scottish literature that differentiates their judgment to some extent from that of less national critics – while leaving it essentially the same sort of judgment: for English and often Anglo-Scottish critics have the same sort of piety for English letters of the more *passéist* schools. The literary output of his own country during the period of his activity is very often an index to the quality of a critic, Sir George, as the preface to his 'Minor Scottish Poetry' shows, is fully aware of the straits to which distinctively Scottish literature has been reduced, and of at least some of the causes; but he is impotent – he has nothing originative to say. He can point to our historic values, but he can suggest no lines along which we can recover and continue them, meet our modern situation and its requirements more adequately, and even advance more safely towards the opening future. His work opens no fresh outlooks, clearer discussions or further initiatives. He has given the Scottish literary tradition of which he has written and lectured no new lease of life, but simply preserved a moribundity of outlook which characterises an ever-diminishing class who have provided themselves with no successors: and, far abler and better-equipped and less puerile and provincial than all but a few of the moving spirits in the Burns Movement to-day, he has failed to do or even to assist them to do what they have done – build up a world movement which despite its present discreditable and futile enough condition is not perhaps incapable of ultimate transmutation into a genuine cultural force, distinctively Scottish in its provenance and directive personnel; and, more recently, initiate a Vernacular Revival Movement, the tremendous literary potentialities of which are unapparent to the vast majority of the workers in and for it who, indeed, belong in every respect to an inferior category of our people to the class of which Sir George is at least a picturesque if ineffectual figurehead. Sir George has 'cut no ice.' Compare him with Brandes, who has achieved a world-wide reputation despite the fact that he is a citizen of a country with only two and a half million population, and writes in a language rarely studied by foreigners. As Ernest Boyd has said:

> The life of Georg Brandes has been one of challenge and combat, of criticism that is creative and constructive, and the record of his accomplishment is the final answer to his opponents. As the intellectual mentor of his own country he can claim for his disciples such men as Holger Drachman, J.P. Jacobsen, Erik Skram, and Sophus Schandorph, and as the interpreter of Scandinavian literature abroad he can point to his championship of Kielland, Strindberg, Ibsen, Björnson; his writings on Oehlenschlaeger, Holberg, and Andersen. There is hardly a writer in the Scandinavian countries about whom he has not had an effective and timely word to say. He translated John

Stuart Mill; was the first to recognise Nietzsche; and his studies of Renan, Taine, Lassalle, and the French Realists, his classical study of Shakespeare, show him as the intellectual bridge between Scandinavia and the rest of Europe.

Who are Sir George Douglas's disciples, whom has he championed against odds, what has he done to bridge the gulf between Scotland and Europe? It is not a question merely of his being a pigmy compared with Brandes – but of whether he might not have achieved more if he had had a different conception of the critic's function, a conception that it is to be hoped some Scottish critic in however small a measure will soon begin to show! Sir George certainly does not deserve the forgiveness to which those who have worked hard are entitled: and if he would have done more had the Scottish press afforded greater facilities – then it is relevant to ask if he ever attempted to increase these facilities. As matters stand he leaves them scantier and poorer than when he began his career: and any emerging Scottish Georg Brandes on even the smallest scale would to-day have to create his own press, or become his own publisher even.

An appreciative article on Sir George Douglas appears in Mr Parker's *Modern Scottish Writers*, and I agree with a great deal that it says. But my acquiescence with almost everything of a flattering character that can be said of his work – when it is considered in relation to what any other of his contemporaries have done in like fields of letters – vanishes when I measure him according to the European scale. At the same time there are poems of his – one or two – that should not be lacking from any such anthology as *The Edinburgh Book of Scottish Verse*, and I have a lively affection for certain studies of old Border life which he has written. '*Rarement un écrivain est si bien inspiré que lorsqu'il se raconte,*' said Anatole France, and it is certainly true that Sir George Douglas is far and away at his best in certain pieces of personal reminiscence, and it is by the quality of these in their interpretation, and, almost, reproduction, of vanished or vanishing aspects of Scottish life that he deserves to be remembered. And in *The Fireside Tragedy* before the emergence of the present movement towards a Scottish National Drama, he showed himself for once *en rapport* with the becoming tendencies of Scottish Arts, and wrote a drama that in some respects compares not unfavourably with any that has yet been produced by the new – and only – school of Scottish playwrights, and might perhaps with a little adaptation suit the boards of the Scottish National Players.

Sir George Douglas's books are: – *Poems*, 1880; *The Fireside Tragedy*, 1886; *The New Border Tales*, 1892; *The Blackwood Group*, 1897; *Poems of a Country Gentleman*, 1897; edition of *Scottish Minor Poets*; *History of the Border Counties, Life of James Hogg*, 1899; *Diversions of a Country Gentleman*, 1902; *The Man of Letters*, 1903; *Life of Major-General Wauchope*, 1904; *The Panmure Papers*, 1908; *The Border Breed*, 1909; *Scottish Poetry (Drummond to Fergusson)*, 1911; *The Pageant of the Bruce*, 1911; and *The Book of Scottish Poetry*, 1911.

See also W.M. Parker's *Modern Scottish Writers*, and article on 'Sir George Douglas' by present writer in *Scottish Nation*, November 13, 1923.   [7.8.25]

9. Frederick Niven; J.J. Bell

Writing in the *Northern Review* of May, 1924, with regard to the novels of Mr John Sillars, about which I shall have something to say when I come to discuss the younger Scottish novelists, Mr A.R. Williams observed that: 'The novel as a Scottish genre seems almost to have gone out of existence. There is evidence in plenty in the catalogues that novels are being written by Scotsmen, but they are not writing Scottish novels, not even those who place their story in a Scottish setting, and the whole trend of things literary and economic seems to indicate that a Scottish Renaissance will find the novel its most difficult obstacle to surmount. The only encouragement one can obtain is to note that here and there are Scots writers of the younger generation – Mr Blake, for example – who are trying to move towards a novel which in treatment and spirit shall be national. Among these is Mr Sillars.' If Mr Blake is, indeed, making an effort to achieve anything of the kind, it is high time that he recognised that *Mince Collop Close* is a *cul-de-sac*, and, questions of literary value apart, about as Scottish as a Polish village in Lanarkshire or the Annual Meeting of the Confederation of Scottish Ice-Cream Merchants – but a year ago I would nevertheless have been in substantial agreement with what Mr Williams said as to the prospects of a genuinely Scottish school of fiction. I would have been emphatically of the opinion that a pre-requisite to the emergence of anything of the kind would be the re-establishment of a Scottish Parliament in Edinburgh, with powers not less than those of the Free State Government in Ireland. Only such a political development, I would have said, can carry in its train that reorientation of journalism and book publishing which will provide the necessary media of publication and that separation of interests tending cumulatively to create a public with a different response to the English public for which such a school will naturally cater. Now I am not so sure. It may be that effective cultural devolution will precede rather than follow political devolution. If so, the latter will, of course, inevitably follow, and not until it does will the former be freed of very serious and otherwise insurmountable handicaps. But since Mr Williams wrote there have been many signs that the Scottish Renaissance movement is making more rapid headway in this particular direction than could then have been reasonably anticipated. There has been the emergence of what has already been labelled the Glasgow School – represented in such novels as Mr Cockburn's *Tenement* and Mr Carruthers' *The Virgin Wife*. I shall deal with this more specifically in due course. But, having made this initial point, I must promptly qualify what I have said. By claiming such phenomena of recent publishing as the novels of this young 'Glasgow School' as evidence of the headway that is being made by the Scottish Renaissance movement, I do not mean that they are contributions to a definite programme for the creation of a distinctive Scottish literature comparable in every respect to the literatures of other countries – which is the aim of the Scottish Renaissance movement, properly so-called – but rather that they are proofs of the widespread movement, taking many different forms at the present time, which those concerned with the express propaganda on behalf of a Scottish Renaissance during the past four or five years, have partly divined to exist and brought to a knowledge of itself, and partly created, even in some respects in opposition to the ideas put forward. In other words, the promoters of the Scottish Renaissance movement have all along realised that their ends could be achieved best by attracting some of their compatriots and antagonising others, their principle in this respect has been that embodied in the lines

> Speak weel o' my son
> Speak ill o' my son
> But aye be speakin',

and they believe that in the balance of these opposite effects will be achieved that all-round national awakening which is their objective.

I am personally of the opinion that the work of writers such as Messrs Blake, Cockburn, and Carruthers, for example – and of any other contemporary Scottish novelist so far except Mr Neil Gunn – must be regarded as the products of antagonisation to the radical principle implied in the propaganda of the Scottish Renaissance movement, a quickening, a readjustment to suit a keener national spirit of criticism of Anglo-Scottish elements rather than the breaking through of something generically Scottish. That is, a defensive movement of the very elements that any literary movement of the slightest value must be attacking. They are in the position, to take a political analogy, of offering this or that form of devolution in place of sovereign independence. They have not yet effected a perdurable compromise, if any compromise can be perdurable with the elements involved – they have not come to effective terms with the basic considerations. The novel is a distinctive form in France, in Russia, and in England, for example – the younger American writers are moving towards the discovery of a distinctively American form of the novel. In Scotland, if the work of the writers I have mentioned – or the novels of older writers of more completely Anglo-Scottish times, such as Frederick Niven and J.J. Bell – is to be regarded in any measure as moving towards 'a novel which in treatment and spirit shall be national,' we are restricted to priding ourselves upon naively trying to do in and for Scotland to-day what every other country in Europe has long since achieved, more fully and more finely. The significant fact about the contemporary novel of literary consequence in every European country to-day is the endeavour to get away from the commercial recipe – the size the publishers have stereotyped – the set number of chapters which have no correspondence whatever with the incidence of vital experience; and so forth. No contemporary Scottish novelist appears to be sufficiently modern to have been infected with this desirable experimentalism – to have the faintest realisation that the orthodox novel convention is a demoded form for which an effective substitute is being seriously – and necessarily – sought by artists whose mere realisation of this in itself gives them a significance beyond that of the most diligent and successful adherent of the old thirty-six chapters formula. Not only are they thus technically belated or impotent: but none of them is sufficiently Scottish either to come to grips with the whole problem of the 'novel as a Scottish genre.' It is nothing of the kind – it is an alien importation that has so far only shown itself susceptible of very intermittent and partial naturalisation. The problem therefore for a would-be novelist of the Scottish Renaissance is to devise a form of the novel that is specifically Scottish – as different in form and method from the English or the French novel as Scots psychology is from English or French – or to devise a specifically Scottish form that will successfully anticipate, so far as Scotland is concerned, the issue of the present widespread search for a substitute for the novel-form. The latter, I would submit, is the likelier ambition. If Scotland is to re-enter the stream of European letters it will not be on the strength of *Piper's News* either in matter or manner – and, although it would have its uses, the translation into Scottish form of the various kinds of the novel that have already been fully developed elsewhere would be no achievement from the point of view of creative art. Scotland, like any other country, must have its contribution to *welt-literatur* assessed in respect of its independent creative values and vehicles – not by what it has in common, technically and otherwise, with other literatures: but by what is peculiarly, or, at any rate, primarily its own. To anyone *au fait* with world-literature the achievements of Mr Blake and his successors – as of their predecessors like Messrs Niven and Bell – are but 'cauld kail het again,' however appetising that may be to the less cultivated tastes of the unprofessional Scottish reader – and none the more tolerable because the *rechauffé*, which formerly passed under this or that German or French name, such as *Naturalismus*, is now served up as Mince Collops, or, cannibalistically, Virgin Wives, and has stood for too long before being reheated.

Both Mr Niven and Mr Bell came to the fore before the present conceptions of a distinctively Scottish literature began to be canvassed, and though neither is superannuated there are reasons for believing new departures on their part – at any rate new departures of any particular consequence even in the restricted field of Scottish letters as at present constituted – improbable. They are, in Mr Williams' phrase, Scotsmen whose novels, despite Scottish settings, are certainly not Scottish. On the other hand, any interest that does attach to their novels is a Scottish interest, for as novels – so far as any wider field than that of contemporary Scottish literature is concerned – they are not of the very slightest consequence. In the issue of the *Northern Review*, to which I have already referred, in a useful if superficial and scrappy article on 'Some Scottish Novelists' since Scott, Miss Agnes Stewart remarked that 'it may be worth noticing that the novel in Scotland has followed an opposite course from that in France. In the latter country, writers like Réné Bazin and Maurice Barrès have made a powerful effort to turn the attention of readers from the intrigues of town life, and to fix it upon the peasant life of outlying districts, whilst in this country the novel is only now becoming conscious of the town. It is surprising that the metaphysical Scot, with his love of moralising and his tendency to introspection, has not produced work of the realistic and problematic kind found in France and Russia. The crowding of our Highland and Lowland populations into busy commercial centres, with the introduction of an Irish element, has created conditions which should lend themselves to dramatic treatment. Still, we have no work of fiction resembling Dostoievsky's *Crime and Punishment*?' That 'still' is, I am afraid, sadly typical of the quality of Scottish literary criticism. It is as if we observed that we had numerous diligent tombstone-makers in Scotland, and yet, curiously enough, no Sphinx or Pyramid – or that while we lack a Taj Mahal, on the other hand we have our own Gleneagles Hotel and the Waverley Station. And again, in any sound generalisation on the comparative state of the novel in France and in Scotland, Réné Bazin and Maurice Barrès are scarcely the writers to be taken as representative of the former. Both these Russian and French references, indeed, are all too illustrative of the inanity of even the most progressive contemporary Scottish outlook on the field of comparative criticism. It is not by such amateurish references and haphazard analogies that an adequate conception of *welt-literatur* – and the present relation and future potentialities of Scottish letters in regard thereto will be secured. I do not make these observations captiously. I believe that it is largely due to the poor quality of literary criticism in Scotland that the general ineptitude and indistinction of modern Scottish letters is attributable: and on the other hand I believe that Scottish writers such as the two I am presently dealing with and their younger followers I have mentioned suffer very greatly from being insufficiently 'literary' – from having inadequate conceptions of the technique of their craft. In literature, as in science, I deem it essential – in so far as any contribution to creative art is concerned – to be as thoroughly abreast of contemporary world-developments as possible. Both Messrs Niven and Bell – and, happily to a decreasing extent, their younger successors now emerging – have suffered, too, from being born into a bad period so far as Scotland itself is concerned. Miss Stewart's remark regarding the absence of realistic and problematic work in Scotland resolves itself into the fact that Scotland has not yet been realised as Scotland – Anglicisation has thrust its problems out of the sphere of practical politics, and as a consequence created a public opinion which, aided by the Anglo-Scottish Press, finds them unreal and negligible, while irrelevant issues assume the guise of reality and monopolise the public mind. And, as part of the same complex process, while the actual conditions and problems of contemporary Scotland go largely undiscussed and are made to appear irrealistic, typically Scottish mentalities, instinctively realising the lack of something essential to them in this Anglo-Scottish 'ethos,' find compensation in a ridiculous romanticisation of the past or in a piddling sentimentalism. Both Niven and Bell, in their attitude to Scotland, share these conditions: this transmogrifying film of unreality comes between them and Scottish realities and affects the quality of their reporting and largely determines the type of issue that presents itself to such selective faculties as they possess. A spark of genius in either would have broken through this film and got down to fundamentals: it is a radical defect of their inspiration itself that has rendered it unable to reject merely the aspects which the existing system has thrust forward and to insist upon 'the whole story.' The essence of their failure lies in the fact that they have attempted to deal with matters which their preconceptions unconsciously falsified – in a way that the subject-matter of great, or even real, art can never be falsified – and, therefore, technically, in a manner not determined by the truth of the matter – the only legitimate determinant of form.

I am afraid, too, that both of them have suffered from that subtle subversion of such talents as were once, if not still, potentially theirs, which affects writers of a certain facility and of inadequate originality when they find that certain kinds of work they do are more readily saleable than others and more popular – if only immediately so. At the same time, while yielding to commercial suggestioning, in this way, the popularity and commercial success of both has been less than that of many inferior writers of substantially the same type simply because these elements of their work were not the most natural to them – for even best-selling stuff demands a singleness of purpose, and no intrusion, even in inverse form, of elements appertaining to other categories. Both Niven and Bell are partially conscious artists – not sufficiently conscious to make good in a purely literary sense, and yet just too conscious to sink to the level appropriate to the Big Public. They have fallen between various stools. Yet I am not sure that either of them would have gone *very* much farther than they have done in the purely literary sense had this dichotomy been resolved. Neither of them have a fundamental attitude to the art of letters essential to work of sufficient quality in any genre to command the slightest international attention. Both suffer from an inferiority complex. This is most marked in Niven – as witness the following passage from the prologue to *A Tale That is Told:* 'Arabesques and whorls, lightenings and convolutions are all very well to make a thin theme and paltry days seem a *tour de force* in the telling. I always suspect writers like Meredith and Carlyle of wishing to seem sages because of the violence they do to language.' 'What I have to do is to tell my story.' Confessions such as these are sufficiently illuminating as to the root trouble in this writer's case. He does not escape the consequences of his puerile attitude to art – product, as it is, of an inner sense of inadequacy to his ambitions rather than to any counter-theory. The pretentious references to all sorts of writers – Bridges, Vernon Lee, Francis Thompson, Crashaw, Patmore, Wordsworth – in *A Wilderness of Monkeys* are evidence of the same disease – a green-sickness of the intellect. Bell is not subject to such blatancies and inequalities – his work, in such books as *The Whalers* (compare this with Hermann [*sic*] Melville's *Moby Dick*) and *Thou Fool*, is more 'of a piece,' more consistently worked out, mainly as a consequence of more thorough documentation. But, even so, how negative an achievement – how far from the exactitude in detail, the apparent omniscience, the inexhaustible interest, the complete relation of a Balzac, and at this time of day we are surely not to forget the limitations of mere photographic realism – or how a single touch of genius can make the best organisation of facts intolerable. Nor are either Bell or Niven really realistic: their work is slabs of sentiment masquerading as slices of Life. Of Niven's *Justice of the Peace*, the *Graphic* reviewer declared that it was 'stronger than anything that has appeared since *The House with the Green Shutters.*' It would have been difficult to hit upon a phrase which showed a more horrible incapacity for literary criticism. *The House with the Green Shutters* will remain a landmark in Scottish literary history for two reasons – its timeousness and the enormous power with which it realised, and affected, taste and tendency. *Justice of the Peace,* or Bell's *Thou Fool*, though in some ways substantially of the same kind as *The House with the Green Shutters,* had no such timeousness and completely failed either to align themselves with and carry further – or to interpose against and controvert – any stream of taste and tendency. In the strict sense of the terms they were both impurposive and impotent – and the inability of their authors to ensure effect and create a position in the way Douglas did is the exact measure of their inferiority to him; for, if they had had the profounder intuition they lacked, the sense of opportunity, the conjunction of purpose and power, that in itself would have lifted their style to a higher plane and evoked the best of which they were capable. But they have never been moved to anything of consequence. They have nothing to say – only as Niven says, but in a different sense, 'stories to tell.' Or, as another critic has said of their type elsewhere, 'however they function, their activities are *in vacuo,* and have no effect on the people – unless it be a lethal, financial one.' They have never reached behind, as it were, the productions displayed on the nearest railway bookstall to the *ground* of their art. Both have written a certain amount of verse – of a type suitable to the collections of the Glasgow Ballad Club – but of not the slightest ultimate value. The traditions of the Glasgow Ballad Club, indeed, are such that not one of its members has contributed to it a single poem that will live in Scottish literature while the great bulk of the work contributed to its collections, or published elsewhere by its members, is of a kind that amply illustrates the pass to which poetry in Scotland had been reduced – not among the Kailyaird school, but among those who fancied themselves and were accepted as our literati – for several decades before the new movement emerged some five or six years ago, and at once exposed the utter inadequacy alike in technique and motivation that was being assiduously cultivated and cherished in such circles, and nevertheless still is.

Niven now lives in Canada – but it must be said that Canada has not quickened his art in any way. Rather the reverse. Despite the extent to which Scots emigrants have influenced most of our colonies, their cultural effect has been, if not negligible, at least non-creative. They have contributed practically nothing to the movements now discernible in all the colonies to create independent literatures. Nor if their exile from Scotland has increased their affection for it has that feeling found creditable literary expression – any more than it has resulted in a realistic preoccupation with Scottish affairs, such as, for example, that of the American-Irish in the fight for Irish freedom. Niven's Canadian work, such as *Penny Scot's Treasure* is a mere commercial product – vastly inferior to Jack London's work, for example. And the difference between a genuine cultural reaction to Canada and Canadian life, and such a localisation of a stock-form destitute of real creative impulse and artistic integrity can be seen by comparing that novel with Louis Hémon's *Maria Chapdelaine: Récits du Canada français* – just as, in the sphere of poetry, Niven's verses can profitably be compared with Louis Fréchetté's *Fleurs boréales*.

Bell's output has been much greater and much more varied than Niven's – and he has achieved one outstanding success – his creation of *Wee Macgreegor*. This had an immense – and well-deserved – vogue for a while: and seems to have fallen into quite undeserved oblivion. It is worth all the rest of Bell's output – and the whole of Niven's put together. Much of Bell's subsequent writing, alike in prose and in drama, has been in the form of variations or cyclic permutations of this lucky hit: but none of these have recaptured that 'first fine careless rapture.' It must not be thought that I am overvaluing *Wee Macgreegor* – on the contrary, I realise its inability to stand against the great comic creations of other literatures: and yet although it is merely superficial comedy and fails to realise the tremendous *vis comica* resident in

Scottish life and every now and again disappointingly adumbrated by writers of insufficient stature to cope with it effectively – one of the great tasks that still awaits the man and the hour – I am of opinion that it, far more than merely proportionately to the literary stature of modern Scotland compared with other European countries, provides a Scottish equivalent to the best humorous literature that has been produced anywhere in the twentieth century. *Wee Macgreegor* is worth a bushel of Peter Pans, Wendys, and the like – and, although it may seem to have enjoyed merely a passing vogue, I believe that it will always continue to find its readers and that it will be recognised as one of the few really distinctive and valuable products of its period in Scotland and occupy a place in the literary history of Scotland that would vastly surprise those who – including perhaps its author – regard it as a mere trifle not to be compared with solemn work such as *Justice of the Peace* or *Thou Fool*, for both of which and a whole shelf of similar productions by the same and other authors (respectable enough work in many ways although they are, and certainly the best of their kind contemporary Scotland has so far yielded), I would not barter a page of *Wee Macgreegor* – though I am in no danger of overestimating the importance of that engaging youngster either!

John Joy Bell's books include: *Wee Macgreegor* (1902); *Clyde Songs* (1906); *Thou Fool* (1907); *The Whalers* (1914); *The Little Grey Ships* (1916); etc. etc. For full list see *Who's Who*.

Frederick John Niven's books include Novels, *A Wilderness of Monkeys, Ellen Adair, Justice of the Peace, Two Generations.*, etc.; Short Stories, *Above Your Heads, Sage Brush Stories*; Verses, *Maple-leaf Songs*, etc. etc.   [14.8.25]

10. Sir Ronald Ross; Ronald Campbell Macfie

Sir Ronald Ross was the only Scottish poet – legitimately so called, for Edward Shanks although a Scotsman is no more a Scottish poet than Stuart Merrill is an American one – who was included amongst the contributors to the first volume of *Georgian Poetry:* and at that time, except Lord Alfred Douglas, Douglas Ainslie, and Ronald Campbell Macfie, whom else had we that could have been so included without gross anomaly? He was – and any of the other three I have mentioned would have been – sufficiently equal in accomplishment and similar in manner to fit in with the other members of the group. At all events the pieces by which he was represented were worthy of their inclusion and amenable to the spirit of the collection generally – and pieces could have been chosen from any of the other three with a similar result. But apart from this quartette of little-known poets – little-known by their poetry at all events – there was at that time no other Scottish poet deserving of inclusion, or work, if represented, could have sustained comparison with the average level of the other poems given in respect of technical accomplishment and plane of poetry involved, let alone identity of tradition. A great deal has happened since then. Of the third series of *Northern Numbers* even the *Times Literary Supplement* admitted that 'the Scottish Georgians are in every way the equals of their English contemporaries.' This is not, however, a claim that I would put forward myself – the English Georgians have severally an address, a range, a body of work, and a representative status and influence that not one of the Scottish Georgians has yet reached. The latter may and I think do – attain an equal level in isolated poems: but taking their output in all, the work of any of the former is still both qualitatively and quantitatively greatly superior to that of any of the latter. I am thinking as I write this, however, of the fundamental Georgians – Walter de la Mare (who owes, I think, his most distinctive qualities to his Scots blood), J.C. Squire, Edward Shanks, Lascelles Abercrombie, W.H. Davies, W.W. Gibson and one or two others – not of such later and slighter recruits as Mrs Shove, William Kerr and Richard Hughes, whose inclusion was simply unaccountable, on literary grounds at all events, and certainly unjustified. But if certain of the 'Scottish Georgians' – George Reston Malloch, Edwin Muir, Muriel Stuart, and F.V Branford, say – were to be asked to join with their English contemporaries in a new volume of *Georgian Poetry,* it would be much more difficult, if not impossible, to cull from their work poems which would 'go with' the others than it would have been ten to twelve years ago to secure such an amenable selection from the work of Ross, Macfie, Ainslie and Douglas: while, if really representative examples of their work were chosen, the relation between them and their fundamental difference from the others would, I think, be clear enough to create the feeling of 'a school within a school' at least. As I shall try to show later, these differences derive in unbroken descent from the Old Makars and constitute and perpetuate the independent literary traditions of Scotland which, on close analysis, have always been discernible even when Scottish letters have seemed most submerged in English – better preserved there, indeed, than in the Kailyairdism which ostensibly exemplifies them. My point is that our independent Scottish traditions are becoming better accentuated – displaying their basal differences from English traditions more clearly – than they did ten, let alone thirty, years ago. The radical difference in 'direction' is once again unmistakably asserting itself. Saltatory developments impend.

Ten years ago Sir Ronald Ross and Ronald Campbell Macfie were exemplifying Scottish poetical genius in the medium of English in a manner similar – but less Scottish externally, at any rate – to that of their predecessors like Robert Buchanan, John Davidson, and 'Fiona Macleod' behind whom in turn, spaced out with many minor figures, tower such comparative giants as Sir Walter Scott, Thomas Campbell and, still further back, Ben Jonson. This is the Scottish element in English poetry. In my opinion it is once more on the upgrade: and under an identity of technique and superficial similarity of subject-matter and tendency it may yet accumulate sufficient strength to split English poetry into two separate schools, if not to subjugate in turn the predominant tradition and assert the supremacy of another that has long been subordinate to it, and indeed, for the most part negligible. In this connection what Gordon Bottomley said in his *Poems of Thirty Years* as to the difficulty now of writing great poetry in the English central tradition and of the extent to which essential repetition and imitation have become inevitable, is a clear pointer to some such development. In the possibility so conceived, at any rate, there is surely sufficient to fire the laggard ambition of the Scottish muse to unprecedented effort. The emergence of a major Scottish poet at this juncture, effectively subsuming (in the medium of English) the tendencies latent in the difference of Scottish psychology from that of our 'predominant partner,' and more especially so if his work in subject-matter and setting were defiantly Scottish, would be a welcome reversal of the state of affairs which has existed so long – whether it opposed to the central English tradition a new canon which would dominate the future as long and as powerfully as that has done the past, or, whether, as the *Glasgow Herald* in advocating literary devolution contends, it was merely destined to have the salutary effect of giving a more spacious balance to English letters at a time when over-centralisation has induced a species of cultural vertigo.

Neither Sir Ronald Ross nor Dr Macfie (to return *à nos moutons*) have yet received anything like their due at the hands of contemporary criticism. I have already indicated that in my opinion they are figures of equal importance to all but the major Georgians – and yet while innumerable essays are devoted to the work of most of these and full-dress volumes to Walter de la Mare and John Masefield, and scarcely anything

can be written about modern English poetry without involving a definite
attitude to their work, it would not be in the least surprising if set studies
of the period failed to include any reference to these two. Why is this? Is
it because despite their command of all the external shibboleths there is
at the base of their work an undisguisable difference – a subtle diathesis
of subversion – the fact that their work is, despite all its appearances, not
English but Scottish, and, in the last analysis, directed to ends at variance with any possibility of complete assimilation? I can account for it in
no other way, and this explanation is in keeping with the whole history of
English and Scottish literary, and cultural, relationships. Look at
Binyon's recent anthology designed to supplement Palgrave where
Scottish poetry, in English, receives the scurviest and most unjustifiable
treatment. Look at any other anthology of modern British verse – in
none of them do Scottish poets receive proportionate representation.
The seriousness of this lies in the fact that – as an inevitable consequence of the Union of Parliaments – publishing and literary journalism
have become almost entirely centred in London, with the result that the
whole machinery of publicity is in the hands of those who are inevitably
most anxious for the complete assimilation of Scotland to England and
most opposed to any nationalistic developments in the North likely to
seek, and in the end secure. a reorientation. I do not say that literary
journalism and publishing under the existing conditions are the
monopoly of Englishmen – or, to a large extent, dominated by successive
relays from Oxford and Cambridge; I am well aware that the Scot is
ubiquitous and always 'amang the heid yins' – and that many of the brilliant intellectuals Cambridge and Oxford send down annually are Scots.
But I raise the question as to whether the existing state of affairs is equi-
table as between English and Scottish writers – and the further question
as to whether, even if the apparent unfairness to Scottish writers of
which I complain is not necessarily attributable to the system but to
other and subtler causes, such an independent Scottish press and
publishing trade as would inevitably accompany the establishment of an
independent Scottish Parliament, would not positively promote Scottish
letters in a fashion impossible under existing conditions and location in
Scotland benefit Scottish writers, by freeing them from the necessity of
certain kinds of protective camouflage. However these questions may be
answered, a formidable body of evidence can be adduced to show that a
comparatively inferior English poet can secure an amount of appreciative notice, a status as one of the poets of his time, a place in the
anthologies, and the other concomitants or sequelae of recognition

which are invariably denied to Scottish poets of superior calibre writing in English. If there were no Scottish poets of a moment equal to those contemporary English poets whom what is really English, although it purports to be British, literary journalism regards as in the first rank, then that would point to there being something in the existing system facilitative of English and inhibitive of Scottish poetical talent, and would, at any rate, accentuate the fact that there is a difference between them and that they respond differently to substantially the same stimuli. If there are Scottish poets of equal moment who are comparatively neglected, then obviously Scottish cultural interests are being systematically subordinated and sacrificed to English. In my opinion the actual state of affairs is partly due to each of these causes. There are no contemporary Scottish poets writing in English equal, and, therefore equally deserving of critical consideration, to the best contemporary English poets (who are not all Georgians) – largely because English is not a language in which any Scotsman can adequately express himself, but even more because of the provincialisation of Scotland and the consequent inhibition of the highest potentialities in Scottish culture. On the other hand, there are Scottish poets equal in every respect to the majority of those after the first five or six whose names would leap to the mind if the subject of contemporary English poetry were raised: but while the latter are thus well known the former have had practically no 'press' at all and their successive books are practically still-born. Of the older generation of these, the two poets with whom I am dealing – along with Lord Alfred Douglas and Douglas Ainslie, with whom I shall deal later – are the most important. In Scotland itself, they are to all intents and purposes unknown outwith a very restricted class of reader – a class, at that, which largely if not entirely accepts the current English valuations, and would be indistinguishable from the general body of British readers of contemporary poetry were it not for a tendency to attach rather more importance to such Scottish poets as these two than the literary journals accord them – and the term 'Scottish Poetry' both at home and abroad certainly conjures up something in which they have no part. 'Scottish Poetry' in this sense remains a 'country cousin,' a very poor relation, of English. I do not refer to the plethora of our local bards. But imagine Buchan or Violet Jacob or Neil Munro – at their very best, in English – in any of the Georgian series! It is not so much the difference between Scottish and English poetry that would be then revealed and thrust into devastating relief – as the difference between poetry of a comparatively high quality and verse of so low a kind as to be comparatively non-poetry.

Both Sir Ronald Ross and Dr Macfie are not only poets but scientists. Dr Macfie has written a large number of popular science books; Sir Ronald Ross's name is imperishably associated with the discovery of the mosquito cause and cure of malaria: he was awarded the Nobel Prize for Medicine in 1902. Despite the fact that Sir Ronald Ross is the editor of *Science Progress*, however, and two of his volumes of poetry are respectively entitled *Philosophies* and *Psychologies*, his ideology is of what may be called the Right Centre. Modern scientific conceptions and their terminology have no more affected his poetry than they affected Tennyson's: a process of syncretism reconciles it to conventional morality and orthodox culture to such an extent that it might easily be the product of the Victorian Age, or still more easily of the Elizabethan. He has passages in which the Keatsian quality shines more magically than anywhere else outwith Keats himself: and passages, again, which Shakespeare might have signed. Dr Macfie is even more destitute of the cachet of contemporaneity – in form and content his work belongs to the mainstream of poetry written in English. This can never be said of really great poets – they are at once of their time and of all time – their best work rises like a rock above the mainstream, resisting all levelling. Both Ross and Macfie pay the penalties of this conventionalism: their work too frequently becomes facile, is too like this, that, or the other thing that has gone before: they are not engaged in the essential task of poetic genius – the ceaseless effort to extend the range of human consciousness. There are real dangers in not sharing the significant preoccupations of one's own time – in relying more upon what an age has in common with the past than upon what differentiates it from any that has gone before – and neither of these poets has been adequately aware of them. The major content of their work is over-generalised – insufficiently specific: and in form they have held aloof from the experimentalism of the age. In other words, both in manner and matter, they have taken far more than they have given: it is always the opposite case with genius. They have taken their talents too easily, evading the test of *le bloc resistant*. Perhaps this is because poetry has been rather a recreation to each of them, preoccupied with 'more serious matters'! At any rate they have been both so sporadic in their 'attack' that I feel that all that either of them has lacked to become a really great poet has been that continuity of impulse which is only to be had when a man makes poetry the main business of his life – as all the great poets have done. Both Dr Macfie and Sir Ronald Ross have served at least two masters throughout.

A writer in the *Glasgow Herald* summarising Mr I.A. Richards' most important essay, 'A Background for Contemporary Poetry,' which appeared in the *Criterion*, said,

> Since the sixteenth century what Mr Richards calls the 'magical view' of the world has been gradually giving place to the scientific. Nature, that is to say, has been neutralised. It is indifferent to us. In contemporary British poetry, therefore, we ought to learn how we are taking this momentous change in the world-view. Mr Hardy, Mr Richards thinks, is the only living British poet who refuses to be comforted by beliefs that derive from the dying (but still strong) magical view of nature. (The magical view, by the way, implies the immanence of a controlling spirit or spirits in nature congenial to the emotional needs of man.) Mr Hardy has achieved a 'self-reliant and immitigable acceptance' of an indifferent universe. The other major poets of the age – Mr Yeats, Mr de la Mare and Mr D.H. Lawrence – have all fled from the necessity of accepting the world-view of science, and have taken refuge in fabricated emotional universes of their own: Mr Yeats, first in folk-lore and latterly in the visions of the Hermetist; Mr de la Mare in a world of pure phantasy for which the distinction between knowledge and feeling has not yet dawned; and Mr Lawrence in a world of the 'Golden Bough' – that is, in the primitive mentality of people like the Bushmen. Mr Richards thinks that poets will have to face the issue in bolder fashion, and, that the first result of that endeavour will be a poetry of nausea. Mr T.S. Eliot, Miss Moore, and some French and German poets have already voiced the feelings aroused by the sense of a world in ruins.

I substantially agree with Mr Richards but Sir Ronald Ross in Harley Street can scarcely be expected to do so, and, as I have already said, Dr Macfie is a populariser. Sir Ronald's pamphlet *Science and Poetry* deals with no such issues: and in their poetry if he and Dr Macfie have been affected at all by the force that has sent their greater contemporaries into the ends of the earth, both of them have solved the problem to their own satisfaction, not by any attempt, such as might legitimately have been expected of poets and scientists, to introduce Euterpe to the new world-view that science has disclosed, but by burying her head ostrich-fashion in the sands of conventional culture. In other words, both in their attitude to science and to poetry, what is lacking in both these poets is – not mere topicality but the creative principle – the flair for 'the unknown,' Rimbaud's phrase – the sense of need to be, if not 'in advance,' at least fully abreast. But considerations such as these do not affect the fact that as practitioners of what is universally regarded as

Poetry by cultivated people, save for the minority given to ultra-modernism, neither of them is one whit more *passéist* in content or technique than the Georgians at all events. Sir Ronald's poetry is 'purer' than Dr Macfie's: but the latter has a much bigger body of work of quality and has addressed himself to major forms eschewed by the former who has to a large extent confined himself, like the majority of contemporary poets, to short poems.

It was well said in an excellent article on Dr Macfie – and a good deal of it applies equally to Sir Ronald – in *The Scottish Nation*, that,

> Dr Macfie is perhaps of all modern Scottish poets, the most character-istically Scottish. He does not write in dialect, but dialect – though still a vital means of expression when used by, let us say. Dr Pittendrigh Macgillivray – tends to become more and more a matter of fancy dress. Indeed it often serves to conceal a complete denationalisation of thought. Dr Macfie's peculiar Scottish quality lies deeper than that. It is rather a habit of mind – a manner of thought which belongs pecu-liarly to Scotland – though even in Scotland it is found less often than one might expect. It is, after all, in such a habit of mind that the true meaning of nationality lies; this peculiar angle of vision which interprets life in different parts of the world, in slightly different terms, in one way and in no other. When the underlying thought gets blurred the sense of nationality declines also, and there is nothing left to take its place except an ugly cosmopolitanism – dreary and banal as cosmopolitan hotels. Modern journalism and cheap travel are doing their work pretty thoroughly, and I see nothing much on the other side to counter this standardisation (or cinema-sation) of the world. Desperately as a few of us may struggle against and resent it, in spite of ourselves, we are all caught in the same web and no man can change at will the colour which generation and environment has given to his soul. Yet a few remain comparatively untouched. There are some whose nationality is so strongly woven into the very woof and web of their thought that no alien influence could ever more than superficially change them. Of these is Dr Macfie.

Of these, equally, is Sir Ronald Ross. That they should be compara-tively unknown – that Scottish Poetry should connote in its generally accepted sense something so unutterably inferior – is the measure of our denationalisation. The same writer in a sentence brings out what I was saying about their unbroken descent from the old Makars, when she says of Dr Macfie's work:

He embodies in his work all that is best in Scottish mentality – its integrity, its singleness of thought, its tenderness, and *that curious practical quality which would allow a Scotsman to converse with angels in a perfectly matter-of-fact way without losing for one moment the sense of their mystery.*

There could be no better description of one of the most distinctive features of our independent Scottish literary traditions from Dunbar downwards.

And so despite what I have said of the non-contemporaneity of these two poets, there is an element of truth too in another critic's questions respecting one of them: 'Is he not sadly out of time with the age? But is he not greatly in time with the ages?' This balance is in favour of both: but to have become great poets – instead of merely the equals of all but a few of their best English contemporaries – they would have required to have been in time with both. But what differentiates them both from the ruck is that, dissent how even an ultra-modern may from their ideology or their technique, they both have, at their best, within the convention to which they adhere, an uncommon *maestria*, a *virtuosité*, of execution and have attempted high things, greatly conceived and greatly wrought.

Sir Ronald Ross's poems include, *Philosophies, Psychologies*, etc. He contributed to *Northern Numbers* and *The Scottish Chapbook*. His novel *The Revels of Orsera* is an interesting experiment which deserves more attention than it has received.

Dr Macfie's books include, *Granite Dust, New Poems, Validmar* (a play), *Titanic Ode, Quarter-centenary Ode, War* (an Ode), *Odes and Other Poems*. He has also published *Fairy Tales* in collaboration with Lady Margaret Sackville.

Mr Richards' article referred to appeared in the July *Criterion*, 1925.   [21.8.25]

11. Sir Herbert Maxwell, Bt; Sir Ian Hamilton

'Sir Herbert Maxwell is now the doyen of Scottish writers,' W.S. Crockett wrote recently.

He has given sixty years of a devoted life to public affairs, and at the moment of writing his fellow-Galwegians propose to honour his distinguished services not only as a local magnate, but also as a national asset. Sir Herbert entered the field of authorship somewhat late in life, his first book, *Studies in the Topography of Galloway*, having been published when he was forty-two. Since then – from

1887 – his pen has not been idle. He has at least half a hundred volumes to his credit in all departments of literary activity. Antiquities, natural history, general history, biography, fiction, have each claimed his attention, and it must be said that he has adorned whatever he has touched. It is, however, as an essayist that Sir Herbert has shone most conspicuously, and he may be remembered in that sphere when much of the other work is forgotten. His *Memories of the Months* (seven series) are among the finest things he has written – perhaps the best.

Sir Herbert is certainly the oldest living Scottish writer, but *doyen* implies rather more than mere seniority – and age is unfortunately his principal claim to respect. Apart altogether from the younger writers to whose existence only an exceedingly limited circle has yet awakened, there is a considerable group of Scottish writers who take precedence of Sir Herbert in every other way – some of them so much so that it conveys an entirely false impression to term him the '*doyen* of Scottish letters,' as if he were *primus inter pares*. Mr Crockett's remarks are typical of the slovenliness alike in expression and in thought which are so characteristic of Scots of his generation. What is the use of claiming that Sir Herbert has adorned every section of literature he has touched? What has he added to the art of the novel? Has he made any distinctive contribution to the art of biography? Is it not true that he has been a comparatively undistinguished worker in these and other fields, and that his long tale of books has only what interest attaches to their subject-matter – not to their form and manner? It is nonsense to aver that he has shone as an essayist. The essay in Scotland has indeed come to a bad pass if we have only Sir Herbert to set against Chesterton, Belloc, and a dozen others in England, to go no further afield. Fortunately, we have Cunninghame Graham, Buchan, and one or two more to mitigate our radical inferiority. Sir Herbert Maxwell is not an essayist – if the word essay means more than an article in prose, a definition which may mean anything or nothing. It would be better to say – not that he is the *doyen* of Scottish letters – but that, for the comparatively small section of our people who are cognisant of his work at all and attach the slightest importance to it (a class constituted mainly of those who share in some degree his antiquarian and other subsidiary prepossessions) he is a 'Grand Old Man.' And in this connection, Professor Saurat has recently written:

> *Contrairement à nous* [the French], *les Anglais* [who include the Scots] *ont plutôt des habitudes que des institutions. Ainsi, leur institu-*

tion de poète lauréat ne persiste guère qu' à l'état squelettique. Il y a un poète lauréat; on sait son nom. Il est peut-être le meilleur des poètes mais, des qu'il est nommé poète lauréat, tout le monde prend à son égard un ton de commisération et presque de mépris. Pour la partie vivante du monde littéraire il devient anathème. Il aurait beau être aussi avancé que les plus futuristes, il est automatiquement transformé en bourgeois désuet. Par contre les Anglais sont en train de prendre l'habitude d'avoir un [grand old man], un grand vieillard des lettres, qui se transforme en idole nationale. On l'adorait... Il mourut. On l'oublia. Le prestige du [grand old man], c'est d'être vivant. Quand il meurt, comme pour les rois de Frazer, son pouvoir passe à un autre.

A national idol in the more genial air of England, but in the dowier atmosphere of Scotland an old man of the sea!

I can imagine no more conclusive give-away of our cultural pretensions than his *The Making of Scotland*. It consists of a set of lectures on the War of Independence delivered in the University of Glasgow in 1910. It is actually a concise rehash of the salient features of the period as conceived by orthodox historiography; and inferior in its organisation and presentation of facts to any higher-grade school history book I know. It is a mere stereotype: the trail of the rubber-stamp is over it everywhere. It says little for the quality of Scottish study to-day that the imprimatur of the University of Glasgow should be given to hack-work of this kind. Scottish history has suffered deplorably from the parochialism of its exponents: few of them have been able to rise to the stature of their subject. It is another evidence of the extent of our denationalisation that the history of our country should have become so largely a preserve of the mediocre. After all, there is no history but contemporary history: and the poverty of our historians is the measure of the small extent to which 'Scotland – A Nation' prevails in current thought. The true criterion of history is its power of making history – a faculty of which Sir Herbert Maxwell's work is wholly destitute. To treat our national history as he and his like have done is to confirm and accentuate the provincialisation of Scotland. The dreary cast of 'local history' is over their work. Not that Sir Herbert is by any means the worst of his type. Although he is an amateur historian he has a cultural equipment in some directions as ample as that of the majority of professional historians: and, by way of compensation, is even more academic than many of them, qualifying his amateurishness (which, frankly exhibited, might have stood him in better stead) with the worst faults of academicism. Here and there one sees him divided between consciousness of his intellectual duties and the duties imposed upon him by his traditions; but for the most part the latter monopolise his services. Scottish history as a department of national activity or art is as far behind that of any other European country as one would expect in view of Scotland's subordinate position. Sir Herbert Maxwell has done nothing to make up the leeway: and, in my opinion, it can only be done as a definite contribution towards the recovery of Scottish independence in the fullest sense of the term. So long as Scotland remains subordinate to England, Scottish history will remain subordinate to English. There has lately been a welcome extension of the teaching (albeit insidiously Anglicised) of Scottish history in our schools, evidence of the rising tide of nationalism again, but it still occupies an altogether inferior position in our curricula to the teaching of English history. Surely it is grossly anomalous that the history and literature of a foreign country should be thus given priority over our own – a priority which is largely responsible for the desuetude of Scottish literature and history, the poor quality of our attention to affairs, and our muddled and mediocre response to the arts. 'Each nation must be conscious of its mission,' says Tagore. 'There are lessons which impart information or train our minds for intellectual pursuits. These are simple, and can be acquired and used with advantage. But there are others which affect our deeper nature and change our direction of life. Before we accept them and pay their value by selling our own inheritance, we must pause and think deeply.' Scotland has paused on the verge of this surrender. Complete assimilation to England seemed a few years ago only the matter of a very little time – now a halt has been called. An effort is being made to determine what we would lose and what we would gain. Sir Herbert Maxwell and his school have done nothing to help us to answer these questions. The issue will be decided one way or the other without them: that is the extent to which Sir Herbert is a 'national asset.' Nothing that he has written throws the light we require on the consequences of selling our national inheritance. He himself indeed asks: 'What more effective equipment can be had for dealing with human circumstance than an accurate knowledge of the events and individuals by whose agency the world and its separate nationalities have been evolved out of primitive and vigorous conditions and moulded into their present form and relations?' and he proceeds to quote

> Breathes there a man with soul so dead
> Who never to himself has said –
> This is my own, my native land.

But to what effect? In *The Making of Scotland* he assembles certain facts and names certain names in exactly the same way as similar historians in other countries might use other facts and other names – but he says nothing to show how Scotland became Scotland. The facts are lifted out of their vital context; the names are not used to conjure up living figures. He tells us that this is how Scotland was made – but he does not show us that Scotland and no other country was the inevitable consequence of the circumstances he describes, nor does he tell us what Scotland is. He deals, in other words, with only that fraction of the stream of occurrence which is usually diverted to turn the wheels of the academic mills, while the vast flow remaining rushes past unused. He has nothing to say of Scottish psychology, of Scottish arts and letters, little of industry, or climate, or the consequences of mere geographic position. And he sedulously avoids the deeper issues of nationalism. In other words, the essential background to any study entitled to call itself *The Making of Scotland* is awanting, and, lacking it, the course of events described is a singularly dispurposed and meaningless procession. This, indeed, is the fundamental fault which vitiates all Sir Herbert's work – as it vitiates practically all Scottish history – essential meaninglessness, the lack of purpose in all but the most myopic sense, the absence of any sense of destiny, an incompetence to deal with the issues without which the formal facts and acts are fortuitous and imponderable. His work lacks national consequence and validity, because he brings to it an anaemic and superficial conception of history and of nationality. He is alike deficient in synthesis and analysis, and inhabits a Tom Tiddler's Ground between the two. There is nothing definitive about his work: and inadequacy of intention and poverty of treatment relegate it to a category far below that of the art of history.

A lack of imagination – and of humour – is at the root of his creative impotence. Witness his claim in the introduction to *The Making of Scotland* – 'The narrative has been told and retold very often, varying in accordance with the prepossession, prejudice, and historical insight of different writers; yet it remains a fact that, while many Scotsmen desire to have a definite understanding of the cause for which their forefathers made such heavy sacrifice, few can give the time necessary for the examination and collation of conflicting authorities. I have attempted, therefore, to put the essence of the matter into these lectures...' If Sir Herbert Maxwell had had the power to correct the deficiencies of all his predecessors in the way he insinuates, he would indeed have rendered a great service to his countrymen, and to world-history in general, but, in the light of the result, this over-confidence in himself is seen as a natural consequence of his amateurish attitude to his theme. He had at least, however impartial he was otherwise, a prejudice in favour of himself which the present writer does not share in the slightest degree.

Structurally even *The Making of Scotland* is a slip-shod indeterminate thing – reflecting in its form, or lack of form, its author's lack of *nous*, of *savoir faire*. It is full of loose ends: and, as both Dr Hay Fleming and Mr Crockett have pointed out, erroneous in detail. This want of artistry afflicts all Sir Herbert's books: and is attributable to the inadequacy of the spirit in which he undertook the writing of them: the dilettante attitude – the too-easy assumption that he was equal to the tasks he set himself. The little sketch of the gable-ends in Karel Capek's *Letters from England* – to say nothing of the letterpress, a paragraph or two which sums it all up in the most remarkable fashion – tells far more about Edinburgh than the whole of Sir Herbert's *Edinburgh: An Historical Study*. The fact of the matter is that from false conceptions of the various kinds of literature he has attempted or from a lack of the necessary industry to *master* his themes, or from the negligence of self-conceit – or a combination of all three – he has failed to raise anything he has tackled into its potential art-form even in the lowest degree. His work remains a species of journalism, with practically no affinity to literature – produced, indeed, by the very antitheses of the processes by which literature is produced. His work in forms dependent upon personality suffers from his temperamental dryness and colourlessness and for the rest 'antiquarianism for antiquarianism's sake' pretty well defines his achievement. In the latter respect he is the best of a type which Scotland during the past fifty years and more has produced in abundance – fungoid phenomena. As a naturalist compare his work with W. H. Hudson's or E.L. Grant Watson's or, to take a very different type. the late W.N.P. Barbellion's. The difference is between literature as represented by these three and the old stupid sentimental unimaginative approach to Nature typified in 'Nature Notes' to the *Scotsman*, or, with a super-sterility, in the unreadable work of Seton Gordon: this *wrong* attitude to Nature, and manner of writing about it, is simply to be found in a slightly more tolerable form in Sir Herbert than in the majority of Scottish naturalists. Sir Herbert has had no influence on contemporary Scotland outwith a small class whose social and material conditions predisposed them to likemindedness to himself, but to whom the whole of the remainder of the population are essentially impermeable. That is to say, he counts for nothing really – and I cannot see the slightest reason for imagining with Mr Crockett that he is likely to be remembered for his work in the sphere of the essay any more than for his work in other spheres. If he is, he can only in the nature of things have what Borrow called a 'very short immortality.'

Sir Ian Hamilton is in rather better case – his comparative ineffectuality (as an artist) being due to the opposite causes to Sir Herbert's for the most part, although his attitude to the concept of 'Scotland – A Nation' is sufficiently similar to give in itself one fundamental reason for the vitiation of his gifts, his failure to employ them dynamically. Sir Ian, however, is not deficient in imagination, nor, altogether, in sense of style. His despatches from the Dardanelles were models of their kind – far and away superior to those of any of our other Generals, and, for the matter of that, to the communications of most special correspondents. He has a brilliant aliveness – a wide knowledge of, and interest in, affairs – almost an ubiquity. But that a man so brilliantly endowed, so advantageously circumstanced, should have become largely a voice crying in the wilderness argues an essential defect at the very basis of his diverse powers – a disorganisation of his personal force that can only be attributable to an infirmity of the will, a moral impotence. In my opinion, this is due to the fact that his tendencies, his criticisms, begin too late – after a too-great acceptance of 'things as they are.' He does not dig down far enough. Dynamite that should have been devoted to blasting operations is utilised for mere pyrotechnics. He swallows camels – and strains at gnats. His conclusions are frequently right – brilliantly right in comparison with those of the majority of his contemporaries in this country – but his premises are utterly wrong and render his conclusions no matter how brilliant they are pointless and nugatory. His heart is in the right place: but his head only hovers round it. In other words, he has an effective imagination, but lacks logic – he is creative but not constructive. Kitchener detested him and used to refer to him as 'that b——— y poet.' It is easy to understand this. There could be no catalysis between Kitchener's junker spirit and Sir Ian's gallant embodiment of the finest elements of the Scottish military tradition. The war may have been for the British War Office a war to save civilisation – Sir Ian was one of the very few of our military leaders who had that civilisation himself in a degree worth saving. Practically all the others had fourth-rate minds: and came to occupy the positions they did by virtue mainly of their limitations. Sir Ian is a poet – one of the contributors to *Northern Numbers* (an indication of his interest in, and identification of himself with, Scottish letters as such, and the conception of Scottish nationality behind its recent developments, just as his campaign on behalf of the Caledonian Canal showed his nationalistic attitude to affairs) – but his poetry suffers like his practical influence from lack of 'significant form': he has the materials of poetry – but lacks effective technique – just as he has a lively sense of affairs, but no dynamic powers. Here again he has failed mainly from an inability to dig into himself deeply enough – he has accepted the traditions of his caste too fully, despite the differentia of his vivid and restless personality, and the traditions of his caste do not permit more than a nodding acquaintance with the art of letters. And as to Scottish affairs, the traditions of his caste do not permit an undue preoccupation with these – an occasional point, perhaps, just sufficient to differentiate a Scottish member of it from an English member of it: but no going thoroughly into the matter – as if it were really of fundamental importance: that would be 'bad form'; Sir Ian came pretty near that over the Caledonian Canal scheme – he felt ridiculously strongly on the question. Happily nothing happened; the matter has now died down – largely, I believe, because of Sir Ian's failure to realise that the opposition to the scheme was related to the question of the whole relative position of Scotland to England to-day. Sir Ian's propaganda was not the Fiery Cross; it was only fireworks. But they were certainly very pretty while they lasted.

But compare Sir Ian's publicism with the stock-stuff of the Anglo-Scottish Press. Writing of Russia (in *The Friends of England*) he has the unusual courage to say:

We also are under a propaganda spell; the propaganda of capitalists who are really afraid the Bolshevists' propaganda will penetrate and smash theirs if the two forces come into contact. Is not that rather timid? Is not that the defensive attitude which invariably is defeated in the end? If, as I believe, we are right from the point of view of humanity; if our capitalist system is on the whole sound and capable of readjustment where it is unsound we ought not to be so frightened; we ought to establish as close relations with the dupes of the Bolshevists as the Soviet will allow, and let them see with their own eyes what's what. But we don't. We seize on any old excuse to keep them at arm's length. Even now we are barely on speaking terms. Why? Because they execute bishops? That would be absurd. We've done a bit in that line ourselves; our own Queen Mary burnt off four live bishops and fifteen priests in one year. The crowds which assembled to witness those bonfires were quite a hundred years ahead of the Moujiks who patronise the new martyrdoms. That is not the reason then. We get nearer to it if we say it is because the Russian Government must first formally admit her debts. We want the Communist system to acknowledge the capitalist system. A very happy thought, but we should stand on firmer ground if the Capitalistic States paid their own debts to one another. Those Bolshies won't admit their debt and won't pay; the French do admit their debt and won't pay; so 'Hats off to France!'

The whole book is full of such pieces of brilliant commonsense and freedom from conventional clap-trap: but it 'cuts no ice' politically. Why not? Why, despite all his experience, his clear view of world-affairs, his brilliant – if a bit slap-dash – style, is Sir Ian practically destitute of political influence, exercising less influence than any parrot of an anonymous leader-writer the mere divulgence of whose identity would show that he was incompetent to deal with the matters on which he presumed to speak, from lack of first-hand knowledge of the facts, inexperience in affairs, provincialism of outlook, and defective education? Simply because the strength of his convictions has not been sufficient to override the traditions of his caste – to compel him to effective action, and, as a first step, to force him to re-examine his whole position *de novo*. His pre-conceived ideas prevent the effective – *i.e.*, the dynamic, the influencing – presentation of what he has observed and felt. Had he not thus occupied an untenable position himself – had he let himself go wherever not the assumed but the tested truth led him – he might have been a tremendous force in contemporary world-politics. And the majority of our orthodox politicians would certainly have detested the politician as Kitchener detested the poet – and for the same reasons. Unfortunately, he has kept himself as soldier – as politician – and as literary artist, in different compartments, and in so doing restricted his power in each of these capacities to no more than a third of that which was potential.

Sir Ian's analyses of the personalities of Lenin, Trotsky, Chicherin, Litvinoff, and Lunacharsky compare only – so far as any writer in English is concerned – to Frank Harris's; a significant fact. Posterity will give Sir Ian credit for a penetration immune to propaganda – a sufficiently unusual distinction; and for a sportsmanly fairness sadly to seek – in such connections at any rate – in Great Britain to-day. A fairer and more humanly sensible statement of the case for the Russian leaders has not appeared anywhere else outside the fourth volume of Harris's *Contemporaries*. And in all his other chapters – as he traverses Germany, France, America, Italy, Bulgaria, Poland, and so on – he has something vivid and vital, just and helpful, to say. But it is when he comes to the big principles that underlie the facts and figures – the world movements, the conflicting theories – that he is at a loss. His work remains journalism, not literature, for this reason: and for the same reason he remains a personality rather than a power.

But the diversity of Scottish temperament and tendency today, even in the restricted class to which these two belong, could not be better illustrated than by thus juxtaposing Sir Herbert and Sir Ian. They typify the two stools between which Scotland has fallen so deeply.

Sir Herbert Maxwell's books include *Passages in the life of Sir Lucian Elphin, A Novel*, 1889; *The Letter of the Law; A Novel*, 1890; *Meridiana, Noontide Essays*, 1892; *Post-Meridiana Afternoon Essays*, 1895; *Scottish Land Names*, 1894; *History of Dumfriesshire and Galloway*, 1896; *Bruce and the Struggle for Scottish Independence*, 1897; *The Making of Scotland*, 1911; *Trees, a Woodland Note Book*, 1914; *Edinburgh, an Historical Study*, 1916.

Sir Ian Hamilton's books include *The Friends of England* 1923; *Staff Officer's Scrap Book*.

See *Who's Who* for the careers of both.   [28.8.25]

Letters

CONTEMPORARY SCOTTISH STUDIES

Sir, – The current issue of The Border Standard *prints a substantial extract from an article recently published in your journal and referring to myself. I have not seen the article, and am not here concerned with the opinions expressed in it, but solely with what are there stated as facts. The writer, supposing him to be correctly quoted, says: 'Nothing of literary criticism has been produced by Sir George that would have been found capable of acceptance by* The Nation and Athenæum, The Spectator, *the* New Statesman, *let alone* The Fortnightly *or the* Edinburgh.' *As a matter of fact* The Fortnightly *for October 1918, contained an article on 'The Peasant in British Poetry,' signed by myself, whilst the issues of the* Edinburgh Review *for October, 1906, and January, 1910, respectively contain articles written by myself, though in accordance with the practice of the* Review *unsigned, on Border Ballads and on Edgar Allan Poe. It is unnecessary to say more. – I am, etc.,*

Springwood Park, Kelso,   *George Douglas.*
August 19th, 1925.   [28.8.25]

12. Edwin Muir

Comparing Sir George Douglas and Georg Brandes, I questioned whether Sir George might not have achieved more, if he had had a different conception of the critic's function – 'a conception,' I said, 'that it is to be hoped some Scottish critic in however small a measure will soon begin to show.' But as a matter of fact we have that already in Edwin Muir – a critic incontestably in the first flight of contemporary critics of *welt-literatur*. He differs from Brandes and from the Brandes-like critic I desiderated for Scotland, however, in that he has not yet become effective in his own country. That will come. Muir is still a young man: and the problems that have to be solved before a Scottish Renaissance can be got thoroughly under-weigh have already been engaging his attention. His interest lies there: but the movement has not yet reached the point at which it can give him a sufficient – and sufficiently suitable – audience to make it worth his while (I do not mean merely financially – though the matter of *modus vivendi* is involved) to devote himself either wholly or in large measure to it. Muir's critical apparatus is not designed for the spade work that has yet to be done. Infants cannot profitably be sent direct to the Universities: and, relatively speaking, interest in literature in Scotland is infantile, while Muir is a Pan-European intervening in the world-debate on its highest plane. The number of readers in Scotland capable of following his arguments is extremely limited – proportionately to population much smaller than in any other country in Europe, or in the United States: as is indicated by the fact that it is only within the last two or three years that his name has become known to any extent at all in what may be called our uppermost class of readers, whereas his outstanding ability has long been recognised in London, he is known in Germany as the translator of Gerhart Hauptmann and as a thoroughly qualified international interpreter of German literature, he has a big following in America, where he has contributed a great deal to most of the leading literary periodicals. A prominent French critic writing on the Scottish Renaissance and remarking on Muir's connection with the movement, is careful to add *nota bene* after his name, as if that in itself were a sufficient guarantee – as it is – that, however unknown the names of the other prime movers in this 'News from the North' may be, 'there is something in it.' And so forth. In short, he has already the makings of a world-reputation, which he is rapidly consolidating. His name is to be encountered everywhere – in *The Nation and Athenæum* almost every week, in *The Calendar of*

Modern Letters, in *The Adelphi*, in *The Saturday Westminster Gazette*, in *The North American Review*, in *The Dial*, in *The New York Nation*. And always over distinctive work – work that, however diverse in its point of departure, is obviously making irresistibly for that common rendezvous where ultimately it will be found to be assembled as a four-square body of criticism challenging comparison with the best of its kind produced by any contemporary – and by all but two or three forerunners – in the English language. Since the collapse of *The Scottish Nation* and *The Northern Review* – to both of which he contributed – Scotland has ceased to offer any suitable medium for his work. There is nothing for him in Scotland – and not until Scotland can maintain at least one organ that can house such work can such a writer as Muir devote himself even partially to the exploration of these problems upon the successful solution of which the re-emergence of Scotland into international letters depends – devote himself, that is to say, in such a fashion as might be most speedily successful in producing an effective movement and guiding it in the best way, functions he is exceptionally qualified to exercise. In another sense, of course – in his own creative work – he must be to a great extent continuously occupied with these problems: and, indirectly, his guidance lies to be found in everything he writes – by those trained, or qualified, to detect it. But it is implicit, not explicit. It is available for an infinitely smaller number of Scots than it might otherwise be, if Scotland could place adequate media at his disposal. And I am not sure that the extent to which the present organisation of British literary journalism compels him to be an English critic rather than a Scottish critic in international appreciation is not inhibiting him to some extent creatively as well as critically (terms that are to some extent, but not wholly, interchangeable). It is significant, at all events, that he 'found himself' most convincingly as a poet not in his work in English, but in his Braid Scots ballads: and in my opinion he would have done better work still if he had not contented himself with conventional ballad Scots, but had employed a full Braid Scots canon of his own devising based upon a *de novo* consideration of the entire resources of the language on the one hand, and its tractability to the most significant processes and purposes of ultra-modern literature on the other. However that may be, it is deplorable that when for the first time in its history Scotland produces a literary critic of the first rank it has no organ to offer him in which he may express himself, and a reading public of which only an infinitesimal portion can follow, or profit by, what he writes, so that he is compelled to devote himself to English or American periodicals where his subject-matter seldom has reference to Scottish interests, and in which he is practically debarred from a creative Scots propaganda of ideas. Nor can he even live in Scotland. The cultural facilities it offers are comparatively beneath contempt. The ordinary amenities of civilised intercourse are almost entirely to seek. Muir can meet his intellectual equals in London, in Paris, in Salzburg, and Italy – but there are probably not a score of people between John o' Groats and Maidenkirk who do not stand culturally to him in the relation of the veriest country-cousins. The atmosphere of the country would rapidly ruin the wonderful critical apparatus he has succeeded in perfecting during the years since he fled from Glasgow, and, in turn, from London, to breathe the *plein air* of the Continent.

But it is part and parcel of the whole theory of the Scottish Renaissance that any sufficiently well-equipped 'watcher of the skies,' surveying the field of European letters, was bound a year or two ago to prophesy that something of the kind was due to show signs of emergence. I have myself pointed out elsewhere that it is in accordance, for example, with the theories Oswald Spengler expounds in his 'Downfall of the Western World' – and along these lines I have been driven to see a potentially-creative interrelationship between such ostensibly unrelated phenomena as the emergence of the 'Glasgow Group' of Socialist M.P.'s; the intensification of the Scottish Home Rule movement; the growth of Scottish Catholicism; and the movement for the revival of Braid Scots. As soon as I began to interest myself in the possibilities of a Scottish Renaissance I found that I was by no means alone in doing so. The matter was definitely 'in the air.' Individual Scots here and there in Scotland itself, in England, and in all sorts of places abroad, suddenly mainfested themselves to me as being engaged simultaneously in the same process. Muir was one of these. He and his wife, and A.S. Neill and others, had, I found, been engaged in debating the self-same issues with each other in Italy, Austria, and elsewhere, before they heard of *Northern Numbers* and *The Scottish Chapbook*, and learned that there was a movement on foot in Scotland itself. A sporadic simultaneity of speculation of this kind is, as every student of literary history knows, a highly significant – if not infallible – phenomenon. In Muir's case it has already led to his remarkable essays on Burns, the Scottish Ballads, and George Douglas Brown, and to his own Scots Ballads. But there was something even more significant than this simultaneity of tendency to me – and that was the astonishing calibre younger Scots were beginning to manifest in every department of art. Take three of them. In literary criticism – Muir, incomparably the finest critic Scotland has ever

produced, and the only one who has achieved an international reputation and influence. In music – F.G. Scott, the only Scottish composer of
international calibre in the whole of our history; and in art – Professor
M'Cance, a profound critic and creative theorist, and a brilliant artist of
the latest school. The two last-named I shall deal with subsequently. The
point here is that all of them – in their knowledge of their arts – have a
European range. They are European in their experience of life. They are
thoroughly 'founded' and intellectually abreast of all that is going on in
world art and world-affairs. They have been successively struck with the
potentialities of a Scottish Renaissance. There is surely more than mere
coincidence in this. Their emergence after the almost complete provincialisation of Scotland is a striking and salutary phenomenon. And the
completely national character of the underground movement that is now
throwing up such significant figures cannot be better illustrated than by
the fact that Muir comes from Shetland [*sic*][1], Scott from the Borders,
and M'Cance from Glasgow. This showed that the diathesis of renaissance was nation-wide. Each of the trio named were 'left-wing men,' too
– aligned with the 'becoming' tendencies in world-culture. They had
each by one means or another succeeded in relieving themselves of the
inhibitions that have so long made the Scottish approach to art so intolerably flatfooted, heavy-handed, and generally *gauche* and ungainly. In
other words, they were capable – as soon as they felt it necessary to their
own artistic development – of viewing Scottish cultural requirements –
the pre-requisites of any Scottish Renaissance worthy of the name –
from an adequate standpoint: and of applying to the task of reintro-
ducing Scots art into the European stream a full knowledge of the relative temporary position of the Arts in other countries, and of employing
all the available technical resources. They could come in on the 'ground
floor.' The main thing is that all three have become – after becoming
thoroughly 'good Europeans' so far as their several arts and their general
cultural equipment is concerned – conscious Scots: and have thus
resolved – potentially at any rate – the basic difficulties which, unresolved in the past, have made the work of practically all Scottish writers
'ill-founded' and comparatively impure, and when written in English,
irrelevant to the main English tradition. In exploring and exploiting their
artistic potentialities – the basic constitution of any work they can do –
they have to reckon consciously with the fact that they are Scots, not
English, and with the variant limitations and opportunities that fact

[1] See 'A Note on the Text' – Ed.

carries with it. One of the main preliminary aims of the Scottish Renaissance movement, therefore, must be to bring every other Scottish writer of any consequence to a like conscious confrontation of the fact that he is Scottish and that his work cannot be proceeding along the lines calculated to enable him to express himself and realise his artistic potentialities most fully unless it offers an unmistakable practical equivalent – in contrast if not also in form and language – of the difference in psychology and cultural background between any Scot and any Englishman. And, while inducing that realisation and enjoining that first practical step, the movement must go further and make it clear that this difference due to being Scottish is not – as it has been generally (but not perhaps consciously) treated in the past – a handicap to be got rid of by deliberate assimilation to English standards, but the primary ground for hope – the outstanding opportunity that presents itself to them. While Muir has not systematically applied himself to the elucidation of these issues, he has – as it were by accident, in the course of other work – illuminated some of them in no uncertain fashion. Such work of this kind as he has already done makes it all the more regrettable that our press is so Anglicised, and so debased, that it has little room for literary matter for the most part – beyond the most flagrant publishers' puffs – and that, even so far as that little is concerned, London fashions in opinion are slavishly copied by reviewers and special article writers whose anonymity would only require to be withdrawn to reveal their incapacity for literary journalism in any responsible sense of the term a little more completely even – if that is possible – than the text of their articles and reviews already does.

Since I have myself been a literary critic of *The New Age* I must let another speak of its peculiar merits. Gerald Cumberland says of it (at the time of A.R. Orage's editorship):

> Tens of thousands of people have been influenced by this paper who have never even heard its name. It does not educate the masses directly: it reaches them through the medium of its few but exceedingly able readers. *The New Age* is professedly a Socialist organ, but the promulgation of socialistic doctrines is only a part of its policy and work. Its literary, artistic, and musical criticism is the sanest, the bravest, and the most brilliant that can be read in England. It reverences neither power nor reputation; it is subtle and unsparing; and, if it is sometimes cruel, it is cruel with a purpose. All sleek money-makers in Art have reason to fear Orage... I have never known an

editor more jealous of the reputation of his paper than Orage is of
The New Age. No consideration of friendship would induce him to
print a dull article, however sound, and when one of his contributors
becomes sententious, or slack, or banal – out he goes, neck or crop.

Now, Muir was on the staff of *The New Age* under Orage's editorship –
and continued to contribute to it until comparatively recently, some
considerable time after Orage ceased to edit it. Cumberland's tribute to
The New Age will be endorsed by any writer or reader of intellectual
integrity: and the fact that Muir was a regular contributor to it during
Orage's time shows that he qualified for – and completed his training in –
the hardest school for critics Great Britain has ever had to offer.
Compare the standards of *The New Age* with those of any existing
Scottish periodical. The former set a level and was inspired by principles
illimitably higher than even the best of the latter – which is to say, the
Glasgow Herald – has achieved. This is the measure of our journalistic
decadence: and the crux of one of the problems of the Scottish
Renaissance. Young Scottish literary aspirants are too apt to plume themselves enormously upon achieving the acceptance of an article or a poem
by the *Glasgow Herald*: but the level of work acceptable by the best
existing Scottish periodicals must be beneath contempt from the point of
view of a Scottish Renaissance. If the former is the pitch of a writer's
ambition he has nothing to offer to any movement of consequence. But if
he aims beyond that – where is he to find a medium for his work? The
answer is that unless his work conforms to English literary fashions –
nowhere in the meantime! A writer in the *London Mercury* recently took
me to task for asserting that English literary periodicals discriminate
against Scottish work. I, of course, never asserted anything of the kind.
What I do assert is that if Scottish creative impulses tend – as all but the
most minor ones must – to develop in forms incompatible with established literary fashions, there is no medium in Great Britain to print
them. This is tantamount to an embargo in distinctively Scottish productivity. And the boycott is completed by the fact that, while this is the state
of affairs appertaining to the literary journalism centred in London, the
Scottish press itself has so far degenerated that it will only accept work so
written as to have a mob-appeal – *i.e.*, both in subject-matter and treatment beneath contempt from a purely literary standpoint. Good Scots
work – comparable to the best contemporary English work – falls
between these two stools. England has quite a number of periodicals
open to experimental work – the excellent *Criterion*, the *Calendar of*

Modern Letters, the *Adelphi*, not to mention every now and again such ventures as *Blast* or *The Tyro*. These are in addition to the whole range of literary periodicals such as *The New Statesman*, the *Nation and Athenaeum*, the *Spectator*, the *Saturday Review* down to the *Bookman* and *T.P.'s Weekly* – all of which are predominantly or at any rate largely concerned with literature, while in all of them Scottish literature is, proportionately to the educated reading publics of the two countries, relegated to almost complete neglect. Even Ireland is better off than Scotland – with the splendid *Irish Statesman*, the scarcely less admirable *Dublin Magazine*, and older organs such as the *Dublin Review* and *Studies*. All of these are on a plan far beyond anything yet devoted to Scottish Arts. Apart from nationalism altogether, compare the leading daily papers of Holland with ours in Scotland. The former devote two or three columns each week to German, French, and English (British) literature respectively – not silly reviews that might be written by their office-boys, but substantial criticisms, by competent writers belonging to the nations in question. Imagine *The Scotsman* doing anything of the kind! Are we so far behind the Dutch, then? Or is it the policy of our papers that is wrong – are they grossly misconceiving the duties of representative journals? They will say that the number of Scots interested in foreign literatures is infinitesimal – not worth catering for – compared with those interested in say, whippet-racing. Quite. But who is responsible for that? What becomes of the power of the Press? Can the Press not elevate public taste? The answer lies mainly in the personnel of our contemporary newspaper proprietors and editorial staffs. There were not so very long ago sound if not great journalists in Scotland. Scarcely a Scottish paper has not deteriorated greatly during the past twenty-five years. More recently there has been a regrettable increase of control over the Scottish Press by English combines. The present degeneracy of the Scottish Press is a natural concomitant of the accelerated assimilation to English standards with its resultant provincialisation of Scotland. Both countries suffer in various ways: but Scotland suffers most – and by far most obviously. Compare Glasgow and Manchester: and then compare the *Glasgow Herald* and the *Manchester Guardian* – the latter with such men as (and I do not overvalue any of them) Allan Monkhouse, C.E. Montague, Professor C.H. Hereford, J.E. Agate, and so on, while the former has – William Power, of course; but who else?[1] Nobody. Literally nobody. And then, as Cumberland boasts, Manchester has its younger

[1] The 1926 edition reads: 'William Power, Robert Bain; but who else?' – Ed.

men 'who formed the Manchester Musical Society, who wrote plays, who organised the little Swan Club which worked with such extraordinary pertinacity and secrecy to create an ampler intellectual life' – men like Iden Payne, Stanley Houghton, Harold Brighouse, Jack Kahane, Lascelles Abercrombie, W.P Price-Heywood, Ernest Marriott, G.H. Mair. Who are Glasgow's young men – and women? There are none... For the credit of Scotland it is high time that Glasgow put itself in a position to be able to offer sufficient inducements to retain in it, or regularly attached to its Press and social life at all events, men like Muir and M'Cance, both of whom have fled it in horror and despair like Karel Capek's; and set about creating an atmosphere in which, as in Manchester, young men and women could cultivate their intelligences and dream their dreams. This much must be said for Glasgow. It is the only city in Scotland where there is the slightest possibility of that ever happening to all appearances. Edinburgh, Dundee, and Aberdeen are beyond hope.

Muir has now three volumes to his credit – *We Moderns* (published under the pseudonym of Edward Moore), *Latitudes* (published by Huebsch in America and Melrose here) – a volume of critical and philosophical studies – and *First Poems* (Hogarth Press). No young Scot should fail to read all three – and everything else Muir writes. His recent essays on the Sitwells, Joyce, Lawrence, and Lytton Strachey will probably be published soon: and he has another volume of poems in preparation which will probably include, in amended and extended form, the wonderful 'Chorus of the Newly Dead,' which appeared in *The Scottish Chapbook*.[2] 'I believe he is also engaged upon a novel of Glasgow life – designed to serve as a dynamic counter-foil to George Blake's work and the other novels of the so-called young 'Glasgow School.' 'Inspiration is not peculiar to the artist,' says Croce. 'It comes to all of us, whatever our walk in life. And it is not a substitute for will, but depends on will. It is a sort of grace from on high that descends upon those who allure it, inviting it by daily effort, preparing themselves to welcome it, and sustaining it, when it has come, by new efforts.' It is Muir's will that has lifted him out of our Scottish provincialism and is making him an international force. My complaint is that there exists a condition of affairs that makes it excessively difficult, if not impossible, for any conscious artist to apply his will-power in distinctively Scottish directions to-day: the Scottish Renaissance move-

---

[2] The 1926 edition reads: 'His recent essays on the Sitwells, Joyce, Lawrence, and Lytton Strachey will probably be published soon: and, as I write, the Hogarth Press announce his "Chorus of the Nearly Dead", one of the most remarkable poems written in English for many years.' (The poem was not, in fact, published in *The Scottish Chapbook* – Ed.)

ment is out to remove that barrier and to make it no longer necessary to work through English or other media with the loss of force that involves in order to influence Scotland and to create Scots Art. 'The Unconscious within us, which "doeth the work," is quite unyielding,' says another writer, 'in its insistence on being equipped with a perfect intellectual technique. If it is baffled by clumsy thought, insular vision, and unpractised craft, it is likely to give up in disgust the effort of expression, and the poor individual who might have been the vehicle of that revelation is torn by the agony of frustration.' The majority of Scottish writers during the past hundred years have been entirely destitute of intellectual equipment adequate to work of international calibre, or even of national calibre comparatively considered. Scotland has consequently become insular and has 'fidged fu' fain' on the strength of work that reflected only its national degeneracy and its intellectual inferiority to every other European country. The majority of the Scottish writers held most in esteem by contemporary Scots were (or are) too 'unconscious' even to experience the sense of frustration. They were too completely destitute of artistic integrity. It is in this that Muir is so significantly differentiated from the great majority, if not all, of his predecessors back to the time of the Auld Makers – both as critic and creative artist. 'Reviewers,' says Alan Porter,

> think they are to be praised if they read a book casually, react naively, like a child, and spin out a few hundred words of comment, easily and without self-adjustment. Indeed, they are rather proud of their little idiosyncrasies and obsessions. 'At least,' they will tell you, 'we are honest. We put down what we felt as we read. It is one man's testimony, and we do not pretend that it is more.' Honest? They have no conception of how far a man must dig into himself before he can lay claim to honesty, and is it any better to deck prejudices in pompous words, to attempt to convince readers that a personal opinion is an absolute judgment? No; that is both charlatanism and disrespectfulness. The critic, before he sets down a word, must beat himself on the head and ask a hundred times, each time more bitterly and searchingly. 'And is it true? Is it true?' He must analyse his judgment and make sure that it is nowhere stained or tinted with the blood of his heart. And he must search out a table of values from which he can be certain that he has left nothing unconsidered. If, after all these precautions and torments, he is unable to deliver a true judgment, then fate has been too strong for him: he was never meant to be a critic.

These are the tests Muir applies to himself – and which the reader may apply to his work – and he emerges triumphantly. He is a critic – almost the only one our singularly uncritical nation has ever produced. Compared with him all our reviewers and special article writers and literary historians and lecturers on literary subjects are discovered as hopelessly shallow and dishonest. He has dug down into himself sufficiently far to find honesty – and many other things – so far, indeed, as to rediscover the fact that he is a Scot, and as such vitally differentiated, a fact than which few things are more deeply concealed to and by the vast majority of his countrymen. Once thus rediscovered it is a fact that must be reckoned with. What Muir is going to make of it remains to be seen; but in his Ballads and in certain of his critical essays he has already made a great deal – and a great deal that may be the cause of a great deal more in himself and in others. I cannot conclude better than by quoting the passage in his essay on 'The Scottish Ballads,' which to anyone who has pride of race and is unwilling to be subordinated to any other people supplies in itself a sufficient *raison d'être* for the Scottish Renaissance movement in general, and the attempt to revive the Scots vernacular in particular: –

> Since English became the literary language of Scotland there has been no Scots imaginative writer who has attained greatness in the first or even the second rank through the medium of English. Scott achieved classical prose, prose with the classical qualities of solidity, force, and measure, only when he wrote in the Scottish dialect; his Scottish dialogue is great prose, and his one essay in Scottish imaginative litera-ture, 'Wandering Willie's Tale' is a masterpiece of prose, of prose which one must go back to the seventeenth century to parallel. The style of Carlyle, on the other hand, was taken bodily from the Scots pulpit; he was a parish minister of genius, and his English was not great English but great Scots English; the most hybrid of all styles, with some of the virtues of the English Bible and many of the vices of the Scottish version of the Psalms of David; a style whose real model may be seen in Scott's anticipatory parody of it in *Old Mortality*. He took the most difficult qualities of the English language and the worst of the Scots, and through them attained a sort of absurd, patchwork greatness. But – this can be said for him – his style expressed, in spite of its overstrain, and even through it, something real, the struggle of a Scots peasant, born to other habits of speech and of thought, with the English language. Stevenson – and it was the sign of his inferiority, his lack of fundamental merit – never had this struggle, nor realised that it was necessary that he should have it... The other two Scots-English

writers of the last half-century, John Davidson and James Thomson (the author of 'The City of Dreadful Night') were greater men than Stevenson, less affected and more fundamental; but fundamental as they were, they lacked something which in English prose is fundamental, and the oblivion into which they are fallen, undeserved as it seems when we consider their great talents, is yet, on some ground not easy to state, just. The thing I am examining here, superficial in appearance, goes deep. No writer can write great English who is not born an English writer and in England: and born moreover in some class in which the tradition of English is pure, and, it seems to me, therefore, in some other age than this...

That is the choice – either to go back to Scots; or to be content to be indefinitely no more than third-rate in an English tradition which is declining, and to the declinature of which no bottom can apparently be set – one of Spengler's 'exhausted civilisations' giving way to 'the stones the builders despised.'

See also three articles on Muir as critic in *New Age*, by the present writer, in May, 1924, and one on Muir, as poet, by Hugh M'Diarmid in *New Age*, June, 1925.   [4.9.25]

Letters

CONTEMPORARY SCOTTISH STUDIES
Sir. – I am obliged to Sir George Douglas for his note of 19th ult. I drafted the sentence to which he refers rather hastily, and it ought to have read not 'Nothing of literary criticism, etc,' but 'Has anything of literary criticism, etc.' My point was that when we think of the Fortnightly *or the other periodicals mentioned we do not think of Sir George Douglas. – I am, etc.,*

C.M. Grieve
[4.9.25]

13. Francis George Scott

The position of Scottish literature compared with that of any other European country is deplorable enough: but that of Scottish music is

infinitely worse. In music as in drama we are unique in the fact that we
have entirely failed to develop any worth considering at all: and in both
cases this is due to substantially the same causes – first of all, the
Reformation; second, the comparative material poverty in our country
which has developed that 'eye to the main chance' which is the salient
and too often the sole characteristic of our people; and, third, our subordination to England. The arts are still to a large extent under Calvinistic
suspicion, and this has borne more heavily on music, the drama, and
dancing than on literature and art. The vast majority of our people over-
whelmed in drudgery are inevitably preoccupied with something very
much more get-at-able than music: and frankly unless the present
economic system (of which our education and our religion are appurte-
nances) can be radically altered a really civilised life must remain out of
the question so far as the majority of our people are concerned. Music
more than any of the other arts demands rigorous intellectual application. Owing to our subordination to England we are cut off from our
own 'sources'; obliged to think in an alien and unsuitable language; and
denied many of the facilities for self-expression and development that
would otherwise have been available. It is impossible to give adequate
consideration to the position of the arts in Scotland unless full account is
taken of our economic and political circumstances; and when these have
been taken fully into consideration it is not surprising to find those who
are most vitally concerned with the absence in Scotland of arts comparable to those of any other country in Europe conjoining to a new propaganda of cultural nationalism a demand for a Scots Free state on the one
hand and, on the other, a faith in what is loosely called 'Socialism' as the
only programme that is likely to give the whole population access to the
highest and best things that life can offer.

If the religious and political courses to which we have been
committed have not come between us and the realisation of our finest
potentialities, it is impossible to account for our comparative sterility.
The case in regard to our music is particularly clear and permits of no
other conclusion. It may be – although I do not think so – that there is
something in Scottish psychology so antipathetic to drama as to account
for our failure to develop that form to any extent worthy of a moment's
consideration. But in music it is otherwise. Obviously forces have
intruded here which have precluded the due development of splendid
beginnings. The future of Scottish music depends upon the resolution of
the religious and political complexes which have inhibited our natural
musical genius. This resolution must be a conscious process – not an

event to be attended Micawber-like. What signs are there that any such conscious effort is being made? The answer to that question is the only material of the slightest consequence with which we can address ourselves to any query as to where Scotland stands, so far as music is concerned: everything else is irrelevant, and depends either upon a misconception as to what music is or as to what Scotland is or both. Apart from some entirely preventable and entirely deplorable suspension of natural musical faculty in Scotland, there is no reason why our exploitation of music should not have kept pace with that of any other country in Europe, judging by the volume and quality of Scottish Folk Song, which is undeniably one of the finest in the world. On this incomparable basis – calculated to sustain an inimitable superstructure – we have built literally nothing. Why? Other countries with poorer bases have magnificent achievements to their credit. We delight in these – but give nothing in return.

That so splendid a tradition – manifestly replete with inspiration as soon as the right psychology approaches it with adequate technique – should have proved, and still be proving, so barren in tendency is obviously an issue of such crucial importance from the point of view of the value of creative activity to any people that the apathy towards it, nonrecognition of the opportunities so created, and failure to concentrate upon it as the most vital problem of our national being, of all who have claimed or claim to be Scottish musicians is the best proof of either their lack of integrity or their lack of capacity. They have exchanged their birthright for a mess of pottage. The whole of the recent musical history of Europe reproaches their impotence, or their incomprehension. That the latter is mainly responsible must be the conclusion of all who are unable to concede the radical spiritual inferiority of our people to all other Western nations.

The position in Scotland to-day is that we have, on the one hand, the great mass of our population given, owing to their material circumstances, practically no opportunity for acquiring a culture: and, on the other hand, a comparatively small section whose culture is practically little more than a mere inversion of the condition of the masses. This means that so far as music is concerned there has never been any carrying-over from purely folk-expression into an art-product – *i.e.*, expression as art – the process which has built up the musical traditions of every other country. There does not seem to be even yet in Scotland, except in a few isolated quarters, the slightest inkling as to what this process is or the means of initiating it. Even those Scots who are actively interested in musical matters and must necessarily be perfectly familiar with this process at work in the music of other countries – or at least with its results in new art-products – seem incapable of applying it to our Scottish sources or of discerning that its introduction and application is the only way out for Scottish music – the only means whereby it can ever emerge on to a plane comparable to that to which music has long attained in every other country. Scotland is their 'blind spot,' as it were: and this is due to their cultural and political preconceptions, suggestions superimposed to the frustration of their natural powers – but it should be at variance with their artistic instincts. That it is not, consciously at all events – and that they should be driven to 'compensate' themselves for this radical 'want' after the fashion in which an inferiority complex inevitably operates – amounts to a 'specific aboulia.' On the other hand, it means that Scotland is to-day a country full of unparalleled potentialities – a country, the only country in Europe, in which literally everything remains to be done. Magnificent opportunities await any Scotsman who has the fortune to be free, or can free himself, of the common inhibitions, and pierce with intuitive genius to the core of this tangle. We hear a great deal about the Scots being a musical people. It is difficult to come to grips with what this means. If it has any reality it would make it all the more inexplicable – indeed, it would have made it impossible – that a people possessed of a Folk-Song that has probably no equal in the world and so extremely appreciative of it (the fact to which the loose phrase really refers) should have become so completely disoriented and precluded from the natural exploitation of it. I do not believe that this is due to any inherent incapacity of the Scottish nation even as it now exists, but wholly to political and economic causes which have the incidental effect of inhibiting our natural genius, and that therefore the removal of these is a first essential – or at least a concomitant – of any Scottish National Renaissance worthy of the name.

Whatever the causes may be – fortuitous or fundamental – when we come to examine the state of affairs in regard to music that actually obtains in Scotland to-day, we find that while it is thus taking credit to itself for possessing a highly intelligent and musical people, it simply has so far altogether failed to find any musical expression for itself worth mentioning, and has no existence at all as a musical nation. Scotland has no place in the map of music. Let alone 'Scottish music,' no Scottish composer finds mention in Landormy's *History of Music*, and references to Scotland or to Scotsmen in any other musical history or dictionary of music and musicians are exceedingly few and far between, and of negligible value at that. Scotland's position comparatively to any other European country is adequately represented by a state of affairs which gives the latter an interesting array of names and a record of historical development and the former nothing. 'Facts are chiels that winna ding,' and people who 'blaw' about Scottish music would be well-advised to perpend its relative position. We have certainly no justification for a 'guid conceit o' oorsel's' in this connection.

The end of last century saw Scotland putting forth its first attempts to find musical expression. The technique of the time was an easy one. It was not an experimental period. Such men as Mackenzie, Learmont Drysdale, Hamish MacCunn, and J.B. McEwen – two of whom are still living – can only be claimed as Scots composers in the sense that they had acquired a technique that was then common all over the world and applied it to Scottish subjects. In other words, their technique was an imposition from the outside. Their achievement can be summed up by saying that it almost entirely consisted in the application of German teaching to Scottish themes. Their technique could have been just as well applied to an English or an Irish theme. Any English or other foreign composer could have applied the same technique to Scottish themes in exactly the same way as they did. They had no impulse impelling them to create specifically Scottish music – to carry on from our native Folk-Song and derive art-products from it. Scotland musically has had no part whatever in the new nationalism that arising after the decline of the great German classics has in turn affected almost every other country in Europe – beginning in Russia with Glinka, Balakireff, and Moussorgsky, and culminating (if what is merely its latest manifestation to date can be referred to as its culmination) in the English Renaissance of Vaughan Williams, Gustav Holst, and others, of which even Ernest Newman is beginning to take some notice, although he did nothing to help the movement in its earlier stages. Most of these national movements are now in their third, fourth, or fifth stages; Scotland is only perhaps coming at last to the threshold of her first. Or rather not Scotland, but a few Scots are feeling their way towards it. Any incipient Scottish music will certainly receive no more encouragement from our orthodox – and self-appointed – arbiters in musical matters than the English movement in its earlier stages received from Newman. The provincialism which the average Scot has to the art of music – and by average Scot in this connection I mean the great majority of Scots who know anything about music at all – is due to the 'inferiority complex' already referred to: he is perfectly willing to accept every kind of music except his own – as is evidenced in the concert programmes of the Scottish Orchestra, which, reflecting to a certain extent although they have done the advantages derived from the national movements in other countries, have apparently failed to create any realisation of the underlying lesson for ourselves. Scotland has still to learn the truth of what Cecil Forsyth says: 'It must be confessed that in almost every generation there are two classes of men working and talking in opposition to each other – the nationalists and the denationalists. And the artistic health and productivity of any community increases exactly with its proportion of nationalists. The denationalists almost invariably have rank, wealth, and fashion at their backs. Indeed, but for the fact that they are a race of artistic eunuchs, the other party would never make any headway. But the people who do, generally get in front of those who *talk*.' So far as Scotland is concerned, the trouble is that the denationalists have thus far had it all their own way, and that what nationalists there are have failed to do anything. But it is impossible that such a state of affairs can be indefinitely prolonged: the increasing national consciousness of Scotland cannot remain much longer unreflected in the sphere of music – subordinate to other people's nationalisms. Of men like Mackenzie, Forsyth well says:

A man of this sort often begins with great natural talent, and if it were possible for him to exercise that talent in a vacuum he would no doubt achieve much. But he does not live in a vacuum. He lives in a closely-packed continent throbbing with the highly developed and strongly differentiated groups of men which we call nations. As a rule he goes to Germany – the country whose technical proficiency is beyond question. There he masters all that the Germans can teach him. But when he returns home he does not ask himself whether after all his musical attainment is merely a brilliant sleight-of-hand, which anyone can pick up with cleverness and application. He does not say: 'I have learned so and so from the Germans: how did *they* learn it?' He accepts the German art of his day as a boy accepts a Christmas present of a box of conjuring tricks. He never honestly knows *why* the tricks are done and so is never able to invent a new one.

Forsyth goes on to show that the effect of nationalism in music was 'to awaken, as I have said, some half-a-dozen nations to the possibility of imitating – not the German music – but the Germans.' This is the lesson that Scotland has still to learn: until it is learnt Scotland can have no music of her own that is not mere translation of foreign idioms.

This brings me to F.G. Scott – the exception who proves the rule I have indicated – the only Scottish composer who has yet addressed himself to these issues and tackled the task of creating a distinctively Scottish idiom – a bridge-over from folk-song to art-form. The bulk of his work is still unpublished: and what is published is little known. I do not think that the musical critics of any of our dailies have so much as mentioned him yet in any connection: the only articles concerning him I have encountered are one by Miss Isobel Guthrie on 'Contemporary Scots Composers: F.G. Scott, Joseph Halley, and Harry Hodge' in *The Scottish Nation*; another by the same lady on 'Scottish Music and Mr Scott' in *The Northern Review*, and, in the same magazine, an account by Edwin Muir, of a 'two-handed crack' on fundamental issues between Scott and himself at Salzburg. Scott's importance lies in the fact that he is the first and apparently the only Scottish composer to appreciate the existing position. Owing to our almost equal lack of any effective literary tradition he has naturally found himself handicapped on that side, too. Practically nothing out of Burns or from the post-Burns period is susceptible of being 'worked up' into art-form: for the simple reason that it has not sprung from the well-springs of the Scottish consciousness. It is miscegenate stuff. It is necessary to go right back to the fundamentals of Scottish mentality and to explore and exploit these, not in any jejune and superficial fashion, like Mackenzie and the others I have already mentioned, but in a thoroughgoing fashion that realises that the new wine cannot be put into the old bottles, or, in other words, that foreign forms will not serve to contain the material so found, but that it necessarily demands new forms distinctively its own – distinctively Scottish. The arts in Scotland are in a curiously interdependent state: they must advance almost simultaneously: music in particular must to a large extent wait upon poetry. Scott is essentially a lyric composer, and has suffered all the more from the latter fact. His early training was practically in the school of McEwen, and he was still almost entirely under the same influence, and had substantially the same 'direction' right up to 1910. Almost everything he wrote prior to that date was in that tradition – in the tradition of Wagner, Strauss, and so on – but it is safe to say that he does not attach the slightest value to these tendencies now, and that it is extremely improbable that the compositions in which he exemplified them will ever be published. It is by such indirections that artists find directions out. In the work that he did next he went definitely back to the folk-song time – working under the literary influence of the Auld Makars and, in particular, of Dunbar – and his originality and value lies in the fact that he attempted to find expression, on the basis of our Folk-Song, through purely modern technical media. In other words, he belatedly and single-handedly set himself to the very task that would have been discharged in large measure long ere this had Scotland not been so inexplicably destitute of all sense of musical opportunity and so oblivious to every consideration of national self-respect in this connection. Albeit thus belated and obliged to do the 'donkey-work,' the mere brute pioneering, that at his time of day he ought to have found done for him by a little host of predecessors in a fashion that would have enabled him to commence on a plane upon which he would not have been so utterly at a disadvantage with his Continental compeers, all of whose 'fathers lived before them,' Scott, at least, has the advantage of having nothing to undo, and, thoroughly *au courant* with the whole field of contemporary music, and thus able to appreciate the uses to which nationalism in music has been put in other countries and the means whereby the varying difficulties in each of them have been successively overcome, he was enabled to approach his own task with a wealth of relevant experience of other people's and the accumulated advantages of several decades of musical development – *i.e.*, other things being equal, he was at least as much better equipped in certain directions coming to his task in 1910 as McEwen and others would (had the task challenged them as it would have done if they had been *en rapport* with the becoming tendencies of their times) have been twenty to thirty years earlier as he was handicapped, relatively to his European contemporaries, by the absence of forerunners in his particular field. He threw himself into his task with appropriate energy, and the results are pretty well embodied in his two volumes of *Scottish Lyrics* (Messrs Bayley and Ferguson) which certainly contain all the distinctively Scottish music that has so far been published – music in which the melodic line is perfectly Scottish and the technique perfectly modern.

It was, however, he soon found, impossible in the particular cultural circumstances of Scotland to continue along these lines. Owing to the desuetude of the Doric – or, rather, the tardiness of its revival – the necessary material is not available. Nor will it ever be: a Scottish Renaissance worth bothering about must necessarily elide this stage altogether. It is too late now. The trouble is that most people who are beginning to think about a Scottish Renaissance are envisaging the creation of work in music and the other arts at some indefinite time in the more or less immediate future that will, when – or rather would, if – produced be hopelessly *passéist* compared with the contemporary work of other countries. This is to take it for granted that Scotland must always be in the position of the cow's tail – that it can never 'draw level.' This is the negation of any true Renaissance spirit, which must necessarily be intent upon discovering short cuts to make up for lost ground. So far as music is concerned that is what Scott has been doing. While his 'Scottish Lyrics' are still too advanced for our musical nation, he has perforce abandoned the lines upon which he was then working as pyrrhonistic and unprofitable, and set off across country, as it were, to join issue at an intuitively anticipated point with the current of European musical development. In other words, Scott found that on the one hand there was not a sufficient *corpus* of Scottish lyrics available to make it worth his while to continue further along that particular line, and, on the other, that there was not only no guarantee but an increasing improbability that if he did he would be achieving his purpose – of bringing Scottish music, while it remained distinctively national, abreast of European tendency. His researches into the literary history of Scotland afforded him little help. In the two volumes in question he was concerned mainly with Burns: and they practically exhausted Burns so far as his purposes were concerned. He took Burns at his least popular – or, in other words, at his most specifically Scottish – and in the Burns *corpus* that is an extremely limited element. On the one hand, therefore, he found himself driven back to Dunbar, and on the other, the paucity of Scottish literary lyrics – *i.e.*, not 'wood notes wild,' but art products – has practically confined him latterly to the use of Hugh MacDiarmid's poems: and consequently he has been obliged to abandon the folk-song idiom and employ a modern international technique appropriate to contemporary world-consciousness. That is to say, he has now reached the stage at which he is doing work at once European and essentially Scottish which is too ultra-modern to find acceptance as music in Scotland and too Scottish to be acceptable as Scottish anywhere in our present denationalised condition. He is facing precisely the same difficulties on the musical side as have already been encountered on the literary side of the Scottish revival movement. It is significant that so far none of Scott's songs has been included in our Festival programmes – despite the fact that Mr Roberton has given it as his opinion, in one of his Orpheus Choir programmes, that he (Scott) is likely to profoundly affect the future of Scottish music. (Incidentally it should be said that practically any opportunity that Scott has had to affect the *present* of Scottish music has also come through Mr Roberton and his choir – notably Miss Boyd Steven – although here again it must be remembered that they have only got to the stage of being able to appreciate and utilise elements of Scott's work that he has almost completely outgrown.)

Just as on the literary side of the Scottish Renaissance it has been expressly declared that 'we must make our own Continental affiliations

irrespective of London, in accordance with the propensities and requirements of our own distinctive national psychology,' so, so far as music is
concerned, Scott's radical variance from the *ethos* of most contemporary
Scottish musicality is due in great measure to the fact that he does not
wait for news of Continental developments to filter down to him *via*
London. He is on the spot all the time. He establishes direct connections
with Bartók in Hungary or Stravinsky in Switzerland as the case may be,
and is alive to whatever is afoot as rapidly and directly as any of his
English contemporaries. The importance of this cannot be over-stressed.
It is the only way in which our cultural subordination to England can be
overcome. As long as we are content to receive our information at
second-hand from London we necessarily remain provincial. The
deplorable condition of Scottish music is largely due to the poor quality
of our contemporary musical criticism, which is wholly derivative, non-
creative, and apparently unconcerned with the underlying realities.
Over-Anglicisation has played a great part in bringing about this discreditable state of affairs. How many of our leading musicians in Scotland
are, in fact, Englishmen – men like Professor Donald Tovey, Arthur
Collingwood, and Professor Sanford Terry? And think of the Scottish
Orchestra (that proud recourse of the Glasgow business man), which has
never had a Scottish conductor in the whole course of its history –
indeed, this year, it is not to have even a British one at all!

How far is the condition of the arts in Scotland due to the 'moralic
acid' to which our boys and girls are subjected during the most impres-
sionable period of their lives? Our absence of all tradition or sense of
tradition in these matters must be largely attributable to the fact that
(until comparatively recently) practically no Scot has been trained as a
professional artist, whether in music or in any other department. Scottish
parents have wanted their children to be anything but that. The consequences of this cannot be easily if ever overcome. Ezra Pound was not far
wrong when he advocated the establishment of Poets' Schools, in which
boys and girls could be trained to become poets. In Scotland we can
connect this with our own history by deploring the cessation and advocating the restoration of the old Bardic Colleges. It is certainly true that
at the present time there is no place in Scotland where any of our young
people can secure the higher branches of musical training along nationalistic lines. What is wanted is not academic but creative training. It is
presently proposed to establish a Chair of Music in Glasgow University.
Will we be any the better of that? Not a bit. The proposal is entirely
supererogatory as far as musical realities in Scotland to-day are

concerned. It merely means a closer affiliation with the Royal Academy and the Royal College of Music – a further step in the effort to entirely assimilate Scottish to English tendency. The English Renaissance exemplified in such men as Vaughan Williams, Bridge, Bax, Ireland, Holst, Bliss, Berners and Goossens, is largely the product of the intensive training of these institutions – largely the result of the work of Stanford and Corder: but to connect Glasgow more closely up with them is to subject Scotland to the backwash of the English movement in lieu of that genuine movement of our own which is so long overdue. It is irony, indeed, that our 'denationalisers,' as Forsyth calls them, should be using the English nationalists in this way, and that the latter should be the instruments of an intrigue – conscious or unconscious – to prevent Scots following their example and doing for Scotland what they have succeeded in accomplishing for England. But Scott is apparently the only Scottish musician who is alive to the irony involved and concerned to create any counter-movement. One of the first things Hungary did when it reacquired its status as a separate nation was to appoint Bartók and Kodály as its head instructors in the Conservatoire at Budapest. Czecho-Slovakia acted similarly. The recent history of music in these countries attests the prescience of the step Scotland cannot hope to emulate either of them as long as it entrusts musical education in Scotland wholly or mainly to non-nationals. As for the Musical Festival Movement (to which I shall recur) it claims to be an educational movement, and so it is, but not in the sense with which I am presently concerned. It is to some extent educative of interpreters, but not of creators. The musical vitality of any country is to be estimated by the latter, not by the former – and of the latter whom have we, or have we ever had, except F.G Scott, whose deficiencies as a representative composer are largely attributable to the cultural condition of the country to which he happens to belong, but whose work, despite all the handicaps with which he has had to contend in a virgin field, is nevertheless far more than any other artistic product of contemporary Scotland comparable to the best products in its kind of any other country in Europe?   [11.9.25]

14. George Reston Malloch

Who are the twenty principal Scottish poets? It is easy enough to name the first ten, not of a size, it is true, but comparable enough, without being driven to such an extremity as would place, say, Fergusson, or, even worse, Tannahill in the list – without, that is to say, considering as poets rhymesters of a kind customarily so considered in Scotland but in no other country. Of these three would be Gaelic poets – Alexander Macdonald, Duncan Bàn MacIntyre, and Dugald Buchanan. But it is impossible to add to the ten without suggesting names obviously incongruous – making mountains of comparative poetical molehills, such as one-song singers, or stretching the term 'poet' in the peculiarly Scottish fashion I have referred to – so long as you stick to the past. But coming to the present it is not difficult to complete the twenty. In other words, Scotland to-day possesses at least ten poets superior to all except the greatest ten it has had in the whole course of its literary history. I waive discussion in the meantime of their comparability with – or with any of – the first ten. That is to say, it is not my present purpose to attempt to arrange the list of our twenty greatest Scottish poets in order of merit. I will only say that in certain respects – as 'pure poets,' as conscious artists – some of these contemporaries are, in my opinion, greater than any of their predecessors, and simply because they are our contemporaries, all of them should have our attention to a greater degree. But, apart from that, that we should have living to-day a group of poets superior – and for the most part immensely superior in many if not all ways – to all but the ten greatest poets our race has ever produced, is an astonishing fact and probably without parallel in the literary history of any other country in the world for many centuries. Two further remarks must be made – first, that nevertheless this does not mean that the group in question equals or even compares favourably with other contemporary or past groups of poets in other countries – any more than the greatest ten poets Scotland has produced compare favourably, let alone equally, with the greatest ten English, or French, or Italian, or Russian poets: Scotland has not overcome its radical inferiority in this and every other art – and, secondly, there is every likelihood that the group in question is simply fore-running a succession of major Scottish poets, writing either in English or Scots or both, destined to appear within the next half-century, and to transcend the present group as completely as they transcend all but an infinitesimal proportion of their predecessors. Of this second ten to make up the desiderated score, the subject of the present essay, George Reston Malloch, who also claims attention as a dramatist, a critic, and a short-story writer, is emphatically one. The others are – of the older school of our contemporaries – Dr Ronald Campbell Macfie, Sir Ronald Ross, Lord Alfred Douglas and Dr Pittendrigh Macgillivray;

and of the younger school, Muriel Stuart, Edwin Muir, F.V. Branford, John Ferguson, and, I think, William Jeffrey, with Professor Alexander Gray and Rachael Annand Taylor as 'runners-up.' I do not say that there are not other living Scots poets in addition to these who transcend all their predecessors but the foremost ten: there are – I think I could name at least another ten – but I simply assert that these at any rate *do*, and challenge any critic to name more than ten Scottish poets not now alive – including Sir Walter Scott, Byron and, if you like, Ben Jonson – in a superior category to any one of these. This may not mean a great deal: it may only mean that we have never had more poets of any appreciable size than can be counted on the fingers. It is purely an internal measurement – a question of domestic precedence, and throws little light, if any, on the relative stature of any of these whom I have named as *poets*. But what I am concerned about in setting out the issue in this fashion is the fact that even of the extremely limited poetry-reading public in Scotland to-day probably not ten per cent are cognisant of these names or at any rate most of them; that 'Scottish Poetry' is a term which does not connote a corpus of which their work is an admitted, let alone an appreciated, element, but almost wholly implies something vastly inferior; that our Scottish press and platform have entirely failed to accord due recognition to any of them; that there are no media in Scotland through which most of them can publish their work; and that there are all sorts of societies and organisations at work for the perpetual glorification of comparative pigmies whose claims to even that sort of immortality any other country in the world would long ago have turned down in no uncertain fashion even if they had had nothing better to put in their place. Read their names over again. No Scottish paper or periodical (except the short-lived organs of the Scottish Renaissance movement) has ever printed a considered article on most of them; their books have been reviewed as of no more consequence than the ruck of contemporary poetry publishing: articles are devoted instead to Helen Adam, to John Smellie Martin, to Gilbert Rae and other nonentities. Most of my list live outwith Scotland and perforce write for English periodicals and the English public. In my opinion this compulsory denationalisation – this divorcement from their natural public – this immersion in the milieu of a different and largely antipathetic culture – has prevented most of them from reaching their full poetical stature: and none of them has it inhibited or subverted more in some ways and developed in others than Malloch, although Malloch is so constituted by temperament and so situated in point of age that he may yet win through by reorienting his efforts on intensively nationalistic lines. He has indeed begun to do so. In subject-matter and purpose much of his recent poetry is more positively Scottish: he has even been experimenting – not unsuccessfully – with the Braid Scots medium: but it is as a dramatist perhaps that he will yet have proved to have recovered himself most effectively by his receptivity to the Renaissance ideas.

Of Malloch's *Poems and Lyrics* (1917), the distinguished Dutch litterateur, Roel Houwinck, said, 'Malloch, a true lyricist, gives a clear expression to his comparatively variable moods. Yet they all have, even in the simplest rhythms, the troubled background of the changing spirit of to-day. The construction of the verses and their intricate music are excellent but behind are such wild and frightened echoes that all brilliancy of form is lost... This poet is close to an interior revolution; he will not be able to maintain for any length of time the beautiful outward balance of his verse.' And then in 1920, apropos Malloch's new volume of *Poems*, Houwinck wrote:

> I am sorry that Malloch is beginning to fall off. Not that this book is worse than the former one, but it is no better. If he were not in every respect a young poet we should perhaps pass by these faults with a shrug of the shoulders in the belief that we were confronted with the tragic but harmonious decay of a mistaken talent or attribute them at best to slovenliness of workmanship. But the fact that Malloch has in him the germ of originality which appears so extraordinarily seldom in literature obliges our judgment to be very strict. Every generation has its ideals, and they hold as well on aesthetic as on moral grounds, when it is a question of realising one's full responsibility, or a case of performing a difficult duty and putting the interests of culture before personal considerations. The critic especially is far too ready to put his hand upon his heart and to avoid all unpleasantness by letting a witty or a general review suffice. But just at this time when we stand at the turning of the tide the critic's task is sharply defined: to preface the way for the new, in so far as this is manifested in forms intelligible in terms of time (the educational element); and in the same way to appraise the old in so far as this is manifested in forms intelligible in terms of time (the historic element). This two-fold duty of criticism can be properly performed only so long as it abstains from primitive and negative personal concessions, which can in the long run be of no use to the parties concerned.

These extracts from Houwinck's critiques are of extraordinary import from the point of view of the Scottish Renaissance. Houwinck detected in Malloch a state of affairs – a looking for something – which the instinct that created the movement towards a Scottish Renaissance believed must be equally present in every other Scottish writer of Malloch's age and under, and which could only be satisfied by its programme. This 'interior revolution' properly consummated should have resulted in a new nationalism of purpose – a new and inspiring real-isation of the potentialities latent in being Scots. 1917-20 – The destiny of Scottish literature – no less than Malloch's own destiny as an author – indeed stood at the turning-point then: and the two were intimately connected. Only in so far as Malloch could react with increased creativity, with improved art – either for or against, be it remarked – to the 'becoming' tendencies of Scottish consciousness as a purposive factor in world-culture then – could Houwinck's hopes be realised; and the same is true of all Malloch's generation and of the younger genera-tion at that time – they only had, and had a chance of expressing, signifi-cance so far as Scottish literature (or the other arts) is concerned, to the extent to which they were conscious of 'something in the air' in those years – of some imponderable problem affecting the basis of their creative constitution about to be resolved – and succeeded in reacting profitably to it. That Houwinck should have intuitively realised all this is a tribute to his extraordinary perspicacity: and confirms what I have said elsewhere of the simultaneity of anticipation affecting Scottish writers at that juncture and of the pervasive power of the factors which were then moving to bring Scotland into line with the new nationalism which was developing simultaneously in so many countries, and to initiate the Scottish Renaissance movement. Malloch did, I think, as a poet and certainly as a dramatist – and has continued to – react profitably to his own artistic integrity, and therefore success. I think his next volume of poems will give Houwinck ample reassurance. 'She dissects a Flower,' for example, which appeared in *The Scottish Chapbook,* is an especially convincing bit of work, and certainly deserves a place in any anthology of the finest post-War poems in the English language.

Writing of Malloch's poetry in *The Scottish Chapbook*, I said that

It is a very considerable record of subtle but important spiritual and technical experiences, and whatever ultimate values it may have in itself, it represents a course in feeling and experimental expression which every Scottish poet who is to be of consequence must take somehow or other. The quickest way for most of them would be to read Malloch's poems in the candid light of questions such as these: – 'Malloch is a contemporary Scot: so am I. How do my psychological resources compare with his? Can I similarly extend my 'awareness' – or am I definitely confined to the lower plane of consciousness upon which Scottish poetry has hitherto moved? How does he secure his effects? What background of imaginative apprehension or actual experience, and of culture generally, is necessary before one can even conceive such effects?' In short, a study of Malloch's work shows the irremediable poverty in accessibility to ideas and sensations and in spontaneous suggestionability of the average Scottish versifier's consciousness, and when these preliminary questions have been answered, secondary questions arise – in how far has Malloch by getting rid of the general repressions of his race become denationalised, or, on the other hand, realised the submerged potentialities, not only of his own personal but of Scottish national psychology? How is his work differentiated from that of his English contemporaries, and is that differentiation due to the fact that he is a Scotsman or to other factors?... Too many Scots regard Scottish literature as, in effect, a 'country cousin' of English literature, comparatively pedestrian and provincial, subject to severe technical limitations, destitute of cultural associations, confined to a certain set of themes and of a narrow mental and moral range. These cannot be expected to regard Malloch as really a Scottish poet any more than they regard Ben Jonson as a Scottish poet. They will say, 'He may be a Scotsman, but for all practical purposes his poetry is English poetry.' They cannot be expected to appreciate the subtle spiritual differences which distinguish all that is Scottish from all that is English even where (often most acutely where) superficial appearances convey impressions of absolute identity... 'For all practical purposes' is a temporary phrase even though the period to which it is applicable may be the whole of our subsequent history as a United Kingdom, and I unhesitatingly assert that the psychological difficulties which are innumerously resolved in Malloch's work are, save where they are difficulties with which modern consciousness in general is dealing (*i.e.,* present to every contemporary consciousness above a certain level), Scottish difficulties as distinct from English ones, although the differences can hardly be appreciated without a comprehensive apprehension of the psychological histories of the two peoples. Little prejudices are discernible here or there (or the facts of little prejudices having been overcome); spiritual atmospheres are created; moral tendencies reveal themselves, instincts are in evidence; minutiae

of personality; shadows of old controversies, which cannot be mistaken
by anyone who has ever gazed into the heart of Scottish history. These
are most essentially different from the corresponding prejudices, affectations, instincts, sense of background, etc., appreciable in English
work; the psychological content is entirely different; the savour of separate traditions, of diverse destinies, is disengaged... Malloch is claimed
as an English poet, but – with a difference; and because of that difference critics have a difficulty in placing him, of dealing comprehensively
with him. They do not refer back his subtle distinctions to their demon-
strable origins. One or two critics indeed appreciate Malloch's true
qualities as an individual poet. 'Alike in depth and reality of sentiment.
as in technical originality and interest,' says Arthur Waugh, 'Mr
Malloch is very clearly a Georgian to be reckoned with among the most
suggestive of his time.' And *The Times Literary Supplement* says that
he is 'a poet whose work has many merits which call for a careful and
sympathetic study, who is not afraid to discover in life more than an
artistic seriousness, who is hurt by the discords of his time and finds it
hard to reconcile them with an inner and absolute harmony of which
he is aware, who is capable of that craftsmanship which is implied in an
exact, appropriate and economical expression of what he has to say. We
move here, then, in a region of sincerities, away from the affected
manufacture of form or formlessness which is the sign of unsubstanti-
ated invention, away from the mannerism which is the mark of indolent
habit, preferring to repeat a metaphor rather than originate one, from
the display of cunning and casuistry which is the profitable weapon of
every trade but the poet's'.

Of how many Scottish poets past or present can the like be said – how
many of them have done work than can be discussed on that level at all?
Malloch as a poet is, as I have said, unquestionably one of our greatest
twenty: I agree, too, with Waugh that as a Georgian he ought – despite
his subtle fundamental difference from the others – to rank in critical
esteem with Walter de la Mare and J.C. Squire and other leading
English poets of the day – but he is too Scottish, albeit elusively, for
English taste, perhaps, and too truly and purely a poet for Scottish taste
– but his day will come. In the meantime, perhaps the best of his work is
still to come. Whether or not, he will rank as one of the first score of
poets in English in the first quarter of the twentieth century. He is
worthy of far more consideration than he has yet received, alike from the
point of view of English (or British) and of Scottish poetry.

As dramatic critic of *The Scottish Nation* he showed a technical knowledge, an independent standpoint, and a wide sympathy which make his articles one of the outstanding features of that periodical, and showed by contrast the comparative worthlessness of the shallow gossip that passes for dramatic criticism in the small paragraphs from time to time given over to such a negligible matter in the majority of Scottish papers. As the critic of English literature attached to the Amsterdam *Hagensblatt*, Malloch has shown himself an able liaison officer between Dutch and British culture.

Finally, as a dramatist, Malloch has recently shown himself one of the few dramatists yet connected in any way with the Scottish National Players who are of any real promise. Two of his plays have been published by the Scottish Poetry Bookshop, and one of these, *Thomas the Rhymer*, has been produced both by the Scottish and the Lennox players. It, and *The House of the Queen*, a beautiful little allegory of the ideal at the base of the Scottish Renaissance movement, are a fine first contribution to a Scottish drama of ideas, and slight although they are, have no little significance and may have no little influence. Both are consummately wrought. Of what other plays in the history of Scotland can this be said? Of exceedingly few. If Malloch could apply – as he may – his technique to a really dynamic theme in a full-dress drama he might vitalise the whole movement towards a Scottish national drama. No other Scottish playwright has yet appeared who is in the least likely to do anything of the kind.

Writing of Malloch as a dramatist in *The Northern Review*, Alan Wylie has said:

> I do not go so far as to say Mr Malloch is the dramatist for whom we have been waiting – it is not fair to judge from two short plays – but I do say he has it in his power to be. There is something in them despite their experimental character that is new to the Scottish stage, something which reminds one of the early days of the Irish revival. For one thing they are unmistakably Scottish, and that is what cannot be said of the Moffat school, just as Yeats or Synge is specifically Irish. That in itself is an achievement... *The House of the Queen* may yet be the *Kathleen ni Houlihan* of the Scottish movement. At least I know of no other play to which to compare it. The two are exactly parallel, but Mr Malloch is no imitator. The call of nationalism is universal, but it takes in each case its own form. Mr Yeats' Queen demanded battle – no Celt could demand other. Mr Malloch asks that

we build. Could the basic distinction between the two have been better revealed? These two plays give Mr Malloch a new significance and our country a new hope. Nearer and nearer comes the dawn.

Mr Malloch has published: –

Poems – *Lyrics and Other Verses* (London: Elkin Matthews, 1913); *Poems and Lyrics* (Heinemann, 1917); *Poems* (Heinemann, 1920).

Plays – *A Night with Burns* (produced Lyceum Theatre, Edinburgh, 1910, and subsequently on tour); *The Birthright* 1912, *Arabella*, 1913; *Thomas the Rhymer* and *The House of the Queen* (Scottish Poetry Bookshop, 1924) and since the above was written *Soutarness Water* to which I refer in a subsequent chapter.

Contributions to *The Scottish Chapbook*, *Scottish Nation*, *Northern Review*, *Northern Numbers*, and many other journals and newspapers. [18.9.25]

Letters

CONTEMPORARY SCOTTISH STUDIES – EDWIN MUIR

Sir, – In your issue of 4th inst. Mr C.M. Grieve asserts that Mr Muir 'comes from Shetland.' May I point out that Mr Muir had the honour to be born in the Orkney Islands? The Orkneys and Shetlands are, for Parliamentary purposes, bracketed together, but the people themselves are quite distinct. There is a great deal of Scots blood in the Orcadian. while the Shetlander still uses many thousands of Norse words in his dialect. Otherwise they are very good friends. – I am, etc.,

15 King Street   D. Horne
Kirkwall

SPELLING OF SCOTS

Sir, – Sir James Wilson has issued an appeal and a series of suggestions with regard to Scots spelling. As this is a matter of moment to the movement for the revival of the Vernacular, may I crave space to briefly rebut his recommendations and to suggest that if our developing movement is given the course he suggests, it will merely run to waste in the unprofitable sands of philology and orthography. To save space I put my points as follows: –

(1) Sir James suggests that all Scots writers should write in the dialect with which they are most familiar, and should in any case keep their dialect pure and not mix it up with any other dialect or with standard English. In reply I would suggest that the partition of the Scots language into dialects is an aspect of its degeneration; that instead of confining

themselves to any one dialect, Scots writers should adopt the idioms, vocabulary, etc., of Dunbar and Henryson and the other old Makars; that by so doing they will be avoiding the degeneracies inherent in all later Scots whether in what remains common to all the dialects or distinguishes one from the other (distinctions, as John Buchan has pointed out, mainly visual); and that in any case they will only so obtain a language adapted to every form of literary expression and not suitable for kailyaird purposes only. In other words, I suggest the use of the greatest common factor of true Scots (as presented in the corpus of Scottish literature worthy of the name) and the employment, where necessary, of genuine dialectical differences merely as, for example, foreign (even Scots) phrases are employed in English.

(2) Sir James suggests as the basis of rendering the dialect the actual pronunciation of old people who have spoken it all their lives in daily converse. This again is to 'found' on decayed and corrupt forms, and is moreover to make the most plebeian and illiterate usage the criterion. You will no more get good broad Scots that way than you could get a good literary medium of English starting from the colloquialisms of a group of Cockneys or Westmorland farm-servants. You might preserve the 'pure impurity' of a given dialect as it existed amongst a given class at a given time in that way, but you could not proceed on that basis to create a national medium of expression adequate to contemporary cultural needs.

(3) Sir James suggests that the same word should always be spelt in the same way, I would not give orthography any such decisive place. There may be good reasons in Scots as there are in English for variant spellings of the same word in different contexts.

(4) Sir James pleads for what amounts to the application of phonetic and simplified spelling to Scots. In my opinion, there are as weighty reasons against this in Scots as in English. Literature appeals to the eye as well as to the ear, and there are traditional and associative values not to be lightly discounted.

(5) Sir James suggests that when a word in common use is pronounced differently from the corresponding English word this difference should be carefully shown in the spelling – e.g., 'un' (and), 'oa' (of), and so forth. Any such disfigurement of the text could profitably be obviated by a short note on pronunciation either in a preface or as an appendix.

In short, I think Sir James's whole scheme is designed to put a premium on local abnormalities (often the results of illiteracy or misun-

derstanding) instead of moving towards an effective canon or synthesis of Scots; and whereas dialect writings have a very circumscribed expressive range and low literary values and a comparatively restricted public, a movement towards a good generalised Scots might put us once again in possession of a distinctive national medium in which we might emulate the old Makars, in whose hands Scots was a literary instrument in the fullest sense of the term.

Scottish writers will be well advised to trouble no more about dialectical integrity, orthographic consistency and the like than Burns and the Auld Makars did. Let those who have nothing of real consequence to write or say delude themselves with these pedantries; those who have will put 'first things first' – and both spelling and philological propriety will be very subsidiary, if not entirely irrelevant, considerations so far as they are concerned – I am, etc..

16 Links Avenue   C. M. Grieve
Montrose   [18.9.25]

15. Frederick Victor Branford

The lamentable plight of current literary journalism in Great Britain cannot be better illustrated than by the *Bookman*'s treatment of F.V. Branford's latest volume of poems: *The White Stallion*. It was reviewed in the May (1925) issue of that periodical by the well-known Irish poetess, Katharine Tynan, and this is what she said of it:

> *The White Stallion* ought not to come after any volumes of verse, however good; it should stand by itself in its own class, or with its peers. If it is anything at all it is great poetry, in a manner we have grown unaccustomed to. One is not surprised to find Mr Branford saluting Francis Thompson. I do not find anywhere in *The White Stallion* the enchantment of Francis Thompson in, for example, *Dream Tryst*, but I do find his magnificence. There are no 'isms,' no freaks and fashions, nothing of its day only. Mr Branford is of the great day that is always with us. He has an apocalyptic vision and an inspired vocabulary. I give no specimens of his work. They cannot be detached. He is in the great line of English poets.

Now the *Bookman* is not scant of space. Many columns of the same issue were – as in every issue – devoted to negligible comments on negligible publications, to trivial personalia, and publishers' puffery of various sorts. It is not every month surely that any literary journal has the opportunity of hailing the advent of one who 'is in the great line of English poets.' Such a phenomenon might well be given the whole issue to himself. If the *Bookman* is to be accounted a literary organ – if its readers are intelligent people interested in literature – such a course would be a natural and widely approved one, and would redound to the credit of the periodical that took it and build up a reputation for it. It could always claim that 'at any rate we recognised Branford for what he was at first glance and gave him something like his due.' But no! the *Bookman* and Mrs Hinkson took no such course. What I have quoted was all that was said of Branford and his book. Had I been Mrs Hinkson and felt as she did, I would at least have seen that my review of *The White Stallion* did stand alone. It would, I think, have been a perfectly simple matter to arrange with any editor. A contributor of Mrs Hinkson's standing would surely have had no difficulty at all events in getting her own way in a matter of this sort. Instead of that, in a whole-page review of seven books of poetry, it was dealt with fourth and received precisely fourteen lines – less than a seventh of the space at Mrs Hinkson's disposal. The only other volume of the seven that was not utterly negligible from every point of view was at all events comparatively negligible compared with Branford's: it would not have mattered if no mention had been made of any of them, so far as the critical status of the *Bookman* was concerned, but the latter would have been enhanced had the entire space been devoted to Branford. And as to the editor – does he know what is going to appear in his periodical before it actually does, if then? If he does – if he saw Mrs Hinkson's paragraph – I may be excused the naiveté of asking why in the name of all that is inexplicable he did not get excited and cry, 'In the great line of English poets? My dear Mrs Hinkson! Are you sure? But, of course, you wouldn't say so unless you were. I know that I can trust your judgment. Well, this is a great discovery. We must make the most of it – just by way of showing that the *Bookman* at least can do a little now and then to counterbalance the contemporary neglect that has been the unhappy portion of so many of our greatest poets. I have written for a copy of Branford's poems for myself. I wish you had devoted all your article to him, but since you didn't I want you to write a long article – a detailed study of his work – for our next issue. I am arranging for photographs, etc., to accompany it, and a personal sketch by someone who knows him. And I think I shall get half-a-dozen or so of our leading *litterateurs* to contribute to a symposium on the precise quality of his genius and the place he is likely to take in the long run. That seems to me the least we can do. What is a literary periodical for if it cannot rise to such an outstanding occasion as this? '

But I am not so naive as to imagine that the editor of the *Bookman* did anything of the kind or, in fact, thought anything about it, or that Branford's name has since crossed Mrs Hinkson's mind at all – or that her portentous utterance so ludicrously spatchcocked into the usual reviewer's gossip carried the slightest conviction to anybody or even raised the curiosity of a single reader. It is a well-known fact that the great bulk of reviewing of books which do not boom for extra-literary reasons scarcely sells a copy more than would sell in any case: and that reviewing fails to exercise its natural functions is no wonder when reviewing is done in this way. And Mrs Hinkson is by no means the worst offender. Apart from an article on Branford I wrote for the *New Age* – and one by the Dutch poet, Wilhelm Klemm, of which I published a translation in the *Northern Review* – I know of no other article as distinct from a mere review, devoted anywhere to him so far. And yet consider the reviews of his first book, *Titans and Gods*. The *Daily News* said: 'A first volume so memorable that it must mean the establishment of a new poetic reputation.' The *Bookman* said: 'It is a long time since the tree of English poetry has put forward such a tremendous branch.' And the *Saturday Review* said: 'It reveals his inspiration to be more exalted than we have been accustomed to since the death of Francis Thompson.' And so on. The fact of Branford's genius is recognised by nearly every reviewer – but they are not really interested and cannot interest the public. They have no words appropriate to such an advent: all their superlatives have already been used and re-used on worthless work – they can only say once again the pontifical nothings they have already said *ad nauseam* of a multitude of comparatively negligible writers. It is impossible that all these reviewers can be other than destitute of all sense of literary integrity and can feel the natural disinterested thrill of discovery their words should connote, so long as they say what they do and rest content with the inability to do no more for genius when for once they do encounter it than as publishers' hacks they do habitually for scores of poetasters, the mere publication of whose work on the usual terms is neither more nor less than a form of fraud.

Mrs Hinkson and the other reviewers I have quoted, in statements that must, I am sure, strike the average reader as necessarily grossly exaggerated, announced no more than the bare truth. Branford belongs, despite the fact that he is a Scotsman and that in intellection and 'direction' as apart from form and vocabulary he is demonstrably Scottish rather than English, to the central English tradition. In previous articles I have quoted Edwin Muir's statement that no Scottish imaginative artist has risen in the medium of English to the second or even to the third rank, and expressed my agreement with it. Branford is no exception to this rule. Looking to the long line of English poets he will not be found to be of even third-rate calibre – but if he is of fourth-rate or fifth-rate he will yet belong to a very small band and be a poet of outstanding consequence and one of an exceedingly small number of like or greater stature Scotland has contributed to *welt-literatur* in the whole course of its history. And though so considered he may be found to be only fourth rate that does not mean that he is not of first-rate consequence to-day – ours must be an exceedingly rich generation, indeed, if he is not; and while on the general balance of all the factors that go to comprise poetical stature he may fall far below giants such as Milton and Wordsworth and Shelley – it is nevertheless such comparisons and no lesser ones than he challenges, and in certain respects – in some one quality or technical gift that is his own, the quintessence of his genius – he may transcend all his predecessors however much they in turn transcend him in other and more important qualities. Branford's relation to English poetry put him as a Scottish poet in very much the same position so far as the generation of Scots is concerned as Lord Alfred Douglas's in respect of his generation. The work of both is almost completely assimilated to the best English models in its own kind. Branford is more fortunate than Douglas – he lives in a greater age. Flawless in form Douglas's sonnets – among the most consummate in the English language though they are – belong to the eighteen-nineties, to the *fin-de-siecle* school, in subject-matter, in vocabulary, in their whole tone and texture. Branford's work is not so 'dated' – can never so 'date.' It has, as Mrs Hinkson says, 'nothing of its day only.'

'Poets "in the true line,"' I wrote in the *New Age*, 'generally have a sure intuition of their place in relation to their forerunners and contemporaries. They "know themselves." The verses in which they explicitly assume the sacred mantle are always worthy of note. Poetasters may try to ape them in this respect – but their claims can never ring true. The test is almost infallible. Let a poet define in a poem his relation to poetry as a whole (or to a certain great succession) and he cannot but measure himself exactly. I remember in this connection (apart from the famous

instance of Milton's set purpose) certain assured verses of Charles
Doughty's. I remember Flecker's 'To a Poet a Thousand Years Hence': –

> Read out my words at night, alone:
> I was a poet, I was young.

And Branford, inveighing against Colour Prejudice, Imperial lust,
"Patriotism," "demons of contention that enhavoc nations," can declare
in a passage that reduces practically the whole of Georgianism to an
impertinent journalistic babble: –

> Against those dark Dominions the great doom
> Of song pours down the aeons. Rank on rank,
> Through futile fields to fertile victories,
> In truceless war the white battalions press;
> *I least and latest marching am yet mailed*
> *Greatly,* and weaponed from a forge whose might
> Passes the hands of Vulcan, for I wield
> Engines invincible dreamed in the brain of God.
> Loud is my lyre, and great in labour grown
> With strains, committed to its nervous charge,
> Of harmony and fruitful toil between
> Nature and Man, the Mortal Deities;
> Unconquerable Antagonists, that bleed
> Blindly in barren battle to no end,
> Bearing the banner of the common fate
> And common weal o' the world, I hold at bay
> Night and the horded rabble of her priests.

There speaks no "idle singer of an empty day," but one conscious of
power, purpose, and place. His lyre may be occasionally too loud; but he
attempts nothing common or mean; and, addressing himself solely to
major issues and boldly dealing with entire integrity with the difficulties
of art to-day and the problem of its functions in the contemporary world,
his failures are infinitely more victorious than the petty triumphs of the
vast majority of those contemporary English poets who have achieved a
little ephemeral reputation.'

I went on to discuss his stature as a poet in comparison with certain of
his contemporaries. 'The *Times Literary Supplement*,' I said, 'recently
devoted a column to Robert Graves's "Mock Beggar Hall" and dismissed
"The White Stallion" with a short paragraph. "Mock Beggar Hall" is
certainly in the current English fashion; but we are told that "the solu-

tion of the conflict between sense and idea, the finite and the infinite…
is condensed very finely into such lines as these: –

> Yet beyond all this rest content
> In dumbness to revere
> Infinite God without event,
> Causeless, not there, nor here.
>
> Neither eternal nor time-bound,
> Not certain, not in change.
> Uncancelled by the cosmic round
> Nor crushed within its range.

Compare this with Branford's song of the "Spirits of the Heavens" in
"Wonderchild": –

> Who returneth whence he came,
> Through Night of Nothing to Thy heart.
> By the Bridge of Sin and Shame
> He shall know Thee, who Thou art.
>
> Who hath died so deep in life
> That Death disdain him for his dart,
> Shall turn in fierce and loving strife
> On Thee and know Thee who Thou art.
>
> Who shall prevail, in awful grace
> Of love, o'er Thee, shall surely run
> With fire and wind before Thy face;
> He is thy Beloved Son.
>
> Who this secret shall acclaim
> He the Many, Thou the One,
> Through doubt, and fear, and sin, and shame
> He is Thy Beloved Son.

The difference clearly shows Branford's relative stature. Despite all their
technical accomplishments, the majority of the Georgians are, by definition, minor poets. Branford, however serious his inequalities, is unmistakably a major poet, and as such is a phenomenon of sufficiently
infrequent occurrence to merit at least a page where small fry like
Graves command a column. One final comparison. Take Sir William
Watson's *Lacrimae Musarum* (Tennyson's Death) with lines such as
these: –

And thou, the Mantuan of this age and soil
With Virgil shalt survive
Enriching Time with no less honeyed spoil.
The yielded sweet of every muse's hive;
Heeding no more the sound of idle praise
In that great calm our tumults cannot reach
Master who crown'st our immelodious days
With flower of perfect speech.

And set against it Branford's *Novissima Verba* (in memory of Francis Thompson) with lines such as these: –

For when the steep and single beam his trinal
Ray shoots brightening here in sound and flame
Through finite forms that wither in the final
Truth, Rarity and Beauty they proclaim;
Then zealous of Himself, the Sacred Fire
Not lavish of the immortalising light,
Himself unto Himself from his own pyre
Draws fairly in proud secret splendour home to Height.
Saint of High Song, of Him thou dost inherit
Whom Height assumed from cross as thee from curse...

But who am I to brave that dread dominion
In zones our faint songs fear and fail to soar,
Uranian Eagle, towering on a pinion
Serener than the Swan of Avon bore?
I do but dare to touch thy tomb as one
Of those sad heathen priests in Asian night
Who made audacious offering to the sun
Of fire and fruit with faltering hand and veiled sight.'

These extracts amply justify Mr C.K. M'Kenzie's declaration that

there is no other Scottish-born poet who is so significant as Mr
Branford. Modern in his whole outlook, he is artistically the legitimate successor of Francis Thompson, for he holds against the
modern schools that a poem can contain as well as provoke thought,
can express a philosophy as well as induce a sensation. His inspiration
is the combination of intuition and reflection; it controls him, but in
its expression is controlled, and so he belongs to the great succession
of our poet-thinkers. One does not say that defines him, for he can
drop philosophy for the lyric as well as any but... even the balanced

music of the *Novissima Verba* addressed to Thompson's memory are
overshadowed by 'The White Stallion' and 'Wonderchild.' Both are, it
is explained, symbols – the one of 'the transcendental, yet indestruc-
tible, incarnation of all Nature,' the other of 'the creative spirit in
spiritual energy pressing forward in conflict with the power of negation,' and the philosophy they teach is that 'the intuition of change
which is Art and the intuition of stability which is Religion are both
visions of reality, valid each in its own right.' That sentence alone
indicates how far he differs from his legitimate ancestors, and into
what new realms of thought his spirit travels. Some day learned men
will explore these realms with slower feet and write learned work on
Mr Branford's philosophy... I do not think Mr Branford has fully
found himself, at least to the extent of simplifying himself to others,
but of the originality and tremendousness of his verse there is no
doubt whatever. He is at once a portent and an example.

Mr Branford has published: –
Titans and Gods (Messrs Christophers); *The White Stallion* (Messrs Christophers); *The
Iron Flower and Other Poems* (Porpoise Press Broadsheet).   [25.9.25]

Letters

MR GRIEVE'S STUDIES

*Sir, – In common doubtless with many of your readers I have been
following Mr Grieve's observations on his chosen theme with lively
interest, and with a keen sense of the justness, of most if not all, of his co-
related criticisms. With his main contention of the necessity of a renaissance which shall be as well political as literary and artistic in the effects
of it, all must be in agreement who deplore, as he does, modern conditions in Scotland, and who have an eye, as he has, to the general
tendency of affairs in contemporary Europe. Mr Grieve does well to
emphasise the importance of the latter, and to plead for them a closer
scrutiny and a more understanding mind than we are used to devote to
the consideration of those objects. The war has brought about a complete
'turn-over' in respect of human values. The old feudal civilisation and
culture are everywhere passing quickly away. Under-dog is in rapid
process of becoming top-dog; and that momentous revolution means that
the world is in for a new orientation, which, though it may not be an
improvement on the old, yet we may be sure will be something very*

different to it. The immediate effect of the political and other forces now at work in Europe will doubtless be to depress the fine arts under the incoming dispensation even more than they are depressed at present, or have been so ever since the departing regime was set on foot, since the first effects of 'popularising' art and literature are, seemingly, always to vulgarise and debase those values. But as regards the ultimate effect of any movement of that kind, there should be room for hope, unless indeed those are in the right who assert that the original sin of mankind consists, not in the sources in which that matter is commonly laid but in a stupidity and a grossness of mind and vision which is at once all-embracing and ineradicable. It seems to me, therefore, that Mr Grieve's eloquent optimism is, on the whole, justified. At all events, truly may it be said of it that, at the present conjuncture, it is necessary; since there exists no alternative to it save the black despair into which theoretical pessimism must plunge us, were we so misguided as to give a loose to that forbidding creed.

I could wish much that Mr Grieve devoted more time and attention to Gaelic affairs than we have heretofore been privileged to witness evidence of in his interesting and understanding studies of contemporary Scottish letters. Perhaps the treat to which I here refer is yet in store for us; but it seems to me that, though that should be the case, yet the true precedence in this matter belongs not to the so-called 'Doric' and its latter-day disciples, but to the originators of Scottish letters, and to the models they left our nation. On every conceivable ground it is more proper and important that, assuming there is to be a Scottish Renaissance, it should draw its first principles in politics and art and literature from native than from foreign sources. – I am, etc.,

R. Erskine of Marr
[25.9.25]

16. John Ferguson

There are three John Fergusons in Scottish literature to-day. It is John Ferguson, the sonneteer, with whom I am presently concerned, and not the John Ferguson, the dramatist and novelist, author of such plays as *The King of Morven* and such novels as *The Dark Geraldine*, nor the third John Ferguson, who wrote that fine historical novel, *Mr Kello*, and subsequently published a *History of Witchcraft*. My Mr Ferguson's total output probably contains fewer words than either of the others have used in half-a-dozen of the hundreds of pages of description or dialogue they have written: but apart from the fact that he has confined himself to a category of literature into which the others have not penetrated – the sonnet-form – and that their work is therefore not easily comparable, he is by far the most important of the three. All of them have done work of excellent quality and of real value to contemporary Scottish literature: but the author of *Thyrea* – the title of Mr Ferguson's one book (his only other published work, apart from a volume of juvenilia, is an edition of the sonnets of David Gray) is one of the most extraordinary figures of the world of poetry to-day, and is certainly assured of a measure of immortality. His restraint is perhaps his most remarkable attribute. He has confined himself exclusively to the sonnet and has achieved a complete, quite distinctive, extraordinarily popular, and probably perdurable expression in a minimum of sonnets even. It seems an impossible accomplishment at this time of day. His total tale of published work is fifty sonnets. His book originally consisted of seven sonnets, and attracted immediate and widespread attention. It is no ordinary poet who has the self-confidence to come before the modern public with so slight a production: and yet on that basis Mr Ferguson has erected an ever-increasing reputation, which has never tempted him into over-production in the very slightest degree, or led him to essay any other form. His book is now in its twelfth edition – a most unusual, if not unique, achievement in the long history of sonneteering, and assuredly one that has no parallel in modern British literature. All of these have been strictly *editions*, although four of them were at one time erroneously described as reprints. The author has made alterations every time his book has gone to press. 'Thyrea: A Sonnet-Sequence from a Sanatorium' itself consists of only seven sonnets: the rest of his output is grouped as 'Other Sonnets.'

The second edition contained an introduction by Dr W.L. Courtney. After a reference to the first form in which the little book appeared and to the fact that it reminded certain critics of Henley's hospital poems – which, however, it only to some extent resembled in subject-matter and setting and certainly not in tone or tendency – Dr Courtney observed that: 'Mr John Ferguson has an individual note which gives distinction to his work. He confines himself to the sonnet-form, which he handles with considerable ease and skill, and I think he is at his best when he deals with solemn themes. Read, for instance. "L'Envoi," or "Chopin's Marche

Funebre" or "Beethoven," and you will recognise the dignity of Mr Ferguson's muse and his capacity for august harmonies. But he has another aspect of his work to give us, a modern, up-to-date quality which comes out in "A Chorus-Girl," "Smith – Bank Accountant," and "A Low Comedian." In this mood he does not hesitate to write a line like "Twice nightly thus, for thirty bob a week," or "His 'biz' and 'cackle' done he gets a 'round,'" in which he deliberately sets himself to be at all hazards realistic. What precisely a sonnet should include and what is its essential character are, of course, vexed questions. In the practice of the best poets it is usually confined to the analysis of a situation, the exploration of a mood, the dissection of a personality, or the vivid rendering of a strong impression. Our author extends its scope, including, here and there, mere narration. Each reader, I hope, will find his own favourite in this charming collection of pieces, but to my mind the author has never done better than in the last six lines of the sonnet dedicated to David Gray.' And Dr Courtney concludes his austere commendation by expressing the hope that the last couplet of Mr Ferguson's sonnet in question may apply to *Thyrea* as well as to *The Luggie.* The sonnet is as follows: –

Others have poured forth loftier strains than thine,
And Fame has placed her laurels on their brow:
Not Shakespeare's vision, Shelley's flush of wine,
Nor Milton's organ voice thou hadst; but thou
Didst sob thy soul in sorrow through the years.
And swan-like, sang'st thyself to Lethe's wave;
And obstinate Fame, that spurned thy passionate tears
Reluctant laid her wreath upon thy grave.
But while the fern-fringed Luggie flows along,
And Bothlin sings herself into the sea;
While lovers stray Glenconner's glooms among,
And storied Night holds Merkland's dreams in fee,
Fragrant thy memory, and thy star shall be
Luminous among the lesser orbs of song.

The late Mr T.W.H. Crosland, in his fine provocative book on *The English Sonnet* laid it down that 'when great poetry is being produced, great sonnets are being produced; and when great sonnets cease to be produced, great poetry ceases to be produced.' It is certainly an excellent augury for the position the present time will occupy as compared with any previous time in the literary history of Scotland, when it can be viewed in historical perspective, that we should have two living masters of the sonnet in Lord Alfred Douglas and Mr Ferguson. These are the twin – if very dissimilar – peaks of Scottish accomplishment in this form: and, what is more, it is only within comparatively recent times that Scottish literature has thrown up sonnet-work of any consequence at all, apart from theirs. But already a little anthology of Scottish sonnets could be compiled that would compare favourably – not with English, not with Italian – but with that of almost any other country, I think. Robert Buchanan wrote some great sonnets; John Barlas deserves more recognition in this respect than he has yet received; Lewis Spence has written at least two sonnets in Old Scots which ought to have been included in *The Northern Muse*, and are certainly not only by far the best, and indeed almost the only, sonnets in our Doric literature but, apart from the language question altogether, two fine sonnets.

Mr Ferguson's dignity and capacity for august harmonies may appeal most to Dr Courtney, but, from the point of view of modern Scottish letters, a great significance attaches to his comedic work. A Catholic fun, the humour of the saints, is at the basis of it. No one who realises the enormous *vis comica* latent in Scottish life can fail to appreciate the true inwardness of Mr Ferguson's profane usage of the form at this juncture in our cultural development. Mr William Jeffrey was right when he recognised in Mr Ferguson a leading spirit in the long overdue effort to deliver the Scottish spirit from its Genevan prison house. 'Bolts and bars do not a prison make' – and it was symptomatic of a great deal that has happened since to find Mr Ferguson disporting himself so defiantly within the strictest limits of his chosen form. He is one of the few poets who have succeeded in producing really comic poetry – poetry that is none the less poetry of a high order, although it contains elements of the ludicrous. And although as sonnets some of his dignified work may rank highest, his most distinctive quality is to be found in others such as the following, which is in his favourite and most frequent vein: –

The Property Man

Unbilled, unnamed, he never gets a 'hand,'
He never 'takes the curtain,' though he plays
The augustest part of all, and nightly sways
A rod more potent than a wizard's wand;
Cities as magic-fair as Samarcand,
He summons forth to front the footlight's blaze;
His Jovelike nod the hurricane obeys,

And the long thunder leaps at his command.
Custodian of treasure without end,
Impartial arbiter of woe and weal,
Bidding the joy-bells chime, the requiem toll…
He doffs his sceptre when the 'tabs' descend,
And hurries homeward to a midnight meal –
A mug of porter and a sausage roll.

Heterodoxy, if not rank heresy, runs through the whole of Scottish poetry in any way worthy of the name since the Reformation. It has always – and necessarily – maintained a guerilla warfare against the mass of national opinion. But Ferguson's poetry is symptomatic of more than that – of the recovery of the Scottish spirit from that blight of Protestantism which has so largely inhibited our poetry. Quite a number of his sonnets – like those of Lord Alfred Douglas – are wholly Catholic: sonnets like 'Stella Maris' and 'Ad Majorem Dei Gloriam.' And in others his satire against puritanical humbug and current religiosity is vitriolic. Witness the forthright opening of 'Miserrima,'

A fair-haired harlot on a city street –
Her purple sunshade smutched with sludge and rain,

with this conclusion: –

Now she is dead, poor child; and now to-night –
Forgotten pious spleen and cruel jest,
The scornful brow, Propriety's cold stare –
I see her sleeping in the land of light,
Soft-pillowed on the Magdalene's breast,
And no reproach nor any pain is there.

Or the savage but justified satire 'On a Street Preacher,' or the polished ridicule of 'The Orchard and the Soul.'

… in his orchard-garden, trim and neat,
I saw the Vicar, rubicund and brown,
Netting his plum trees as the sun went down –
A husbandman – but not of wayside wheat.

Scottish Art is at last avenging itself for the outrages perpetrated upon it as a consequence of the Reformation, and the new spirit is nowhere better exemplified perhaps than in Mr Ferguson's 'Christ at "Aladdin,"' which, no doubt, innumerable smug and sanctimonious Scots continue to find blasphemous: –

> The house is crammed, the overture is done;
> The curtain rises o'er the lowered lights;
> Across the stage swing troops of tinselled sprites,
> And round and round the comic policemen run;
> The Widow Twankey dances with her son,
> The debonair Aladdin, brave in tights;
> Within the magic cave what dazzling sights,
> And in the enchanted palace, oh! what fun.
> The childish flotsam of the neighbouring streets,
> Long breathless wondering, from the topmost seats
> Sends sudden laughter rippling through the air;
> O marred yet merry little ones, I know,
> The Christ who smiled on children long ago
> Himself hath entered by the gallery stair.

An Aberdeen critic, 'A.K.,' wrote some years ago in a review of a new edition of *Thyrea*;

> The sonnet has never been popular with Scottish poets. I do not recollect an instance of a vernacular sonnet. The voluminous Drummond of Hawthornden, it is true, wrote sonnets innumerable, but for two and a half centuries thereafter the form does not appear in Scottish poetry, and no great Scottish poet employed it to express his thoughts. In more recent years, James Thomson, Andrew Lang, John Barlas, and several others, have written sonnets, some of them distinguished, many of them ephemeral. Of all poetic forms the sonnet, in its true excellence, is more exacting, and since its invention by delle Vigne in the 13th century few of its practitioners have maintained their productions at an equal height of worth. Some have excelled in form, some in thought; yet it is significant that in the former class none has reached the perfection attained over half a century ago by Dante Gabriel Rossetti in England and José Maria de Heredia in France.

This is a confused utterance, all too typical of current Aberdeen criticism. What the last sentence means it is difficult to say – and the idea that the sonnet is a more exacting form than other forms is, of course, absurd. But far more than in proportion to the relative stature of Scottish to English or to French literature is Mr Ferguson a sonneteer comparable to the two mentioned. Scotland has given England one of her greatest sonneteers in Lord Alfred Douglas, who, indeed, is the peer of either Heredia or Rossetti, but Ferguson she keeps for herself. Lord Alfred stands in the central tradition of English literature – assimilated to it as no other Scottish writer, save F.V. Branford, has ever succeeded in becoming – but in his intransigence, his experimentalism with new sonnet-content, his use of slang, his ideological tendencies generally, Mr Ferguson belongs to the very different tradition of Scottish literature and is very peculiarly and powerfully a Scot of these times when old inhibitions are being overcome and a new outlook is manifesting itself in the North.

Thyrea and Other Sonnets is published by Mr Andrew Melrose. who also publishes *In the Shadows*, Mr Ferguson's edition – to which he supplies a preface – of David Gray's sonnets. See also articles on Mr Ferguson by the present writer in *The New Outlook*, 1920, and *The Scottish Chapbook*, 1922; and by 'A.K. ' in *Aberdeen Daily Journal*, March 26, 1921; and by the same writer on him, and Miss Violet Jacob, under the heading of *New Scottish Poetry* in the same paper on October 27, 1921. [2.10.25]

Letters

ORKNEY AND SHETLAND

Sir, – Writing from 15 King Street, Kirkwall, in your issue of 18th September, Mr D. Horne is at some pains to point out to your literary contributor, Mr C.M. Grieve, how Edwin Muir escaped the distinction of being a Shetlander (accorded to him by Mr Grieve) by the accident of being born an Orcadian. Mr Horne was quite right in correcting that slight slip on Mr Grieve's part, but he would have been wiser to have stopped there; for, in going on to give your contributor some gratuitous instruction in the history and geography of these outlying parts, Mr Horne writes somewhat carelessly himself.

It is true that the people of Orkney and Shetland are 'quite distinct' in that 40 or 50 miles of ocean roll between the two halves of this island-county of the north-east; but in every other respect they are no more to be regarded as distinct or separate peoples than, say, the good folks of Arran and Bute, the island-county of the south-west, are to be so regarded.

If I were Mr Horne, I should not insist too much upon the Orcadian's being a cross-bred Scot, any more than I would continue the common mistake (seen in the same sentence) of speaking as if ethnology and philology were identical. However, unless I knew exactly what Mr Horne

*implies by 'a great deal of Scots blood in the Orcadian,' I do not feel at
liberty either to condemn his statements entirely or to approve them in
part; but, taking as the easiest interpretation 'an admixture of people
from the mainland of Scotland,' I should like to know whether Mr Horne
is prepared to maintain that Orcadian 'blood' has been appreciably
altered from its primitive Nordic purity thereby. Whence came these
Orcadian-Scots? From Caithness and Sutherland perhaps, from the
Moray Firth, from the Hebrides? Perhaps the engrafting was just as
Norse as the original stock. If Mr Horne means, however, the traditional
'Scots of Dalriada' I think he will derive much profit from consulting Sir
Arthur Keith as to who and what the 'Scot' of history really was, and as
to what overwhelming claims can be put forward for the Nordic origin of
the great majority of Scotsmen. If he desires to go further afield, I need
only remind him of the Danes of Lothian and the Vikings of Normandy:
while, if he is thinking of peoples descended from aboriginals like the
Picti and Kymri, I must ask him if he assumes the total extinction of
those primitives by the Nordic settlers in any of the regions already
named, and whether, therefore, any marked distinction would be subsequently introduced by varying degrees of immigration from any of the
so-called Celtic areas of the mainland. I am afraid Mr Horne will find it
extremely difficult to draw any ethnological distinction between
Orcadian and Shetlander.*

*Philologically the difference is even less. Wherever I have met an
Orcadian who was not ashamed of his own dialect. I have found his
speech as thickly larded with old Norse roots and idioms as my own
native tongue; but Mr Horne's estimate of the richness of the
Shetlander's Norse vocabulary is, unfortunately, as Mark Twain said of
the rumours of his own death, 'greatly exaggerated.' I only wish it were
true that we had 'many thousands of Norse words' in daily use, for it is
in them that the strength, beauty, and richness of the Shetlandic lies; but
alas; of them the same tale can be told as of Manx and other island
tongues. Orcadians and Shetlanders alike should join in the preservation
of the last fragments of the old Norn speech in Scotland, or to postpone,
at least, the day of its disappearance. This can best be done by a realisation of their kinship and common heritage, and not by the augmentation
of petty and imaginary distinctions.*

*Speaking from personal observation, and after careful consideration, I
would concede to Mr Horne only one distinction that may be drawn, one
that is temperamental, and due, very probably, to the influence of
surroundings. The average Orcadian, no matter how intellectual or*

artistic, is always of a placid nature, and apparently as void of changing moods as his flat landscapes and the almost undeviating nature of his native rock-strata; but the Shetlander seems to me more variable, as full of ups and downs as his rugged and hilly outlook, and, in short, a trifle less stoical.

Mr Horne's concluding remark is the most surprising of all: 'Otherwise they are good friends.' I never knew we were anything but the best of friends, in every respect, and there is no 'otherwise' needed, nor has Mr Horne's letter shown any reason why it should ever be. It is such a pity that distance divides. I should esteem it a privilege if it were possible to run along to 15 King Street, Kirkwall, of an evening, after a hard day in school, and refresh a jaded intellect by discussing, perhaps, 'Contemporary Scottish Studies,' from which this present discussion emanated. But the ocean rolls between. and who knows but that it is our chief bond of friendship, for do we not say 'freends 'gree best at a distance?' – I am, etc.,

Sandwick   *Robert W. Tait*
Shetland   [2.10.25]

17. William Jeffrey

When William Jeffrey's poetry first began to appear some five or six years ago, it commanded attention for several reasons. It was not the sort of stuff in subject-matter or in vocabulary – or even in form – that any of Mr Jeffrey's contemporaries were producing: but it was unmistakably, if somewhat unplaceably, reminiscent of such great poets as Milton, Blake, and even Dante. Mr Jeffrey was definitely attempting large utterance through the medium of famous forms at a time when the majority of his contemporaries were concerned with lesser matters and experiments with new forms or with what may be called 'various forms of formlessness.' In other words, Mr Jeffrey was apparently entirely outwith, if not oblivious of, the spirit of the age: and endeavouring, however unsuccessfully, to align himself with the mightier figures of the past. He was signally concerned with what John Buchan comments upon as having been so completely lacking in Scottish poetry since the days of Dunbar – 'the long perspective and the "high translunary things" of greater art.' He had obviously courage, originality, and lofty ambitions. But to 'build the mighty line' calls for more than that. It demands an adequate subsumption, intuitive or otherwise, of all that has gone before. The question was – had Jeffrey that or could he acquire it? And no one who was aware of the cultural background out of which the art-products of contemporary Scotland must emerge would have ventured an affirmative. An insufficiently systematised knowledge or intuition of what relevant to the purpose in hand has gone before – an inadequate tradition or sense of tradition – is what has so long delimited and is still (to an at last perceptibly decreasing extent happily) delimiting Scottish artists and restricting them to minor matters and an inferior plane. The antecedent conditions to the production in effective degree of the kind of poetry to which Mr Jeffrey was addressing himself were lacking in Scotland; but the fact that a Scottish poet had emerged who was constrained to address himself to that kind of poetry and none other – and that other compatriots of his were beginning to manifest a reorientation of Scottish genius towards matters of a different nature and an immensely higher plane than those with which it had so long been almost exclusively preoccupied – gave ground for hope, and it became a speculation as to whether Jeffrey would develop the strength of will to contend successfully against an unfriendly environment and make good his deficiencies to such an extent as to enable him to produce work of permanent value along his chosen and most difficult line, whether, perchance, the development of the sympathetic movement would be swift enough to reinforce him from without, or whether in the absence of such timeous support and the lack of adequately determining perceptions on his own part the *lacunae* in his equipment would prove untraversable and engulf his struggling aspirations. Scottish education – our spiritual and social background – does not equip our young people for such high emprises. We are given a very hit-or-miss and haphazard founding – and great art depends upon adequate foundations. A 'half-baked' intelligence cannot address itself to the major tasks of art – and it seemed highly improbable that any one educated in modern Scotland and subjected almost wholly to the influences of contemporary Scottish life, without being specially favoured by wealth or social position, could transmount the innumerable difficulties and reach and maintain himself upon that altitude of the spirit, that vantage-ground over mortality, essential to such work: nor, unless endowed with unlikely attributes of endurance, could such an one plumb the corresponding profounds. The whole tendency of such a society as is to be found in modern Scotland is towards the average, the lukewarm, the mediocre. Any Promethean opposition to the vast tendency of the time in such a society is a mere 'charging of malaria with a bayonet.' Contrast the conditions in which any modern Scot is brought up with those under which the young Milton was reared; as Professor Saurat says – 'He wrote verses which were considered marvellous in the home circle when he was about ten years old, and he was thenceforward brought up deliberately to be a man of genius. What colossal pride must have been latent in a family where such a thing was accepted as normal, where such an enterprise was carried through successfully, to the complete satisfaction of all participants in this unique conspiracy... In 1632 he retired to Horton where, with the full approval of his father, he devoted himself to deliberate preparation for his high mission. A few years later he wrote to Deodati: "Do you ask what I am meditating? By the help of Heaven, an immortality of fame."' It is, I think, safe to conclude that there is no family in Scotland conspiring today on behalf of one of its members as Milton's conspired for him: and that there is no retreat in Scotland to which any young man in Scotland has been encouraged or permitted to retire under such conditions as Milton enjoyed at Horton.

One wonders how Milton, if he had been born in humble circumstances, with few facilities of completing his education, in Scotland towards the end of last century, and the necessity of earning his living as a member of the editorial staff of *The Glasgow Evening Times* would have fared – and on the whole I am inclined to think that his greater natural genius if compelled to such conditions could scarcely have produced better work than Jeffrey has done in just such circumstances. Jeffrey is certainly a poet of the Miltonic type and, all things considered, what he has already accomplished redounds as splendidly to his strength of character as it unquestionably reflects the inadequacy of his times to facilitate the best development of his potentialities.

Approaching the problem of Mr Jeffrey from a somewhat different angle, Mr Edwin Muir in the *New Age*, apropos *The Wise Men Come to Town*, said:

> He is a mystical poet: he strives for great effects at a time when almost everybody else is trying to secure neat little ones; he is, in other words, at direct variance with his age, completely out of the current of his time. The natural thing for young writers at present (I set it down simply as a fact) is to distrust greatness, to be impatient of greatness, as if in some way it had let them down. They strive for quite a number of things, and for the truth, no doubt, among these! but they do not attempt greatness

of utterance. Mr Jeffrey does. He had better be careful. He had better be careful, for if disillusion, hatred, cynicism, are part of the portion of the present generation of poets, there must be a necessity of some kind in them; and if Mr Jeffrey has escaped them he has been either very fortunate or very blind. The volume proves that he has been very fortunate; but it proves also, I think, that he relies too much on his good fortune. His utterance at its best is large utterance: but it is careless utterance, even uncritical utterance. It is never the utterance of a minor poet, but it is often the utterance not of a poet at all. I say this reluctantly, for Mr Jeffrey had the promise of great gifts. He has vastly more abundance than any of the Georgians; but for lack of discipline and of a more severe technique it only carries half the way. But having important things to say he should at least have as much sincerity and conviction in his voice as the poets who have hardly anything to say at all: yet very often he has not. It is not natural endowment which fails him, but discipline, and once more discipline. He has a fine capacity for striking out exact and vivid phrases, and that is as good a proof as any of genuine imagination: but he is frequently content to accept the second-best... What displeases one in Mr Jeffrey's poetry is a frequent too-clear echo from the past, an original one cannot name, but which on that very account is not less displeasing. What Mr Jeffrey chiefly needs, it seems to me, is a more severe questioning of his inspiration. As it is, the book is a remarkable work.

In these remarks Mr Muir pierces to the root not only of the trouble with Jeffrey's work, but the trouble with Scottish arts and letters as a whole; what we are suffering from is an utter lack of tradition, a want of standards. That is why it must be a close coterie movement that will redeem our position, if anything can. Referring to what Mr Muir had said, and writing of Mr Jeffrey's later poem, *The Nymph*, I expressed the view that he had profited by Mr Muir's advice. 'He has attained to a greater clarity, a deeper sense of congruity,' I wrote. 'This purification has entailed no diminution in the "speed" of his work, that sense of "first-time" success which was the notable characteristic of his previous poems. Otherwise put, Mr Jeffrey's previous visioning was like that of a man possessing, very intermittently, "normal" eyesight in the Shavian sense, and the rest of the time suffering in rapid succession from a choice selection of common ophthalmic ills. In *The Nymph,* for the first time in a poem of any length, he maintains normal vision throughout. It is "all of a piece." It places Mr Jeffrey indisputably in the first flight of our younger British poets.' Here is the closing passage of *The Nymph*:

The cavalcade's celestial horde
Comes nearer, nearer, nearer;
Fiercely the chariot shines, and clearer
Than heaven's lightenings dragged from rest,
Or a thousand stars in one bulk prest.
Majestic, terrible, fiery in speed
Apollo passes... He pays no heed
To that weak pillar of white flesh
The waves have caught as in a mesh.
He passes westward over the hills;
And as his turning axle fills
The air with dying thunder, prone
Upon the sand the nymph lies lone;
Of strength and joy she is bereft,
From hope her heart is ever cleft,
And now the breeze around her sighs
And soft waves close her fear-filled eyes
While from a wood, to outwit death,
A satyr runs with panting breath.

By the time Jeffrey had published his first book of poems he had at least a clear realisation of the need for one of the objects which must be part and parcel of any Scottish renaissance movement – in his own words, the necessity of liberating the genius of Scotland from 'the Genevan prison house' – and an appropriate detestation of the 'Kailyard school' and of that kind of literary mosaic work which has so often been substituted for poetry by members of the Glasgow Ballad Club and the like. And he rapidly developed to the realisation of his 'direction' embodied in the following passage from an article on 'Blind Georgians' which he contributed to *The Scottish Nation:* –

Unfortunately many of the Georgian poets regard the poet as being one who describes things in rhythmic language, a sort of glorified descriptive journalist who wears coloured spectacles; or indeed as one who takes a Dionysian Cook's Tour of the sensations... The Georgian poets have evinced fine powers for associative musical thought only, and little for the energies of poetic imagination. They have worked with material things: not with the baseless winds of starry vision... Such poetry lacks vitality and creativeness, and is of little import to our present age, which needs writers who are well-springs of living water. Even Abercrombie, perhaps the biggest of the Georgians, whom skygazers had once thought to be a comet of wondrous portent, now makes but a lanthorn-splash in the night. In the poem *Ryton Firs* he introduces many lines about the mole, telling how it takes burrowing jaunts abroad, and does all manner of remarkable things. That is not the method of true poetry. I can find all I desire to know about the mole in a naturalist's book. But if a man tells me how he saw in a vision a mole burrow into the earth, meet a skull, and converse with that skull about human fate, time, and God, then I should say that that man is uttering potential poetry... In his apology Hardy calls upon the poet and the saint to do battle once again for beauty and truth. Shall we turn to him a deaf ear? We in the North here, where many, many hills are gloomy as Egdon Heath, are not deaf of ear; and we may perhaps relieve that over-striding Colossus of the Georgians of his task of pondering upon the balancings of the clouds and upon frustrated aims of life. Let us at least attempt the noble task.

Elsewhere in *A Note on Yeats* he wrote: –

> Those passages of Shakespeare or Dante which are the greatest are also the most easily understood – provided, of course, the reader be naturally moved to poetry... I have a fancy that the poet, when feeding the purest flame of his inspiration should employ only those images which are of an immemorial and eternal nature. Such images are the naked human body, earth, air, fire, and water, the elements of life and matter.

While in his later work Jeffrey has overcome many of the inequalities of his earlier poems and achieved a finer congruity and clarity, it must be observed that he has latterly increasingly restricted himself to minor forms. I would fain hope that this is a case of *reculer à mieux sauter* – because, if not, it must be attributed to the power of an adverse environment to delimit his creative efforts. In the first flush of his inspiration he turned to blank verse and to great subjects demanding long poems – in this he undoubtedly displayed the true disposition of his genius. It will be singularly unfortunate if he is now disposed to subject his efforts to the Procrustean bed of contemporary journalistic requirements in verse. It is at all events the case that his most finished efforts are all short poems; and that in many of his short poems he harps on the same strain and reintroduces identical imagery to such an extent that it loses its imaginative force, while behind it sense – I do not mean mere meaning, but vital significance and genuine creative effect – is often to seek. These short poems, nevertheless, place him in the first rank of modern Scottish poets, and several of them will be indispensable in any future anthology of Scottish poetry – yet his main interest, his outstanding promise, does not lie in that direction. He is only secondarily, however exquisitely it may transpire in the long run, a lyricist. He will miss his true metier if he allows any consideration to tempt him away from concentrated effort to 'move the noble numbers' which were his initial prepossession. Rossetti declared that 'sheer brains were a pre-requisite of any work of great art' and many of Jeffrey's shorter poems, however interesting and delightful in themselves, are of a kind that suggests that he is dallying dangerously with the path of least resistance – that he is not applying himself as he ought to be applying himself, in scorn of such smaller successes, to the *bloc résistant*. Only unremitting intellectual effort will enable him to realise his great potentialities – he must be on the alert to allow no other process to substitute itself for fundamental brain work as the dominant element in his output. Words for words' sake – mere repetition – will not avail him – and too often his poems of late have a hallucinatory quality, a dreamlike inconsequence, which – whatever may be said for it – is not one of the elements that go to build up great fabrics of poetry. His symbols are not moving to the construction of a world of thought or feeling of their own: they are falling like the debris of some *monde interieure* which has disintegrated before it could be described in its entirety.

But whether Jeffrey succeeds or not – and external circumstance is unfortunately likely to have the determining say in that – in bending the great bow and shooting the inerrable arrows to which his strength should be dedicated, he has already enriched our poetry with numbers, which, if they are unrelated pipings and not movements in a complete harmony of creation, are beyond question among the most remarkable products of Scottish genius. Of his work, it may be asked, as Jethro Bithell asked of Peter Baum's: 'What mathematician shall reduce to plain terms, what poet's soul shall fail to understand,' such a vision as this: –

> I saw an old man sitting still
> Upon a granite rock;
> There were no lines upon his face
> That did not mock.
>
> I asked a furrow on his cheek
> What its decision was;
> And shrilly like a reed it said,
> 'All love doth pass.'

I asked a furrow on his brow
What had mislaid its trust;
And like a wind in March it said,
'All thought is dust.'

And then I gazed with courage bold
Into his snow-white eye;
And lo! God and His chariots
Like swift red deer passed by!

Or, again, 'to what category shall the critic of literature assign the heroic landscape,' which he calls 'Nocturne': –

Thou shalt see, my love,
At some future hour
Thine own sweet planet
And the dawn in flower.

Now through the darkness
Of turning spheres
Behold what a marvel
In heaven appears!

Where the outmost curves
Of heaven lie
The untameable lions
Of God go by!

Jeffrey has published: –
Prometheus Returns (Erskine MacDonald); *The Wise Men Come to Town* (Gowans and Gray); *The Nymph* (Porpoise Press Broadsheets); and numerous contributions to the *Glasgow Herald*, *The Dublin Magazine*, *The Scots Magazine*, etc.   [9.10.25]

Letters

POETRY AND CRITICISM

Sir, – Burns alleged that 'Freedom and whisky gang thegither.' Americans may not agree. One thing is certain, however, and it is that politics and literature do not go together. Mr C.M. Grieve would have it that they do, and Mr R. Erskine of Marr lends his support in this regard. Sir Walter Scott was an excellent patriot, and he was a true blue Tory and Unionist. Burns had strong aristocratic leanings and was not a

Home Ruler. It is not necessary to subscribe to the creed of any political body to become a lover of one's native land, and feel the inspiration of what some call 'nationality.' Scotland is sharply divided. The Gaelic tradition is not quite the Lowland tradition. Mr Grieve may refer to MacDonald and Duncan Ban Macintyre, and think Dugald Buchanan (the Calvinistic poet and writer of hymns on a level with Watts) is worthy to be mentioned with these and others he does not seem to know about, but his views on Gaelic poetry are worthless. Neither MacDonald nor Macintyre can be classed with any Lowland poet.

As for Grieve's 'Great Ten' living poets and the possible eleventh, they are easily surpassed by several others. John Ferguson, author of Thyrea and Other Sonnets, *is an exception, but apparently it is necessary to mention one eminent writer, or two eminent writers, to provide a basis for the others. George Reston Malloch, for instance, has only to be quoted so that an antidote may be provided for Mr Grieve's long, gushing article – far too long to be convincing, for methinks he protesteth too much. Take, for instance, any verse from Malloch's poem entitled 'She Dissects a Flower,' which Grieve singles out for special praise. Here is one: –*

> *For he who talks of wisdom tires,*
> *And he who brings me passion stales,*
> *The ebb and flow of my desires*
> *Upon some iron barrier fails.*
> *The cup of my Circean wine*
> *I give, and heroes sink to swine,*
> *The flame of spirit give, and none*
> *Can bear the vivid soul alone.*

The verse is mechanical and undistinguished and prosy. As a whole, the poem has no particular merit.

It appears to be necessary to abuse such artists as Robert Fergusson, whose 'Auld Reekie' and 'The Farmer's Ingle' are really great poems, Neil Munro and others, to make way for some of Mr Grieve's literary darlings. But I refuse to be convinced by mere assertions, and expect reasoned criticism with examples of the poems so highly praised. The 'Great Unknown' in literature, etc., 'boomed' by Mr Grieve, have yet to prove their worth. If modern Scottish literature is to be promoted, and if there is to be a Scottish Renaissance (so far we have had the posters only), 'log-rolling' is not what is required. We want not merely 'something attempted,' but 'something done.' As one of the alleged 'back numbers' in the Edinburgh Book of Scottish Verse 1300-1900, *I solemnly and sincerely enter my protest against much that has been written by Mr Grieve in the name of 'criticism.'*

What we seem to need most at the present time is another Pope to deal with the literary Pretenders in England and Scotland who have nothing to learn in the gentle art of self-advertisement. Never in the history of literature were poorer 'wares' more highly lauded. But the public is as heartily sick of 'log-rolling' as it is of 'shell-shock' verse, and it refuses to see merit in bad craftsmanship and neurotic sentiments. It still prefers poetry with music and inspiration. – I am. etc.,

Donald A. Mackenzie

THE SCOTTISH SONNET

Sir, – An anthology of sonnets by Scottish poets could be made, as Mr Grieve suggests in his illuminating article on John Ferguson (author of Thyrea). *May I suggest that the enterprise be undertaken by some native publishing firm – preferably by the Porpoise Press? The precision of form and pregnancy of thought required by the sonnet are elements most valuable to writers of the younger generation. As we have entered an age in which the Einsteinian cosmos is replacing the Newtonian, and Jesus of Nazareth and William Blake are replacing the blood-sacrificial symbol of an institution and the philosophers of the absolute, it is inevitable that the poetic expression of the age must be cast in moulds suitable to clarity and subtlety of thought and to visionary ecstasy and beauty. The sonnet is one of the suitable moulds in which a poet who keeps abreast of the advancing spiritual wave of the age can profitably express himself. In Scotland this advancing wave is taking us away from what I once termed 'our Genevan prison.' Evidences of the forces working towards this liberation are seen in Mr Hugh MacDiarmid's* Sangschaw, *a collection of remarkable Doric poems. Of one of the lyrics in this book, 'O Jesu Parvule,' I had occasion to write thus recently: 'A splendid lyric, one of the few Scots cradle songs worthy of the epithet "Christian" that have been written by Scotsmen since the blight of Calvinism fell upon the land.' The revision of the Scottish Hymnary that the Presbyterian Churches have now under consideration is also an evidence of liberation; but, alas! from the reports of the various Presbyteries it seems that the bulk of the bad music and vulgar verse contained in the present hymn book will be retained. – I am, etc..*

Glasgow
Oct. 3 1925

William Jeffrey
[9.10.25]

Letters

ORKNEY AND SHETLAND

Sir, – When I pointed out that Edwin Muir was born in the Orkney Islands it did not occur to me that my letter would raise any controversy. Certainly it was penned in no churlish spirit, and I do not regret anything said therein if it has found me a friend. In going beyond the mere correction itself, all I desired to do was to emphasise the fact so often forgotten by many that 'Orkney' and 'Shetland' are not synonymous terms. The Orcadian, like the Shetlander, is a distinct type, but this distinction carries no sting with it, and must never be allowed to intervene between their common interests. On the contrary it adds to the charm and variety of life. It would be sad indeed to venture forth of a morning, only to find all the clouds cut after one pattern; the sky an unchanging monotone; everybody wearing the same smile, or frown; men, women and children looking, dressing and thinking alike. No beauty and no poetry. Horrible!

Mr Tait admits a temperamental difference in the Islanders. This is no negligible factor, and must tend to produce an art and literature peculiarly its own. If anyone cares to examine a poem in the Shetland vernacular with one in Orcadian this will be at once apparent. Or compare the Shetland skiff with the Orkneyman's small boat; or the great Shetland Festival of Up-Hellya with the New Year's Day Ba' of Kirkwall. In mentioning Scots blood and the Norse language I did not forget for a moment that these matters are not identical.

The Orcadian Scot did not come first of all from Caithness, Sutherland, and the Moray Firth and the Hebrides. Instead, from about 1230 and for centuries afterwards, he came from the Lowlands – the Lothians, Fife, Forfarshire, and other Scottish counties that lie outside the 'Highland Line.' According to J.G.F. Moodie Heddle 'The people of Orkney therefore must be put down as in the main an amalgam of Norse and Lowland Scots.' In the 'Proceedings of the Orkney Antiquarian Society,' volume II (1923-1924), Mr J. Storer Clouston arrives at the same conclusion in his article on 'The People and Surnames of Orkney.' From ancient remains scattered over the county it is quite evident that Orkney was peopled in the dim and prehistoric past. Wave after wave of invaders must have swept over the islands, leaving enduring marks upon the population.

As to language, 'The humblest Orcadians have for centuries past spoken English more correctly and naturally than was at all common *among the lower orders… A few Norse words, mostly nouns, survive embedded in the local speech, whether English or Scots' – Mr J.G.F. Moodie Heddle.*

The estimate of the richness of Norse words in the Shetlandic is not mine. My authority for the statement is Mr T. Mainland, F.E.I.S., Head-master, Bressay Public School, in 'Cambridge County Geography,' the Cambridge University Press, 1920. He says 'The spoken language is a Scottish dialect with a mixture of Norse words – many thousands, says Jacob Jacobsen – with accent and pronunciation distinctly Scandinavian…'

I quite agree with Mr Tait that Orcadians and Shetlanders should join in the preservation of those fragments of old Norse still remaining. As I have previously said, any individuality of the Orcadian and the Shetlander must never be the cause of petty jealousy, instead, let there be a healthy and friendly rivalry and co-operation wherever possible. While I may be a perfervid Orcadian and a patriotic Scot, I aspire to something greater still – the universal brotherhood of man. For the peace of the world it cannot come too soon.

Whether or not our surroundings have influenced the character and temperament of our people I am unable to say, but the roaring seas have certainly cut us off from a great deal of social and other intercourse. I do not for a moment admit that we "gree best at a distance,' and if Mr Tait ever manages to visit Kirkwall I shall endeavour to prove the fallacy of the saying. I warn him, however, that one of the finest sights visible from my windows is Kirkwall Secondary School, from which many splendid young men and women have gone forth into the great world lying in the magic South, including Edwin Muir. – I am, etc.,

15 King Street   David Horne
Kirkwall

THE 'NORDIC' ORIGIN OF THE SCOTS

Sir, – Your correspondent, Mr Robert W. Tait. says, in your issue on October 2, 'I think he (Mr Horne) will derive much profit from consulting Sir Arthur Keith as to who and what the Scot of history really was, and as to what overwhelming claims can be put forward for the Nordic origin of the great majority of Scotsmen.' I would be much obliged if Mr Tait would tell me (and others) what precisely is meant by this term 'Nordic.' It seems to be very loosely, and carelessly, used: and I have seen it ridiculed in many quarters in which 'light and leading' in *such matters exist. Mr Tait advises Mr Horne to 'consult' Sir Arthur Keith. But is that gentleman really the proper person to consult in this connection? I have yet to learn that Sir Arthur, eminent no doubt as he is in his own line, is an ethnologist of worldwide repute, such as are, undoubtedly, many I could quote, and quote against him. And besides, racial origins cannot be determined by ethnologists alone. Archaeologists must also be consulted. and even the now despised philologists are entitled to their 'say,' to say nothing of political psychologists. Mr Tait evidently thinks that Sir Arthur Keith – whose ukases on divers matters make interesting 'copy' for journalists, no matter how disreputable they may really be – has already disposed of the matter of the origin of the Scots off his own bat; and perhaps he will be more surprised than pleased to learn that, to say the least of it, this is very far indeed from being the case. – I am. etc..*

Buchan

MR C.M. GRIEVE'S ARTICLES

Sir, – Mr C.M Grieve's gallantry is irresistible. Scotsmen cannot but applaud him for Northern Numbers, The Scottish Chapbook, The Scottish Nation, *and* The Northern Review *however they may quarrel with many of his judgments and prepossessions, and lament that thus far his ventures have lacked commercial success. Even his arguable oracles are graced by a 'have-at-you' spirit which is abundantly welcome in contemporary criticism, and his present series of articles in your pages might be a valuable chart for a voyage that every patriot – even if not himself a man of letters – should wish to make. But Mr Donald A. Mackenzie's plea in your issue of 9th October is certainly called for. The abuse of writers of established rank – men like Barrie and Neil Munro, whose little fingers are thicker than even Grieve's head after all – requires to be supported by sturdy, tenacious reasoning if it is to convince. Mere assertion and iconoclasm as often as not suggest only a doubt whether the critic understands these authors and their aims. He pauses not to consider what they have been inspired and called to do, what they have wished and tried to do, but incontinent assails them because they are not archetypes of himself. Even if their fame is local and their vogue bound to pass, their work can only be duly appraised for its own qualities; and Grieve's preference for realism and psychoanalysis does not of itself condemn romanticism or make impossible the realisation of perfect beauty in it or any other medium frowned upon ex* cathedra. *No reader of Grieve's* Annals of the Five Senses *will deny his brainpower and psychological penetration, but there may well be controversy concerning his power of expression and style – matters not altogether indifferent to the art. On the other hand, Grieve's eulogies of lesser-known men also require more adequate support than he gives. Branford is indubitably a considerable poet who has had too little recognition, and Jeffrey and Edwin Muir in their verse work have certainly had – and shared – great moments and bright days. But none of them has given the world quite enough work yet to justify a generalisation about their merits which would elevate them to the pedestals from which the Barries and Munros have been so ruthlessly swept. Nor is any merit they have intensified or made more recognisable by Mr Grieve's ipse dixit. I am indeed readier to 'take his word for' a great deal than Mr Mackenzie seems to be, and am more than willing to come to Grieve's articles as a pupil to be instructed – but his canon of European standard is only declaimed, not revealed or expounded. If indeed his dictum is just that only about a dozen men in Scotland have wide reading in the literatures of Europe – in comparison with which our own idols are so puny and our comparatively young and unknown men so 'promising' (albeit of only fourth-rate rank!) – why does he not show us why and wherein ''tis so'? or why does he not indicate a brief necessary course of reading in these accessible cultures for those of us who are ignorant of them and incapable of using them, and of estimating his use of them, through no fault of our own except that we find ourselves much immersed in the work of other callings which claim us. That is one of the services one free and fit to be a man of letters – apart from creative work – might be expected to do his generation, and assuredly Mr Grieve is capable of it even if it needs unwonted patience. But simply to jibe at our ignorance and bad taste and force his judgments down our throats is neither cricket nor criticism worth while and may soon make Mr Grieve – who has not had mercy on the Andrew Langs and Robertson Nicolls – a damned literary panjandrum of the very sort he despises. It is to be presumed that he writes to instruct the rest of us in these articles, and not merely to pat the backs of the dozen who do know Contemporary European Literature. We are thankful. but we ask for more.*

I should like to second Mr William Jeffrey's suggestion of a Scots sonnet anthology – and certainly some of C.M. Grieve's sonnets stand very high – and with regard to his despairing comment on the Revised Church Hymnary, may I cheer him and myself with the undoubted fact that the Revision Committee is not bound by the fatuous and self-

cancelling casual cavillings of Presbyteries, and my firm impression that while it will yield to the persuasions of great masses of Church members to restore a small number of hymns favoured because of indefinable but not unworthy associations, it will in no wise bow to any outside demand for the removal of the relatively large number of Noble Hymns its members have deemed it right to add to the book simply because some people do not yet appreciate these. The tilt at the 'bad music' is due to a misunderstanding since consideration of the music is only in the initial stage now, but there is good reason to expect that the tunes selected will show a return to majesty and dignity and an abhorrence of saccharine, and also that the ecclesiastical democracy will not be able to deal so harrowingly with the music as it has in some places shown a futile desire to do with the words. – I am, etc..

Greenock   W.H. Hamilton
9th October, 1925

CONTEMPORARY SCOTTISH STUDIES
Sir, – It is time to lodge a strong protest against the continuance in your columns of the articles entitled 'Contemporary Scottish Studies.' Any claim they might reasonably have to attention is forfeited by the indiscretions of the author. His every paragraph is burdened with bombast and self-adulation, and his vague, involved, and irrelevant prolixity renders his deliverances utterly worthless either as appreciations or as adverse criticisms. His style, which is obviously a studied defiance of all that is venerable and reputable in classical English, places his writing outwith the province of literature. His most apparent defect is his want of perception. He is devoid of all sense of humour. He accuses an Aberdeen writer of a want of lucidity – 'This is a confused utterance all too typical of current Aberdeen criticism. What the last sentence means it is difficult to say, and the idea that the sonnet is a more exacting form than other forms is of course absurd.' His next sentence is a brilliant illustration of his own perspicacity – 'But far more than in proportion to the relative stature of Scottish to English or to French literature is Mr Ferguson, a sonneteer comparable to the two mentioned.'(!) Emboldened by the courtesy extended to him in your Journal he has in his latest lucubration made a new departure in Bohemianism. He makes a bitter and unwarrantable attack on Puritanism and the Reformation, and he ardently proclaims himself the apologist of blasphemy. He does so advertently, for he knows that, 'No doubt, innumerable smug and sanctimonious Scots

continue to find – "Christ at Aladdin" – blasphemous.' No one challenges C.M. Grieve's right to speak authoritatively on the canonisation of Magdalenes with besmutched purple sunshades, but exception must be taken to the prostitution of The Scottish Educational Journal *from its legitimate purposes. In the exercise of that liberty he so often vaunts, C.M. Grieve might commiserate those benighted souls who are not able to discern anything but filth where he sees 'high art.' If he cannot patiently tolerate the scrupulosity of those who conscientiously continue to discriminate between the sacred and the profane, he ought to find some other medium than the pages of an educational journal for his vituperation. Probably he will find in* The New Outlook *or elsewhere more suitable environment for his invective. – I am, etc.,*

Edinburgh   T. Robertson
October 7, 1925

POETRY AND CRITICISM

Sir, – And what is Mr Mackenzie's letter but log-rolling and self-advertisement? The crux of his complaint is revealed in his description of himself as 'one of the alleged "back numbers" in the "Edinburgh Book of Scottish Verse".' I haven't devoted a study to him. Hence these tears. If I had there might have been more of them.

He condemns my 'mere assertions,' and his own letter is full of them. He says that my views of Gaelic poetry are worthless. Are his to be taken at his own valuation? I imagine that Anatole France knew a thing or two about literature as well as Mr Mackenzie, and he devoted a long exposition to the intimate relationship of politics and literature. Mr Mackenzie's fifth, sixth and seventh sentences are a stupid non sequitur. Besides he is apparently criticising my critical ability without having read my arguments. So far from arguing that a writer must be a Scots Home Ruler to do any good work for Scottish literature to-day, I have expressly stated that the Renaissance movement must cut both ways – by stimulation, on the one hand, and antagonisation on the other... His whole letter is a tissue of palpable absurdities.

I know the true cause of Mr Mackenzie's 'solemn and sincere' protest too well to take it seriously. But I imagine that I can throw an amusing light on questions of log-rolling and self-advertisement and 'the abuse of such artists as... Neil Munro, and others' if Mr Mackenzie will give me permission to print extracts from certain letters of his.

Can there be any better proof that the Scottish Renaissance movement

is making rapid headway, and in the right direction, than the fact that
Mr Mackenzie's increasing chagrin at being left out in the cold has at last
forced him into open controversy. – I am, etc..

C.M. *Grieve*
[16.10.25]

18. Muriel Stuart

There is a wide-spread idea that Scotland has been especially rich in
songstresses. This is not so: and those we have had have been, as in other
countries, almost without exception definitely inferior in accomplishment and not markedly different in tendency to the fourth and fifth rank
of their brother-poets. Few have risen above the merest mediocrity at
all: and those who have generally by only one poem or at most two or
three poems. The total output of our poetesses of any quality at all has
been exceedingly slight. The position to which women were so long relegated accounts, of course, to a very large extent for this; and consequently one would expect to find a different state of affairs manifesting
itself in these days of comparative sex-equality, and of feminism – and
one does indeed, find it. Scotland has a group of songstresses to-day of
far greater consequence than any of their predecessors: and the women
poets – while the best of them produce work very different in content
from that of their male contemporaries – compare as a whole very fairly
with the men poets. Two living poetesses stand head and shoulders
above all the others – these are Muriel Stuart and Rachel Annand
Taylor. Jessie Annie Anderson, a personality of much greater compass
and more abundance, only falls below them in artistic force and finish. A
succession of fairly sincere and individual artists such as Christine Orr,
Janetta Murray, Mabel Christian Forbes, M.E. Graham, Bertha
Cruickshanks, Hilary Staples, and Brenda Murray Draper come at
varying intervals behind. Mrs Violet Jacob heads the older section of a
different category specialising in the vernacular, in which Miss Anderson
has also done excellent work, while the younger section of it is undoubtedly headed by Miss Marion Angus, to whose work I shall recur.

It is amusing to recall, in view of such a group, that Mr D.T. Wood,
writing in *The Thistle* of February, 1914, could remark that 'even the
lyre of Jeanie Morrison, who earned Whittier's praise, does not seem to
have been taken up by any Scotswoman who is desirous of adding

another name to the list of Scotland's women poets.' Jeanie Morrison, forsooth!

In my opinion, Muriel Stuart is the greatest woman poet Scotland has so far produced. She is less superficially Scottish than Rachel Annand Taylor. She never uses the vernacular or Scottish subjects and settings: the latter frequently does – and is, to my mind, best when she does. Her other work is too mannered and Italianate. But there is no attitudinising about Muriel Stuart's poetry. It is blazingly forthright and sincere – an irresistible tide that carries away the bulwarks of conventional female reserve. Mr Herbert Palmer, in a recent contra-Georgian article in *Vox Studentium* (Geneva) singled her out as perhaps the greatest woman poetess writing in English today. I think he is right. Who shall be put against her? Both Rose Macaulay and Helen Parry Eden are definitely minor poets: Edith Sitwell has a unique stylistic interest, and her work is extraordinarily vivid and witty – but, as someone said, her work is like 'devilled almonds' and certainly she presents the extras to a repast, not the repast itself. I can go over all the others – but none of them have Muriel Stuart's amplitude and sweep: she alone, too, is writing poetry which, whatever its faults, is almost always on the major plane. And in content, if not in its more obvious concomitants, she is far more modern than most of her sisterhood in Scotland. Her power derives from her complete individuality of perception and her forthrightness of utterance. She stoops to no trimming or concealing. Her concern is predominantly with the innermost emotions of Woman in the typical predicaments of her sex, and here she regains a directness of statement that has nowhere in Europe been more singularly to seek than in modern Scotland – a recovery relating her work anew to her greatest predecessors in Scottish Poetry and, by emphasising the gulf between her and the soul-destroying sentimentalities of the Kailyard School, revelatory of her especial significance at the present juncture of Scottish letters.

It is particularly interesting at the present moment to note that in her first book she anticipated one of the most significant characteristics of subsequent Scottish verse – the emergence of a new mysticism and the stressing of the Christ-motif. This reveals her effective relationship with the most significant of our younger poets, and the whole 'becoming' re-orientation of our literature, just as her other qualities as I have indi-cated mark her as at complete variance with the inhibiting Puritanism with which the Renaissance movement is openly contending all along the line and demonstrate her fundamental relationship with the Auld Makars. It is easy to understand on both counts why her poetry is

comparatively little known and little appreciated in contemporary
Scotland: but Posterity will put that right.

> 'How knowest thou Christ?' I answered.
> 'By the thorn.'
> 'Nay, but the thorn tree grows in every wood.
> For any brow forsworn!'
> The other whispered: 'Thou art tempted here
> For my sake,' but the beggar's voice came fleet
> As pain: 'Three crosses did that hillside bear,
> Not Christ alone hath wounded hands and feet;
> Dost thou believe
> That every pierced hand stretched to thee is Christ?
> Shall not some thief impenitent deceive…'

The quality of that – the plane of its utterance, the acuteness and
freedom of its ratiocination, the profundity of the issues it raises, the
blend of beauty and wit and dramatic daring and deliberate simplicity of
statement – is undeniable: but it does not do justice to Miss Stuart. It is
torn from its context in a long and closely woven poem. All her best work
is in long poems – too long for reproduction here, too subtly knit to be
dissevered in quotation. But some of her single lines show her power:

> 'A stopped stream smelled of Death.'
> 'A thin hail ravened against the door of dark.'
> 'To feel the mighty stars, streaming to meet me.'
> 'And no dew lies in the dead Morning's eyes.'
> 'Christ's hand that tips the blue-rimmed porridge bowl!'

This last has scarcely been glimpsed in Scotland since the days of the old
Makars, but our vision of Him is renewed as delightfully, as humanly, in
Miss Stuart's work as in John Ferguson's sonnets.

Writing of Miss Stuart and her work in the *Scottish Chapbook* of
November, 1922, I said: –

She is our Scottish equivalent of René Vivien – of Else Lasker-
Schüler, that flame of chaotic passion, consuming and consumed, of
whom Peter Hille has said that she is 'the black Swan of Israel – A
Sappho whose world has yawned asunder' – of Agnes Miegel – of
Jean Dominique. 'Hectic?' – But as someone wrote when a similar
criticism was levelled against Francis Thompson: 'He revels indeed in
'orgiac imageries' and revelry implies excess. But when excess is an

excess of strength, the debauch a debauch of beauty, who can condemn or even regret it? Would we had a few more poets who could exceed in such imagery as this!'...

Our Scottish 'critics' have not hastened to acclaim Miss Stuart. Their praises are bestowed elsewhere. Annie S. Swan can write 'I think you possess a fine poetic feeling.' The Rt. Hon. Ian Macpherson: 'I am glad you are publishing a new edition of your poems. Their homely charm, simplicity, fidelity to life and gracefulness have always appealed to me. Many of them arouse memories which are a priceless possession.' Sir Harry Lauder: 'Let me say how much I appreciate your writing. Your verses in your mither tongue are grand and simple and most effective, and should be widely read.' Sir William Robertson Nicoll, the late General Booth (just before he died!) and many others in similar strain. All these appreciations not of the work of a poetess such as Miss Stuart, needless to say, but of the unutterably wretched effusions of a syco-phantic lady, of a type almost as numerous in Scotland to-day as littera-teurs of the kind from whom I have been quoting, the quality of whose work is fairly illustrated by such a passage as this: –

> Don't make my life so very bright;
> My eyes should blinded be –
> Give me the sunshine after rain
> That sets earth's fragrance free –
> For balmy showers refresh the flowers,
> And spread their fragrance wide;
> So free my life by sun and shower
> From arrogance and pride,

or this, composed on the death of Edward VII.,

> A king of greatest credit and renown,
> Who kept unspotted, shining pure, his crown
> Has crossed the Bar, and laid his sceptre down.
> In Heaven he reigns and wears another crown.
> His mother, waiting at the other side,
> With outstretched arms, and eyes fixed on the tide –
> 'Come home at last! My well-beloved son!
> With honours crowned and duty bravely done.'

Ashamed and impotent in the face of such preposterous 'poetry' and praise, the handful of living Scots who do know what poetry is and recognise to some extent the significance of Miss Stuart may well say to

her, in the words of her own poem to Charles Bridges in her first volume
'Christ at Carnival and Other Poems' –

> Thou knowest at what cost
> Thy sleep was taken on those awful hills –
> What thou hast gained, and lost;
> Thou knowest, too, if what thou art fulfils
> The pledge of what thou wast.
> And if all compensates the poet's wreath
> That wounds the brow beneath.

Muriel Stuart has published: – *Christ at Carnival, and Other Poems* (Herbert Jenkins, Ltd., 1916); *Poems* (Methuen, 1918); *Poems* (Heinemann, 1922).   [23.10.25]

Letters

POETRY AND CRITICISM

Sir, – Your correspondent, Mr Donald A. Mackenzie, says that Mr Grieve's 'views on Gaelic poetry are worthless.' The event may or may not prove Mr Grieve's opinions on that head negligible; but until he has uttered them I see no reason why Mr Mackenzie or any one else should sit in judgment on Mr Grieve, much less condemn that gentleman unheard.

Mr Mackenzie's precipitancy does not encourage general confidence in his regard. Very dogmatically he asserts that letters and nationalism 'do not go together.' What precisely does Mr Mackenzie mean by this odd expression? If he means that nationalism and letters have no connection the one with the other, in that event it is obvious that he has read European history to singularly little purpose.

'The Gaelic tradition,' says Mr Mackenzie, 'is not quite the Lowland tradition.' Obviously it is not, yet the resemblances between much Gaelic poetry and not a little of the Lowland muse are many and striking, which is not to be wondered at since no question of a racial distinction is here involved, but only the accident of a difference of speech. Mr Mackenzie affirms that neither 'MacDonald nor Macintyre can be classed with any Lowland poet.' I find Mr Mackenzie's language lacking in clarity and precision, which should not be the case having regard to the very settled nature of the 'views' he entertains, and his dogmatic way of uttering them: but if by classed he means compared, then I crave leave to inform him that the thing which he considers as impossible to be done

has already been done. Not long ago Dr Calder published a revised text of Macintyre and took advantage of the occasion to draw a close comparison between the work of that bard and the poetry of Robert Burns.

Mr Mackenzie will find much that is interesting and possibly helpful to him in some of the late Donald MacEchern's critical observations touching Gaelic poetry. The essay on the subject of Omar Khayyám (which Mr Mackenzie will find in Am Fear-Ciuil*) is more than commonly deserving of mention (and study) in this connection. – I am, etc.,*

Oct. 14, 1925   R. Erskine of Marr

Sir, – It is less embarrassing to be abused than to be praised by Mr C.M. Grieve. His characteristic letter in answer to mine contains all the faults I find in his journalistic efforts which invariably have more assertion than argument. It may not be impossible for Mr Grieve, when he is somewhat older, to become a serious and sincere critic of literature, instead of a writer of 'stunts.' Men of his type have usually a lot of 'wild oats' to sow before they settle down to sensible journalism. But I refuse to believe he is, or ever will be, a 'thought reader.' He says of me: 'I haven't devoted a study to him. Hence these tears. If I had there might have been more of them.' I am not shedding tears of sorrow for myself. If I were to shed any, they would be tears of pity for Mr Grieve's victims who have been compared by him to Milton and Keats and placed in a very false position indeed.

If my literary work is so deserving of censure, why were contributions to Northern Numbers *solicited from me by Mr Grieve, and why was my name advertised as a contributor in several of Mr Grieve's* Chapbooks *although I never sent in a single line of verse?*

I do not recognise Mr C.M. Grieve as a literary leader or guide. I do not wish to be associated with his movement, and my contributions to Northern Numbers *were given before I knew that Mr Grieve intended to 'run' that 'stunt' of his.*

I have never met Mr Grieve, and anything of mine he has used was sent in response to appeals for contributions to what I understood to be simply an anthology of contemporary verse. No man can accuse me of 'log-rolling.' I do not belong to, and have never attempted to found, a little mutual admiration society. If Mr Grieve and his friends will take my advice, they will drop their 'stunt' and settle down to serious work. They will, no doubt, find their proper places in good time. May I remind

*them of the following most appropriate Biblical adage which they appear
to have forgotten.*

*'Let not him that girdeth on his harness boast himself as he that
putteth it off.' – I am, etc.,*

Donald A. Mackenzie

CONTEMPORARY SCOTTISH STUDIES

*Sir, – Barrie and Neil Munro may be suffering as Mr Hamilton suggests
from digital elephantiasis; my work is certainly not comparable to theirs
in another very different sense, and that Mr Hamilton should imply that
it is weakens his claim to criticise me and counter-criticise them. As to
their being 'established authors' I cannot agree, except in so far as they
command a certain public – a smaller one than the late Nat Gould's or
Annie S. Swan's. What critic of any consequence has conceded their claim
to serious regard, and what relative stature has been ascribed to them? I
am not concerned with what they have 'wished or tried to do' but with
what they have done – and left undone; and with their relation, or lack of
relation, to the main elements of the* Zeitgeist. *I have expressly iterated
and reiterated in the course of my articles that I am surveying my
'subjects' from a special and carefully defined angle: and I am well aware
and have clearly indicated that from other and commoner angles they
appear quite differently. My purpose and the space at my disposal in
these columns, and in the volume my articles are to make, does not permit
of all-round treatment. A critic's function in my opinion is, theoretically,
to criticise; practically I recognise the need to give a certain amount of
reason, explanation, incidental information, etc. – but I cannot agree that
any criticism is invalidated because the 'working' is not shown.*

*It is nonsense in any case to speak of my 'abusing' Munro – I was
myself the first to point out that unless my special point of view was
remembered what I had said would appear basest ingratitude. As to the
relatively small output of some of the writers I have praised 'guid gear
gangs in sma' buik' sometimes, and certain names hold an indisputably
high place in the literatures of various countries, and in world literature,
on the strength of no more. I quite recognise the difficulties my references to a European standard present to readers who have little or no
acquaintance with European Literatures: but I do not see how I can
surmount these so far as the present articles are concerned. Where am I
to draw the line? I have already defined my position in my previous
series of articles on 'Towards a Scottish Creative Criticism' in these*

columns. My critical writings elsewhere include dozens of articles on many contemporary European literatures and other arts. Those who know the languages in question can investigate them for themselves; those who do not will have little difficulty in securing lists of such translations, primers, etc. as exist in English. My attitude is that those who have not a comprehensive knowledge of welt-literatur *are incapacitated from comparative criticism and should be correspondingly modest and refrain from using such terms as 'established authors' etc. where these imply more than a temporary popularity with a certain public as to whose discrimination there may be diverse opinions. I do not despise the sort of literary panjandrum Mr Hamilton seems to indicate. On the contrary I find it necessary before commencing to write to presuppose a certain level of knowledge and intelligence on the part of my readers-to-be. But it is no condemnation of my criticism to say that it is insufficiently self-explanatory or detailed and abounds in references to unknown literatures – that is rather a criticism of my readers and of my perhaps too generous presuppositions regarding them. I am unwilling to believe that the foundation I have taken for granted for these articles (unsuitable enough for* The People's Friend, *I admit) is non-existent on the word of Messrs Hamilton and Mackenzie, against whose letters I can set many letters of appreciation and concurrence from others.*

As to Mr Robertson, he talks of my 'bombast and self-adulation,' but his subsequent sentences imply that he is himself an infallible judge of English style, that he is a connoisseur of perceptual values, and what not. I am at least as much entitled to a good conceit of myself as he is. Most writers on Scottish literature – e.g. John Buchan, Professor Gregory Smith, Sir George Douglas, etc. – have commented on its progressive provincialisation and ascribed this largely to the Reformation. Many others – e.g. Lord Haldane, Professor Phillimore, etc. – have discerned with me that we are to-day outgrowing the worst consequences of the Reformation. Is the policy of the Educational Journal *to be that the sectarian prejudices of its least enlightened readers are to act in censorship of its contents? I am, of course, not concerned with religious foibles as such, but with their improper operation in dictating the response or lack of response of certain types of reader to work like some of Ferguson's sonnets. I may be devoid of a sense of humour but I certainly cannot help feeling something suspiciously like amusement that the charge should be made by one obviously so much further removed than myself from any participation in the saving grace. – I am, etc..*

C.M. Grieve

POETRY AND POLITICS

Sir, – Mr Ruaraidh Erskine has espoused the Gaelic cause in a most practical way, for he speaks, reads and writes the Gaelic, but he and other enthusiasts must be reminded that there is no essential connection between a race and a culture. Two branches of the same race may come under the influences of two distinct cultures. We know, for instance, that the Celts who settled in Asia Minor abandoned Celtic modes of thought. Hieronymus of Cardia, quoted by Pausanias (VII., 17), informs us that they became worshippers of Attis and ceased to eat pork. They thus abandoned old Celtic religious traditions and Celtic habits of life. The Celts of the Lowlands have long lost their old language and acquired the modes of thought and the traditions of another language. Is it not the case that the chief argument in favour of the teaching of Gaelic in schools is that the Highlanders should not suffer loss of identity – that their Gaelic traditions and modes of thought should not perish?

Dr Calder may compare Duncan Ban to Burns, but to me it is a surprising thing to find the Highland poet of the mountains compared to a Lowland bard who never mentions the mountains.

Burns is our greatest and, some think, the world's greatest love-lyric poet, and I once heard Sir Chihchenlo-feng-luh, when he was Chinese Ambassador in London, declaring that Burns was as well understood as such by a Chinaman as by a Scot. But the same could not be said of Duncan Ban Macintyre, who cannot be appreciated properly except by Gaelic speakers. Burns may have used Gaelic airs for some of his songs, but his models were not Gaelic models, and he knew nothing of Gaelic literature and tradition. He admired and followed Robert Fergusson, whom he regarded as a greater poet than himself, and also Alan Ramsay ('Canty Alan') and his other literary 'gods' were Pope, Shenstone, Gray, etc., as we gather from his own poems.

The attempt to class the Gaelic with the Lowland poets is quite futile. The severe formation of Gaelic poetry is absent from Lowland poetry; the themes and modes are quite different.

In Scotland the Gaelic movement is kept out of politics, and I have Irish friends – well-known Gaelic scholars – who wish they could say the same about the Gaelic movement in Ireland.

The man who prostitutes Art by making it the handmaid of a political clique is, in my opinion, on a level with one of sordid soul who quotes Burns to advertise a blend of whisky, or similarly draws upon Shakespeare to assist in promoting the sale of patent medicines.

The Muses must not be disfigured with the posters of any political *party. May I remind young writers in this connection that when politics come in at a study window, poetry flies out at the door. – I am, etc.,*

Donald A. Mackenzie
[23.10.25]

19. Hugh Roberton and the Musical Festival Movement

'When the Glasgow Musical Festival started in 1911,' wrote Mr Roberton in a recent article,

> there were pessimists who gave it a couple of years to burn itself out. There were optimists, too, but none daring enough to predict the position as it is to-day. If we who were in at the beginning had been told that within 14 years Scotland would have 32 Festivals, representing at least 60,000 competitors, we should have smiled. But it is so. Glasgow was not the first Festival. Aberdeen has that honour, although even this must be qualified, for the Co-operative Movement had been working along the Competitive Festival lines for some years before. Glasgow, however, may claim to be the spearhead of the movement. In the early days, when Glasgow was still working on a bank overdraft, her promoters went forth spreading the gospel in Renfrewshire, Dunbartonshire, the Borders, Stirlingshire, Perth, Dumfries, Inverness, Elgin, Lanark, Wishaw, Cambuslang, Wick, the Monklands – these and others all owe their origin, one way or another to Glasgow. More, the British Federation which links up the whole movement is largely a Glasgow conception. It superseded the old Festivals Association, a useful but less democratic body, which up to 1920 had existed to co-ordinate the work. That body was largely English in character and outlook and rightly so, for it was in England that the movement as we know it to-day originated. When the movement started here we had the advantage of English experience extending over a generation to draw upon. And we profited. Unlike England we have never had to go through what might be called a pot-hunting or prize-hunting period. In the Scottish movement the educative rather than the competitive side has always been emphasised. To-day there is no prize-money of any kind at any affiliated

Scottish Festival, and many of them have even discarded medals. Not the prize but the honour is the thing.

By an amusing chance, alongside Mr Roberton's article, there appeared one on 'The Dilemma of British Music' by our foremost musical critic, Ernest Newman, in the course of which he found it necessary to say that

> on the whole I cannot help thinking that, in spite of all our musical activity, the average Briton of today knows less, at first hand, of what is going on in the musical world than his grandfather did. The situation is a curious and disturbing one. It means that certain contemporary movements will pass completely away before the average man has had a chance to become acquainted with them.

[This was what I was driving at in my article on Mr Francis G. Scott when I stressed the need for eliding certain stages altogether in the composition of Scottish music if the products of a Scottish Renaissance in this respect were to be other than absurdly anachronistic, and this is why I rank the *Forscherblick* quality of genius; the divination of tendency, as the paramount desideratum in Scottish mentality today.]

> For this singular state of affairs there are no doubt several reasons. The improvement in orchestral playing and the rise of the virtuoso conductor inevitably lead to a certain standardisation of the repertory. No one cares to risk his reputation on the production of a difficult new work that cannot be given adequate rehearsal. As regards the smaller forms we have to admit a breach between the generality of new composers and the generality of great performers. The latter prefer the old music because its beauty of line gives them opportunities to display their special art, which is founded on a tradition of linear beauty. It is almost impossible, for instance, to get the great violinists to take up the newest violin music. As one of them put it to me once: 'A Viotti concerto may not be first-rate music, but at any rate I can express myself, my conception of beauty, through it; whereas such a work as Bartók's second violin sonata, interesting as it may be in many ways, is not only alien to my ideas of beauty, but seems to me alien to the spirit of the violin.' The pianists say much the same thing; the greatest singers will not touch the newest songs. What is the way out of this *impasse*?

Whatever may be said for the Musical Festival Movement on other grounds than those of purely musical interest, it cannot be gainsaid that

its whole tendency is to prolong and to worsen this *impasse* – that as a
condition of its existence it is necessarily bogged in a very narrow and –
not stationary, but as the movement extends, actually contracting –
repertory far below the level of contemporary creativity in all the kinds
of music concerned. Its educational value in one direction by no means
compensates for its anti-educational tendency in another – it may be
developing thousands of executants, but it is certainly widening the gulf
between the progressive creator and the public – if only by interesting
the mass of those who would normally constitute the musical public in
their own fiddling little abilities as singers or players in such a way as to
make them prefer to emulate each other instead of listening to really
great artists and trying to understand and enjoy really great music. The
logical conclusion to the tendency is a 'musical' parallel to that state of
society in which everybody lives by taking in everybody else's washing.
This is not confined to music, of course. We have the same thing in
poetry. Hundreds and perhaps thousands of doggerel-mongers have
reached the stage of being far more interested in their own and in
kindred productions than in real poetic effort and, regarding the latter as
'highbrowism' and alien to their ideas of beauty and, indeed, alien to
what they regard as the spirit of poetry, they have banded themselves
together into an Empire Poetry Association and live by buying each
other's brochures of verse and anthologies in which they can appear by
paying a guinea a poem or thereabouts. This is mediocrity on the offensive with a vengeance; and raises big questions as to culture and democracy, Socialism and the Servile State, and so forth. To revert to the
dilemma of British music, the only way out Mr Newman sees is via
'mechanical' music – gramophone, piano-player, wireless – despite all
their defects, and he contends that the purveyors of these are not enterprising enough. 'They will tell me, no doubt,' he says, 'that they know
their own business best, but I cannot help thinking that if they would
leave the accepted things alone for a little while and make it possible for
the man who is curious about Stravinsky and Schoenberg and Bartók
and other much-discussed composers of the day to hear their music
instead of only reading the critic's wrangles about it, it would pay them.'
Personally, I have no reason to suppose that it would. I think it is highly
improbable. The fact that even Glasgow has not got the length of organising a branch of the Contemporary Music Society does not conduce to
expectations of large sales for reproductions of the works in question.
Nor do I think it at all likely that any of the purveyors in question will
make the experiment. And yet to resist this strangling circumscription of

the repertory – to get away from this mania of imagining that increased volume of mediocre competence is educational progress – to reverse the overwhelming preference for quantity to quality – to get back to really musical considerations and away from these Yankee nostrums of uplift and mass-music and being 'a' Jock Tamson's Bairns' – to realise the negligibility of everything else in comparison with that contemporary creativity which is moving forward into the unknown from the furthest frontiers musical genius has yet reached and to endeavour in our day and generation to subsume the achievements of the past and move, however little, beyond them – these are the requirements of our musical salvation. And they are not to be found in the Musical Festival Movement. The multiplication of mutual admiration societies – the alarming increase of brotherly love – the devastating piety and platitudinarianism of all such manifestations of the inferiority complex of popularly-educated mass-mediocrity in full blast are diametrically opposed to, and irreconcilable with, the interests of Art, and therefore, if Art has any value, ultimately harmful to the masses subjected to their influence and subversive of whatever latent expressive or appreciative faculties they have. I fully share Dr Adolph Weissman's view that the growth of middle-class culture has choked the sources of inspiration – in certain directions. At the same time it is true that apart from the increase of economic lets and hindrances and the increasing unsuitability of the surrounding cultural atmosphere, a man born to compose will compose whether the masses are sufficiently well-educated to appreciate his work or not, and the question of whether the next great creative phase is, as Dr Weissman will have it, to annul the existing divorce between cultured art and folk art will probably not concern him. But I am at one with another writer who says that 'if the *general* interests of art can only be served by one of two things – bringing genius down to the folk or lifting the folk more nearly to the level of genius – by all means let us get on with the lifting. It will be worth while if its only achievement is the hastening of genius's natural reward.' But once the horde of adjudicators of one kind and another are satisfied it does not seem to me that there is likely to be in Scotland much of the reward left over – even in the shape of opportunity – for mere genius. The whole movement is rather like the Socialist Art Circle, which lays far more stress on the fact that such and such a perpetration is the spare-time product of a self-educated bill-poster's labourer than on any cognisable artistic criterion. Defective opportunity is erected into a canon. Multatuli has well said that the opinion of one incompetent person is of as much value as the opinion of a million incompetent people, and Mr Roberton and his associates need to be reminded that to evolve a multitude of singers and players, all of whom are comparatively mediocre at the best, is no artistic benefit. 'The calm reading of a passage of Scripture by one whose lit face is eloquence itself, or the sprightly saying of "Up the Airy Mountain" by a wee bobbed-hair girl, or the singing of "O Saviour Sweet" by a "through-ither laddie,"' have no more to do with musical progress than 'the flowers that bloom in the spring tra, la.' Tosh of that type is the true giveaway of the movement – it is known by the ideas it keeps company with.

The whole business of music in Scotland is in a deplorable condition. Musical Festival education is an exceedingly shallow and superficial thing at best. Mr D.A. Anderson, President of the Dundee Musical Festival, has recently written – and surely the second sentence is a masterpiece of unconscious humour and a *reductio ad absurdum* of the whole position – 'Music is essentially universal and is also most democratic and human. The message-boy, as he whistles or sings on his rounds, provides ample evidence of all three, and every encouragement ought to be afforded for the extension and development of such ordinary gifts which are common to all. No unusual gifts are required, and there is no reason why the refining influences and advantages of music should not be enjoyed by every class of people.' That is true – except that in His divine wisdom God did not make everybody anything like equally accessible to these influences or disposed to take equal advantage of their opportunities. The whole field of music lies open to everybody – who will put himself to the trouble of going over it – and his achievements need only be limited by the extent to which his industry fails to make good his essential natural limitations which even the Festival Movement cannot enable him to transcend. The Musical Festival Movement puts a premium on the vast mass who will not put themselves to the trouble of learning any more than is necessary to impress audiences who know less than they do themselves – aids and abets them in the ostrich-like policy by which they ignore everything they cannot easily acquire and fit in with their preconceived ideas, and imagine that they have become musical by shutting their eyes to almost everything really worth bothering about – encourages them to value their ordinary gifts to such an extent that they become oblivious – or remain indifferent – to the extraordinary gifts of the few who alone are capable of carrying on the great traditions founded by a like few, but for whom the mob could never have reached their present level of dangerous complacency. Education – not true prescience – is the only solution: and so far as music is concerned in Scotland at any rate anti-educational influences, in all but the narrow senses which concerns the merely executive development of great numbers not even a perceptible minority of whom will ever reach a level justifying what is being lost in other directions, have for the time being the field to themselves. Our fundamental difficulty – explaining our lack of genuine musical progression in a distinctively Scottish sense on the one hand, and our vulnerability on the other to 'Festivalitis' and similar diseases – is our entire absence of tradition in this country, our lack of perspective and sense of proportion. Imagine *Eisteddfodau* and Musical Festivals in France. Imagine the French reaction to such a devastating phenomenon as community singing. All these things are the symptoms and stigmata of that condition best known as 'half-bakedness.' They are the antithesis of every tendency or aspiration that is artistically valid or salutary. And they press most hardly on the creative artist. That is why these things in Scotland and elsewhere are run mainly, if not wholly, on other people's music or on atavistic and infantilist 'resurrected' stuff of our own.

The low standard of criticism in Scotland is largely responsible. The motto of it seems to be – praise everybody: no adverse comments. Pupils always do the utmost credit to their teachers. Every local singer or amateur actor or organist or violinist invariably does full credit to himself or herself. No doubt they do – whatever that means. The leading Scottish critic is perhaps Mr Percy Gordon, of the *Glasgow Herald*. Here is an example of *Glasgow Herald* musical criticism well up to its average quality (the italicisations are mine) –

> The current issue of *The Scottish Musical Magazine* contains in the editorial section some rather pessimistic utterances regarding music in Scotland. They arise, *curiously enough*, from a reference to the recent institution of a lectureship in music at Aberdeen University... the institution of the Competitive Festival is *the greatest thing that has been done for the cause of music in our history*. The writer of the article goes on to say that 'what Scotland is indeed badly in need of is something that will stir her up in no uncertain manner. A "music week" organised on the right lines should certainly do so – but it must be done thoroughly and comprehensively!' An earthquake would stir up Scotland in no uncertain manner, but I am no believer in the power of its aesthetic equivalent to do much towards furthering any branch of Art. Art is long, and while a music week, whenever it may be held, will not be without benefit, it would be wiser to measure our

progress in the art by 'Music Decades.' And I think it hardly fair that
the writer should stigmatise as 'merely a trade boom' the music week
which is being organised by the Scottish Music Merchants'
Association. As purveyors of *all things necessary* to the study and
enjoyment of music, the music merchants have a definite and very
important contribution to make to the advancement of the art in
Scotland, and an inevitable outcome of an organised attempt to boom
their trade will surely be *improved business methods, from which the
consumer will benefit.*

Anyone who does not instantly 'tumble' to all the iniquitous and
excruciating inwardness of that paragraph should cease forthwith to
imagine that he has the slightest capacity for gauging the position and
prospects of music in Scotland. To quote a recent *Dundee Advertiser*
review, 'The faithful bonniness of it is enough to make us feel wae.' So
far as music in Scotland is concerned, one is inclined to be like the saxo-
phone player who let the whole thing slide.

And imagine the pessimism of the *Scottish Musical Magazine* of all
papers. It is what *Morning Rays* is to the *Hibbert Journal* to any other
musical periodical I know at home or abroad.

Of the excellence of the Orpheus Choir – and Mr Roberton's genius
as a choir conductor – there are no two opinions: but the limitations
referred to by Ernest Newman must be kept in mind – and the
'Orpheus' takes no risk and never fails to throw a suitable sop to the
'gods' in the way of 'The Road to the Isles' as a wind-up or something of
that kind. Neither the choir as such, nor the individual members of it,
are in the least likely to do anything for the genuine advancement of
Scottish music. At the same time, while the precise character of Mr
Roberton's special abilities must be recognised and found to reside in a
narrow technical gift unsupported by any wide or really good knowledge
of music or fundamental artistic integrity, it cannot be gainsaid that he is
a remarkable and forceful personality and has rendered notable social
services if the direction these take reacts detrimentally on true creativity
in some ways. A long, fully particularised and very laudatory article on
him by H. Orsmond Anderton appeared in *Musical Opinion* for October
1921, and while I agree with much that it contains – bearing in mind the
reservations that I have set down and the fact that once he steps beyond
his own proper, and very narrow, sphere Mr Roberton's enterprising
figure is all too apt to disguise itself impenetrably in shoddy or even, at
times, sanctimoniousness, demonstrating that his is essentially a

commonplace mind apart from his choral flair – I must dissent from the pervading idea that a kind heart takes the place of a thorough education or that social sympathies and a humanitarian outlook excuse a lack of artistic rigour and an occasional playing to the gallery. But perhaps it is inevitable in Scotland that a musical movement must have an evangelical flavour (and an 'elder') and that one who strays so far from the straight and narrow path as to occupy himself mainly with singing and playing should insist in season and out of season that cultural considerations are to his mind entirely subordinate to social services and uplift in general. The unfortunate thing about Mr Roberton is that there is no expedient pretence about all this. His tongue is insufficiently in his cheek: and he takes himself far too seriously for the wrong things as a rule.

See also article 'The Glasgow Orpheus Choir,' by Harvey Grace in *The Music Times* of May 1st, 1925. [6.11.25]

Letters

GRIEVE AGAIN

Sir, – My knowledge of modern Scots literature is very small. Some of Grieve's heroes and villains I never heard of. But the fact that I thoroughly enjoy reading his articles suggests that he can make the unknown interesting. It is not what he says; it is the attitude behind his saying that is of importance. His individual criticisms of individuals may be good or bad... Not having read Neil Munro, for example, I cannot judge Grieve's judgment of him. But the attitude that Grieve takes up, his attempt to valuate Scots literature as a part of welt-literatur; this is the most interesting and most valuable piece of journalism that I have seen in a Scots paper. It seems to me that Grieve is simply trying to look at Scots literature from a window in Prague or Vienna, or Paris. I once showed an old Scots woman the ancient parts of Nürnberg. 'Beautiful,' she murmured, 'but I think I like the Canongate better.' Grieve's critics make me think of the old lady.

It is true that in writing Grieve must give the impression that he is a superior person. Any criticism postulates a superior attitude, and Grieve's criticism is damnably superior. He cannot mention men of note in European literature without appearing to be a superior person. His critics are really incensed at his superiority. Why they should be I do not know. I don't feel that Grieve is my superior because he juggles with literary names I never heard of. Here is a man who knows European literature – I forget how many languages he can read – a man with a decided attitude, a man with something new and bracing to say – and between the lines of the Scottish Educational Journal *I read the words: 'Stop him! Drop his articles.' Are the correspondents timid, or do they lack the sense of humour that they accuse Grieve of lacking ? – I am, etc.*

A.S. Neill

THE EUROPEAN STANDARD OF CRITICISM

Sir, – Mr C.M. Grieve informs us that he writes his 'criticisms' from 'a European standard,' and refers to his own 'comprehensive knowledge' by denying it to those who differ from him. Is he a superman? Or has he lived for over a century? No ordinary man can possibly be a sound and safe critic of half-a-dozen literatures.

In my opinion, the 'European standard' is a delusion and a sham. In France Shakespeare is appreciated by very few, although Germany 'raves' about him. Byron is more thought of on the Continent than Shelley or Keats. I am not one of those who think Byron is a mere minor, but there can be no doubt that his position on Parnassus is lower than the positions occupied by Keats and Shelley. Macpherson, the author of 'Ossianic epics', interspersed with genuine fragments of Gaelic lays, was for long the rage in Europe from Portugal to Russia, and the Highland poet undoubtedly exercised a greater influence on the Continent than ever did Milton.

The 'European standard,' indeed! To a Frenchman, a Spaniard, a German, or a Russian, much of Burns is incomprehensible. A few love lyrics only can be understood. But Burns, the artist, is not appreciated. A French critic translates this snatch of lovely word music: –

> *O wert thou in the cauld blast*
> *On yonder lea.*

as

> *Say if you were in the cold tempest*
> *In the meadow down there?*

In the poetry of every country there are beauties whose appeal depends to a large extent upon association. The foreigner cannot possibly feel the thrill of lines like

Ca' the yowes to the knowes…
Whiles o'er the linn the burnie pours.

What does a Parisian or a Berlin scholar know of a 'burnie' and all that
it means to a Scot? What would a Russian, Italian, German, Frenchman,
or Spaniard make of

Bonnie wee thing, cannie wee thing,
Lovely wee thing, wert thou mine,
I wad wear thee in my bosom
Lest my jewel I should tine.

Are we to dethrone our Scottish lyric lord because the foreigner cannot
appreciate him as an artist? Are we to set up in Scotland a 'European
standard' and cast the poetic gems of Rabbie to the wind ? Apparently
Mr Grieve is ready to do something like that. We've had curious views
from him regarding Burns and regarding Robert Fergusson, 'the marvellous boy' minstrel of Edinburgh – another great artist in the Doric.

I have already given my opinion regarding the poetic fare provided by
Mr Grieve's 'darlings.' My view of the 'movement' is that it is decadent.

Would you, Mr Editor, permit me here to voice my protest against the
attitude taken up in an Educational Journal with regard to John Knox,
the man who wanted to have a school in every parish ? He was no enemy
of culture.

We have heard, too, of the 'Geneva prison house'. But that was the
'prison' from which Milton's organ notes were poured – the 'prison' from
which John Bunyan sent us his matchless prose.

Read Milton's 'Comus' and search for prison bars! Read the early
writings of Barrie and Ian Maclaren, for that matter of it, and what do
we find in these to bring the blush of shame to the cheeks of any true
Scot or any true artist? Our young literary swashbucklers are ashamed
of the 'Kailyaird school.' It is apparently not theatrical enough for them.
But the Reformation gave us the grand old doctor of Ian Maclaren and
the real old weavers of Barrie – the type of men I knew as a boy. Judged
from Mr Grieve's 'European standard,' they may be of little account.
They are no less admirable for all that – these 'nails that held the world
together for us. Barrie is a great artist, but he has never been greater
than when he 'bided' in Thrums. When one thinks of the putrid themes
of so many modern novelists, Thrums smells sweet as new-mown hay.

It is not necessary to be vulgar to be strong, to be indecent to be
vigorous, to be bizarre to be original, to be violent to attract attention, to

strain after effect to be artistic. But it is necessary to be sincere to be convincing and to worship Beauty to be a true poet. The more the poet loves Beauty the greater he becomes. His views on Darwin, Newton, Einstein, Freud, John Knox, Calvin, the Popes, etc., are of very secondary importance. If he is a true poet, he will shut his text-books and his various 'languages-learned easily' books, and consider the lily, the buttercup, and the daisy, hear wisdom from the lark and find 'sermons' in stones. It is the poet's experience of Beauty that really matters in poetry. His views on what poetry should be are 'not worth a snuff,' unless he is capable of producing poetry which appeals to the innate sense of beauty possessed in varying degrees by all and sundry. The sincere poet cannot consciously sing to Europe: he cannot tell whether Europe can understand or appreciate him. It may. or it may not, although he chances to attain great stature. But he can sing to his 'ain folk', and he may leave them deathless strains which foreigners cannot read or care for. If Mr Grieve's poets are singing to Europe, and not to Scotland, that may be one reason why a lover of poetry like myself cannot discern the greatness and charm they appear to hold for their 'shepherd'.

In my last letter I wrote regarding 'the severe formalism' of Gaelic poetry. My small handwriting caused our friend, the printer, to make me say 'severe formation.' – I am. etc.,

Donald A. Mackenzie

CONTEMPORARY SCOTTISH STUDIES

Sir, – Mr C.M. Grieve's reply to my complaint is studiously fair except at one point where he attempts to fasten on me the statement that Scottish readers sufficiently acquainted with contemporary European literature to appreciate and ponder his judgments are non-existent. It was his own statement in his study on Sir George Douglas (August 7) that prompted my most respectful request for more reasoned instruction and less assumption. He then wrote: 'The number of contemporary Scots thoroughly abreast of welt-literatur cannot exceed a dozen at the outside,' and although that is not perhaps exactly the same thing it justifies a plea for more expository light and a trifle less heat, especially when the plea is accompanied by a provisional acceptance of the instructor's dictum. – I am. etc.,

Greenock　　　　　　　　　　　　　　　　　　　　*W.H. Hamilton*
30th October, 1925

P.S. – *Mr Grieve asks. 'What critic of any consequence has conceded their claim (i.e., Barrie's, etc.) to serious regard?' Miss Storm Jameson's* Modern Drama in Europe *(Collins) certainly cannot be pooh-poohed, and although I should argue some of her verdicts as well as Mr Grieve's (whose trenchancy they exceed) her judgment of Barrie is wholly appreciative and firmly reasoned at that, and Miss Jameson certainly knows European literature of to-day. But is it the critic – any critic – who has the last word about any creative effort after all? Have European critics given, e.g., Hardy his due?*

THE 'NORDIC' ORIGIN OF THE SCOTS

Sir, – *When Mr Horne and I entered into a little friendly discussion as to the racial history of Orkney and Shetland, I do not suppose we contemplated anything of the nature of a three-cornered contest; but having chosen to do so in public print we cannot be surprised at 'Buchan's' joining in at a point that is undoubtedly of general interest. However, I am sure we should have welcomed him more had he come in a more amiable mood, and without concealment of his identity. If, instead of saying nasty things about Sir Arthur Keith, quite undeserved too, he had endeavoured to show where and why that eminent authority is wrong, in his opinion, it would have been more to the point. For my own part, while I should never insist that Sir Arthur Keith is infallible, I am satisfied that I quoted no mean authority on the subject. It was a fortunate coincidence, that, just twelve days after my letter appeared in your columns, your English contemporary* The Teacher's World, *devoted its front page (and more) to this 'gifted scientist,' whose 'profound acquaintance with the pre-history of mankind' constantly enables him 'to suggest fresh angles of vision applied to the world as we know it.' I do not think I need add more on that point.*

As to the meaning of the term 'Nordic,' I may say that I have seen it used in three different senses: (a) to designate a tall, fair, long-headed race founded in the northern parts of Europe; (b) the Teutonic peoples generally; and (c) the northern branch of the Teutonic. It was chiefly in this last sense that I used the term; but since the greater must include the less, 'Buchan' may quite well adopt any of the three in reading my letter, without altering its purport in the least. – I am, etc.,

Robert W. Tait

ORKNEY AND SHETLAND

Sir, – *Permit me to say how much I appreciated Mr Horne's reply in your issue of 16th October, and to remark how pleased I am to notice how very little there now remains at issue between us. Only one point is really in need of clearing up, and that is with regard to linguistic differences. Had it occurred to me that the substance of Mr Horne's first letter was mainly a condensation of two paragraphs from Messrs Heddle and Mainland's book, 'Orkney and Shetland,' as is now apparent, I should not only have understood his point of view better, but, without modifying in any degree the views I expressed, I should have phrased them differently so as to be equally well understood by him.*

I had the great privilege of being personally acquainted with the late Professor Jacobsen and know something of his methods; and, having observed with what care and caution he would move towards even the simplest conclusions, I would agree that any estimate of his is practically beyond question. It is a fact that in his efforts to preserve the old Norn speech (it is to be sincerely hoped that this term does not annoy our friend 'Buchan,' but it is Jacobsen's own preference, so I offer no apology) the great philologist gathered an amazing amount of material in the Shetland Isles – literally 'many thousands' of words; but it must not be forgotten that the great bulk of these were obtained from very old people, who in turn had got them, in their younger days, from still older people, and that what Jacobsen thus rescued from oblivion was, in great measure, a dead language. Jacobsen's praiseworthy efforts have done much to prevent further loss, and may even have helped towards a restoration; but, when dealing with the everyday speech *of the people, which was what I particularly referred to, a few hundreds would be nearer estimate than the 'many thousands' so carefully gathered by the kindly professor. If Mr Horne ever allows me to reciprocate the hospitality which he so graciously offers, he will not take long to discover the truth of my words. It is a regrettable fact that the decay of the old Norse tongue, which he would assure me has advanced so far in Orkney, is proceeding in Shetland just as surely, and very little more slowly.*

I always knew that even 'the humblest Orcadians' speak English (and a very beautiful English it usually is) when occasion demands – as can the Shetlander – but it, fortunately, is as well to correct the impression, so often given, that the average Orcadian habitually speaks 'pure English.' There is a distinct Orcadian dialect, which is no more Scots than it is English, but peculiar to the islands. An Orcadian acquaintance of mine, who hailed from Westray (and who, when I last parted from him, announced that he was going 'abaird o' th' bôt') would willingly bear me out in this if it should happen to meet his eye; but I am sure Mr

Horne will not wish to deny it. The 'broad Orcadian' is a picturesque tongue; and, while differing from the Shetlandic in some interesting points, resembles it in having eliminated nearly all the harsher-sounds of the three parent languages (Norse, Scots, and English), and in still retaining more than 'a few Norse words' in daily use.

As regards racial history, little room is now left for any difference or misunderstanding between Mr Horne and myself. We both recognise a pre-Norse substratum (regarding which the authority whom he quotes wisely says, on p. 35, that it is 'unsafe to dogmatise'), a Norse colonisation, and later admixtures from the Lowlands of Scotland and from the nearby north of Scotland. All this applies to both groups of islands, in equal degree except as regards the 'later admixtures' which have been more plentiful in the case of Orkney; and I must repeat my contention that since the people of the Lowlands were, unless history lies, 'Anglo-Danes,' and since the extreme north of Scotland was commonly referred to as 'lands of the Norsemen,' it is impossible to establish any appreciable degree of racial difference between Orcadian and Shetlander. because of varying streams of immigration from these regions.

In conclusion, I wish to say that I quite understood that Mr Horne's first letter implied no invidious distinctions; but I felt that, without a little explanation, it might give rise to misconceptions. Mr Horne says 'I do not regret it if it has found me a friend', and while I would seek to assure him on that point, I should like to add that I am sure that the frank and friendly tone of his second letter would bring into that category every one who read it. – I am, etc.,

Robert W. Tait
[6.11.25]

20. R.F. Pollock and the Art of the Theatre

Within a stone's throw of the Covent Garden Opera House, one of London's largest places of entertainment, the world's smallest theatre is to be opened shortly – in an old hay-loft. It will seat only 96 persons and, under the name of 'The Gate Theatre Salon,' is to be run pretty much on the lines of a proprietory club. The project is under the direction of Mr Peter Godfrey, who explains that the theatre is intended to be a nursery for the 'Communists of the art world.' 'Pure art' is the object of the promoters. Mr Godfrey is of the opinion that the nightly audiences will not as a matter of fact exceed about twenty-five. I would fain gather from this that he intends to debar the merely curious and confine admission to those who are seriously interested. 'The Gate Theatre Salon' may profitably follow the lead, too, of Vsevolod Meyerhold, the most iconoclastic of contemporary Moscow producers, in dispensing with a curtain and having the actors appear in their ordinary work-a-day clothes. I do not know whether there are ninety-six Glaswegians sufficiently interested in the problem of creating a distinctively Scottish drama to enable the Gate Theatre Salon method to be followed there: but I am perfectly certain that it is only by some such means that the task can be carried through. It may be necessary to make concessions to secure the requisite number to launch a little Experimental Theatre movement. Projects such as Meyerhold's and even Godfrey's may be too drastic for the douce intelligentsia of Glasgow. On the other hand the problem of creating a distinctively Scottish drama is one that may well engage the minds of all who can appreciate a first-rate intellectual opportunity bristling with difficulties of every imaginable kind. Whether the necessary number of enthusiasts can be rallied round him, or not, Mr R.F. Pollock's significance in relation to Scottish arts and affairs at the present moment is precisely due to his realisation that this is the *via sola* of Scots drama. He is the only Scotsman I know with the necessary flair and the necessary knowledge of Contemporary European Drama to create, if he is given the opportunity and suitable dramatic texts, a new theatrical technique in accordance with distinctively Scottish psychology. The whole trend of his mind is at variance with the point of view of the Scottish National Players in their approach to the matter. Three years ago the present writer wrote, apropos the announcement that during the previous two years 150 Scottish plays had been submitted to the Scottish National Theatre Society, of which 17 had been found fit for production and four were then awaiting production, that

> this spate of alleged plays is indicative of nothing but the spread of *cacoethes scribendi*. Even the small percentage deemed worthy of production may have had commercial possibilities but were certainly utterly devoid of literary significance. Technically nothing has been done to differentiate Scottish drama from English. It is at once pitiful and amusing to read that this precious Society is determined to prove that there is a distinct Scottish drama on the strength of such plays as Mr Neil Grant's. A Scottish drama cannot be created in that way. This

so-called 'movement' is doomed by shallowness of purpose, the absence of research, conscience, and imaginative integrity, and the mistake of thinking that it is possible to secure a Scottish drama as a mere offshoot of the contemporary English stage in its most ephemeral and trivial aspects; a freak of hybridisation, resembling the stoneless plum, is all that can be so secured.

About the same time, the Hon. R. Erskine of Marr, in the *Glasgow Herald*, in words as applicable to Scots drama in English or the Vernacular as in Gaelic, was pointing out that:

There has come down to us no example of Gaelic literary talent in true dramatic form, and such modern plays as have been written do not support the notion that the authors of them are conversant with any stage, save perhaps the English, or as well grounded in ancient Gaelic literature. We must, therefore, set aside these modern Gaelic essays of playwriting. and, firm in the conviction that, for a variety of reasons into which it is not necessary here to penetrate, these are not those that should come, we must look for others... I mean, of course, such a choice as a true Gaelic craftsman would make, who knows the history of his race and literature, is conversant with the psychology of his people, and has a sound knowledge of the European stage, especially with the dramatic writings of those countries the genius of whose inhabitants is near to our own, such, for example as France, Spain, or Italy.

Alter the word Gaelic to Scottish, and that sentence describes the equipment Mr R.F. Pollock is bringing to this task. He is the first Scottish producer who has manifested a dynamic realisation of the prerequisites of a Scots drama *sui generis*. In this respect he unfortunately remains in advance of the playwrights: but that he should be revolving the specific problems of a Scots theatrecraft in anticipation, and that a line of criticism such as his, supported by technical experience and the will to produce, should be manifesting itself against the policy of the Scottish National Players, are matters of prime moment at this juncture of the movement towards a Scottish drama.

In the course of an article on the subject of 'Scots Stage Production,' Mr Pollock observes that

it may be that not until we evolve a new dramatic form of expression in setting, gesture, and intonation will the capabilities of dramatist and actor produce distinctive virile result... There must be a definite first step, so let us dispense with conventional scenery. Instead, let us be frankly negative and use simple dark drapings. That is at least sincere... It is characteristic of the Scot that he thinks a lot but says little. This feature is seen in the diversity of intention that may be signified by the word meaning broadly 'Yes,' but spelt phonetically 'Ughugh.' Facial expression and gesture are used so aptly that a conversation may sometimes be continued largely by use of this word or its synonym 'Aye.'

Were an experimental Scots little theatre begun – and twenty-five enthusiasts could do it in Glasgow if twenty-five can do it for London – its repertory might very well start with a play confined to one word in that way. It would at least be an adequate departure from the sort of thing that has hitherto called itself a Scottish play, and would far better deserve the title. From that point the movement might very well develop – educating its playwrights as it went along by imposing upon them a method of collaboration with the producers and the players with mere suggestions instead of concrete plays to work from – into attempts to adapt, with additions giving the material to hand contemporary gagging, allegorical effects and so forth, some of the extraordinarily dramatic work of Dougal Graham, the Skellat Bellman of Glasgow (the nearest thing to a Scots drama yet evolved) and some of his fellow 'flying stationers,' or to expand into full-size *divertissements* some of the splendid suggestions latent in the games and nursery tales to be found in Robert Chambers' *Popular Rhymes of Scotland* and elsewhere. The current type of Scots drama, and stage conceptions of Scottish character like the Scotch comedian in the music-halls, can only be supplanted by an effective use of the *vis comica* latent in Scottish psychology. Genuine manifestations of it will make short work of such 'wut.' It is not for nothing that Meyerhold's plays are usually satires on old Russian life and literature and burlesques of its masterpieces. This is the line that must necessarily be followed in Scotland too. Due consideration of the quality of the *Bunty Pulls the Strings* or *Courting* sort of thing, passing itself off as Scottish drama, in relation to contemporary European developments in drama will make this clear. It is even truer of the concept of the Auld Licht Elder or the figure that goes about with a Balmoral bonnet on, a bottle of whisky in one hand and a bulgy 'gamp' in the other, and of the other lay figures of Scottish kailyaird drama, that these are the elements of a pitiably diminished myth – a myth deplorably attenuated and ineffectual compared with the myth which is potential in the same material

– than it is true of the degenerated national myths in the commercial theatres of other countries, while in Scotland alone this prevailing myth is not being opposed or emulated. But that is what is really needed if headway is to be made towards a genuine Scottish National Drama, for as T.S. Eliot has said, 'the modern dramatist, and probably the modern audience, is terrified of the myth. The myth is imagination and it is also criticism, and the two are one.' A new myth must rise like the jinn out of the bottle of a little theatre. It is absurd to imagine that Scotland can be supplied with what it has never had – and does not want, although it badly needs it – by means of a Society appealing to the general public. If creative tendencies in countries with great traditions in drama are nowadays being forced out of the great playhouses into little theatres, the Scottish movement should anticipate the inevitable by beginning there.

That, I fancy, is the gravamen of the charge Pollock would bring against the Scottish National Players, although he admires their work in some ways and would wish them success – that they have become a social institution at the expense of their original purpose. They have gained a following and failed to follow the gleam. What hope is there for a play that does not please their members? Obviously their efforts are restricted. Their movement as they have shaped it depends upon popular fancy and therefore is not free to pursue a creative purpose. And none of the plays they have produced have represented a distinctively Scottish form, the dramatic equivalent of the *differentia* of Scots psychology. They have all been alien in form, although they have been Scottish in subject, setting, and, to some extent, in speech. Not being new and peculiar to Scotland, they have not demanded more than conventional production and acting.

Mr Pollock's Lennox Players differ from the National Players in that, under his influence, they clearly realise what is wanted and are already elaborating a technique that will correspond to it as soon as it is forthcoming. Their work on such plays as Lady Margaret Sackville's 'When Andra Smith Cam' Hame,' Alexander MacGill's 'Pardon in the Morning,' and G.R. Malloch's 'Thomas the Rhymer' (a significantly different production this last from the Scottish National Players' production of it) – despite the fact that these plays are not the Scots drama that is being awaited – showed the effects of this forethinking on problems of national technique, and to some extent preluded the technical developments that can only manifest themselves with full effect as dramatic forms in full accord with Scots psychology are forthcoming.

It is pioneer work that Mr Pollock is applying himself to and fashioning his Players to further; and its importance is derived from the fact that they are the first group, and still the only group, who realise that, in the words of *The Scottish Chapbook*. 'It is futile to speak of a Scottish National Theatre until a start has been made to devise a national theatrecraft. At best the Scottish National Players will help indirectly by disseminating the idea that there is (or rather should be) a difference between Scottish and English drama, and intelligent people who witness these productions will see that nevertheless no such difference exists and ask why. Once a sufficient number of these intelligent people begin to ask why with sufficient urgency, the problem of producing a really Scottish play in a manner which represents a definite effort to create a genuine Scottish National Theatre, will cease to be insoluble.'

Mr Pollock and his Players will then have acquired a sufficient number of enthusiasts to enable them to start a creative studio along the Gate Theatre Salon lines and to become what they are – the spearhead of the movement temporarily *manqué* towards a Scots national drama.

The Lennox Players have produced: –
Scenes from *The Tempest* and *Twelfth Night* – 16th January, 1924.
Scenes from *Macbeth* and Gordon Bottomley's *Gruach* – 14th February, 1924.
Till Something Happens, by R.F. Pollock.
When Andra Smith Cam' Hame Again, by the Lady Margaret Sackville.
The Eve of Saint John, by J. Saunders Lewis – 20th March, 1924.
Pardon in the Morning, by Alexander MacGill
Thomas the Rhymer, by G.R. Malloch – 12th February, 1925.
Cameron o' the Track, by Jean St. C. Balls – 31st March, 1925.
And play readings:
The White Headed Boy, by Lennox Robinson.
The Tragedy of Nan, by John Masefield.   [13.11.25]

Letters

THE BROAD SCOTS MOVEMENT

Sir, – With regard to your leader in the last issue of the Journal I am behind none in my admiration of Dr Murray's genius: he has rendered a signal service to North-Eastern Scotland not only by helping to preserve the Buchan dialect, but also by enshrining in literary form customs, beliefs, and types of character that have all but disappeared from that area.

The stimulation of a deeper interest in Scots song, literature, and history in our schools (and elsewhere) is a commendable ideal, but the teaching of Broad Scots as a regular part of the curriculum is another

*question. What substantial advantage is to be reaped from the achieve-
ment of national bi-lingualism, even if it be practicable? Much greater
than the difficulty of multiplicity of dialects at present prevailing, and
the false shame referred to on the part both of parents and of teachers is
the difficulty of time. Under the present regime even the indispensable
subjects simply jostle one another for attention in the Time-table, and the
hours assigned for the teaching of English, which is, inevitably, the
keystone of the whole educational arch, are already fully occupied with
its ever-widening field. Most of us have a struggle getting rid of the
dialect from the speech and compositions of the pupils: the teaching of it
could only heap up confusion. The recognised test of an educated child
(or adult) is his ability to write and speak the English language, and that
is not learned in a day. English is the medium of business, social intercourse, of the platform, pulpit, and Press even on this side of the Border,
and the ratepayers and parents have the right to insist that more and
more emphasis be placed upon correct and beautiful (if you will) expression of English on the part of the children educated. Most Scotsmen have
to contend all their lives with dialectical tendencies in pronunciation and
colloquial habits of speech, and regret their lack of opportunity to master
such defects during the school period*

*The child must certainly be introduced to the native song, literature,
and history (as time may permit), but these must not interfere with his
mastery of English, not only that he may worthily take his place in the
world, but also that he may be able to appreciate the much larger and
more magnificent fabric of English literature. This will be more than
ever necessary if we are to realise our desire to keep England perpetually
supplied with Archbishops, Prime Ministers, and Professors, and the
Dominions with capable administrators.*

*Our job as teachers – poor, patient asses – is already big and difficult
enough. Leave the preservation of dialects to poets, gentlemen of leisure,
philologists, and literary societies. – I am, etc..*

Lenzie   *John Cook*
9th November 1925

CONTEMPORARY SCOTTISH STUDIES

*Sir, – Unless Mr Grieve deems A. France beneath his notice, he must feel
rather perturbed at repeated protests from readers against the all but
insurmountable obstacles to their understanding his rheumatic prose.
My struggle with his effusion on the Musical Festival Movement reveals*

to me a bundle of inconsistency and misunderstanding.

'The low standard of criticism in Scotland is largely responsible,' he says, for our present musical dilemma; 'the motto seems to be – praise everybody: no adverse comments,' a Festival Association being one of the 'mutual admiration societies.' It is quite evident Mr Grieve has never been a Festival competitor with a Newman or a Roberton adjudicating on his efforts! For him, the fumbling, money-making Press and its reporters are synonymous with adjudicators' sheets and adjudicators.

Newman in writing is valid support for our critic when it suits his purpose; the same Newman at the adjudicator's desk is anathema. What has so mysteriously charmed away his artistic integrity? Grieve and Newman may be at one in deploring the state of British music: luckily they are as the poles apart in their attitude to the Festival.

Again, Mr Grieve for long enough has been exhorting would-be creative artists in Scotland to cultivate a European outlook and so attain a true perspective. 'Go to England and the Continent, thou sluggard, and learn something!' has been his advice; but when he meets a Scots Festival singer, he shouts: 'Stay at home! Shun Festivals run mainly on other people's music!' Which Grieve (if either) are we to take seriously?

'Musical Festival education,' says the pundit, 'is an exceedingly shallow and superficial thing at best.' Who said it wasn't? Our critic himself in the same article denounces the movement as anti-educational. How then can he talk of Festival education at all? But do the French, whose good sense in this matter Mr Grieve admires, debar a youth from juggling with equations or toying with a composition, on the grounds that he may never be a Kelvin or – a Grieve? 'Imagine Eisteddfodau and Musical Festivals in France,' he sneers. I can't – after having heard French school choirs!

Such misfortunes as Mr Grieve's inability to understand massed singing and to distinguish it from solo singing are not at all surprising. They are the natural outcome of that solitude to which the chosen few are condemned!

It seems that the Festival Movement has 'done those things it ought not to have done, and left, etc.' Who can believe with Mr Grieve that it has widened the breach between composer and public, and restricted repertory where before was none; or that it should be censured for not doing what common sense indicates it should never attempt, and acquaintance with the facts shows it has never attempted? I borrow for the occasion a little of Mr Grieve's monopoly of asseveration, and answer, 'Nobody of any consequence.' And what message has this same

Mr Grieve for the twentieth century when, in his view, the creative artist should look upon the mass, the 'mob' (ugly word!), as dirt; and when he does condescend to recognise those poor one-language illiterates, it should merely be to upbraid them for their lack of support in not buying his music or his books?

Man's inhumanity to man, forsooth! How often it is the reward of Justice! – I am, etc.,

Wishaw   *W.M. Brownlie*

THE HEAVYFATHERHOOD OF MR DONALD A. MACKENZIE

Sir, – The other day I experienced in these columns somewhat of the heavyfatherhood of Mr Donald A. Mackenzie. I was commended for espousing the Gaelic cause. but at the same time as he laid the rather weighty hand of his epistolary approval on my head, and gently patted it, he uttered words of solemn warning. I and 'other enthusiasts' he said 'must be reminded that there is no essential connection between a race and a culture.' Thus in effect were I and other espousers of the Gaelic cause bidden to run away and play with it, but on no account to wax too enthusiastic about it. I have been warned before now in similar fashion, and generally (I have noticed) by persons who disliked the arguments I employed without their being able to make any very appreciable headway against them. But, no matter: there are other things in the philosophy of the heavyfatherhood of Mr Mackenzie with which I prefer to deal briefly on the present occasion, instead of this matter of enthusiasm.

Mr Mackenzie says that I and other enthusiasts must be reminded that there is no essential connection between a race and a culture, and to prove this assertion of his he quotes the case of the Asiatic Celts 'who ceased to eat pork.' In the first place I am not aware that either here or anywhere else I have made bold to affirm that the connection between race and culture is essential. I am however quite willing to accept Mr Mackenzie's word for it that once upon a time these Asiatic Celts gave up pork, though why on account of this (to me) most reasonable abstention they should be held to have turned their backs on their race and culture passes my comprehension. I am aware, however, that Mr Mackenzie has written learnedly and extensively on pork; and, of course, it may be that through the channel of his friend and confidant, Sir Chihchen-lo-feng-luh (whose name, by the way, had it been Gaelic, instead of Chinese, had been denounced as impractical long ago), he has learned a deal in addition about pigs and pork, as well ancient as modern; for, if my memory serves me right, it was one of that distinguished person's countrymen who first practised roasting the animal. But, assuming that Mr Mackenzie is right in thinking that abstaining from pork involves an absolute exclusion from race and culture, so far as the Celts are concerned, what about apple-sauce, to which most pork-eating Celts of to-day are partial? I have read somewhere that the eating of apple-sauce with roast pig is a comparatively modern custom, and further that the home of the former invention is Germany. How, therefore, do we now stand with regard to this matter? The Celtic purists who on racial and cultural grounds refuse to take apple-sauce with their pork can be but a handful, and are obviously not worth considering. The general custom among Celts is for pork (Celtic) and apple-sauce (Teutonic) to go, and go down, together. What happens then in those numerous cases in which these symbols of Celtic raciality and culture on one hand, and Teutonic raciality and culture on the other, are mixed, and taken inwardly together? Does one force invalidate the other to the extent of an absolute exclusion of it from the physical and intellectual economy of the consumer, or may it be held – which on the whole seems the thing that is the more reasonable to believe – that Mr Mackenzie on pork is far too imaginative a writer to be a sure guide with regard to racial and cultural themes?

But Mr Mackenzie on pork by no means exhausts Mr Mackenzie otherwise. Appropriately enough he keeps the richest product of the vineyard of his heavyfatherhood till the last. In the concluding paragraph of his letter on 'Poetry and Politics,' he begs leave to 'remind young writers in this connection that when politics come in at the study window poetry flies out at the door.' In other words, Mr Mackenzie is persuaded that the connection between politics and letters is imaginary, and that his bounden duty is to warn 'young writers,' out of the boundless goodness of his heavyfatherhood, to beware of harbouring any so dangerous a doctrine as the reverse of this axiom. But surely the eternal intimacy and co-relationship of cause and effect were never more clearly demonstrated than when the Italian Risorgiamento followed the Italian Renaissance, and the French Revolution the writings of the Encyclopedists and Libertins? Mr Mackenzie appeals to sentiment in the shape of absent friends in Ireland who, he says, desire as much as he can do that the Gaelic movement should be 'kept out of politics.' There would appear to be a deal of the late Mrs Partington in Mr Mackenzie, besides his sterling heavyfatherly qualities. In any event, I venture to regard his counsel as impertinent. It is impertinent because both movements have *made use of political means in order to open the schools to Gaelic, and it is impertinent because the history of language movements in general shows that their sources are political, no matter what the blindness of some and the timidity of others may cause both to allege to the contrary. – I am, etc.,*

R. Erskine of Marr
[13.11.25]

21. William and Agnes M'Cance

These names are still practically unknown in Scotland and only known in England to a very limited public and on the Continent in certain advanced art-circles. But the existence of two such personalities – and their recent awakening, or return, to a sense of their distinctive potentialities as Scots and of the unique opportunities now offering themselves for a Scottish Renaissance – are unquestionably the most promising phenomena of contemporary Scotland in regard to art. If that divination of opportunity which five or six years ago led to what has since become known as the Scottish Renaissance movement, was well-founded – if, indeed, the psychological moment had arrived for a national awakening (and that was the preliminary assumption which has led to many of the subsequent activities and aspirations which I have been describing) – it was obvious that personalities of this very kind must speedily become active in Scottish art and so complement and confirm the manifestations of the new spirit already evident in literature, music, and other developments of our national life. This anticipation fulfils itself in Mr and Mrs M'Cance, and the lines along which they are now thinking and acting adumbrate the future of Scottish art – the effect of the Renaissance spirit in this sphere as it will be appreciated in retrospect. It is confirmatory of the genuine character of the whole movement that its direction in art like its direction in other departments is seen to depend upon three main factors – (a) alignment with ultra-modern tendencies manifesting themselves internationally, (b) in accordance with a new or renewed realisation of fundamental elements of distinctively Scottish psychology, (c) which have hitherto for the most part been misunderstood, misapplied, or otherwise denied free play through the operation of the various factors, political, religious, or economic, which have, until their recent setback, been conducing to and, if unarrested and reversed, would obviously have culminated in the complete assimilation of Scotland to England and the permanent provincialisation of our country.

Both Mr and Mrs M'Cance belong to the Glasgow district, and are in their early thirties. Prior to leaving Glasgow, Mr M'Cance gave a lecture to the young 'Society of Painters and Sculptors' on modern art which was received with a certain measure of hostility to say the least of it. They went to London, where he did a certain amount of illustrating and lecturing. At present he is art critic of *The Spectator*. In writing of their own work one is handicapped by the fact that probably none of one's readers have seen any of it. Exceptions may perhaps be made of Mr M'Cance's portrait of Mr J. St Loe Strachey and of the fifty-foot panel he painted for the *Daily News,* which has been described as one of the best examples of progressive unity in modern painting. Both, however, are highly productive artists, concerned exclusively – and this is the measure of their artistic integrity – with the basic problems with which progressive artists everywhere are to-day preoccupied and not with the commercial application of established, that is to say effete, techniques. And they are necessarily approaching these problems, and resolving them, as Scots – that is to say that the psychological factor is so directly involved and dominant in work of this kind that the difference between the effects they are securing and the effects their French or German contemporaries are securing gives the precise measure of what is distinctively Scottish in this connection. The traditions of what is called 'Scottish art' mean nothing to them – but in so far as these were not the products of acquired techniques incapable of relating Scottish psychology to art products in a specifically effective fashion correspondences will be discernible in retrospect. In the meantime their work is probably unintelligible to the great mass of those who look to find a 'likeness' in a portrait (and are at sea with a psychological criticism expressing itself in terms of the inter-relationships of planes) or who demand of a picture that it reproduces a recognisable place or embodies a pleasing conception or 'points a moral or adorns a tale.' And the number of those in Scotland who have got beyond the stage of making such demands of any work of art with which they may be confronted is extremely small. Indeed the proportion which has yet been confronted with any work of art which does not conform to such preconceptions is extremely small. The whole course of modern art in all its amazing and absorbing developments is a sealed book to all but a mere handful of the population of Scotland. All they know about it is derived from the cheap

witticisms or indignant attacks – as on Epstein's 'Rima' – which occasionally diversify the popular press. And as a consequence to speak or
write of art in Scotland to-day is almost inevitably to find oneself in a
position similar to that so well described by Lord Dewar when, as he
says, 'I, once, during an after-dinner speech, used the word Lipton when
I was treating of Milton, but soon found that my audience were with me
in spirit.'

But M'Cance's ideas on the subject of Scottish art can be bluntly set
forth without reference to the history and relative aspect of ultra-
modern tendencies in general. If he were interviewed on the subject he
would probably say – and I, for one, would feel that the declaration gave
a lead to Scottish Art which it has long awaited, however ruthlessly it
traverses the prevailing conceptions on the subject – something like this:

The sooner the Scots realise that they have never had a culture the
better. We have merely had a few good names. We have had a certain
amount of folklore and we have a great amount of inherent vitality.
We must accept the fact that we are a young nation (with tremendous
elemental potentiality), which is not worn threadbare by precedent.
England is on the verge of collapse, France is senile. Their culture is
lacking in vitality – is dispassionate and clammy. They have no belief
in posterity because there will be no posterity for them. They hark
back to the past; they get hysterical because St Paul's is crumbling.
They have no confidence in their own capacity to rebuild St Paul's.
Scotland must dissociate itself from English culture. Scotland being a
young nation has sent out feelers throughout the world, extracted
what it can use to advantage, and is now in a position to start its
culture, being still vital and elemental. It can even resurrect English
culture – give it new impetus and life. Now that we are about to
expand culturally, let us examine our attributes. *So far there has been
too great a cleavage between Engineering and Art.* Actually what has
taken place in Scotland up to the present is that our best constructive
minds have taken up engineering and only sentimentalists have practised art. We are largely (the world has assessed us rightly) a nation of
engineers. Let us realise that a man may still be an engineer and yet
concerned with a picture conceived purely as a kind of engine which
has a different kind of functional power to an engine in the ordinary
sense of the term. Here then is what we Scots have – a terrific vitality
combined with a constructive ability unequalled by any other nation.
What more do we need? – merely sufficient analytical power to clear

away the maze of sentimentality and accepted 'artistic' values which obscure our ideas of art. Let us no longer alienate our engineers from art. Let us advise our sentimentalists in art to migrate to 'spiritualism' or let us equip an expedition for them to explore the possibilities of Celtic Twilight in some remote corner of the world where they will not disturb us in our work. Let them give up cumbersome paint and canvas and take to photographing fairies on uninhabited islands. Anything. Anyhow now is the time for a real Scottish culture.

Thus, roughly and readily, I imagine M'Cance would express himself on the subject, and whatever may be thought of sentiments such as these there is no denying that they suggest a means of affecting a long-overdue union between what is ungainsayably one of the dominant aptitudes of Scottish genius – (hitherto divorced from art and confined to 'practical' affairs as a consequence of that self-same materialism which has so largely conditioned the cultural desuetude of Scotland, prompted our union with England and been since generally invoked as the main, if not the sole, justification of its denationalising sequelae; and evolved the stultifying concept of the canny Scot at variance with our real, if suppressed psychology) – and one of the strongest tendencies in world-art to-day, the necessity of coming to terms with the Third Factor, the Machine, and no longer confining ourselves to that overpast condition of affairs in which only two factors had to be reckoned with – Man and Nature. M'Cance might have further strengthened his case if he had invoked not only our engineering genius but our metaphysical flair: just as the former has been confined to machinery, so the latter has been largely devoted either to theology or the law; and just as the former is now a quality *par excellence* for the tackling of some of the most difficult problems of progressive art to-day, so is the latter in significant accord with the prime requirements for the exploration of abstract form and the 'pure' conveyance of states of mind. And the recent work of Mr and Mrs M'Cance is the best proof of the validity of their theories.

Compare the trend of M'Cance's mind with what Jane Heap says in a recent *Little Review* apropos the Machine-Age Exposition organised by that organ of *l'avant-garde*:

It is inevitable and important to the civilisation of to-day that he (the engineer) make a union with the artist. This affiliation of artist and engineer will benefit each in his own domain, it will end the immense waste in each domain and will become a new creative force... The snobbery, awe and false pride in the art-game, set up by the museums, dealers and second-rate artists, have frightened the general public out of any frank appreciation of the plastic arts. In the past it was a contact with and an appreciation of the arts that helped the individual to function more harmoniously. Such an exaggerated extension of one of the functions, the extension of the mind as evidenced in this invention of machines, must be a mysterious and necessary part of our evolution. The men who hold first rank in the plastic arts to-day are the men who are organising and transforming the realities of our age into a dynamic beauty. The artist and the engineer start out with the same necessity. No true artist ever starts to make 'beauty'; he has no aesthetic intention; he has a problem. No beauty has ever been achieved which was not reached through the necessity to deal with some particular problem. The artist works with definite plastic laws. He knows that his work will have lasting value only if he consciously creates forms which embody the constant and unvarying laws of the universe. The aim of the engineer has been utility. He works with all the plastic elements, he has created a new plastic mystery, but he is practically ignorant of all aesthetic laws. The beauty which he creates is accidental. The experiment of an exposition bringing together the plastic works of these two types has in it the possibility of forecasting the life of to-morrow.

Granovsky, the Russian constructionist, who made the decor for Tzara's *Le coeur à gaz* expresses himself along analogous lines when he writes:

The term aesthetic has been so outworn by long usage that anyone employing it runs the risk of being easily misinterpreted. I propose to employ it in a strictly scientific sense, disregarding entirely its now fashionable and casual association with intuition as a criterion of plastic qualities in an object. Unfortunately the sequence and interrelation of forms and their effect on the spectator have not as yet been established with any exactitude... Were all the proportions of plasticity better known, art would pass from the confines of purely personal appreciation on to the road of original invention.

In Scotland – in art as in letters – we are still in precisely the same position as was Holland, prior to the emergence of the 'De Stijl' group in 1917 – a country of pretentious and vigorous conservatism, 'constantly warming up the egg of the 80's,' as Theo Van Doesburg has put it, although 'this celebrated movement only defended a tendency which had already lapsed in France' – a fight for the cast-off clothes of other nations.

But in the ideas of M'Cance and his wife and one or two others Scotland may soon acquire not only an equivalent to the 'De Stijl' development, but, thanks to the unparalleled strength of our engineering and dialectical aptitudes if these can be reoriented and applied in cultural directions, transcend it and at one step make good the long inhibition or subversion of our most distinctive powers and become the vanguard of the art of the future.

M'Cance is presently engaged in a new book on aesthetics, the nature of which may be gauged from the following synopsis: – (1) Introductory. Three stages in artist's development: (a) undisciplined intensity; (b) conscious awareness of problems; (c) with background of organisation regaining intensity. (2) Analytical: (a) story picture: replaced by cinema; (b) portrait: inadequacy of one static visual image to portray psychology of sitter; (c) naturalistic picture: dead replica in paint always inferior to actuality; (d) impressionism: psuedo-scientific form of naturalism in painting. (3) Design in the other arts. e.g., novel (probably on final analysis concerned with conduct or dynamic moral values). (4) Design and life, e.g., engineering (economy of force), domestic, social functions, etc. (5) Psychological. How design evolves in artist's mind. (6) Technical. Part played by senses in technique of art, habit formations, importance of tactile and kinaesthetic imagery. (7) Abstract design, arbitrary form and lighting in painting. (8) Different kinds of design resolved by different ratios of imagery. (9) Speculative, inherent impulse to art, etc. (10) No standard of art – only qualities. (11) Place of colour. (12) Painting centrifugal – sculpture centripetal. (13) Fascination of double line in drawing. (14) Importance of subject-matter as a releasing influence to the subconscious. (15) The spectator or public.   [20.11.25]

Letters

THE 'NORDIC' ORIGIN OF THE SCOTS

Sir, – I must apologise for 'butting in,' uninvited, to the pleasant little conversation 'twixt Messrs Horne and Tait, though to be sure the correspondence columns of a newspaper is an odd place to choose for an exchange of views about public matters apparently designed to be private. However, my more immediate object in writing is to invite Mr Tait's attention to a singularly scathing and damaging attack on the 'Nordic' theory which has been recently published. He will find it in Sir Leo Chiozza Money's The Peril of the White, *a book which is well worth reading on general grounds, though I say it who am not the publisher of it. Doubtless, the author of the book I name is not a recognised man of science, but in that part of it which relates to the 'Nordic' theory he has consulted those who are, and, with their aid, sair is the drubbing he gives it. It is no exaggeration to say he fairly turns it inside out, showing in addition how mischievous it is in a political way.*

I have said, and say here, nothing about Sir Arthur Keith to which any reasonable man can take exception. In his own line – anthropology – Sir Arthur is doubtless a good enough guide, but my point is that as ethnologist he is none at all. His support of the ridiculous 'Nordic' theory is the measure of his credibility so far as Scottish racial origins are concerned. If Messrs Tait and Horne desire authoritative information on this head let them consult the two fine appendices to Rice Holme's books about the conquest of Gaul by the Romans and the latter's invasion of these isles. In neither of these sources does the name of Sir Arthur appear, though both appendices are based on the works of the leading European ethnologists. – I am, etc.,

Buchan

CONTEMPORARY SCOTTISH STUDIES

Sir, – Mr R. Erskine's letter is almost wholly irrelevant, being occupied chiefly in an attempt to ridicule Pausanias for having shown that the Celts who settled in Asia Minor changed their modes of thought and life. He is certainly not at his best when he 'jokes wi' deeficulty.' Apparently he would like to confuse the issue by involving me in an anthropological dispute, but he does not appear to know enough, even about Celtic mythology, to waste one's time over. For instance, he would have it that the pork diet is Celtic and that apple-sauce is Teutonic. In the Celtic Paradise called Avalon, etc., after its 'apple tree of life,' there is always, however, a pig a-roasting, and the departed Celts are supposed to feed on pork and apples. A dilettante like Mr Erskine should be the last to pose as a critic of men who engage in serious anthropological research.

I found fault with Mr C.M. Grieve for including three Gaelic poets in his list of 'Ten Scottish Poets.' In doing so, he posed as a competent critic of Gaelic poetry and one possessing an intimate knowledge of the Gaelic language. Mr Erskine at once rushed to the rescue, and made statements to which I have already replied. Having now no case, he must abuse the plaintiff. But we have long been accustomed to find Mr Erskine a fiery but ineffectual espouser of lost causes.

Mr Erskine will have nothing of art for art's sake or of learning for learning's sake. Poetry and Gaelic must have for him a substantial foundation of political utilitarianism. Duncan Ban Macintyre, in his 'Beinn Dobhrain,' adopted three distinct measures to which are applied terms taken from corresponding strains in 'piobaireachd.' The poem is a product of art for art's sake, and there is conscious pride in the art and slavish adherence to its canons. There is absolutely no trace in that great poem of the nostrums insisted upon by Mr Erskine – no trace at all of his special brand of political particularism. Duncan Ban sang gloriously because he was an inspired poet and a lover of nature. He did not help to turn a 'party' mill to please any self-chosen leader – to help any 'cause' or promote any 'movement.' What a waste, from Mr Erskine's viewpoint, of political horsepower!

I am 'impertinent', according to Mr Erskine, because I do not approve of the attempt (a futile attempt, indeed) to make the Scottish Gaelic movement, and any modern Scottish literary movement which may exist, or come into existence later, the bondmaids of a political party great or small, old or new. But, then, I am a native Highlander, and a native Highlander who refuses to be exploited by alleged Celts is a sinner of the deepest hue. Mr Erskine may raise his standard on the 'Braes of Marr' (one 'r' would do), and Mr C.M. Grieve may erect at Montrose a paper Parnassus, but I prefer to give both a wide berth, refusing, as did my ancestors before me, to be 'herded' by any self-appointed leader from outside into any set of opinions or actions.

I have accused Mr Grieve of 'log-rolling,' of praising with exaggeration writers of small merit, of introducing politics into discussions about art, of sneering at men of old whose names are revered by the great majority of Scots, and of attempting to set up a 'European standard of criticism' which is a 'delusion and a sham,' because, when it is applied, we are expected to admit that Ossian Macpherson is a greater poet than Milton and that certain small fry 'boomed' by Grieve are greater than Burns, or Fergusson, or Barrie.

Mr Grieve's prolonged 'pooh-pooh!' Mr Erskine's quibbles and irrelevancies, and Mr Neill's confessed ignorance of matters under dispute, should be sufficient to convince the cultured readers of an educational journal that the cause promoted by these, the 'Great Three,' is, indeed, deplorably weak.

In a small mysterious 'poem' by 'Hugh M'Diarmid' (Mr C.M. Grieve) entitled 'The Lone Shore,' the 'sea' and a 'bird' are the leading characters. I think of the former as Mr Grieve and of the latter as Mr Erskine. There are only ten lines in the 'poem,' and six of these are: –

> *Sea – Boomflapswirlishoo.*
> *Boomflapswirlishoo.*
> *Bird – Weewee. Weewee.*
> *Sea – Boomflapswirlshoo.*
> *Swirlshoo. Swirlshoo.*
> *Bird – Weewee. Weewee.*

Mr Grieve may, on his very 'lone shore,' continue to 'boom,' 'flap,' etc., and Mr Erskine may 'weewee' in response, but I refuse to take either of them too seriously in discussion regarding the Scottish Arts. – I am, etc. (in the most 'fatherly' spirit),

Donald A. Mackenzie

THE BROAD SCOTS MOVEMENT

Sir, – Mr Cook, in his letter of 9th November says much that we agree with. His main contention that English is the keystone of the educational arch no one will gainsay, but he overlooks one or two very important points. To a very large section of our school children English is almost a foreign tongue; in the learning of any subject they have two problems to face, the subject-matter and the language. The idea is more important than the method of expression; granted ideas, expression will come later.

I quote one of his own sentences, 'Most Scotsmen have to contend all their lives with dialectical tendencies in pronunciation and colloquial habits of speech, and regret their lack of opportunity to master such defects during the school period.' Without admitting for one moment that there is any great need to be apologetic for a Scots tongue, I can use this admission as an argument against Mr Cook's whole contention. Scotsmen retain their faulty(?) speech simply because they have never been taught to distinguish between Scots and English. Our mother tongue has so long been looked upon as a mere debased English – a corruption of the current literary medium – that few have troubled to study the dialect at all seriously, with the result that the youngster looks upon his everyday speech as merely mispronounced English, and what he does do is to change 'richt' into 'right,' 'rins' into 'runs,' when very often the change should be 'rightly' and 'run.' The teacher has not shown that the Scots, like the German, lacks a definite adverbial ending, and the 's' ending in the Present Indicative Plural is a regular Scots form, and that the relative 'that' is always followed by a verb ending in 's' so long as it refers to the present. These are examples of a very limited kind; an adequate survey would fill a respectable volume. If we are not to teach Broad Scots, should we not clearly show what is Scots? According to Mr Cook our teaching of English has been a failure, and I am unaware that any other method, except the one he advocates, has been adopted. Might we not approach the language question from another angle by starting with the child's tongue and building up from that? Let me assure Mr Cook that a good knowledge of the dialect does not spoil a man's English. From a fairly wide experience of preparing dialect contributions for the press, I can assure him that the best dialect was contributed by those whose English was least exceptionable, and the least satisfactory work came from those whose attitude towards the dialect was the patronising one. That, perhaps, was to be expected in the tongue of a people whose national emblem is the thistle.

Even if Mr Cook is not urged by a perfervid nationalism, he may find that it will pay to make the dialect a study, and a subject of tuition, for many difficulties in the reading of Middle English are non-existent to the student of even present-day vernacular. Let him list the usual deviations, from the literary form made by our pupils, and he will find that these can very well be classified, and are not the result of haphazard lack of thought or carelessness, but follow definite laws of grammar. Knowing these deviations, he can then take definite steps to eradicate Scotticisms from English composition. Let him take examples. The Scot prefers the definite article, e.g., so much the ton; there are no plurals in measures, 'seven pound the ton'; there is preference for the strong verb; double prepositions are usual: 'in over the cart'; the preservation of the old meaning of words, 'wit' for sense or knowledge; the past participle after 'would not,' 'could not,' and 'should not' where the 'have' has been elided in 'widna,' 'cudna,' 'sudna'; the nominative absolute forms in personal pronouns, 'him and me went home.' Even where English vocabulary has been adopted, these forms crop up, just as in the Gaelic-speaking parts we have Gaelic idioms and construction with English vocabulary, e.g., 'I am just after doing it.' Our children think in Scots and translate, often with very funny results, as for example when the servant-lass of a northern dominie said. 'I cannot call this wall no more' – i.e., 'I cannot work this pump any longer.'

We may curse the dialect as a hindrance to good English, but, however soothing that may be to our feelings. it does not cure the disease. Treat it respectfully and we may get both good dialect and good English, and Mr Cook will agree with me in this, both are badly needed. – I am, etc.,

W. *Cumming*
[20.11.25]

22. The New Movement in Vernacular Poetry: Lewis Spence; Marion Angus

It is an extraordinary thing that the great majority of vernacular enthusiasts should be seeking to promote a revival of Braid Scots and at the same time endeavouring to stereotype the very things responsible for its deterioration and disuse. Nowhere is any creative reapproach to the Doric likely to be more bitterly resented and opposed than amongst those who are clamouring most vociferously for its resuscitation. So conservative is the movement headed by the Burns Federation under Sir Robert Bruce that they have committed themselves merely to an attempt to perpetuate the debased dialects still more or less current and disavowed any intention of recreating the national language *in toto*. Along with this absurdly fractional aim they conjoin an enthusiasm for these debased dialects in their written form which practically nowhere approaches the lowest planes of literature; and inveigh against any attempt to depart from the traditional and deepening rut of post-Burnsian Kailyairdism. Dr James Devon, for example, says:

> Under the name of preserving the vernacular there were people who wrote more or less cleverly in imitation of their fathers and they used words that were as foreign to usage as modern slang. The true line would be to encourage young people in the use of expressions they had heard from their elders in so far as these expressions were fitting. There could be no Scottish Renaissance until people had something to say and were bold enough to say it in the tongue with which people were most familiar. Burns had written for his contemporaries and for the people who shared the same kind of life as he. His language was not an artificial one – he had expressed for them in the words they best understood and with which they were most familiar their feelings and his own. A circle had been formed in Glasgow for the preservation of the vernacular, and its object should commend itself to all lovers of Burns.

But why form a circle if the way towards a Scots Renaissance is *via* the most common speech and understanding? – as if almost every literary movement of any consequence were not a small coterie affair to start with and carried through as a rule amidst the indifference, if not against the opposition, of the generality. Is literary English coincident with spoken English – and do the majority of the most significant and important writers of England or any other country write for the mass of the people? Is popular taste and the mass of contemporary understanding not invariably intent on the products of mediocrity and averse to the best products of its period? Any literary language would be deplorably mutilated and devitalised if it were confined to terms in every-day use amongst the rank and file of the people. Dr Devon's contentions – and they are shared by the majority of the so-called 'leaders' of this movement – will not stand a moment's examination by anyone familiar with the prerequisites and methods of literary creation. No literature of any consequence has ever been produced in any country under such limitations as Dr Devon suggests young people in Scotland should impose upon themselves. Happily, young people in Scotland are manifesting quite different ideas and intentions. And they know that Burns did – and that every other writer must – employ an artificial language. Mr John Buchan has said: 'Burns is by universal admission one of the most natural of poets, but he used a language which was, even in his own day, largely exotic. His Scots was not the living speech of his countrymen, like the English of Shelley, and – in the main – the Scots of Dunbar; it was a literary language subtly blended from the old 'Makars' and the refrains of folk poetry, much tinctured with the special dialect of Ayrshire and with a solid foundation of English, accented *more Boreali*.' And it had its limitations. It fell far short of the stature of the potential canon of Scots. Mr Buchan says, for example, that Burns was kept from one special kind of magic: 'the only instance I can recollect where he attains it is in the solitary line

"The wan moon is setting behind the white wave."'

It is certain, at all events, that all the best poets of to-day and to-morrow who write in Scots must be out to obtain effects which were not within the compass of Burns or of the instrument of Scots he fashioned to other and – since achieved – surpassed ends. The true line is not that indicated by Dr Devon: but a synthetic Scots gathering together and reintegrating all the *disjecta membra* of the Doric and endeavouring to realise its latent potentialities along lines in harmony at once with distinctive Scots psychology and contemporary cultural functions and requirements. A similar feat has been accomplished elsewhere – in Norway, for example; and all the arguments which Dr Devon, Mr Alexander Keith and others have brought to bear against the proposals for a synthetic Scots have already been disposed of in Norwegian practice. The only thing we lack in Scotland – and it was that which mainly conduced to the success of the Norwegian movement – is a sufficiently intense spirit of nationalism.

Objection has been taken in other quarters to the use in such experiments as have already been made towards a synthetic Scots of such obsolete words as 'eemis stane,' 'amplefeyst,' and 'yow-trummle.' It is suggested that little is gained by their use. But the objection springs for the most part from the same spirit that leads to one of Blake's most celebrated lines being generally printed: 'Tiger, tiger, burning bright.' 'But,' as Mr Lytton Strachey says,

> in Blake's original engraving the words appear thus – 'Tyger! Tyger!
> burning bright'; and who can fail to perceive the difference? Even
> more remarkable is the change which the omission of a single stop
> has produced in the last line of one of the succeeding stanzas of the
> same poem:

> > And what shoulder, and what art,
> > Could twist the sinews of thy heart?
> > And when thy heart began to beat,
> > What dread hand? and what dread feet?

> So Blake engraved the verse; and as Mr Sampson points out, 'the
> terrible, compressed force' of the final line vanishes to nothing in the
> 'languid punctuation' of subsequent editions – 'what dread hand, and
> what dread feet?'

Ford Madox Ford in his book on Conrad tells how they used to drive

> over a country of commonplace downlands and ask ourselves how we
> would render a field of ripe corn, a ten-acre patch of blue-purple
> cabbage. We would try the words in French; *sillonné, bleu-foncé,
> bleu-du-roi*; we would try back into English; cast around in the back
> of our minds for other French words to which to assimilate our
> English and thus continue for quiet hours.

It is only by like methods that Braid Scots can be resuscitated and lifted
out of the deplorable pass to which it has been reduced. But nothing is
further from the minds of those who are agitating for the revival of the
Doric and forming vernacular circles in Glasgow and elsewhere. What is
in their minds? A correspondent writes:

> On Thursday night I attended the meeting to form a vernacular circle
> for Glasgow, and I was never so disappointed in my life for the
> interest of Sir Robert Bruce, Sheriff Blair, Mr A.M. Williams, Mr
> George Eyre Todd, etc., lay in memorising Burns and Johnny Gibb o'
> Gushetneuk, but none of the speakers ever referred to the vernacular
> unless to laugh at it. They were all more concerned about telling a
> funny story than about revealing the literary potentiality of the
> language. They were not concerned about the future of the tongue at
> all. They denied it a future and pooh-pooh'd the idea of its use as a
> national vernacular. They even ridiculed one west-end lady who uses

nothing but Scots even in her drawing-room...

Nevertheless the true creative approach to the vernacular is being made: and is adequately illustrated in the work of Lewis Spence and Marion Angus. Both represent a radical departure from the methods of Kailyairdism. Their poetry is most interesting where it has most of those qualities which recently led another critic of the old school to say of a certain contemporary Scots poem that he did not deny its beauty, but thought it fair criticism to suggest that it *added nothing to the thought* it took as its *point de départure*. This sort of criticism – and the attitude to poetry from which it springs, the general attitude to poetry, be it remarked, of the great majority of Burns enthusiasts and admirers of Charles Murray and the lesser lights of post-Burnsian pedestrianism – has the same defects that vitiate much in Dr Johnson's *Lives of the Poets*. It is a like attitude that led him to declare *Lycidas* 'easy, vulgar, and therefore disgusting,' the songs in *Comus* harsh and unmusical, Gray's work nothing but 'glittering accumulations of ungraceful ornaments,' Donne's merely absurd, and leads the *Aberdeen Free Press*, Dr Devon, and others to demand 'sensible poetry.'

> Such preposterous judgments, [says Lytton Strachey of Johnson,] can only be accounted for by inherent deficiencies of taste; Johnson had no ear, and he had no imagination. These are, indeed, grievous disabilities in a critic. What could have induced such a man to set himself up as a judge of poetry? The answer to the question is to be found in the remarkable change which has come over our entire conception of poetry since the time when Johnson wrote... Poetry to us means primarily, something which suggests, by means of words, mysteries and infinitudes. Thus, music and imagination seem to us the most essential qualities of poetry, because they are the most potent means by which such suggestions can be invoked. But the eighteenth century knew none of these things... In such a world, why should poetry, more than anything else, be mysterious? No! Let it be sensible; that was enough.

And in his essay on Beddoes the same writer says:

> Sir James Stephen was only telling the truth when he remarked that Milton might have put all that he had to say in *Paradise Lost* into a prose pamphlet of two or three pages. But who cares about what Milton had to say? It is his way of saying it that matters; it is his expression. Take away the expression from the *Satires* of Pope, or from *The Excursion* and though you will destroy the poems you will leave behind

a great mass of thought. Take away the expression from *Hyperion*, and you will leave nothing at all. To ask which is the better of the two styles is like asking whether a peach is better than a rose, because, both being beautiful, you can eat the one and not the other.

So far as Braid Scots is concerned, however, 'the brave translunary things' have been so long completely lacking – all but the most common-place elements of the language have been so ruthlessly inhibited – that if neither of these styles is better than the other in this sense, certainly there is no question as to which is most important at the moment and most in need of intensive cultivation. Mr Spence and Miss Angus are bringing back the roses of the Doric and re-establishing our contact in bonds of beauty with the old Makars for whom the Doric could encompass 'the full circle of poetic material.' As to the others peaches are few: it is the homelier turnip, at its best wholesome and not uncomely, which is in general cultivation.

Mr Spence is one of the most resourceful, versatile, and engaging of contemporary Scots. It is impossible to do justice here to the many aspects of his work. He is a recognised authority on the mythology and religions of ancient Mexico; lately he has devoted two most interesting, able, and stimulating volumes to the Atlantean problem; he is an ency-clopaedist of occultism, rich in curious lore, brilliantly collated and brought thoroughly abreast of modern international research; he is a playwright and a short story writer, he is a forcible writer on current affairs, national and international. He is perhaps the finest rhetorician in Scotland to-day – in a Scotland that has, unfortunately, become so sensible and prosaic as to be dangerously inappreciative of rhetoric. As a poet his earlier work, in English, was a little too obviously influenced by French decadence; it was written to a fashion, and the writer had still to find himself. In his later English poetry he has obviously done so. Intricate music, recondite allusion, wonderful colouring, subtle intellec-tion are the characteristics of his work. He stands alone – belonging to no school. But it is in his vernacular verse that he has found himself most effectually, bringing to it the same exquisite sensory and intellectual equipment (an equipment not shared by another poet writing in Scots for five hundred years), and finding in the word-music and sound-suggestiveness of the Doric an even better medium than in his complex and colourful English. This will, I fancy, rank as his most signal achieve-ment – that he was the first Scot for five hundred years to write 'pure poetry' in the vernacular. The achievement is unquestionably related to his nationalism; it was that which made him realise so clearly the causes of the sorry pass to which Braid Scots had been reduced and, following upon that, revealed to him what ought to be done, and, in part, how. He has performed that part perfectly, and some of his work will live. It is amazing that it is not represented in Buchan's *Northern Muse*. But it will yet come to its own. Space only allows me to quote one sonnet, but it amply bears out what I have said. Where, without going back to Mark Alexander Boyd, can it be paralleled in our literature, and who will deny that it is entitled to stand alongside his 'Cupid and Venus' and that it contributes to Scots verse elements of high poetry which it has singularly and almost wholly lacked since that was penned?

Portrait of Mary Stuart, Holyrood

Wauken be-nicht, and bydand on some boon,
Glaumour of saul, or spirituall grace,
I haf seen sancts and angells in the face,
And like a fere of seraphy the moon;
But in nae mirk nor sun-apparelled noon.
Nor pleasance of the planets in their place,
Of luve devine haf seen sae pure a trace
As in yon shadow of the Scottis croun.

Die not, O rose, dispitefull of hir mouth,
Nor be ye lillies waeful at hir snaw;
This dim devyce is but hir painted sake,
The mirour of ane star of vivand youth.
That not hir velvets nor hir balas braw
Can oueradorn, or luve mair luvely make.

Miss Angus' work must be mentioned alongside Spence's; it is notable for similar reasons, although her vein is a narrower one. She achieves, however, a higher plane of poetry than Mrs Jacob ever reaches, although her work may be lacking in certain popular qualities and an associative 'body' to be found in the *Songs of Angus*. Here again – in view of what I have already said – the proof is in the 'preein',' and those who know the hum-drum, flat-footed sentimentality of most vernacular verse will welcome so pure and poignant a note as this: –

Mary's Song

I wad ha'e gi'en him my lips tae kiss,
Had I been his, had I been his;
Barley breid and elder wine,
Had I been his as he is mine.

The wanderin' bee it seeks the rose;
Tae the lochan's bosom the burnie goes;
The grey bird cries at evenin's fa:
'My luve, my fair one, come awa'.'

My beloved sall ha'e this hert tae break,
Reid, reid wine, and the barley cake,
A hert tae break, and a mou tae kiss,
Tho' he be nae mine, as I am his.

The only effect a poem of that kind has amongst the great majority of vernacular enthusiasts is to start a controversy as to whether 'tae' is permissible, meaning 'to' or whether it should be reserved to mean 'toe.' The flat-footed prosaicism which has so long dominated Braid Scots letters will not be overcome without a stiff struggle. A writer on Mr William Robb's *Book of Twentieth-Century Verse* (Messrs Gowans & Gray) points out that in it 'the Scottish Chapbook is so sparsely drawn upon that the latest phase of northern verse is practically unrepresented. The book is thus, in the main, true to a type so long established as to have become almost a convention... Apparently Scottish dialect poetry, *as shown here*, cannot rise above its environment. The one hopeful sign is that there is evidence of a desire to do so, a desire to escape from the trammels of the past. And henceforth no one in Scotland has any excuse for not knowing exactly how we stand, poetically; the fifty or so poets whose work in the vernacular is exemplified here tell us plainly what we can do. What we have not done is immeasureable.'

But the new movement has accomplished a great deal more than Mr Robb gives it credit for. True, he includes poems by Dr Macgillivray and Miss Angus: but they should not be in that gallery. It is significant that such an anthology of the vernacular verse product of the past twenty-five years should so unscrupulously boycott the 'growing end' of its subject, and illustrate the tactics of mediocrity on the defensive. Those who wish to read what is really of consequence in modern Scots verse must look elsewhere.

Mr Spence is presently preparing a collection of his recent poems for publication. See also his *The Phoenix and Other Poems* (Porpoise Press Broadsheet, Dec. 1923) and his 'Modern Tendencies in Scotland' (*Nineteenth Century and After*, October, 1925). For Miss Angus see her *The Tinker's Road* (Messrs Gowans and Gray, 1924). Attention may also be drawn to George Dickson's *Peter Rae* (Messrs Allen and Unwin) – incidentally of special interest as an attempt to deal with industrial civilisation, machinery, the War, and other contemporary problems in poetry, and partly in Scots; William Ogilvie's *The Witch and Other Poems* (Porpoise Press); and Thomas Sharp's *New Poems* (Messrs Macmillan, 1925). Other poets using Scots to some extent along individual lines and clear – or occasionally clear – of the Burns rut are 'Tamar Faed,' Miss Hilary Staples, Mr William Soutar, Miss Jessie Annie

Anderson, Mr Robert Crawford, Mr Joseph Lee, Mr Andrew Dodds, the Rev. T.S. Cairncross, and Professor Alexander Gray. The principal figures in the conventional groove after Charles Murray – a long way after – are, perhaps, Miss Mary Symon, Thomas Morton, David Rorie, W.D. Cocker (*Dandie and Other Poems*, Messrs Gowans and Gray, 1925), John Smellie Martin (*Scottish Earth*, Messrs Hodder and Stoughton), and Gilbert Rae (*Mang Lowland Hills*, Messrs Collins, 1923). R.L. Cassie's work (*The Gangrel Muse*, Aberdeen Newspapers, Ltd., 1925, etc.) has a dialectical richness and interest which compensates to some extent for its poverty as verse, and the same author's *Heid or Hert* (1923) is one of the few contemporary efforts in wholly vernacular prose.   [27.11.25]

Letters

MR GRIEVE AND THE KING'S ENGLISH

Sir, – I have tried to read some of the articles of your correspondent, C.M. Grieve. May I be allowed to suggest that, instead of dabbling in foreign literature, he would be well advised to make a closer study of his mother tongue? Many of us are apt to be carried away by the study of foreign languages, but surely we should try to perfect the knowledge of our own before attempting to indulge in pedantic comparative studies such as Mr Grieve indulges in.

His last article in particular may give some indication of what I mean. There are at least eight expressions, acknowledged by italics or mentioned under inverted commas, that are quite un-English: – via sola, cacoethes scribendi, sui generis, divertissements, vis comica, wut, differentia, manqué. And is douce intelligentsia *not a quaint combination for good English prose?*

In addition, his use of the word flair *is quite wrong. I do not dare to suggest that this is due to his imperfect knowledge of French: the mistake has probably arisen through the faulty construction of the sentence in which it occurs, or perhaps through a printer's error. 'He is the only Scotsman I know with the necessary flair and the necessary knowledge of Contemporary European Drama.' Again, could not an expression more English than* gravamen *have been found ?*

The alleged reputation of Mr Grieve as a literary critic hardly justifies recourse to 'I would fain…,' 'It is not for nothing that…,' and the quite illogical 'obviously.' And can we calmly accept as good English 'It may be necessary to make concessions to secure the requisite number to launch a little Experimental Theatre movement'?

The constant repetition of clichés like 'It is absurd to imagine that…,' 'It is futile to speak of…,' 'It is at once pitiful and amusing to read that…,' is frankly weak writing: the use of phrases such as 'The problem… will cease to be insoluble' shows a poor sense of word economy.

His general style is cumbersome and old-fashioned. There is at least one sentence of more than 120 words in the article I speak of (and you know what sort of words Mr Grieve uses!). Plain, straight-forward writing seems to be foreign to his nature. His constructions are loose, awkward, and inconclusive: his words have a volume of sound and a grotesqueness of appearance out of all proportion to the sense they are intended to convey: while obscure allusions like 'jinn out of the bottle' and 'spearhead of the movement' seem to be his peculiar hobby.

In short, sir, don't you agree that Mr Grieve might do worse than leave welt-literatur *alone for a time and return to (or at least begin) the study of 'The King's English' or Thomas Browne? He might then improve a style of writing (I almost wrote 'English') that is, to borrow his own expression, 'a freak of hybridisation, resembling the stoneless plum.' – I am, etc..*

R.B.M., Greenock

THE MUSICAL FESTIVAL MOVEMENT

Sir, – Mr Brownlie might have less difficulty in understanding my articles if he did not read into them so much that isn't there. French school choirs versus Musical Festival effects on the one hand; yes, but, on the other hand. French music versus Scottish! Personally I would exchange all our Festival competitors for two or three Aurics, Poulencs, or Honeggers, and, though I am under no delusion as to the stature of these composers, I am confident that the Muse of History would approve my preference. As another writer has said, there is a widespread tendency to entertain

> *the fallacy that the study of music means to learn to sing or to learn to play. Does the study of Shakespeare mean learning to act or learning to write dramas? One person in a thousand can sing to the pleasure of his hearers: one person in ten thousand can play the piano without discomfort to her listeners. But all persons who are supposed to be 'educated' should be trained to understand music. Such understanding comes only from much hearing of music and from some instruction in the language, grammar, and historic development of music. Even our best Scottish schools and most of our Musical Festivals busy themselves with increasing the number of skilled soloists, select choirs, and expert executants. It is a limited aim, but does not touch the great stream of a nation's life. The educator's aim is to spread as widely as possible an*

intelligent understanding of music, to secure for music a place in all minds, and to make the appreciation of music a source of intellectual stimulus and a deep fountain of joy.

As to Ernest Newman, I have still to learn that to concur with a writer in one particular is to identify oneself with all his other deeds and dicta, or incur a charge of inconsistency. I advise our would-be creative artists to cultivate a European outlook, in order to create distinctively Scottish arts; I condemn festivals run mainly on other people's music, because the repertory is narrow and third-rate, because sound musical knowledge is neither a preliminary nor a consequence, and because the movement is obviously not conducive to the creation of distinctively Scottish music. Where is the inconsistency? My objection is not to foreign music: but to boasting of our Scottish musicality on the strength of it.

I did not say that the Festival movement was entirely anti-educational – I said that it was educational in some directions (inferior ones) and anti-educational in others (all the more important ones). Whatever may be thought of my style, I said this so plainly that Mr Brownlie's misunderstanding is obviously due, not to my inability to write, but to his inability to read.

It is not my view that the creative artist should look upon the mob (which is quite as good a word as mass, pace the sentimentalists) as 'dirt,' but simply that the views and tastes of the generality are negligible from the point of view of any specialism – and that genuine creative work has generally to be done despite their indifference and often in the teeth of their active opposition, and that of the demagogues who pander to them. If a writer on certain subjects about which, either because they are unilingual or for other reasons, most folk know nothing and care less, ventures to point out that it the case, that neither makes these subjects unworthy of study nor does it imply that the writer in question regards the mass as 'dirt.' Nor can I see that anything is to be gained – even in the twentieth century – by pretending that the mass is better educated or otherwise inclined than it obviously is.

The debauching of public taste and subversion of popular education by commercial, political, religious and other interests engages my indignation as much as it does that of any one in Scotland, and I am as determined as anyone to do what I can to secure the removal of the economic and other handicaps which stunt the great majority of the workers. But even were these removed, the mass would remain relatively negligible for every creative purpose. – I am, etc.,

C.M. Grieve
[27.11.25]

23. William Power; W. Sorley Brown

Of the critics who write for the Scottish press and sign their work either with their name, initials, or pseudonym, only two require to be considered in these studies – William Power, of the *Glasgow Herald* and W. Sorley Brown, of the *Border Standard*. Mr William Jeffrey has done a certain amount of useful and creditable critical work and played a timely role as the fugleman of the new movement in Scottish poetry heralded by the publication of *Northern Numbers:* but he is primarily a poet and as such has already been dealt with. Reference will be made later on to the work as playwright and novelist of Mr George Blake: but his work as literary editor of the *Glasgow Evening News* was as undistinguished and ephemeral as his subsequent essays in *John o' London's Weekly*, on which curiously enough he succeeded Mr Sidney Dark, have been. Its level was rarely above that of trivial gossip, and topicality and the exigencies of contemporary journalism were its conditioning factors. Even within these limits, however, good work can be done: but the fashion set by Saint Beuve has not found an effective exponent in Scottish journalism yet. The main objection to what chit-chat does appear is that it is not concerned with pure letters, but with book-publishing: criticism is subservient to commercial considerations. So far as Scottish literature is concerned advertising and other interests convert most of the 'book notes' into Anglifying propaganda and dictate a subtle contempt for Scottish letters as such, which generally finds its expression in the assumption that a frank acceptance of permanently provincial limitations is the only proper attitude in a Scots writer. The same interests – and the sort of talents which go to secure their possessors' positions as literary editors on most of the daily papers – account for the general acceptance of popular London standards, and the absence of any differentiation in taste between Glasgow, Edinburgh, Dundee and Aberdeen as compared with London. Blake's work, however, at its worst has always been infinitely superior to the inane lucubrations of some of our London Scots – Mr James Milne, for example, or Mr Brodie Fraser. Dr J.M. Bulloch is on a higher plane as a book-reviewer and occasional essayist, while he has a refreshing regard for some, at any rate, of the differentia of Scottish life and literature. His principal claims to regard lie in other directions, however – in particular, genealogy, a field he has made peculiarly his own. Mr Alexander Keith, of the *Aberdeen Free Press and Journal*, belongs to a bygone age: and his extraordinary ineptitudes in dealing with contemporary cultural phenomena have probably not been paralleled anywhere since Keats was told that 'this will not do.' His complete inability to understand modern developments of all kinds gives his essays priceless qualities of humour of the kind H.L. Mencken treasures up in the 'Americana' section of the *American Mercury*. He is a Rip Van Winkle giving vent to anachronistic *gaffes*. Consider the following extract from one of his recent articles, for example; –

> At odd times in the history of literature – as of everything else – new 'schools' of writers emerge and new 'movements' are initiated. As a rule, when we have got accustomed to the novelty, and had time to investigate its qualities, we discover that there is nothing so very new in it after all… Studious comparison, then, and a little adjustment end in revealing to us the superficially extraordinary fact that Sophocles, Aeschylus and Euripides cherished substantially the same philosophy and expounded substantially the same doctrine, not only as Hardy, Conrad, and Galsworthy, but as the most eminent of those whom we are pleased to term the 'modern' novelists. The angles of approach are slightly different; that is all.

Verb. sap.

'The Critic on the Hearth' (Mr Norval Scrymgeour) of the *Dundee Advertiser* is a genuine lover of literature of an old-fashioned type, but he is handicapped in three ways – by the paucity of space allotted to him, the need to devote that space to noticing as many as possible of the books that come in (with due regard to a fair division amongst the various publishing firms), and the necessity of saying a good word of one kind or another for all, or practically all, of them. As a consequence he is seldom able to devote more than a short 'stick-full' to any one book. His heart is in the right place, however, and not infrequently his head too. The deterioration of such papers as the *Dundee Advertiser* in their attitude to literature within the past decade or so cannot be overlooked. It has accompanied a general transvaluation in the scale of news values which followed the inception of Northcliffe's 'New Journalism.' Not so very many years ago the *Dundee Advertiser* was a solid organ of an excellent type. Literature in these days was accorded something like its due space. Now the death of a Conrad or an Anatole France has news value for little more than half-a-dozen lines: and the whole field of literature only commands about one column per week as against at least two pages devoted to football. The *Scotsman*. on the other hand, continues to devote a considerable amount of space to book reviews, and has occasional quasi-literary articles and leaders as well: but the *Scotsman's* literary journalism has always been a byword. The *Dundee Advertiser's* one column is certainly worth ten times as much as all the space devoted to books in the *Scotsman* in the course of a week put together.

The *Border Standard* is a local weekly, but the personality of, its editor, and proprietor, Mr Sorley Brown, has given it a literary quality and influence second to that of no paper in Scotland save the *Glasgow Herald*, and it is a remarkable fact that it not infrequently devotes more space to purely literary articles than the *Glasgow Herald* does in the course of a week. It was, for example, the only Scottish paper that deemed that the life and work of Roger Quin, the Tramp Poet, deserved, on his death, as much notice as is commonly given to a cup-tie: and whereas the majority of Scottish papers seldom give more than a short lyric in any one issue, the *Border Standard* reproduced as a special supplement the whole sequence of Lord Alfred Douglas's prison sonnets. Mr Sorley Brown himself is a trenchant writer and an acute and fearless critic, but he is less often concerned with purely literary than with moral issues. Of his essay on 'The Genius of Lord Alfred Douglas' (1913), John Buchan wrote: 'It is very well done – sound and acute criticism, and it wanted doing, for A.D. has never had proper recognition. I agree with you that he is a far greater poet than Wilde; indeed there is no living man or woman who can equal his best sonnets.' This year (1925) Mr Sorley Brown has made another 'heroic foray against the attitude of neglect and contempt for true genius' by publishing an able and illuminating brochure on T.W.H. Crosland.

Mr Power's work is on an entirely different plane: and both in form and substance demands – and commands – more attention than all other 'literary writing' in the Scottish Press today. He is a true critic, concerned with the fundamental factors in art, and confines himself to no one field, writing, as the mood prompts or occasion demands, on literature, the drama, art, the music-hall, travel and what not. He is, indeed, too *ondoyant et divers* and the superficial range of his work could profitably be contracted to increase its depth. On the whole, however, he is as clever and stimulating a journalist of arts and letters as can be expected in the present condition of provincial journalism even on such a paper as the *Glasgow Herald*; and the Scottish Renaissance movement owes a great deal to him. He is practically the only critic in Scotland who has recognised the true inwardness of the post-War phenomena in Scottish arts and letters, and his position enabled him to secure for these developments a sympathy and following – what is called a 'good press' – in the only quarter where a 'good press' was likely to be of the slightest use. I am in a position to know just how slight that use was even in Glasgow: but that was not Power's fault. In a recent article on 'John o' Badenyon,' for example, he makes bold to say that

> the best things by far for Scots children to learn are Scots songs... And the very best hobby for grown-up Scots, one that will last them as long as their senses endure, is a study of Scots literature... For a potent spirit lies within those volumes of Scottish poetry and song, a spirit which, when liberated, will prove stronger than industrialism, latifundia, and the sporting system. We shall see 'a dead man win a fight.' The Makaris will re-make Scotland.

When practically all the inferior papers of Scotland are jeering at the very idea of a Scottish Renaissance or misconceiving the issues in the most hopeless fashion, it is significant that so robust a piece of vaticination should be pronounced in what is incontestably Scotland's greatest organ today – by a critic, who, owing to the plane upon which his paper is conducted, is necessarily head and shoulders above those who discharge equivalent functions in Edinburgh, Aberdeen and Dundee. It is, in other words, noteworthy that the whole essence of the plea underlying the movement for a revival of Braid Scots should be so unequivocally championed by the only literary journal in Scotland which has a public for literary work on a level similar in expression and ideation to that which appears in Manchester, Liverpool, Dublin, or Belfast. The necessity of expressing himself on a certain level can sometimes save a man from the *gaucheries* and *gaffes* to which those of whom lower standards are required too readily succumb.

An earlier essay of Mr Power's, however, is one of the most important documents in the development of the Scottish Renaissance movement. A certain type of critic is apt to say that the movement so far has consisted only of propaganda – only 'of the posters' – that the actual work has still to be done. This is a mistake. The Scottish Renaissance has taken place. The fruits will appear in due course. Earlier or later – that does not alter the fact. 'For the Scottish Renaissance has been a propaganda of ideas, and their enunciation has been all that was necessary. Mr Power is one of the few who have realised that, and he does not hesitate to say so in the article to which I have referred. He says, for example: –

> For over a century Scotland has attempted to put her past definitely behind her, except for tourist purposes, and to devote herself exclusively to large-scale industry, the letting of shootings, the breeding of

prize-stock and the export of whisky, Empire builders, and heids o' depairtments. There is something not unalluring about this decline into complacent provincialism. Gear-gathering and purely individual aims make smaller demands upon the average mind than a full national life. Literary renaissances are bothersome things. Best to assume that Scottish history ended with Scott, put your feet on the fender, 'ferlie at the folk in Lunnon,' and turn with a tranquil mind to the chartularies of Pluscarden, the fluctuations of the price of fish at Leith in the sixteenth century, the witchburnings of James VI, Lockhart's *Scott*, and the history of the U.P. Church. Nations, however, do not retire from business quite so easily. The past has a propellant power undreamt of by antiquarians. Ghosts from our emptied countryside flit through the industrial areas where two-thirds of the population are bunched. They squeak and jibber quaint Babylonish nonsense about land values, municipal this and that, and the exploitation of the proletariat. What they really want to say, but they have lost the language for it, is that a nation in which three-fourths of the population are divorced from the land and from the sanative variety of rural life is not in a healthy state. The same idea haunts the mind of the middle-class Scot who has not been drugged by an English public-school education. Also, he begins to feel the personal need for a spiritual centre of national life. He wants to give a present and a future tense to the things that constitute the real soul of the Scottish nation. Our young men have visions, and our old men dream dreams... The signs of a national literary renaissance are plainly evident. Our poets and essayists have definitely moved away from the flat-footed moralising, maudlin sentiment, chortling 'wut' and cosy prejudice that degraded so-called Scottish literature in the period between Scott and Douglas Brown. They have realised that art is not an evasion of life but a brave and closely studied attempt to get at its essentials. It is *la vraie vérité...* The champions of provincial slumber and facile imitativeness who put up their umbrellas in Edinburgh when it is raining in London, find it easy to pour cold water on the idea of a Scottish literary renaissance. Art, they say, should be spontaneous. A literary renaissance that tries to root itself in a national impulse is like a tree standing on its head. But the Scottish literary renaissance has already begun to root itself in Scottish life, which includes the whole history of Scottish literature.

His point of view in regard to Braid Scots can be profitably compared with that of the majority alike of the opponents and enthusiasts for its revival (although in view of the success of the *landsmaal* movement in Norway I am not prepared to concede that, given an adequate nationalistic spirit, Braid Scots cannot be revived as a prose medium, too, or rather – since little or no Scots prose yet exists – be made into one): –

> What of Gaelic and the Scottish vernacular? Gaelic is dying as a spoken tongue. *Tu l'as voulu, Georges Dandin,* we may quote to the Highlanders. But as a subject of literary study, along with Irish Gaelic, it is of priceless value. Really good translations of Gaelic poetry, by a Scottish Douglas Hyde, would send a rich tributary stream of inspiration into Scottish literature. Glasgow ought to be the world-centre of Celtic scholarship. The Scottish vernacular is also dying from popular speech. For that reason it can have no future in prose literature. *Johnny Gibb* is a unique *tour de force.* It lacks transparency and melodic flow; it is a conglomerate of quaint opacities that cloud the sense and hold up the narrative; it is everything that good prose is not. Like German, only more so, Scots is chaotic in prose and spontaneously formful in verse. It is loaded to the muzzle with gnomic, homely, comic, tragic and romantic suggestions. It is an arsenal of spells and evocations. Its inspirative power was manifested two centuries ago when a small group of vernacular poets in Scotland brought about the Romantic Revival and the Return to Nature in Europe. The power of Scots is still undiminished... It has become that unique phenomenon, a language unspoken but sung and felt, and alive with all the elemental forces that lie behind the huge mechanism of intellect and civilisation. Reproaches about resort to Jamieson need not trouble our Scottish poets; accuracy and an approach to standard Scots are the first essentials; localisms should be banned; if a word is 'felt,' and the feeling of it is conveyed to the reader, then its use was justified. With Dr Craigie to keep them right in verbal detail, the poets will go ahead in Scots, never fear. *They are handling something bigger and more vital than Provençal, Catalan, or even, in some respects, modern English.* And the English prose of Scottish authors will derive strength from the stream of vernacular poetry that flows beside it; not so much by the taking over of savoury words and expressive phrases as by the inspiration of perpetual contact with the elemental soul of a nation.

Note the sentence I have italicised. Mr Power is alive, too, to the larger hope of the Scottish Renaissance, first seized upon by Professor

Denis Saurat in his brilliant article on the Scottish Renaissance Group in *La Revue Anglo-Americaine*, and says: 'Europe, wounded and weakened and disillusioned by the War, is a prey to parasitical influences of morbidity, spiritualism, freakishness, pseudo-psychology, and deadly materialism. Her aeroplanes cleave the clouds, but her soul remains below. Once again as two centuries ago, after the dreadful wars of Louis XIV, she looks around for springs of healing. May she not find them once again in the waters called forth by Scottish poets from the rocks of their native land?'

Mr Power has published *The World Unvisited* (Gowans and Gray, 1922). See also 'The Drama in Scotland' (*The Scots Magazine*, April, 1924): and numerous articles in the *Glasgow Herald, John o' London's Weekly*, etc.   [4.12.25]

Letters

THE MUSICAL FESTIVAL MOVEMENT

Sir, – Mr Grieve in slippers for a defensive letter is no whit more impressive than Mr Grieve in buskins for a bombastic article, though in the former guise the comparative absence of empty pomposity is a welcome feature. He will not, I hope, take this opinion amiss, aware as he is of my inability to read; but is it merely a coincidence that in his articles, his lucid moments almost invariably open and close with quotation marks?

I am not particularly anxious that Mr Grieve should identify himself with all Newman's deed and dicta. I am anxious that he should not identify Newman with all Grieve's dicta. The point is important – for Newman's sake. The charge of inconsistency remains, aggravated rather than otherwise, witness the following: (1) the tastes of the mass are negligible from the point of view of creative purpose – it is the same negligible mass which, because of their interest in festivals, are taken to task for not fostering the creation of Scottish music; (2) 'Festivalitis and other diseases' are rife in Scotland because of our lack of tradition and perspective – Mr Grieve has graciously credited England with both of these, yet 'Festivalitis' is English in origin; (3) 'the alarming increase in brotherly love' – this from the writer whose pious professions are enshrined in the closing paragraph of his letter. Only Mr Grieve's apparent earnestness restrains us from using a word less polite than 'inconsistent.'

The limits our writer imposes upon the educational value of the Festival movement are so narrow as to restrict it to the work really done by tutors and teachers on the executive side; his concession is therefore valueless, and for him the movement remains anti-educational. It is more. For him and 'another writer,' Festival effects, except for one part in a thousand on the vocal side, and one in ten thousand on the instrumental, are positively painful.

Mr Grieve is fond of logical conclusions. He sees as a result of the Festival a musical parallel to everybody taking in everybody's washing. The logical conclusion to his creative obsession is everybody taking in their own washing and nobody else's.

The Festival, he says, monopolises the attention of those who would normally constitute the musical public for his creative artists. What a sin Festivalitis has to answer for! We are grieved to think that our comparatively late birth has denied us experience of those palmy pre-festival days when the creative artist's public has not been lured away by puny Bachs, quack Elgars and third-rate Scots folk songs! These were the days! But what has befallen their creative products?

Mr Grieve may hope to open our eyes in the time necessary to read this article: Festival promoters do not expect to work miracles quite so speedily. They realise that they have only begun their work. They have already altered concert programmes beyond recognition. Their repertory is not restricted and cannot be standardised. If music exists which on Mr Grieve's assessment is first rate, they will introduce it – provided their idea of first rate coincides with his. We should not be surprised if it doesn't. The creative work he demands will be encouraged not by letting things slide nor by destructive criticism, but by widespread improvement in technique and interpretation, lecture and reading courses in appreciation (which come within the scope of Festival Associations), constructive criticism of work that is the result of study and demands some knowledge of musical language and grammar. No festival competitor ever carried away anything without having first brought that knowledge with him, and the stimulus to the acquirement of such knowledge came from the Festival.

We agree with Mr Grieve that the study of music does not mean learning to sing and play; but we also believe, unlike him, that learning to sing and play is conducive to an understanding of music. While he is pleading for his Aurics and Poulencs, the Festival movement is preparing, slowly but surely, the public that will yet ensure for all such an appropriate measure of attention. – I am, etc.,

Wishaw   W.M. Brownlie
                                              [4.12.25]

Letters

Sir, – May I record my appreciation of, and entire agreement with, the feelings of our correspondent 'R.B.M.,' whose letter, in the Journal of November 27th, on the subject of 'Mr C.M. Grieve and the King's English,' is quite the most sensible of all those called forth by that gentleman's very extraordinary articles. Week by week, with growing impatience, I have wondered how long readers of an 'educational' journal were to endure without protest, 'literary' criticism couched in a style which violates almost every possible rule of good English writing. For one thing at least, Mr Grieve deserves the gratitude of teachers of English – he provides a 'gold-mine' of passages to be held up to advanced classes for correction! Besides the faults that R.B.M. mentions, others, even more elementary, constantly shock us. From Mr Grieve's last study I quote this: – 'Some of his (i.e., Mr Lewis Spence's) work will live. It is amazing that it is not represented in Buchan's Northern Muse. But it will yet come to its own. Space only allows me to quote one sonnet but it amply bears out what I have said.' Such careless and inaccurate English would not be tolerated in a sixth form essay. We do not suggest that any one who sets out to criticise literature must himself be a great stylist; but surely the power of clear and correct expression – if elegance be too much to hope for! – may fairly be demanded of one who wishes his literary judgments to be taken seriously.

But indeed, these judgments of Mr Grieve's are hardly such as to compensate, by their wisdom and insight, for the labour of trying to fathom the obscurities of his style. A typical example is his verdict on Mr Lewis Spence, whose sonnet, 'Portrait of Mary Stuart,' he quotes with such high praise. No one will deny that Mr Spence possesses a certain vein of poetic inspiration, but what impression does that sonnet make on the impartial reader? Does one not feel that the writer has spoiled what might have been a poem of haunting charm by choosing as his medium of expression a strange jargon which is neither English, any living Scottish dialect, nor even correct Middle Scots? No one but a student of Middle Scots could understand forms like 'bydand' and 'vivand' – such expressions can only tease the general reader; and the scholar would be irritated and repelled by Mr Spence's inaccuracies and inconsistencies. An acquaintance with, and a real love of, the works of the older Scottish poets – recollections of the Prologues of Gavin Douglas, and of the strange charm of Henryson's Testament of Cresseid, with its most *perfect of all epitaphs –*

> *Lo, ladyis fair, Cresseid of Troyis toun,*
> *Sumtyme countit the flour of womanheid,*
> *Under this stane, lait Lipper, lyis deid –*

these only make one sure that the day of the 'makaris' is past, and that any attempt to revive their language can be only a sort of literary pose, essentially artificial, and can never produce great poetry. The genius of Spenser himself did not wholly justify his use of a curiously compounded poetic diction, full of archaisms and pseudo-archaisms, and even Mr Grieve will, I think, admit that Mr Spence is a little lower than Spenser. One hopes that Mr Spence will continue to write – not, like the great Elizabethan, who, 'in imitating the ancients writ no language,' but, as he can, in English; and one could wish that Mr Grieve had chosen to quote a poem that would have brought out to better advantage the real powers of a writer whom he obviously desires to honour. – I am. etc.,

Alison E. Foster

MUSE OF SCOTTISH POETRY

Sir, – Transfusion of blood is accepted to-day as a chirurgical method, and I have therefore been much impressed by Mr C.M. Grieve's recommendation that the Muse of Scottish Poetry should have injected into her veins some of the ichor of her medieval ancestresses. I submit for your consideration my own experiment at such re-invigoration, premising that every word is to be found in Gavin Douglas or William Dunbar. – I am, etc.,

Gavin Dunbar

P.S. – I prefer Lewis Carroll's "Twas brillig and the slithy toves.' – G.D.

> *Quhan okkeraeis and capellis cast*
> *And catclukes stint and swye,*
> *And bladyeanes blaiknit blaitmowit maghs*
> *And Port Jaff blent on skye.*

> *The skuggis of the sichand blonkis*
> *Gart bismyng bismeiris pingill,*
> *Til rebaldis rigbanis crynit fast*
> *Jow-jordan-heidit at the ingle.*

The sterne superne glemand on garthe
Made gekkis at this paukkis,
Thir mangit myrth gart gledaris grane
As paddocks under rakkis.

During this quhile I nurnit sair,
On mensk to menzie gane,
And dasyt in my dowy dowte,
Panssit of lufes peirt pane.

MR GRIEVE'S CREED?

Sir, – It is becoming clear that Mr Grieve is not simply a warlike crank with a turn for slashing, but a constructive idealist with a reasoned creed. If he would state this creed once for all, instead of leaving us to gather it gradually from his criticisms, those of us who were not alert enough to make his acquaintance before reading his contributions to the Journal would be in a better position to appreciate his articles. I think I am beginning to grasp his position, but as my impression may be quite wrong, I submit a short statement of what I take to be his creed, and invite him to correct or supplement it as he may think fit.

1. Man's chief end is to develop a culture which shall extend his consciousness and guide his behaviour.

2. Culture is the concern of the human race as a whole, and should be pursued by the joint efforts of all nations.

3. Each nation must make its independent contribution to world culture along lines determined by its distinctive psychology.

4. Scotland is a single indivisible cultural unit independent of England.

5. The main characteristic of Scottish psychology is an intense consciousness of the great mysteries, combined with a matter of fact attitude to them.

6. This is due to the instinctive endeavour of the hypersensitive Celtic spirit to stiffen itself by adopting the cultural instruments of tougher minded races.

7. Scottish culture is therefore essentially derivative, so that though the people are mainly Celtic, their language is Saxon, their polity Norman, their ethics Hebrew, their law Roman, and their theology Swiss.

8. In adopting the English language Scotland was wise, and at one time she seemed about to make it the basis of a real culture.

9. In adopting the narrow sectarian Calvinistic theology Scotland was

unwise, and her independent national culture, being cut off from Catholic world culture, withered away.

10. The object of the Scottish Renaissance is to create out of the wreck a new culture, which shall be a living force in Catholic world culture.

11. It is impracticable and undesirable to rear this culture upon a Celtic foundation.

12. Neither is it desirable to found it upon modern English culture, which is decadent.

13. Nor can it be founded upon Post-Reformation culture, which is hopelessly provincial.

14. What is possible and desirable is a creative modern development of the interrupted Scots-English culture of the fifteenth century.

15. The effective force in the Renaissance will be an intellectual aristocracy consisting of those in whom the distinctive characteristics of Scottish psychology are naturally powerful, and carefully cultivated by a thorough study of Scottish cultural history and contemporary international creativity.

16. The duty of the relatively uninstructed multitude is to recognise these finer spirits, and follow their lead.

H. Brown
[11.12.25]

24. The New Movement in Scottish Historiography: George Pratt Insh

It has been said that 'Happy is the country that has no history.' Scotland is practically history-less so far as the last century or so is concerned at all events: but whether it is happy or not is a matter that may be left to politicians and others to debate. Mr William Graham, M.P. for Central Edinburgh, has commented on the tremendous leeway that has been allowed to develop in Scottish economic and social documentation. Scottish scholarship has been advertently starved of its due financial facilitation: Scottish records, as Professor R.K. Hannay and others have complained, have been largely mis-kept and are in chaos. On no single Scottish political or economic issue is there a single book of a thoroughly up-to-date, thorough, and comprehensive kind capable of giving a lead to intelligent people. The necessary facts and figures for coming to definite conclusions in regard to any Scottish question are practically inaccessible to the man-in-the-street, and popular conceptions in general – when there are any (and usually there are none) – are wide of the mark. It follows that Scottish politics are largely opportunist, based on no fundamental conceptions, having nothing like adequate information or an adequate national attitude behind them, and destitute of continuity and coherence. Scottish issues emerge adventitiously and sporadically in British politics and journalism from time to time, and occasionally loom importantly enough for a little: but the attitudes adopted towards them seldom include any dictated by principles derived from an exhaustive consideration of Scotland as an independent entity; but are, as a rule, casually and incidentally adopted. There is, generally speaking, no coherent conception of the course of events in Scotland – as distinct from England – during the past century at least. The whole field has been obscured by masses of extraneous material, by British, Imperial, and international considerations, which have served to overwhelm and thrust out of sight all the specifically Scottish data – all the information which, had it been properly related instead of being 'divided and over-come,' would have served as a ready touchstone and test of, for example, the gain or loss to Scotland through the Unions of the Crowns and the Parliaments. To isolate such information now is exceedingly difficult.

The history of Scotland as a whole, apart from that merely of the last century or thereabouts, has suffered greatly through the increasing Anglification of our school curricula, and of Scottish life and letters generally. The Editor of *The Scottish Educational Journal*[1] has recently been pleading for the devotion of more time and a different spirit to the study of Scottish History in Scottish schools – but he has required to finish up his plea by admitting that a prerequisite of any such development must be the provision of appropriate text-books. So far they do not exist. They have still to be written. Another recent writer on the subject has pointed out that those responsible for the raising of the question of the better teaching of Scottish history in Scottish schools are very largely

> under the impression that all that is required to be done is to increase the time at the disposal of teachers for Scottish history. Much more than that is required. There are few teachers at the present time capable of teaching Scottish history, and it is imperative that we should have, what we have not now, teachers properly qualified to teach the subject. The position at present is as follows: – Trained

---

[1] For full report on this important address see 'Scottish Home Rule' (Vol. 6, No. 6. – December, 1925). [MacDiarmid's note. – Ed.]

teachers with Chapter V. qualification to teach English – that is, who have studied at the University in the classes of English literature, Anglo-Saxon (or Latin, or Moral Philosophy), with a little British History, or Italian literature, plus any two other subjects, are considered by the Education Authority as qualified to teach English. In many cases they have not studied or read a word of history of any kind, still less history from a Scotsman's point of view, from the time when they left the intermediate school at the age of 14 until they return as recognised teachers of the subject. At the University there is a class devoted to Scottish History and literature. Surely the obvious solution of this problem is for the authorities to select teachers whose honours English degrees include the degree in this subject. This would at least ensure that Scottish history is taught by teachers who know something about the subject they teach... But, after all, the crux of the matter is not the mere teaching of Scots history, it is rather the point of view from which it is taught. Our present school histories present it not as a national thing, but as an unfortunate and sometimes not at all necessary prelude to English Imperialism.

Arguing along similar lines, in my inaugural address to the Edinburgh University Historical Association, I suggested that one of the criteria of history was its power of making history – a test that would certainly play havoc with practically everything that has been written with regard to Scottish history – and that to rewrite Scots history in Braid Scots (at any rate, the history of a period when Scots was in general use) might prove a valuable corrective and supply us, if the task could be carried out with true genius, with a work whereby we could adequately test the denationalised character of the vast bulk of the literature on the subject. I declared too that no distinctively Scottish philosophy of history had yet emerged nor had any modern Scottish historian written on his subject on a plane corresponding to that of the foremost living historians in other countries, while most of the historical work that was being done was Scottish only in subject-matter and was lagging far behind contemporary European scholarship in its psychological penetration, in its 'economic realism,' in its accurate recreation of atmosphere. Stylistically and in almost every other respect Scottish history remained provincial, inadequate to the conception of 'Scotland – a Nation,' and, to a large extent, over-Anglicised. Some of these points have been underlined – and the whole point of view has been effectively related to the present world position of historiography – in a very interesting article on 'The

Psychological Interpretation of History' by Mr W.H. Marwick, which appeared in *The Scottish Educational Journal* of 16th October, and which can hardly fail to exercise a very important influence on Scottish historiography in the immediate future.

The existing position is very well described by Mr Henry Lamond in a letter to *The Times* of November 11th, 1925, in the course of which he says that

the best way Scottish scholarship can acknowledge its indebtedness to the Faculty of Advocates for the transference of the Advocates' Library to the National Board of Trustees would be the combined effort of Scottish scholars to present to the new National Library a real 'History of Scotland' based on the results of modern research. Never has Scotland been so fortunate in the number of scholars of competence resident within her gates. Never has Scotland stood more in need of such a work. In the light of modern research her whole history needs rewriting from the earliest time till 1603, while from the latter date onward till the present day it is time that those Scotsmen who remained in Scotland should receive recognition of the part they played in developing their native country during these three eventful centuries. To-day Scotland has less public spirit and courage as a nation than a Balkan republic.

But the very emergence and expression of sentiments such as these – and they are emerging and being more emphatically expressed on all hands throughout Scotland to-day – is a sign of a change in the national spirit; and, as a matter of fact, the supply has already been anticipating the demand – the Renaissance spirit has been manifesting itself in Scottish historiography during recent years, and its developments are already strongly marked. The general outlines of our national evolution have been traced by Hume Brown, Andrew Lang and Law Mathieson. Recent books which represent the new tendencies which are now at work and indicate the lines upon which our historians have now begun to move are (a) *Domestic Life in Scotland, 1488-1688*, by John Warrack (1920), which represents the effort to get beyond the dull and mummified details of the text-book of political history and to attempt the reconstruction of the life of a past age in a fuller fashion; and (b) Alan Orr Anderson's *Early Sources of Scottish History, A.D. 500 to 1286* (1922) which represents the movement towards tracing the international aspects of Scottish history, Mr Anderson, in his two volumes having gone to the Irish and Scandinavian chroniclers to supplement his earlier study of Scottish history as it appeared in the English chroniclers and in the Scottish sources available. It is along these two lines that Scottish history must develop if there is to be any hope of its aspiring to follow in the great traditions of the older Scottish historians. It naturally follows that, in the general evolution of Scottish history, we shall pass beyond all that has been done by Hume Brown and Andrew Lang and others, so that it is not necessary to single out here any particular historians whose work remains to be challenged. But what does want to be challenged is the idea that history in Scotland was a negligible thing before the advent of English professors in our midst about the end of the nineteenth century, and this is the third line that, in conjunction with the other two, is presenting itself to Scottish historians to-day – the need to emphasise the fact that we have an old and great tradition of history in Scotland. Knox and Bishop Lesley, Calderwood and Archbishop Spottiswoode, Woodrow and Father Innes, Hume and Robertson, and so on – names such as these refute the assumption that Scottish historical scholarship is a recent growth, transplanted from south of the Border. Another point is that Scottish history has been written very largely from the Presbyterian standpoint. This attitude has met with incisive criticism from Andrew Lang and others: and it is to be hoped that we shall soon have full justice done to the Roman Catholic and Episcopalian standpoints and their traditions of scholarship just as in political and economic respects we may hope to counterbalance the fact that the great majority of Scottish historians have come to their task pre-committed to favour the existing relationships of England and Scotland and the existing state of society.

As regards the more immediate tasks awaiting accomplishment in the field of Scottish history, there must be a general move forward. The vast stores of manuscript material in the Register House must be adequately catalogued and the work of issuing printed calendars ought to go steadily on; this work of documenting research must be attended by an effort to incorporate its results in fresh, well-written volumes that will appeal to the general public. Some effort should be made to bring typical extracts from the Scottish records before the public in a cheap and handy form (as in Dr Insh's *School Life in Old Scotland,* Educational Institute of Scotland, 1925, 2s. – a model of its kind in every respect). The records contain much that is of surpassing human interest, and the Scots in which they are set forth is virile and racy – a magnificent prose instrument.

Four men, in particular, are shaping this new and humane school of Scottish history. These are the subject of the present study, Dr George

Insh, Principal Lecturer in History at Glasgow Training Centre; Professor J.H. Baxter, of St Andrews, whose researches in European History will ultimately revolutionise our attitude to mediaeval Scots history; Alan O. Anderson, whose work is preparing the way for a clear understanding of the main factors in early Scottish history; and Professor R.K. Hannay, whose enthusiasm and insight have done a great deal to strengthen and expand the School of History founded in Edinburgh by the late Professor Hume Brown. Attention must also be directed to the Historical Association of Scotland's new series of pamphlets – Dr W. Douglas Simpson's *The Scottish Castle* (1924) and Miss Mary G. Williamson's *Edinburgh Between the Unions*. Both of these were discussed in an article entitled 'Tower and Town' (*Scottish Educational Journal*, June 26, 1925) by Miss Irene F.M. Deane, in an article valuable alike for its scholarship, its point of view and its sense of historical values. In Miss Deane we have obviously a writer of very great promise.

To come from the general aspect of affairs to Dr Insh, I have chosen him because he best exemplifies the new spirit in Scottish history and is exerting, by his position at Jordanhill, his addresses to various bodies, and his published books and articles, a more general influence than any other contemporary Scottish historian. All the lines of development I have indicated are present in Dr Insh's work. Of his *Scottish Colonial Schemes* (Messrs Maclehose & Jackson, 1923) Professor C.M. Andrews of Yale University, writing in the *American Historical Review*, well said:

> Quite apart from its value as a contribution of exceptional merit to the history of Scottish emigration to America in the seventeenth century, Dr Insh's volume is significant as marking a new and growing interest among British writers of to-day in their colonial past. Furthermore, both because the work is written by a Scotsman from the standpoint of Scotland, and because to a considerable extent it is based upon materials in Scottish archives, from which frequent quotations are made, it has a racy flavour all its own and a character essentially and peculiarly Scottish. No one but a Scotsman could create the atmosphere that distinguishes this book.

Dr Insh has edited for the Scottish History Society a volume of papers illustrative of the voyages of Scottish ships to the Isthmus of Darien and to the Eastern seas; and is at present engaged in a study of the Darien Scheme in its relation to the social, economic, and political history of Scotland; while in the article from which I have just quoted, Professor Andrews expressed the hope which all who realise the importance of the subject and the value of Dr Insh's work and his special equipment for this particular task will share, that once he shall have completed his Darien volume,

> he will be interested to pursue his subject into the years following the Union, even on to that period after 1760, when there began the Highland emigration which lasted until the Revolution, and brought thousands of Scotsmen to America and the West Indies.

Happily, Dr Insh is still a young man – in his early forties, and much may be expected from him. The University of Glasgow have already fitly recognised the value of his work by conferring the degree of D.Litt. on him in 1922, and some six months later – in the same year – the jealously guarded and seldom bestowed honour of Research Fellow.

Dr Insh finds time to take a many-sided interest in Scottish cultural activities, apart from his own particular work. He has taken an active interest in the work of the Scottish National Theatre Society both as a member of Council and as a member of the Play-reading Committee, while his essays in dramatic criticism based upon the Scottish National Players' productions have evidenced his knowledge of the theatre and insight into the various arts that are tributary to it. His services as a lecturer are in great demand, and he has lectured under the auspices of the Workers' Educational Association, the Royal Philosophical Society of Glasgow, the Glasgow Bibliographical Society, the West of Scotland Branch of the Historical Association, and numerous other bodies, while he has taken a lively and helpful interest in all the manifestations of the Scottish Renaissance movement, and was one of the associate editors of the short-lived *Northern Review.*

An admirable sketch of his career appeared in *The Bailie* (October 17, 1923), and the writer of it began by saying:

> At the present day the study of Scottish history is passing through an interesting phase. With the broadening and deepening of the spirit of historical scholarship there has come a period of intensive study and research. The days when an individual historian could attempt the task of writing by himself a history of Scotland seem now in a far distant past; the days that will see the production of a history repre-senting the combined efforts of Scottish scholars exist as yet only in the vision of a few ardent enthusiasts; in the meantime the work of investigation and exploration of research and formulation is being steadily carried on by a small band of Scottish students.

And in the forefront of that band stands the quiet, genial, unassuming and yet resolute and extraordinarily resourceful form of Dr Insh.

[18.12.25]

Letters

MR GRIEVE AND 'THE KING'S ENGLISH'

Sir, – If the attitude of the majority of Scottish teachers to 'the King's English,' and their conception of style generally is like R.B.M.'s that must largely account for Scotland's comparative literary puerility and provincialisation. As a Scots Republican, I have no particular interest in English, whether of the King's variety or otherwise, and would immensely prefer to write my articles in Braid Scots, or even in French or Russian. It is part of my case that English is psychologically unsuitable as a medium for Scots, and it is absurd that I should be told that 'plain straightforward writing is foreign to my nature' – which I admit – and yet recommended to adopt it. But while I disbelieve in English as a medium of expression for Scots, I must add (in all modesty) that I have, upon occasions, used English, both in prose and poetry, in a way which has won the encomiums of much better judges than any of your correspondents, while none of them, to my knowledge, has done anything of the kind. I have now practically ceased, in so far as my creative work is concerned, to write in English, simply because I believe that other media will serve me better, and enable me to obtain the special effects I am out for in a way that English (overwhelmingly adscripted, as Professor Saintsbury has pointed out, to certain purposes to which as a Scot I am almost wholly antipathetic) cannot. In this belief I am again supported by numerous critics superior in every way to any of your correspondents.

I need not refer here to the 'Beyond Meaning' movements in contemporary welt-literatur, experiments in the balling-together of words, and other elements of Futurist and Expressionist technique save to admit that I am committed to many of them (and regard my own style, despite all the strictures it has evoked, with the most deplorable complacency) to an extent which really renders me a hopeless subject for the fatherly advice of your correspondents. They bring their qualifications as critics under grave suspicion by their persistent failure to recognise this, and to see that for this and other reasons, practically all their comments are impertinent in at least two senses of the word.

I may point out, however, that even R.B.M. is driven back upon the use of the term clichés instead of some English equivalent; even in his short letter he, too, repeats himself in a way that 'shows a poor sense of word economy', and his third sentence is very clumsily constructed.

But I have no fault to find in his arithmetic. – Yours, etc..

C.M. Grieve

Sir, – I have swithered long, but have ettled sorely to express my mind regarding Mr Grieve's articles. I like a gallant fighter even when I disagree with him. He has submitted to us a whole series of articles. I have done him the honour of trying to read them all; I have even attempted to get a little sense out of them, perhaps an inexcusable lapse on my part. Might I be permitted to give my general summing-up? I believe the writer is a Scotsman; he betrays, at least, one characteristic feature, a pungent pen in fault-finding. I may be wrong, but I cannot recollect one single instance of really cordial commendation; all our Scots writers are but indifferent creatures, and none are worthy of a place except in fourth-rate literature. That may be very true – my criterion may be terribly low, but, he must excuse me – never once has he made himself intelligible in his reasons for placing them so low. Somehow they have not caught the Zeitgeist, they have no standing in welt-literatur. I am not quite sure what the Zeitgeist of the present may be, but I believe 'I am not quite sure of anything' epitomises it fairly well. Might I congratulate him in having absorbed that spirit? If he were only quite sure as to his aim I give him the credit of believing that he could express it clearly in vigorous Anglo-Saxon without borrowing horrible words like aboulia. Is there cant among literary critics as well as among quacks and schoolmen? I am very forcibly reminded of Dousterswivel; also of an old miller who lived near us at one time. He was both farmer and miller, and once he was supervising the thatching of some ricks. His foreman was a very capable man, but old Sandy did not think he was fixing a 'bag-raip' as it should be fixed. 'That winna dee, Rose: that's nae the wye te dee't.' 'Weel, will that dae?' came the impatient query. 'Na, na, tak' it the ither wye,' said he. 'Here, come up an' lat me see foo te dee't,' said the angered Rose, and down he came. The old man took up the challenge, mounted the ladder, fumbled for a few minutes and then said, 'Oh, ye war deein a' richt: come awa up again.'

Now, it does not perhaps need an expert to tell when a rick has been tidily finished, nor need a critic be a very fine writer, but when one ventures so far as Mr Grieve has done, I think we might ask him to cease the purely destructive in his criticism, and let us know clearly what he and others ought to aim at, and if by his study of foreign literature he has got a little gleam of light, he might please share it, instead of merely making darkness mirker. Many of your correspondents have already made this request. He has retorted by saying that he assumes he is writing to enlightened people. I can only speak for myself, but I do not mind confessing that I am not so enlightened as not to be in need of straight-forward plain writing. Nobody wishes to wander in a mist. If Mr Grieve really desires us to attain any goal, why should he act the squirt and cover his retreat in ink?

One other point of criticism: he desires a Scottish Renaissance, and all the time he is urging the need, not for anything distinctive, but for a Scotch imitation of what is being done elsewhere. Is that so? Either my reading or his writing is at fault. At any rate I can hardly imagine anything distinctive in mere mimicry.

If he should confess like ordinary wayfarers, 'The God of our fathers is gone: our gods have feet of clay: we know not whether we wend, and lacking faith we hesitate, we grope, we fumble,' a decent fellow-feeling would make us charitable. As it is, he has chosen the part of showing the way, but not one glimmering styme has yet been vouchsafed us, and we are getting impatient. – Yours, etc.,

New Byth

W. Cumming.
[18.12.25]

25. Stewart Carmichael

In one of my poems I say

> Dundee is dust
> And Aberdeen a shell.

And in the dust that is Dundee Mr Stewart Carmichael, if he is nothing so startling as a trumpet, is at least an elfland horn, serving to maintain an all-too-easily missed but yet never wholly vanquishable note of beauty in the dreariest waste of materialism that contemporary Scotland possesses. Carmichael's studio in the Nethergate is like an oasis in a desert – one of the very few spots in Dundee where there is any spiritual life. There are others: a few; but they are all cultivated but non-creative, passive, not active. Not that Carmichael's makes any headway or does more than maintain itself. It is at any rate quite imperceptibly, if at all, that (to vary the metaphor) it is 'leavening the lump.' But how extraordinary that it should even contrive to preserve itself with undiminished purity throughout the desolating years in so utterly antipathetic an environment. Dundee has always been almost a cipher culturally. Practically no good thing in any of the arts has come out of it. Within the past few decades it has become more than ever sterile and degenerate. It only requires a comparison of the files of its papers for the past year or two with those of, say, quarter of a century or half-a-century ago to demonstrate the declines, in range, in tone, in all respects: and as with its journalism so with all the other aspects of its life. The extremely low wages that always obtained in its staple industry, and the consequent general debilitation of the community, are largely responsible. Dundee to-day has a population of poorer physique, with a higher incidence of illness and mortality, than any other place in Scotland. Incredible conditions prevail in it. One tenement has no fewer than three stories below the level of the street: and these stories are divided up into the one-roomed houses of which there are so many in Dundee. There are, indeed, numerous cellars occupied as one-roomed houses. Under such conditions the general mental level is correspondingly low. And the complement of such a state of affairs is certainly found in the Municipal Art Gallery, with its almost incredibly vulgar Herkomer, its fatuous Henry Kerr, its 'Magazine-Art' display of Grey's 'Neuve-Chapelle,' and its blatant portraits of all manner of local nonentities cheek-by jowl in the most extraordinary fashion with a minority of works of genuine – a few of really high – merit. There are a few wealthy private 'patrons of art' in Dundee, but most of them are commercial collectors rather than genuine connoisseurs or picture-lovers, and, in each of these categories, the 'inferiority complex' is generally in full blast. This accounts for the fact that there is a market, however limited, in Dundee for modern French stuff, Cezanne, Van Gogh, and the like. But between plutocratic extremes and proletarian nescience there is practically no public interest to sustain native art-products. Stewart Carmichael has been content with poor pickings, and that has enabled him to maintain himself where many another would have failed. Happily, too, he has more than one string to his bow. There used to be quite a little group of artists in Dundee some years ago – in it but not of it – but Carmichael is almost the only survivor now. The others are dead, or have gone to Edinburgh or London. Their places have not been filled by any younger men. One of the few still within close call is

Alec Grieve, Carmichael's brother-in-law, who lives at Tayport. He is a landscape artist of individuality and power; and used to contribute very powerful cartoons to *The Labour Leader.*

The work whereby Stewart Carmichael makes his living – the work that sells – and that finds acceptance most readily at the Royal Scottish Academy and elsewhere is his architectural work – his water-colour drawings and lithographs and etchings of old buildings in this country and abroad. These are admirable of their kind. Mr Carmichael's early architectural training has stood him in excellent stead for this type of work. At his annual exhibition this year he displayed exceptionally fine water-colours of Furnes and Louvain and the Abbey of Arbroath. Earlier Italian studies of the same kind, and pictures of Edinburgh and of Balmerino Abbey and many others. all carried, as these do, a fine sense of architectural values and a capacity for bodying forth the nature and effects of buildings with verisimilitude and power. All these, of course, were purely 'representational' and romantic instincts were evidenced in the choice of subject and angle of approach. Such documentations of the contemporary scene at a remove – but not too great a remove – from the man-in-the-street's habitual view has values of its own, apart from the purely artistic, and these exercises of Carmichael's skill should be in greater demand than they are. There is quite a considerable public who could quite well afford to buy such work, but who still prefer types of art with, at once, less associative and less aesthetic value. While he executes them with rare skill, however, of none of these works could it be said: 'This is quintessential Carmichael – none other but he could have contrived just this effect.' It is therefore unfortunate, perhaps, that he should devote himself, perhaps require to devote himself, so largely to this type of work, which, when all is said and done, many another artist in Europe (if comparatively few in Scotland today) can or could do equally well. Nor is there anything distinctively Scottish in Carmichael's approach to architecture in art. In his choice of colour – in his choice of subject, even – there may be little *differentia*; a foreign artist might differ in such details, but, fundamentally, nothing distinctively Scottish transpires in this category of his art.

And Stewart Carmichael is very notably and entirely a Scot, combining within himself both poles of our country's culture. He has subsumed the whole of our national past to an extraordinary degree and is equally at home in Gaelic and Braid Scots. The traditional disjunction between, even antipathy of, the two, which has done so much to prevent Scotland integrating itself effectively, does not exist for him. His personality is his greatest asset. He stands for all things that are noble and of good report.

He is the very antithesis of the stock-conception of a Scotsman. Contact with so fine and vital a Scot in these degenerate days carries one back to pre-Reformation Scotland, to the days when Scotland was one with Europe in life and faith. By some miracle of personal synthesis Carmichael has transcended the provincialism to which the Scots nature has so largely become subjected and preserves unabated in himself the high old qualities of our people in full communion with the culture of Europe. That he is a man of his own generation, and almost wholly unaffected by such recent technical developments and experimental tendencies as we expect in *les jeunes*, is no condemnation of his work nor any reflection on the quality of his continuing vitality. But in so far as the nationalism in his work is concerned, and the purity of his own raciality, he has been the gainer. If the newer techniques are to naturalise themselves in Scotland – or if the Scottish genius is to develop independently along lines analogous and complementary to recent European tendencies – art such as that of Stewart Carmichael's must be reckoned with and its significance as nation-alism understood. All the art products of Scots – and particularly Scots living in Scotland and depending wholly or mainly on the Scottish public – must be reckoned with from this point of view, as a means of finding why certain forms of artistic expression have hitherto been favoured by Scottish artists and the Scottish public, and thus what lets and hindrances, psychological and commercial, have determined the course of art in Scotland and what general attitude or capacity of response to art – in a word, atmosphere – has been developed. But Stewart Carmichael's work offers far more positive answers than these to creative investigation seeking to found itself securely in national tradition. If his architectural studies offer little that is seizably national, it is otherwise with his portraits. Here his consciousness of what is distinctively Scottish finds scope. There is no mistaking some of these faces for other than Scottish. His insight into Scots character is inerrable. In his recent exhibition his 'Mrs J. Smith, Aberdeen,' was a painting of this kind and, as one critic wrote,

> It is not so much a 'speaking' subject as a subject that with difficulty refrains from speaking, and one could imagine that very wise, witty and pawky observations would be heard if this kindly-faced old lady spoke her mind.

Again an attitude of consequence – constructive and comprehensive – informs his splendid friezes of Scottish History, the Makars, Scottish Women (with Jenny Geddes – not Queen Mary – in the centre) and so forth. Here then is an artist who has maintained a many-sided relationship with the genius of his country at a time when that was being more and more obscured by an overwhelming pressure of assimilation to English standards. He has unobtrusively but subtly and persistently maintained the national traditions in his particular field of art, and deserves ampler recognition in these days when the cause of 'Scotland – a Nation' is once more in the ascendant.

But his most distinctive vein is represented by his symbolical compositions. Here the poet side of his nature emerges. It is not surprising that these pictures should be held in little esteem to-day and their real value missed. But as manifestations of the Scottish Psyche – as glimpses into the soul of Celtic imagery – they stand in a category of their own. They are very different from the ornamental designs of John Duncan – another fine Scot of the older generation. Carmichael is less concerned with outward trappings. His visions are more profound, and personal to himself while distinctively Scottish in quality. He cannot manifest them in terms of the old myths – no language of symbol exists in which they can be readily expressed. Paintings such as 'Birth,' 'The Friends of Genius' (Poverty and Disaster), 'Chance,' 'The Wife of Judas,' and a score of others confront us with this aspect or that of a powerful imagination that has difficulty in compressing cosmic conceptions or remote spiritual problems into terrestrial or human terms at all. These are wild, weird designs, full of unique psychological interest. If I was asked 'What is a Scotsman?' I could scarcely do better than show my interrogator one of these compositions: for that is what they are – so many revelations of that mystery of faculties and inhibitions complex beyond most, the Scots soul in its Gaelic aspect, or in the occultation of Judea. In them we have the quintessential Stewart Carmichael; manifesting himself in pictures that could only have been painted by a Scottish artist and by no other Scottish artist than himself.

[25.12.25]

Letters

MR GRIEVE'S CREED
Sir, – So do I prefer Lewis Carroll's 'Ballad of Jabberwocky,' but that is not to say that a reinvigorated Scots to-day cannot be used to like ends as successfully as English – if one knows how.

H. Brown sets down my general position very clearly. I will not quibble about the use of the phrases 'the English language' in Clause 8 or

'Scots-English culture' in Clause 14: before 'Celtic foundation' in Clause 11 I would insert the adjective 'purely', and in Clause 7 after 'derivative'- I would add 'like practically every other culture. ' Otherwise his Sixteen Points admirably describe my position and programme. – I am, etc.,

C.M. Grieve

THE NORDIC ORIGIN OF THE SCOTS

Sir, – I feel that I owe 'Buchan' an apology for taking so long to send in this reply to his last letter, all the more because my delay may have been misunderstood as betokening an unwillingness to follow his line of discussion, either from a churlish resentment at this 'butting-in uninvited,' as he put it himself, or from fear of venturing further because of the difficulties he had put in the way, in the shape of quoted authority. However, I must explain that pressure of my duties has been my only deterrent; and, with your permission, I should like to take up the discussion again where 'Buchan' left it.

I can scarcely believe that 'Buchan' is so obtuse as he pretends to be. He must have known that the snub I attempted to administer was not on account of any intrusion on his part, as he affects to believe, but on account of his mode of entrance and general demeanour. His first contribution to the discussion was not, to say the least of it, remarkable for either sweetness of temper or nicety of feeling; and though he has since with more amiability endeavoured to soften the tone of that first deliverance, I must state plainly my objection to him in that, behind the protection of a nom-de-plume, he made an attack upon a great living British scientist, characterising him as a man who periodically gives to the public Press conclusions which cannot be proved by facts, and as a man whose aim, or at least whose only effect, is to provide attractive material for journalists. If 'Buchan' really thinks that in thus resorting to aspersions instead of legitimate arguments (an offence aggravated by withholding his own name), he has done nothing that 'any reasonable man ' could object to, then I can say no more to him on that point. Our ideas of right and wrong are hopelessly at variance.

I am pleased to see that 'Buchan' now has the grace to admit that Sir Arthur Keith is at any rate a recognised authority on anthropology – of which ethnology is but a prolific branch – but that Sir Arthur can be so on a certain main section of a science, and at the same time so unreliable on its chief sub-section as to merit no consideration (in 'Buchan's' opinion), strikes me as rather funny. The situation, however, becomes positively comic when 'Buchan' dethrones Sir Arthur Keith and sets up Sir Leo Chiozza Money! I am reminded of a phrase of 'Anthony Farley's' (S.G. Hobson) – to 'fall to the level of amateur statisticians of the Chiozza Money kidney' and I have no doubt that one who performs such astonishing feats with figures may be an equally expert conjurer with ethnological data which others have gleaned; but I cannot accept either his testimony, or 'Buchan's' admiration of it, as any weighty evidence against the Nordic origin of the Scots. The other work which 'Buchan' recommends I hope to have an early opportunity of consulting, but I must say here and now that I do not expect a work with such a title to do more than to treat very indirectly the special subject we have under consideration.

It would have been more to the point had 'Buchan' accepted my hint, and, instead of merely ridiculing those who uphold the Nordic theory, had given one or two main reasons which lead him to speak so contemptuously of 'the ridiculous Nordic theory.' To my mind, nothing could ever be half so ridiculous as the pan-Celtic doctrines supplied to us in our school-books for generations – stuff which 'Buchan' has doubtless swallowed and found comforting – consisting chiefly of conclusions based on linguistic affinity, by which means one might, with equal ease, postulate an Anglo-Saxon origin for American negroes! Almost any theory would be better than that which classes such distinct types as the Highland Scot, the South-Western Irishman, and the Welshman, all as members of one happy family, and the egregious Sassenach as practically the only 'fremd' member of the household.

As we are still left to guess what it really is that 'Buchan' finds so ridiculous in the Nordic theory (though, to be sure, any theory is liable to be pushed to ridiculous extents by well-meaning enthusiasts, and it is hard to say what 'Buchan' may have come across on the subject), I propose to set the example of definiteness by abandoning Nordic theories for the present, and giving him a few Nordic facts instead. We may leave Sir Arthur Keith out of it, now. and take what may fairly be termed the beginning and end of the matter.

In 1842 the great Retzius, a Swede, found that Swedish skulls could not be distinguished from those of the Highland Scots. He went over to Scotland, and found that but for dress and speech it would be impossible to pick out a Swede from among a group of Scots. Not only in the skull, but in every noteworthy characteristic, the resemblance was striking; and, after all, if two races are really distinct, or really akin, the main points of divergence or similarity should be obvious to the eye, while the rest should be ascertainable without too great difficulty. The resemblances between Scot and Swede, and the differences between the Scot and other members of the 'Celtic family' are too many and too obvious to be lightly set aside. The aphorism: 'Skulls are harder than consonants' is still the best guide to the investigator; and it would seem that one must insist upon it still, with as much emphasis as when it was first uttered.

To come nearer home for the conclusion, I understand that Professor Robert Reid, of Aberdeen, has published the results of a long enquiry into the racial characteristics of the Scots ('Celtic' and Saxon) material which I believe to be the very latest on the subject. I have not had an opportunity of reading it myself (though 'Buchan,' if his pen-name has a geographical significance, may find it easy to get into direct touch with this source of information), but I know that the Professor's verdict is that he finds the Scot, whether Celtic or Saxon in speech, more like to the Swede – the Nordic type – in physical characteristics than to any other people on the Continent of Europe. If 'Buchan' wishes to upset that, I presume he will have to try to trace a closer resemblance to the Breton or the Walloon; and I fancy he is up against a very difficult task. – I am, etc.,

Sandwick   Robert W. Tait
Shetland

SCOTS AND THE DORIC

Sir, – In a recent letter of Mr Grieve's there are one or two remarks which call for some comment. Allow me to make it. He says he finds English no suitable medium for a Scot. I quite agree. English is a foreign tongue to our race, but if we use it at all we should use it correctly. But Mr Grieve says he would prefer to use the Doric or Russian or French. It is singular he should omit Gaelic from his list of preferences. Gaelic is the original Scots, and one would think that the first thoughts of any patriotic and intelligent Scot like Mr Grieve would turn to the language of his race, instead of to the Doric, or French or Russian. Regarding the Doric, I fear that horse has been dead some time, and to flog it as some are doing nowadays is sheer waste of time and effort. And was Doric ever a horse, much less one worth flogging? For my part, I encourage all I can the Doric movement, not because I think that dialect an end in itself, but because I think it a means to an end. The growing interest in it is a sign that numbers of our countrymen are beginning to think nationally, a wholesome and necessary reaction after the surfeit of imperial imaginings in which they have indulged far too long. The Doric then will *teach them to think nationally, and from so thinking I hope they will come in course of time to think still more so, which, if they do, should lead them, one and all, to the Gaelic, which is our true national tongue and the one in which the Scot can best express himself. And, Sir, is he likely ever to do that in this poor apology for a language styled the Doric? I think not: I don't want to say here anything uncomplimentary about the Doric, because I want the movement so styled to spread, but God knows, I could do so on very abundant and very excellent authority. All I will here say therefore is this, that the Doric never was, is, or ever will be in all human probability, a language fit for literary men to use. Why, Sir, not the simplest philosophical proposition could be propounded in the Doric; and he would be a bold 'Greek' who should charge that upon the Gaelic. Without turning a hair, so to speak, I will undertake to put into understandable Gaelic in this place – provided I have your permission to it – any passage from any modern or ancient philosopher which may be chosen for that purpose. And this I should be able to do because Gaelic is a polite language, with an immense tradition of learning behind it, and a vocabulary corresponding thereto, not because I flatter myself that I am learned above others in that language, or that I have any especial gift for the sort of undertaking I glance at. Doric is rich in a kind of homely imaginativeness, and in a power of expression which is essentially of the folk, but considered as a suitable vehicle or medium of expression for educated men and women it is, compared with Gaelic, as chaff to wheat. Its roots do not lie in learning and politeness, as those of Gaelic do, but in rusticity of utterance and bumpkinisity of thought. It will serve its turn as a means to ends, but as an end in itself it is simply unthinkable; and the sooner Mr Grieve and his friends grasp that fact, and act on it, the better. – l am, etc.,*

Buchan
[25.12.25]

26. Towards a Scottish National Drama: John Brandane

The 'facts' in regard to Scottish drama can be readily ascertained by reading Alexander MacGill's 'The Theatre Before the Union' (*Northern Review*, August, 1924); William Power's 'The Drama in Scotland' (*Scots*

Magazine); Dot Allan's 'The Scottish Theatre: A Call for Municipal Effort' (*Review of Reviews*, January, 1924), and Reah Denholm's 'The Scottish National Theatre Movement' (*Scots Magazine*). These four articles bound together would form an admirable history of Scottish Drama from the earliest times to the present day – apart, of course, from the drama in Gaelic.

> Scotland alone, [Miss Allan observes,] has no real drama of its own... Given this sense of poetry, this hero (Bonnie Prince Charlie) and this heroine (Mary Stuart) ready-made, why has Scotland evolved no drama of its own? To find the answer to this, one must go back to Mary Stuart's own time. She it was who was responsible for the introduction to the Court of Holyrood of the masque, a form of entertainment which provoked the ire of John Knox. But the Queen's reign was brief and her influence was not a lasting one. The spirit of Knox, on the other hand, lived after him. It was the survival of this militant spirit that incited a group of fanatics in Glasgow only a few decades ago to burn down one of the earliest playhouses erected in Scotland as a protest against the visit to their city of the celebrated Mrs Bellamy... In one way, the visit of Mrs Bellamy created a bad precedent. It served to establish the dependency of the Scottish theatre upon that of London, a dependency which to the great detriment of Scottish national drama has endured with occasional bright intervals ever since. In this respect our Scottish cities, it may be retorted, are no worse off than Manchester, Leeds, or many of the other English provincial centres. This argument is, however, beside the mark inasmuch as, save for a matter of mileage, Manchester and Leeds may be regarded as part of the integral whole of the metropolis. What London laughs at, Leeds usually laughs at likewise. This is not so with Scotland. What moves London to mirth moves, on occasion, Edinburgh to tears. Nowhere, in fact, is the difference between English and Scots mentality more sharply defined than in the theatre. It is the failure to recognise this difference that is accountable for a great deal of the bad business done by touring companies in the provinces today.

Dealing with the same question, Mr Power says:

> Why is it that the Scottish mind, so analytic, individual and sharply picturesque – and Scottish life, so dramatically intense and racy of the soil – have never found expression and reflection in that most charac-

teristic, most spontaneous product of an independent, highly self-conscious race – a national drama? Professor Gregory Smith's theory of a natural impediment needs only to be stated to be instantly dismissed. The Scots, as Froissart remarked long ago, are fonder of pageantry and splendour than the English. When their crust of reserve breaks down under stress of emotion, they reveal themselves as natural actors, quick to exploit a dramatic situation and set it off with vividly picturesque phrases and richly expressive gestures. Nor did Scottish drama perish in the shadow of the great Elizabethans. In the Scotland visited by Ben Jonson there were possibly not half-a-dozen people who had heard of him or of Shakespeare. Scottish drama had already perished. It had been strangled in its cradle by the 'grim Genevan ministers,' the kirk session, and the puritanical and churchified town councils. Both in England and in Scotland puritanism was relentlessly hostile to the stage. But in England it was foiled by the diversity of social interests, the humanist traditions of the universities, the culture of the aristocracy, and, above all, the influence of a monarch who was head of a State Church that represented a successful compromise. In the narrower field of Scotland, clerical puritanism, seconded by aristocratic greed, gained a rapid victory and captured the life of the Capital. The Court stood for everything that the mass of the people disliked. The stage was involved in the discredit and defeat of the Court. Along with art, music, dancing and everything intellectual that did not redound directly to the greater glory of Calvinism, the theatre became associated in the popular mind with prelacy, alien aggression and monarchic absolutism. This fatal 'complex,' to use the Freudian term, held the Scottish mind in bondage until the middle of the eighteenth century.

I agree with all this, but would go a little further to account for the absence of any breaking-forth of the long welled-up faculty since the middle of the eighteenth century – a long enough time to recover from the effects of inhibition and make up for lost time. Professor Gregory Smith is not so easily dismissed as Power would have it: the facts he puts forward are 'chiels that winna ding'; but they can be taken into account and reconciled with very other conclusions than his.

We must not assume that Puritanical inclemency was the sole cause of disaster. No zealotry could suppress lyric freedom, and the Muse, whether true-love, or light-o'-love, or frankly ribald, inspired the Scot when she willed, and by feebler pens than Burns's, even when the laws of the Righteous were most severe. In Scotland, as elsewhere, drama would have defied all interference, had it outgrown its infant weakness. Though an epidemic Puritanism carried it off, it was from the first, and was destined to remain, even if fate had been kinder. a 'puir shilpet cratur.' The problem is one of family history, rather than of rough handling by the Assembly of the Kirk... It is clear that when the tyranny was least strong, or when, during that tyranny, rebellion was most active, Scottish drama did not find its opportunity... If, therefore, the effect of this superimposed Puritanism may be disregarded, what arguments can be brought forward that the conditions for the growth of a national drama were unfavourable? There is, in the first place, the general consideration which is connected with what has already been said of the familiar and retrospective habits of Scottish literature. These are even less of an aid to the dramatist than to the epic poet. if they are not accompanied by what is after all the dominant characteristic of drama, the sense of movement and the presentation of that movement in a coherent and, it may be, single action.

Meeting Professor Gregory Smith on his own ground, we can accuse him of having a conception of the drama based mainly on its past exemplification in English – or, at any rate, a conception of the drama at complete variance with that which is emerging in Europe to-day, when those very propensities and tricks of the Scots mentality which were admittedly of little or no use in the creation of drama as hitherto conceived, are in most demand and are rapidly foreshadowing an entirely different *kind* of drama than the world has yet seen – a saltatory development unpredicated in the past evolution of Drama. It is my belief that the time is only now coming when the Scots psychology can express itself in distinctive and dynamic drama – that it contains forces which can only emerge when the factors which have built up European civilisation as it presently exists exhaust themselves and require to be replaced by the very different forces which they have so long inhibited. In other words, the Spenglerian hypothesis seems to me to fit the facts far better than either that of Mr Power or that of Professor Gregory Smith. Let us see what other evidence is available for anticipating that the psychological moment for Scottish drama has not yet come but is imminent.

The first point is that in the absence of a radical departure from the

existing conventions of the theatre, as developed in England and elsewhere in the past, no Scots dramatist has produced drama of the
slightest note or in any way other than most superficially differentiated
from English drama. This tends to confirm our theory. All the other lets
and hindrances to Scottish drama Mr Power and others refer to have
disappeared except this psychological deadlock which defies effective
resolution along all the customary lines. The fact of the matter is that the
very qualities of the Scottish genius which have hitherto warred against
its emulation of England in any of the arts are precisely qualities which
to-day are in the most significant alignment with all the newest and most
promising tendencies in *welt-literatur.* Professor Gregory Smith analyses
them admirably in his opening chapter 'Two Moods,' in which, *inter alia*,
he says:

> There is more in the Scottish antithesis of the real and fantastic than
> is to be explained by the familiar rules of rhetoric. The sudden
> jostling of contraries seems to preclude any relationship by literary
> suggestion. The one invades the other without warning... If a formula
> is to be found it must explain this strange combination of things
> unlike, of things seen in an everyday world and things which, like the
> elf-queen herself, neither earth nor heaven will claim. This mingling,
> even of the most eccentric kind, is an indication to us that the Scot, in
> that medieval fashion which takes all things as granted, is at his ease
> in both 'rooms of life,' and turns to fun, and even profanity, with no
> misgivings. For Scottish literature is more medieval in habit than crit-
> icism has suspected, and owes some part of its picturesque strength to
> this freedom in passing from one mood to another. It takes some
> people more time than they can spare to see the absolute propriety of
> a gargoyle's grinning at the elbow of a kneeling saint.

The Scottish National Theatre movement seems singularly blind to
the most important thing with regard to its own intentions which a study
of Scottish psychological and cultural history has to show; and the
majority of those who are setting themselves out as Scottish dramatists
to-day are at the furthest remove from that *Expressionismus* through
which lies the only possibility of liberating any Scots Drama worthy of
the name.

The lesson is plain enough for all who run to read, and has recently
been most pointedly emphasised by one of the most brilliant of our
younger Scots, Professor Allardyce Nicoll in his history of *British
Drama.* (Messrs Harrap, 1925.) His last chapter may well be read by any

would-be Scots dramatist in conjunction with a careful re-reading of the chapter from Professor Gregory Smith I have just been quoting. It shows the only way out for the ultimate manifestation of Scots genius in drama of a major kind – the only way to prevent that relegation of the Scottish contribution to future arts and letters to the minor role Professor Gregory Smith confidently prophesies for it. Surveying contemporary tendencies, Professor Nicoll observes in serious drama and in comedy the union of actual life with something outside the ordinary world, literally supernatural or imaginatively fanciful, and expresses the opinion that drama will turn from naturalism towards fantasy, and an imaginative treatment of real life. Herein undoubtedly lies the great opportunity for Scottish genius.

'John Brandane' (Dr John McIntyre) has won wide recognition as the finest dramatist the Scottish National Theatre movement has as yet produced – and he is. There could be no shrewder condemnation of the movement. For precisely the same reason that most people commend his plays, I am constrained to condemn them as manifestly unScottish – marking not a salient accomplishment in the movement towards a Scottish drama, but, on the contrary, proving a grave misdirection. Brandane's work has neither of the two characteristics of Scottish genius (let alone both of them) – excessive particularism or unpredictable fantasy. If it had shrewdly got at the factors which have so long inhibited Scottish genius, and are still so largely inhibiting it, there would have been extreme resistance to it. But it has occasioned no indignation. In other words, it has not touched the roots of our national being. Mr Lennox Robinson accounts Mr Brandane one of the first half-dozen playwrights of the younger British school, along with Noel Coward, Sean O'Casey, and others. Perhaps he is. Coward and one or two others of Mr Robinson's team seem to me exceedingly small fry. But there is one thing the other five all have in varying degree that Brandane lacks – and that is contemporaneity. They all represent recognisable movements in drama, related to the Zeitgeist, observable internationally in all the arts. The content of Brandane's work on the contrary is negligible save for the purposes of entertainment. He originates nothing: he makes no intriguing departures: he says nothing that is not superficial: he never comes to grips with real life: there is nothing that one can seize on and say 'this is quintessential Brandane – there is no mistaking it.' As a matter of fact his plays might have been written as far back as 1875; they reflect nothing that has happened since then in human life and thought or in the evolution of the drama, save perhaps in a little trick here and there of stage technique – which is a very different thing from dramatic technique. It is just here perhaps that we come to grips with Brandane. He has a sound knowledge of the theatre – but has no great dramatic gift; he is a better stage-technician than he is a writer. He has nothing to say – but he knows how to say it. His work is extremely thin, conventional and unimportant – but it is put together in a thoroughly competent and business-like fashion. It is in point of literary quality precisely equal to that – not of people like Bernard Shaw, Granville Barker, Galsworthy, nor yet of the newer men like Richard Hughes, Caradoc Evans, and so forth – but of that intermediate type of dramatist who is never named in any serious discussion of tendencies, who really does not count except at the ticket-box, the undifferentiated purveyor of assorted entertainments to the mass – men like (it is difficult to recall their names) the authors of *Charley's Aunt* and *When Knights were Bold,* and a score of other quite successful, if less sensationally successful, productions. And it is precisely a playwright of this kind we would expect to be at the head of the Scottish Players' efforts. These efforts are directed simply and solely to produce the same sort of thing as is being, or has been, produced in English Repertory Theatres, or at the Abbey Theatre, give it a little Scottish local colour, and call it Scottish National Drama. But it is not in this way that anything of national consequence is done. Nothing the Scottish Players have done has given the slightest impression of a long-inhibited faculty suddenly asserting itself – no issue has been forced with the national consciousness – no bearing upon the national life has been developed. I am not pleading for propagandist plays: but for something deeper than propaganda – a sense of destiny realising itself, an effect of influence, the consciousness of a radical difference because we have at last obtained what we have so long, inexplicably and unfortunately lacked, a feeling that fundamental factors are at work. Brandane's plays disengage nothing of the kind. It is not on the strength of such plays that Scotland will regain a place in any study of the tendencies at work in contemporary drama. There are no tendencies at work in Scottish drama so far as Brandane's plays are concerned (and Brandane is our greatest dramatist): Scots psychology remains outwith the scope of drama in any sense worth mentioning.

Brandane's work may, however, serve as a reminder that mere technical competence, mere acquaintance with Scottish history or Scottish life and character in this district or that, mere clever dialogue and so forth will not suffice to create Scots Drama – unless there is a powerful impulse at work, expressing itself through the distinctive factors of Scottish psychology, in its own inimitable fashion, at the right time.

Given the latter all the attributes of the clever craftsman may or may not be found also; that is a matter of comparative unimportance. As a matter of fact Brandane has almost all the qualities or accomplishments of a perfect dramatist according to the textbooks. He merely lacks the smallest glint of genius, and the slightest element of topicality – not topicality in the usual sense, but timeliness with reference to the real needs of the national life, those requirements, conscious or unconscious, which a real Scots National Drama would help to meet. As it is, I am of the opinion that despite all its technical finish, Brandane's work signifies the futility of seeking to find Scots National Drama along the lines the Scottish Stage Society are going. It is, of its kind, a fine enough performance, but it is destitute of promise. One has only to think of the kind of ideas any great dramatist deals with – their tremendous germinative power, their relevance to the major problems of humanity, and, generally, to the deeper and more particular problems of a given people, their originative and tendencious power – to see Brandane in his true light, and to see the justice of St John Ervine's remark that 'the best that Glasgow can do in the way of a repertory theatre is an occasional performance by the Scottish National Players, whose title is a trifle grandiloquent, considering the extent of their operations.'

Mr Alexander MacGill, in an article on 'The Plays of John Brandane' (*Northern Review,* May, 1924) showed that a healthy dissatisfaction exists in certain quarters; 'Unfortunately, it is not the big play which the theatre is looking for – a little amateurish touch here and there would have been forgiven for the sake of some body or strength in the play,' he observed of Brandane's four-act Highland comedy, *Full Fathom Five*, and concluded however that 'we must admit that John Brandane is the biggest man the theatre has produced, but that his biggest work is *The Glen is Mine.*' I do not think there can be any difference of opinion as to this – but *The Glen is Mine* stands in no dynamic relationship to the Scots Soul and the psychological moment – it makes an excellent entertainment but sets no leaven to work in the national life. And I frankly disbelieve in its 'exquisite Celtic idiom, as pure and expressive as Synge's use of the Anglo-Irish speech,' as H.N. Brailsford calls it. Is it more than the language of the 'Celtic Twilight' Scoticised – a derivation from Ossian, Fiona Macleod and Neil Munro and various Irish writers rather than from real life or first-hand imagination?

Mr Brandane's novels resemble his plays – they are readable, and Scottish in subject and setting, but in nothing deeper, and belong, to my mind, to a great body of books of a very workmanlike kind which perish annually for lack of any deeper quality than the many excellent but yet unavailing qualities they possess.

Mr Brandane's novels are *My Lady of Aros* and *The Captain More*. Two of his plays are published in a volume issued by Messrs Constable – *The Glen is Mine* and *The Lifting* (1925).   [8.1.26]

Letters

MR GRIEVE'S CREED?

Sir, – Mr Grieve's acceptance of my statement of his position, subject to a few corrections which with a little more care I might have anticipated, encourages me to touch upon a subject which I shirked in my last letter. I am anxious to avoid giving any possible ground of offence, or stirring up the odium theologicum, *but I do not think we can reach common ground until the matter is cleared up. I therefore submit the following additions to my former statement: –*

17. The core of every sound culture is its theology, understanding by theology a comprehensive imaginative vision of the nature and meaning of the universe, resting upon our total experience, and directly applicable to the conduct of life as a whole.

18. A catholic theology is one which can form the permanent living core of a world culture, which can be modified to suit the varying psychology of peoples and ages, and which contains in itself the justification of such modifications.

19. The supreme task of the Scottish Renaissance is to achieve an appropriate modification of catholic theology.

20. The Scottish genius is eminently theological, but to reach catholicity it must enrich its imagination by closer contact with its own spiritual sources and with contemporary spiritual life.

21. To reach catholicity it is often helpful, but never necessary, and not always sufficient, to make submission to the Roman Catholic Church as it now is. – I am, etc.,

47 Brisbane Street   H. Brown
Greenock

BRAID SCOTS AND GAELIC

Sir, – 'Buchan' is evidently 'ploughing a lonely (Gaelic) furrow' in a fast-

ness of the Scot's mither-tongue in its most vigorous form. He is good enough to admit that Scots is helping us to think nationally, but he claims that Gaelic has even superior merits in this aspect. I cannot follow this latter contention, but I agree with the first, and go much farther.

The parent of Braid Scots was the Anglian and Jutish dialect of Primitive Norse. Professor Bugge's monumental work on the earliest Runic inscriptions, read in conjunction with the oldest Northumbrian memorials, makes the connection quite clear. This idiom has been displacing Gaelic in Scotland since the eighth century or before, and has profoundly affected our Scottish psychology. Language and national character act and react upon each other. The direct and virile Germanic speech united with the racial blending to change the mode of thought – to infuse more of action and achievement into the Celtic contemplation and dreaminess. The Celtic tongues have always been misty and elusive, while the Germanic languages combine a rich under-current of poetry with lucidity of expression, rigid word-economy, and pitiless common sense.

Scots is not an offshoot of the Saxon pre-Conquest English, but an allied idiom that had its oral literature – the song and story of the camp-fire – long before it was implanted upon our eastern shores. It super-seded the Celtic speech of the Picts and Scots, founding a composite national mentality through the unceasing interaction of character and its verbal expression.

From the anthropological comparisons made by Sir Arthur Keith, Retzius, and others, as cited by your correspondent. Mr Tait, it would appear that the superimposition of Germanic tongue upon Celtic race or speech dates from before the dawn of history. In any case, the physical correspondences of Scot and Scandinavian are remarkable. In language, the original seed of primitive Norse – not far removed from Common Germanic – was reinforced, in the north and east of Scotland, by the distinctive newer Norse of the Viking Age. The Northern occupation and raids need not be here discussed; they are mentioned merely as an important source of enrichment of the Scottish language.

Our tongue is now popularly confused with 'English' or 'English dialect.' This is the natural result of the unpatriotic and snobbish attacks that have been launched upon it for centuries past. Masses of our compatriots are abandoning their sense of nationality, and substituting an apish Anglicism or a vague enthusiasm for something called 'Empire' – really a League of British Nations. These States will take care of themselves, but Scots must see to Scotland, or her very name will die.

Our tongue has languished, too, from lack of literature in the pure medium. The spoken forms have become corrupted or unetymological in mutually intolerant areas. But the experience of Norway, Friesland, the Faroe Islands, shows that united and patriotic effort will do wonders in the regeneration of neglected idioms. In my humble opinion, all our local forms are equally sacred, and their literary furbishers should command the delighted attention of lovers of the tongue owre Braid Scotland. But what do we see? Mostly petty squabbling. A production is not Scots because some district cannot easily read it, or because it does not sufficiently conform to the habit of 'mealin' in English words.

I do not decry the Gaelic or the Highlanders. Some Gaelic counties have added much to the lustre of our annals. But the clansmen have a habit of confusing national and tribal issues. May we hope that they will accept the offered hands of their non-Gaelic brothers, so that we may close our ranks and work together for Gaelic, Braid Scots and other national ideals? 'Scotland owre a'!'

Scotland, as a nation, will never re-adopt the Gaelic language and mode of thought, but if the outlook be national, there should be complete reciprocity in the promotion of Doric and Gaelic.

Although no novice in languages, I do not try to waste your space by answering 'Buchan's' strictures on the Doric, or pointing out some elementary drawbacks of the Gaelic, as admitted by Highland grammarians. Unity should generate tolerance.

Buchan has not spoken Gaelic since the days of the Book of Deer. Your correspondent, therefore, must be nearly as lonely as I am in this English village. I think I know who he is, but venture to hope that our mutually helpful propaganda would benefit if he would discard his nom de plume. – I am. etc..

Potters Bar

R.L. Cassie
[8.1.26]

Letters

THE 'NORDIC' ORIGIN OF SCOTS
Sir, – I had meant to reply to Mr Tait's letter before now, but the holidays and one thing and another conspired to defeat that good resolution. However, late is sometimes better than never. Mr Tait should read a

good paper in the Forum *by Professor Boas, of Columbia University, U.S.A. It is entitled 'This Nordic Nonsense,' and is very entertaining reading from my point of view, though hardly so I fear from that of Mr Tait and his prophet, Sir Arthur Keith. I note that Mr Tait cultivates a sense of humour. He says I 'become positively comic' when I 'dethrone Sir Arthur Keith' and 'set up Sir Leo Chiozza-Money' in his room. But if Mr Tait will have the goodness to refer to my letter he will find that I referred to Sir Leo Chiozza Money, not as an authority, but as one quoting those who, on this matter, have it. Consequently, Mr Tait's sense of humour is here misapplied. He has made his joke, but alas! it has no point. As for Sir Arthur Keith, touching whom Mr Tait is so touchingly solicitous – and credulous – I repeat what I said before about him, namely, that he is doubtless a light unto the Gentiles in his own particular line, but, judged as ethnologist, well – almost am I persuaded to prefer Mr Tait.*

Mr Tait alleges – through someone else – that the skulls of Highlanders cannot be distinguished from those of Swedes. Doubtless both are round, like the swede of the vegetable kingdom; but if Mr Tait and his 'great Retzius' – scarcely an up-to-date authority on craniological matters by the way – mean to affirm that all Highland and all Swedish skulls are alike, I fear that the only just reply to that assertion is that both are talking nonsense. Doubtless, there are Scots and Scandinavian skulls which are alike. Having regard to Norse invasions of Scotland, and settlements therein well within historic times, it would be surprising indeed if the resemblances I speak of did not exist. But though they exist they do not exist in sufficient number to justify Retzius or anyone else in affirming that there is no ethnic difference between the average Scot and the average Scandinavian.

Finally, Mr Tait calls to his aid Professor Robert Reid, whose book however he acknowledges not to have read. To be equally candid neither have I read it; but if the conclusion to which the author comes in it is to the effect ascribed to him by Mr Tait on report or hearsay, in that event I can but say, in conclusion, that I fear that Professor Robert Reid has written to singularly little purpose. Possibly he, too, is a disciple of that very shaky ethnologist, Sir Arthur Keith. – I am, etc.,

January 4, 1926   Buchan

A CELT'S PROTEST

Sir, – I think it is about time that a mere Celt, with a name as 'tartan' as mine, entered a protest against the gross libels on his people and their

literature which have of late appeared in your correspondence columns. H. Brown, who is assisting Mr C.M. Grieve to decide how future literary geniuses must think, feel and write, alleged recently that the Teutons had 'tougher' minds than the Celts. I don't pretend to know what a 'tough mind' is, but I hope it has no connection with what my old schoolmaster used to call a 'wooden head'. Perhaps, however, H. Brown wanted to flatter the non-Celts. Now, R.L. Cassie (his surname sounds as Celtic as the one translated 'Brown') grows lyrical over 'the direct and virile Germanic speech,' which helps 'to infuse more of action and achievement into the Celtic contemplation and dreaminess.' He goes on to allege that 'the Celtic tongues have always been misty and elusive, while the Germanic languages combine a rich under-current of poetry with lucidity of expression, rigid word-economy, and pitiless common sense.' Evidently Mr Cassie is still living in the world of Freeman and Green.

A very typical Anglo-Teutonic poem is Beowulf. *When the old warrior of that name is about to die he delivers an appropriate oration which reveals the stage of civilisation reached by the Teutons who invaded England. Lines 2,735 – 2,740 of the poem read: –*

> *In my own home I (Beowulf) awaited what the times destined for me, kept my own well, did not pick treacherous quarrels, nor have I sworn unjustly any oaths. In all this may 1, sick with deadly wounds, have solace;* because the Governor of men may never charge me with the murder of kinsfolk, *when my life parts from my body.*

Here we have 'lucidity of expression,' indeed. But what about the Teutonic ethical standard? The warrior boasts that he has never murdered his relations, and consequently regards himself safe with his God. Alas! poor Beowulf.

The 'noble' Teuton acquired a nobler outlook on life, however, after King Oswald learned Gaelic during his sojourn in Scotland (as Bede informs us), and became a convert to Christianity. On regaining his Anglian kingdom, Oswald sent to the Scottish Church for a Bishop, because 'he desired,' Bede explains, 'that the whole nation over which he began to rule should be imbued with the grace of Christian faith.' Bede and others tell that when Bishop Aidan preached to the Angles in Gaelic, King Oswald translated his sermons. Other missionaries from Scotland followed Aidan and the famous monastery of Lindisfarne was founded. Evidently the Celtic tongue, in which the message of Christianity was delivered, was neither 'misty' nor 'elusive'. The Angles were rescued from Paganism and a low code of morals.

When the Celts raided Rome and 'held up' the citadel garrison, their language was not in the least 'misty.' They made themselves perfectly well understood, and they set an example to their descendants (not forgotten in the Scottish Education Department in our own day) of making a collection of valuable Roman coins. The Celts in Italy, who terrorised the Romans for a few centuries, those who fought for Carthage, for Pyrrhus, etc., those who plundered Delphi, those who held a great part of Europe and part of Asia Minor in tribute (as a Greek writer reminds us), those who fought against Caesar in Gaul, and those of ancient Britain, from whom so many of us are descended, had never any difficulty in making themselves understood, and they were fairly 'tough.' According to Julius Caesar, the Gaulish Celts were much more cultured and had a higher standard of living than the Germans. The Celts are quite respectable in history.

Celtic literature is not 'misty,' and it is certainly not 'elusive' and it is less 'dreamy' than many suppose. The old Gaelic bards dearly loved a satire – one that (as they said) 'raised blisters,' and many modern Highlanders are very satirical fellows and are not lacking in 'pitiless common sense.' One of the literary needs of our time is, I think, a little satire in the typical Gaelic manner.

Celtic literature is also very dramatic. Diodorus Siculus, quoting Poseidonius of Apamea, who visited certain Celtic areas, tells us of the Celts that 'their appearance is awe-inspiring; their voices are deep and very gruff... Their speech is threatening, strained and dramatic. They are nevertheless acute-minded and apt in receiving instruction.' Evidently Celtic literature reflects the Celtic character.

It was a Celt who acted as tutor to Julius Caesar and taught him much, including Greek, which resembles the Celtic languages in several respects. The Celts were not all soldiers.

As for the mental equipment and practical tendencies of modern Celts, I need say little. A few names from my own native county (all of Black Isle stock or birth) may, however, convey much to my readers. These are Hugh Miller and Sir Roderick Murchison, the geologists; Sir Hector Macdonald, the military genius; Sir George Mackenzie, the statesman; Sir Thomas Urquhart, the great translator; and Alexander Mackenzie, the renowned explorer, whose surname is printed across a large area in Northern Canada. They were all able and resolute Celts and not dreamers of misty dreams with minds in a complicated state like Fiona Macleod's curious folk.

During the late war many Highlanders proved that they had inherited the valour and dourness of their Caledonian and Gaulish ancestors. My mother's clan, The Mackays (known to Caesar as the Aedui in Gaul) showed up well among other Celts.

The Celts of Scotland are neither weak-kneed nor weak-minded, and their literature reflects their innate characteristics – their modes of thought based on their modes of life. If Teutonised dreamers like H. Brown and R.L. Cassie would only read some translations of genuine Gaelic literature, they would be less inclined to write about a large section of the inhabitants of Scotland with as little knowledge as if they were dealing with the inhabitants of China or Timbuctoo.

It is, many feel, about time that the German propaganda, which was intended to prepare Europe for a brutal war and the ascendancy of the 'blonde beast,' was stamped out of existence. All our national virtues were for long proclaimed by Germanised writers as 'Teutonic': all our failings were alleged to be 'Celtic.' Dribbles of Teutonic intruders were supposed to have transformed us body and soul, although, as I have shown, the 'Father of English history' tells a very different story. A change of language does not necessarily transform a Celt into a Teuton, or a Red Indian into an Englishman.

The nineteenth century nonsense about the 'Celtic temperament,' the 'Celtic gloom' and 'Celtic dreamers' should be flung into the nearest ash-bin with other rubbish.

In many of our Scottish schools young Highlanders have been taught to be ashamed of their ancestors. I was ashamed of mine until I learned something about them, including those who supplied large ships in the thirteenth century for the French and the Normanised Lowlanders. As a result of my forty years' residence in the North and West Highlands, which has enabled me to write of Highland Celts with some knowledge, I have studied Celtic history and Celtic literature, and now I am extremely proud of my ancestors. But if they resembled the Fiona Macleod folk and the 'Celtic' folk imagined by Matthew Arnold and others whose writings reek of racial effrontery, I should have changed my name and adopted that of a French lady in my family tree, or else emigrated and pretended to be what a young anthropologist, who met me in Manchester, once alleged I was – a 'typical Englishman.' One cannot help shrinking from acknowledgement of any kinship with the 'typical Celt' created in the imaginations of certain pseudo-Teutons who have dreamed very misty dreams indeed. – I am, etc.,

Donald A. Mackenzie
[15.1.26]

27. Other Dramatists

Mistaken – fundamentally mistaken – as I believe the policy of the Scottish National Players to be, it must not be assumed that I question the integrity, the genuine enthusiasm, and the patient courage of some of the promoters of the movement. For Mr D. Glen Mackemmie, the Chairman of the Scottish National Theatre Society, at any rate, I have the highest respect. He has done splendid service in this and other directions in relation to Scottish national effort over a long period of years, and has never had anything like the backing and recognition he should have had. Although the claims that have been made in certain quarters for the Scottish National Players (including the claim embodied in the name) are hopelessly unwarranted, what they have done has, in contrast with the bulk of the other dramatic fare on offer in Scotland, deserved, for its own sake apart from its nationalistic appeal altogether, ten times the support it has received; and if the title assumed is exceedingly hyperbolical it must, at any rate, be conceded that there is no other combination that has anything approaching the same claim to it on actual performance – yet. At the very lowest estimate the Scottish National Players' enterprise may transpire to have initiated in regard to Scottish Drama those indirections by which directions may ultimately be discovered. Their work will have its alterative value for more radical experimenters. From this point of view, if from no other, it may be wished that a greater measure of achievement and popular attention had attended these efforts, and that a more substantial repertory had accrued to their credit. As matters are, however, they have scarcely provided an effective point of departure for their successors. In almost every respect, they afford negative rather than positive grounds for difference. Possibly, after all, the greatest service they have done is simply to have given currency to the words 'Scottish National Drama' – a service not altogether set off by what they have provided in name thereof.

Nothing need be said of any of the players themselves. The measure of their achievement – or lack of achievement – is that none of them has become a name outside a very small circle. To Scotland as a whole – to furth of Scotland still less – has any of them become what the brothers Fay and others quickly became for the Abbey Theatre. The Scottish National Players remain an anonymous body. No histrionic any more than any dramatic genius has emerged. Nor has any recognisably distinctive Scottish school or mode of acting been built up.

'Spectator' in a recent *Irish Statesman* recalls

> a conversation I had recently with a youthful friend who was sternly critical of the manifold imperfections of Irish drama. I forget what particular brand of expressionism he favoured, but to clear the way for it he made plain to me, in the wholesome fashion adopted by youth for the chastening of middle age, that the gods of my dramatic idolatory were fit only for the scrap-heap. Synge was too obvious and Yeats too remote, and while he grudgingly admitted that Lennox Robinson and Sean O'Casey knew something about the theatre, he had no hope that they would lead us into the promised land. In despair I urged that if the Abbey playwrights were not so good as they ought to be they were at least an improvement on what had gone before. 'Isn't it something,' I pleaded, 'to have delivered us from the stage Irishman?' He looked at me with a puzzled air. 'What was the stage Irishman?' he asked. If the coming-of-age performances included a specimen of the sort of drama the Abbey superseded I think critics of the theatre would see in truer perspective the reality of the revolution effected by the Irish dramatic movement.

May be! But nothing of the kind can be urged yet in favour of the Scottish National Players. They have not delivered us from the stage Scotsman. They have only subtilised him a little, and made him thereby the more difficult to get rid of.

Apart from Brandane and Malloch no other playwright claims any attention, but several plays do. I am not to concede here that any writer who writes a play or two plays – even if they are very good plays – becomes *ipso facto* a dramatist. On the contrary. The production of one or two plays, however good in themselves, may prove precisely that their writer is not a dramatist. Malloch and Brandane have both a sufficient number of plays to their credit to entitle them to be regarded as contemporary Scottish dramatists: but each of them has done far less in this direction than a writer requires to do in most countries before his pretensions can hope to secure serious consideration. The comparatively little they have done, all on a minor scale at that, is in itself a proof of the meagreness of their inspiration: and in respect of quality nothing either of them have done would lift them above a densely populated ruck of playwrights in any other civilised country. In Scotland, however, they stand out as positive phenomena. Graver even than their deficiencies in quantity and quality is the fact that their plays are of kinds in which sheaves of better plays have been done almost everywhere else, and that fundamentally there is little that is distinctively Scottish in them. Nor do they – Brandane's at any rate; Malloch is a little better in this respect in *The House of the Queen* and *Soutarness Water* – represent any real effort to deal with the basic difficulties of establishing a distinctive and dynamic Scots drama. Having thus 'scaled down' Brandane and Malloch to their real proportions, and found them of exceedingly puny stature, our other dramatists, proportionately reduced, become scarcely discernible.

J.A. Ferguson is the author of three plays: and on the basis I have been indicating that makes him, other things being equal, entitled to be accredited with rather less than half the stature of Brandane or Malloch. Other things, however, are not quite equal. Both Brandane and Malloch have quite a tale of work to their credit on a higher plane (in like categories) than Ferguson's *The King of Morven* and *The Scarecrow*. But *Campbell of Kilmohr* (produced in the spring of 1914) is, in its way, as good as anything either Brandane or Malloch have produced. No anthology of the Best Contemporary Scottish Plays could omit it – any more than they could omit Naomi Jacob's 'The Dawn.' But Naomi Jacob is even less of a dramatist than Ferguson. George Blake's *The Mother* would be included in that volume, too, but what else? Robert Bain's *James I* (which William Power has well said is next to John Davidson's *Bruce* – which ought to be revived – our best historical play) and the same author's *Punch Counts Ten* and G.W. Shirley's *The '45; Prince Charlie at Dumfries*. These six, with perhaps three each by Malloch and Brandane, would produce a volume which compared with a similar volume of the twelve best plays by contemporary authors of any other European country would be – just presentable and no more, excusable on the ground that the evolution of a Scots National Drama is just commencing, and that there are still many factors to stunt and delimit and emasculate it which have to be contended against in no other country. These twelve just emerge into the region of what can be admitted as nationally representative – as slightly better than nothing – and as internationally presentable in company where Scotland's special lets and hindrances are understood and due allowances are made. Either as nationally representative or internationally presentable, all the other plays that have been written during this first quarter of the twentieth century are negligible. At the same time, I may hazard the view that the source of the next advance towards Scots Drama will be from the growing mass of village dramas which are being produced – crude, unsatisfactory as yet but racy of the soil – from these, and from the sort of thing, a medley of fantasy and realism, Mr Bain has initiated in *Punch Counts Ten*, rather than from any of the others.

Of Mr Shirley's play – and here again a fertile and promising vista is disclosed – the *Glasgow Herald* justly said:

> Perhaps the greatest interest of the play is to be found in the successful use which the author makes of the old vernacular, in which he has chosen to develop his theme. The problem of appropriate speech is one of the oldest difficulties of the writer of historical drama. Where the claims of complete realism demand the employment of words and forms of speech which have gone out of general use, the solution of the problem must always be a compromise in a work designed for effective stage production. Mr Shirley has not permitted himself so much licence in that respect as has been generally allowed dramatic writers, but his solution is still a compromise. He uses a form of Scots sufficiently old to help him to secure his atmosphere, but not so antique that it cannot be readily understood by most of his present-day townsmen at least, although a few words and phrases may have escaped some of the audience at the first performance of the work. Any loss of dramatic effectiveness which was thus caused is, however, counterbalanced by the value which his work may have in the stimulation of the movement for the study of the Scottish vernacular, of which the drama can be a potent instrument.

The importance of this language issue cannot, in fact, be over-emphasised. No doubt Mr Shirley had many wise counsellors who advised him to tone down, or eliminate, his archaisms. Probably he had difficulty with some of the members of the Dumfries Guild who produced it. But he was well advised to stick to his guns and, in so doing, he may well, unobtrusively but yet effectively, have helped to mark a very necessary turning-point in the movement towards a Scots drama – a turning-point which I hope the announcement of the Scottish National Players that they are shortly to produce Malloch's *Soutarness Water* – its writer's finest play and his first in Braid Scots (is there no relation between these facts?) – means has now been definitely taken.

In another respect the production of *Soutarness Water* may mark an important turning-point in the development of the movement – a break with the stultifying respectability that has hitherto characterised it. The Play-Reading and Selecting Committee have obviously been in the throes of a crisis in connection with it. But the right side has triumphed. From what I know of the composition of the Committee in question I am frankly surprised. In this connection, Gordon Bottomley says:

> There is no doubt about this play. It is probably the most important and significant thing that has happened in Scottish literature since *The House with the Green Shutters*, and it is much better than that because its intention is less predominantly sensational. It is an admirable work by a man who is going to count. I believe that the Scottish National Theatre Society cannot turn such a play down without discrediting itself in the eyes of the future and disqualifying itself in the eyes of those Scotsmen in whom its deepest hope lies at present.

Mr William Power also says that it is

> in all respects one of the most powerful dialect plays I have ever read... If the Scottish National Players cannot present this play, it were better that they should disband forthwith; and a Society that can be kept together only by the support of the kind of people who object to this play is of no conceivable service to Scottish drama.

There is no need to make such a mountain of such a molehill. The play is not a great one – except in relation to the present state of Scottish drama. It would not deserve a couple of lines in Huntley Carter's great survey of the Contemporary European Theatre. But the rout of its moralitarian opponents, and the decision to produce it, are welcome and unlooked-for signs of vigour. The Scottish National Players may yet find themselves. This is practically a first step in the right direction – and one that helps to counterbalance so far as Glasgow is concerned the recent stupid banning of *Theism and Atheism* from the public libraries.

I do not like Mr Power's commendation of *Soutarness Water*, however, on the grounds that 'the language is direct and picturesque – there is no padding.' That is precisely what is wrong with it from the point of view of the possible new kind of drama which shall address itself to Scots psychology. In this connection straight technique will not help. Chekhov is the dramatist who should be studied. He has more than any other to teach the true Scots playwright. His indirect method – his oblique dialogue – his use of irrelevancies consist with the complex, cautious Scots mind. The future of the Scots theatre lies in practically actionless drama, and the employment of expressionist technique to express the undemonstrative monosyllabic subtlety of the Scot.

It is to be hoped, however, that the production of *Soutarness Water* will lead to an explosion of opinion. It will help to clear the air. It will force the leaders of the movement into the open in a decisive national way, and put an end to 'hole-and-corner methods' and the tendency to remain a species of Tooley Street Tailor which has hitherto characterised them. It is time those of them who have any weight were making it felt against real odds.

A Braid Scots dramatist of promise is Alexander MacGill, whose *Pardon in the Morning* has been produced by the Lennox Players and whose *Tribute* shortly will be. Both of these are in the Renfrewshire dialect. Neither deserve inclusion in the anthology of which I have spoken: but they are both sufficiently good – sufficiently above the great mass of Braid Scots plays which have been written in recent years – to justify the hope that here we have developing a dramatist in Scots who will come to bulk largely in any view of our subject in this second quarter of the century.

MacGill's *Pardon in the Morning* appeared in *The Northern Review* (June-July, 1924) and Naomi Jacob's *The Dawn* in *The Northern Review* (August, 1924). Miss Irene F.M. Dean contributed an informative article on 'J.A. Ferguson: Dramatist and Novelist' to *The Scottish Educational Journal* (September 4, 1925), and Dr G.P. Insh had an article on Robert Bain in the same journal on July 10, 1925.   [22.1.26]

Letters

TOUJOURS GRIEVE

> (*Paraphrase from the French of Fabien Pillet.*)

> 'Wee dramatist,' Grieve calls me,
> But there's nothing there that galls me;
> For while I await
> Till someone state
> If he really is as tall's me,
> Him by his rancour I estimate
> And his stature then appals me.

> John Brandane.

A CELT'S PROTEST

Sir, – I regret having aroused the ire of your esteemed correspondent, Mr Donald A. Mackenzie. I made no aspersions upon Celts. Nothing in *my letter conveys the impression that they are 'weak-kneed' or 'weak-minded'. I distinctly stated that 'some Gaelic counties have added much to the lustre of our annals,' and I fully endorse Mr Mackenzie's remark that their literature reflects their modes of life and thought.*

Of course, it is common knowledge that their early acceptance of Christianity gave them a great cultural advantage over the heathen Germanic tribes. So far, we are on common ground.

But I must adhere to my view regarding the qualities of the Celtic languages. Apart from the fact that they have been receding for many centuries before adaptable and progressive European idioms, my personal study of Gaelic encounters phonetic and grammatical peculiarities that seem to cloud the thought, and completely differentiate it from the mental processes common to the great majority of Scots. Aspiration, the harmony of broad and narrow vowels, and the combinations of silent and sometimes sounded letters, set up bristling ramparts of initial difficulty before the learner. Then we have false analogies sanctioned by usage, the tendency to vary the spelling of silent or decayed consonants and excessive synthesis or close composition, making the elements difficult to recognise. These are only a few of the initial hindrances to the acquisition of the tongue.

In my opinion, however, the chief drawback is the arrangement of words – the basis of the mode of thought – which differs fundamentally from other European tongues of wide currency. The absence of the verb 'to have' compels a radical change in the formulation of simple ideas. I may perhaps quote an example or two.

> *Thuit mac an tàilleir bhig.*
> *(Fell son of the tailor little.)*
> *Has the boy not a knife?*
> *(Is [a] knife not at the boy?)*

Most of these difficulties are fully admitted by the enlightened and broad-minded author of Scottish Gaelic, *issued by* An Comunn Gaidhealach.

These facts, in themselves, warrant me in calling the tongue misty and elusive, although its beauties do grow upon one in the course of study. After having devoted a great part of life to dabbling in other tongues, I make little headway with Gaelic in my declining years.

I understand, however, that many fluent speakers are unable to write the language correctly. There is much newspaper controversy about forms and derivations, and there seems to be a standing difficulty in maintaining the needed supply of efficient Gaelic teachers for Highland schools. Do not these facts bear out the contentions of my previous letter?

I have referred to Beowulf for the translated lines that Mr Mackenzie quotes. The expression 'morthorbeals maga' (archaic sign for th transliterated) would not, in my opinion, refer to the killing of near relatives. As Mr Mackenzie knows, the tribe (mægth) was a Germanic parallel of the earliest known Celtic clan or petty state. This is evidenced by the names, 'Scylfingas,' etc. The appellation of the chief or founder of a ruling line was often extended to include his people. I think Mr Mackenzie will agree that Celt and Teuton of the Beowulf epoch were alike compelled to rely upon the arbitrament of the sword in the struggle for life. Quarrels and 'murders,' even among kinsfolk, were merely normal incidents of those fierce days.

Mr Mackenzie hints that I must be steeped in English influences. Although I cannot accept extreme Celticism as synonymous with Scotland, I am a Scotsman first, last, and always. I believe in Scottish unity as the first step toward Scottish freedom – our emancipation from the very English influences of which I am suspected. That unity will not be found either in undiluted Celticism or Lowlandism, but in the mutual aid and toleration of Gaelic and non-Gaelic-speaking Scots.

I may be allowed to state that I am of Highland descent on both sides. The earliest record of my name yet traced is of Aberdeen, in 1478. One of my tribesmen, Andrew Cassie of Kirkhouse, Traquair, fought for the Chevalier in 1715, and his son or grandson for Prince Charlie. My mother's family, the Lawsons of Speyside, were Gaelic speakers, though probably of Norse descent. Like Mr Mackenzie, I am very proud of my ancestors.

I cannot abandon my view as to the role played by the Germanic blend of language in moulding the mentality of its users in Scotland. This fact cannot be dissociated from the preference of the Gaelic Celts for English as a medium of public expression, 'Fat ails them at Braid Scots?' The action and interaction of language and national character is apparent in every civilised country of the world to-day.

It is my earnest hope that Highlander and Lowlander, while cherishing and cultivating their special ideals, will loyally help each other, and work earnestly together for the welfare of the Scottish nation. – I am, etc.,

R.L. Cassie

Sir, – I do not seem to have made it clear to Mr Mackenzie that the statements in my recent letters are not intended to express my own opinions,

*but what I take to be those of Mr Grieve. Before making up my own
mind, I am doing my best to follow his.*

*But, in any case, I do not think that my remark about the 'hypersensi-
tive Celtic spirit' and the 'tougher-minded races' contains any real
ground for offence. Certainly none was intended by me. In spite of my
surname, I am at least three parts Celt myself, and if Mr Mackenzie can
show that the Celtic spirit contains within itself a perfect balance of all
possible excellencies, I shall be only too pleased. But if each race has its
own glory, it is no disparagement of one to deny to it the peculiar glory
of another. If, then, I say the Celtic genius is unusually rich in fire and
air, and consequently to that extent deficient in the earthly element. my
statement may be untrue, but I do not think it is insulting, at least to the
Celt.*

*I am sorry that my clumsiness of expression, in which of course Mr
Grieve has no share, though he has adopted the general sense of my
statement, should have given annoyance to Mr Mackenzie or any other
Celt. – I am, etc..*

H. Brown
[22.1.26]

Letters

CONTEMPORARY SCOTTISH STUDIES
*Sir, – I assent to Mr Brown's additional propositions, but with the rider
that he may find it ungrateful work – in the long run sharpening other
people's conclusions. The first requirement of logic has been disregarded
– there has been no definition of terms. What he means by 'culture,' etc.,
may be quite other than what I mean. It is impossible for me to explicate
more precisely here many of the issues I have touched upon in my articles; or the more or less related issues raised by Mr Brown and other
correspondents. I am not avoiding any controversy, but cannot expect to
be permitted to monopolise more of your space than is already allotted to
me. But Mr Brown – and possibly others – may be interested to know
that I deal pretty comprehensively with the political and religious implications of a Scottish Renaissance in* The Irish Statesman *of 16th inst.
That article will form the first chapter of a short book descriptive of the
tendencies-in-play in Scotland to-day and the pre-requisites of a distinctive Scottish culture of international moment. The volume will probably*

appear in the autumn. [1] *Elsewhere I hope to deal comprehensively at an early date with the political, economic and social conditions of Scotland to-day from a Separatist standpoint.*

Mr Brandane's doggerel shows him to be even smaller in another respect than I rate him as a dramatist. I am sorry he has committed himself to 'grieve toujours.' His momentary chagrin was perhaps natural but unfortunate. He knows perfectly well that I wrote without rancour and I defy him or anyone else to point to anything of a rancorous character in my article. To differ, however trenchantly, from his own estimate of his achievements as a playwright – and the estimates of certain other critics – implies nothing of the kind. My stature, relatively to his, is irrelevant to the matter: but Mr Brandane himself, in a saner moment, has, I am glad to say, expressed his warm appreciation of (what he was pleased to call) the 'Left Wing's' propaganda and products; and I still retain a forlorn hope that that was not conditioned by an undue assumption of reciprocity.

Mr Wm. Cumming can accept my article 'Swatches o' Hamespun' in lieu of any other reply to his letter. – I am, etc..

C.M. Grieve.

JOHN DAVIDSON'S 'BRUCE' AND MR C.M. GRIEVE
Sir, – It may be hoped that Mr C.M. Grieve's wish that the Scottish National Players should tackle the production of this great Scottish Drama will not fall on deaf ears. It is a work of noble beauty and splendid in poetry and, like the rest of its maker's work, has not had the honour due in its own country. Indeed, one who is puzzled only by the meagreness of praise that Mr Grieve will allow to any product of the creative Scottish mind is wholly with him in the desire to revive interest in the best masculine work of the past and to have it appraised on high aesthetic grounds, as the best way to release the shackled potencies of the present and to beget a virile Scottish renascence. I know nothing of the councils of the National Players, and can only speculate – a trifle sceptically – as to what Mr Grieve means by a triumphant rout of moralitarians in the production of Soutarness Water. *But such a play as that, and such work as Davidson's, appear to myself as things of a burning moral loveliness even if I hold very strongly to other conclusions concerning truth than the passionate self-styled materialism of the latter. Some of us do agree with Mr Grieve that, for us, Truth appeals from the aesthetic*

---

[1] This book was never published. – Ed.

side far more divinely than from the ethical (the conventionally ethical, anyhow) – but surely there can be no dichotomy in either Truth or Beauty, and in the end of the day there will be overwhelming conviction surely that what is ethically fair and aesthetically true are wholly and sublimely one. Anger at morality or at any of the supposedly mistaken manners of its effort to find its true self – seems to me to be a needless surrender on the part of those who seek truth in the holy, haughty and equally errant spirit of the aesthete. Nothing but the positive, constructive contribution of each school can evolve light and fire.

Synge's dictum that art must become 'brutal' again before it can become great is a truth that is dangerous to the literal-minded. Neither his own work, nor Davidson's – though proudly violent – argues that truculence, however sincere and convinced, is necessary or sufficient. Beauty is not to be restricted by any dictator and will appear in barbaric dress or cramasie and hodden-grey or in more delicate fabric as she wills – hence the pettiness of decrying, e.g., Barrie to glorify Synge or Davidson, and the sheer petulant folly of any critic laying down any law for her rebirth in Scotland or elsewhere. Chekhov is no doubt very great and cleansing – but there are others, quite different, equally stimulant (to vary the figure); and I am disposed – with all admiration – to cavil at Mr Grieve's attempted limitation of the Spirit of Beauty in the movement he contemplates, as it is revealed in his reiterated insistence on the element of violence as necessarily predominant everywhere in the art of the new age, e.g. his praises of The House with the Green Shutters, or of the songs of Burns (set so thrillingly by Francis George Scott) which affect or avow a callousness concerning certain domestic arrangements, are undoubtedly parts of a salutary reaction in the imperious service of creative art: but a reaction is not a renascence, and I see little hope of renascence if its leaders, inspirers and champions are to plume themselves on anti-moralitarianism, or confine their recognitions to art that – instead of claiming a freedom wider than the universe – confines itself to a specialism of this sort. There is not a single major poet or creative artist who could ever have been predicted from aught that went before him – that is why each in turn dazzles us with wonderland seems for a little to have rung the last possible changes on the bells of beauty, till another rises, a de la Mare after a Yeats and so on – or who could have been produced or synthesised by any school or rule. And one's furious enjoyment of Mr Grieve's articles is not to induce submission to his admirable browbeating, however wide his reading and superior his intelligence, concerning a fundamental like that.

Davidson's Bruce (for attention to which we both plead) has not much of the quality which seems to be perilously near to an obsession with Mr Grieve – not nearly so much as his Testaments; but it is neither because of that, nor in spite of that, that it is worthy of honour. At all events. I – who do not care tuppence for the criticism that sees glory in any smack of rebellion and in little else. and whose view of the universe is certainly vastly different (even apart from our difference of endowment) from Davidson's – still find on well-nigh every page of that poet a majestic blaze of spiritual beauty, that is in the last analysis no more defiant than Job or Calvary itself, but pregnant with theology and morality and tragedy alike from beginning to end; and for Art, and the renascence of Art, that passion transcends any poor view, or difference, of conclusions as to doctrine or convention – but it also pours contempt on the pride that chortles over a rout of moralitarians in the production of a work of Art! I do not write, let me remark, as a moralitarian, Lord knows. – I am etc..

W.H. Hamilton
[29.1.26]

28. 'Swatches o' Hamespun'

Observing that the present century has witnessed a remarkable revival of interest in the Scots Vernacular, which has taken several forms, lexical, dramatic, and poetic, a writer on the subject of 'A Scottish Renaissance' in *The Times Literary Supplement* (January 7, 1926) rightly points out that there is nothing to prevent the successful revival of Scots as a general literary instrument, given a sufficiently strong nationalistic impulse. But that is the great *sine qua non.* Unfortunately the great majority of those who are concerned in the movement to revive Braid Scots have not come to understand this: and those who endeavour to point it out to them are accused of mixing up politics and letters.

> In our own time, [says the writer in question], Norse, Frisian, Afrikaans, not to speak of Welsh and Erse, have shown what a few resolutes can accomplish when carried forward on a strong wave of national or local sentiment. But such a wave there must be. The literary severance of Norway from Denmark was due to the same forces that presently brought about its political separation from

Sweden. Without such forces – and there is little sign of them in Scotland – the aspiration after a *general* revival of literary Scots will remain a dream.

I do not agree with him that there is little sign of the generation of such forces in Scotland to-day. I believe, on the contrary, that saltatory developments are impending. But, whether or not, the fact remains that no one who is chiefly concerned with the problems of transcending the present limitations of distinctively Scottish letters – no one who is unwilling to see Scottish genius permanently subordinated to English, and Scottish psychology prevented from expressing itself save indirectly through an alien medium arbitrarily interposed between it and the world – can remain indifferent to the political implications of any movement worthy of the name, to revive Braid Scots. A Vernacular revivalist who is not also a Scottish separatist is a contradiction in terms. But the fact remains that the majority of our self-styled Vernacular revivalists have failed to think out the prerequisites to the success of the movement which they think they are promoting by their negligible sentimentalisms, and they are actually in the anomalous position of paying lip-service to the 'mither-tongue' at the very same time that they are stereotyping the conditions which have led to its desuetude. The same writer reveals another radical inconsistency in their position when he points out that

> Unhappily, Scots has kept humble company so long that it has not only suffered impoverishment in its vocabulary, but contracted associations too homely, too trivial, sometimes too vulgar for high poetry. If it is to be used again for that purpose, at least on a grand scale, it must break these low associations and form new. In other words, he who aspires to reform Scots poetry must first do what Spenser did for English; he must create a new poetic diction… The example of Burns does not greatly help. It is true that Burns, by reinforcing traditional Scots from his own 'hamely Westlan' dialect. did not apply it to new purposes.

He goes on to show that the only way is to, quite arbitrarily, create a synthetic Scots, founding on the traditional Lothian Scots, but admitting good Scots words from any quarter. 'This was how Aasen went about it with Norse… Obsolete words revived have at first neither meaning nor associations except for the scholar; yet if they are good words they may take root and blossom afresh; there is nothing for it but time and use.' And, in conclusion, he refers to 'the faith without which there can be no conquest: the belief that Scotland still has something to say to the imagination of mankind, something that she alone among the nations can say, and can say only in her native tongue.'

In these sentences he has penetrated to the heart of the whole issue. But the majority of our vernacular enthusiasts, especially those in the north-east corner, think otherwise. They are humble people – who have resigned themselves to the belief that only the lowliest literary rôle confronts the Doric – not too lowly, however, for such despisers of highbrowism as themselves, who, indeed, have so little interest in or knowledge of literary matters as such that, as by the hand of one of their leaders, Dr J.M. Bulloch, they have declared, their principal reason for desiring to revive the Buchan dialect as a literary medium is simply because it is only, so far as they know or wish to know, capable of being used in a fashion that is beneath criticism. They do not wish to say anything to the imagination of mankind. All that they want is a little private 'stunt' of their own, that demands nothing beyond an average hind's sensibilities, in the prosecution of which they can forget that feeling of inferiority with which they are afflicted when genuine artistic considerations are being canvassed. This is the worst form of highbrowism inverted. It is indeed worse than any form of highbrowism, for highbrowism does make certain demands on its devotees. It is natural, therefore, that the majority of Buchan vernacular enthusiasts should be successful London Scots who, under a guise of local patriotism, are glad to make a virtue of their constitutional incapacity for culture of any kind, and so, in the company of their kind, get rid of the oppressive sense of spiritual inferiority, so galling to those who have been merely commercially successful, which afflicts them in the presence of those incomprehensible people they encounter on all hands who are really artistic. The strain of living in an educated world makes them glad to relapse from time to time to the levels of the ploughman or the fishwife. The accuracy of this diagnosis will be apparent when it is remembered that the stock argument of these people is that the desuetude of the vernacular is due to 'superior people who consider it vulgar.'

Mr William Will, for example, has recently been telling the Vernacular Circle of the London Burns Club that the Doric was not dying from natural causes, but was being bludgeoned out of existence by miserable purse-proud specimens of our fellow-countrymen. I am convinced that on the contrary more harm is being done to Braid Scots by some of its supposed friends, and the poverty-stricken stuff they laud in the name of it, than by those who are openly contemptuous of it. The leaders of the London Vernacular Circle (who are wealthier than nine-tenths of the poets and prosewriters of Scotland from Dunbar to Burns inclusive put together) are doing nothing to help such efforts as are being made in various quarters to revive Braid Scots as an instrument of literary expression – least of all are they bringing any worthy sense of literary values to bear on the matter. They are not concerned with anything so un-Scottish as literary values. On the contrary they are intent upon stereotyping the very ideas and attitudes to art that have been mainly responsible for its deterioration and desuetude than about reviving the Doric *per se*. The Doric will only revive if the very opposite spirit to theirs can be brought to bear, and if it can be made a fit medium for all-round expression of the modern Scottish mind. If it cannot we must reconcile ourselves to permanent cultural subordination to England and the progressive distortion and falsification of our faculties of expression. But it unquestionably can – given the right spirit. It is absurd to try to tie down the Scottish mind at this time of day to the groove of Johnny Gibb o' Gushetneuk. If Braid Scots is to become a living thing again it must be developed to correspond to the suppressed elements of Scottish psychology in ways of which English is incapable, and not be identified exclusively with the cult of mediocrity to which Aberdonians in particular have so largely committed themselves. Any young Scot with literary powers which he wishes to dedicate to his native country can have no more disheartening experience than to come in contact with the kind of ideas on cultural matters entertained by the London Vernacular Circle and their equivalents in Scotland, and will certainly receive no encouragement from these people unless he falls in both with their petty moral prejudices and lack of interest in anything that is not of a wholly kailyaird order. From the Renaissance point of view, on the contrary, it is claimed that it is utterly wrong to make the term 'Scottish' synonymous with any fixed literary forms or to attempt to confine it to any particular creed or set of ideas – let alone to such notions as are really part and parcel of Scottish degeneration and provincialisation. That is to deny it the very characteristics of a living and sovereign thing; and yet that is what the majority of our so-called vernacular enthusiasts are doing.

The Scottish Renaissance movement, on the contrary, sets out to do all that it possibly can to increase the number of Scots who are vitally interested in literature and cultural issues; to counter those academic or merely professional tendencies which fossilise the intellectual interests of most well-educated people even; and, above all, to stimulate actual art-production to a maximum. Obviously one of the ways in which this can be done is to attack and break up the preconceptions responsible for the existing state of affairs, whatever they may be – religious, political, commercial, social or otherwise; and to those who resent our doing this in one direction or another all we say is – 'Prove to us that this or that convention or moral prejudice or political interest is of more ultimate consequence to the people than that spiritual liberation which the production and enjoyment of art involves, and we will refrain from our attack upon it.' The Renaissance demand is simply that, whatever the causes of the stunting and provincialisation of the Scottish arts may be, they must be removed, and forces must be substituted for them which will have the contrary effect of stimulating the art-producing and art-enjoying faculties of our nation to the uttermost. Scotland may be, let us concede, all that it should be morally and politically and educationally – but it is emphatically not so artistically, and it is necessary to experiment fearlessly to find out why, and apply the necessary remedy.

Carlyle said that if Burns had been a first-class intellectual workman he might have changed the whole course of British literary history. The question is whether that cannot still be done – whether it is not even necessary in the interests of English, let alone Scottish, literature. It depends upon what you think of English literature, and particularly the present position and prospects of English literature. The thing that mainly interests me is the extent, as Professor Saintsbury has pointed out, to which English has been adscripted to a certain broad attitude to things which has its own great merits, but also its own demerits, and which certainly acts as a sort of censor to prevent the successful exploitation in English letters of the particular kind of moral and psychological and aesthetic issues with which the Scottish genius is best fitted to deal, and the canvassing of which is the most significant feature of certain other literatures to-day – a feature which brings the literatures in question into much more vital alignment with the trend of science, and life, to-day than English literature is. The ambition to thus reorient English literature – to give the Scottish partner in the unequal alliance that predominance which has hitherto been the prerogative of the Southern partner – may seem to Englishmen an impertinent and unwarrantable one; but surely no Scotsmen can deny that it is infinitely more in keeping with Scottish national dignity than the cultural subservience we have hitherto shown, and generally excused on materialistic grounds – an excuse which affords singularly little satisfaction to-day when the state of our industry and commerce suggests that a reconsideration of the bargain is long overdue.

But the enthusiasts in the North-East corner will have none of this. All they want is 'Swatches o' Hamespun.' Their ideas are beyond the wildest farrago with which Mencken has ever enriched his delectable *Americana.* Here is an example – part of a protest against the attempts that have been made to bring Scotland into fresh relationships with the culture of Europe. As Professor Hugh Walker has put it:

> People who keep pigeons have discovered that from time to time they must bring eggs from a neighbouring dovecot if they wish to keep up the excellence of their birds. If pigeon fanciers are too exclusive, and refrain from all exchange of eggs, their stock will weaken and ulti- mately die out. A like fate, De Quincey thinks, awaits the literature of any country which is preserved from all foreign intercourse. He says that every literature, unless it be crossed by some other of a different breed, tends to superannuation. Writing nearly a century ago, in 1821, he asks what, with this example before our eyes the English should do, and answers, 'Evidently we should cultivate an intercourse with that literature of Europe which has most of a juvenile constitu- tion.

Sound advice – and precisely what is now being advocated and attempted in regard to Scots literature. But the North-Easterners cannot distinguish between this and imitation – as if each nation had not, as Professor J.H. Morgan puts it in his book on John Morley, 'its own *Zeitgeist* which assimilates in its own way the ideas it borrows from else- where. This "time-spirit" is forever transforming what it works upon. A people's power over an idea is limited by its own past.' Scotland's past is such that we can intromit very actively with all manner of foreign litera- tures for many decades to come without jeopardising our 'ethnic substance.' But the enthusiast to whom I have referred writes:

> *Tolstoi, Dostoyevsky, Gorki, etc., etc., are either decadent or impos- sible.* I am not speaking at hazard, and have read enough of them, in the original, to know that the Scottish national ego, new or old, is as far as the poles from them. No rapprochement is possible. There are not – and cannot be – any points of contact between Scottish and Russian cultural feeling or, rather, national soul. In spite of the abundant nonsense written every day about the Auld Alliance, etc., the Scots and French brains are as unlike as can be. The French brain works in a unique way. This is well evidenced by their *total inability to grasp* [the

italics are his own here] elementary canons of gratitude, the discharge of obligations, and other things that right-thinking nations associate with *honour*. Their literature is great in beauty, in cosmopolitan value in many directions, but the precept 'It is righteousness that exalteth a nation' will forbid Scots, I hope, from ever getting permeated with the Gallic sexual streak.

Comment is superfluous.

It is not surprising to find, in conjunction with such an attitude, the feeling that 'surely from the vernacular point of view such a line as

> For a daidlin', toitlin' sharger, an' an
> eeseless, smearless smatchet

is hard to equal.' I would fain hope that it might prove so. The same writer says (in the preface to the first series of *Swatches o' Hamespun* (1921, *Banffshire Journal Limited*) 'The subjects dealt with are homely – the dialect is not suited for the handling of subjects other than these.' English as used by chaw-bacons might be confined to like subjects and not seem suited for anything else – but it would not be the fault of English. Nor is it the fault of Scots that the New Byth people make the poverty-stricken use of it that they do. In the preface to the Third Series we are not surprised to read: 'The people who use the dialect are douce, decent folk who do not pose as humorists...' But they will not be the only people in Scotland who will fail to see the joke in these quotations!   [5.2.26]

Letters

CELT AND TEUTON
Sir, – I am afraid Mr R.L. Cassie's criticism of the Gaelic language is really based on his own difficult experiences as a student. But, surely it is unfair to find fault with Gaelic, or with any other ancient language, because it does not happen to conform with English. Why complain of the Gaelic idiom? The richer and more individual a language is, the more idiomatic it is bound to be. Why complain of the Gaelic system of spelling? Is the English system perfect? Ask any foreigner who has had to wrestle with 'cough,' 'doff,' 'enough,' 'stuff,' etc. Gaelic can be quite as clear and direct as English. Take, for instance. the opening line of a fairly old poem, 'The Desire of the Ancient Bard,' as an example:

> *O caraibh mi ri taobh nan allt.*
> *O lay me by the side of the streams.*

Here is a characteristic specimen of descriptive Gaelic from the ancient Cuchulain epic, which is older than Beowulf:

> *Not often is a warrior seen more handsome than the warrior that is in the front rank of that company. Bushy, red-yellow hair he wore; his countenance comely, ruddy, well formed; his face slender below and broad above; a deep blue-grey, beaming eye, and it flashing and laughing in his head; a well-set, shapely man, tall, slender below and broad above; red, thin lips he had; teeth shining and pearl-like; a clear ringing voice, a white-skinned body; most beautiful of the forms of men; a purple cloak wrapped around him; a brooch of gold in the mantle over his breast, a hooded tunic of royal silk, with a red hem of red gold.*

A detailed description of his weapons follows.

My readers will note how like the Gaelic style was that of Thomas Carlyle, who wrote as he talked, and talked as his ancestors did before him in Gaelic.

We find in Gaelic poetry and prose vivid word pictures, light and shadow, humour and pathos, simile and allegory, dramatic incidents and stirring, rapid narratives. Withal, there is much 'atmosphere' and colour and many flights of imagination and lyrical outbursts.

When, on the other hand, we turn to Anglo-Saxon literature we are immersed in sadness and dullness – in the gloom (miscalled 'Celtic'); and there are frequent obscurities. Worst of all, there is a shocking lack of humour. Dr Clark Hall, who cannot be accused of being pro-Celtic or anti-Teutonic, writing on Beowulf, *tells us that its particular obscurities were caused by the inability of the poet to express himself clearly at times – 'he does not always know how to say it' – and Hall notes further that in the* Beowulf *epic there is an 'entire absence of humour.' but an occasional 'grim specimen' of 'unconscious humour,' The same scholar reminds us that 'simile and allegory are foreign to the genius of Anglo-Saxon poetry,' and that Anglo-Saxon poetry is 'sad,' the 'sadness' of* Beowulf *being 'unusually prominent.' Although Mr Cassie casts doubt on the accuracy of the translation I gave in my previous letter, Dr Clark Hall, the translator, writes:*

> *We may dismiss the darker side of Beowulf's character with a very few words. In some respects it is evident that his ethical standard was*

low; he takes great credit to himself for not having sworn false oaths or murdered his relations.

Compared with Beowulf, the Gaelic heroes like Cuchulain. Ferdiad, Fergus, etc., are almost 'moderns.' They are certainly chivalrous, humorous, gallant and generous, and they do not slay their relations or make any references to broken oaths. We pass from gloom to sunshine, from a prison house to green fields, when we pass from Anglo-Saxon to Gaelic literature. In the Cuchulain epic we are in quite a Homeric atmosphere:

Then was the grave of Ferdiad dug by the Gaels and his funeral games were held.

Cuchulain and Ferdiad serve different sovereigns, and when these are at war, the warriors find themselves on opposite sides. They had in their youth attended the same 'military college' in Skye, and are sorry to find themselves chosen to fight in single combat, Cuchulain exclaims:

As my soul liveth, I would prefer to fall by the hand of that warrior than for him to fall by mine.

Then another says of Cuchulain (who slew Ferdiad in the end):

It is not fear of Ferdiad that caused his anxiety for the fight, but his love for him.

Here we have a fine dramatic situation – two former friends forced by stern duty to be enemies.

The rules of Gaelic chivalry were exacting and were invariably honoured. Treachery was unthought of. A man would rather die than break a single rule of chivalry. After the first day's combat, the warriors meet as friends. The modern boxers, similarly strict observers of 'the rules of the game,' shake hands in 'the ring.' Of Cuchulain and Ferdiad it is related:

Each of them put his hand on the other's neck and gave three kisses in remembrance of his fellowship and friendship.

It is evident that mediaeval chivalry was of Celtic origin. No trace of it is found in Teutonic literature. Nor do we find Celtic-like loyalty in Anglo-Saxon writings – the loyalty that in later days made the Highlands safe for Prince Charlie.

Mr Cassie asks, 'Fat ails them (the Gaelic Celts) at Braid Scots?' In my native place the change from Gaelic was to Braid Scots, and my first *language was really a dialect of the Doric. As a bairnie. I said my 'good wordies in my goonie.' I often read Robert Fergusson with ease and relish because so many of his old words and phrases are familiar to me. In my boyhood I also heard spoken, by a community of fisher folk, a very archaic form of Braid Scots. The 'thou' and 'thee' are in use and the 'h' and even 'wh' are dropped by these people. Here's a swatch:*

> *First boy – 'A polled thee?*
> *Second boy – Bubba.*
> *First boy – Did thoo get ony sclafards?*
> *Second boy – A feow.*

That beats 'Hugh MacDiarmid' even when he is in 'full sail.'

I have heard exasperated fisher mothers calling their daughters 'limmers,' 'smatchets,' and 'trollops,' and when I go north I remark to a fisherman that it is 'a yagach mornin!,' and he understands. A fishwife once remarked to me on a wild April day, when the sea was lashed into a fury by a gusty 'soo'-wasterly':

> *Ech, sir, 'an Gentle Hannie is skyawlan roon' the 'eel o' Ness wi' a w'ite futhur in 'er 'at, she'll be 'arryin' the crook.*

Some recent articles and letters on Braid Scots by alleged experts who are trying to acquire it, have amused me, and I leave these gentlemen to tackle my specimens of a genuine dialect still spoken in a corner of north-eastern Scotland. It has quite a rich vocabulary.

To many Gaelic Celts Braid Scots is a difficult language. But there are areas in which 'Gallickers' (as we were called) understand and speak it. I used to translate the fisher folk's Braid Scots to a Gaelic-speaking school chum who came from the landward part of the parish.

I have to thank Mr Cassie and Mr Brown for their courteous letters. but I am still prepared to fight on so as to help towards a better understanding between all sections of Scots. Let us, in fair play, get rid first of all of the caricature which has been labelled 'Celt,' and remember instead the gay lad of other days who wore bright tartan, danced the Highland fling and inspired the Lowland lassies to sing, 'A Hielan' lad my love was born' and similar ditties.

John Buchan, in a recently-published book, told us that to him a Highlander is a 'foreigner.' This surprised and shocked me greatly, especially, coming as it did, from a man who was born in Fife and reared in Glasgow, where Highlanders are not strangers or regarded as aliens. Buchan would have it that the 'brethren' of the Borderers are really the folk their ancestors referred to as 'the auld enemy.' But I refuse to take him seriously as an ethnologist or, for that matter of it, as a Border bard. He enjoys deserved popularity as a literary baker of wholesome soda scones and pan loaves, which I prefer to the poetic hard biscuits provided by Sir George Douglas.

An anti-Celtic bias is not creditable to prominent Scots and especially to Lowland Scots with Gaelic surnames. Perhaps that bias has prevented the able writers in question from producing richer and more artistic poetic cakes and pastries to adorn their literary shop windows. (It is a historical fact that before the intrusion of Angles in the Eastern Lowlands, the inhabitants were British Celts (P-Celts), and that after the expulsion of the Anglian military aristocrats the Gaelic (Q-Celtic) Scotts, Douglases, Maxwells, etc., were 'planted' there by King Malcolm as lairds, etc. These west coast Highlanders did not become Teutons because they adopted the language of their tenants who had previously adopted the language of the Anglian lairds. The new language had been fostered by commerce, which was diverted by the Anglians towards England.

Ethnologists remind us that the intrusions of minorities, especially minorities of males, never alter a race. The law of 'reversion to type' operates as a result of intermarriage, and ultimately the alien males are 'bred out.' Highland and Lowland, we are in the main 'a' Jock Tamson's bairns.' The fact that Lowland songs and ballads reveal no trace of Anglo-Saxon influence, but are very Celtic in metres and modes of thought, indicates clearly that the literary genius of the Borders has drawn some of its inspiration from the auld, auld stock whose place-names still survive, as they do also in Lochaber and Moray, in Inverness and Ross, and in Argyll and the Isles.

We have in Scotland no 'Ulster question,' and it behoves all Scots patriots to 'wage war' against the Separatist party, which has been attempting to erect an imposing artificial barrier between the Highlands and the Lowlands. The Gaelic language has lingered longer in the Highlands than in those parts of the Lowlands in which it was spoken till the 17th century, and the British (Welsh) language of the Lowlands has long been forgotten. Into the Lowlands came literary influences which did not touch the Gaelic area. Man, however, does not live by literature alone, and during the Lowland bi-lingual period certain influences and ideals passed from one language into another, just as folk customs and folk tales passed freely, as we know. A Teutonic language has not trans-formed the Celtic Lowlanders body and soul. It appears to have exer-

cised less influence on their character than some suppose. In the late war Highlander and Lowlander were similarly brave and steadfast and reliable, and they mutually admired and trusted each other. The pipes and the tartan meant much to both. They knew well they were really 'Jock Tamson's bairns,' and little did they heed the theories of the men who would have it that the 'braw, braw lads' and other Lowlanders are Teutons, which, of course, they are not. – I am, etc.,

Donald A. Mackenzie

SCOTS AND 'BRAID SCOTS'

Sir, – As some remarks of mine on the subject of Scots or Gaelic have been criticised by Mr R.L. Cassie perhaps you will indulge me with a little of your space in which briefly to reply to that gentleman. But first allow me to compliment Mr Donald A. Mackenzie on his spirited answer to Mr Cassie, whose zeal on behalf of 'Braid Scots' seems inclined to carry him far beyond the bounds of historical accuracy. For instance, he affirms that 'Buchan has not spoken Gaelic since the days of the Book of Deer.' I do not know what particular 'days' Mr Cassie had in mind when penning this passage of his letter; but what I do know is that Gaelic was widely spoken in the province he names long after the Battle of Harlaw. Mr Cassie also affirms that 'this idiom (Braid Scots) has been displacing Gaelic since the eighth century or before.' A Germanic dialect of sorts was certainly introduced into the province of Lothia in the wake of the Germanic tribes who conquered and settled it; but as for Scotland proper and Galloway (wherein Gaelic survived until the eighteenth century), the displacement he speaks of did not begin to take effect till centuries after the period he names. Malcolm III, says Robertson, left his kingdom as Gaelic as he found it. William the Lyon ruled over a mainly Gaelic-speaking people; and even as late as the reign of the third Alexander the predominant speech be-north the Forth and in Galloway was not 'Braid Scots' but Scots. The University of Aberdeen was founded in the year 1494: but in the ordinances detailing the languages permitted to be used at that seat of learning Mr Cassie will find no mention of 'Braid Scots,' though true Scots or Gaelic is certainly enjoined. When Mr Cassie shall have explained away these facts I will be pleased to supply him with others quite as pregnant and to a similar purport.

In a second letter to your columns Mr Cassie finds fault with the Gaelic language. Doubtless Scots is not perfect. but I beg leave to remind Mr Cassie that none of the inventions of man is so. Most assuredly,

English is not perfect, nor French, nor Spanish, nor indeed any other tongue uttered by human lips. Even 'Braid Scots' might be objected to on this score. For example, it has a poor vocabulary, a worse literature, is culturally 'impossible,' and to polite ears sounds uncouth. Mr Cassie must pardon these asperities, my excuse for them being that he has deliberately provoked them.

For my part I think that if your several writers and correspondents – beginning with Mr C.M. Grieve and ending with Mr R.L. Cassie – would devote more time and attention to Gaelic matters, and less to 'side-shows' like Braid Scots and the perpetuation of Scandinavian and Germanic influences in Scotland, the more would the prospects of the Scottish Renaissance improve, and the day of its advent be hastened. – I am, etc.

Buchan

TOWARDS A SCOTTISH DRAMA

Sir, – The recent performance of Malloch's Soutarness Water by the Scottish National Players aroused considerable attention. It was universally felt by the critics that in this play a real attempt had been made to dramatise certain basic traits of the Scottish character. But the play failed as a whole because of heterogeneity of content and weakness of construction. We are driven, therefore, to re-examine the grounds for the hope that Scotland can produce a distinctly native drama of cultural importance, and to reconsider the question of the form that possible drama should assume.

The historical fact that no first-rate native drama has ever flourished in Scotland is currently attributed to clerical and bourgeois antagonism to the theatre as an institution. But might it not be the case that the genius of the Scottish race does not naturally lend itself to expression in the dramatic form that has ruled the roost in the post-Renaissance theatre up to within recent years? This type of drama – fundamental in England – is one of episode and action; and we have come to think that this type is not one ideally suitable as a foundation for native Scottish drama.

The plays so far produced under the aegis of the S.N.T.S. convince us that the Scottish mind loses grip of life and imaginative reality when it works in the medium of the popular 'narrative' form of English drama. The majority of these plays have suffered from looseness of construction and prolixity of sentiment. The instance of Barrie does not negate our contention. Barrie's plays depend more upon the nice manipulation of *sentiment and fancy than upon episodic action. Indeed, the Barrie type of drama is in its comfortable way an approach to the ideal form for Scottish drama that we are now coming to visualise. The achievement of this new drama will be the work of years and of the combined effects of many people.*

What the nature of this new drama is may be best understood by a consideration of ballad poetry. This poetry, starkly realistic in style and highly imaginative in conception, is the natural mould into which the dramatic imagination of the Scottish race was thrown during its period of greatest vigour and turmoil. Intensity and brevity are its most characteristic features, and these are likewise features of the Scottish imagination at its best. Indeed, the ordinary Scot thinks and feels a great deal but seldom expresses himself volubly. He understands, therefore, the brief flashes of vision and of psychological insight revealed in the ballads.

We feel that he could likewise understand and enjoy a form of drama that is more a commentary upon an action (like the ballad) than that form, traditional in England and copied by Scotsmen like Brandane and Malloch, that is an episodic account of an action an account that is mostly a sort of shorthand note for a romantic novel. The literary urge of the Scot towards an imaginative life of action reached its zenith in the novels of Sir Walter and its decline in the novels of Stevenson, Munro, and Buchan. The life of the episodic romance as a vehicle for the expression of the Scottish soul has come to an end. The Scottish soul is now in the grips of an 'inward-seeking' phase. Carlyle (whose best work is most stupidly neglected to-day) first directed the soul upon its new path – or rather 'revived' path, for the great 'Makars' entered upon the same path 400 years ago.

The form of drama required to express this soul upon the stage will be like that fashioned by Chekhov, Pirandello, and Balieff (of the 'Chauve-Souris'). The conversation will be directed towards revealing psychological truth rather than outlining episodic action. As a general rule the dramatist will aim at producing plays or ballets that express the thoughts and feelings of certain chosen people, under stress of emotion, in tense imaginative language or suitable dances and music.

Pirandello's form, moreover, would give a great measure of freedom to the imaginative and alert-minded dramatist. For instance, a play could be constructed in which characters famous in Scottish literature – Bailie Nicol Jarvie, Tam o' Shanter, and others – would appear upon the stage searching for, say, the living people who are their incarnations. By

*means of a form modelled on or derivative from Pirandello a philosoph-
ical and satirical drama could also be evolved. As the cinema is more and
more drawing to itself the drama of action, it is the bounden duty of the
legitimate stage to keep the spoken drama of thought and feeling alive. –
I am, etc.,*

William Jeffrey
[5.2.26]

Letters

THE NORDIC ORIGIN OF THE SCOTS

*Sir, – In reply to 'Buchan's' letter of 4th January, I must assure him that
I am not greatly exercised in 'cultivating a sense of humour.' That is
something which neither needs nor tolerates much cultivation if only
Nature has implanted it as a liberal vital influence, and I have never had
to complain of any meagreness of endowment in that respect, while on
the other hand 'Buchan' unconsciously affords melancholy evidence that
no amount of cultivation will ever produce more than the sorriest imitation of what has not been so implanted. He exhibits a constitutional
inability to see the point, which is only augmented by his pathetic insistence that therefore there can be no point to see. In my last letter I
suggested that some of his obtuseness must be assumed, but I am
wondering now if it really is. Such a failing is certainly not a Nordic
characteristic, and, as there is always a certain number of exceptions to
every generalisation on racial questions, I willingly concede to him the
probability that the thought of a Nordic origin, which has vexed him so
much, need no longer be regarded as a matter for personal worry.*

*Since 'Buchan' missed the point of the joke, I must explain that it did
not depend on the assumption that he was putting forward his 'amateur
statistician' as an authority on ethnology; the whole humour of the situation lay in that he did not, and could not! For, after saying, quite unwar-
rantably, that the writer I quoted was no authority on ethnology, and
after boasting of the 'eminent authorities' whom he would quote against
him, he brought forward only a political figure-grinder. That his cham-
pion had formed his conclusions after reading certain of those eminent
authorities is beside the mark for present purposes; if there was any
substance behind 'Buchan's' boasting he should have made direct use of
his material according to promise and threat. Did 'Buchan' find that his*

'authorities' would not at all suit his purpose unless when suitably arranged by his 'prophet'?

It is quite in keeping with 'Buchan's' ideas of what is fit and proper that, after proffering me his 'authorities' at second or third hand, he should have the ill grace to write, 'Mr Tait alleges – through someone else – ' forgetting how trenchantly the remark could be turned back on himself; and when he would fain raise a sneer by saying that I quote Professor Reid 'from report or hearsay' he is not aware that I was doing, with some definiteness of statement, what he is so fond of doing with characteristic vagueness, namely, making use of material obtained through an intermediary, for my reference to Professor Reid was supplied from the writing of another scientist, who had cited him as a personal investigator of the very facts we have under discussion. A saving sense of humour would have prevented him from laying himself open to a tu quoque. *I trust that in future 'Buchan' will remove the beam from his own eye before he starts searching for the mote in mine; but there is another proverb which says that it is difficult for the hunchback to see his own hump.*

A sense of humour would also save him from the folly of constantly reiterating that a theory must be absurd merely because he does not believe in it (for he has never even attempted to show wherein the absurdity lies), or from saying that because he does not appreciate a certain publication it must have been written to little purpose. Who is this 'Buchan' that we must accept his word without any explanation of the reasons underlying his conclusions? His logical sense must be as deficient as his sense of humour. He would be better advised to turn his attention to the 'cultivation' of the useful 'swedes of the vegetable kingdom' (I have to thank him for the phrase) whose roundness has appealed to him, remembering, while so engaged, that it is precisely in the departure from that 'neepy' rotundity that Swedes (of the human species) and Highland Scots exhibit their most striking craniological resemblances, and that therefore his one pitiful attempt at a joke miscarried woefully through his very ignorance of the subject on which he presumes to write so autocratically.

Worse, still, however, than his lack of humour and logic, is his inability to play the game along straightforward lines. I promised to give him the 'beginning and end of the matter, ' in fulfilment of which I had to start with Retzius, who, though 'Buchan' may not have known it, was emphatically a 'great' man and the founder of a national study of the skull. My thanks for this is that he must needs criticise me for quoting one who cannot be called an up-to-date authority. Presumably he would raise the same objection if I quoted Darwin on evolution! What value he put upon the evidence of two 'up-to-date' scientists we have already seen. It seems to me that 'Buchan' is in the position of one who, having been led to say, by the necessities of his argument, that white is black, is determined to throw mud from a safe distance till he- makes it appear *black.*

I do not know if it is another instance of his continued reluctance to come to grips on a definite issue, or a mere chance omission on his part, but I must point out that now when at long last he has produced, in the person of Professor Boas, someone with presumably some claim to scholarship who has definitely declared against the Nordic theory, he should either have given the number or date of the journal in which his article appeared, or, better still, he might have presented a brief summary of the Professor's contentions. So much is being written and published nowadays that one must not expect one's opponent to be either omniscient or omnivorous as to all that is written on any subject; and when reference numbers are not furnished we expect instead a quotation, or a reproduction of the arguments employed. Under the circumstances I am having to ask a friend, more favourably situated than I am geographically, to hunt up the article for me. When I have read it and have discovered more about 'Buchan's' point of view, which I presume it represents, I may have more to say to him; but in the meantime I must cultivate patience as well as (good) humour in this matter. However if 'Buchan' does not wish to prolong unduly this already too lengthy discussion he has the advantage of knowing the name and address of his opponent and if he cares to post me his copy of the Forum *containing the article referred to I shall return it to him as soon as possible through the office of this paper with a refundment of postage. – I am etc.,*

Sandwick, Shetland   *Robert W. Tait*
Jan. 29, 1926

MR GRIEVE'S ARTICLES

Sir – I shall eagerly await the appearance of Mr Grieve's promised books, and in the meantime I must thank him both for his articles and for his replies to my letters. It seems almost impertinent to give praise to one whose valiant spirit seems to need it so little, but in view of the large amount of adverse criticism he has received I can do no less than say that his ideas seem to me extremely interesting and suggestive. He has certainly given me a sympathy with the spirit of the Scottish

Renaissance, and a vision of its possibilities which I never had before. I believe many other teachers would be willing to say the same. – I am etc.,

47 Brisbane Street   H. Brown
Greenock.

TOWARDS A SCOTTISH DRAMA

Sir – In the hope that the very interesting letter from Mr William Jeffrey, in your issue of 5th instant may invite response I venture to contribute the following opinions on the practical aspect of production.

When it is considered that hitherto the method of interpreting the basic traits of Scottish character has been on alien principles all attempts to evolve a distinctly native drama have virtually stopped short when the ink dried on the paper. They could not be tried in practice.

A new form of drama and stage technique must be evolved that will be distinctive not merely different. And the distinction may broadly be defined as, whereas English drama concerns itself with episode and action, Scottish drama seeks to convey thoughts and feelings. The Scot in intercourse either expresses his thoughts in a few words or else uses a superfluity. But both are means to the same end: to avoid being definite. Hence thoughts and feelings must be interpreted by minute externals to convey their meaning and intention across the footlights.

Present methods of production fail to express these. The working out of a psychological situation becomes crude and incoherent when, at the expense of realism, episode and action are emphasised.

The only safe means of getting a response that is certain is to rely upon thoughts and feelings. To an audience the appeal will be individual and the effect will be more or less according to emotional receptiveness.

We must concentrate on the observation of externals. Before a word is spoken there is the mental process in arriving at the decision to speak. By a carefully planned scale of emphasis and exaggeration this can be translated to the restrictions and conventions of the stage in order to present thoughts in the process of being worked out. How often has it happened that the finesse of a situation, the consummation of a cleverly conceived psychological crisis, is coarsened beyond recognition by the actors adopting heroic and grandiose methods that may impress for the moment but become ridiculous on reflection.

In presenting our plays we must lead the audience as individuals to think with us. The dialogue to be spoken should be carefully analysed, each sentence divided into compartments of mental development. The pause should be used judiciously to mark each step in thinking. Between the several characters there must be a definite display of gesture, adjusted to presage a crucial point balanced to create the crisis by emphasis, contrast and speed of action.

This may appear intricate but it is quite capable of practical interpretation if only the methods of planning movements on the stage be extended to include gesture. Plays repeated night after night follow a definite plan of exits and entrances. This gives definite groupings to present episode and action. By developing the plan to include gesture, facial expression and intonation, the salient features of the Scottish mentality can be faithfully presented on the stage.

These principles belong to the theatre and are related to its conventions. They seek to link the brains of the actor with those of the audience. They aim at being intimate, vivid and sincere.

On these lines the development of our drama would be given the fullest freedom for the expression of native characteristics. They afford a means of interpretation not alien as hitherto, but founded on the features we are justly proud of sincerity, restraint, and simplicity – I am etc.,

R.F. Pollock

CONTEMPORARY SCOTTISH STUDIES

Sir – I would like to make some remarks in reply to the interesting letters of Mr Donald A. Mackenzie and 'Buchan,' if not encroaching excessively upon your valuable space.

Mr Mackenzie makes an able comparison between Celtic and Germanic literary style and chivalric standards. I did not intend to doubt the accuracy of the translation of the Beowulf *passage given by him. I merely desired to draw attention to the probability that tribal quarrels would often lead to bloodshed among kinsfolk of varying degree. While appreciating the fine spirit of mutual loyalty shown by Cuchulain and Ferdiad, I would instance the devotion of Wiglaf to his dying chief. And I am sure that Mr Mackenzie fully recognises the lustrous chivalry of Beowulf's crusade, in which he achieved the destruction of the monsters Grendel and his mother who had terrorised Hrothgar's folk for many years.*

There is, too, a great deal of the joyous or 'gleodream' spirit in Beowulf *as in some of the Icelandic sagas. The bard was the tribal or national historian, story-teller and humorist, though the latter function was nearly eclipsed by the stern conditions of existence.*

Are not the obscurities of style in Beowulf *largely motived by the alliterative form of the verse? The need for alliteration in each line seems to have helped towards the enrichment – and occasional darkening – of the language by masses of synonyms. But if I mistake not, the same alliterative fashion existed in Celtic verse. One must marvel at the poetic gift displayed by these oral* litterateurs, *who must have often improvised their compositions.*

I am delighted to read Mr Mackenzie's reminiscences of his home Doric. Apart from the context the first two remarks of the loons are rather puzzling but I find the key in 'sclafards' – our Buchan 'sclaffert.' 'Yagach' is strange, but I get the meaning of the fishwife's little speech except the idiom "arryin' the crook.' It would appear that Ross-shire Scots has much in common with the tongue of Caithness. which differs from Aberdeen, Banff and Moray mainly in the use of d for t, and a larger number of genuine Norse survivals.

If Mr Mackenzie ever cares to read Swatches o' Hamespun *(with which I am not entirely unconnected) he would find many correspondences with his mither tongue. Its condemnation in various quarters I consider as a fine testimonial. Northern Scots, in all its trifling variations is pulsating with virile life.*

I am at one with Mr Mackenzie in hoping for a better understanding among all sections of Scots. I am opposed to 'Buchan's' local intolerance just as I am compelled to differ from those Highlanders – happily few and decreasing in number – who hardly accept the Lowlander as a fellow-countryman. As Mr Mackenzie says. 'We're a' Jock Tamson's bairns' and there is a strain of Celtic blood in most of us.

I am not a Separatist in a sense disruptive to Scotland. I would like to see us all united in the effort to secure for our country her just status as a member of the British Commonwealth.

Nothing is truer than Mr Mackenzie's remark that, during a period of bi-lingualism certain ideals and influences were transferred between tongues. My theory of the interaction of speech and national character puts the matter in a more extreme way, perhaps, but there seems to be no difference of principle.

I am all for co-operation between Highlander and Lowlander in the preservation of language and vital Scottish interests. This mutual action need not take the form of proselytising in separate linguistic territory. In my view, the best results would come from the folk being bi-lingual when possible, and working together for the promotion of local literature or drama in the homes of each tongue. Though these experiments might at first produce no better results than the despised 'Swatches,' 'we maun creep ere we gyang.'

Regarding the approximate epoch of the lapse of Gaelic in my native district, I have no doubt that my reference was substantially exact. At the moment I have no access to libraries, but (through the kindness of a friend who is very enlightened upon these matters) I had the opportunity of reading some chronicles of Ellon, indicating the absence of Gaelic records, and quoting local specimens of old Scots dating from about 1400.

Regarding the general question, I prefer to think of the frontier of to-day, or even the greater Scotland that once extended far south of the present Border. The south-eastern Celts received the Germanic speech from the invaders, and spread it among their countrymen. Their descendants have been good Scots for many centuries, and cannot be shut out in any comparison of language based upon a restricted 'Scotland proper.'

The Ruthwell Cross (about 700) is good evidence in support of my moderate assignment of the eighth century as an early period of the linguistic displacement. 'Buchan' would say that Dumfries was not then in Scotland, and that the tongue was not Scots. But the district and language were to become Scots, the dwellers speaking originally a form of Celtic.

I am sorry that 'Buchan' is so displeased with the speech of the folk around him. His poor opinion of its vocabulary, literature, and cultural value is refuted by a long line of writers from Barbour to Charles Murray.

'Buchan' must feel out of his element among folk whose simple speech is so redolent of 'bumpkinisity' and jarring to polite ears. I love these brainy loons and bonnie lassies. I am yet ane o' their ain, and am proud to use their tongue when I go among them. Yes, I love them, even when they wallow in the mud of local tale or play, and thus incur the biting contempt of the pioneers of the new Scotland. – I am, etc.,

R.L. Cassie
[12.2.26]

29. The Hon. Ruaraidh Erskine of Marr

The same type of person as fought for the freedom of the Press is to-day recognising the need for its regulation in the interests of the integrity of thought and public opinion. The claim that newspapers are private businesses to be run in any way their proprietors think fit is untenable. To a very large extent to-day capital is being used through the medium of newspaper proprietorship to debauch the public mind in the most unscrupulous fashion and with the meanest motives. In a real sense there is no freedom of the Press in Great Britain today. A government which spends scores of millions of pounds annually on compulsory education cannot remain permanently indifferent to the extent to which that expenditure is stultified by 'the New Journalism.' At the same time that the Press is exercising an utterly unwholesome influence in certain directions – and on certain sections of the public – it is largely ceasing to exercise – or to exercise effectively and in a desirable fashion – what ought to be its principal functions! Its news is as bad as its views. It is dominated not by journalists with any professional code, but by 'the commercial side': and its claim to decide what shall or shall not be reported solely by what it calls its 'sense of news-values' is undermined by the fact that that 'sense' itself is dictated nowadays by anything rather than a broad concern for the public good. This base making and manipulation of public opinion must be terminated. Democracy is practically divisible to-day into the unthinking mob moved this way and that by the stuntist Press on the one hand and, on the other, the almost equally large proportion of the population who have ceased to 'pay any attention to what the papers say' and made up their minds on the main issues in current affairs independently of them, and, for the most part, in spite of them. It is, for example, an utterly anomalous thing that practically the entire Scottish Press should be anti-Socialist and engaged upon continuous misrepresentation of the Socialist position, while a third of the population are Socialist voters. It is again utterly anomalous that practically all the Scottish papers deride the Scottish Home Rule programme as the farcical demand of a handful of fanatics, while Bill after Bill to confer measures of self-government upon Scotland again have been thrown out of the House of Commons by the English majority despite the fact that they have been supported by an ever-increasing majority of the Scottish representation of all parties. Do the Scottish people want home rule? The papers, which tell us that they do not, are the very papers whose columns are closed to any debate on the subject and which have studiously refrained for decades to do what the Press of every other country does – hold a watching brief for the national interests and maintain a continuous audit into all the departments of the country's affairs. Who has ever seen in any Scottish paper competent articles, with detailed statistics, into any phase of our industry or commerce *from a purely national standpoint* – that is to say, so set out as to discriminate between Scottish and English (or, if you prefer it, Scottish and British) interests? Anyone who is in the habit of writing to the papers on Scottish issues knows what the taboos are. 'Thus far and no further' he may go – and 'thus far' falls short of the distance at which he would be in a position to deal effectively with the continual ridicule to which the very idea of Scottish Home Rule is persistently subjected. The fact of the matter is that the existing Press has its vested interests in the maintenance of the *status quo* – it is a product of the existing state of affairs – and under the present economic order it is practically impossible to establish a free Press. It cannot contend against the Press that already exists as a product or accessory of business interests dependent upon the present order. Business so dominates the matter that a detached multimillionaire to-day might readily sink his entire fortune in endeavouring to run a daily paper in favour of, say, a Scots Free State, even supposing it got at the outset, and maintained as long as it lasted, more readers than any two other daily papers in Scotland combined. Established business to-day has a power to which public opinion is practically irrelevant. It cannot prevent the growth of public opinion in directions to which it is opposed but it can prevent or indefinitely delay the effective organisation of the public opinion in question. That is the position of the great mass of Scottish nationalist opinion in Scotland to-day: and how to enable it to express itself when all the means of expression are monopolised by the English or Anglo-Scottish opposition is the problem.

These considerations, baldly set forth, come to my mind as I start to write of the Hon. Ruaraidh Stuart Erskine of Marr. His significance arises from the fact that he embodies in himself the antitheses of all the tendencies which led to the Union and have since fostered the inherent tendency of the Union – the complete assimilation of Scotland to England. It is easy to understand to what an extent such a phenomenon has become the target of all whose enmity is aroused by the slightest divergence from the normal. He has been persistently derided and insulted and denounced by all the anonymous nonentities who staff the Anglo-Scottish Press. But despite them, and the overwhelming odds confronting his programme (the restoration of Scottish independence, and of Gaelic culture in Scotland), he has maintained decade after decade a propaganda which the Press might keep subterranean, but to which they could not deny an ultimate ubiquity. He has never lacked the courage of his convictions; his consistency has been unimpeachable, and his tenacity marvellous. To-day he is beginning to reap the reward of his labours. Already popular opinion in Scotland has veered round to a very large extent to the attitude he adopted to the War, for example. His persistent propaganda has at last taken shape in what is the most promising nationalist organisation that has been formed in Scotland since the Union – the Scottish National League. At present he has no organ of his own. His journalistic enterprises have been many – annuals, quarterlies, monthlies, weeklies. They have served to keep the fire of Scottish nationalism alight. The two most important were *Guth na Bliadhna,* a beautifully produced Gaelic quarterly and practically the sole repository of contemporary Gaelic arts and letters of the slightest consequence; and *The Scottish Review*, the files of which are indispensable to students of Scottish affairs and hold masses of information inaccessible or very difficult of access elsewhere. Both were heroic examples of the art of swimming against the current. In both cases the literary resource of their editor and proprietor was outstandingly evident. He was the founder, too, of Ard-Chomhairle na Gaidhlig (the Gaelic Academy) and Comunn Litreachais na h-Albann (the Society of Scottish Letters). It is interesting to observe that just as the latest organisation with which he is identified, the Scots National League, is by far the most promising and powerful, so, just at the moment when he has again suspended the last of his periodicals, it is becoming increasingly clear that tendencies in contemporary newspaper trustification are leading to a reorientation of the attitude of certain Scottish newspapers to Scottish nationalism – a tendency attributable in part, too, to the effect other recent amalgamations of English and Scottish interests, with centralisation in London, have had upon the business of the papers in question. These newspapers are not insensible to the conjunction of the adverse effect of recent tendencies in affairs on Scottish interests with a rising tide of nationalism in the minds of the people as a whole. The result of this, at the very least, will be to make Scottish nationalist journalism and periodical enterprise easier than it has hitherto been. The result may also be that in quarters that ten years ago would have seemed exceedingly unlikely, Mr Erskine may at last be accorded some recognition for what he is – one of our ablest and most disinterested publicists; one of our most distinguished litterateurs; a man of wide knowledge, versatile accomplishment and great charm and fineness of character; and, above all, a Scot who has maintained intact in himself, if nowhere else, the indefeasible unity of Scotland, its sovereign independence, and a centre in which the 'Anima Celtica' has lain in no spell-bound trance, but continued to function, if not freely, faithfully. I account him one of the

most remarkable personalities of modern Scottish history, the very core
and crux of the *Gaeltacht*. It is too early yet to see his political and
cultural activities in proper perspective, but I am confident that an
adequate lapse of time will serve to correct the general view as to the
validity and value of his views on all matters affecting Scottish interests
just as the post-War period has already slewed round large bodies of
opinion, very differently disposed at the time, to substantially the same
position as Mr Erskine adopted to the war while it was still being waged.

But there is another respect in which he is remote from the generality, despite the rapid decay of materialism within the past few years.
'He has attempted' (as Professor Mackinnon said of the Highlander, in
his inaugural address on his succession to the Celtic Chair at Edinburgh
University), 'not unsuccessfully, to live not for the day and hour alone,
but, in a true sense, to live the life of the spirit.' Apart from a steady
stream of political articles and correspondence, he has maintained a
regular flow of imaginative prose studies, plays, etc., both in Gaelic and
in English. Gaelic letters have been cut off, pretty much as Braid Scots
have been but to somewhat different effect (there is a difference
between Kailyairdism and Celtic Twilightism) from contact with
European culture on the one hand and the practical life of the people on
the other. The bulk of the Gaelic movement, as represented in the
various Highland Societies, etc., is a purely sentimental thing, divorced
from reality, and headed by the very people who have eviscerated the
economic life of the Highlands and Islands, or acquiesced in its eviscera-
tion, while maintaining a pseudo-patriotism in their coteries in grotesque
contrast with the actual conditions obtaining in the districts they claim to
represent. There is no genuine cultural interest among these people and
the bulk of what they cherished as Gaelic literature, art, or song is either
old stuff ineffectively related to conditions to-day and vitiated by the
false attitude that prevails towards it amongst them, or a psuedo-culture
derived from it but amenable to a state of affairs against which any
authentic Gaelic culture would necessarily have to strive unceasingly.
Even at its best it is only folk-art that is cherished, nowhere rising into
high classicism and art-forms. In other words, the general regard, where
there is any regard at all, is for old forms merely, devoid of the old
substance: little new wine is available and, where any is, it is of so poor a
vintage that the old bottles serve it. In Mr Erskine, and a few of the
contributors to *Guth na Bliadhna* and other organs he has provided from
time to time, alone has any effort at experimental Gaelic arts and letters
been sustained: and in him, if in no one else, has that effort been in

some measure related to appropriate elements of European culture elsewhere – to the Spanish of Eugene D'Ors, for example. He has made independent affiliations without regard to English interests; and, on the other hand, he has succeeded in preserving conceptions of Gaelic policy and some little interest in the potentialities of Gaelic culture in Scottish communities abroad – especially in certain areas of Canada and America. But few of those who echo the sentiments of the 'Canadian Boat-Song' have more than a vague sentimental regard for the old country and fewer still any concern over the practical elimination of Gaelic genius from the sphere of practical politics and the substitution for it of alien tendencies.

It is unfortunate that no English translation of Mr Erskine's Gaelic dramas has yet been published. Even in translation something of their quality would transpire (although a great deal would be lost) and that would be sufficient to show that in him Scotland has a representative dramatist of no little distinction. A vein of real genius manifests itself in them, and they are on a higher level – and emerge more indubitably as an authentic expression of hitherto unexpressed faculties of distinctive Scots psychology – than any Scots drama yet written in English or the Vernacular.

All his creative work in Gaelic, too, is characterised by a quality generally lacking in work in a lapsed or languishing language. 'Braid Scots' has entirely lost it for centuries, for example, and that constitutes the greatest difficulty now confronting those who would seek to revive 'Braid Scots' as a literary medium for a work above a Kailyaird level. This is a sort *of hauteur*, an absence of rustic coarseness – what, dealing with the same rare quality in Aodhagán O Rathaille, Séumas O h-Aodha happily calls 'literary pride,' *uabhar na litriochta*. A well-known Gael (himself a writer of parts) once remarked to Mr Erskine, 'You have restored to us "gentleman's Gaelic."'

Circumstances have compelled Mr Erskine to devote most of his time to work of an ephemeral nature – although its influence will be far from ephemeral and much of it will retain a documental value. But his powers would have been better displayed if, instead of being scattered through a mass of newspapers and other periodicals, his political and cultural propaganda had shaped itself into book-form. Now that younger men are at last coming forward eager and willing and, to some extent at least, able to take over the 'donkey work' of the movement, Mr Erskine may perhaps find leisure to give his manifold opinions on Scottish affairs substantive and definitive form.

Stuart Mill was right when he said that: 'If all mankind minus one person were of one opinion, and only one person were of the contrary opinion, mankind would be no more justified in silencing that one person than he, if he had the power, would be justified in silencing them.' To the extent to which the Scottish Press tends to ignore, suppress, or misrepresent Erskine's views on Scottish matters does that Press partake of the nature of a dangerous and intolerable conspiracy. 'Thought,' as Ramiro de Maeztu says, 'is not only a social function, but one of the most important. If it is a function, like that of railway service, it ought to be acknowledged and organised' – and not made dependent upon the commercial interests of a few newspaper proprietors and their hirelings. And even if it were true that Scotland had benefited materially from the Union with England it would still be true that for many a long year now Erskine of Marr has stood – and stood practically alone – for things of far more importance, for, as Walt Whitman said of the commercial and industrial development of America, 'I too hail those achievements with pride and joy; then answer that the soul of man will not be satisfied with such only – nay, not with such at all finally satisfied.'

[19.2.26]

Letters

CONTEMPORARY SCOTTISH STUDIES

Sir, – It is perhaps useless to answer Mr Grieve's criticism of Swatches o' Hamespun. *It may be just as well, however, to convince him that I am not one of these 'dum dogs quha... dar not only nocht barke, bot maist schamefullie poyit with staff and sting, dar nother quhryne nor quhyng.' I do not intend to 'quhyng.' One who has the temerity to embark upon the sea of publication must face criticism with the best grace.*

Might I call attention to the title of the booklets? I do not think it is pretentious – it sums up pretty accurately the contents. To the man who wishes something of fine texture and with pretension to style, the output of the homely hand-made loom must necessarily make little appeal. Such a loom is best suited in these days for the production of 'clooty coverins' perhaps abhorrent to such supersensitive critics as Mr Grieve.

Might I also point out, what he has evidently failed to note, that the whole intention was to produce, 'dialect, literature if possible, but dialect first and foremost'?

His ability to criticise Aberdeenshire dialect has already been displayed by his remarks rewarding Hamewith's *language; he is entitled to keep to his own views of art. But to quote from the old author (in whom he will no doubt delight) 'Sen ze haif harpit sa lang on that ane string... we exhorte zow to schaw it justlie toneit, or ze leif it. Quhilk geue ze may do, and assuir the peple and vs heirof, it is the radiast waye to persuade al zour aduersaries to delyte in the rest of your melodie.' Mr Grieve's views on our dialect are unworthy of consideration: he is entitled to express opinion as to whether it is a happy literary medium.*

Furthermore, when an architect proceeds to plan a but-and-ben, he is entitled to kick when he is told that his building is unsuitable as a kirk. His views as to his intention must be considered. Mr Grieve applies a literary standard to a linguistic effort.

He has shown by his articles how much stress he lays upon the suitability of the dialect for the expression of thought – away from the merely homely – by very carefully eschewing it, and thus confirms my statement, which he holds up to ridicule.

His reference to chaw-bacons – our local 'caup-clawers' – betrays a standpoint of contempt for the very people he would fain lead. I always thought love of the humble was the necessary precedent of reverence for the great. Burns evidently made a bad break in choosing the little things around him as subjects for his muse – but far be it from me to quote him as my exemplar.

If it be any satisfaction to Mr Grieve, might I tell him that this little effort at recording the dialect as it is, has met the same fate as others with literary pretensions of which Mr Grieve knows something? Both have failed to secure a reading public – not to be wondered at perhaps in both cases. Evidently the 'spaad' of my humble characters is as wersh as the 'bloody shovel' of his was repugnant. – I am, etc.,

W. Cumming
[19.2.26]

Letters

Sir, – Mr Robert W. Tait's last to your columns is an admirable specimen of what is called 'writing round a topic.' In the course of a column or two of closely packed type he manages to say next to nothing, certainly nothing in the least degree calculated to diminish my scepticism touching the ethnological creed, and the prophets thereof, in which he appears to lodge a truly child-like faith. But, so far as I am concerned, I must now leave Mr Tait to ramble alone. I am sorry I cannot oblige him by sending him a copy of the Forum *in which appears the article entitled 'This Nordic Nonsense.' The copy I read I saw in the hands of an American friend of mine. I borrowed it, and – contrary to custom – returned it; and my friend has now left this country. But if Mr Tait is seriously desirous to examine the foundations of the faith on which he leans so heavily in an ethnological way he should make some special effort to procure a copy of that* Forum. *It might have the effect, if not of working a perfect conversion in him, at all events of rendering him a little less positive in his pro-Nordic affirmations than he is at present.*

With regard to Mr R.L. Cassie, there was really no need for him to use the rather ponderous irony he employs in order to express his disapproval of the 'pioneers of the new Scotland'. I think that most Gaelic-speaking 'pioneers' are sympathetic towards the 'Doric' movement; but the false history and pretensions as vain and ill-founded, in which the zealots of 'Braid Scots' are apt to indulge, among them, and lead to a measure of plain speaking on their part which the advocates of the 'Doric' were wiser did they their utmost to avoid. – I am, etc.,

Buchan
[26.2.26]

30. A.S. Neill and our Educational System

At the last Annual Congress of the Educational Institute of Scotland, Mr James Maxton, the Socialist M.P. for the Bridgeton Division of Glasgow, delivered an address on 'A National Aim in Education,' in which he advocated the substitution of the tweedledum of an educational policy amenable to Socialist desires as opposed to the existing tweedledee of an educational system subservient to the established order of things. He pointed to the fact that various powers, Japan, Germany, Sweden and Denmark had made up their minds to achieve certain objectives – commercial, technical, financial or military – and had shaped their educational machinery and inspiration towards achieving these ends. Turning to Great Britain, he asked if there was any such general purpose running through their national life, and answered in the negative. 'The people of Scotland and the teachers of Scotland,' he continued, 'had a duty to do what was done in Japan, what was done in Sweden, what was alleged to be done at Oxford, Cambridge, Eton, and Harrow – to discover definite national ideals – ideals which would not be contradictory of national traditions, which would not clash with national characteristics, but which would be complementary to these and inspire them with new life and vigour.' And he proceeded to suggest that suitable ideals for Scotland in this respect were independence, thrift, courage and so forth. Beyond illustrating the puritanical bias of a large (perhaps the overwhelming) element in the Scottish Socialist and Labour movement, his remarks really begged the question at issue. They were illustrative of the general state of mind in regard to education in Scotland to-day. Almost everybody would share Mr Maxton's sentiments: but, in actual application, there would be a tremendous diversity in the connotations attached to such words as 'independence,' 'thrift,' 'courage,' 'character.' etc., while 'contradictory of national traditions,' and 'not clashing with national characteristics' – what do such phrases mean? Mr Maxton professes to believe that the Scottish people, not the British House of Commons, should manage its own education. But are our national characteristics to be those our denationalised race manifests to-day – are our national traditions to be deduced from post-Union manifestations of Scottish life or from what? Despite the fact that Scottish Education remains at the mercy of a preponderantly English legislature – hardly an example of our business capacity and those capacities for fighting against the tide and mastering not only our souls but our environments, which Mr Maxton believes to characterise us – he disagreed with the Master of Baliol's view that we are a dreamy, impractical race. His conclusion, moreover, that the ideal system should advance 'that sense of values which meant that everyone should get the best possible value out of life' may mean anything or nothing. Well might Dr MacGillivray who followed him remark that he differed from Mr Maxton in regard to the aim not mattering and contend that 'the aim is the whole thing – if we go in for a national system of education, let us see that it is a natural system of education, one that will develop the real nature and the real good of the individual.' But here again what is a natural system of education, what is anybody's real nature and real good?

The type of idea on educational matters held by Mr Maxton and shared to greater or less degree by the bulk of the Socialist and Labour movement, and, perhaps, by Progressives generally, in Scotland to-day, expressed in the best possible way (which Mr Maxton's address by no means exemplified) certainly supplies a much-needed corrective to the hitherto prevalent attitude which it is rapidly supplanting; but it is only relatively better in certain details. It does not throw us back upon first principles nor do away with the anomaly of speaking of 'education' when we are referring to a system which imposes far more than it educes and is designed for – or, rather, owes its design to – a multitude of extra-educational factors, lets and hindrances, in which whatever pure educational impulse there may be is almost wholly nullified. What Mr Maxton was trying to say has perhaps nowhere been better expressed than by another Scotsman, Mr G.W. Thomson, in his book, *The Grammar of Power* (The Labour Publishing Company, Ltd., 1924), where *inter alia,* he says:

> It is obvious that the control over education possessed by a relatively small section of the community enables it to dictate not only the conditions of labour, but the very ideology of the common people, whilst giving a thin and false veneer of culture to the classes and an essentially wrong view of history and social dynamics... One important step in human emancipation would be a large grant of self-government to the teachers, who possess at present virtually no control over the form of education or over the conditions which they know are absolutely essential to the efficient discharge of their duties. When the teachers are free themselves, they will quickly educate scholars for liberty.

I agree with Mr Thomson that this would be a vast improvement on the present state of affairs; but it does not touch the heart of the matter. After all, there is no guarantee that any consensus of opinion is better than any individual opinion – democratic control is not necessarily better than class-control or a dictatorship. 'By their fruits ye shall know them.' But from one pole to the other of what I may call the orthodox position – from the point of view which, say, regards the Scottish educational system as it exists to-day as perfect, through positions such as Mr Maxton's, to the point of view which regards it as a branch of capitalist machinery – one thing is taken for granted, and that is that it is right to make children means to ends, whether the end be that they shall become efficient wage-slaves or class-conscious proletarians. That, it seems to me, is blasphemy against the Holy Ghost. It may be unavoidable in the circumstances in which humanity is presently placed, or is ever likely to be placed, and it may be laudable then since such a system is inevitable to make it as good a system of the kind as possible – to defend it that is, in practice: but there should always be the reservation that it is indefensible in theory. So with all such talk as that of inculcating patriotism, independence, 'truth,' thrift and of 'making good citizens.' All these are irrelevant to the real business of education – which is simply and solely to 'educate,' to enable the individual to realise himself or herself to the fullest possible degree, without giving him or her any vocational, political, moralistic or other bent or bias of any kind. It may be impossible to embody that ideal in any system of education in the world as it is organised to-day or as it is ever likely to become organised, but there is nothing in principle to chose between an ideology dictated by a relatively small section of the community, by the community as a whole, or by any individual, and short of the realisation of the ideal of complete self-realisation as the sole objective in education, it is futile and misleading to talk of 'educating for liberty.' The idea of 'indelibly printing' anything on the character of any child – as Mr Maxton ironically enough wanted 'the spirit of independence' to be printed – is a monstrous one. Bernard Shaw is right when he defines Education as a form of assault, depending for its only sanction on the fact that might is right. Nor can 'good intentions' be successfully pleaded in extenuation.

While it is practically impossible then to hear any idea on education matters which is not vitiated by incredible presumption, objection may also be taken to Mr Maxton's prelections from a nationalist point of view. It is the sorriest Chauvinism to imply that there is anything distinctively Scottish about independence, thrift or courage. These qualities are to be found in – and are honoured and extolled by – every people under the sun. The national spirit is something apart from any such qualities – it can manifest itself now in them or now equally well in their opposites. Nothing that Mr Maxton said shed any light on the peculiar qualities of the Scottish national spirit – although his speech as a whole perhaps showed some of the main reasons why the Scottish national spirit has so largely lapsed into ineffectuality.

Principal Maurice Jones of Lampeter College was on sounder lines when he recently declared that 'the higher standard of knowledge and culture which now prevails amongst the Welsh people was illustrated in the literary and dramatic movements which now characterise the Principality.' He strongly criticised the utilitarian conception of education which was so common and which regarded education mainly as an avenue to a 'job' and did not value it as a treasure in itself, and as something destined to create citizens adequately prepared for life in its wider sense. The result of this conception had been that, in spite of the almost unequalled education in Wales, she had not yet produced a cultured democracy. He traced the mischief caused by a system of education which since 1870 had ignored the existence of a separate nation in Wales with its own language, genius, history and traditions, and which, in spite of many recent improvements, was still far from what it ought to be as a Welsh national system of education. I do not quite share Principal Jones' evident high opinion of the recent literary and dramatic tendencies in Wales – but what he says certainly applies to Scotland with far more force. Only recently have tendencies manifested themselves to improve our educational system in this particular nationalistic sense – and we have been subjected to denationalising influences far longer, far more insidiously and intensively, and far more 'successfully,' than Wales. Recent writers to the *Scottish Educational Journal*, for example – to show how little we have even yet progressed – have been emphasising the desirability of good plain straightforward English, which is, in fact, the language which is principally taught in our Scottish schools. The connection between that fact and the comparative poverty and inefficacy of Scottish letters must be very close. I believe that the use of English cramps the Scottish style and falsifies and inhibits the Scottish consciousness to an extraordinary degree, and that first-class work by Scotsmen in English is a practical impossibility. This hypothesis at all events fits the facts of our cultural history and supplies a reason for what is otherwise inexplicable unless you are prepared to admit that Scottish psychology is destitute of creative potentialities equivalent to those of other countries – an admission that would have to be qualified by one or two striking exceptions and recognition of the fact that it was not always thus. The fact that there is no effective differentiation between the Scottish and English use of English on the face of it implies an uncon-scionable suppression of the distinctive elements of Scottish psychology. There is room for a great deal of national activity such as that recently begun to introduce the study of the Scots Vernacular into our schools and to increase the place given to Scottish rather than English history (even the Secretary of Scotland the other day deplored that while he derived so much benefit from history at school he was given so little 'pure Scottish history') – and for a good deal of political activity to secure Scottish control of Scottish education, and the liberation of our system from financial dependence upon English wishes – but, as Mr Thomson elsewhere remarks, the great bulk of politics is concerned with exceed-ingly unpolitical and generally artificial considerations and rarely gets down to fundamentals, and the same would remain true of Scottish education so reoriented, relatively better in all but purely educational respects although such a re-orientation would make it. Bergson's theory of the two selves gives us perhaps the easiest method of describing what differentiates any educational system from a real education (*i.e.*, the thing that happens to an artist when he 'finds himself').

> Fundamentally the mind is a flux of interpenetrating elements which cannot be analysed out. But on the surface this living self gets covered over with a crust of clean-cut psychic selves which are separated one from the other and which can be analysed and described. This crystallisation into separate states has come about mainly for the purposes of action and communication in life. (T.E. Hulme)

The present educational system in Scotland – like every other educational *system* – is concerned with the superficial self. Real education – upon which everything that is vital in life depends – is concerned solely with the fundamental self; it is in direct opposition to everything that tends to create the superficial self, beyond the working minimum of sanity, and especially, to anything that tends to so harden that crust as to inhibit or handicap the fundamental self, or give a direction to life from without rather than purely from within. The only Scottish educationist to-day of the slightest significance from the point of view of real education is A.S. Neill, the author of A *Dominie's Log* and the other *Dominie* books, the latest of which is A *Dominie's Five*, an account of some of his further experiences in his international school at Hellerau. Mr Neill is now in England and is running his school at Lyme Regis. His importance arises from the fact that he alone, or practically alone, amongst educationists in this country has had the courage to follow the newer ideas which are everywhere leavening the educational world to their logical conclusions. Most other educationists go so far and no further; they are pulled up by moral or religious or other extra-educational considerations. But so far as Mr Neill is concerned education is simply and solely a matter of psychology. He does not acquiesce in the interposition of any political, moralistic, religious or other extraneous influences at all – least of all does he come to his task *parti-pris* in favour of any such meaningless abstraction as 'independence,' 'thrift' or 'courage' or as an instrument for the perpetuation of existing conventions of any kind or the facilitation either of the assumptions whence the existing order of industrial civilisation derives its workability or any alternative assumptions which might in any way replace that order with another. He is not concerned with any of these things. In other words he is nothing but an educator – one who draws out, not one who takes it upon himself to 'imprint' anything. This may seem far enough from Scottish nationalism, but in so far as there is any nationalistic quality as apart from things which short-sighted people like Mr Maxton mistake for it that cannot be inculcated – it can only be allowed to show itself, or prevented in this measure or that from showing itself. The present system largely inhibits or distorts it. Mr Neill's methods alone can give it the freest possible scope.

Mr Neill has a genius for understatement: and his *Dominie* books have by no means 'pulled the weight' which their brilliant, common-sense, shrewd knowledge of life, complete integrity of attitude and simplicity of form deserve. People judge largely by appearances. Serious work in psychology and pedagogics is still almost indisseverably associated with either a pompous platitudinous style, or a dreary waste of solemn 'scientific English.' Neill ruled himself practically out of court altogether by his blasphemous preference for a semi-fictional form and a snappy medium, liberally larded with slang and enlivened with irreverences of all kinds. His books are, nevertheless, the most stimulating and suggestive on their subject by any Scotsman and disclose a singularly modest but yet extraordinarily candid and courageous personality; and, in the opinion of the present writer, express a point of view in regard to the functions, rights, and most advantageous methods of the educationist which will be the only creditable or, indeed credible, type of opinion at the end of another quarter of a century, while, in contrast to them, the sentiments almost unanimously expressed to-day by teachers or educational administrators, and exemplified throughout our whole system of popular education will seem like a nightmare of the distant past. The ordinary headmaster of a school to-day may pride himself on being so much better than Mr Wackford Squeers. In the light of what is already known (and so unanswerably demonstrated in Mr Neill's books) the distance advanced seems to me incredibly small, and I am confident that from looking back from the middle of this century it will be imperceptible and they will seem to stand shoulder to shoulder, equally barbarous. But the way Mr Neill expresses this in his new book, *The Problem Child* (where, for the first time, he abandons story-form and simply sets forth his principles and methods, with an invaluable mass of first-hand experience) is 'Psychology since Freud's genius made it alive has gone far, but it is still a new science. It is merely mapping out the coast of an unknown continent. Fifty years hence psychologists will very likely smile at our ignorance to-day.'

The quality of this fine forthright book, which has established Mr Neill's title to be regarded as an experimental educationist of the first rank, to whose pioneer work the world will subsequently owe a great deal, can be gauged from such sentences as these: –

'An atheist can ruin his family by imposing a code of morality just as effectively as a Baptist can.'

'No teacher has the right to cure a child of making noises on a drum. The only curing that should be practised is the curing of unhappiness.'

'The over-wrought parent of the "bad boy" does not as a rule challenge his or her own code of morals... I cannot say the truth is, but I can declare my strong conviction, that *the boy is never in the wrong.* There is no original sin, there is only sickness.'

'There may be a case for the moral instruction of adults although I doubt it. There is no case whatever for the moral instruction of children. It is psychologically wrong. To ask a little child to be unselfish is wrong.'

'Not long ago I visited a modern school. Over a hundred boys and girls assembled in the morning to hear a parson address them. He spoke earnestly to them advising them to be ready to hear Christ's call. The head asked me later what I thought of the address. I replied that I thought it criminal. Here were scores of children with consciences about sex and other things. The sermon simply increased each child's sense of guilt. Christ's call was in each case suppressed effectively when the mother first began to teach the child to be good. Christ's call was surely the call to love your neighbour as yourself, and by suppressing God's given instincts the mother taught the children to hate themselves. To love others while hating yourself is impossible. We can only love others if we love ourselves.'

These are mild in comparison with much that is in this book. I share every opinion it expresses. I am conscious, however, that the bulk of Mr Neill's book would seem blasphemous heresy to the overwhelming majority of my fellow-countrymen and fellow-countrywomen, and that the majority of the Scottish teaching profession would share their view. It is futile for Mr Maxton to plead for 'courage in thought, in facing truths, however unpleasant.' The Scottish teaching profession will not face this book. But a few teachers here and there will, and gradually it will triumph, until all the great mass of the teachers who regard it as a hideous travesty of all they believe in will dwindle in historical retrospect to a mob of incredible figures belonging to a barbarous age.

In the meantime those who plume themselves on Scottish education to-day may reflect on the absence of Scottish arts, letters, and cultural activities of all kinds; on the progressive denudation of our countryside; on the appalling problems presented by our great cities; on our progressive denationalisation and provincialisation – and justify their self-gratulation. Whither is Scotland drifting? Our educational system does not seem to be communicating any 'direction' to our course. Is our inchoate state not due to the prostitution of our schools to materialism and morality, and to a stupid misconception and maltreatment of the Scottish spirit?   [5.3.26]

Letters

DORIC AND GAELIC

Sir, – I regret some want of clearness in the last sentence of my previous letter, which seems to have been misapprehended by 'Buchan.' In that sentence I was alluding to the criticism of Swatches o' Hamespun *by my friend, Mr Grieve, whom I consider a real pioneer, because he is making war upon outworn beliefs which are clogging our national life. It is true that he and I look at various Scottish problems from different angles, but that is not the present question.*

If 'Buchan' be a pioneer of the Gaelic movement in his district, he is working in a sterile field. Converting the Buchan folk to Gaelic may be likened to 'ploughing the sands.' 'Buchan,' as a Gaelic scholar and lover, could probably achieve far more by putting his shoulder to the wheel in aid of local effort in some Highland county where the language is being threatened.

'Buchan's' first letter is the genesis of the whole correspondence. In this communication he first patronised the Doric, and then – comparing it with Gaelic – attacked it in slighting terms, improvising the word 'bumpkinisity' to express his opinion of its users. In my mildly defensive reply and a subsequent letter I ventured to make some criticisms of the Gaelic, but I must disclaim responsibility for 'Buchan's' initial tone, continued all through the discussion. I can only suppose that, in putting the onus of his

'asperities' upon me, he had overlooked the terms of his first letter.

'Buchan,' as Mr Tait has ably pointed out, seems to have a habit of confusing unsupported assertion with argument. Thus, he easily demolishes my references to the early Ellon chronicles and the Ruthwell Cross (epochs in the gradual recession of Celtic) by a vague remark about 'false history' and a few more words in the same genial spirit.

In taking leave of 'Buchan,' however, I would like to thank him for his first letter, as it opened the way for an interesting discussion that may prove helpful to both the languages. – I am, etc.,

R.L. Cassie
[5.3.26]

Letters

NORLAN' DIALECTS

Sir, – The swatches of Norlan' fisher dialect which I gave in my last letter have puzzled even Mr Cassie and must therefore have been 'Greek' to some others. "A polled thee?' means 'Who cut your hair?' and 'Bubba' is 'grandfather.' (It is, a Hindu friend informs me, the Sanskrit word for 'elder brother'.) 'Sclafards' are 'slaps.'

The fishwife's "arryin the crook' refers to the pot which was suspended from a hook over the fire. In wild weather the fishermen cannot put out to sea and the pot is empty; the demon-goddess of the south-westerly gales of spring has 'harried the crook.' This deity is called 'Gentle Annie' and is apparently the Gaelic Anu of the place-name 'Paps of Anu,' whose name is also given as 'Danu,' her worshippers having been the 'Tuatha de Danann' ('the tribe of the goddess Danu'). As Ana and Annis ('Black Annis'), she was remembered till recently in Western England. The 'white feather in her hat' is the foam, and the 'heel of Ness' is the point of a little promontory which is dangerous to sail round during a 'soo'-wasterly.' The full translation is: 'When Gentle Annie is shrieking round the "heel of Ness" with a white feather in her hat, she robs the (pot) on the (chimney) hook.' The 'saying' is quite poetic.

'A cowld and yagach morning' is 'a cold and raw (shivery) morning.' Another interesting word is 'yaw.' The 'yaw-line' is the line coiled up and thrown from an incoming boat so that the rope may be hauled in and made fast. One who interrupts a conversation is said to 'yaw in.' I remember a witness in a court Case once declaring of another, 'He yawed in and laid a' the barm (blame) on me.'

As I have said, the fisher dialect differs greatly from the 'toon' dialect which favours diminutives as greatly as did the dialect of Chaucer to whom 'showers' were 'showeries,' a 'son' a 'sone' (sonny), a 'mill' a 'millie' and so on.

My verses which follow are put into the mouth of a 'loonie' and will illustrate my native dialect. They refer to an old baking custom. The female bakers made from the remnants on the baking board a small bannock with a hole which was supposed to protect the baking against fairy attack, evil eye, etc. This small bannock was given to a child who carried from a magic well water which was sprinkled round the hearth to complete the charm. It was believed that the child should not be told what the water was wanted for, but it was necessary that an innocent child should provide the water willingly. If he grumbled about being sent to the well, the water-charm would not be effective. No part of the baking was given to the youngster before the water was brought. The 'grannie' first tempted him with the cake, and then diverted his attention to something else before sending him to the well which in this case had a 'stroop' and was called 'stroopie well.' The boy knew he would get the 'charm bannock' on his return. (I have no doubt many of my readers have in their childhood seen the little bannock with the hole, but they could not have been aware why it was baked.)

Granny's Baking

When granny bakes her oaten cakes
   I aye drap in to news a whiley.
If she should want a messagie,
   She'll ken that then I'd rin a miley.
My grannie's cakes are groff [1] and sweet,
   She'll aye mak' ane for her 'wee mannie';
Oh! aroon' Cromarty there's non'
   Can bake sic cake as my ould grannie.

'An' whit's yer news the day?' she'll speer,
   As I sit on my ain wee stoolie;
'An' div ye like my bonnie cake?
   An' wad ye hae a bittie, mooly? [2]
'Och! grannie, aye,' I'll mak' reply.
   She'll smile, 'Jist hear yon moosie rakin'

---

[1] 'Groff' is 'thick.'

[2] 'Mooly' is Gaelic and means 'my treasure.'

Ahint the press thof[3] *grannie's here –*
   The little roguey smells my bakin'.'

She'll bake ilk cake as roon's the moon,
   Wi' soople thoomb and nev[4] *so knacky;*
Then whip it ower and clap it doon
   Upon the girdle in a crackie.
She'll cut a crossie wi' her knife,
   An' leave fower farlies saft as jelly;
An' then she'll sigh, 'I'm done, but I
   Maun bake a cakie for yerselie.'

She'll say, 'Noo, tak' the pailie doon
   An' bring a stroopie drink for grannie –
You'll mind and row yer hankie roon'
   The han'lie or't 'ill hurt yer hannie.'
The weaver's wife draps in to crack
   Wi', 'Bless yer he'rt and hoo 's yer body?' –
I ken my cakie's toastin' fine
   As I ging up the stroopie roadie.[5]

Alang the hedgie linties sing,
   I keek for nesties ha'din eggies;
I'm gleg and tentie as I ging
   For fear the nettlies scam my leggies.
The wudden stroopie's on the dreep,
   I leave the pailie hingin' canny,
And buttercups and daisies plick
   Far up the Kirky Brae for grannie.

'Ah, me the day!' as she wad say,
   A' this is owld-warld crack, I'm thinkin'; –
The stroopie water's no thocht noo
   So cool and clear and sweet for drinkin'.
Nae grannies bake sweet oaten cake
   For bairns wha think they're geyan quirky;
And mine so dear this mony a year
   Lies sleepin' near the Gaelic Kirky.

---

[3] 'Thof' is 'though.'
[4] 'Nev' is 'fist'.
[5] Pronounced 'roddie.'

Verses of this kind may not appeal readily to those for whom old words and old customs have no real associations, or to those who imagine that violence is strength and that one must needs use the 'muck rake' to make appeal to crouse and couthy folk wha hae a crack roond the ingle o' an evening. Lovers of their native dialect, 'wha've gane oot to the frame,' have aye, when they hear it or read it, dinlin memories that winna devall, and to such the old diminutives sound sweet as the lintie's sang. They sigh (they dinna rage like the bauthrin blawarts of the new artificial-dialect school of verse-makers) because to their dool the diminutives are dwynin in the speech of the folk. When, therefore, one completes an e'enin' stent by giving expression in a genuine dialect to genuine emotions treasured by many, is one necessarily writing unpoetic verse? My own answer is in the negative.

Mr Cassie has kindly sent me, through the Editor of this Journal, the 1923 Swatches o' Hamespun, which is a treasure trove to lovers of the Doric. Apparently some of the contributions jar on the untrained and unaccustomed ears of city-born Scots who have of late been dabbling in auld wirds that have apparently little meaning to them and no associations at all. 'Bit,' as the delightful 'Swatches' poetess, Jessie Coutts, puts it, 'Countra' fouks ken brawly weel foo bantarn cocks can craw.' Publications like 'Swatches' should help to prevent the misuse of words which are so familiar to those who formerly spoke daily or still speak the Doric. It is unscholarly and inartistic to misuse words picked out of dictionaries, and the vernacular movement will never be advanced by linguistic blundering. The 'couthy mither tongue' must be accurately acquired. It is a free and living thing, and it would be disastrous to put the branks on it by tampering with its rich vocabulary.

That the north-east dialects are capable of great things in literature has already been demonstrated. As a writer of melodious and imaginative verse, William Thom, for instance, is worthy to be ranked with Shelley and Coleridge, as I hope to show later. There has always been sweet music 'whaur Gadie rins at the back of Bennachie.' Mr Grieve's sneers at norlan' dialects make one feel sorry for him. He has no idea what he has missed and is missing. – I am, etc.,

Donald A. Mackenzie

GAELIC AND DORIC

Sir, – Circa 1430 practically the only language spoken in the Garioch district of Buchan was Gaelic. We have this information on the authority

of John Harding who, about the year I name, visited Scotland, and there-
after composed a metrical account of his travels. Mr R.L. Cassie,
however, opines that no Gaelic was spoken in Buchan later than the
period of the Book of Deer, the Gaelic entries in which date from the
twelfth century. I could adduce other evidence similar in effect to that
which I have set forth above, and applying some of it to Aberdeenshire,
and the rest to other parts of the Lowlands in which to-day Gaelic is not,
though yesterday, as it were, it was, and was, too, in a very lively
manner. But arguing with those who are minded neither to hear nor see
that which conspires to make themselves and their contentions look
foolish is ever saorachadh gun bhrigh; *and so I beg to be excused. – I am.*
etc.,

Buchan
[12.3.26]

31. R.E. Muirhead and Scottish Home Rule

This is not the place in which to attempt even a summary of the Scottish
Home Rule movement or any analyses of the personalities in whom it
has mainly been embodied. That such a movement in any country
should not have become a factor in affairs which – though it might
remain very much a minority element – could not be ignored would be a
surprising fact, implying material for a curious psycho-political study;
but that this should have happened in Scotland, with its antecedent
traditions and tendencies – especially in view of the fashion in which the
Union of the Parliaments was contrived – is scarcely credible at all, and
certainly quite incredible if the common generalisations as to Scottish
character (love of country, capacity for affairs, tenacity, high education,
and so forth) are accepted, as they are even by the majority of Scotsmen
themselves. Conjoin to this the fact that a majority of the Scottish representation of all parties at Westminster has supported Bill after Bill to
restore self-government to Scotland, only to accept defeat at the hands
of the overwhelming English majority. It implies either that in this
particular matter the majority of the Scottish representation were
conscious that they had not a proportionate following of the Scottish
people behind them or sufficiently behind them to warrant other steps
to end what can only have been, if they were really convinced of the
need for devolution, an intolerable state of affairs – or an extraordinary

incapacity on their own part for leadership. Indeed, it implies both of these – because even if a majority of the people were not sufficiently behind them, only a radical defectiveness in their own qualities as leaders would have prevented their speedily acquiring an adequate following if their cause was good. The latter can be assumed from the fact that a majority of all parties of our M.P.s registered their conviction to that effect from time to time and, however incapable they may have been, it must be conceded that on the whole they were in the best position to know. Nor is it reasonable to assume that in acting as they did they did not represent at least a very substantial body of public opinion. A reverse at Westminster should at least have been marked by a definite intensification of Scottish home rule propaganda in the speeches and writings of the members in question. That would have evidenced their good faith and the determination which they owed to themselves in the circumstances. On the contrary they have always accepted defeat in a manner incredible in men really in earnest. We fall back, then, upon the real explanation of the lack of anything cumulative in the advocacy of Scottish Home Rule in and through the existing political parties. An inveterate habit of thinking of Scotland in terms of the existing situation has stultified for all practical purposes whatever there was of genuine conviction of the need for Scottish home rule in the minds of these gentlemen. The same thing accounts for the static state of electoral opinion on the matter. To this in the case of the M.P.s must be added to some extent, their natural tendency to concentrate on 'practical politics,' as they are called, instead of real politics – really fundamental issues – and, in the case of the electorate, the sense of impotence created by the lack of leadership and the lack of much of that special knowledge of the neglect of Scottish interests of which, owing to their almost entire preoccupancy with the actual issues arising at Westminster, the M.P.s have failed to make proper use. In other words, both the M.P.s who have voted in favour of home rule and the majority of those of their electors who, if asked, would have expressed themselves in favour of their action in so doing are too much the products of the existing system to develop, in the absence of a campaign coming from an entirely different point of view, any attitude towards the question capable of yielding a real dynamic.

This 'unreal' demand for Scottish home rule is mainly maintained by the Scottish Home Rule Association, the mainspring of which is – and has for many years been – Mr R.E. Muirhead. The great majority of the members of the S.H.R.A. envisage in demanding Scottish home rule no radical divergence from the existing English situation. The constitution of the Association calls for Scottish self-determination but, apart from the fact that the existing situation *is* Scottish self-determination in the sense that it can be terminated as soon as an effective proportion of the inhabitants of Scotland make up their mind to terminate it (not that the people of Scotland are to blame for not so making up their minds, in view of the English and Anglo-Scottish monopoly of all the main means of propaganda and publicity), the majority of the members do not contemplate any self-determination which would mean a break away from existing standards. They are not animated by a deep-seated sense of national difference. What they want is the devolution of the adminis-tration of purely Scottish affairs: and their arguments in favour of this are mainly based on relatively trivial considerations. The congestion of business at Westminster, for example, is not the kind of issue to set 'the heather on fire.' The great majority of such political issues as would be affected by devolution of this kind find the bulk of the people apathetic. It is certainly absurd that the Scottish question of Church Union should be 'enabled' by a predominantly English Assembly, rather than in accor-dance only with the expressed majority wish of Scotland – but the majority of the Scottish people are utterly indifferent to the question of Church Union, and protest on such a score is consequently a waste of time. It illustrates the misconception of reality which vitiates the whole propaganda of the S.H.R.A. In the absence of an effective grievance they are making mountains of molehills. But the real grievance is not so much in anything that England has done as in what our association with such a disproportionate partner has enabled her to prevent our doing. Mere action and reaction within the range of existing British politics holds us to a plane upon which it is impossible to generate an effective political principle to secure anything really worth working for in relation to Scottish nationalism. What is wanted – what alone will yield a real dynamic – is a separate conception of 'Scotland – a Nation' in accor-dance with purely Scottish psychology. This, if acquired, will still accom-modate Tory, Liberal, and Socialist. That is to say, it could still be urged on a non-party basis. Whence is it to come? It can only arise out of a renewed sense of nationality fed on a re-reading of Scottish history and a delineation of new opportunity. Bickerings as to the neglect of Scottish interests, the disproportionate incidence of imperial taxation, the commercial and industrial disadvantages of bank amalgamation, the cost of sending deputations to London instead of to Edinburgh or Glasgow, and so forth will never develop it. They are mere reflexes of the *status quo.* If a live issue is to be created it must be in another sphere alto-gether. Mentally, morally, economically and even psychologically the great bulk of the Scottish people to-day are unconscious of having any potentiality of different 'direction' to the English. The impotence of the S.H.R.A. is due to the fact that it has concerned itself almost wholly with issues below 'nation-size' – issues that have no bearing on the core of nationality, but are the merest superficial trimmings. But it has embodied no vital manifestation of Scottish culture opposed to the prevailing ethos. It has been bogged in mere 'politics.' In any national movement politics are a very subsidiary matter – effects not causes. Develop a national consciousness and if the existing political institutions are at variance with it they will be altered. The S.H.R.A. have put the cart before the horse. The only way in which the objects of the S.H.R.A. can be realised is by concentrating mainly on undoing all the effects of national subordination and increasing Anglicisation; and that, first of all, in the sphere where it is most vital – not the national purse but the national soul. Merely material considerations, even if they are urged in terms which pay lip-service to larger national ideals, will be ineffective. Sentimentality is useless – and lip service to Scottish nationality and the great figures of our past is futile if Scottish nationality to-day cannot create distinctive tendencies of an adequate character, and embody them in personalities of sufficient force.

There is nothing so creative about any of the members of the S.H.R.A. In other words, they are not sufficiently Scottish themselves to advance their cause. At the most they are only sufficiently Scottish to maintain themselves – not to make any headway – against the continual pressure of an alien environment. Their propaganda has never become more than a very minor element in British politics. Neither in spirit, in method, or in tendency, has there been anything specifically Scottish about it. 'Seek ye first the Kingdom of Heaven, and all these things will be added unto ye.' This text embodies a great realisation of what must be the core of any achievement. All the grievances with which the S.H.R.A. occupy themselves will disappear precisely in proportion as the Scottish national soul is recovered and Scotland begins to 'stand for' anything again in the comity of nations.

Incompetent diagnosticians of public opinion, the S.H.R.A. propa-gandists lack alike that proleptic sense of how things will strike people in the mass sometimes found in first-rate journalists, and the further gift, essential to their avowed purpose, of originating the mode or policy, planning the ways and means of its execution, and judging its political reactions in advance and to a T. The absence of the first of these is undoubtedly reflected in the poor quality of their propagandist writing. Surely no national cause was ever advocated in poorer 'literature.' Is it not something in their attitude to life itself, and to culture, that is at fault – democratic methods, a bourgeois spirit incapable of effectively embodying a claim to sovereign independence, of advancing their point of view on the level of the affairs involved? Lobbying in Westminster and in Co-operative Society committee rooms is a poor imitation of the manipulation of affairs. The lack of an 'uncontented care to write better than they can,' the disabling absence, even hatred, of extremism, indicates a subordination of temper incompatible with their political aims and claims. It is not an easy thing to develop these faculties, but nothing less will suffice. The whole question of Scotland's position will become one of moment only in proportion to the commanding power that can be acquired in the statement of it – and probably the only way in which such a change can be encompassed is by deliberately generating attitudes and reactions in regard to Scottish affairs, and a style of communicating them, at variance with the whole atmosphere alike of the great mass of Scots apathetic to the issue, and that other body which, while desiring Scottish home rule, manifests such an invertebrate readiness to accept defeat, to serve merely as a safety valve for the *status quo*, or, at best, to continue indefinitely in the role of Sisyphus.

While, therefore, I believe that the methods of the S.H.R.A. have been essentially futile, and the personnel almost wholly ineffective for the objects of the Association owing to their lack of essential 'vision,' it is, after all, by indirections that directions are discovered and in this sense the S.H.R.A. have perhaps done valuable service. They have explored all the ways in which Scottish Self-Government cannot be secured – except perhaps one: the granting of a certain measure of devolution, which might not only mean nothing for the recovery of Scottish nationality in any real sense of the term, but might actually tend in the opposite direction. There are signs, however, that in the S.H.R.A., as in other more important, if perhaps less well-known, groups, the danger of this is now being realised or, perhaps, they are being affected by the development of the necessary dynamic elsewhere. It has taken a long time to realise that the British Parliament cannot grant or withhold Scottish Self-Determination – that that lies wholly with the Scottish people; but apparently the fact has at last struck home.

The main redeeming feature of the S.H.R.A. has been Mr Muirhead – and that largely by his capacity for personal self-sacrifice and his extraordinary tenacity. Even the S.H.R.A. with its anaemic and largely Anglicised ideas contains many members prepared to sacrifice time and energy. It contains fewer who have got away sufficiently from the stock-conception of the Scot to sacrifice money. Mr Muirhead is the principal of the latter. It has so far been a remarkably poor investment. Within the sphere to which he has unfortunately almost wholly confined himself he has maintained a persistent pro-Scottish propaganda with a resource in debate and a factual efficiency and equipment over a long period of years of a most notable kind. If only as one insisting upon a distinction even in the absence of any real difference. Mr Muirhead has thus perhaps, however exiguously, contrived to keep a semblance of Scottish nationalism at work in the minds of large sections of his countrymen too Anglicised to be in any degree amenable to the more truly Scottish propaganda of the Hon. R. Erskine of Marr: and has thus kept them to a greater degree than they would otherwise have been available for the influence of new fundamental manifestations of Scottish nationalism if, and when, these develop. To those who know 'Ronnie' Muirhead and his singularly selfless devotion to the cause he has at heart, his unwearied energy, and his extraordinary patience in the face of continual disappointment (a patience as of Bruce's spider), this may seem a grudging tribute. It is not meant to be so. I am only trying to see him as he will be seen in the perspective of history. 'By their fruits ye shall know them'; but to judge Mr Muirhead – and one or two others of his leading associates – Miss A. Milne, Helensburgh; Rev. Walter Murray and 'R.E.'s' brother, Dr R.F. Muirhead, in particular – by the absence of real effect on affairs of the Association, and still more so by the unfortunately sentimental and myopic type of opinion that predominantly characterises it – would be extremely unfair. Nor can I feel that it may be said of them: 'They built better than they knew.' They have practically mistaken the shadow of Scottish nationalism for the substance – but, at least, believing it to be the substance, it can be said that they have pursued the shadow with a wonderful assiduity and disinterestedness for which they deserve all credit. However misled, they are people of high character, if none of them have capacities of leadership or any dynamic attribute of personality. The majority of the other active workers for the Association are negligible. They address a great many meetings and write a certain number of articles and letters – but they have nothing to say. In this they do not differ from the great majority of politicians of other parties, but the leaders of the latter do more on a plane of prolepsis and *savoir faire*.

If I assume the rôle of 'diminisher' to discontent them with their busy ineffectiveness and reveal them as the nugatory factors they are, it is with the hope that they may reorient their activities, transcend their infirmity of will, acquire a technique of development in place of their introvert defeatism, and emerge at length on a plane of effective nationalism. They must oppose the prevailing forces in politics with counter-conceptions of equal magnitude, seeking not the devolution of Scottish affairs from Westminster, but the restoration of Scotland to an adequate place in the sun.

The S.H.R.A. publish the only existing organ of Scottish Nationalism – a monthly newssheet entitled *Scottish Home Rule* (30 Elmbank Crescent. Glasgow). Other publications are – *Home Rule for Scotland: the Case in 90 Points*, by Rev. Walter Murray. B.D.; *Self-Government for Scotland*, by R.B. Cunninghame Graham; *Self-Government for Scotland*, by Mrs Annie Besant and others; *Scotland Yet*, by Rev. James Barr. M.P.; *The Deer Forests, and How They are Bleeding Scotland White*, by J.M. MacDiarmid. [19.3.26]

32. Neil M. Gunn

Practically the only young Scottish prose-writer of promise manifesting himself today is Mr Neil M. Gunn, whose first novel, *The Grey Coast*, is published by Messrs Jonathan Cape, Ltd. – the only Scottish prose-writer of promise, that is to say, in relation to that which is distinctively Scottish rather than tributary to the 'vast engulfing sea' of English literature. As a writer of short sketches and short stories, he has contributed largely to the *Glasgow Herald*, to the *Scottish Nation* and *Northern Review*, to *Chambers' Journal*, to *The Dublin Magazine*, to, above all, the *Cornhill*, and many other periodicals: and is our nearest equivalent to the Irish Liam O'Flaherty. All that mass of contributions (none of them yet collected in volume form) have had beyond their competence and consequence saleability tentatives of a curious kind – hints of a casual attitude to his output only occasionally interrupted by the need to resolve difficulties of kinds which lie outwith the *gebiet* of magazine-writers. No doubt these passages have often stirred doubts in the minds of editors as to the acceptability of his MSS. – doubts hardly, in some cases, subdued by the perfect normality of the rest. I do not mean 'purple passages.' I mean sudden breakings-through into dimensions in which the editors and readers of popular periodicals of even the best kinds suffer from incontinent agoraphobia – declaustrated thus unexpectedly from the given conventions. It is curious to see pedestrian journalese become mucronulate in this fashion, and it was precisely these uncovenanted developments that aroused speculations as to his further development. Would he thrust out into the atmosphere of originality altogether – throw spikes, not like the 'fretful porcupine,' of mere uneasy conscience, but 'beyond himself' entirely – random arrows into the unexplored with which all imaginative writing of more than social consequence is solely concerned? He must have had the desirability of excising these passages suggested to him often – he must have had difficulty in placing his MSS. precisely in proportion to the frequency of their occurrence. This, to those who were thinking of his work with non-commercial hopes, argued a commendable thrawnness in him – a sense of something really to say disputing with his mere facility. And it is precisely this 'stalk of earle hemp' that has been obtruding itself more and more significantly in his recent work. There is an allied reason for his special significance from a purely Scottish point of view – a double-barrelled reason. His un-Scottish preoccupation with pure technique; and his constant endeavour to apply it to the purely Scottish scene. In other words, he is showing an ever-lessening tendency to subscribe either in style or in subject-matter to the un-Scottish conventions of all British editors and almost all British publishers. He is, in fact, tending in the opposite direction: and having got rid of the attitude at once to life and to letters which has characterised the period of Scotland's nationalistic and literary nadir, his artistic integrity is bringing him into unmediated relations with Scottish nature, human and otherwise. The process is not yet complete. He has not wholly found himself nor has Scotland reacquired entire autonomy in his consciousness. His work remains unequal – now almost anonymous in its resemblance to 'current fiction' in the mass, now falling into a Kailyaird rut, now tinged with the Celtic twilight. Above these levels, at its second-best, it manifests a point of view not dissimilar to George Douglas Brown's, but more humane, more *divers et ondoyant* than his, but, at the same time, less organic. It is this style – of attitude to life, not of writing – which comprises most of *The Grey Coast*. But the best things in the book are pure Gunn – something new, and big, in Scottish literature; and they intermittently steep the book in a further dimension of the spirit than the author of *The House with the Green Shutters* ever reached. In the light of them mere realism – inverted Kailyairdism – becomes dated and loses the force it might still retain if these other elements were absent. In other words, another novel of exactly the 'House with the Green Shutters' kind may yet be written. The writer of it will be a bigger figure than any other that Scotland has produced since George Douglas Brown died. But Gunn, if he can maintain himself exclusively, for the length of time it takes to write a novel or a sequence of short stories, in the rarer air to which he rises for brief moments every now and again in *The Grey Coast* and elsewhere – will not be a second George Douglas Brown or a second anybody – he will be an originative artist in his own right; he will have circumvented the alien atmosphere that transmogrifies almost all fictional treatment of Scottish life either into a provincial parody of what it should be or a miserable shadow of English genres, and broken clear through into the Magna Scotia in whose ample and distinctive air Scottish novels can comport themselves in as comely and comprehensive a fashion and with as unqualified an independence of provenance and inimitability of kind, as can the very different novels endemic to the diverse traditions of Russia, France or England. At his best Gunn gives no mere reflexes or inversions of the forces that have provincialised Scottish literature. Nor in his complex psychological understanding is he imitating later novels from other European literatures than have hitherto been naturalised in our rheumatic atmosphere. His technique and his subject-matter are elements of each other not to be analysed out into imitations, conscious or unconscious, of anything else: but break in an unpredicated fashion from the denied core of our national genius with a promise of effective uprising against the alien culture which has inhibited it so long.

Gunn writes mainly in English, although there is a dialectical colouring in *The Grey Coast* and a psychological patterning of the style which he may yet develop into a purely Scottish use of English. His subtle evocative and 'troubling' power is well illustrated in such a passage as this:

> There is a quality in this half-light that is at once a folding of wings and an awareness. Colour intensifies, 'runs,' so that the ditchside of tall kingcups at hand becomes a deep still flame of gold, and the field of 'half-sphered scabious' beyond the bank swoons in a veritable ravishment of 'purple mist.' Into the silence creeps gradually a listening stillness. The bleating of a sheep or far barking of a dog dies out in ears that continue to hear the echoing forlornness. Upon the body itself, squatting stiffly, steals that subconscious alertness which, if a sudden hand were to descend on a shoulder, would cause a jump with the heart in the mouth.

And (in the same story – earlier writing than *The Grey Coast*) comes this significant evidence of his creative trend:

'Iain Mackay', I thought, deliberately, 'epitomised in himself this particular sea-coast. He knew with an intimacy of the marrow its uttermost essence. He merged again with that essence willingly or unwillingly, but in some way *wittingly*.'... The harbour basin fills. Boat-decks, rigging, masts slanting to rest in their crutches, figures moving about, at first dimly, then more distinctly; a face, faces; sounds: all coming before the staring eyes through stages, as it were, of imperfect focusing, till the picture lives, moves, throbs. A species of 'movies,' if you like – for away from the influence one must needs jest about it to keep balance. But under the influence – my father's stride, a trifle quicker than the others, the face a trifle more alert; the tongue with its ever-ready shaft. And there the men from the Lews – the heave-ho! chant of the Gaelic voices, the *krik! krik!* of the halyards... An ache comes to the soul, the lips stir to an old savour, saline, brimful of life. Something here of the marrow, ineradicable. School-keeping, shop-keeping, book-clerking, all the pale, anaemic occupations of landsmen and citymen... teaching children all day long so that they may 'get on,' may be successful in attaining the clerical stool or pulpit, or measuring, at a profit, so many yards of red flannel for a country woman's needs... a throw-back, am I?

Or again (writing of Fiona Macleod, Yeats and the others):

Intellect strives and flashes towards some final revealing illumination – till the effort inevitably expends itself like a twopenny rocket attempting the work of a sun. And when failure thus rushes down in a renewed darkness, swamping all meaning and logic – dream poetry is there, a glimmering half-light, beckoning. Not an interpretation of the Ultimates: a refuge from them. The man of action, with his raw grip on the realities, ignores it – till he finds the sphere of his activities dissolved like some unsubstantial pageant, till (for this is the thought) the routh of life that swarmed the Seaboard and clothed the very salmon poles is left a ghostly greyness and a calling of gulls. Then poetry casts its net, its iridescent net, and the silvery fish of the intellect is meshed in the music of lost days and beauty forgone... Perhaps the making of all great poetry has involved this fight – and this admission. Perhaps the men who have written greatly of the half-light have known the stark realities of the light. Let me say as much, even if I don't believe it yet, for, after all, what do I know of the Ultimates that I should talk of a refuge from them?... There the fading light on the breast of the sea, there the dim-glowing West facing me as arm and body cleave through: and haunting my brain hypnotically the saying: 'And the symbol of Murias is a hollow that is filled with water and fading light.'

The nature of the study Mr Gunn undertakes in *The Grey Coast is* indicated in this passage:

> The voices settled to a drone again in the margin of Maggie's consciousness. Now and then, as she drew out a needle and prepared for another row, she would glance from under her black lashes at the wag-at-th'-wa'. The glance, returning, would take in the figures by the fireside, and for a moment a subtle appraisement would gleam in it and die. The expression on her face, however, never varied from its indifferent calm: as though the secret life of the mind could go on of its own accord, without touching immediate material existence at the surface at all; indeed, so remote from it that even the gleam of appraisement betokened rather a criticism by the unconscious than a disturbance in her positive reflections. Silence, the long brooding hours altogether too long to be filled by thought, the wakefulness wherein no word is spoken, the vague self-hypnosis: it may be that under it all the mind of its own volition pursues hidden ways of dream and thought, to be revealed outwardly in a gleam, an unconscious gesture, a decision positive as unexpected. And of all places, such a grey strip of crofting coast, flanked seaward by great cliffs, cliffs 'flawed' as in a half-sardonic humour of their Creator to permit of the fishing creek, was surely the place for the perfect growth of this duality of the mind, whereby the colourless, normal life becomes at once a record of the stolidly obvious and of the dreamlike unknown.

This co-existence of incompatible appearances and realities – the antitheses between what the characters choose to be and ought rather to be – the fact that ostensible character is a subtly-manipulated disguise behind which nature seeks to deceive life until, in most cases, it becomes a mere reflex of the disguise – the 'monstrous joy of soiling the ideal' – the algoniac alternate yielding to and fighting with brute circumstance – these and such as these are the themes, subtly developed, of this sincere and searching novel, and it is part and parcel of Mr Gunn's promise that they present themselves with more unanalysable reality and momentum in his dialogues than in his descriptions, intimate and telling as these are. Just how in the simple sentences of these conversations the multiple forces contending behind the words, and, for the most part, just below

the level of consciousness communicate themselves with such complicated comprehensiveness of effect and yet such vital conviction is the
secret of Mr Gunn's art. It is enough to say that if he can rid himself of
his remaining inequalities – sustain himself wholly at the pitch of the
best elements in this book – and bring the method by which he encompassed them to full maturity, he will rapidly take rank as the foremost of
living Scottish novelists – a George Douglas Brown come to magna-
nimity and endowed with all the knowledge psychology has acquired
since Brown's day. As it stands, *The Grey Coast* is more significant
achievement than all the novels of the so-called young Glasgow school
put together.   [2.4.26]

Letters

GAELIC AND DORIC

*Sir, – 'Buchan' is refreshingly certain regarding the pedigree of the men
of that ilk, and to the coming of Braid Scots. Watt has it that by the end
of the fourteenth century 'the new population had supplanted or
absorbed the old Celtic inhabitants.' Dr Giles dates the coming of Braid
Scots as following the 'Herschip o' Bowchane' in 1308. In 1402 a list of
forestallers in Aberdeenshire is completed; among the sharks are named
'John Oute with the swerd' at Deer; 'Simo Curst,' 'Litil Wil' at Foveran –
not one of them Gaelic names. (Mair's 'Ellon.')*

*In the 'Querula domini Malcomi (Arbroath) aduersus dominum de
Meldrum pene Cerras vocatas Cautey in baronia nostra de Tarwas'…
there appears a pun upon the word Caute. The complaint itself is in the
vernacular which establishes nothing so far as the language of the
district is concerned, but it states how 'ane common smyth was tholyt tyll
bigg ane smyde in the moss.' The said smyth vas callit Ade of Caute and
in skorne with nychtbowris vas callit lard of Caute in derisioun because
he sett in the myddys of ane cauld moss and throwe that skorne the land
was callit Caulty' (Cosmo Innes). Evidently the people of Tarves of 1460
knew the meaning of cauld – and Tarves is not far out of Garioch. And in
the very centre of the Garioch, a charter granted by David, Earl of
Huntingdon and the Garioch, is granted to the first of the Leslies and is
addressed to vassals 'Franks and English, Flemings and Scots' so that
even then four different tongues had been spoken including Scots (i.e.
Gaelic). It takes some faith, therefore, to swallow the statement that*

'circa *1430 practically the only tongue spoken in the Garioch was Gaelic.'*

And is *'Harding'* quite a dependable witness? In 1908 some Buckie men were travelling in an English train; a stranger was in the compartment and, evidently much interested, he asked if his companions were speaking Gaelic. And he was quite an intelligent Englishman too.

Would *'Buchan'* kindly explain the following points? Why is it that English, spoken by once Gaelic-speaking peoples – e.g. Invernessians and Irishmen – is full of Gaelic turns and idioms while in our particular *'nyeuk'* these are entirely absent? And why, on the other hand, are all the intimate idioms and turns of phrase almost purely Teutonic? And why have practically all Gaelic words disappeared from our vocabulary except terms of vituperation, e.g. cyard, eeshan, ablich, clort? The terms of endearment in Gaelic might well have been preserved, but they have disappeared, much to the loss of our dialect. In the late war French children picked up Tommy's lingo – the kind not used in the drawing-room. Can this also be the explanation of the presence of Gaelic *'cuss-words'* in our vocabulary? Is it a relic of the feud between the natives and the *'ootlins'*? I am concerned with truth; I have no pet theory about skulls or their contents, so *'Buchan'* can be expository instead of explosive if and when he answers. – I am, etc.,

Buchan Humlie
[2.4.26]

33. Mrs Kennedy-Fraser and the Songs of the Hebrides

Mr Hugh Roberton, writing, very appropriately, in the *People's Journal*, in the course of a series of articles entitled, equally appropriately, 'Crotchets and Quavers,' devoted a column to *Songs of the Hebrides*, in which he expressed his opinions so dogmatically that it must be concluded that they belong to the former of these two categories.

It is not so very long ago since Burns died, [he said,] … the spark of genius still burns in Scotland. To-day, the newly-published fourth volume of the *Songs of the Hebrides* came into my hands. In turning over the pages and finding here and there a gem of purest ray serene and everywhere the stamp of the pure gold of achievement, my heart went out to that patient grey-haired woman who lives under the shadow of Edinburgh Castle, and who over many years has laboured so fruitfully in this field of her own choosing. Strolling into a music shop in an English city the other day, I saw scores of Hebridean songs on display. 'Do they sell?' I asked. 'Of course they do,' the manager replied. 'They are not just for Scotsmen; they are for every serious-minded student.' There you are. The name of Scotland carried furth of Scotland, and honoured. And that is only a small part of the service Mrs Kennedy-Fraser has done to her native country. What a strange people we are! In some respects how curiously uncivilised! Were gold or precious stones to be found in the Isles what a terrific rush there would be! The financiers would put on their thinking caps and set companies on foot, and bargain and corner. The Press would shriek. There would be questions asked in the Commons. And yet that was a small thing in comparison with what is contained in those four volumes of Hebridean songs. For Mrs Kennedy-Fraser has discovered and reclaimed what is more precious than gold, rarer than rubies, more enduring than institutions or systems of philosophy... What is there within knowledge that is likely to outlive 'The Eriskay Love Lilt' or 'The Seagull of the Land-Under-Waves'?... Many of these Hebridean songs fall easily within the category of 'great.' That they are not all exactly as they fell from the lips of the people is not the sound argument many well-meaning Gaels think it is. Nor does it take us further to say that some of the songs, like the 'Twa Sisters' have been pieced together. Both statements may be true, but might be adduced more fitly as testimony to the art of the composer. Again, some folk are fond of reminding us of the invaluable collaboration of Kenneth Macleod... I mention these matters here because I have heard such arguments put forward quite seriously. The fact is Mrs Kennedy-Fraser has done what only a fine artist can do. She has put the songs into what seems to her (and what seems to many competent judges) the most artistic and permanent form. Furthermore she has given to the songs a background of pianoforte accompaniment which in itself is a work of genius. A brilliant technician, a keen student, an original thinker, she never for a moment lets her pen run away with her. A clumsy hand or a clumsy mind could easily have ruined every song in the four books. As it is, there is not a commonplace bar in one of them. Many of them are supreme works of art... I feel proud of this opportunity of paying tribute to the genius of a great Scotswoman, and to the genius also of her colleague. When the generations to come are able to get this work into focus two names will shine out very brightly in our national story... The matter cannot be settled in our lifetime, but it will be settled and, whoever wins, Marjory Kennedy-Fraser and Kenneth Macleod are not going to be on the losing side.

I have quoted the above *in extenso* for various reasons – because it is a choice example of the mixture of 'sob-stuff,' invincible ignorance, and conceit which characterises nine-tenths of the pronouncements of those who are to-day regarded as authorities on the arts in Scotland; because to anyone who is *au fait* with the international musical position to-day it gives itself away so completely and proves up to the hilt the very opposite conclusions to Mr Roberton's as to the precise nature and value of Mrs Kennedy-Fraser's achievements: and because it affords an admirable pretext to do what Mr Roberton and his kind are all so anxious to avoid – argue the matter out.

'Ah, if Burns were alive to-day how we should honour him!' You will hear enthusiastic sentimentalists talk in this way. It means nothing. If he were alive we should treat Burns pretty much as our fathers did, for it is not given to a generation to get the work of great genius into right focus. We can stand and understand the effulgence of lesser lights; the fierce white light of genius blinds us. No. Burns alive today would just be a heap o' trouble and the great multitude would not know him. Eat haggis, therefore, and drink whisky if you will, but do not flatter yourselves. You are not discoverers.

How comes it then that Mr Roberton is so certain that he has contemporaneously got 'great genius into right focus'? Is he a discoverer? But, if so, what has he discovered? Only what a great mass of the people have already discovered. *Songs of the Hebrides*, on his own showing, have a great sale in England and elsewhere. How does he reconcile his unmeasured encomiums of Mrs Kennedy-Fraser with the great popularity of her work in her own day? In view of his own statements he can neither be convicted of modesty or consistency. The fact of the matter is that he knows, or ought to know, that it is all tosh to write of 'Songs of the Hebrides' as he does, and that, even in Scotland to-day, intellectually and artistically null as it is in comparison with any other country in Europe, infinitely better work than Mrs Kennedy-Fraser's is being done – and that her work and the associated activities of the Festival movement are standing in the way of that better work – that spirit of genuine integrity, that long overdue development in Scottish music – as inferior work almost invariably stands between genius and the public. The difference in other countries is that there is always an adequate intelligentsia to recognise genius from pseudo-genius and to counter-balance the facile demagoguery of their Mr Robertons. In Scotland there is not. 'We're a' Jock Tamson's bairns.'

What is the truth about these *Songs of the Hebrides*? In the first place they are not Hebridean songs at all. They are in no way essentially Scottish even. And above all – so far from belonging to the future as Mr Roberton would have us believe – they do not even belong to the present; they are definitely 'dated' – they belong to the '90s and have the appropriate artificiality and decadence. The readiness with which they have found widespread popularity – their success in 'playing to the gallery' – is, in itself, the strongest evidence against them. Mr Roberton may airily brush aside as of no moment the criticisms that 'they are not exactly as they fell from the lips of the people' and 'some of them have been pieced together,' and dismiss, as airily, any disposition to enquire too closely into the nature of Mrs Kennedy-Fraser's collaboration with Kenneth Macleod. But a great deal more will be heard of these and allied issues, and they are of fundamental importance. Already questions are being asked in quarters to which even Mr Roberton cannot affect a sublime superiority. Mr Ernest Newman, for example, feels 'that the application of cold scientific tests to the whole body of Hebridean song would yield some quite positive conclusions.'

It would, [rejoins another controversialist,] but perhaps not the expected. The first stage in that work, were it to be undertaken, would require to be the establishment by strict scientific principles of a reliable basis on which to found the theories that were to follow. That could not be done with the *Songs of the Hebrides* as issued to the public by Mrs Kennedy-Fraser and her collaborator. Their work is not done on scientific principles, cold or otherwise; and anyone undertaking research or study in Hebridean song and music as revealed in them would be wasting time and effort. The music given to us – at least in some of the more popular items – is adapted to the accompanying English words and the original Gaelic ones are disre-garded. The tunes would have to be taken out of their settings, which are not in keeping with the melodies and the original words. The English words would have to be relieved of all camouflage which tends to delude the unwary. For instance 'Kishmul's Galley' would have to be tamed down to 'MacNeill's Boat.' 'The Reivers' would have to disappear altogether, and some title substituted which would be suggestive of womanly affection for husband or lover which had gone forth on a stormy day 'to rive the sea' (the English idiom being 'to plough the ocean') and not at all to 'reive' argosies on the high seas. The putting of the *Songs of the Hebrides* in condition for the exercise of scientific study on them would be a huge task in itself, and the last persons to commit the work to are surely those who made the task necessary.

Evidence along these lines – and it can be adduced *ad infinitum* and is quite ungainsayable (the examples mentioned will be in themselves sufficient to show most people that we have here again something not dissimilar to the mongrel work of Ossian or 'Fiona Macleod' in the literary sphere) – in no way impugns the artistic quality of the Kennedy-Fraser work; but it proves that to call it Hebridean is misleading and unwarrantable and that if, through it, 'the name of Scotland is carried furth of Scotland and honoured,' Scotland is accepting bouquets on false pretences.

The important thing, of course, is not whether the songs are Hebridean or miscegenate productions but whether they are, as Mr Roberton avers, in many instances supreme works of art and in most instances great art. But before going on to that, since so much is heard of Scotland's incomparable wealth of Folk-Song, it may be suggested that insular enthusiasts of Mr Roberton's type before they begin talking about discoveries 'more precious than gold, rarer than rubies, more enduring than institutions or systems of philosophy' should endeavour to get Mrs Kennedy-Fraser's achievement into proper perspective by comparing it with what has been achieved by other workers in like fields. Let them, with due solemnity, for example, put Mrs Kennedy-Fraser's four-volume collection alongside Mr Béla Bartók's 'finds' as the result of twelve years' painstaking labour – Hungary, 2,800 folk-tunes; Rumania, 3,500; Slovakia, 2,600, Biskra. With his colleague, Kodály, he has collected 4,000 more Hungarian melodies. If Mrs Kennedy-Fraser had made her collection on a scientific basis, as Newman wished, it would have enabled us to tell how far they had been stylised. Bartók, unlike Mrs Kennedy-Fraser, prints the melodies on one page without harmonies of any kind and then follows his treatment of them. It is in regard to his methods of treating folk-song that he may most profitably be compared with Mrs Kennedy-Fraser. A recent writer on Bartók (Frank Whittaker, in *Musical Times*, March 1, 1926) puts it thus:

He had begun to employ folk-tune themes, but with the penetration of genius realised that he was not building on solid foundations… I am dealing with this phase of Bartók's career in some detail because of its close bearing on the ever-recurring controversy about the influence of folk-songs on 'national' composers. A few months ago, in the *American Mercury*, John C. Cavendish attacked the premise 'that folk-tunes in general lend themselves most aptly to musical treatment, and have thus proved a source of valuable inspiration to the greatest of composers.' In support of this, Mr Ernest Newman wrote 'No one denies the value of good folk-song in itself. All that some of us have denied is that a "national" school of music can be created by composers of the present day taking the folk-music of their own country as their model.' In the narrowest sense this is no doubt true, although I think Bartók, who is certainly helping to create a national school and who frequently employs actual folk-tunes, only just escapes the proscription.

But he goes on to show how after winning wide recognition – as long as he was doing work of a folk-music character – after he really began to find himself he was ridiculed, boycotted, maligned, hooted – for years he had to stand alone. The same thing will happen in Scotland, whenever a serious effort is made to cut clear of the old 'mumbo-jumbo' and create a Scottish national school of music. Whoever tries that on will stand very severely alone so far as Mr Roberton and all his Festival friends are concerned. They are not discoverers – they are determined that there will be no discoveries – and certainly Mrs Kennedy-Fraser is none. She is exactly in the position that Bartók abandoned when he began his fight. She has made no fight. Hers has been a case of capitulation all along the line.

It is interesting to find another writer in the *Musical Times* for March saying of Bantock's Hebridean Symphony (which F.G. Scott has well described as 'a welter of sound where the tunes borrowed from Mrs Kennedy-Fraser's collections float about like sprigs of heather'): 'It was a disappointment to find how unimpressed one was on rehearing this work after so long a period (ten years).' Let Mr Roberton revise his prediction of immortality for Mrs Kennedy-Fraser's work in the light of that. The truth seems to be that no technique applied to our native productions can raise them to art products of a first-rate order – these can only be attained by a Scotsman who has completely assimilated their content, *lived it*, in fact, and has a technique for that expression and no other.

True art is the balance between technique and expression. Wherever there is not that balance the result is artificial and inartistic. The matter can be set out in a table, as follows: –

Technique=Expression.	I. Folk-Song and Dance.
Technique greater than Expression.	II. Utilisation (as by Bantock) of above. Never arrives at balance.
Technique=Expression.	III. Pure creation as in I, creating as the primitives did but using modern means and modern matter.

Mrs Kennedy-Fraser is only at Stage II, and has not sacrificed her popularity, as Bartók did, by passing on to Stage III to achieve anything worth while either for music or for Scotland. 'We have reached a point,' as F.G. Scott put it in his recent address to the Glasgow Centre of the English Association, 'in European musical history when it is hardly any longer possible to utilise folk-songs as leading themes in music. We must seek rather to get at the spirit which animates our native songs and dances and make our music as the primitives made *theirs,* a reflection of our environment and spiritual needs. This is what I understand by the description of music as being a language – a universal language, not merely a universal notation, able to meet all contingencies.' Bartók's use of folk-song would shock all Mrs Kennedy-Fraser's admirers. She is carrying on the old tradition. 'Peat-Fire Smooring' is really a smooring of Scottish intelligence. Or, to quote Scott again, 'It is not necessary that Scottish music should flatter Scotsmen – they have lived on flattery long enough – at present they need a music that will tell them what they are – a very different matter.'

The modern Italian composer, Casella, gives the following divisions in his 'Evolution of Music': –

   I.   The Diatonic Period (Primitives, Renascence, Classics, Romantics).
  II.   Transition Period (Post-Wagnerians, Neo-Classics, Precursors of Modern Era).
 III.   Present Period (Polymodality, Tonal Simultaneity, and Atonality).

Where does Mrs Kennedy-Fraser come in there? Her future is ancient history: she is a Rip Van Winkle of Scottish musical development. E.J. Dent says that 'the function of art is to strike a balance between the "romantic" and the "classic" sides of human personality – what common parlance calls the "heart" and the "head".' Any sort of music can do this to suit somebody; it depends on the state of the 'heart' and the 'head' of the hearer in question; but, if work is going to be put forward as of national significance and permanent artistic value, then we are entitled to demand that the national standard of heart and head involved in the choice is of a comparatively creditable kind, concerned with work capable of appealing to men, as well as to seals, and dependent upon something of more consequence than scarlet robes for its vogue. [9.4.26]

Letters

GAELIC AND DORIC

Sir, – John Harding is a sufficiently respectable witness. He is quoted by the late Professor Hume Brown, a painstaking and accurate historian, if not a very lively one: and other writers of parts have accepted his word as good. Harding states that in his day Marr and the Garioch were peopled by 'wild Scots.' The 'wild Scots' spoke Gaelic, and had little, if any, English. Watt, on the other hand, is no authority. He condemns himself when he says that by the end of the fourteenth century 'the new population had supplanted or absorbed the old Celtic inhabitants.' There was no 'new population' – within historic times, at all events – the turnover from Gaelic speech and manners and customs to the corresponding English entities being due to social and political causes, and not to any change of blood. It is hard to get Lowlanders to realise this, though the process has been going on for centuries under their very noses, many a 'country' which formerly was Gaelic-speaking having become English-speaking within living memory, and of course without involving the smallest racial change. The charter evidence 'Buchan Humlie' quotes in this connection is valueless. It was the common practice in those days to address charters to 'Franks and English, Flemings and Scots.' The Scots, of course, were the vast majority, the others being, relatively to them, a mere handful of the nation, but the Scots were mentioned last because they did not hold to the charter, and because the official tendency was to feudalise forms and institutions as much as possible. The reason why the folk of Inverness and district speak English rather than any Scottish dialect of it is that their English is a comparatively modern acquisition. Had they dropped Gaelic at the same time as the men of the Garioch began to desert it they had doubtless spoken a form of Braid Scots. But the turnover I speak of occurred when the Doric was decayed, decaying, and discredited; so, in preference to turning to it, they very sensibly and naturally acquired good English. 'Buchan Humlie' says that in his particular nyeuk Gaelic terms and idioms are entirely absent from the Doric. I require proof of that assertion from your correspondent; but I warn him beforehand that I am not prepared to accept him as judge unless he is himself a Gaelic scholar, or has presented his Doric as an object of study to some one who is. Loose (and often wild) statements by perfervid Braidalbans darken the controversial air far too much as it is. Some years ago, Mr Lachlan MacBane – editor of the Fifeshire Advertiser *– published an article (Gaelic) in* An Ròsarnach *in which he unmasked a great number of Gaelic words figuring as pure 'Doric'! In that paper, however, he but touched the fringe of the no less important and interesting question of the influence of Gaelic on current Lowland idiom, but from the little he then let fall on that head it was easy to collect that here again Gaelic influence was very strong – stronger by far than the Doric pundits dream of, or are prepared, seemingly, to admit. About the beginning of the nineteenth century Gaelic ceased to be the vernacular of the folk inhabiting the country of Cromarr in Aberdeenshire. Nowadays, there is not a word of Gaelic spoken throughout its length and breadth, though the people that there inhabit are of course of the same racial stock as their forefathers, who spoke Gaelic, and knew no English. Nowadays the peasantry of Cromarr speak the Braid Scots that obtains in that part of Aberdeenshire, and their social superiors English, with next to no accent. The implications of these facts, so far as they relate to the matters raised in controversy by 'Buchan Humlie' (and others of your Doric confidants) should not be difficult for them to digest, and set forth in their minds in clear and ordered fashion. – I am, etc.,*

Buchan
[9.4.26]

34. Various Poets (I) Douglas Ainslie

The late Professor W.P. Ker, in his address to the Philological Society on Jacob Grimm, observed that the Brothers Grimm

had not much taste for romantic excursions and inventions; their temper is just the opposite of that empty romantic craving, like the hunger of lean kine, which sent the poets and novelists ranging over the universe in search of subjects, properties, and local colour... Jacob Grimm, [he continues,] is of the same mind as Wordsworth; his romance is at home. He puts it finely in the dedication to Savigny: 'True poetry is like a man who is happy anywhere in endless measure, if he is allowed to look at leaves and grass, to see the sun rise and set; false poetry is like a man who travels abroad in strange countries and hopes to be uplifted by the mountains of Switzerland, the sky and sea of Italy; he comes to them and is dissatisfied; he is not as happy as the man who stays at home and sees his apple tree flowering every spring and hears the small birds singing among the branches.'

His dissatisfaction need not be conscious, however, and it is in a somewhat different sense than the surface one the word implies that his poetry may be less 'happy' than it might have been if he had stayed at home. Scottish poetry has suffered a great deal from this cause. Of Douglas Ainslie, in particular, we must lament that, like Ephraim, he has 'joined himself to strange gods,' and that he has in the process so completely denationalised himself as to have practically ceased to be a Scottish poet in any sense of the term without becoming either a European or an English one in any effective fashion.

From his five volumes of poetry, all out of print, he has now selected eighty poems for publication as his *Chosen Poems* (Hogarth Press, 1926), and the volume has an interesting introduction by Mr G.K. Chesterton – himself, as are Walter de la Mare, Gordon Bottomley, and other contemporary English poets of note – partly a Scot. No one perhaps has written more pregnantly, with more concentrated understanding, of Scottish landscape and Scottish life, and more particularly of Scottish letters, than Mr Chesterton. No student of Scottish literature should overlook his introduction, for example, to Dr Greville MacDonald's life of George MacDonald (1925). Here again, in his comments on Mr Ainslie's poems, he hits the nail upon the head. Observing how lightly we pass in Mr Ainslie's poems from translations from Italian to translations from Sanskrit, from purely classical and Hellenic pictures to Chinese scenes, he says:

Yet I have happy doubts about all this universality of culture. I suspect Mr Ainslie of being something better than a citizen of the world. I suspect him of a secret nationalism, and of wearing, so to speak, a plaid under his pilgrim's gown. Nobody ever yet got Scotland out of a Scot; and I do not believe that the author, in his heart, allows Scotland to descend to an equality with trifles like Athens and India and China. I had the first hint of this when I turned the page containing that most spirited and spontaneous lyric addressed to a lady descended from the great Cameron of Lochiel. This is not pretending to be a Buddhist or an ancient Greek or an ancient Chinaman. A lyric ought to be like a gesture. This Lyric has in it the very gesture of a man giving a toast on impulse at the end of a banquet, lifting his glass with an outward thrust and speaking words that come to him. Even something irregular in the rush of the simple metre resembles exactly the rush of words that would come with such a movement. Sir Walter Scott would have been glad to have drunk the toast – or to have written that poem. And this impression increased in my mind when I came to the longer poems about Scottish history. Their very length is in this sense a sort of betrayal. Rapid as are the events they describe, they have an air of leisure as the verses of Scott had an air of leisure. It is the spirit of leisure that rests on men when they are writing about the things they really like. It does not in any sense follow that they are the things they do best, or even that they think they do best. It is a question of liking the subject rather than liking the result. But we know by this atmosphere when a man does like a subject; when he would like the subject even without the result. Sir Walter Scott probably got more pleasure out of the rhymes and legends he collected than out of the poems and novels he made from them; and was more fresh and spontaneous as an antiquary than as a poet. It is this pleasure in the subject itself that I feel in this case in the ballads about the battles of Scotland. And it is this fact that confirms my suspicions that the author is something better than a cosmopolitan.

There is a great deal of truth in all this. But in my opinion it is also true that the few Scots poems in it are also among the very best poems in the collection. Mr Ainslie's work would have reached a higher level if he had been content to be first and foremost the Scot that he so seldom – but then so successfully – permits himself to be. There is no gainsaying the quality of 'The Stirrup Cup' to which Mr Chesterton refers: –

> Lady, whose ancestor
> Fought for Prince Charlie,
> Met once and nevermore,
> No time for parley!

Yet drink a glass with me
'Over the water':
Memories pass to me,
Chieftain's granddaughter!

'Say, will he come again?'
Nay, lady, never.
'Say, will he never reign?'
Yea, lady, ever.

Yea, for the heart of us
Follows Prince Charlie;
There's not a part of us
Bows not as barley.

Under the breeze that blew
Up the Atlantic
Wafting the one, the true
Prince, the romantic.

Back to his native land
Over the water:
Here's to Prince Charlie and
Lochiel's granddaughter!

For two or three more such lyrics a great proportion of the 'Amiel's Thoughts,' 'Calypso,' 'Stecchetti's Lyric,' 'Sapphics at Versailles,' and the like which comprise Mr Ainslie's collection could gladly have been dispensed with. He goes everywhere but really gets nowhere – except when he returns home. The other Scottish poems are 'From the Prelude to the Song of the Stewarts,' 'Battle of Largs,' 'Coming of William Wallace,' 'Last Adventure of Wallace,' 'The Mother of Robert Bruce,' 'The Coming of Robert Bruce,' and 'Death of the Douglas.' No Scottish anthologist can afford to overlook them – especially perhaps the last, with its splendid ending: –

... the bones of the Douglas repose
In the Church of Saint Bride 'neath the granite.
Where yet ye shall view, and ye please,
Eighth marvel of seven on our planet,
The Douglas at peace.   [23.4.26]

35. **Various Poets (II) Rachel Annand Taylor**

Mrs Taylor is in like case to Mr Ainslie – only she is a greater poet, and the loss to Scottish poetry in her alienation has been greater. The extent to which she has estranged herself – largely Italianised herself – is curiously illustrated in the following extracts from her *Aspects of the Italian Renaissance*, in which we have the curious spectacle of a Scotswoman coming to look at Scotland with the eyes of a foreigner and seeing things remote from reality.

It may seem strange, [she says,] to pass to a little and barren kingdom (*i.e.*, from Florence, that 'city of the red lily of the vine and the olive, of the tenderest Campanile and most daring Dome'). Yet it is natural enough, for Flodden Field was only one of the red love-tokens that Scotland wore for France. The French Renaissance crossed the sea most definitely with Mary; and if the bitterness of political strife rent and spoiled the gift it was French building, French personality, that affected Scotland, as the French royalty had already dyed her mood; and it was a French reaction that ruined the burthen of beauty, for Scottish Protestantism came from the lucid and terribly definite Calvin, not from the compromising Luther. In this country, where Celt, Norman, Latin and Scandinavian have never really mingled, there were, and are, deadly contrasts. As great spaces of barren moor and sighing fires and grey mysterious waters give a heightened value to certain natural things, like birchwoods rare as illusions of jasper and silver, spring branches with the buds set like patterns, cherry-blossom singing like an epithalamium, green lakes like water-lilies set in cups of barren rock, exotic, Egyptian, wild pure sunsets, and the miraculous western seas – so the stretches of brooding, seldom-speaking, ironic and tragic people are broken constantly by the leaping up of personalities compact of pride, passion and imaginative charm, red flowers in a barren and sea-tempered land.

Of 'the most famous of Renaissance ladies,' she writes –

Marie Stuart, lover of love and verse and personal liberty, wonderfully red and white, flower-like and flame-like, whose name still creates an impression as of clashing steel, whom it seemed necessary either to adore or to kill, the anger of her enemies being only an inversion of the idolatry of her lovers! She came with her French songs and music and dances, her Italian secretary and her

Renaissance tolerance but to a land already half-Catholic, half-Calvinist, preying violently upon itself, like the Celtic snake-symbol. The Calvinist won for a while this barren, beautiful land of legend, ballad, and song, eager for the exotic, hungry for extremes. But the religious difference, fiercer and more sincere than in any other country, and therefore more devastating, yet had a Renaissance origin on either side; and the spirit of the great period still lingers in the land where the Latin Chair of a University is the Chair of Humanity, and where proud poverty is yet in love with antique learning.

Would it were true!

Mrs Taylor's poetry suffers even more than her prose from this want of truth, this heady hyperbole, this fantastic over-colouring. It is mostly very preciose, very far-fetched, very mannered, very unreal. The reasons are not far to seek for her failure – as for Mr Ainslie's failure – to acquire a place of the slightest consequence in English poetry. The best of her work, like the best of his, is the most Scottish: and she counterbalances herself even more effectively in this way than he does – swinging back from floreate affairs of a very Italianate order to – actually – bare little stanzas in Braid Scots. The latter are often sufficiently good to show that an unprofitable prepossession with the Italian Renaissance has robbed the Scottish Renaissance movement of one whose true place should have been at its head. Take 'The Princess of Scotland' as an example of Mrs Taylor's Scottish poetry, not in the vernacular: –

> 'Who are you that so strangely woke,
> And raised a fine hand?'
> *Poverty wears a scarlet cloke*
> *In my land.*
>
> 'Duchies of dreamland, emerald, rose
> Lie at your command.'
> *Poverty like a princess goes*
> *In my land.*
>
> 'Wherefore the mask of silken lace
> Tied with a golden band?'
> *Poverty walks with wanton grace*
> *In my land.*
>
> 'Why do you softly, richly speak
> Rhythm so sweetly-scanned?'

Poverty hath the Gaelic and Greek
In my land.

'There's a far-off scent about you seems
Born in Samarkand.'
Poverty hath luxurious dreams
In my land.

'You have wounds that like passion-flowers you hide:
I cannot understand.'
Poverty hath one name with Pride
In my land.

There are several little ballad-fragments, and many interesting attempts to present Scottish subjects in new forms in *The End of Fiammetta*, which no Scottish anthologist should overlook, and which have their significance in these days when there is a wide-spread feeling of discontent with the old ruts to which Scottish poetry has been so long confined, and through the whole transpires an attitude to Scottish history, psychology, and nature, human and otherwise, which has a peculiar interest at the present juncture and may be a means – if it has not enabled Mrs Taylor to free herself and become the Scottish poetess she was surely intended to be – of freeing others and may exercise a great and beneficial influence on the immediate future of Scottish poetry as a whole.

Mr Ainslie is best known as the translator of Benedetto Croce. Messrs Macmillan published his translation of Croce's *Philosophy of the Spirit* (4 vols.), and Messrs Chapman and Hall, *European Literature in the 19th Century*. Mr Ainslie's own books of poetry are: *Escarlamonde*'(G. Bell and Sons); *John of Damascus* (Messrs Constable); *Prelude to the Song of the Stewarts* (Messrs Constable); *Moments* (Messrs Constable); *Mirage* (Elkin Matthews); and *Chosen Poems* (Hogarth Press).

Mrs Taylor's books are: *Poems* (1904); *Rose and Vine*; *The Hours of Fiammetta*, *The End of Fiammetta*; and: Prose *Aspects of the Italian Renaissance* (Messrs Grant Richards, Ltd.).

[23.4.26]

36. Various Poets (III) Male Voice Choir

Well over 1,000 poets who have published at least one volume of verse are living in Scotland to-day, and there must be several times that number alive and contributing to various periodicals who will yet do so. To put the total numbers of versifiers at round about 5,000 is probably well within the mark. I have read, I think, all the volumes of verse that have been published by Scottish rhymers in or furth of Scotland within the last quarter of a century, with the exception of some privately printed or obscurely printed work. The great bulk of it all is without a single redeeming feature. The task of hunting for the slenderest yield of anything in any respect meritorious is a veritable searching for needles in an endless succession of haystacks. Only a very few of the writers in question have succeeded in evolving a single set of verses, or even a single verse, of the slightest value. The whole of this output falls into two main categories – work that is indistinguishable from the great mass of mediocre verse in English that is being produced everywhere else throughout the English-speaking world, and work that is, however mediocre, distinguished by specifically Scottish subjects and settings, and, in a very considerable proportion of this category, by being, more or less, in what purports to be Braid Scots. I only intend to refer here to poets who while inferior to those with whom I have already dealt singly, and in most cases greatly inferior, yet rise above the ruck and whose work presents some aspect or other of value, however modest. And I take the men first. Peter Taylor has not yet published any volume, but he has done work well above the average, both in English and in Scots. Both in choice of subject – as in some admirable verses which first appeared in *Punch* descriptive of the passing of a motor-car – and in an absence of stock-reactions, 'rubber stamps,' he displays a modern intelligence at work, alert if not penetrating, while in his Braid Scots poems he is one of the very few whose verses might not equally well be the work of any other of an almost countless army of vernacular rhymers. He has not, however, succeeded in liberating himself from the Kailyaird pressure to any vital extent. Rather he hovers still just within its penumbra, but not too far within to be unaffected by the pleasanter prospects beyond to which, albeit, he cannot wholly win. As Robert Bain said in an admirable article on 'Scottish Poetry of To-day,' in the *Burns Chronicle* (1926):

> In the poetry of both Charles Murray and Violet Jacob there is some-thing from which the coming Scottish poets must liberate themselves. They must cease singing for ever about a day that is dead – not because I say it, but for their own salvation. The home hills, the old days at school, the places hallowed by sentiment, country life seen in retrospect – these have been the themes of innumerable verses that differed in nothing but geography. Now the yearning for home is one of the most vital of human instincts, the love of it at the root of all

true patriotism. If these feelings are, however, a mere sentimentality, and not a deep passion, they tend to a slackening of thought. Artistry grows flabby as the emotional impulse fails in power, and when neither passionate art, nor a passionate heart is driving the poet, poetry trickles out into thin verse. So the local poet comes into his pale kingdom and rules in thowless state. What oppresses me in reading all this poetry of place is that it seems to be written by old men or exiles; even its humour seems a chuckling over ancient humours, which take on a romantic charm when regarded through the rosy-tinted glasses of memory. But the great emotions, pride and love or contempt and hate, do not sweep through one in a thousand of verses – so – inspired, must I say? – and only old cronies are kindled, and even these to but a momentary flicker of fire. Scottish poetry, if it is to come to anything, must cut the painter that binds it to the past and sail out into the deeps of the living world around it. The apron-strings of even the kindliest mother will fetter the growing son, but the poetic cords of the finest past are a hangman's rope. To be worthy of Scotland her poets must create her afresh, seeing her as she is, accepting her past as a driving force or as a stimulus to rivalry in new fields of endeavour, lighting their own torch at the ancient fires, not merely holding up a mirror to reflect these.

But I am afraid that, for the most part, Mr Taylor is rather reflecting alien fires. New to Scottish poetry as some of the notes he strikes are, they are not new to English poetry, and he has not succeeded in blending them effectively with his background. His poetic faculty is working pretty much on the old lines of Kailyaird conventionalism; what difference there is is superimposed by an intellectualism trying to get out of the old ruts but unseconded in its endeavour by the profounder factors upon which the quality of the poetic result depends. Mr Taylor has written nothing of permanent value: but two or three of his poems would deserve a place in any anthology of contemporary Scottish poetry not circumscribed, say, to less than a hundred examples by perhaps half as many different writers; and his work as a whole, both in its little successes and its larger failures, has a special interest at the moment as evidencing the difficulties and dangers of the transition through which Scottish poetry is passing. The same may be said of the work of Alister Mackenzie – a slim sheaf of which has been published by the Porpoise Press – only the English influences to which he has responded have been different. So also in the case of George Rowntree Harvey, David

Cleghorn Thomson, and Thomas Scott Cairncross – the last an older and more accomplished poet than these others, whose English work has approximated much better to the best of its models, and who in it is much more of a Scottish poet, in the essence of his work as in the externals of preoccupation with the Scottish scene and with Scottish themes, while, curiously enough, in his Braid Scots work he is irremediably poor and actually less Scottish. Lauchlan Maclean Watt is a voluminous versifier in English, but his work is a wholly nondescript welter on the surface of which the Scottish externalities of subject and setting are jostled hither and thither like so much flotsam and jetsam. His prose writings on Scottish literary subjects show that he has no intuitions of value of either a critical or creative character. There is perhaps little or no fury about his overwhelmingly pietistic and sentimental output, but it is at least mainly sound, 'signifying nothing.' At his rare best, like Taylor and the others I have mentioned, he might deserve inclusion in an anthology of such a character as I have predicated. All six, while they have a certain technical ability, are incapacitated from acquiring the other elements which, in association with that technical ability, might produce work of a still minor enough character, but equivalent in value, to, say, that of the English Georgians, the least of whom (in all the volumes except the last one, at any rate) is a giant in comparison to any of them, by a fundamental indistinction of spirit, a sheer lack of *nous* – of creative purpose. Their work is essentially meaningless. They nevertheless represent the next flight in contemporary Scottish poetry to such poets. in English, as Malloch and Jeffrey, if a long way behind them or, in Scots, to Charles Murray.

Along with them may be mentioned W.H. Hamilton, Duncan Macrae, Will H. Ogilvie, and Cecil Taylor. Hamilton's work is almost wholly imitative in manner and to a large degree in content too. He is best when he is most personal. But he has at least a sense of form – an ability to seize upon and reproduce modes, generally of the more musical kind – which is lacking to all the first-named five, except Cairncross, and the result is that, slight as is the poetical value of his work, it bears the impress of a spirit that is keenly sensitive to the poetry of others (as, indeed, his study of John Masefield and innumerable critical articles in diverse periodicals, amply attests). Perhaps for this very reason he has had all the more difficulty in 'finding himself.' Macrae is an older man and writes in older modes with a species of Parnassian effect. Will H. Ogilvie is one of the most prolific of modern versifiers, and perhaps over-facility has been his ruination. Miss Palmer, in her succinct and valuable account of *Modern Australian Literature*, points out how the pioneers of Australian poetry in the nineties of last century were

> joined by a brilliant colleague, Will Ogilvie, who in his *Fair Girls and Grey Horses* ended by destroying their simple craft. With more skill than the others, he had less real simplicity, and imparted into the bush themes a light romanticism and a touch of facile sentiment. Where the bush ballad had been like a man striding across open country he made it into a waltz in a barn, with lamps and flowers. As far as mere form went, this meant the substitution of smart stanzas lit by epigrams for the long loping lines and sparse rhymes. But in spite of the troubadour easiness of most of his work, there was a hint of real poetry in it.

It has, despite his long tale of books, remained at most a mere hint, and, in his case, as in that of the previous two mentioned, there is nothing specifically Scottish, even when Scottish subjects or scenes are taken. It is all a case of the superimposition of alien and second-rate techniques – not any technique growing out of the subject itself or dictated by those elements of these writers in which whatever real poetic faculty or real nationality of spirit they have resides. This also applies to Cecil Taylor, except that his work at its best depends more upon vital observation and genuine reaction. There is no mistaking the gleam of real poetry in the following verse from a poem entitled 'Frost' – as clear a gleam as is to be found anywhere in the work of any of these poets, although Taylor cannot manifest it for more than a line or two at a time anywhere and his average quality is lower than that of some of these others –

> No living thing is nigh;
> Only a robin comes
> Begging with bright round eye
> The world's crumbs.

So slight a gleam as that, nevertheless, entitles Taylor to be ranked among the foremost twenty of the great five thousand.

E.R.R. Linklater deserves honourable mention in a subsection of the above category as a humorous poet – a *rara avis* in Scotland. There is, of course, a perennial crop of light-verse writers in our school and college and university magazines and elsewhere. Linklater rises sheer out of the ruck of these and has developed an 'angle' of his own which he exploits with great technical dexterity. Along with him may be bracketed R.

Watson Kerr, who has rendered service in other directions to modern Scots letters as the conductor of the Porpoise Press. Kerr's recent Hudibrastic verse has had certain merits which give it a niche of its own. Whether he will develop real satiric power remains to be seen. The need for work of that kind is so great – and the knack of producing it apparently so rare – that further developments may be eagerly awaited. Kerr's war poetry – at its best among the best of its kind – certainly the best produced by any Scottish soldier (Sorley's and Joseph Lee's was of quite another kind) – I shall deal with elsewhere: in it a savagely realistic reaction employed the same technical means as are now being engaged to sarcastic purpose. Of the other younger poets represented in *Scottish University Verses, 1918-23*, who have written verse of a quality above that of the great bulk of the general output by all Scottish poets during the same years but who, apart from such isolated successes, have no title yet to be considered as 'practising poets' may be mentioned Angus Macrae, W.S. Morrison, and Kenneth M'Cracken. These three have manifested a potential ability which Scottish Poetry can hardly afford to let go without further exploration. In like case are William Soutar, Alasdair Alpin MacGregor, and A.D. Mackie.

Murdoch Maclean, the author of *Songs of a Roving Celt* and other volumes, is a versatile and voluminous versifier of the Will H. Ogilvie type, but with a broader hint of real poetry in his work and a robuster nationality of sentiment, while his Gaelic affiliations differentiate him from those I have already mentioned, contrasting favourably with the Celtic twilightism of Lauchlan Maclean Watt and the more conventionalised and, in other respects, much slighter Hebridean work of Alasdair MacGregor. Maclean is, on the whole, the truest poet yet named; and his work should certainly not escape Scottish anthologists. Despite the strong Gaelic element in much of his work, he handles the Doric equally well in other poems, while he develops romantic or realistic themes with equal facility and a general effect of artistic integrity – that is to say, of varied but always authentic and well-personalised impulses finding appropriate forms. James Roxburgh McClymont is another ready writer with a large and varied output, but he falls into quite a different class, being, like a far more diffuse Douglas Ainslie, a cosmopolitan poet to whom everything is grist. Robert Crawford published a series of sonnets on 'Eve' in the *Scottish Chapbook* which entitle him to mention here. None of his other work has, however, approached the same plane.

Professor Alexander Gray performed a real service to Scots letters by his translation of the songs and ballads of Heine into the Doric. These renderings are, at their best, a splendid series of demonstrations of the potentialities of development in Vernacular verse, and take rank as amongst the best translations of Heine yet effected into any language. In his original Doric verse, Gray seldom, if ever, approaches the level of these translations in his manipulation of Scots, while, in content, they are, for the most part, on a pedestrian Kailyaird level. In his English verse, while the quality of the poetic spirit at work is invariably very thin, that is sometimes offset by an epigrammatic sparkle and is generally manifested in neat and economical forms. Of all these and a few other writers – say a score out of the whole number – it may be said, as Bain said at the close of the article to which I have already alluded, that they

> have written single poems or a few indicative of a changed outlook, a bolder presentation of reality, and a genuine eagerness to catch the spiritual significance of life today… But they have still, in my opinion, to make good their claim to be regarded as poets of national standing.

Two of them who are very popular amongst certain (different) classes of readers and are in their way 'national figures' – Will H. Ogilvie and Lauchlan Maclean Watt – owe that position entirely to extra-literary causes or to popular confusion as to the nature and functions of poetry.

Representative selections are given in *Northern Numbers* of Peter Taylor (3rd Series); Lauchlan Maclean Watt (2nd Series); Thomas Scott Cairncross (1st Series); W. H. Hamilton (3rd Series); William Soutar (3rd Series); Will H. Ogilvie (1st and 2nd Series); Alexander Gray (2nd and 3rd Series); R. Watson Kerr (1st and 2nd Series). Gray's Heine translations, and Cecil Taylor's *The Secret Flower, and Other Poems* are published by Messrs Grant Richards; D. Cleghorn Thomson's and Robert Crawford's poems by Basil Blackwell. Oxford; J.R. McClymont's by Messrs Ouseley; Hamilton's book on Masefield by Messrs Allen and Unwin; Dr Maclean Watt's *Scottish Ballads and Ballad Writing* by Gardner, Paisley; and on *Gavin Douglas* by the Cambridge Press; and Murdoch Maclean's *Songs of a Roving Celt* by Messrs Deane's Yearbook Press.   [21.5.26]

Letters

HISTORY IN SCHOOLS

Sir, – There are many signs which make it clear that our nation has grievously declined from the national standards created of old. In every department of national life this decline is evident, but in none more so than in literature, and particularly in history and historical composition. Mr C.M. Grieve's papers have done us much service in this respect. In piece after piece he has ably exposed the decline I speak of, and the causes of it. But there are other witnesses, and some of these have lately appeared in your own columns. I refer more particularly to the draft schemes for the teaching of history which some of your readers have contributed to your pages. Judging by these, national sentiment and national science could not well be at a lower ebb than these documents prove that both have already reached.

If history is to be taught at all in Scottish schools the viewpoint of those who teach it, as that of the manuals they employ for that purpose, should surely be primarily Scottish. In other words, the intellectual 'jumping-off ground' as it were should be native, not foreign. I believe this is the invariable custom throughout Europe. Necessarily, in all cases the native history comes first, and thereafter – that is to say when the pupil has acquired the atmosphere of his own national story – the various points of contact of it with the history of other peoples are taken up, expounded, and the pupil duly versed therein. A synthetic process or method may be, and often is, preferred by some. The points of contact I refer to are tackled as they occur, and the pupil is drilled in them at the same time as he is taught the more essentially native parts of the historical course. But in any event – be the method what it may – the reasonable and the well-nigh universally followed plan in respect of the teaching of history in schools is for the native and his country to hold first place. In this sorry kingdom of Scotland, however, this does not occur. Native history is relegated to a back seat. It is not made the intellectual 'jumping-off ground' for the pupil. English history is used to introduce such slight glimpses of Scottish as the course allows; and continental history is ignored save when and where it happens to interfere with the current of hum-drum English affairs. Greater signs of native degradation than these I think it would be hard to find.

But this method of expounding history in our schools is a cause of ignorance in the unfortunates who are subjected to it, besides being a sign or symbol of fearful national degeneration. Take, for instance, the 'teaching' that circles round the exploits of, say, Simon de Montfort, whose name bulks largely in our so-called Scottish historical courses. Of course Simon de Montfort is historically interesting; but that he should be used, as he is used in our native schools, to puff up a decaying and discredited institution like the English Parliament is, to my mind, monstrous. It may not be so as regards the English, whose fatuous adulation of their boasted 'Mother of Parliaments' may reasonably be indulged them, since we must be tender where native institutions are concerned, but that is no reason why the Scottish youth should be asked to toe the *line of the gross superstition I refer to. Our young nationals should be taught the truth of matters in the light of past history and current tendencies; and the truth of the particular matter to which I refer is that the day of the single national parliament is over, and that the future of political mankind rests with decentralisation and regionalistic councils as means to tackle and solve the many complex social questions by which modern society is everywhere faced. Take again all this antiquated blether and bosh about 'Good Queen Bess' and Drake and Raleigh, and other high-sea cut-purses of the time. How on earth can such historical 'teaching' profit us? What have we got to do with the figures I name and others of their sort, save to take that moderate and reasoned heed of them and interest in them which is just proper so far as the demands of international science are concerned ? Judging by the way these personages and their like suck our historical courses you would imagine that the England of that time ruled the whole European roost, whereas the plain fact is, as any historical student (be he Scot or Dutchman) knows, that England was a potty and pettifogging little country, scarce able to pay its way along, before a certain turn of European events took it in hand, and it emerged from this obscurity it had been in ever since the conclusion of the Hundred Years War.*

Grant me permission to revert to this topic some other time. There is a great deal to be said about it that positively screams to be said, especially in a journal which appeals in a very particular manner, as yours does, to the teaching profession; but for the present I think I have said enough: I fear I have greatly exceeded reasonable space as it is. – I am, etc.,

Aboyne   R. Erskine of Marr
29th April, 1926   [21.5.26]

37. Various Poets (IV) Ladies' Choir

To turn from the Male Voice Choir to the Ladies' Choir and do for the small percentage of our poetesses who are in any measure perceptible above the rut what I have just done for their brothers, I must, first of all, single out the name of Jessie Annie Anderson. She is to be praised in very much the same way, despite very similar defects, as Croce praises Fernan Caballero – for her abundant femininity, her many-sided interests, her spontaneity, and, along with these, her carelessness of artistic elaboration.

She attempted no blandishments, [says Croce of Caballero,] she paid no attention to arranging in such a way as to excite or to seduce the imagination of readers, she did not expand and falsify feelings and passions, nor raise them to the rank of theories, but was animated with a pure and serious conviction, and possessed sound judgment. And above all a spring of poetry was bubbling in her heart.

As much may be said of Miss Anderson; she is an equivalent figure on the much smaller scale of Scotland. Writing of Robb's *Book of Twentieth Century Scots Verse*, Thomas Henderson has said: 'Of examples of the complete mingling of the universal and the personal that makes the true lyric we have not many. Jessie Annie Anderson almost gives it to us in 'At Sweet Mary's Shrine' –

> Luve broke my hert, an' got within –
> He only tried tae pain it; –
> How could Luve brak' sae saft a hert?
> I never socht to hain it.

That certainly comes within measurable distance of the magical simplicity of

> I sighed and said among them a'
> Ye are na Mary Morison!

but it is by no means an isolated occurrence, but a very frequently recurring one, in the very considerable bulk of Miss Anderson's work. But she never gets beyond that 'almost.' Bathos follows hard on the heels of Beauty; scarcely anywhere does she maintain for a whole verse – let alone a complete poem – those pure perceptions which illumine so many phases in otherwise unhappy contacts, and which, so maintained only a few times, would have given her a much higher place than with all her abundance she has attained. That is why she must be graded so far below Marion Angus, for example – although Miss Angus works only the slenderest vein and Miss Anderson has ranged over the whole field of poetry and essayed innumerable modes. The present writer devoted a short study to Miss Anderson's work in *The Scottish Chapbook* (January, 1923), in the course of which I said:

Miss Anderson has learned no parlour tricks. Coteries cannot capture her, nor stunts corrupt. She has never exploited herself, nor does her work lend itself to exploitation by others. She has never been tempted to be clever. She is catholic in a fashion which is permanently unfash-

ionable and essentially Christ-like. A glimpse of her working creed is
caught in lines such as these: –

> ... we did agree art is a gift
> Not to be tricked in light, fantastic ways;
> Not to create nor catch a common craze;
> Nor to be used in mart in tradesman thrift;
> Nor as a tranquil lake whereon to drift
> By pleasant thoughts through fair and easeful days;
> Nor to be used as power to win sweet praise;
> But as a trust, God-given, to uplift
> The whole creation to the Higher Law
> By truth's unsparing sight, who sees the core,
> By strenuous effort, sympathies which draw
> The lives of men together more and more...

She has an abiding anticipation of 'the Unimaginable Light of God,'
which makes her sonnets like 'a night of stars triumphing towards the
Dawn.'

It is a great pity that with her big heart and many gifts she lacks that
faculty of achieving significant form, in the absence of which all the rest
is so largely wasted. She is also a busy writer on Scottish issues in
numerous papers and periodicals and, curiously enough, a sound and
discriminating critic of the work of others. I know few more interesting
books on subjects connected with Scottish poetry than *Lewis Morrison
Grant: His Life, Letters, and Last Poems*, which she edited. It should not
be overlooked by any student of modern Scottish life and letters.

I also wrote an article on the sonnets of Miss Hilary Staples in *The
Northern Review* of May, 1924, and need say no more here than that,
like Miss Anderson, her work should not escape any anthologist of
contemporary Scottish sonnets, while of her work as a whole pretty
much the same may be said as of Miss Anderson's save that she has a
smaller range and, even within it, less height and depth. More recently
she has written to a considerable extent in Braid Scots: and her work
reflects the new tendencies which are applying the vernacular to fresh,
imaginative purpose. A poetess of a very different type is Brenda Murray
Draper, who writes for the most part in free forms to an effect that is
largely (but excellently) journalistic, although at its best it rises into
genuine poetry in which, however, there is nothing distinctively Scottish
either in the expression or in the fundamental intellection. Muriel E.

Graham is a more diverse and finished versifier; she has a sense of form far superior to any of the three. already mentioned. The content of her work is too often *cliché* and commonplace; the impression it gives is of a writer who has a very considerable measure of dexterity in the manipulation of words and verse-forms, but who has little or no poetical gift of her own. Yet here and there she achieves an excellent imitation of a good poem. She reminds me in this respect of the American lyricist, Sara Teasdale. Janetta W. Murray is a versifier of the same type, but with a different orientation. Whereas Miss Graham confines herself for the most part to what is popularly regarded as poetical – natural description, noble sentiments – Miss Murray's is largely an urban muse and she utilises 'realistic' scenes – with, however, very much the same effect as Miss Graham secures by her more conventional adherences. In other words, the fundamental conception of poetry is much the same in the minds of each, although it leads the one to describe country scenes and the other to graphic reporting of Glasgow streets. Along with these two, as competent versifiers who seldom rise above 'magazine verse' level into anything deserving of inclusion even in such an anthology as I postulated in my preceding article – and who, even so, are certainly above the great ruck of living Scottish 'poetesses' – may be mentioned Agnes Falconer, Christine Orr, Orgill Cogie, Anne Milne, May W. Fairlie, and, in Braid Scots, Penuel Ross and Barbara Ross M'Intosh.

A niche of her own must be accorded to Mabel Christian Forbes. Her slender output is always peculiarly distinctive and has a different provenance altogether to the great mass of facile verse. It is intensely personal and proceeds from a remote angle of consciousness. It seldom succeeds in carrying complete conviction or achieving full expression – but it has always been profoundly felt and, even where the problem of 'communication' has not been solved, an authentic, imaginative faculty is obviously in operation. Mabel Christian Forbes, who was, prior to the War, one of the Editorial Committee of *The Blue Blanket*, edited the posthumous volume of Maitland Hardyman's poems.

Isobel W. Hutchison has a much larger tale of accomplishment, and here again there is always a distinctive note. Her books include *Lyrics from West Lothian* and the cantafable, *How Joy was Found* (Messrs Blackie), while a long poem, 'The Calling of Bride' appeared in *The Scottish Chapbook*, and, more recently, Miss Hutchison has written plays and prose of note. Her quality is indicated by the following: –

For Those at Sea

The shining starfish and the inspirèd weed
Shall clamber in your fingers unafraid.
Your bright astonished eyes shall take their meed
Of leviathan and the treasure that is laid
On the floors of ocean. Ye shall never see
Through the green arteries of the watery deep
The tedious growth of earth, yet shall ye be
Charged in her charge, and lapped in Protean sleep.
Your sympathetic hands shall softly move
With the music of her tides in their ebb and flow.
Ye shall be part of all that ye did love;
Mid strange new-fangled dreams lulled to and fro
In the wake of moons and stars outnumberèd
Until the unplumbed sea restore her dead.

Along with Miss Hutchison as one of the few contemporary Scottish poetesses who can handle the longer poem to any effect must be mentioned Mary E. Boyle, who also deserves especial mention as by far our best writer of children's verse. There has been no more delightful book of its kind by any Scottish writer since R.L. Stevenson's *Child's Garden of Verses* than Miss Boyle's *Daisies and Apple Trees* (Aeneas Mackay, Stirling) – or, at any rate, it must be bracketed with James Guthrie's *A Wild Garden* (Messrs Selwyn and Blount). Miss Mildred Lamb's illustrations to it are equally delightful. *Herodias Inconsolable* (Chelsea Publishing Company) substantiates my first assertion and shows that Miss Boyle can use blank verse to fine and sustained effect.

The twelfth poetess I would mention (claiming for these twelve that they form the second group amongst contemporary Scottish poetesses, the first being confined to Muriel Stuart, Rachel Annand Taylor, Violet Jacob, and Marion Angus) is Helen Cruickshank, who has not yet, I think, published her work in any collected form. The last of my twelve, she is by no means the least, being a vivid versifier with a brilliant colour sense and lively, dramatic intuitions. I agree with a friend who says of her Braid Scots poems 'the same type as Violet Jacob's and not far behind – maybe with a more sincere basis' (in the sense of applying the Vernacular to her contemporary experience and not in exercises merely in historical accord with the *milieu* in which, ere it almost entirely lapsed from use, it continued to be spoken). And the same friend points out that she is considerably younger than Mrs Jacob.

I have only excluded Miss Barbara Drummond from my twelve because she is younger than any of the others, and her output, so far as it is known to me, is confined to a few poems. But the high promise of these is indubitable; and while the quality of thought they evince is much stronger and deeper than in the work of any of the others, the choice of subject – the old Gaelic myths, treated in no 'Celtic twilight' fashion but in a deep Catholic spirit as if Miss Drummond had somehow renewed within herself the traditions of the old Bardic Colleges – suggests that she may yet become a very considerable figure in the Scottish Renaissance Movement. At the opposite pole of our nationality may be mentioned the little handful of poems in Braid Scots which is all that I have seen of the work of 'Tamar Faed.' They manifest unquestionable promise.

Much younger than Miss Drummond – and one of the most voluminous of contemporary Scottish poetesses – is the Dundee prodigy, Helen Adam, whose much-boomed 'Elfin Pedlar' was published, with illustrations by the author, by Messrs Hodder and Stoughton in 1923 in a big volume of nearly 150 pages, including an introduction by Dr John A. Hutton. Miss Adam was then twelve years of age. I shall be exceedingly surprised if what poetic faculty she has develops in a fashion leading to work of the slightest real value after the absurd praise lavished on this unfortunate production. She is a Scottish counterpart of the American Hilda Conkling: but it certainly cannot be said of her, as Louis Untermeyer says of Miss Conkling, 'Even if with maturity, Hilda never writes another phrase, or worse, writes thousands of them in the prescribed manner, she is to-day a definite and original figure in contemporary poetry.' On the other hand it is certainly true that her work, while of the same kind, is, of that kind, a great deal better than that which the great majority of contemporary Scottish versifiers in English write and what the majority of the reading public regard as poetry and often describe as 'beautiful words'. That is what it is – words, words, words! The beauty is a matter of taste and definition of the term beauty. But while Miss Adam has written yards of verse of a sort, she has still to write a poem. This in no way detracts from the curiosity of her achievement even as it is at so early an age, but it can be no service to her to describe what she has already done in misleading terms – if she has any real poetic potentiality at all.　　　　　　　　　　[4.6.26]

38. Newer Scottish Fiction (I): Norman Douglas; F.W. Bain

It will be the business of one of its protagonists when the Scottish Renaissance Movement begins to make general headway to deal thoroughly with the Kailyaird School of Novelists – Barrie (to whose work I have already referred), 'Ian Maclaren,' S.R. Crockett and the others down to Joseph Laing Waugh, and so put an end to it. The disease has never been properly diagnosed, and although its evil effects have been recognised and certain steps have been successfully taken to abate them, it is still working widespread if more subterranean mischief. And the direct reaction from Kailyairdism exemplified in George Douglas Brown's *House with the Green Shutters* and J. MacDougall Hay's *Gillespie* and the like will then be recognised as a mere reversal, the same thing disguised as its opposite. The intuitive, unargued recognition has merely resulted in developments in which the essential characteristics of each of these schools have been modified and made more or less innocuous, as in the work of Dr R.W. MacKenna or 'O. Douglas.' In other writers an appearance of difference, an illusion of progress, has been secured by a mere change of location in time and place – to the contemporary Scottish city from the rural parish of half-a-century or so ago. This is all that has happened in such a novel 'by one of the new Glasgow school' as John Cockburn's *Tenement*. Such real genius as Scotland has produced has kept clear of the whole degrading entanglement (except in the case of Brown, whose genius is indubitable and whose novel is carried beyond its genre by its stupendous and salutary savagery) – and, unfortunately, almost entirely clear of Scotland too. I have already dealt with aspects of this issue in my essay on Cunninghame Graham. There are three other very diverse Scottish writers who are unquestionably among the most interesting of imaginative prose-writers in English to-day. The greatest of these is Norman Douglas; the other two are F.W. Bain and Kenneth Grahame. These last two might as easily be Martians as Scots, so far as all the superficial elements of their work is concerned. Douglas's work bristles with entertaining *aperçus* on Scottish life and character, which only a Scot, bitterly and bafflingly entangled in his nationality – and, paradoxically, the more bitterly and bafflingly, the more he succeeds in transcending it in most directions – could write. But, as a matter of fact, they are each of them merely fulfilling to the letter what Professor Gregory Smith prophesied Scots genius would contribute to English literature – nothing 'central' but strange mosaic work, curious *pastiche, tours de force*, stylistic exercises in the absence of that essential (indefinable but yet very definite and always recognisable) substance which is the stuff of great literature in English. They have not fought out their problems in their proper field (Scotland), but have flown them, with the consequence that in the ends of the earth the Thistle clings all the more grotesquely to others and is in no way to be shaken off. They may sublimate it – transform its *bizarre* form into the subtlest spiritual exaggerations or tricks of style – but they cannot minify it. The greatest of such Scots was Herman Melville now belatedly come to his own. 'From insanity,' said Plato, 'Greece derived its greatest benefits.' 'But,' says Raymond Weaver, one of Melville's biographers,

> the dull and decent Philistine, untouched by Platonic heresies, justifies his sterility in a boast of sanity. The America in which Melville was born and died was exuberantly and unquestionably 'sane.' Its 'sanity' drove Irving abroad and made a recluse of Hawthorne. Cooper alone throve upon it. And of Melville, more ponderous in gifts and more volcanic in energy than any other American writer, it made an Ishmael on the face of the earth.

That America was largely Scottish. Mr Bonney, the American Consul in Edinburgh, has recently been lucubrating about the identity in ethos, despite superficial differences, between America and Scotland. Mr H.L. Mencken has a good deal to say on the same subject – but he does not share Mr Bonney's gratitude to Scotland. Nor, as a Scot, do I welcome Mr Bonney's utterances. It is precisely what America and Scotland have in common of this sort that the best elements in both countries are trying to destroy. 'The essential thing,' says Mr Bechhofer in his *The Literary Renaissance in America*,

> about the recent American literature with which I propose to deal is that it represents a revolt against the intellectual standards that have for so long dominated American culture. One may accept the current phraseology and label the official philosophy 'Puritanism,' or 'Philistinism'; but the name does not matter. The standards are there.

They are at least equally in evidence in Scotland, too, and are practically indistinguishable from their Yankee equivalents. The Scottish Renaissance Movement is tackling with squibs from the other side the same stupendous and unspeakable bond between the two 'cultures' as all the younger American writers of the slightest literary consequence are dynamiting from theirs, Calvinism, however 'perverted,' however snubbed and relegated to the rear, obtrudes as irrepressibly in Norman Douglas's erudite and ecstatic prose as the inveterate indoctrinations of Jesuitism 'kyth' in James Joyce's *Ulysses*. Douglas is, in fact, a Scottish equivalent of Joyce, operating less demoniacally and on a smaller scale. Unlike Joyce, he had no Scottish literary movement, as Joyce had the Irish literary Renaissance, for a spring-board. But, much more amenably to prevailing morality, Douglas's *South Wind* is a kind of miniature *Ulysses* – if for the Iliad which was Joyce's base we ascribe to Douglas a Ruritanian model. In the inner essence of their styles, if less in the forms of expression in which they clothe them, Douglas and Joyce have a great deal in common – as is not surprising when we remember the kinship of the Scots and the Irish, the Gaelic basis they have in common. They have both the same sensuous interest in the formation of ideas, the same inexhaustible concern with mental processes. Ezra Pound once said: 'Most good prose arises from an instinct of negation: the best prose writers choose the only means left them of eliminating (by exact diagnosis) something (the typical mediocrity of contemporary existence) too hideous to be tolerated.' That is true – but only of writers belonging to nations in which what intelligentsia it has developed suffers from an inferiority complex. It is not true of writers belonging to nations which have succeeded in developing major literary traditions of their own. Pound's mistake arose from his being an American himself. But his dictum explains Irish and Scottish epiphenomena like Joyce and Douglas. Douglas, however, comes from what is predominantly a Protestant country; Joyce from Catholic Ireland. And Douglas out of a country that has been at a literary standstill for the best part of a century so far as the production of work of European consequence is concerned – and Joyce as the end of a renascent movement in Irish literature which, before his emergence, in Yeats and others, had established itself continentally. The stagnancy of Scotland, and its Protestantism, is reflected in the fact that Douglas is largely a product of the Nineties. Gilbert Seldes puts the matter compactly when he says that

> it was as Old Believers, the last of Rousseau's faithful in an age corrupted from the pure faith, that the Nineties first appear. With them his melancholy turned at times to pessimism, his doubts to a sceptical languor; one swooned with love of Nature only while walking along the Strand and knew the purity of love only in Leicester Square; and the hysteria which a kindly providence

bestowed on Rousseau the last disciples found could be safely and artificially induced. They fled him down the labyrinthine ways, but they embraced him at the gate. For in essence their faith was the same, and the same and most significant in this; that they had faith and believed in the possibility of having faith, and believed in the triumph of whatever fate they held.

And then, turning to what we inherit from the Nineties, he says, 'We have substituted analysis for introspection, irony for satire. and a spirit of huge, bitter, passionless mockery seems so exclusively appropriate to us that we sometimes overstrain to achieve it... The difference is that for the most part their disillusion hurt them and ours does not.' And he goes on to declare that Mr Eliot's *Waste Land* and Joyce's *Ulysses* are the only complete expressions of the spirit which will be modern for the next generation. Douglas is almost completely modern for this one – a wonderful achievement for a Scot. His countrymen who wish an object-lesson on how to 'carry over' the unfaced problems of their national consciousness – only to be solved by the production of a centripetal literary tradition of their own – into the literary tradition of another nation in such a fashion as to transform their angularities and lacunae into positive assets, peculiarly attractive at least to the few and for the time being, should take a course in Douglas's writings.

The swifter momentum of English letters to which they have trans-ferred themselves has also carried Bain and Grahame further forward than any Scottish writer in the narrower sense – Bain is perhaps as modern as anything Oriental ever can be; Grahame has brought Arcady down to – not this generation – but certainly last one. The three of them rank in relation to each other in direct ratio to their comparative contemporaneity.

But from the purely Scottish standpoint it is extremely interesting to see how they have carried over into English literature distinctively Scottish qualities – the old 'antithesis between the real and the fantastic,' to which I have already referred, 'intermingledons,' as Burns called them, those fine frenzies, all that Edwin Muir means when he says that the Scots are less 'sane' than the English, the lust of ratiocination, that almost mystical devotion to detail, that delight in 'playing with the pieces' they have, who,

> unable to comprehend an ordered and lovely system [or rather unable to belong to it or to devise its like to suit themselves in accordance with their inmost needs] find their compensation in an abnormal sensitive-

ness to its momentary and detached manifestations, absorbed in the interest of disparate phenomena, delighted with individual things.

In such conditions great art is impossible: but the art of these three is at least alive – and obviously preliminary to a synthesis which will not be achieved within the field of English literature, since its achievement, if it ever is achieved, will automatically establish Scottish literature in a field of its own.

[Algernon Blackwood, E.L. Grant Watson, the Bones, James and David and 'Benjamin Swift' (W. Romaine Paterson) are other cases in point: and Rebecca West's *The Judge* remains – unfortunately – the best *Scottish* novel of recent years.]   [25.6.26]

39. Newer Scottish Fiction (II): Others

But – to turn to newer Scottish fiction in the proper sense of the term (for the work of the authors of *Pagan Papers, Hair of the Heifer,* and *South Wind is* not quite recent, and, as I have just indicated, is in lieu of Scottish rather than Scottish work – and the only thing that brings them under my heading is really the novelty of remembering that they are Scots and of considering their work from the point of view of the separate Scottish literary tradition that might have been) – Harold Nicolson, in his monograph on Tennyson says that 'what the early twentieth century demands from poetry is a reality of emotional impulse.' I would add that this, compactly put, is what it demands from prose, too; and that none of the younger Scottish writers, with the single exception of Neil Gunn (with whom I have already dealt) is producing work in fiction of the kind that is most distinctive of, and natural to, this generation, or seems to have the slightest inkling of the issues I raised in my last article and in many of my previous ones. All they are doing is repeating in a more or less (and generally less) Scotticized form what the last generation, or previous generations, of fictionists in England and other countries did. None of them are abreast of their times – responding to the current movements in the world of creative art. They are following old-fashioned formulae – filling old bottles and generally with stale wine, or, at the best, with very thin beer of their own brewing.

Mrs Virginia Woolf, in an admirable essay on 'Modern Fiction,' gets right to the roots of the matter. Writing of Wells, Bennett, Galsworthy, and others, she says:

No single phrase will sum up the charge or grievance which we have to bring against a mass of work so large in its volume and embodying so many qualities, both admirable and the reverse. If we tried to formulate our meaning in one word we should say that these three writers are materialists. It is because they are not concerned with the spirit but with the body that they have disappointed us, and left us with the feeling that the sooner English fiction turns its back upon them, as politely as may be, and marches, if only into the desert, the better for its soul... If we fasten, then, one label on all these books, on which is one word 'materialists,' we mean by it that they write of unimportant things; that they spend immense skill and immense industry making the trivial and the transitory appear the true and the enduring... The form of fiction most in vogue more often misses than secures the thing we seek. Whether we call it life or spirit, truth or reality, this, the essential thing, has moved off or on, and refuses to be contained any longer in such ill-fitting vestments as we provide. Nevertheless, we go on perseveringly, conscientiously, constructing our two and thirty chapters after a design which more and more ceases to resemble the vision in our minds. So much of the enormous labour of proving the solidity, the likeness to life, of the story is not merely labour thrown away, but labour misplaced to the extent of obscuring and blotting out the light of the conception. Look within and life, it seems, is very far from being 'like this.' Life is not a series of gig-lamps symmetrically arranged; life is a luminous halo, a semi-transparent envelope surrounding us from the beginning of consciousness to the end. Is it not the task of the novelist to convey this varying, this unknown and uncircumscribed spirit, whatever aberration or complexity it may display, with as little mixture of the alien and external as possible? We are not pleading merely for courage and sincerity; we are suggesting that the proper stuff of fiction is a little other than custom would have us believe it. It is, at any rate, in some such fashion as this that we seek to define the quality which distinguishes the work of several young writers, among whom Mr James Joyce is the most notable, from that of their predecessors... In contrast with those whom we have called materialists, Mr Joyce is spiritual; he is concerned at all costs to reveal the flickerings of that innermost flame which flashes its messages through the brain, and in order to preserve it he disregards with complete courage whatever seems to him adventitious, whether it be probability, or coherence, or any other of these signposts which for generations have served to support the imagination of a reader when called upon to imagine what he can neither touch nor see.

In Scotland we not only provide similar impossible fits in vestments, but we worsen matters by stocking these solely in foreign styles to which the psychology we wish to don them can never become reconciled in any degree whatever. We have evolved no distinctive form, no prose rhythms, no vocabulary adapted to the specific nature of Scottish psychology in its differences from English. The denationalisation of Scottish life and our educational system – the lack of any cultural centre – the absence of literary movements of any kind – the tremendous puritanical and practical bias that afflicts us – all these and other associated factors have prevented the development of any 'sense of Scotland,' any comprehensive or creative attitude to Scottish life and destiny. They have obtruded between us and our country – between us and our own psychology – a more or less opaque, but always distorting and dimming and minifying film of alienation, of ineffectiveness, of apathy. We are inspissated with hazy and misleading generalisations, which prevent us from seeing clearly and relating effect to cause in any dynamic or vital way. And they have provincialised us. Our best writers in this or that of the various demoded forms we have imported and to some small extent succeeded in naturalising in Scotland are small fry even in comparison with relatively mediocre exponents of the same forms still practising in the South. No contemporary Scottish prose-writer is 'taking his country anywhere,' or having the slightest real effect. What novels and volumes of short stories do appear have a very temporary and very slight recreative value during the season in which they appear and subsequently in a degree that diminishes to vanishing point in two or three years. There is no progression – no purpose or, at any rate, no result. Of 'spirituality' in the sense in which Mrs Woolf uses it – or creative integrity as Joyce exemplifies it – there is not a vestige. None of our young fictionists have anything to say. I am not pleading for propaganda or didacticism – some of them manifest one or other or both of these in various directions – but deploring an utter absence of significance, of fundamental purpose. And as to their outlook on their art, and the methods upon which they construct their novels or their sketches, almost without exception they seem to me to have taken some correspondence course in the 'Art of Fiction' ('Make money while you learn') or to have set out deliberately to produce a best-seller, pandering to what they thought the public wanted – as if best-sellers were not always the purest of flukes! In short, there is a hideous mixture of imitativeness and commercialism, with an utter absence of aesthetic consciousness.

I do not propose to enumerate all our younger novelists and short-story writers. Perhaps the most important was (I put it in the past tense because it was an importance of promise which has not been since realised) Mr James Bryce, whose extraordinarily unequal *Story of the Ploughboy* showed at least a man with a personality of his own and a deep experience of various kinds of life, and which contained, amongst much that was stilted and completely unreal, passages of altogether uncommon power, quite equal to the best in George Douglas Brown. The thrashing of a lice-ridden 'loon' by a hind under the excitation of a sadistic young woman remains in my memory after several years for its sheer completeness: and there were other elements in that book – a getting away from stock-conceptions, an independent attitude to Scotland, a knowledge of and ability to describe aspects of Scottish life and scenery which had not been used before – which make it well worth the while of young Scots to read. I have already alluded to Mr Cockburn's *Tenement* – a purely 'machine-made' naturalistic 'study' of Glasgow of the kind that old-fashioned people still call, and regard as, realistic. It was a first novel, and the author may yet do better work, if he realises the need for sincerity, acquires a measure of maturity, and ceases to try to shock people or to simulate tragedy by piling 'atrocities' on top of each other. Any genuine attempt to see Glasgow as it is, and to put down the results in fictional form or otherwise, is certainly to be welcomed. The overwhelming urban developments of Scottish life have scarcely yet given rise to any attempted literature. The late Sheriff Lyell's Edinburgh novels, *The Justice Clerk*, and the *House in Hanover Square* are restricted – in so far as they have any contact with life at all – to a very narrow class of character. Miss Agnes Stewart may be right when she says that 'there is some good film-stuff in *The Justice Clerk*.' That certainly indicates the level of the work. On a much higher plane was the novel, *The Virgin Wife* (1925) by John Carruthers – like *Tenement* a first production – an ill-constructed story, full of immaturities, but distinctly promising. 'The author,' as one critic pointed out,

> has wisely cast to the winds the foolish old convention that the last page should gather up all the loose threads, kill off all the unsavoury people, and marry the hero to his divinely-matched affinity. Peter Trevena's marriage occurs in the middle of the novel, and the end of the story, although it marks the close of one phase of his life, no more

settles all the problems which have arisen during its course than would any given moment of actual life... As a study of one aspect of Glasgow life, the picture of Trevena's lodgings could not well be bettered.

Along with Mr Carruthers and Mr Cockburn, as belonging to the new Glasgow school, may be mentioned Miss Dot Allan, with *The Syrens* (some of her more recent work in the form of short sketches has reached a much higher level); Mrs Catherine Carswell with *Open the Door,* a deft but superficial study in personalities; John Ressich, a short story writer and occasional essayist of power; George Woden, whose *Little Houses* had real literary merit of an unobtrusive sort; and Patrick Miller, whose *The Natural Man is* one of the best 'realistic' war novels we have had. Edinburgh may be credited, alongside these, with Augustus Muir and Bruce Marshall; St Andrews with Gilbert Watson; and Aberdeen with Agnes Mure Mackenzie. As précieuse the latter is the most distinguished of the lot and has a volume of studies of 'Shakespeare's Women' and another of verse to her credit. But none of them are really 'sizeable' yet, or, in any way, showing signs of becoming representative national figures.

There are two others who may be classed as belonging to the Glasgow school, but deserve rather fuller mention. These are George Blake and J.M. Reid. Robert Angus, writing in *The Scottish Nation*, put the whole issue in regard to contemporary Scottish fiction very succinctly when he said:

Setting aside the purely commercial type of fiction, the novel in Scotland is to-day limited to a few followers of the Stevenson-Neil Munro tradition, and the series of women writers like Mrs Carswell. Miss Allan and O. Douglas, who derive all from Annie Swan, without her 'uplift' and her genius for banal narrative, though with considerably more conscious, if not always successful, effort after psychology and style. There is no one to-day writing a Scots novel even of the very questionable merits of Crockett's, Ian Maclaren's, or Barrie's for the simple reason that, with the mobilisation of output under the now commercialised system, the novel writer has to write for a buying public, and as eighty per cent of that public is English or Anglicised, the novelist must avoid like the devil anything that would look real, any attempt to depart from Scottish types as fixed by English humour or exiled sentiment... To me, [he continues,] George Blake's *Mince Collop Close* is simply inexplicable. If it were the work of the confessed mass-producer of fiction one would silently condemn it to the limbo recognised for such. But Mr Blake is a notable figure in

Scottish literature. He has some extremely fine prose to his credit, and he has written *The Mother;*

and he proceeds to expose the hopeless crudity, the incredible melange of impossibilities in *Mince Collop Close.* He then turns to J.M. Reid's *Sons of Aethne* – a story of Scotland in the days before Kenneth Macalpine

> but it is all in shadowland amid the half-lights in which puppets play; not all Mr Reid's art will persuade us that they are real; they elude us, incomprehensible because there is nothing to comprehend – where the old legends scored so heavily was that they came out of the earth strong and vital; they were universal. primary, essential – Mr Reid's recension is book-learning, precious, pretty, artistry not art.

I have nothing to add to these extracts; both Mr Blake and Mr Reid ought to be potent figures in the Scottish literary movement. Neither of them is. Why: 'Both,' says Mr Angus,

> are afraid and so both are insincere. Mr Blake ran away from the facts. Mr Reid never had any facts at all… If there is to be a Scottish novel, let it be Cowcaddens or Cathcart, Carnoustie or a clachan in an outer isle,. but let it .be the real, which is not merely the actual, but its spiritual interpretation. It won't sell that type of novel, it won't be praised, and it won't make its author any more popular; for half Scotland today, the Scotland of Harry Lauder and Burns's orations, is unreal and will fight to the death for its unreality, but it will be worth doing.

No more than that need be said, save perhaps to add that, in the Stevenson-Neil Munro tradition, the best work is being done, perhaps, by John Sillars in his increasing – but scarcely progressive – tale of Arran novels; while excellent historical novels of their kind are Edward Albert's *Kirk o' Field* and Winifred Duke's *Scotland's Heir*, a striking picture of the days of the '45 Rebellion which has evoked an encomium from Hugh Walpole. But it is not merely historical novels that are wanted but novels which, whatever their location in time and place, will be distinctively Scottish in the deepest sense (and, apart from externals of Scottish chronicle either of the above might have been located anywhere else in Europe or written as they stand by a writer of almost any nationality) and will *make history* in a fashion that the whole tale of Scottish novels since *The House with the Green Shutters* has completely failed to do. [2.7.26]

Letters

THE LATE LEWIS MORRISON-GRANT

Sir, – I have just received from a literary friend a copy of Mr C.M. Grieve's article, 'Ladies' Choir,' which appeared in your issue for the 4th ult., and as the article contains an allusion to the 'Life of Lewis Morrison-Grant' I send you herewith a cutting on the subject of L. Morrison-Grant which appears in the current number of the Brechin Advertiser. Those of your readers who are interested in poetry written by Scots within the last two or three decades, may be interested in the paragraph should you be able to give it space.

Allow me to add that I am exceedingly pleased to find that Mr Grieve placed the names of Rachel Annand Taylor and Marion Angus where he did. Both poetesses are too little known, although – or is it because? – their qualities are very high indeed. – I am, etc..

Jessie Annie Anderson
Editor of Lewis Morrison-Grant:
His Life, Letters, and Last Poems

The following is the paragraph referred to: –

Lewis Morrison Grant, the 'Scottish Keats',
Appreciated in Poland.

It is now over thirty years since the Brechin Advertiser in the course of its review of Protomantis and Other Poems, by Lewis Morrison-Grant, said 'the high order of thought and powerful diction are marvellous for one so young'. Since then many little reputations have flashed up and died out in Scotland. but the Advertiser has pride in recording that the genius which it then recognised grows steadily in the recognition of other authorities – if still chiefly outwith Scotland. During last winter, in the course of his lecture on Keats to his students, Dr Roman Dyboski, Professor of English Literature, the University of Cracow, alluded to the late Morrison-Grant as also amongst the great 'inheritors of unfulfilled renown.' Dr Dyboski has both a British and a Continental reputation as an authority on literature. He is at present engaged on a work on Byron, and he is proud of the fact that he was the first to remind his countrymen of the achievements of Scottish genius in the history of British civilisation.

It is, he says, twenty years since his enthusiasm for the great qualities of Scotland was awakened in him by his German teacher, Professor Schipper of Vienna, an editor of the works of Dunbar, and an ardent admirer of Burns. Many readers of the Advertiser will welcome this testimony to Mr D.H. Edwards's early insight into the genius of 'Scotland's Keats,' whose wonderful volume was published while the youth was barely 19. [2.7.26]

Letters

CONTEMPORARY SCOTTISH FICTION

Sir, – In the course of an interesting little essay on contemporary Scottish fiction your correspondent, C.M. Grieve, has been good enough to award me 'distinction as a précieuse' on the strength of two books which he specifies. One of them does exist, most manifestly, for it was a doctorial thesis and has the bulk incumbent on its kind. The volume of poems, however, I have not seen, though I hear of it now and then in my Press notices, and I had the pleasure lately of reading an interesting critical account of it in a Scottish paper.

May I take this opportunity of laying its ghost, so far as Mr Grieve and your readers are concerned? I am a little weary of explaining why it is not to be had from The Times Book Club. – I am, etc..

Agnes Mure Mackenzie
[16.7.26]

40. The Burns Cult (I)

Mr Robert Bain put the matter very mildly in the opening sentence of his admirable article on 'Scottish Poetry of To-Day' in the *Burns Chronicle* (1926) when he said that 'Many genuine lovers of Burns see little distinction between what is good and bad in their own Poet's work and, consequently, cannot win from his best the highest pleasure that it gives.' To start with – who *are* the genuine Burnsians? Burns clubs are not literary societies – that is to say, the opinions of the great majority of their members on any literary matter are not worth a moment's consideration, they are incompetent to form any. A considerable experience of Burns clubs has shown the present writer that the Burnsian element in them is exceedingly small; the great majority of the members do not know their Burns even – the accepted Burns (that is to say the Burns as conceived on the basis of his most popular songs and satires) even – and are practically destitute of knowledge of, or interest in, literature apart from his work. The bond of membership is a social and not a cultural one. And as a rule it is an exceedingly exiguous bond – manifesting itself for the most part only for a few hours once a year. The bias of the inner circle of enthusiasts has led them in the past to concentrate on bibliographical and genealogical pursuits, preservation of place interests, establishment of 'shrines,' erection of monuments – anything and everything connected with the externalities of Burns and his work rather than upon appreciation of the man's true character and significance and the continuance of his work and the attempt to perpetuate his spirit and realise his ideals. The excessive futilities which have accompanied this cult are without parallel in the history of the world. Nations whose history has been starred with relays of men of poetic genius as great or greater than Burns have not allowed their significance to run to sand in this way – even if, at the very worst, they have had, in respect of this or that poet, a crop of antiquaries and bibliographers and biographers and marginalists of all kinds, at least all of them have had a powerful cultured class, a dominant intelligentsia, able to secure for each genius in turn his proper setting and an adequate valuation based on the essentials of his work, and thus to ensure his due influence. Their quality is not obscured and their force dissipated by hordes of mediocrities. Literature in these countries has its standards and its definite sphere and functions. It is only in Scotland where there are no cultural standards – where there is little love or appreciation of literature – that so grotesque a travesty of literary honour could have developed itself. What would Burns himself think of it all? What, for example, would he think of the latest amazing manifestation of the cult – the provision, in a handsome oak case, of a plan of the old Mauchline kirkyard, showing the location of the graves of the poet's contemporaries buried there, and the further provision of artistic name-plates for the graves themselves, seventeen of them, including those of James Hamilton, Burns's message boy, Gavin Hamilton ('the poor man's friend'), Robert Wilson ('the gallant weaver'), Mary Morrison, 'Auld' Nance Tannock, William Fisher ('Holy Willie'), 'The Godly Bryan,' Janet Gibson ('Racer Jess'), John Brown ('Clockie'), the Rev. William ('Daddy') Auld, John Richmond, Andrew Noble, James Humphrey ('The Bletherin'), 'Laird' M'Gaan, William Patrick (Burns's gadboy); James Whiteford (brother of 'Maria of the Catrine Woods'), and Burns's infant children. What an appalling interminable business! The humourlessness, the unimaginativeness, the sheer imbecility of it, are simply indescribable. It is not too much to say that if all the money that has been spent on the Burns movement had been offered as a prize to any Scotsman who could produce a poem which a Board of international literary critics of standing would have agreed was an addition of genuine consequence to world-poetry, Burns would have been infinitely better honoured and the money infinitely better spent. Prizes do not encourage poetry, of course, and the fact of the matter is that no conceivable effort to do so that the united world membership of Burns clubs can embark upon could, of itself, do anything to enhance Scottish literature; these people as matters stand can, and do, hinder – under no circumstances can they directly help. But there is one way, perhaps, in which they could facilitate the doing of a task which is long overdue – they could commission a writer of the calibre of, say, Mr Lytton Strachey or the Hon. Harold Nicolson to write a study of Burns – of Burns the poet as poet. Nothing else matters.

A judiciously-selected anthology of extracts from the innumerable orations on 'The Immortal Memory' is another long-overdue task which would tax the resources of the most competent wit. A volume could undoubtedly be compiled which would be an immortal scream. Mr Mencken's selected *Americana* pale in comparison. In a selection of the world's worst criticism – on lines similar to those Mr J.C. Squire proposed to adopt in respect of the 'best bad poetry' – the Burns section would be by far the biggest and the most excruciatingly funny. In a country like Scotland where there are no literary traditions and where no special fitness but rather social considerations have always dictated the selection of the 'orators,' the inevitable result is that all manner of essentially non-literary persons – ministers, schoolmasters, law lords, and what not – have, year in and year out, conspired to bury Burns under an ever-increasing cairn of the most ludicrous and inapposite eulogy. The enormities of praise that have been heaped upon him beggar description. They are peerless products of people with no sense of proportion – no intuitive appreciation of literature – no sense of literary latitude and longitude to guide them – floundering from one fatuous misconception to another, almost as if they were trying to excel each other in saying the last word upon something of which their first word, their very angle of approach, showed that they were constitutionally incapable of saying anything that was not the very essence of irrelevance and fatuity. Nor would a series of selections chosen without regard to the tit-bits of utter egregiousness but rather to represent the general run of these orations fairly – the type of sentiment, the attitude to Burns and to literature generally, that has overwhelmingly characterised the Annual Suppers everywhere, be different in kind however much they might be in degree. In sum these orations are a terrific indictment of the whole cult – and of Scottish 'culture.' It is an appalling thing to reflect that of the thousands and thousands of columns of these speeches all but an infinitesimal fraction is utterly valueless save for purposes of satire. To hunt through them for a single critical *aperçu* of the slightest value – for any illuminating comment – is a hopeless task. One thing will strike anyone who does try to analyse them – the extent to which they are paraphrases of each other, the absence of independent approach and genuine personal reaction, the conscienceless perpetuation of the conventional commonplaces and clichés. All this spate of essentially meaningless verbosity – the product of a stupid conventionalism reinforced by no first-hand authoritative re-study of the poet and his work, still less by any consciousness of the history, functions and problems of Scottish literature – would not matter, or would not matter so much at any rate, if there was a single strain of a different kind of activity maintaining a real criticism or seeking to relate the poetry of Burns effectively to the changing needs and tastes of the world or endeavouring to carry on his work for Scottish literature or to preserve his spirit and work for his ideals in contemporary life. But of genuine Burns criticism in this sense there is scarcely a vestige. Burns, as a poet, has long ceased to be taken seriously by anyone really interested in literature. Exhaustive studies of the technique and output of other poets pour annually from the presses. But not of Burns's work. Even the personality, the man himself, has never been maturely studied. There is not a single book upon him – scarcely a single comprehensive essay – that is even passably well written. Most of the biographical matter concerning him has been strung together in a very mediocre fashion, vitiated by a provincial morality and a lack of *savoir faire*. It is high time the Burns legend was destroyed and the man himself, 'in the round,' a credible human figure, rescued from the eponymous proliferation of moralitarian, 'patriotic,' propagandist and counter-propagandist excrescences under which he is buried – a human palimpsest in which all that is significant and immortal has been overwritten with tawdry and trivial scribblings of all kinds. From the strictly literary as against the broadly human point of view the things that principally want doing to-day, amongst all the things which should have been the first concern of the Burns cult, are to resume Burns into his proper historical setting – to see him as he really is in relation to world-poetry as a whole – to consider what effect he has had upon Scottish literature in particular – and to consider his handling of the vernacular. There are, happily, signs just now that each of these inter-related tasks is beginning to be tackled – or, at least, that there is a promisingly increasing appreciation of the need to tackle them; and it is with these signs – and the tasks themselves – that I am going to concern myself here.

One aspect of the matter has recently been very well stated by Mr Lewis Spence.

What we desire, [he says] is to see a new psychological approach manifested in Scottish verse. During the last quarter of a century [Mr Spence ought to have said 'during the last century'] Scottish literature has done little to attract the attentions of the world of culture. It has certainly failed to appeal to European imagination as the Irish or Norwegian literatures have appealed. The crass sentimentalities and undistinguished banalities of the Kailyaird School alienated from the first sympathies of critics of taste and insight. Scotsmen of perspicacity and experience could not but feel depressed at the popular vogue of a cult which they were aware frequently afforded only a base caricature of their countrymen, paving the way for the grosser tradition of Lauderism. Nor to Scotsmen of liberal views did the somewhat artless impulse to concentrate the entire literary thought and homage of the nation upon the achievement of Robert Burns, however admittedly great, appear as likely to be conducive to the healthy or catholic expansion of Scottish literary life and activity. Those of them, more familiar with the genius and tradition of the older and more courtly Scottish poets, Douglas, Henryson, Dunbar and Lyndesay, and with the tradition, magical and intense, of the northern balladeers, recognised in these a spirit as genuinely native and technically more worthy of affection and close study than the work of their successors. While worshipping Burns, 'this side idolatry,' they wholeheartedly detested the host of uninspired plagiarists who succeeded him, and deplored the descent of Scots poetry into an abyss of infamous cliché and mechanical reiteration. It was, indeed, inevitable that the whole race of poetasters should have misconstrued and misapprehended the essentials of the Burnsian composition, confounding as they did an inspired simplicity, a great lyric artlessness, with mere banality. Incapable of discerning the true merits of a tonic gift, the quality of which probably remains unsurpassed, they laboured under the delusion that anything couched in Scots must naturally possess an equal excellence with the effortless cadences of a great natural artist who sang as spontaneously and with all the perfervid enchantment of a thrush in a morning garden. From the death of Burns to the end of the late war may, perhaps, be regarded as the most jejune and uninspired period in Scottish letters. Not only was it parasitical to a great name in a manner that scarcely any other literature can ever have been, its history was almost utterly devoid of those frequent regroupings and reorientations of the literary elements which are regarded by the superficial as the manifestations of originality; for although 'originality' is actually incapable of attainment, the surest sign of artistic vitality is its endeavour. This, within the period alluded to, was almost wholly invisible, and old men, and some young ones, maundered on in the Burnsian tradition. But 'the war changed all that!' It achieved what nothing else could have achieved, because it removed for a while large numbers of Scots from the Caledonian scene, and permitted them a view of a larger world: and this estrangement had the effect it ever has on the Scottish mind – a marked quickening of the patriotic sense, mingled with a desire for new things.   [23.7.26]

41. The Burns Cult (II)

What is the truth about Burns? 'Patriotism and centenaries,' says Philip Guedalla, 'are the two greatest enemies of truth' – and no great writer has suffered more from them (for 'anniversaries' and 'centenaries' are in the self-same category in this connection) than Robert Burns. The tragedy of Burns is that he was a great poet who lived in an age and under circumstances hopelessly uncongenial to the exercise of his art and that, as a consequence, he was prevented from penetrating to an intellectual plane in keeping with his lyrical genius – there is an unspanned gulf between his matter and his manner, between his calibre as a poet and the kind of poetry to which he was for the most part restricted by his want of cultivation, between his powers and the work he actually produced and the influence that work has had. It is one of the greatest ironies – if not an unparalleled irony – in literary history that if not 'a mute inglorious Milton' Burns, at all events, was kept relatively so in relation to his powers. His great popularity is derived almost entirely from the results of the thwarts he encountered, his inability to find appropriate expression for his genius, his hapless compromises. His worst failures have been his greatest success, *e.g.*, the unspeakable 'A Man's a Man.' It is as if a God were to be embodied as a small town citizen and, though his Godhead were apparent, the biological limitations of the form imposed upon him, and the general circumstances of the life he had to accept, betrayed his impulses into forms little better than caricatures of those which, had he been free, they would have found. Burns was no God and elements in his own nature conspired constantly with the adverse circumstances and intolerable environment in which he was placed against the best that was in him. The result is that he is for the most part seen as the poet he was only in the power of his versification; the content of nine-tenths of his work is on an altogether deplorably low level. He was no thinker, no politician, and, except in certain very narrow directions, no realist or observer of nature. Neither was he a Scotsman in any fundamental sense of the term – that is to say, he had no specific 'sense of Scotland,' no vital appreciation of the distinctive functions of the Scottish genius. The bulk of his sentiments are, whether one shares them or not, and no matter how passionately or otherwise in his heart of hearts he entertained them, historically appreciated, either a mere utilisation of certain kinds of political, moral, and social thought current at the time (and by no means either peculiar to Scotland or carried in Scottish life and letters to any degree which invests them with any special national significance) or a like utilisation of literary conventions then in favour. Pope's definition of true wit applies to most of it – it was the current thought of the time better expressed than by all but a few. But that does not alter the fact that the intellectual content of Burns's work is exceedingly meagre – that his expressions of political opinion 'cancel out,' varying with the mood he happened to be in and being obviously used as mere literary 'properties' – that his moral views are hopelessly commonplace and opportunist – that his descriptions of scenery are generalised until they cease to apply specifically to any place – that the kinds of poetry he wrote were generally the lowest and never the highest kinds – that the 'divine voices' are almost wholly absent from his work – and that he is almost wholly destitute of any sense of beauty. His intellection, such as it was, was not typically Scottish, in the sense of carrying forward, or applying in new ways, the most distinctive qualities of the Scottish mind. On the contrary, he was mentally a typical – an archetypal – Scot of his age, inspissated with English influences. He did not inaugurate a new era in Scottish literature. He merely crowned the tendencies which had been long at work. Patriotically we owe little to him. His use of the vernacular was exiguous

– eked out with English. His attitude to women is wholly unreal; his songs to any one of them might as easily have been addressed to any other – or to some abstraction – for all of precise psychology that transpires from them. Like most of his 'descriptions of nature' they are hopelessly generalised. And, worst of all, they are not true to himself – they are a polite fiction. The truer Burns, in his relation to women, is to be seen in *The Merry Muses*. The rest was playing to the gallery. This accounts for the deadly sameness in all of them; it was a mere convention. Most of his work rings psychologically false. This is not to gainsay the technical merits of the poems in question – his power of expression (if only of expressing, not himself, but the stock-conceptions of particular kinds of poetry then in vogue, the orthodox approach to orthodox subjects – forms of expression, albeit, singularly otiose and valueless to-day). Burns is probably the most powerful lyrical poet the world has ever seen. It is in keeping with the cultural history of Scotland that such a Pegasus should have had to work in double harness with the clumsiest of cart-horses – that Burns's wonderful power of song should have been so prosaically shackled, that his unique passion should have had to manifest itself behind such an irrelevant array of trite platitudinisation. And it is in keeping too with the cultural history of Scotland that even yet he should be most esteemed for the orthodox externalities of his work – for all that is irrelevant to, most opaque to, and most disfiguring of his genius rather than for the essence of that genius in itself. Historically, Burns is to be discerned as a safety-valve – a means of 'working off' Scottish sentiment amenably to the tendency to progressive Anglicisation which had set in so strongly by his day. He did little to counter this by creating any realistic Nationalism. It must be remembered too, as explicative of much, that Burns was by no means a representative Scotsman even of his own age – he was only the mouthpiece of a class which became, in him, for the first time fully articulate, a class that was in the nature of things not free and generally least so when it flattered itself on its 'independence.' But all that was best in Scotland lay outwith it – and outwith Burns's consciousness. In a close study of the historical, topographical, personal, and cultural references in his poems as against the body of Scottish life and literature prior to his birth it is curious to find how little of Scotland Burns either inherited or acquired for the purpose of re-expression, and that re-expression was never along the line either of the highest qualities implicit in any part of it or the most dynamic potentialities inherent in it. Burns's intransigence was wholly superficial, and was no more directed at the reversal of the existing tendencies than effective in that direction. As to the morality of

his work, he swung between bowdlerisation and sculduddery; and his
admirers have shared these natural complements of each other. But the
official – the general – attitude to Burns remains even to-day pretty much
that expressed by the Bishop of Derry and Raphoe (Dr William
Alexander) in these ludicrous lines: –

> Smiles for the song that hath such rare beguilement,
>   Laughter and love to win,
> Tears for the dust, and ashes, and defilement,
>   Tears for the shame and sin.
>
> O the wild wit that mars the holy hymning!
>   The stains upon the stole!
> The spray-drops from the sea of passion dimming
>   The windows of the soul!
>
> Hush! the man's sighs, his longings and his laughter
>   Are silent now by Doun;
> The music of the immortal song lives after,
>   A many-mingled tune.
>
> And all at last with solemn sweet surprises
>   In anthems die away,
> And o'er the glee of 'Tam o' Shanter' rises
>   The 'Cottar's Saturday.'
>
> And from a multitude beside the river,
>   And on the mountain sod,
> Sweetly goes up for ever and for ever
>   'Come, let us worship God!'

Who was it who said of this that they 'noted with much satisfaction this
delicate yet full-hearted tribute to Burns, which is all the more acceptable *because the Bishop is an earnest theologian on his own lines.*' He
must have been. They are a numerous breed, however. This attitude
finds its natural complement in those who admire Burns as a 'rebel,' a
Socialist, an immoralist. Both are equally irrelevant to his genius and are
founded on the dreadful literalism that imagines that a great poet had
necessarily 'anything to say' – that his ideas, the content of his work, are
of the slightest consequence. In no poet is this less the case than in
Burns. Apart from sense little of his essential quality resides even in the
sound of his work – his use of words – which is the reason why he did so
little for Braid Scots.   [30.7.26]

362

Letters

THE NEW BARDS AND THE OLD

Sir, – One gathers from Mr Grieve's most recent pronouncements, which are approved of by his admirer, Mr Lewis Spence, that Scotland is to be regenerated (1) with the aid of the swatches of rhymed prose industriously purveyed by those patriots, the monthly, weekly, and bi-weekly bards of the new literary cult, (2) by the total suppression of all Burns functions, orations, memorials, etc., (3) the abandonment of the 'Kailyaird' tendencies, and (4) the return of the literary fashions of Dunbar. Douglas, Henryson, and Lyndesay.

Apparently our native land has, according to Grieve & Co., been lying far too long in a sort of literary bog. 'But the war changed all that!' Mr Spence tells us what the War really accomplished:

> *It achieved what nothing else could have achieved, because it removed for a while large numbers of Scots from the Caledonian scene, and permitted them a view of a larger world; and this estrangement had the effect it ever has on the Scottish mind – a marked quickening of the patriotic sense, mingled with a desire for new things.*

Scotsmen, however, have long been wanderers. They were all over the world long before 1914. Those who suffered and died in France, Belgium, Italy, Salonika, Gallipoli, and Mesopotamia, and on the ocean, saw less of the world than the peaceful adventurers who went forth before them. If the soldiers and sailors learned anything in the literary line, it was to appreciate more deeply than ever before the hamely, simple sangs of their native land. I refuse to blame the War and the brave Scots who fought in it, for the new poetry, the new criticism, the new Doric, or anything else connected with the 'movement' with which Mr C.M. Grieve and Mr Lewis Spence are identified. It is wholly a movement of an organised group of young and middle-aged writers from whom we get more propaganda than art. Not one of them has, in my opinion, yet produced any prose or verse worthy to be ranked with Scotland's best.

I am weary of all the shouting about the 'Kailyaird School' – a term introduced by Henley, who sneered at most things Scottish. Sir J.M. Barrie, the 'founder' of this 'school,' is a genius and an artist. If Mr Grieve and Mr Spence will read (and re-read) Barrie's Little Minister, Auld Licht Idylls, *and* The Window in Thrums, *they will find qualities which they themselves lack – a sense of style and a sense of humour.*

They may dislike what Henley called 'the theological weavers,' but the fact remains that the old Scots weavers and the other Scots artisans were very theological indeed. That essential fact should be faced. The horrors *of the inartistic, long-drawn-out ending of* The House with the Green Shutters *were rarer in the Scotland of my boyhood than were Sunday school soirées and prayer meetings. There is no room in Scotland for a Gorki, because Scotland has little of the wholesale squalor and ignorance and immorality of the terrible Russian environment in which Gorki was reared. The majority of Scots of the generation and area to which Barrie belongs were decent, clean-minded people, who worked hard for little reward and laid up treasure in heaven.*

The 'Kailyaird' fashion did not really begin with Barrie, however. Robert Henryson, for instance, wrote a famous 'Kailyaird' poem entitled 'Robene and Makyne,' and there is 'Kailyairdism' in the ballads. William Dunbar, who sang of London, 'The flour of cities all,' and satirised Edinburgh on account of its weather, who gloried in the union of the thistle and the rose and made his Muse lecture on 'Content,' etc., is the last bard we would expect to have held up as an example to the modern bards of Scottish Sinn Fein. Our modern rhymers, who defy accepted canons of art, are surely not serious when they recommended Gavin Douglas, who could be so artificial –

> *Flaggis of fire, and mony felloun flaw,*
> *Sharp soppis of sleet, and of the snip and snaw…*
> *So busteously Boreas his bugle blew,*
> *The deer full dern doun in the dales drew.*

Here we have 'alliteration's artful aid' carried to an excess found only in the dull performance of Anglo-Saxon poets of the dullest period. Burns (who was more like Dunbar than was any other Scots poet) is like a breath of free wind from the ocean compared with some of our early Scots writers who imitated Chaucer, etc. He had what many of them lacked – spontaneity and inspiration. Douglas, Henryson and Lyndesay are lesser bards than Burns; and, compared with Burns, the post-war rhymers are as grass-blades to elm trees.

It is difficult to deal in detail with Messrs Grieve and Spence. One looks in vain to them for reasoned criticism; they are purveyors of wild assertions and wilder literary prophecies. According to Mr Spence, Scotland has done little in the way of literature during 'the last quarter of a century.' Mr Grieve corrects him with 'the last century.' I have just been turning over the pages of Professor Macneile Dixon's The

Edinburgh Book of Scottish Verse, *and agree with him that 'some of the verses by living writers, are not unworthy of association with Scotland 's best.' If one takes the years in which the Scots poets died during the past century, one can remind Mr Grieve of Baroness Nairne, James Hogg, Sir Walter Scott, Thomas Campbell (a real war poet), Allan Cunningham ('A wet sheet and a flowing sea'). William Motherwell ('A steed, a steed of matchlesse speede'), and several others who similarly dwarf Grieve, Spence & Co. There were also great prose writers, including Hugh Miller.*

Recently we were informed that Mr Spence was a greater bard than Andrew Lang, and I was immediately reminded of two great Lang sonnets with such lines as –

> *The bones of Agamemnon are a show*
> *And ruined in his royal monument…*

and

> *And through the music of the languid hours,*
> *They hear like ocean on a western beach*
> *The surge and thunder of the Odyssey.*

I have never read any verse of Mr Spence worthy to be compared to Lang's.

If there is going to be a Scottish literary renaissance, the Grieves and Spences, and the others associated with them, would be more convincing and more effective if they had less to say in abuse of the writers of their native land, and produced instead something worthy of being called 'artistic'. It is, I repeat, Art we want, not propaganda. Poetry is concerned with Art, not with politics.

Not one of the Grieve-led writers is in the same street with John Ferguson of sonnet fame, who is as well known in America as in his native land. It is absurd on the part of the Grievites to attempt to 'rope him in.' He is not in their movement, nor of it. I refuse to believe that he approves of the new Doric department, or recognises Montrose as the literary capital of Scotland. As a Highlander, I must protest against the whole literary creed of Grieve, Spence & Co. – I am, etc.,

Donald A. Mackenzie
[30.7.26]

Letters

THE NEW BARDS AND THE OLD

Sir, – *In the ordinary course I should not have condescended to reply to Mr Donald A. Mackenzie's unprovoked and amazingly vulgar attack. But as he attributes to me certain views which I do not hold, and as his purpose is openly and characteristically vindictive, it becomes necessary to refute his crazy assertions.*

In the first place, he identifies me with the movement which has come to be known as 'The Scottish Literary Renaissance,' and assumes that I am acting under the leadership of Mr C.M. Grieve, with whom, he suggests, I am working as one of 'an organised group.' It must be a very loosely organised group as far as I am concerned, for I have had the pleasure of meeting Mr Grieve on two occasions only, and have not heard from him by letter for more than a year! When I recently published an article in The Nineteenth Century *on the subject of 'The Scottish Renaissance,' it did not necessarily imply that I was identified with that movement any more than I am identified with the revolution in Mexico, which I have also recently discussed in the Press.*

I certainly admire much of Mr Grieve's work, but to associate my own efforts, literary and propagandist, with his, is fair to neither of us. In a recent leading article, the Glasgow Herald comparing my work with that of Mr Grieve, remarked: 'They are poles apart in language and subject matter... Mr MacDiarmid (Mr Grieve) draws his vocabulary from Scots anywhere and of any time: Mr Spence derives from the old "Makaris".'

That puts the matter in a nutshell. Mr Grieve is engaged in an effort to popularise 'synthetic' Scots, while my own predilections and propaganda strive towards a literary revival of the old Court Scots, which it is not intended should displace. but supplement, the current Doric, providing Scottish poets with a more polished literary instrument. And may I say here that so far from 'defying accepted canons of art,' I am a strict adherent to accepted forms in verse, and have frequently been adversely criticised for my conservative attitude in this regard.

Mr Mackenzie attributes to me a desire to overthrow the Burns cult in Scotland. But is it subversive of the fame of Burns to indicate that a whole-hearted devotion to him at the expense of all other Scots poets ancient and modern is a retrograde sign in present-day Scottish life? Surely the work of Burns is the more appreciated after an intelligent perusal of his forerunners. Both in verse and prose I have tried to maintain the fame of Burns, and it is a particularly cowardly thing on Mr Mackenzie's part to try to arouse indignation against me by representing that I have decried the Bard. Indeed it is worse. It is a piece of calculated mendacity, especially in view of my recent articles in The Times *to awaken interest in the work of the Burns Vernacular Circles.*

On the other hand, I plead guilty to a deep distaste for the work of Sir James Barrie. I confess I can see in him nothing but a mere journalist with a capacity for misrepresenting Scotland in order to pander to the Cockney palate. His writings do not in any sense appeal to me as literature; nor has his work, in my view, the distinction conferred by the artist. But when Mr Mackenzie's savage and stupid censures on the work and personal character of Stevenson are recalled, surely any criticism I have levelled against the myth-maker of the Albany must seem the mildest of cooing.

Nor have I associated my Art with propaganda. I have deliberately segregated it from my Scottish Nationalist propaganda, if not from my efforts to reawaken interest in the language – not the spirit – of the old Court poets, and to revive 'Gentlemen's Scots'.

I say nothing of Mr Mackenzie's remarks on the subject of my verse, as I do not choose to regard him as a critic of insight or scholarly capacity. It is impertinent in him to criticise the work of his betters. He may be entrusted, perhaps, with the scissors and paste of minor journalism, but his mental and educational equipment incapacitates him from the serious discussion of such a theme as Scots poetry, old or new. The circumstance that Mr Mackenzie never contributes anything to newspapers or magazines of standing on the subject of Scots Letters completely invalidates his claim to pose as a critic in this difficult sphere. And why should he protest 'as a Highlander' against my 'literary creed,' or that of Mr Grieve? Has he not his own literary medium, the Gaelic? Or does he know as little of that as he does of the Doric? Let him cultivate his Gaelic primer to better purpose. He will then at least have a language in which to outpour his garrulous spite. At present he has only a patois.

It is obvious that Mr Mackenzie's letter has been inspired by resentment that his own 'swatches of rhymed prose' have not met with acceptance in literary circles, and by the disappointed ambition of one who mistook a pony for a Pegasus. – I am, etc.,

Lewis Spence

Sir, – I have just read with amazement the scurrilous attack by Mr Mackenzie on Mr Spence in the current issue of your Journal. On many occasions has Mr Mackenzie been known to denounce the Kailyaird school in general and Sir J. M. Barrie in particular. Surely he must have a most convenient memory. I don't suppose many people will pay much attention to Mr Mackenzie's ravings, as he makes a habit of running down everyone who does not give him unstinted praise and he is absolutely intolerant of the slightest breath of criticism. Mr Spence's poetry requires no boosting, to true lovers of poetry and to those who understand it. Mr Mackenzie's contribution to your Journal will be recognised as an outpouring of spleen. Now to come to the part of the letter where Mr Mackenzie refers to the bards of Scottish Sinn Fein. Let me take Mr Mackenzie's memory back to the meeting of The Scots National League in the Y.M.C.A. Hall on June 1922, when he, as a member of the audience, got up and made one of the most inflammatory speeches of the evening. Although he was not billed as one of the speakers, he spoke longer and more fiercely than anyone there on the subject of Scottish independence, and that is only one instance of many occasions of the sort. It seems to me that Mr Mackenzie must have some private grudge against Mr Spence, hence the outpouring of wrath. In conclusion, I would like to add that I think the whole attack is unworthy and unmanly. – I am, etc.,

Lover of Justice
[6.8.26]

C.M. Grieve or Hoots, Blethers

'Hail, land o' cakes an' brither Scots
Frae Maidenkirk to John o ' Groats.
If there's a hole in a' your coats,
    I rede ye tent it.
A chiel's amang ye, takin' notes,
    An', faith, he'll prent it.'

Tak' shame, your Continental neighbours
Has ta'en them to their pipes an' tabors:
While you, ye menseless sliplalabors,
    Maun think it teugh
On Scotia's star to spen' sic labours
    As redd the bruch.

The lear to diagnose your ill
He'll gie ye, fegs, again your will –
The Czechs are like a weel-gaun mill,
    Their clap plays clatter;

While twal-pint Scotia's yell's the bill
    An' weak as water.

It's like your Lallan tongue an' Erse
Is yearly gettin' 'worse and worse,'
Sae that to rhyme a single verse
    Is e'en owre kittle.
But pret ye wi sic heich converse,
    Ye'll fin it smittle!

There no' a European nation
But cocks her pow abune her station
Wi' true aesthetic orientation –
    The very Russians
Is leagues an' leagues this side damnation -
    Compared wi' hus anes.

Ye maun gie owre deliberations
On a' extraneous inspissations;
For oh, to them wha hae the patience
    Its nae sic wark
To strip the sawl o' a' the nations
    E'en to the sark!

Ye feckless, gangrel, toom wanwordies,
Ye'se get his crummock owre your hurdies
But an' you'll straucht lea' aff your sturdies
    In thocht to men,
An' a' your heritage whilk smoor'd is
    Ye'll spier to ken.

Robert Macintyre
[13.8.26]

42. Towards a Synthetic Scots

It is amusing to find a few Scots assessors at Musical Festivals and other self-regarded experts – none of them with any work in Scots of the slightest consequence to their own credit – laying down the law, in evident alarm at the new tendencies which are manifesting themselves in recent Vernacular literature, that 'there must be no mixing of different dialects' – *i.e.* (for this is what it amounts to), no working back from the bits to the whole, no effort to reintegrate the *disjecta membra* – but despite these stick-in-the-muds, and no matter how long it may take the great body of lovers of Scots to arrive at any conception of the new position, it is happily obvious that Scots has at last – and not too late – been committed to a synthetic process. This is still in its initial stage, of course. Valuable work has already been done, however, and an increasing body of writers is being attracted to the new possibilities. How far the process can go without those concerned in it meeting and mapping out a definite and comprehensive policy it is impossible to say: but it may be that the latter course will yet be taken by an adequately representative group. There is a great mass of problems to tackle certainly before an ample provisional canon can be established and applied. In the absence of that, a good deal of individual effort is likely to be wasted in ultimately unfruitful channels. The development of the *Landsmaal* movement in Norway – as of the Provençal movement – was coterie work. No coterie of sufficient calibre has yet emerged in Scotland. The few poets and theorists who have so far advanced and the new synthesising tendencies are a very heterogeneous handful – at such different stages of development that useful co-operation between them is scarcely possible; while there is no non-creative worker for Scots with anything of value to bring to such a suggested symposium. Practically all so-called vernacular enthusiasts are still bogged in considerations of dialectical demarcation. Nevertheless the movement has begun, and the ultimate outcome is assured. The history of dialect developments in most other European countries makes it clear that the synthetic principle is bound to triumph in the long run – if complete desuetude is to be avoided; and since the Burns Federation and other bodies are pledged to the revival of Scots, it follows that however improbable any such development may still appear to them, they must sooner or later come round to realise that a synthetic Scots is the only way out. Not only so: but the time is propitious. The peculiar relations now establishing themselves between literature and linguistics make it obvious that a speedy and successful use of synthetic Scots would give Scotland a short cut into the very forefront of contemporary creative experimentalism. Let me illustrate this point by a few references to recent Russian literature, for example.

Compare Burns and Victor Khlébnikov (1885-1922). Burns did nothing to restore Braid Scots. He simply took it at the level at which he found it. But for him, of course, its desuetude would since have been very much more rapid and complete. He arrested its decline. But it was only a ghost of its former self to which he gave a new lease of life – and that on a far higher and wider plane than prior to him it had occupied. He showed that literature of world consequence could be expressed through the medium of Scots even in the decayed forms in which he found and used it. But his vein of Vernacular was a very narrow one and poorly represents the riches of the tongue. Indeed it misrepresents them, and, ironically enough, Burns's achievement instead of being a help now is in many ways a stumbling-block. This is the more ironical in that Burns himself synthesised in his use of words from different dialects with probably a certain percentage of terms obsolete even then. But his whole attitude to words was literal and the reverse of that which must be consciously adopted and applied if the recreation of the tongue instead of its mere conservation at a given level of declinature is to be the objective – if that immensely greater achievement is to be accomplished, in other words, to which Burns might have addressed himself if he had had the attitude to words of a Khlébnikov, for example. Prince Mirsky says of Khlébnikov:

> Words and forms had for him an existence of their own, and his work in life was to create a new world of words. He had a deep primary feeling for the nature of the Russian language... All things were only a material for him to build up a new world of words. This world of words is without doubt a creation of genius, but it is obviously not for the general. He is not and probably never will be read except by poets and philologists, though an anthology *ad usum profanorum* might be selected from his works which would present him more attractively and accessibly than he chose to do it himself. As for the poets they have found him an inexhaustible mine of good example and useful doctrine. They use his works as a granary whence they take the seeds of their own harvests. His work is also of great interest to the philologist, for he was a lord of language. He knew its hidden possibilities and forced it to reveal them. His work is a microcosm reflecting on an enormously magnified scale the creative processes of the whole life-story of the language. Khlébnikov, in his creative linguistics, was true to the genuine spirit of the Russian language; the method he uses is the same as that used by the language itself – analogy. Another Futurist (Kruchónykh) endeavoured to create an entirely new language or even to use a new language, created *ad hoc*, for every new poem. This movement led to little good, for Kruchónykh himself

and most of his followers had no feeling for the phonetic soul of Russian, and their *written* inventions are, more often than not, simply unpronounceable. But when this 'trans-sense' *(zaumny)* language is used in sympathy with the phonetic soul of the language, it produces rather amusing and interesting effects.

Probably Prince Mirsky here does much less than justice to *zaumny*, judging it by auditory criteria, when its primary appeal is visual or to the inner ear – if its appearance on paper is effectively related to the shapes words originally designed for chiefly phonetic uses took, and elaborates and 'spookifies' these, it can be infinitely useful and enriching. Such experimentations as Khlébnikov's and Kruchónykh's, at any rate, represent the two main creative tendencies at work in Russian literature – and not only in Russian literature but in *welt-literatur* generally. A third is the realisation of the necessity for reinvigorating and reforming poetical methods and the prosecution of researches into rhythms and forms, and with it, in its relation to the position and possibilities of Scottish letters, I propose to deal in my next study under the title of 'Race and Rhythm.'

In the meantime it will be obvious that linguistic experiments such as are described above represent the very antitheses of the attitudes which brought Scots to its present low level and stereotyped elements of its disintegration in the gutter dialects employed by Burns and his imitators. It is not only in poetry that the new tendencies in Russian have borne great fruit. Rozanov, a tremendous figure whose speculative genius is only now winning British recognition, in his 'anti-Gutenberg' prose tried to create a more 'spoken' form of written Russian. Remizov, the most influential of contemporary creative writers, has gone infinitely further in this direction.

His prose, [says Prince Mirsky,] is *skaz*, that is to say, it reproduces the syntax and intonation of spoken language, and *of the spoken language in its most native and least literary forms.* He has a keen sense for words, for individual words and for grammatical composition. His prose, often very studious and elaborate, is always new and never falls into *clichés*. He has taught the Russian writer to value his words, to think of them as of independent beings and not to use them as mere signs, or as parts of ready-made verbal groups... His action on the language has been largely parallel to that of the Futurists, who have also applied themselves to linguistic creation and delatinising the language.

It is in like ways that Scots must be re-created (really created – for, for literary purposes, it has practically never been) and de-Anglicised. 'Sense of words' is the keynote to the whole position: but beware of those who lack the necessary *flair* and perpetrate such atrocities as, for instance, Dr Lauchlan Maclean Watt's recent 'Scots poems.'

The Jazz-ification of what generally passes – and is still largely in use – as 'Braid Scots' (the Kailyaird canon) is another hopeful possibility if it can be done along such lines as those adopted in Russia by Mayakovsky, who

> uses the diction of every day in its cruder forms, *deforming* it to *suit his needs in a direction opposite to that of the older poetical tradition.* His language is free from 'trans-sense' elements; but, considered as a literary language, it is a new dialect, a dialect which is entirely his own creation. For the way he puts to use the elements of spoken language makes them sound quite different from the usual... There is a certain affinity between Mayakovsky and Mr Vachel Lindsay. But, apart from the difference of spirit animating the two poets, Mr Lindsay's poetry is essentially musical, intended to be sung in chorus – Mayakovsky's cannot be sung at all; it is declamatory, rhetorical – the verse of an open-air orator. Judged by 'Victorian' standards, his verse is simply not poetry at all; and judged by Symbolist standards, it is no better. But it is largely owing to our Symbolist education, which has widened to such an extent our poetical sensibility, that we are capable of appreciating this rowdy and noisy rhetoric. Mayakovsky is genuinely popular, read by a very wide circle of readers. His appeal is direct and simple, his subjects can interest the most uncultured, while the high originality of his craftsmanship makes him a paramount figure in the eyes of the professional poet.

A Scottish Mayakovsky at this juncture would be a Godsend. The popular verse he would react against is not poetry at all from any stand-point, so there would be no loss in that direction, while a sufficiently uncultured public abounds in our midst.

The ridiculing and non-comprehension of the movement towards a Synthetic Scots – and towards such suggestions as I have just thrown out or as are implied in these quotations – simply shows the grotesque igno-rance of the history of Continental literature on the part of certain so-called Scottish 'critics.' They will do well to 'mark, learn and inwardly digest' in this connection what Laurie Magnus in his *Dictionary of European Literature* (Routledge, 25s.) says of the Spanish writer, Luis de Gongora y Argote, the tercentenary of whose death falls to be observed next year, *viz.*,

Gongora's 'vice' was to play with the words themselves: to introduce strange words; to use forced constructions; somehow, and ultimately anyhow, to cause surprise by unexpectedness, and thus to attain to a style so obscure, so allusive, and so much involved, as to perplex even the learned audience of cultivated linguists to whom his poems were addressed. What was the object of it, in the first place? Plainly, no poet of genius would practise Gongorism out of sheer malice; and Gongora's purpose was clearly enough to supple and diversify the resources of the literary language of Spain. It was capable of extension and enlargement; of Grecisms, Latinisms, Italicisms; of borrowings of vocabulary and construction from languages which had proved themselves capable of a more perfect literature than Spain had yet produced. In a sense Meredith was a Gongorist, as Rabelais had been before him; and though all obscurity is not Gongorism, all Gongorism is obscure. Every great writer who is dissatisfied with the powers of the language which he uses, who finds some words worn by the use and others inadequate for emphasis, and who tries to supply such shortcomings by new formations or new combinations, is doing work which will bear future fruit, however much ridicule it may arouse in the present by its more or less violent breach with current usage. A Gongorist is strictly an altruist, though his conscious motives may be mixed. He is risking contemporary misunderstanding, even personal obloquy, for the sake of enriching the inheritance which he administers in his generation.

The quotations with regard to Khlébnikov and others are from Prince Mirsky's *Contemporary Russian Literature, 1881-1925* (Routledge, 12s. 6d.). [13.8.26]

The Two Hughs

'His forward voice is to speak well of his friend; his backward voice is to detract.' – *The Tempest*.

Duan I. to Hugh MacDiarmid.

Says Grieve to Hugh, 'I'm gled that you
Gae howkin for auld phrases,

I hae nae broo o' the gash crew
    That ca's the gowans daisies.

'Oor auld Scots Muse suld aye refuse
    To pit ocht but a mutch on,
And needna read on ony screed
    Yont Henryson and Huchown.

'Oor Scots ingine has aye sinsyne
    Been smoored and stintit lowein;
To beet the flame, bide you at hame
    And keep the auld bells jowin

'And if a wheen at what ye mean
    Suld girn or gant or swither,
Tell them they gley, since you and me
    Ken mair than ony ither.

'A' wise men ken pipes draw best when
    Ye keep in the auld dottles
Take it as true frae me, dear Hugh
    New wine needs aye auld bottles.'

Duan II. to Hugh Roberton.

Says Grieve to Hugh, 'I' m wae that you
    Should be sae frush a praiser
O' auld-farrant sangs that the muckle pock pangs
    O' Mrs Kennedy Fraser.

'Though 'The Road to the Isles' some folk beguiles
    To ben and glen and valley,
Nae wag o' kilt nor an Eriskay lilt
    Wad get me on Kishmul's galley.

'They may gae that please to the Hebrides
    And bring fakes, like James Macpherson,
But for auld Erse tunes, horn spiled for spunes
    I hae a strong aversion.

'When foreign clans near the far Balkans
    Their forebears' airs gae seekin,
They're braw, braw lads, but nane but jauds
    Gae whaur the peats are reekin.

'Mrs Marjorie ne'er sets doon an air
    As naked as she hears it
And Kenneth's Gaelic, like the Bible's italic
    Is a sign that his verse blears it.

'Lot's auld gudewife fand death, no life
    When she cast looks ahint her
The past is past: east isna wast,
    And spring repeats not winter.

'Bantock and you and Newman too
    Gar me think ye are dottle,
Tak it as true frae me, dear Hugh,
    New wine needs a new bottle.'

Duplex.
[13.8.26]

Letters

THE NEW BARDS AND THE OLD

Sir, – The octopus has achieved notoriety not only because of the number of tentacles it uses in attack, but also its habit of ejecting an evil-smelling, inky fluid when on the defensive. Mr Lewis Spence reminds one of that squirming genus of dibranchiate Cephalopoda. A victim of the Spence finds himself involved in a maze of wriggling irrelevancies and personalities; and, if he shows fight, the waters of controversy are darkened with inky abuse.

I have dared to protest against the literary heresies of Grieve, Spence and Co., and must therefore be made to appear in polluted waters as a sinner of the deepest dye. Meanwhile the lashing and stinging tentacles brand and libel me as 'savage and stupid' and 'impertinent,' as an intruder guilty of 'calculated mendacity' and 'garrulous spite,' as a poor creature who is 'lacking in mental and educational equipment,' ignorant of the Doric, and fit only to use 'the scissors and paste of minor journalism.' When I write of Spence, Grieve and Co., I am 'criticising my betters.' (Alas! poor Yorick.)

Mr Spence's letter is characteristic. It recalls other letters and several articles in which the note of personal vanity has been conspicuous and the note of hysteria not entirely awanting.

Education is usually judged by its results, just as one's ethical stan-dards are judged by one's behaviour. Mr Spence forces me in self-defence to respond not in the manner of a 'new poet' with my own opinions about myself, but with a few indisputable facts. How am I regarded as a writer of verse by really eminent critics? In Professor Macneile Dixon's The Edinburgh Book of Scottish Verse, 1300-1900 *(the standard Scottish anthology), I occupy no fewer than five pages. Mr Spence is not represented at all. Nor is his work to be found in the newly published anthology,* Gems of English Verse, *covering the period from Shakespeare to the present day, in which I am represented by three poems. Even Mr C.M. Grieve overlooked Mr Spence when he himself made his first bid for public attention by compiling, with the aid of writers who were very generous to him, the first issue of* Northern Numbers. *Mr Grieve, however, solicited from me several contributions, being, as he stated and as his action demonstrated, appreciative of my work. My lyrics are much sought after by composers and vocalists, and several have been published with musical settings by Professor Granville Bantock and others. All my lyrics recently printed in this Journal are at present being set to music having been asked for by an eminent composer. One of my lyrics has been translated into French, and published with a musical setting along with the name of a famous vocalist who sings it. There is also a Parisian Russian translation of the same lyric. Evidently I can hold up my face in presence of my 'betters.'*

Readers of this Journal *are aware that I am not ignorant of the Doric. My Doric poem contributed recently to its columns has been quoted in the* Toronto Globe *and in American papers with acknowledgments to this* Journal. *I am, withal, a contributor to the new Dialect Dictionary, my writings being quoted from to illustrate the proper use of certain archaic words still current in the north-eastern area. Mr Spence's reck-less statement regarding my knowledge of the Doric is, after all, the sort of thing one has become accustomed to expect from him.*

My educational and mental equipment serves me fairly well. I am considered good enough to lecture to University education and psychology classes at the special request of the professors. I was invited three years ago to deliver the inaugural extra-mural lecture in anthro-pology at the University of Manchester and to repeat it, and to lecture on the beginnings of art to university classes. The Cambridge editor of that international series, 'The History of Civilisation', has ordered from me two volumes, one of which was published recently in London and New York. My Ancient Man in Britain *is referred to in the leading British archaeological journal as a 'standard work,' and it is honoured with special mention in Trevelyan's new* History of England, *published the other day. Am I as stupid and ignorant as Mr Spence would have your readers believe?*

Mr Spence's letter is followed up (it is a 'coincidence,' of course) by a 'drummer-boy' letter from one of his admirers who poses as 'A Lover of Justice.' This anonymous writer alleges that I delivered in Edinburgh an 'inflammatory speech'. I have always been a Scottish patriot, and I have never used 'England' for 'Britain,' as did Mr Lewis Spence in other days in certain of his sonnets from which quotations were given not so long ago in the Edinburgh Evening Dispatch. *A recent letter from my pen in the* Observer *contained the arguments used in my Edinburgh speech, which was far from being 'inflammatory.' It simply censured those Scots who are anti-Scottish, and insisted that one could be a Scottish patriot without being either anti-English or anti-Irish. I have never been in sympathy with the aims of those who wish to dissolve the Union. In my* Ancient Man in Britain *I insist on the immemorial racial and cultural bonds between Scotland and England. The great masses of the English and Scottish peoples are descended from the same ancient stock.*

It is untrue to say that I have denounced Sir J.M. Barrie and the Kailyaird School, or made unfounded statements regarding R.L. Stevenson. The 'inky' ejections of the literary 'octopus' have occupied me thus far, obscuring, as is evidently the desire of the clique of Spence-styled 'Betters,' the real points at issue. (If there is a parrot among the crows, the fault is not mine.)

I should have liked to have replied at some length to Mr Grieve's further attack upon Burns, because he would have it that the author of 'Scots Wha Hae' was not an exponent of Scottish patriotism, and because he has repeated Henley's ugly word 'skulduddery' and re-echoed some of Henley's libels. I recently wrote of Burns as a lyric poet, and I find Mr Grieve has accepted and repeated my views. He is evidently in need of further instruction regarding Burns's poetic merits in other directions, as well as a lecture on the exercise of charity in dealing with Burns as a man.

> *Bear, bear him along*
> *With his few faults shut up like dead flowrets;*
> *Are balm-seeds not here to console us?*
> *The land is left none such as he on the bier –*
> *Oh, would we might keep thee, my brother.*

These words from a funeral chant by Browning occurred to me when reading Grieve's uncharitable remarks regarding a great man whose virtues outweighed his human failings.

What I dislike most about the new brand of Scots poetry, which is being advertised like a patent medicine by its exponents, is its deplorable pretence. The bards are 'on the pose' and consequently lack sincerity. They strain after novelty for its own sake; and instead of being original, they are simply full of affectations. Defects like these are fatal to artistic achievement. Their poems are exotics, and resemble decadent architecture overloaded with meaningless decorations. The so-called 'renaissance' movement is essentially decadent. Its products are not 'home grown' in the real sense, but faintly and clumsily imitative of the expired and forgotten modes of another Age. They lack present-day inspiration, and are simply a rattling of dry bones covered with the dust of centuries.

The use of obsolete words on the part of the literary 'tomb robbers' is like the use of obsolete designs on the part of architects who erect prisons that resemble old castles, or villas with meaningless and useless parts copied from the ancient buildings which alone required them. To me a 'Hugh MacDiarmid' or Lewis Spence poem, which has been rendered bizarre and obscure by the use (or misuse) of obsolete words. is simply so much jargon. If that 'oracle,' Mr C.M. Grieve, who was reared in Edinburgh, writing as 'Hugh MacDiarmid,' is found using wrongly a word that happens to survive in a dialect unfamiliar to him, he claims he has the right to give it a new meaning or a new shade of meaning. A well-known canon of art is thus violated. If it is essential that an artist should make himself clearly understood, how can 'MacDiarmid' possibly appeal to readers? He is not an artist in words when he simply obscures his meaning. The greatest poets are the clearest poets; they make artistic use of words with full appreciation of their meaning, colour, and musical qualities. Mere imitators provide sound without sense, they have not mastered their medium; they are unable to express themselves clearly and artistically. Withal, they write too much. Men who rush into print with every experiment, every 'trial piece', and rush often, seem to imagine that quantity makes up for the lack of quality. They become bardic hacks, and. as such, suffer loss of a sense of proportion. Burns. Shakespeare, or Shelley could not, were they alive to-day, keep up with Mr Lewis Spence as a producer of 'lyrics'. Once a week; or twice a week, his effusions appear in print. Shakespeare's fame as a lyric poet depends on just a few short lyrics, but they are real lyrics. Mr Spence has yet to produce a real lyric, and so has Mr Grieve. The rhymed pieces they call 'lyrics' are not really lyrics at all.

May I explain that I write as a 'Highlander,' because a Highlander is a Scot, and has a right to have his say when modern Scottish literature is discussed. I belong to a family which has been well represented in literature since the seventeenth century, both in Scotland and in England, and am not likely to show the 'white feather' when threatened with 'brow beatings' from Spence & Co. I shall continue to write on literature with full appreciation of merit wherever found and with ready condemnation of pretence, fearing no organised group and despising unsportsmanlike methods of controversy. In the interests of education, it is necessary that literary critics should be honest and truthful and sincere – not mere 'log rollers'. – I am, etc.,

Donald A. Mackenzie
[13.8.26]

43. Rhythm and Race (I)

In a recent leader in the *Glasgow Herald* (24th July last), under the caption of 'Rhythm and Race,' the writer began by referring to the observations of Thomas MacDonagh in his book on *Literature in Ireland* regarding the differences between Anglo-Irish verse and verse written in what he termed the Irish mode – and quoting or instancing various poems with the 'wandering, lingering movement' in question, contended that the influence of this native speech-rhythm is apparent in well-known poems so far apart in time as Moore's 'At the Mid-Hour of Night' and Yeats's 'Lake Isle of Innisfree,' all the peculiar charm of each being due to its presence, and that this holds good of all Irish poetry that is characteristically native; it appears in no poetry produced on this side of the Irish Sea before Mr Yeats let it fall on the ears of English poets. I rather imagine that the idea that this particular kind of poetry or effect in poetry is characteristically Irish – or more characteristically Irish than certain other kinds of Irish poetry – is a characteristically English (or British) misconception, not unrelated to the attitude which would make Irishry in literature synonymous with Celtic glamour. Daniel Corkery in *The Hidden Ireland* shows very clearly how the metres and manners of Irish poetry have changed with the changing times. In the eighteenth century

in the glowing *Aisling* we find unwitting expression of the darkness that lay upon their life... The *Aisling* poems were all written in stressed metres – that is, the most literary poems of the time were written in metres that the old bardic schools had despised as unliterary, if one may use such terms. The stressed metres of the untrained poets, of the wandering ballad-singers, had now displaced the syllabic metres of the bards, had become the recognised mode of the Courts of Poetry.

And he goes on to compare the Scottish Jacobite songs with the *Aisling* poems:

The differences we notice throw us back on the two worlds in which the poems flourished. The Scottish poems are simple, homely, direct; and if they have life in them to this day, as many of them have, it is because they were written to and about a living man on whom living eyes had rested with affection. The *Aisling* poems had no such close inspiration. The Irish Gaels, since the going away of Sarsfield, whom they loved, were a people without a leader. The Scots wrote of 'My Laddie,' of 'Jamie the Rover,' of 'Charlie Stuart,' of the 'Blackbird.'... Unlike the Scottish the Irish song-writers took none of these affectionate liberties with the names of the Stuarts. They wrote of 'Saesar,' of 'Charles Rex,' of 'The Lion.' So that if one inclines not to the splendour of art but to its intimacy, its warmth of feeling, one turns to the Scottish songs, because of the warmth of feeling in them and the directness of expression. It is far otherwise with the *Aisling* poems. They do not move us; they dazzle us. Or if one is at all moved by them, it is not by or for the cause they sing. What is imperative in these songs is the art of the singer. Indeed their own beauty, not Prince Charlie, is their theme; whereas, in the Scottish poems, to leave out 'the bonnie bird' is to leave out all. It is curious how little else except warm affection for the Prince himself is in these Scottish songs – the poet has but scant thought for anything else, little for Scotland, not much for the Cause. On the other hand, Ireland is all in the *Aisling* poems; and the only lines in them that strike fire from us are those that tell of her sorrows – her princes dead, her strongholds broken, her lands in the possession of churls, her children scattered across the seas... Turn them into prose and they have no longer an excuse for existing. In the *Aisling* poems, content and manner are one, so intimately that to separate them is properly to come on neither. The words live in their sounds, not in their sense; it is the subtle, irresistible witchcraft of their music, and not what they say, that steals away the listeners' brains.

How even the *Aisling* shows the varying pressure of the times – becomes
spirited or lapses into wistful decorativeness as hope rises and falls
between 1684 and 1798, is admirably brought out and, as the writer
claims, in Romain Rolland's words, it would be hard to find a better
illustration of how a people's art 'reveals the true feelings of the soul, the
secrets of its inner life, and the world of passion that has long accumulated and fermented there before surging to the surface.'

A little later Mr Corkery deals with a fundamental consideration.

> Whatever of the Renaissance came to Ireland, [he says,] met a culture
> so ancient, widely-based and well-articulated, that it was received
> only on sufferance; it had to veil its crest and conform to a new order;
> it did not become assimilated, assimilated so thoroughly that its
> features can no longer be discerned, though its effects are felt when
> the subsequent culture of the Gael is compared with the pre-
> Renaissance. The same thing happened, at least in the plastic arts, in
> India. The flamboyant vigour of the Renaissance must not dazzle us
> to the fact that one of its evil effects was to whiten all the native
> cultures of Europe to a common value; it introduced into them all
> common forms and a common factor – the Greek standard of beauty,
> such as the Renaissance understood it – and never since has any of
> these native Continental cultures been really itself.

'It was not so in Ireland,' says Mr Robin Flower in his introduction to
Dánta Grádha. 'There the established forms were too strong... The
question of tradition is the gist of the whole matter. There was not in
Surrey's day a stable tradition in English verse in poetry of this kind. In
Ireland, on the other hand, an old and honoured tradition gave the poets
a firm and steady grasp of style.' The significance of the fact that the
Herald leader-writer speaks of writers so far apart in time as Moore and
Yeats, and ignores what, prior to the eighteenth century Corkery calls
'that great literary tradition that for a thousand years had been moulding
the Gaelic conception of life and letters' will be readily appreciated in
the light of these quotations.

> For good or ill, then, the native colour, the Gaelic tang, has prevailed
> in Irish literature all down the centuries to 1847, and just as one may
> recognise mediaeval sculpture by a certain earnestness that often-
> times looks like fierceness, almost like savagery, so one may always
> know the best poetry in Irish: there, too, is an earnestness, a 'dreadful
> sincerity' that burns away and away the graceful unessential until the

subject emerges keen-edged, stark, and, occasionally terrifying. Less
of this note is found in the poetry of the eighteenth century than of
any other century, for all that poetry is of course only the weak ending
of a great tale; but still it is there, yes, even in the *Aisling* poems
themselves, decorative and all as their nature is.

In this connection it is only necessary to read the chapter on
'Development of Irish Poetry' in Dr Douglas Hyde's *Literary History of
Ireland* to see that what is singled out by our leader-writer as one of the
elements in 'all Irish poetry that is characteristically native' appertains
only to the products after the collapse of the Gaelic cultural tradition,
and is as totally unrepresentative of Irish poetry as it would be to test a
man's normal vigour and bodily habits by his condition in an advanced
stage of senile decay. For what is specifically Irish we must look elsewhere.

> Down to the close of the sixteenth century and during the greater
> part of the seventeenth, verse, with few exceptions, continued to be
> made in the classical metres of Ireland, by specially trained poets,
> who did not go outside these metres... It was during the seventeenth
> century that the greatest change in the whole poetical system of the
> Irish and Scots Gaels was accomplished, and that a new school of
> versification arose with new ideals, new principles, and new
> methods... The Scottish Gaels, if I am not mistaken, led the way in
> this great change, which metamorphosed the poetry of an entire
> people in both islands. The first modern Scottish Gaelic poet to start
> upon the new system seems to have been Mary, daughter of Alaster
> Rua MacLeod, who was born in Harris in 1569. If the nine poems in
> free vowel metres, which are attributed to her by Mackenzie in his
> great collection, are genuine, then I should consider her as the
> pioneer of the new school. Certainly no Irishman or Irishwoman of
> the sixteenth century has left anything like Mary's metres behind
> them,

and Dr Hyde says of the nature of the revolution so accomplished:

> It is impossible to convey any idea of this new outburst of Irish
> melody in another language. Suffice it to say that the principle of it
> was a wonderful arrangement of vowel sounds, so placed that in every
> accented syllable, first one vowel and then another fell upon the ear
> in all possible kinds of harmonious modifications. Some verses are
> made wholly on the á sound, others on the ó, ú, é, or í sounds, but the

majority on a wonderful and fascinating intermixture of two, three or more. The consonants which played so very prominent a part under the old bardic system were utterly neglected now, and vowel sounds alone were sought for.

One other quotation will be useful before I proceed to get to grips with the contentions in regard to Scotland towards which the *Herald* leader-writer was moving when he used the Irish argument referred to, and it is of particular interest perhaps because of its bearing not only on this specific question but on the general question of the relationship of politics to literature, my insistence upon which in previous articles has irritated certain correspondents to this *Journal*. It is from Robert Graves's *Another Future of Poetry* (Hogarth Essays) and begins by quoting Mr Robert Trevelyan's statement in his *Thamyris, or Is There a Future for Poetry?* (Messrs Kegan Paul) that 'the conscious principle according to which English verse has been written from the time of Chaucer until recent years has been that of syllable counting.'

This, [says Mr Graves,] is only true of one of the main strands of English poetry. It is true that this has been the principle of the cultured prosody imposed on English from the Continent, and productive of a great deal of noble verse; but the earlier native prosody which takes small stock of syllables, reckoning instead musically by the stress-centres of the line and the time-interval between them, has never been driven from popular poetry and has frequently been adopted by poets of culture. The readiest examples of native prosody are to be found in nursery rhyme and country ballad. In the earliest English verse these stress-centres (for often the stress is not on one syllable but, as in *how do you* do? and how do you *do?* spread over two or three) are marked clearly by alliteration. Anglo-Saxon verse is all alliterative and stressed, its syllables are uncounted. In the fourteenth century came William Langland, a contemporary of Chaucer's. Though the most famous of the middle English poets to revive the Anglo-Saxon alliterative metre, he was by no means the only one. In the sixteenth century John Skelton, in my opinion one of the three or four outstanding English poets [– by the way, wasn't Skelton a Scot? –] though reducing the alliteration, adding rhyme, and even using the lineal arrangement of rhyme-royal, wrote in the native style as often as in the Continental. In the seventeenth century, Shakespeare, who had been dominated at his first visit to London by the Continental prosody in vogue at the theatres, gradually rediscov-

ered his popular inheritance, and developed the foppish blank verse
that Surrey and Wyatt had brought from Italy into a metre in which
both principles, native and Continental, interacted; it was a metre
capable at times of stresses as turbulent as those in *Beowulf*, while at
others it would still strut syllabically like a fine gentleman. The two
principles of prosody correspond in a marked way with contrary
habits of life, with political principles; the Continental, with the classical principle of pre-ordained structure, law and order, culture
spreading downwards from the educated classes – the feudal principle; the native principle, with what Mr John Ransom calls the
Gothic principle, one of organic and unforeseen growth, warm blood,
impulsive generosity and frightful error – the communal principle,
threatening the classic scheme from below. The rare poets who have
contrived to reconcile the two principles have always had, like Skelton
and Shakespeare, one foot firmly planted in the aristocratic set and
the other equally firmly in the crowd. The future of English prosody
depends enormously on the outcome of the class antagonism that
undoubtedly is now in full swing. A Red victory would bring with it, I
believe, a renewal of the native prosody in a fairly pure form, as the
white domination of the eighteenth century made for pure classicism,
and kept it dominant until the Romantic Revival, intimately
connected with the French Revolution, reintroduced stress-prosody.

We are now reasonably well equipped to proceed to the remainder of
the *Herald* leader, which is in the following terms: –

If we turn to other countries, ancient or modern, we find that while
thought is international, since none has a monopoly of ideas of life
and death and God, rhythm is racial. The Greeks used pitch as a
means of measure in verse, and the Chinese have done so for 4000
years. Latin verse is quantitative, though it is difficult for the English
reader to conceive of language so spoken except chantingly, so
permeated is he with the need of accent to convey those shades of
meaning which the Roman obtained from inflexion. French poetry
bewilders our ear no less, for it is wholly syllabic. Its Alexandrine
breaks into four groups of syllables to which the untrained English
speaker gives almost automatically the lilt of 'Bonnie Dundee,' and
that is fatal. German poetry, by reason of its abundance of double
rhymes and dissyllables ending in e, seems insipid when translated
into corresponding English measures of the mode in which
Longfellow was so ruinously facile; and finally no English measures

can convey the power and rapidity of Dante. Our clanging monosyllables lack speed. From this array of facts it seems conclusive that genuine racial difference is revealed in the rhythm of a nation's poetry. What is the obvious conclusion? That where rhythm is common to two peoples, they are essentially one, however much they pride themselves on their difference. They may differ as brother from brother, but deeper than the qualities which distinguish them is this beat in the blood or the brain which proves them kindred and which compels them to respond to the same rhythmic appeal of speech and music. This is interestingly illustrated in the poetical work of Hugh MacDiarmid and Lewis Spence, both poets familiar to our readers, both acclaimed by some as leaders of the new movement towards Scottish Independence in art or politics, or both. Both are intensely modern Scots; this intensity apart they are poles apart in language and subject-matter, and as poets, have only one thing in common – they are English in rhythm! Mr MacDiarmid draws his vocabulary from Scots anywhere and of any kind; Mr Spence derives from the old 'Makaris,' among whom Dunbar placed Chaucer, the

> Rose of rethoris all,
> As in our tong ane flour imperiall.

'Our tong'! We do not recall any poem by either of the two with a non-English rhythm; we wager that neither has ever heard any alien sound in the rhythm of any English poet from Chaucer to Bridges. To-day, when all poetic forms are in the melting-pot, Scotland is tenaciously English. No political or other conclusion need be drawn from this, save the apparently ironical and humorous one, that any apparently racial antagonism between North and South may, on closer examination, prove to be but a family quarrel, the world-old objection of a younger brother to aggressive personal traits in his elder. We refrain from suggesting which is which.

(To be continued)
[20.8.26]

Letters

THE NEW BARDS AND THE OLD
Sir, – Mr Donald A. Mackenzie's tirade on the 'New Scots' is, I hope, the swan-song of the 'Old Scots.'

Youth is knocking at the door, and, like Ibsen's builder, the old school (as exemplified by Mr Mackenzie) is piling up a huge barricade of worn-out tradition to retard its entry. I say 'retard,' for Mr Mackenzie by his heated insistence in opposing the new movement clearly proves that it is gradually forcing open the door and letting in a ray of light on the darkness of Scottish thought. I cannot say Scottish 'Letters' – for it cannot properly be said that there has ever been any.

The 'greybeards' as, I think, Mr Lewis Spence amusingly called them, hold fondly to what they vaguely call the 'traditions' and 'characteristics' of Scottish literature. But I do not know what these are, nor have I ever seen any exposition of them by those who fatuously use the terms. There has been a considerable body of English literature with certain Scottish characteristics produced in Scotland which many of Mr Mackenzie's way of thinking blissfully imagine is Scottish literature. But after the brilliant beginning with such writers as Henryson, Dunbar, Lindsay, Gavin Douglas, Scottish literature languished and from that time to the present there has been no development – no 'main stream' – and therefore no National Literature. There have been at intervals singers (but few prose writers) who have been essentially Scottish in their outlook and in their medium, but they have been in most cases incidental and have never formed a sequence or built up a tradition.

The poets of the present Renaissance movement are in reality the first direct outgrowth from the Old Makars. They see that the amazing hotch-potch which has existed since the passing of the Court poets, and which some are pleased to regard as representative national literature, must be ignored – that they must get right back to the only real body of Scottish Literature that exists, and from these roots carve their destiny as writers in a medium and an atmosphere characteristic of the Scottish temperament.

How Mr Mackenzie can regard such a movement as 'decadent' I cannot understand. unless he possesses one of those extraordinary conservative minds which regards all forms of progress as 'vulgar.' The attempt is certainly courageous, and both Mr C.M. Grieve and Mr Lewis Spence deserve every credit for the excellent work they are doing, and I think Mr Mackenzie would be doing literature a far greater service if, instead of rushing into print, he sat down quietly to ponder over the reason why Scotland in the past half century (if he will insist that she did before) has turned out no volume of National Literature of even the slightest note. I commend the idea to Mr Mackenzie because I am confident that, unless he has an incurably prejudiced mind, he will completely change his opinions. Writers who have produced such little masterpieces as 'The Watergaw' and the 'Bonnie Broukit Bairn' (Hugh MacDiarmid), and 'The Grey Etin' and 'The Hows o' Reekie' (Lewis Spence) can hardly be called 'bardic hacks' by any man in his senses.

In conclusion, I would like to say that though the 'literary heresies' of Mr Grieve are bound to hurt those who cheerfully accept the inflated reputations of such spoiled darlings as Burns, such literary nihilism is entirely necessary. Scottish Literature must, phoenix-like, burn itself on a pyre of outworn and mistaken 'traditions' and rise renewed from the ashes. Unfortunately the Burns tradition will smoulder like damp firewood. It has by now become almost part of the mental make-up of a certain class of sentimental Scots who worship not the poet but the man – whose 'virtues out-weighed his human failings.' Let the people, if they will, take the man for their patron saint, but for God's sake let our writers and men of intellect regard the poet in the true perspective – I am. etc.,

Norman M. Wilson

THE NEW BARDS AND THE OLD

Sir, – Mr Donald A. Mackenzie's sordid and contemptible letter illustrates more eloquently than could any words of mine the jealous and vindictive mentality which inspired it. He wantonly attacks my work in a spirit of mean and libellous envy, and when I castigate him as he deserves, whimpers in cowardly surprise and discharges a volley of the vilest abuse. Does he imagine that he can launch one of his garrulous diatribes and employ such terms as 'swatches of rhymed prose,' 'purveyors of wild assertions,' and the like, and tell the world that the whole body of my work and effort is so much nauseous rubbish without drawing an indignant retort upon himself? If so, he must be even more provincially naive than I had thought him. But it is not to belabour him further that I write. He has evidently had all the punishment he can take. I desire to bring to public notice his especial modus operandi in achieving a cheap publicity – that self-advertisement of which he has accused me, and which his half-talent assuredly does not warrant.

Mr Mackenzie's stratagem, now familiar to many, is to wait until some literary or scientific contemporary receives that public notice to which he is entitled. Then, animated partly by the most unblushing envy, partly by a desire to trumpet his own petty triumphs, he dashes into the limelight of newspaper correspondence, seeking by Grub Street invective to tear to shreds the reputation he meanly covets. The destructive process is assisted by tireless conversational propaganda among his nodding *acquaintance, in which he seeks to discredit the object of his spleen by every means in his power, and by sneaking little paragraphs in obscure corners of the daily Press. It is a process which Scottish authors have long had to suffer from at the hands of the Scottish journalists of sorts, who, unable to comprehend the methods of the artist, attempt to destroy them by vulgar abuse. But the mud-slinging method is invariably accompanied by a long catalogue of his own accomplishments, the titles of his publications, the manner in which his 'lyrics' have been set to music, details of his serio-comic 'lectures,' and so forth – a list which scarcely the most pushing publicity agent could secure for him in the ordinary columns of the Press, but which he cunningly combines with his 'justificatory' arguments in a newspaper letter. And this is the man who rails against the 'self-advertising tendencies' of others! Personally I have never known anyone who magnified himself in private conversation so nauseatingly. For my part, if I have received 'advertisement,' I can safely say that it has been invariably through the pens of others, not from my own. Perhaps this exposé of his methods may be kept on record for future reference should he attempt similar tactics again.*

Mr Mackenzie's strictures on my 'irrelevancy' are hugely amusing when one remembers that those who know him best are constantly accusing him of an inherent total lack of the logical sense. As regards his absurd remarks on my verse, I am content with the enthusiastic encouragement of real men of letters. Mr Mackenzie's notions of what constitutes poetry are rustical and out-moded, and his own efforts in that sphere bald, undistinguished, imitative and uninspired to a degree. The Crofter in Literature is admirable when he confines himself to the humble lays of his countryside. He may then succeed beyond all the dreams of the more conscious artist. But when he fails through overweening conceit or crass ineptitude, and especially when he adopts the airs of the Higher Critic – he becomes a public nuisance. And who, indeed, is Mr Mackenzie that he should pose as a critic of what he can never understand?

On the last occasion when I was forced to listen to Mr Mackenzie's garrulous eulogies of himself and his malevolent grumblings that he had not been recognised as he deserved, he informed me that he meant 'to give up "littery" work and go out to the fish trade in Australia.' When one recalls his undoubted powers of scandalous invective it seems a thousand pities that some Antipodean Billingsgate should be robbed of such a promising recruit. – I am, etc.,

Lewis Spence
[20.8.26]

Letters

THE NEW BARDS AND THE OLD

Sir, – Mr Mackenzie has referred to me as a drummer boy, but I really must give pride of place to him as he beats the big drum most success-fully.

If he is such an ardent patriot, then why be patriotic under another name? I think it was either Home or Hume he called himself when he addressed The Scots National League in the Y.M.C.A. hall. He will see by this that I am a very observant drummer boy.

On another occasion, when passing through the Meadows, I heard Mr Mackenzie addressing a large crowd and assuring them he had just returned from Russia, and gave a graphic account of what he saw there. So you see he is a much travelled Patriot. (Perhaps!) I have also a good memory when it comes to recalling who was the attacker in this corre-spondence, and I think it is a thousand pities that Mr Spence fell into the trap Mr Mackenzie usually sets for his victims.

His method is to launch a scurrilous attack in one or more journals on anyone who is getting recognition for work well done; this is to Mr Mackenzie like a red rag to a bull; then he waits until his unfortunate victim writes to defend himself and sends along a catalogue of his wares, plus an attempt to tear to shreds the reputation of the person he is attacking. He rather reminds one of the pedlar who calls and empties his wares on the doorstep for one's inspection, even if one has said, 'No, nothing to-day, thank you.'

If any letter could give a man's character away, surely Mr Mackenzie has given himself away. He has absolutely wallowed in mud and would make the most hardened 'octopus' seem like a good fairy.

If Mr Mackenzie is such a very learned person as he would have us all believe, and if he is of the stuff that learned persons are made of, then I shall be proud to remain 'a drummer boy'. – I am, etc.,

Lover of Justice

THE NEW BARDS AND THE OLD

Sir, – For some years now I have noticed a discussion going on in your columns under the above heading. As it is likely to continue for some years more, I feel that I must attempt to put myself in touch with at least the main features of the question. I would suggest, therefore, that, after the fashion of the serial stories in the newspapers, you place at the begin-

ning of each week's instalment of correspondence a summary of what has
preceded and a note upon each of the leading characters. In particular (I
must confess my ignorance with regret), would you let me know: –

> (1) Who is Mr Grieve and what has he done?
> (2) Who is Mr Donald Mackenzie and what has he done?
> (3) Who is Lewis Spence and what has he done?

I can see that they are all very angry and justly indignant with somebody for something, and that people have been very nasty to them, and
that Scotland has been let down again. But it is all very vague, and one
can scarcely tell whether the great conflict is about Scotland or themselves. – I am, etc.,

Philistine

THE NEW BARDS AND THE OLD

Sir, – There is little to reply to in Mr Lewis Spence's latest letter. It is
sadly lacking in argument and deplorably ill-mannered. Abuse is
certainly not convincing and misrepresentation never effective. Mr
Spence's controversial style is hardly in keeping with a serious discussion
of literary topics in an educational journal; it seems more suited for a
'stairhead squabble.'

I insist that there is only one kind of poetry; that there has never been
and that there never will be but one kind of poetry. The 'new poetry,'
which organised mutual-admiration cliques have been industriously
foisting upon the public, is really bad poetry – the work of incompetent
rhymers who set up their own poor performances as a standard of excellence. The so-called 'Scottish Renaissance' school is simply a by-product
of the 'shell-shock poetry' which a healthy criticism has now relegated to
the background. Its products are devoid of vitality and promise and are
undoubtedly decadent, as I have shown.

Mr Spence does not disturb me by referring to my verses as 'rustical.'
The greater part of my life has been lived in the Highlands, and I write
of what I know and as I feel. The great Wordsworth was 'rustical' and so
was the great Burns. There is, after all, more poetry in the country than
in the town.

If some of the so-called 'new poets' had been brought up in the
country, they would be less inclined to say ridiculous things in their
verses. I can't think of a country-bred writer composing falsetto verse
like that of Mr Lewis Spence, or adopting such a curious attitude
towards Nature. Recently, for instance, our sympathies were solicited on

behalf of a river which did so much work turning mill-wheels, etc., that it suffered from a sore back. Mr Grieve alleged in a remarkable poem that honey bees 'milk' aphides. Any country-bred 'loonie' could have told him that he had mixed up the bees with the ants. He also seems to imagine that worms have teeth. At any rate, he has in one of his poems the aston-ishing statement, 'The worms will soon be chowin' anither braw man.' To one accustomed to the Doric as a living language, that is very funny indeed. Mr Grieve's recent reference to words as 'coorse' as 'stots' is really a libel. Stots are often as gentle as they are bonnie, and they are not nearly as 'wull' as 'a wheen kicking colts tearin' up a' the tirf.' I wonder if Mr Grieve could distinguish at sight a stot from a heifer, or a gimmer from a hogget.

I have been making my living by my pen for a good many years and have written more books than I care to confess to. It therefore amuses me to find Norman M. Wilson (his name is new to me) alleging that I am 'rushing into print.' Apparently he is pretty young. 'Youth,' he warns me, 'is knocking at the door,' and to him, I am one of the 'grey-beards.' I see in Who's Who *that Mr Spence was born in 1874, so he is no chicken, although not included among the 'grey-beards.' Youth has, of course, a habit of knocking and of making other noises. It is perhaps as well, there-fore, to remind Mr Wilson that some great work has been done by men of 'middle age.' Scott was 55 when the crash came and we all know what he subsequently accomplished. Milton was 50 when he began to compose* Paradise Lost, *which was published nine years later, and he was 63 when* Paradise Regained *was published. Swift wrote* Gulliver's Travels *when he was 59, and Defoe was 60 when the first volume of* Robinson Crusoe *appeared in the booksellers' shops, Chaucer began his* Canterbury Tales *when over 47 years of age and finished them before he was 60. Pope was 40 when he wrote the* Dunciad *and 45 when he finished his* Essay on Man. *Henry Fielding had* Tom Jones *published when he was 42 and Shakespeare was 38 when he wrote* Hamlet, *47 when he wrote* The Tempest *and 49 when he wrote* Henry VIII. *Sir David Lyndesay's best work,* The Dreme, *was his first poem, and he wrote it at 37. Dunbar, Henryson and Douglas were full-grown men when 'at their best.' Youth 'knocking at the door' need not therefore be impatient. A writer who is in a hurry to be famous is apt to overwork and do an injury to his Pegasus.*

Mr Wilson tells us that the 'new poets' are going to give us something very new by merely imitating the ancients. That is really what his argu-ment amounts to. These ambitious and pretentious 'youths' are going back to the 'Old Makars,' from whose 'roots' (poetry) they are to 'carve their destiny as writers.' They are, apparently, to be great men from the start. I must confess, however, that I dislike 'carved' poems, because they are always poor imitations. Real poems grow up like flowers. The poems he refers to amusingly as 'masterpieces' are of the 'carved' variety.

It is quite misleading to allege that the 'Old Makars' of Scotland gave us a really 'national literature.' The truth is that Henryson, Dunbar, Lyndesay and Gavin Douglas were all imitators of the English poet Chaucer. Indeed, the first is by one prominent critic lauded as 'Chaucer's aptest and brightest scholar,' while Dunbar is, in the opinion of another critic, really 'the most noteworthy of the Scottish disciples of Chaucer.' According to Skeat, Gavin Douglas's style was 'much affected by Anglicisms.' There are few scholars who do not nowadays admit that a great deal of the work of some of the 'Old Makars' is 'mere doggerel.' It is as well that they wrote in what is now a dead language. Ordinary decency prevents me giving modern renderings of the coarse humour of Sir David Lyndesay and of William Dunbar, the ribald priest. Dunbar's 'Billingsgate' is notorious. He detested Edinburgh and its profiteering shopkeepers and innkeepers, was pro-English and anti-Highland, and he is scarcely an example for a modern exponent of that very vague and very elusive thing called the 'Scottish temperament.' Dunbar, however, had genius, and his lurid imaginings and the hilarity of even his most bitter and biting satires raise him as a writer to a level that the gross Lyndesay never reached. At his best he comes nearer to Burns, the satirist than any other Scottish poet, but, as a Lyric poet, he is a pigmy compared to the beloved 'Bard of Ayr.'

In one respect the 'Old Makars' tower like giants above their modern would-be imitators. They were artists who displayed fine craftsmanship in rhyme and rhythm. Dunbar revelled in displays of technique. One can count no fewer than thirty-two rhymes in one of his eight-line stanzas, but some of these rhymes are very disgusting, indeed. If Dunbar had not been a genius, much of his work would have perished long ago on a midden heap.

When Norman M. Wilson dismisses Burns as a 'spoiled darling,' and ignores that great Scottish genius, Sir Walter Scott, he simply makes me shake my head over him as a critic. He has evidently much to read and learn. 'Hugh MacDiarmid' and Lewis Spence are far from being Dunbars, or Henrysons, or Lyndesays. They lack humour, they are poor craftsmen, they have not been endowed to any extent with poetic minds, and their sad attempts to infuse life into a dead language are quite futile.

'How many,' asks an eminent scholar, 'can read Dunbar without reference to a glossary?' When Dunbar was living only a minority of the
people of Scotland used the language in which he wrote. The majority
spoke Gaelic, etc. To Dunbar, Kennedy of Carrick was a 'Gaelic-
speaking beggar bard.' Dunbar's dead language cannot now be thrust
upon all Lowlanders and Highlanders as a genuine national inheritance.
The Scottish people don't want it and they don't need it.

Mr Grieve has been telling us what happened in Norway. If Scotland
were to imitate that small nation, it would revert to Gaelic, or to Old
British, or mix up these languages and 'enjoy' a 'blend.'

Mr Grieve takes very seriously Prince Mirsky's 'literary Baedeker' to
recent Russian literature in which Tolstoy's Confession is amusingly
compared to the Book of Job, and a genius like Chekhov receives rather
curious treatment. Writers of little account, whose Russian works will
never be translated into English, are well represented. As a Baedeker, or
Murray's Guide, the book is undoubtedly of interest and value. But when
one reads what the Prince has to say about Lyeskov's Enchanted
Warrior, one is less inclined to regard him as a great literary critic than
does Mr C.M. Grieve.

If we are to have in the future Scottish poetry of any merit from the
'new poets,' these gentlemen should forget the foreigners and cultivate a
sympathetic interest in the modes of thought and modes of life of their
native land. Mr Grieve is disdainful of the 'common folk' and Mr Spence
thinks it clever to sneer at crofters and fishermen. Burns, Scott, Barrie
and other great Scottish writers are libelled as pretenders. It is really
deplorable to find the 'new poets,' who proclaim that they are Scottish
patriots, so very 'anti-Scottish' in their tendencies. Many city-bred men
do not seem to know or love the real Scotland. Some appear to think they
can create a new Scottish literature by picking archaic words out of glos-
saries and sprinkling their pat, uninspired verses with them. If they were
artists, if they had constructive imaginations, if they had originality, if
they had anything to say and were able to say it well, it would not be
necessary for them to attempt to imitate the 'Old Makars' or, rather, to
pretend to imitate them. Poetry must have a basis of reality; it must
express real emotions, real experiences and be written in a living
language with full appreciation of the meaning, force, music and beauty
of words. Imitative poems are artificial poems. They are shams, and .
worthless as literature.

Poets are born not made, and those rhymers who form cliques and
elect their 'office-bearers' to 'posts' on Parnassus, are doing what no real

poets have ever done, or ever will do. Sincerity is the outstanding char-
acteristic of all great art, and sincere artists abhor pretence and the noto-
riety resulting from intrigue and from conspiracies against 'patient
merit.' – I am, etc.,

Donald A. Mackenzie
(This correspondence is closed. – Ed., *S.E.J.*)
[27.8.26]

44. Rhythm and Race (II)

I am willing enough to concede that there is a sense in which all men may
be said to be brothers, and that the English and the Scots are included in
it but, beyond that, if the leader-writer had proceeded to draw any political or other conclusion from his 'array of facts,' he would have found that
it would not sustain any, not even the 'apparently ironical and humorous
one,' which he suggested. On his own showing the bond which in his
conclusion he greatly exaggerated is only similar in kind to that which
relates the Greeks and the Chinese! I am quite agreeable to take it at that.
It would take up too much space to analyse what he says of French,
German, and Italian poetry, but even if what he said has hitherto obtained
in the literatures of these countries (and that is only partially the case) it
need not do so to-morrow – and yet what is peculiarly French or German
or Italian will remain so. Rhythm does not go deep enough. Like other
manifestations – dominant tendencies in thought, peculiarities in sensibility, the operation of the diverse selective instincts which produce this
ethos or that – it is liable to change. The essence of nationality is independent of it. It may be noted that the leader-writer's references to foreign
literatures 'date' themselves – they ignore modern manifestations which
have largely upset and in many instances transmogrified or thrown over-
board altogether what had been for long the conventionally accepted
'national rhythm' (in most cases the mainstay of the whole post-
Renaissance practice) in each of the European countries, *e.g.*, the
Petrograd ego-futurists' objective – 'to destroy toothless ratio,' or the
'lyrical simultaneities' of the Italian Ardengo Soffici, and so on. Yet these
futuristic experimenters abandoning all the traditional sign-posts and
hand-rails of their respective literatures, are in many cases not less but far
more intensely 'national' in the most specific sense of the term. Of one
after another of them writers belonging to other countries have to confess

that they are sheerly untranslatable for this reason. And there is a sense in which untranslatability into any language other than that in which they were written is a criterion of certain kinds of literature – and these the kinds with which the most vital writers to-day in all European countries are mainly engaged. It is this, as I have already pointed out that shows that the trend towards a synthetic Scots is in alignment with the most significant developments in *welt-literatur* to-day. The extraordinary conservatism and provincialism of English literature has prevented these tendencies making much headway in it – though *skaz* of a sort has had its effects on Dickens, Kipling, and others, linguistic experimentation in poets like Charles Doughty and Gerald Hopkins [sic], and *zaumny* in Joyce, in prose, and T.S. Eliot in poetry, and, before either of them, in Lewis Carroll and Edward Lear. Not rhythm but background is the fundamental consideration, and readers may be recommended to read Prof. H.J.C. Grierson's essay on 'The Background of English Literature' – with its all-too-brief references to the Northern 'might-have-been' over which the Renaissance – the classics – prevailed. Further suggestive matter on the same subject, more sympathetic perhaps to the possibilities of eventual development in that direction, may be found in the late Professor W.P. Ker's essays on Icelandic and other northern literatures; and in this connection, also, interesting sidelights – from the musico-literary angle – were thrown in recent correspondence in the (Sunday) *Observer* apropos Wagner's utilisation – and unavoidable, insidious Hellenisation – of Norse myths. To 'get' what I am driving at here in its most comprehensive bearings, T.E. Hulme's *Speculations* should also be read – in particular, such of his essays as *A Critique of Satisfaction* and *Humanism and the Religious Attitude* in which, *inter alia*, he says:

> In spite of its extreme diversity all philosophy since the Renaissance is at bottom the *same* philosophy. The family resemblance is much greater than is generally supposed. The obvious diversity is only that of the various species of the same genus. It is very difficult to see this when one is *inside* this philosophy; but if one looks at it from the standpoint of another philosophy it at once becomes obvious. A parallel may make this clearer. The change of sensibility which has enabled us to regard Egyptian, Polynesian and Negro work, as *art* and not as archaeology has had a double effect. It has made us realise that what we took to be the necessary principles of aesthetic, constitute in reality only a psychology of Renaissance and Classical Art. At the same time, it has made us realise the essential *unity* of these latter arts. For we see that

both rest on certain common presuppositions of which we only become conscious when we see them *denied* by other arts. In the same way an understanding of the religious philosophy which preceded the Renaissance makes the essential unity of all philosophy since seem at once obvious. It all rests on the same conception of the nature of man, and exhibits the same inability to realise the meaning of the dogma of Original Sin. Our difficulty now, of course, is that we are really incapable of understanding how any other view but the humanistic, could be seriously held by intelligent and emancipated men.

In this connection readers who wish to see what particular bearing this has on the ideology of the Scottish Renaissance Movement may be referred to a controversy on 'Humanism' in *The Scottish Nation*, in which Edwin Muir, F.V. Branford and I took part. Hulme goes on to 'get over this difficulty' in a series of the profoundest and most brilliant notes in British critical literature. The bearing of all this on my quotations from Corkery and Graves last week with regard to the influence of the Renaissance and native prosody will be obvious; and that, so far from Scotland being 'tenaciously English' while poetics are in the melting-pot, the same tendencies are at work here and are part and parcel of the Scottish Renaissance movement, is very appositely brought out by Lewis Spence in an article on 'The Scottish Literary Renaissance' in the July *Nineteenth Century,* where he points out with regard to Hugh MacDiarmid's work that

> what all its reviewers have failed to observe is that it revives the spirit of the Scottish domestic rhyme, of that peculiarly native, unchronicled and now almost discarded body of traditional jingle through which the soul of Scotland shines often more veridically even than in the work of Burns or the balladeers, and which, in turn, and in its manner, derives from the flytings or raggings of the old court poets

– a judgment which confirms Mr MacDiarmid's own opinion of the tendencies of his work, since, in a recent poem, he refers to it as

> ... ratt-rime and ragments o' quenry
> And recoll o' Gill-ha'...

and, again,

> flytin' and sclatrie.

If the Scottish Renaissance movement has not yet become so pervasive as to change the rhythms in modern Scottish poetry in the bulk, that does not mean to say that it will not eventually do so, nor does it prove, as the leader-writer seems to think, that these existing rhythms are really Scottish at all, any more than what passes for Scottish to-day in most other directions. His so-called identity or kinship between English and Scottish rhythms may be a phenomenon due to the fact that the Anglicisation of Scotland dates back further than we commonly imagine. But if this consideration leads to the discovery that to secure already existing Scottish rhythms unparalleled and without affinities in English we must go back to Gaelic, why, that is a position I have already suggested in these studies. The *Gaeltacht* is the ultimate provenance or deriving-ground of the unexhausted evolutionary momentum, one of whose manifestations is, in some of its deepest bearing at all events, the Scottish Renaissance movement.

But the leader-writer's notes do not take us so far down as that. The superficiality of his position is most clearly given away perhaps by what he says of a quotation from Seumas O'Sullivan – 'An Englishman or a Lowland Scot would read these lines quite differently from an Irishman'; I agree; and would ask if there are not poems by MacDiarmid, Spence, and others which any Scot (who could read them – any Scot who is a Scot) would not read quite differently from the way any foreigner, English or otherwise, could. Rhythm in the conventional school-book sense of the term means very little, and is only a rough description of one of the elements or characteristics of any poem. If the other elements are of a kind such as cannot be found in the poems of a given other language, or such as have different values to the people of one nation than for those of another. it is absurd to give priority to this one element and contend that because it is also found in the poems of the other country that implies a deep-seated relationship, against which all the other differences contend in vain. In any case, however, most of such considerations are irrelevant so far as the present and future of poetry is concerned, however important they may have been with regard to the poetry produced between the Renaissance and the beginning of this century in certain countries. [3.9.26]

Letters

OLD BARDS AND NEW
Since the correspondence of this subject was closed last week we have had a communication from Mr Donald A. Mackenzie with reference to the following paragraph which appeared in the letter from 'Lover of Justice': –

'When passing through the Meadows I heard Mr Mackenzie addressing a large crowd and assuring them he had just returned from Russia,
and gave a graphic account of what he saw there.'

Mr Mackenzie assures us that this statement is untrue.

Ed, S.E.J.
[3.9.26]

45. Rhythm and Race (III)

Discussing Professor E.A. Sonnenschein's essay, 'What is Rhythm?' and
its accompanying appendix on Experimental Syllable-Measurement, and
the use of the kymograph, which can exactly measure the duration of
every syllable in speech, Mr Herbert Read in his recent volume of
essays, *Reason and Romanticism* (Messrs Faber and Gwyer) – which
have established his reputation as one of the most significant of living
literary critics – says that

> when this scientific measurement is applied on a large scale to the
> main body of 'refined English verse,' the results show beyond doubt
> that 'quantity is nothing less than a structural element in the best kind
> of English verse, side by side with accent.' Syllables are only relatively
> long or short, and even then may vary with the context; or they may
> be of equal value in a foot (isosyllabic), or protracted, or even, where
> the rhythm demands it, merely imaginary. Professor Sonnenschein is,
> of course, mainly concerned with the analysis of traditional verse
> forms, and no one interested in this aspect of the subject can afford to
> neglect his book. He does not, however, make any attempt to apply
> his definitions and discoveries to the extension of the possibilities of
> poetry. He does not seem to realise, for example, that his definition of
> rhythm is not merely applicable to refined extracts from Tennyson
> and Keats, but that it is equally applicable to 'The Strayed Reveller'
> and *The Waste Land*. In fact, Prof. Sonnenschein's definition, without
> more ado, substitutes the element of proportion in rhythm for the
> element of regularity; and this is precisely what the best *vers libriste*
> poets, in France, England, and America have been contending for...
> If, then, we are to substitute for the concepts of measure (that is, for
> regular, accented feet) a concept of rhythm dependent on nothing
> but its own innate rightness as tested by the ear, we must inquire

more closely into the nature and origins of such rhythms. How are they
come by? The conventional metrist will say that at any rate in the case
of Shakespeare and Milton, and even in the case of Arnold, they are
variations on the basis of a regular measure. But this is casuistry, for all
rhythm, even the rhythm of prose and of speech, is only perceptible by
contrast to a hypothetical norm of regularity – a uniform temporal beat
or simple iambic sequence. Certainly all free verse of rhythmical structure is related to such a norm or basis. But actually no rhythms are
consciously constructed by a system of normal measurements; they are
rather spontaneous sense perceptions. And any comparative study of
rhythms reveals the fact that they are relative. They vary from age to
age and from language to language. Chinese and Polynesian rhythms
are perceptible to us, but they are foreign to our habits. English
rhythms have a good deal in common with Germanic rhythms, but both
are quite different from French or Spanish rhythms. Even within the
limits of our own language, if we observe carefully purely local dictions,
we find surprisingly different rhythms. A man from Newcastle and a
man from Hull speak in entirely different *tempi*. But we must beware
of a loose connotation of the word 'rhythm,' which is better kept for
aesthetic effects. We can, however, resort to the word 'idiom.' A living
language analyses into idioms: idioms are the live organisms of speech –
words are molecules and letters atoms. Now this organic unit, this
idiom, is instinct with rhythm; it has irrefrangible intonation, and poetic
rhythm is but the extension and the aggregation of these primary
rhythms. Even measured, regularly accentuated verse is successful only
in so far as it makes use of or accommodates itself to these idioms. Free
verse, which includes the slightest as well as the widest divergence
from regular pattern, is but the free use of these idioms… We can only
seize the real rhythm instinctively. It *has* been found – in the modern
ballet, in American rag-time music, and in a minute quantity of modern
poetry. But when we have found the rhythm we are only at the beginning of art. We have found no more than the instruments of art.

The *Glasgow Herald* leader-writer's error, therefore, is of the same
kind as would have been a condemnation of such modern poetry in Scots
as he mentioned if he had condemned it in the light of the reference in
the above quotation to 'living language' on the ground that Scots is a dead
language or so debilitated as to have no recognisable pulse of life – a
misunderstanding of the sense in which 'live idiom' is opposed in such an
argument to 'dead idiom' (to the use of which, as of unreal rhythm, Mr

Read rightly attributes 'the sickness of nearly all modern poetry'; it rings false in the actual turmoil of the day), which would have been very similar to that of a recent correspondent of the *Scots Magazine*, who naively contended that all this pother about a Scottish Renaissance was beneath contempt since none of our 'Scottish authors of established reputation' had given it their benediction. How in the world could they be expected to do anything of the sort? Is not the whole point of such a movement a complete reaction against all that they are and stand for – all that they think Scottish even or that is generally thought Scottish, thus demonstrating the vitality of the Scottish spirit in its refusal to be restricted to certain stock-conceptions and manifesting its capacity to break out in new directions! Perhaps the main handicap of a Scottish Renaissance to-day is the contemptible puerility of such counter-criticism as has been directed against the ideas that have been put forward in connection with it. In other words, what we are reacting against may very well prove in the ultimate analysis to have been so low, so spineless, so inert as to be incapable of providing a springboard for any new development worth mentioning. In that case the blame will not lie with the promoters of the Scottish Renaissance movement. I have already contended in these studies that if the Scottish Renaissance movement is to succeed it must operate not only by attracting an effective body of writers and artists to its particular programme, but by effectively antagonising others. So far its antagonising powers have been singularly non-productive. In this connection, students may profitably compare what Professor Whitehead says in his *Science and the Modern World*: –

> There are two principles inherent in the very nature of things, recurring in some particular embodiments whatever field we explore – the spirit of change, and the spirit of conservation. There can be nothing real without both. Mere change without conservation is a passage from nothing to nothing. Its final integration yields mere transient nonentity. Mere conservation without change cannot conserve. For, after all, there is a flux of circumstance, and the freshness of being evaporates under mere repetition... The psychological field, as restricted to sense-objects and passing emotions, is the minor permanence, barely rescued from the nonentity of mere change; and the mind is the major permanence, permeating that complete field, whose endurance is the living soul. But the soul would wither without fertilisation from its transient experiences. The secret of the higher organisms lies in their two grades of permanences. By this means the freshness of the environment is

absorbed into the permanence of the soul. The changing environment is no longer, by reason of its variety, an enemy to the endurance of the organism. The pattern of the higher organism has retreated into the accesses of the individualised activity. It has become a uniform way of dealing with circumstances; and this way is only strengthened by having a proper variety of circumstances to deal with.

Is the Scottish Renaissance movement decadent? Those who have contended that it is may well read what Professor Whitehead goes on to say:

This fertilisation of the soul is the reason for the necessity of art. A static value, however serious and important, becomes unendurable by its appalling monotony of endurance. The soul cries aloud for release into change. It suffers the agonies of claustrophobia. The transitions of humour, wit, *irreverence*, play, sleep, and, above all, of art are necessary to it... An epoch gets saturated by the masterpieces of any one style. Something new must be discovered. The human being wanders on. Yet there is a balance in things...

If the Scottish Renaissance Movement is successful it will profoundly alter the rhythm of Scottish life. The rhythms of the poetry associated with this achievement will follow this new life as it develops and more and more clearly dissociates itself from the old. If these 'rhythms' (taking the narrow conception of rhythm which dictated the *Glasgow Herald* leader) are – in the initiation of this departure – similar to those mainly associated with English poetry, it will only be poetic justice if they supersede those 'distinctively Scottish rhythms' (so-called) which inform the work of poets whose availability to progressive provincialisation is so largely responsible for the present deplorable position of Scotland and of Scottish arts and letters.   [8.10.26]

46. Creative Art and the Scottish Educational System (I)

(From an address to the New Education Fellowship, Glasgow)

It is a useful exercise to try some evening to recall all that you have said and all that has been said to you in the course of the day. You will not be able to recall more than a fraction of it, of course, and even then you will trim it up very considerably – your own side of it anyway. But if you have any capacity for disinterestedness and analysis, and just sit down and assess the value even of that – the degree of purposiveness in it, the quality of the thought, the amount and comparative value of your real self (as you flatter yourself you are) you got across – you will find that in your promiscuous intercourse you are living for the most part in an atmosphere certainly not higher than that of what is still known in certain quarters as 'Family Fiction.' You may then, if you are exceedingly candid with yourself, realise the truth of what H.G. Wells says when he refers to the 'parading attention to the passings and comings of intrinsically insignificant personages, filling the papers, accentuating the extraordinary triviality of human association, stealing dignity from knowledge, mocking progress, and dishonouring all life,' and you may realise, as Wells forgets, that all but a moiety of the people in the background, never in the limelight, are not only no better but almost infinitely worse. Probably there are not a hundred people in Great Britain who could maintain an impromptu conversation for twenty minutes, except on a business matter, which, if reported verbatim, would not read quite incredibly banal. Where ordinary small talk does not quite suffice we fall back upon a camouflaged variant of it consisting of all sorts of generalisations and platitudes. I am concerned here not with fatuity in general, but with fatuity as it particularly affects arts and letters and the relation to these of life and education. So the type of generalisation that concerns my subject is this: 'Everybody knows that Tolstoy ———.' Now, the fact of the matter is that so far from everybody knowing very few do. The influence of literature has always been and remains confined to a relatively small percentage of the population. All so-called educated people pay a certain amount of lip-service to literature and to the other arts, but few know more than shamefully little about them and, if pressed, will admit as much without shame. They will confess to cultural poverty and disfigurements of all kinds with a carelessness at strange odds with their anxiety about their personal appearance or the opinions about them of other people whom in their hearts of hearts they nevertheless recognise to be in every respect as negligible as themselves. Ninety-nine per cent of them – at a very conservative estimate – are confined to a little circle of reading that relatively is so grossly inadequate that to boast on the strength of it of being 'a great reader' – 'interested in literature' – is as if one boasted oneself a mathematician on the score of an average familiarity with the multiplication table. One cannot make a statement like that – one cannot begin to analyse just what the education of most so-called educated people really amounts to – without being grossly offensive and in the main – which is more important – seeming quite irrational and impossibilist. One's very first discoveries so traverse well-nigh universal assumptions as to be frankly incredible. Happily honest people – people of intellectual integrity – will not stick there (and a teacher who lacks intellectual integrity betrays Education from within, 'wounds it in the house of its friends'). So let us be frank. Croce's *European Literature in the Nineteenth Century* consists of essays on Alfieri, Monti, Schiller Leopardi, de Vigny, Manzoni, Berchet, Giusti, Heine, Balzac, Baudelaire, Flaubert, Zola, Daudet, Ibsen, Maupassant, and Carducci, amongst others. How many of the 'educated people' of Scotland to-day have read anything by these men even in translation – how many can flatter themselves that they have assimilated the essentials of their contribution to European culture? And it is a precious poor list. We are talking about something we haven't got the most rudimentary sense of if we mention European civilisation without knowing exactly intimately, what not only these men but scores of others – scores of musicians and scientists and philosophers and artists – stand for. To what extent in relation to such a reasonable test can Scottish education to-day claim that the completed article as it leaves our Universities is cultured? In other words – precisely how anachronistic are we, how far behind creative civilisation does our intelligentsia lag all the time? Are we to fall back upon the general feeling that all these foreign writers are negligible – inferior to our own products – except for specialists?

The case is worse when we come to what may be comprehensively called 'Dada' – ultra-modern arts and letters. When I use the term Dada I am, of course, not thinking so much of the specific little French movement that took that name – I am not even wondering how many teachers, for example, have so much as read lames Joyce's *Ulysses* or T.S. Eliot's *The Waste Land* (which, when all that most people know and esteem has vanished as it had never existed, will, almost certainly, survive as the representative expressions of early 20th century life and thought in the English language) – but of all those manifestations in contemporary arts and sciences which the great majority of people who have ever seen or heard anything of them find hopelessly unintelligible – as if three-dimensional minds were perpending four-dimensional phenomena. The truth of the matter is that in all the Arts, and in Science, the minds of the advance guard today are probably operating on planes which the vast majority of people are never destined to reach at all. Just as we yielded to the old anti-foreign feeling for justification in the former case, are we to join here in the herd-cry of charlatanry, to condemn these people as 'highbrows,' as if there were some peculiar virtue in low-browedness or medium-browedness? Are we sincere in feeling that we do not want to be cleverer than other people, or is it just that we realise that we can't and seek to make a virtue of it? Are we satisfied to share in the contempt for all that is new and different, all that challenges our understanding, with the vast imitative repetitive majority, who are incapable of devising, incapable of realising the stupendous difficulty and transcendent importance of devising anything new either in form or content, and who cannot assimilate anything but the softest of soft pap?

The difference between a Dadaist and a respectable product of the Scottish Education System is that the latter likes something he can understand and the former something he can't. It is obvious that the Dadaist must carry a process of elimination a good distance before he arrives at a point at which he can derive any satisfaction, whereas the R.P.S.E.S. needn't move off the bit. It is also obvious that liking something you can understand means throwing bouquets at your powers of comprehension all the time, while the Dadaist, on the other hand, is looking for *culs-de-sac* to bat his head against. The latter is, of course, a comparatively religious process. From the point of view of Education, the R.P.S.E.S. has little, if any, use for more than the minimum of it he can't evade – the minimum he can practically apply – while the Dadaist doesn't become one till, in some direction of other, he has learned all that can be taught and enters into unexplored territory for himself. Pedagogic interest therefore – on a long view – lies with the latter. Apart from that it is surely a question of personal honour. This stupid insistence on mere meaning, on values that, however idealistic at first glance, are all at best in the last analysis utilitarian, this disinclination for the incomprehensible, for what is beyond us, that should put any mind worth having on its mettle, are all dishonourings of our minds, panderings to what is commonest and basest in us, sloth, the fear to be different from other people.

To what extent, I asked, is the completed article as it leaves the Scottish Universities to-day cultured? We are all familiar with scores of graduates. What do they really amount to? Compare them, for example, with the young German, Otto Braun, killed in 1918 in his 20th year. We find him writing to a chum in 1909 – when he was 12 years old –

Go, dig down into your innermost self, ask yourself whether you do not often force yourself to adopt forms which are not a true reflection of your inner self. Only the form that comes honestly from within is capable of presenting our thoughts in a worthy shape to others.

Again, in 1911: –

> It is a sign of weakness to do something merely out of reaction. Ah! to be able to carry a serene balance of stability and perfection in one's soul! But it is terribly difficult to accept influences which are necessary and yet use them only as a means towards the end of shaping one's own being from within, and not to keep on carrying these elements as foreign bodies in one's system, however enthusiastically one may have accepted them at first.

It is because Scottish children seldom, if ever, have such instincts that Scottish education imposes itself so stultifyingly upon them. At an age when most of our children are being subjected to Band of Hope lectures, consider the maturity of such an utterance as this:

> I am convinced that a physically degenerate age such as ours imposes duties upon us far beyond those of any other, so that the purely sociological aspect of the question forces one to abstinence, since only a small modicum of one's life is lived for one's own self. Were this otherwise, or did we live in a healthy age, I would certainly drink since this has been done by all great men, and in all great epochs, and since the greatest poets have glorified it in song.

Finally, can we imagine any Scottish child we know, or any adult for the matter of that, being able to say:

> This morning so-and-so told me of so-and-so's praise of me. These eulogies always arouse a certain distrust in me – a sense of shame. I shall always bear within me an unpolluted spirit, and a god whom few know, but who, after I am gone, will shine the brighter. I shall have many enemies and experience many attacks during life, but, after my death, I shall be a symbol and a monument to men – one who will be a *beginning* – one who will have progeny.   [5.11.26]

47. Creative Art and the Scottish Educational System (II)

Now let us scale down these considerations to the level of the great mass of our people. What trickle from the great wellsprings of European arts and letters has yet percolated to them? They have not only little Latin and less Greek – what they know of anything is so infinitesimal, so corrupt, so worthless as to be negligible. And they are the product of generations of the best system of popular education in Europe – the heirs of all the ages. Do not imagine that I think they would be necessarily any better if they were all miraculously raised to the D.Litt. level. On the contrary, just as Ernest Newman points out that it is the professional musicians who are standing between the great public and the vital forces of modern music – seeking to impose anachronisms, stereotypes, abracadabras of all kinds on them from which their human qualities naturally find relief in the opposite direction in jazz, so, in my opinion, are the professional educators standing between them and culture generally, arid driving them to find relief in shoddy newspapers and silly cinema and wireless programmes. Lots of people, like Annie S. Swan, are preaching the gospel of work to-day. It is like the thrift campaign, to which most board schools are prostituting themselves. Education as a whole is condemned by the fact that soulless drudgery, the mechanical performance of set operations in which the human instinct to create finds no outlet, remains, increasingly becomes indeed, the inescapable portion of the great majority of people. Educationists cannot be oblivious to what happens, to what under the existing system must happen, to those they educate. All but a moiety of them are condemned to tasks demoralisingly below their education – any education. The whole tendency and meaning of human inventiveness is towards the Workless State, the state in which all human drudgery is eliminated, in which the great majority of people will not require to work at all in the usual sense of work today, but will be able to concentrate on the far more important business of becoming human beings in any real sense of the term. To talk of work as an end rather than a means, to envisage, and adapt successive generations to, the permanence of conditions in which labour-saving devices are ruthlessly restricted, an arbitrary and absurd monetary system prevents the mass of the population deriving any advantage from the almost illimitable increase of productivity operating on inexhaustible natural resources, and prate of the jobs most people are condemned to waste their lives on as if they were capable of yielding that satisfaction that comes from honest essential service and from labours that call for the highest qualities of manhood and womanhood, is sheer blasphemy. The present educational system is part and parcel of the system that propagates this vicious and anti-human Gospel of Work – so much so that it is fair to regard it in the main as a means of prostituting the intellectual and spiritual potentialities of successive generations in a fashion which – for all practical purposes – confines the souls and minds of the population within the sordid ruts requisite to the existing economic order and its inherent requirements. Any overplus after the discharge of that function of providing factory-fodder for Mammon amounts to little more than something similar to the welfare work carried on amongst the employees of certain comparatively 'enlightened' firms. Thus it comes about that teachers who, above all, should be the inspirers and defenders of cultural values in the community, reconcile themselves to the grotesque anomalies of a system in which side-street grocers and petty bourgeois of all kinds dominate the social scene, while poets and artists are despised in proportion to their reluctance to subsist on the crumbs from the rich man's table, or to aid and abet him like the other agencies which maintain him in his ludicrous position by helping to keep the great mass of the public in a state of obfuscation. That is our condition to-day. Creative artists must do their work in the face of general indifference – in the teeth of general opposition even – while nonentities flourish.

Dr Steel has recently been talking about propaganda in schools, and the Press has been discussing his work. To claim that certain entrenched financial interests upon whom accumulated capital, and the complexity of modern industrial and commercial inter-relationships, confer a practically unassailable monopoly of the vehicles of publicity, are to be allowed complete licence, and that this is synonymous with the Freedom of the Press is farcical. It is not to the credit of an 'educated democracy' – of educationists – that organised mis-representation should so easily, so continuously, gull great masses of the people at this time of day. The Press is neither more nor less than an instrument for the promotion of certain private interests and operates in the main under present conditions as a tremendous stultifier of our vast annual expenditure on education. A typical Press comment on Dr Steel's remarks read: 'It is imperative, however, in these days that there should be no attempt by teachers who harbour advanced views to abuse their position and that there should be no qualms in meting out summary justice to those who would be so treacherous.' In my opinion it is far more imperative that there should be no such attempt by teachers who do not harbour advanced views – since they are far more numerous and far more guilty – witness religious education, savings associations, patriotic and temperance addresses, prize-day platitudes, and all the hundred and one other ways in which children are brought to conform, conventionalised, imbued with preconceptions favourable to the *status quo* in morals, economics, and otherwise. It is absurd to contend that teachers should be content to be the blindfold or blinkered, if not the blind, leaders of the blind, that they should confine themselves to displaying only a professional residue of themselves in school and leave the children in regard to all the more intimate and important things of life to the tender mercies of comparatively incompetent and irresponsible people like parents and ministers. If this is the price educationists must pay for a state system, the sooner it is divorced from state control the better. I look forward to the autonomy of the teacher. The growth of free, private and experimental schools is therefore a welcome sign. There are far too many colourless minds in the teaching profession as it is. I would sooner entrust a child to the robust personality of a teacher who was a confessed cannibal than to a mindless and spiritless nonentity. I am entirely opposed to any increase of parental interference with children. Family relationships operate to hold people for the most part to given levels. Whatever may be said of them in other respects they are overwhelmingly anti-educational in their effects. That is why we have a *compulsory* educational system. Scottish education has largely suffered by ignoring the value of anti-social qualities, of minority traits and tendencies. These have meant a very great deal in the history of arts, letters and science – infinitely more than their opposites. One of the main efforts and effects of Education should be to canalise, to clear away, the appalling accretions of futile imitativeness and repetition in which literate humanity everywhere is bogged. Instead of that we find today that the instinctive freemasonry, the contagion, of mediocrity was never more rampant and inescapable. That is the real danger to civilisation – and to education. There is a great deal of justice in the complaint that popular education is making people all of one pattern. The wholesale sacrifice of differences is certainly a dangerous feature of it. It does not value what Professor Whitehead calls that 'state of muddled responsiveness' that generally precedes creative activity. On the contrary, it more and more tends to turn out slick 'booksellers' assistants.' On the effective accentuation of differences rather than resemblances, on the stimulation of whatever elusive tendencies there may be to abnormal ego-centricity, however morbid, however anti-social, rather than upon the inculcation of good manners, social address, civic instincts, a standard of intelligence, and the rest of the formulae for the manufacture of Rotarians and robots, depends the development of artists and thinkers. There is a close connection between the fact that Scotland has had (in the sense in which that is true) the best educational system in Europe, and the poorest output of artistic genius. You cannot serve God and Mammon.

The flow and direction of the newer intellectual forces in post-war Germany has been well described as the 'will-to-significance'. That is what is almost wholly lacking in the products of the Scottish educational system. We need some such vision as Count Keyserling expounds in his School of Wisdom at Darnstadt – based on the ideal of 'being' rather than of 'being able to do'; asserting that personality transcends ability and approaching in this the Goethean postulate that the supreme felicity of man is personality or, as Keyserling puts it, seeking to create full-value human beings *(vollmenschen)*. The educational objective should be the polarisation of personalities. Keyserling calls for a new synthesis of intellect and spirit – no longer with the backward but with the most highly developed elements of humanity. Or, as another writer puts it, Keyserling's efforts are directed against the sabotage of the spiritual-intellectual treasury which mankind has slowly erected in its honour, and against all attempts to prevent its being extended laterally and vertically – and it is a similar attitude I have been trying to manifest here, claiming that in its present organisation Scottish education as is proved by the comparative cultural backwardness and creative sterility of Scotland during the past century, is one of the instruments of that sabotage, and that it is high time it should be reoriented and devoted to the production of poets and artists rather than of 'heids o' depairtments,' whether in the civil services or in multiple stores.   [19.11.26]

48. The Scottish Academy of Music

There is no living Scotsman for the intentions of whose munificence I have more respect, and for the results of whose munificence I have less, than Sir D.M. Stevenson. In spirit he is a Maecenas of Scottish arts and affairs; in effect he is all but negligible. Who can assert that his many splendid gifts have in any corresponding fashion enriched our national life? Sir Thomas Beecham recently asserted that financial stringency in these difficult times was not the cause of the quandary in which all the creative arts are finding themselves to-day in England – one night's proceeds from any of the fashionable night-clubs could subsidise a genuine creative enterprise. If that is so, rightly applied, Sir Daniel's gifts amount in the aggregate to a sum which could have gone a long way to stimulate vital developments in practically every sphere of cultural activity in Scotland. They have done so in none. The life-giving stream has been allowed to dissipate itself in the sands of sterile Academicism. Either Sir Daniel's methods have defeated his motives or the trouble is due to a radical misconception of ways and means. My purpose here is to frankly analyse the process at work; and I can only trust that, so far as Sir Daniel and a few others in whose reactions to my remarks I have any interest are concerned, the disinterestedness and urgency of my concern with Scottish arts and affairs during recent years will acquit me of any seeming impertinence, remembering that while some may give their money others must needs give their lives and that it is with the latter and not with the former that the issue lies in all its most important respects.

A correspondent, signing himself 'W.J.,' has recently written as follows in several Scottish periodicals:

> Money is being collected and plans are being laid for the foundation of an Academy of Music in Glasgow. The correspondence which has appeared in the Press on this important matter seems to be hopelessly scant and insufficient, and the *raison d'être* of the Academy, as set forth some time ago in a public appeal for funds, seems to me dissatisfactory and hopeless as far as the fostering of creative culture in Scotland goes. The true aim of an Academy of Music in this liveliest of Scottish cities should be the creation and development of a school of composition that is racially Scottish and that is technically on a level with the best Continental schools... In Russia, Poland, Germany and France the teachers and schools that shape the professional equipment of the future composer have dominant racial characteristics. However much Tchaikovski and Saint-Saens owed to their natural powers, they owed more to nationality and early training. The technicalities of music, like the technicalities of painting, are international; the creative urge and inspiring idiom are fundamentally racial. Now, the aims of this Scottish Academy, as set forth in the public appeal, take no notice of these vital facts. They seem gratified with the mere granting of degrees and diplomas, and the elimination of the necessity for students to study in London or abroad. If these aims are carried into practice the Academy will become a mere cramming shop for non-creative people, whose only purpose is teaching in schools or playing in churches or orchestras (all very necessary, of course); and it will be a fortress for ideas and practices 20 or more years behind the times. It will, in brief, become a backwash of London schools, and wholly untouched by energising influences from

the Continent. It will, that is, neither improve not alter the nature of musical culture in Glasgow and Scotland in the least.

To that Sir Daniel replies:

The promoters would not have spent, as they have done, three years on trying to bring the scheme to fruition if it were to become what he calls a backwash of London schools and wholly untouched by energising influences from the Continent.

On the contrary they have been advised by the highest authorities in the country that

if the scheme, as foreshadowed, is carried out in its entirety, Glasgow will have far and away the finest musical centre in the United Kingdom, not only for the training of professionals and amateurs and the teaching of the people to understand and appreciate musical works, but will be a conservatorium in the highest sense, where the musical genius of the Scottish nation will be drawn out and fostered.

In several previous articles in these columns I have gone exhaustively into the whole question of the comparative position of Scottish music and pointed out some, at least, of the prerequisites if Scotland was ever to do what every other country in Europe has long since done and acquire a place in the world of music. More recently I have published a lengthy pamphlet on the subject,° with special reference to this proposed National Academy and the related project for a Chair of Music in Glasgow University. I do not propose to go over the same ground here. The facts are not in dispute. But there are several questions which may pertinently be addressed to Sir Daniel thereanent. The first of these is with reference to his use of the phrase 'the highest authorities in the country.' Who are they? If we are told who they are we will be able to gauge the reality of their concern for, and their competence in respect of, anything that is distinctively Scottish. It is curious that they have not been busy heretofore in urging the need for Scotland to begin that national development in music which in every other country in Europe is now in its third or fourth stage of development. It is curious that they have in no way supported either such little efforts as have been made to secure discussion on the subject (efforts which have had to win past an amazing Press censorship operating in the interests of the ever-more-complete assimilation of Scottish standards to English) or succeeded in

° *The Present Position of Scottish Music* (*Border Standard* Office, Galashiels. 1s.)

making or in stimulating others to make, any beginning in the creation of distinctively Scottish music. It is curious in the present almost wholly denationalised condition of Scotland that nothing short of a 'Scottish National Academy of Music,' will suffice them. Is the condition of affairs that our Union with England has brought about to be suddenly and sensationally reversed in regard to music while in every other direction, political, economic, social and cultural, Scottish nationalistic tendencies are minority elements challenging almost-overwhelming opposition? What a pity that these people have so far given no earnest either of their zeal for a distinctively Scottish music or their ability to produce it – no earnest even of their realisation of the issues involved and their relation to other factors in our national life. Jove leaping fully-armed from the head of Minerva is 'not in it' with these people, who are so suddenly (if still anonymously) manifesting themselves in the 'winter of our discontent' and are, if Sir Daniel is to be believed, to resolve problems that are mainly psychological by a provision of external facilities. It would be well worth looking forward to if it were not so inherently impossible. The fact of the matter is that Sir Daniel and his associates are putting the cart before the horse. They are trying to do with money what money cannot do. They would do more for Scottish music, and all the other arts, if they spent what they have to spend on a propaganda to re-create, or to intensify and re-orient, a realistic spirit of Scottish Nationalism. The rest would inevitably follow; it is because of the absence of such a nationalism that we have lagged so far behind. Instead of that they are going to give us another school! As if we had not schools enough of every kind! How much this new school will do for Scottish music may be gauged by considering how much during the past hundred years all our schools and colleges and Universities have done for the creation of Scottish literature. There is nothing whatever wrong with Professor Tovey, for example, but what has he done for Scottish music?

Such an Academy, even if it represents – as it most obviously does not do in Scotland to-day – the crest of a wave of national enthusiasm, speedily becomes a stumbling block to the creative spirit. Even if there were creative activities in Scotland to-day which could be temporarily furthered by the establishment of such an academy in ten years or in twenty years it would, if vital tendencies continued to manifest themselves, become a museum of fossilised conceptions and practices and the butt of the advance-guard. Let Sir Daniel be under no delusion. If it is a social service he wishes to perform that, for what it is worth, this Academy, as planned, may supply; but if he wishes to help Scotland to make up its shameful leeway in regard to music – and thereby ultimately to give a far greater social service – it is inconceivable that it can be done in a completely denationalised atmosphere in this way. The only way in which it can be done is as it always has been done – as every new departure in any of the arts has been effected – by isolated creators working against the indifference and generally against the active opposition of the great majority of their compatriots. Such isolated creators can be helped individually by rich men who understand their needs and sympathise with their tendencies. They may even to some extent be called into being by the provision of prizes for work answering to certain tests. But the whole history of the arts goes to show that it is exceedingly seldom, if ever, that gentlemen like Sir Daniel and his associates can be in a position to detect genius fighting against the stream – until genius himself 'arrives.' Even if Sir Daniel's 'highest authorities' are not those to whom the very first fruits of the long-overdue Scottish musical development would be anathema, the second crop inevitably would be. Scotland has nothing to give musically if what it has to give, so far from securing the assistance and approval of any National Academy, would not evoke its bitterest opposition and that of professional and public opinion generally both at home and abroad – representing, as it must, so radical a break with the *status quo nunc*.

Not only are Sir Daniel's authorities in an unprecedented and entirely unpredicated position if they are able to guarantee any creative development in Glasgow, but they are surprisingly reticent with regard to the *modus operandi* whereby they are to bring about such a revolution in our national relationship to the art of music, and how they are not only to create the creators, but – for the two things go together – get them a hearing. Even if distinctively Scottish music on a plane that would compare favourably with the contemporary products of other countries were being produced, it could not continue to develop, even with the backing of a National Academy, unless there was an extraordinary revolution in Scottish public taste – in a direction which it is the direct interest of not only the majority of such composers as we have but of our music firms, teachers, executants and artistes of all kinds to prevent. If any such music comes along and manages to secure a public it means that all these people will have to take the trouble of readjusting themselves to a very inconvenient degree and that existing vested interests of many kinds will be imperilled. Not only so: but the creation and diffusion of such music would have its repercussion on every other phase of our national life and international relationships in a fashion which, again, would run counter to the *status quo* (that has been developing during the past two or three hundred years) and its inherent implications. It is obvious that if anything of the sort is to be encompassed through an Academy, associated with a Chair of Music in Glasgow University, everything turns upon the personnel of the teaching staff, and the occupant of the Chair. Who are they to be? Are they even to be Scots, or is Sir Daniel to make his miracles still more miraculous by employing foreigners to create Scottish nationalism in music? Nothing in the history of music would be more surprising than – in view of all that has hitherto transpired (or, rather, failed to transpire) – to find the requisite number of Scotsmen to undertake these duties with that precise objective. If such men existed the movement would already be making headway and have something to show for itself. Creative work along these lines, however handicapped (and there are some minor ways perhaps in which these handicaps could be monetarily resolved by a discerning Maecenas) is the only thing that will do anything to remove from Scotland the reproach with regard to music under which, alone of European countries, it presently lies: but in the absence of significant 'small beginnings,' of all the usual phenomena attendant on new creative departures, and in the presence of an overwhelming pressure towards completer Anglicisation and of an actual refusal on the part of our existing Anglo-Scottish Press to insert signed letters from well-known writers on this very subject of a 'Scottish National Academy of Music' (a fact which accounts for the scant and insufficient discussion of which 'W. J.' complains) Sir Daniel's assertion, and the guarantees of 'high authorities' on which it is based, is one that might very well be supported by a detailed statement on their part showing cognisance of Scotland's exact musical position, the causes of it, and how it is to be cured. Let Sir Daniel and his associates take the nation into their confidence and, instead of asking us to assist in purchasing a 'pig in a poke,' tell us exactly how they propose to go about matters. Some of us know how the creation of national music has been gone about in other countries, and by that and out of knowledge of Scottish psychology and Scotland's position generally, we will be in a position to check their proposals, while, if the scheme really deserves its title of 'national,' nothing but advantage can accrue from the fullest threshing-out of all the pros-and-cons.

In conclusion, it may be remarked that 'W.J.,' in the letter from which I have quoted, curiously overestimated the necessity to composers of the sort of teaching and technical training such an Academy gives – even if, in any given country, it has 'dominant racial characteristics.' Balakireff, at first the dominating member of the Russian 'Five' – their educator –

'gifted with a musical instinct, prodigiously sure, was almost entirely igno-rant of the art of composition. He had practically no theoretical knowl-edge, and he taught that experience could be adequately acquired by practice.' When Rimsky-Korsakoff was appointed professor of composi-tion at the Petrograd Conservatoire he admitted that he was almost wholly ignorant of what he was to teach; in particular, he had no more than a very vague idea of counterpoint and fugue. Moussorgsky 'did not learn harmony, never wished to learn it, nor to master the technique of music, and, little by little, he instinctively discovered his own altogether individual form of writing.' Such instances can be multiplied indefinitely. Our inordi-nate respect for education is a national weakness intimately related to our creative impotence.

The heart of the whole matter – and the reason for knowing that little or no good to any creative art can result from the establishment of any Academy – is given by Arnold Schönberg where he holds that music be-longs to the explanatory sciences which teach what a thing is and not how it ought to be done. 'How can we say, that sounds good or bad?' he asks,

> who is judge in this case? The authoritative theorist? He says, even if he does not justify his opinion, what he knows – that is to say, not what he has discovered for himself, but what he has learnt; or what everyone believes because it is everyone's experience. But beauty is not the experience of everyone, being at most only the experience of certain individuals.

As a teacher Schönberg is opposed to premature theoretical formulation:

> He has not technique, [he writes,] who can just skilfully imitate some-thing given; rather he is the slave of technique – the technique of another. Whoever is capable of perceiving aright must realise that such technique is fraudulent. Nothing really fits in properly; it is merely put together with some skill. In such a case nothing is exact, nor develops out of itself, nor holds together; viewed from a distance, however, it seems genuine enough. There is no technique without invention; but invention must create its own technique.

Will Sir D.M. Stevenson kindly explain how the proposed Academy is to prevent itself being other than a transmitter of such fraudulent tech-nique – and how, in the senses I have been indicating, it can possibly be, not only a real creative force but a specifically Scottish one? Or is it all just another case of mistaking the shadow for the substance, the letter for the spirit? [4.2.27]

Appendix

I 'Introductory'
(from Contemporary Scottish Studies, 1926)
by Hugh MacDiarmid (C.M. Grieve)

'Let the Scotsman be content, as I think he generally is, to be a Scotsman,' enjoined the Prime Minister (Mr Stanley Baldwin) recently. But it all depends on what connotation is attached to the term 'Scotsman,' as to whether such contentment is desirable in the interests of Scotsmen themselves and their country, and European arts and affairs generally – or, merely, as some of us think, in the interests of Englishmen and of those Anglo-Scots who have sold their birthright for an (admittedly substantial) mess of pottage. To determine this it is necessary to examine the ethos of Scotland to-day; to enquire into the contemporary and, generally, post-Union contribution of Scotland to world culture; to institute comparisons between the stock-conceptions of things Scottish to-day and the qualities which manifested themselves in Scotland before the Union – even to consider anew what really *is* the chief End of Man and, more particularly, the best possible destiny that Scotland can secure, or, at least, plan and purpose for itself. There is an anecdote of Big Mac, who declared, 'One thing I thank God for – I'm a Scotsman,' and Little Dick, who retorted, 'That shows a nice forgiving spirit anyhow.' For other reasons than perhaps actuate the majority of my countrymen I can heartily enough second Big Mac's sentiment, but, on the other hand, I am not of a forgiving disposition, and there are many directions in which I would fain make sure of being able to accommodate the Deity with a better grace than I can yet command. These essays are part and parcel of an endeavour to encompass that object.

They originally appeared in *The Scottish Educational Journal* (commencing in May, 1925), to the editor of which I here tender the customary acknowledgments. Appearing in his pages had both its advantages and its disadvantages – and, so far as presenting them now in book form goes, the latter greatly outweigh the former. They did not always appear weekly; the General Strike caused a hiatus – these and other causes necessitated a good deal of repetition. The type was kept standing; and the articles appear here practically in their original form.

Nor does this book comprise the entire series of 52 articles embraced in my arrangement with *The Scottish Educational Journal*. Sixteen of these have not yet appeared at this time of writing and are not included.[1] Nor was that series as originally planned sufficiently comprehensive to effect my purpose. I therefore now propose to make this volume a First Series; and to devote a second volume to another series, which will include the sixteen articles above-mentioned and another fourteen which I now consider necessary. Some of the persons or issues which I have thus left over, however, I have touched upon in my concluding chapter, just to show that I have them in mind. In addition to what I say there I must frankly admit here that I regret that I have not had space in this first volume to deal with the art of Duncan Grant, J.D. Fergusson, S.J. Peploe, and one or two others (my regret is mitigated in the cases of Muirhead Bone, James M'Bey, Sir D.Y. Cameron, and several more, by the facts that they are already at least sufficiently well-known and that my criticism of them would have been more adverse than in these other cases); the sculpture of William Lamb and Benno Schotz; the typographical genius of James Guthrie; the terpsichorean genius of Isadora Duncan; the pianistic genius of Frederick Lamond; the place in German, and European, letters of that extraordinary 'translated' Scot, John Henry Mackay; the Credit Reform proposals of Major C.H. Douglas; the personality of Willa Muir, whom I consider to be the most brilliant of living Scotswomen; the polyglot powers of the veteran Principal Sir Donald MacAlister, to whose Russian translations *The Slavonic Review* recently paid a well-deserved compliment; the scholarship and critical power of Professor H.J.C. Grierson; the epigrammatic faculty of Lord Dewar; the anecdotal prowess of the Marquis of Aberdeen and Temair and his peer, Sir James Taggart, and, along with them perhaps, the Marquis of Huntley; the – what can I call it? – of the Countess of Oxford; the philosophies of the Earl of Balfour, Lord Haldane, Professors Pringle Pattison and J.Y. Simpson; the political importance of James Maxton and John Wheatley; the influence of Professor J.S. Phillimore; the diverse work of such men as the veteran Professor Patrick Geddes, Professor J. Arthur Thompson, Professor Allardyce Nicoll, Ramsay Macdonald, J.L. Baird (with his invention of 'television'), Sir D.M. Stevenson, Martin Anderson ('Cynicus'), David Alec Wilson (the monumental biographer of Carlyle), and Allan Barns Graham; the comedic talent of Will Fyffe, if not Sir Harry Lauder – all

---

[1] In the event, forty-eight articles appeared. – Ed.

these, at least, one would fain have taken in at a first glance over the field of contemporary Scottish Arts and affairs. There are many others who bulk largely whose proportions one would fain have reduced to make more perceptible the worthier figures they are obscuring; these I need not mention here.

But while these articles were being written others with whom I would, or should, have dealt have been removed by death and so have fallen outwith my range. I regret especially that a volume of mine dealing so largely with Scottish letters should have had no more than merely passing references to William Archer, W.P. Ker, Roger Quinn, Duncan M'Naught, Hector Macpherson, Theodore Napier, and, to go further back, Thomas Common, the translator of Neitzche – for one of the difficulties I have encountered lies in the fact that a leeway extending over decades has been established so that when men such as some of these (Common, for example) die they do not take the place in our history they deserve – they lapse into a limbo and the impression of Scottish life and letters over the period to which they belonged which any stranger, or, for the matter of that, without independent and difficult research, any Scot can secure is merely one of chaos in which even size-able names fail to appear except from any but the Kailyaird angle, which throws into grotesque disproportion either the wrong people or, infre-quently, the wrong aspects of the right people. Of these more recent dead I should have liked in particular to have dealt at some length with James Mavor, and, above all, James Murdoch, the historian of Japan, that extraordinary man, at one time a Professor of Greek, at another a member of a communist colony in Paraguay, and finally a recluse in Japan (although he died in Australia) but, as a recent writer has put it, 'still the cottar's son, even to the woollen "gravat" round his neck.' As typical, and infinitely more valuable, a Scot than Sir Harry Lauder or the late Andrew Carnegie!

Not only are there such omissions, then, in these pages, but I am acutely conscious that readers who are not Scots – and, to scarcely any less a degree, readers who are Scots – will seldom be able to supply the appropriate background to what I write. There is an unbridged gulf. It is impossible without specialised study to connect up such modern issues as these with which I am dealing with a sense of Scottish continuity. Even in Scotland the history of the country, either in its cultural or other aspects, is almost wholly unappreciated; the most ludicrous misappre-hensions as to the history of slightly more remote periods are prevalent (*The Scottish Historical Review* in one recent issue destroyed no fewer than three long-standing mistakes in regard to Scottish History); and in regard to current affairs, journalism, politics, and other factors are so disposed as to engage Scottish minds with anything and everything rather than a good all-round view of their own national position. The process of assimilation inherent in the terms of the Treaty of Union – and accelerated by means which were in violation of such safeguarding clauses as the Treaty did contain – has made it practically impossible for the majority even of Scottish people, living in Scotland, to 'think Scottish.' Space was not allowed me here to effectively fill in the great majority of these blanks – to relate such things as the so-called 'Irish Invasion' of Scotland (destined in my opinion to be the best thing that has happened to it for over 200 years at least), the emergence of the 'Glasgow Reds,' the depopulation of the Highlands and Islands, the tyrannous and demoralising centripetalism of London, the Rosyth scandal, and so forth, to each other and to a comprehensive national programme – let alone setting them in their historical perspective, a process which, had I begun it, would have led me to fall foul of history as it is taught in Scottish schools, whether as Scottish History or English History, or European History, almost in its entirety. Nor, in so far as aesthetic and cultural issues were concerned, could I use the illustrations or indicate the ideas which I would have used or indicated had I been writing for a public who are not soon out of their depth in the veriest shallows of modern, or, indeed, any literature or ideology. The Scottish teaching profession – to whom *The Scottish Educational Journal* appeals – are on the whole the best educated and most open-minded reading public available in Scotland: but literature with the exception of those writers whom it is educational practice in Scottish schools to regard as classics and a certain proportion of the more popular writers of the day (that is to say English, or in an odd case, French writers, along with a few recollections of chance reading outwith the beaten track in College days) is outwith their ken, and the same applies to art, music, and affairs – except perhaps E.I.S. affairs. In these circumstances I was severely handicapped, and it is only fair to myself that I should say so. Nor was my task lightened by an occasional bit of moral censorship; my article on Muriel Stuart, for example, would have been rather longer but for the excision of a passage in which I examined a quotation from her poems alongside one of Milton's. Both dealt with Sex; and this volume ought certainly to have had an article on The Sexual History of Scotland. The Scottish atmosphere will not be effectively improved until our tacit Comstockery – with which, in a more explicit form in America, H.L.

Mencken deals so effectively – has been dragged out into the light and examined unflinchingly.

Perhaps the greatest omission in this volume is an adequate account of the contemporary Gaelic movement and of contemporary Gaelic literature. On the whole, however, it may be said that Gaelic letters to-day are pretty much in the position of Braid Scots letters – whatever is being done, except in rare instances, has practically no purely literary or artistic value. It is done in the traditional forms and lacks the breath of life – the contemporary application. It is not joining issue with Scottish life to-day in any way. In Gaelic drama recently rather more is being done; and certainly one great play has been produced, far greater than any in Braid Scots or English by any living Scots dramatist – *Crois-Tara!* (*The Fiery Cross*, a play of the time of the '45) by Domhnull Mac-na-Ceardadh, who has also written distinguished verse. Other living Gaelic dramatists are Eachann MacDhughaill, John W. Macleod, Mairi A. Chaimbeul, and John Maccormick, who has also written a Gaelic novel, a real heroic tale, in *Dun-Aluinn*, as has Angus Robertson in his *An t-Ogha Mor* (1913). But I have not dealt with modern Gaelic letters here – or the work of An Comunn Gaidhealach – because to do so would have involved raising all manner of questions which could only have been dealt with adequately in a book devoted to themselves. The position and prospects of modern Gaelic literature can only be appreciated in the light of a knowledge of the cultural traditions of the Gaels and to that – vital as it is to any thought of a big Scottish Renaissance Movement and the re-establishment of an independent Scottish nation – the majority of the issues with which I have chosen to deal in the meantime have only an ultimate relationship. I have, however, dealt with issues which, concerning as they do the majority of the people now living in Scotland, are, in my opinion, preliminary to any effective re-emergence either in the political or cultural fields of the Gaelic elements, or, to use a better phrase, our Gaelic background.

It is in the nature of things, too, that some of the parts of these chapters are already behind the times. Developments have taken place in the interval between their appearance in *The Scottish Educational Journal* and here. William Jeffrey, for example, has strengthened his position greatly with his *The Doom of Atlas* (Gowans and Gray, 1926) and more recent poems. Lewis Spence is heading a new Scottish National Movement which is developing promisingly in certain districts. And so on. Details such as these could be multiplied. Perhaps the most important thing is the successful development of a social side to the Scottish

Renaissance Movement in entertainments similar in kind to those given by the Sitwell Group in the New Chenil Galleries in London. In Burgess Scott the Movement has found an artiste capable of 'putting over' the new products in Scottish Poetry and Music to a wide public. Personal contact is a great solvent of the difficulties of new techniques, and Mrs Scott's singing is likely to evoke an immediate response on the part of the public which may have important results. Hitherto the difficulty has been to get an artiste who would risk novel numbers instead of playing to the gallery with old favourites, and, in the case of F.G. Scott's song settings this was accentuated by their demand for a dramatic rendition running counter to the determination of almost all singers to preserve a 'beautiful vocal line.' Joseph Hislop, J.A. Campbell, Roy Henderson and other Scottish singers who ought to be singing Scott's songs presumably will not do it for these two reasons. So far he has not found a male inter-preter; that is to say that the best of his work has never been sung in public. Miss Boyd Steven sang a few of his songs very successfully; Miss Ursula Greville in New York and elsewhere was even more successful. Miss Helen Henschell, the distinguished auto-accompanist, would prob-ably prove an ideal exponent of them. So does Mrs Scott.

Another development – to the debit rather than the credit side of the Movement – is the reversion of Mr D. Glen Mackemmie from the Chairmanship to the Secretaryship of the Scottish National Players, and the probability that a return to repertory is intended. Little although the S.N.P. have done for Scottish drama – and little though they seemed likely to do – this is unfortunate. It means that those who have hitherto put the object of achieving a Scottish National Drama first have given way to those whose position is that 'We are only too anxious for Scottish Drama – if we can get it – but we are not going to prefer nationalism to art.' It does not seem to occur to these people that that is precisely what they are doing – other people's nationalism, which has produced art, as Scottish nation-alism can do, in its own, probably very different way, only if there is adequate concentration on that object and on the overcoming of whatever has prevented its development in the past.

The whole position, which this book has been written to manifest, is excellently summarised by Mr Lewis Spence in a recent letter to the Press, in the course of which he says: –

> I advocate the employment and teaching of the Scots Vernacular side by side with standard English, not as a substitute for it. All Scottish people should be bilingual. If they were the general verbal stock

would be immensely enriched, and in any case Scots is the true and
natural psychological language of North Britain. It has been observed
a hundred times by competent critics that no Scotsman can ever
acquire an irreproachable grasp of English as a spoken or written
language... What Mr Grieve and I do desire is to see a new psychological approach manifested in Scots verse. During the last quarter of
a century Scottish literature has done little to attract the attention of
the world of culture. It has certainly failed to appeal to European
imagination as the Irish or Norwegian literatures have appealed. The
crass sentimentalities and utter banalities of the Kailyard School
alienated from the first sympathies of critics of taste and insight.
Scotsmen of perspicacity and experience could not but feel depressed
at the popular vogue of a cult which they were aware frequently
afforded only a base caricature of their countrymen, paving the way
for the grosser tradition of Lauderism. Nor to Scotsmen of liberal
views did the somewhat artless impulse to concentrate the entire
literary thought and homage of the nation upon the achievement of
Robert Burns, however great, appear as likely to be conducive to the
healthy or catholic expansion of Scottish literary life or activity. Those
of them, more familiar with the genius and tradition of the older and
more courtly Scottish poets, Douglas, Hendryson [*sic*], Dunbar, and
Lyndesay, and with the tradition, magical and intense, of the northern
balladeers, recognised in these a spirit as genuinely native and technically more worthy of affection and close study than the mark of their
successors. While worshipping Burns, 'this side idolatry,' they wholeheartedly detested the host of uninspired plagiarists who succeeded
him and deplored the descent of Scottish poetry into an abyss of infamous cliché and mechanical reiteration. It was, indeed, inevitable
that the whole race of poetasters should have misconstrued and
misapprehended the essentials of the Burnsian composition,
confounding as they did an inspired simplicity, a great lyric artlessness, with mere banality. Incapable of discerning the true merits of a
tonic gift, the quality of which probably remains unsurpassed, they
laboured under the delusion that anything couched in Scots most
naturally possess an equal excellence with the effortless cadences of a
great natural artist, who sang as spontaneously and with all the
perfervid enchantment of a thrush in a morning garden. From the
death of Burns to the end of the late War may, perhaps, be regarded
as the most jejune and uninspired period in Scottish letters. Not only
was it parasitical to a great name in a manner that scarcely any other

literature can ever have been, its history was almost utterly devoid of those frequent regroupings and reorientations of the literary elements which are regarded by the superficial as the manifestations of originality; for, though 'originality' is actually incapable of attainment, the surest sign of artistic vitality is its endeavour. This, within the period alluded to, was almost wholly invisible, and old men, and some young ones, maundered on in the Burns tradition. But 'the War changed all that.' It achieved what nothing else could have achieved, because it removed for a while large numbers of Scots from the Caledonian scene, and permitted them a view of a larger world; and this estrangement had the effect it ever has on the Scottish mind – a marked quickening of the patriotic sense, mingled with a desire for new things.[1]

It is with these post-War developments – and the way in which what preceded them in regard to Scottish arts and affairs during the past two or three decades appears in the light of these developments – that I am concerned here. This is the first book devoted to contemporary Scottish literature, except a small volume published in 1917 by W.M. Parker devoted to short studies of twelve authors, eight of whom are dead and therefore outwith my range. I would also draw attention, however, to an important article on the subject: 'Le Groupe de "la Renaissance Ecossaise,"' by Professor Denis Saurat, now of London University, which appeared in the *Revue Anglo-Americaine* in April, 1924; to a later and more comprehensive study, which appeared under the title of 'Bokmentavakningin skoza' in the January-March, 1926, issue of the Icelandic quarterly, *Eimreidin*, by Alexander M'Gill, who is rapidly taking the place in regard to Scandinavian studies of the late W.P. Ker, and who has written, in his recent Fanad studies, some of the most delightful descriptive prose by any modern Scottish writer; to the articles in recent (1925 and 1926) issues of *The Scots Magazine* on Contemporary Scottish authors by Marion Lochhead and on recent developments of Scottish poetry by Charles Graves, himself a young poet of distinction, whose first book, *The Bamboo Grove* (Cape) attracted much favourable attention; to the penetrating article on 'The Scottish Literary Renaissance' by Lewis Spence in the (July, 1926) *Nineteenth Century and After*; and to the exceedingly able and dynamic study of 'Scottish Poetry of To-day' in the *Burns Chronicle* (which has taken a new lease of life, and re-oriented itself, to accord with a cult which is rapidly ceasing to be merely convivial and antiquarian and becoming a

[1] Cf. 'The Burns Cult (I)' (23.7.26). – Ed.

literary and nationalist movement, under the editorship of Mr J.C. Ewing) of 1916 by Robert Bain, the Poetry Critic of the *Glasgow Herald*, to which he has long contributed much of the very finest appreciation and analysis of contemporary verse to be found anywhere.

In conclusion here, I would say that I have not been able to ascertain whether Roy Campbell, the author of 'The Flaming Terrapin,' is a Scotsman or not; and that I have been unable to devote any attention to American and Colonial writers of Scottish descent or any consideration to the Scottish elements in such English poets as Gordon Bottomley, Lascelles Abercrombie, and Walter de la Mare.

II 'Conclusion'
(from Contemporary Scottish Studies, 1926) by Hugh MacDiarmid (C.M. Grieve)

I

The Burns Movement – The Next Step? Within the past year or so the Burns Cult, with its world-wide clubs, has been rapidly reorienting itself, and has put the revival of the Vernacular in the forefront of its programme. It is becoming to an increasing extent a Scottish literary and national movement and not just an organisation for maintaining an Annual Dinner and orgy of indiscriminate eulogy, and for the bibliographical and antiquarian study and preservation of Burnsiana. It may be that through a new address to Burns' great ideal of Universal Brotherhood the Scottish psychology will yet realise in an higher fashion that is connoted in mere ubiquity or even in success in commerce and engineering its world-function, and become, not merely cosmopolitan, but – they are part and parcel of each other, and opposed to cosmopolitanism or imperialism – national and international. Alongside this reorientation has come a new attitude to Burns himself – not the old stupid provincial idolatry, but a reconsideration of his place and power on purely literary grounds. The new disposition of the activities of the Cult is attracting a new type of speaker and writer of a higher cultural calibre. It is becoming widely recognised that the day is past for rehashing the personalia – rewhitewashing or redenigrating the Bard – and that the time has come to consider his quality and methods as a poet, his comparative international status, the influence he has had on Scottish life and letters, the way in which he handled the Vernacular, to appreciate his limitations as well as his powers, and to resume him into his proper historical setting and see him in that. The application of modern critical methods to Burns and his work cannot be long delayed. In the meantime, there is a decreasing inclination to abide by his practice in regard to the Vernacular and in regard to verse-forms and subject-matter. So far as Vernacular Revival is concerned, the majority of Scots interested in it are still almost hopelessly handicapped by their ignorance of European literary history. They have a great deal to learn, for example, from the *landsmaal* movement in Norway, the Catalan movement, and the way in which Russian was made a complete, and perhaps unparalleled, literary medium no longer ago than the nineteenth century – and especially perhaps from the *zaumny* and *skaz* experiments of such recent Russian writers as Khlébnikov and Remizov. The idea of a synthetic Scots is rapidly gaining ground, however, amongst the younger intellectuals; it is significant to find School and College magazines begin to appear, wholly or partially, in Braid Scots – this although few or no questions in regard to Scottish literature are set in examination-papers and Scottish classics are not available in handy form for school use. Educational publishers realise, however, that the demand is growing – that increasing numbers of Scottish school children and students are studying the Scottish language and literature outwith school hours – and that it is high time the Scottish Board of Education allocated a compartment in every school and training centre time-table to these subjects. In the meantime, commercial caution is causing them to wait in the hope that some such definite rearrangement will be made and that every examination-paper will contain at least one question on Scottish language and literature. But the movement is developing, and if the educational authorities do not move in keeping with it, the time may speedily come when educational publishers will be prepared to inaugurate series of Scottish national text-books without any such official guarantee. A few 'die-hards,' such as Alexander Keith, adjudicating as Scots assessors at Musical Festivals, are still to be heard enjoining their auditors to 'be careful not to mix their dialects' – in other words, not to work back from the bits to the whole; not to enrich Scots as English and most other languages have enriched themselves. The tercentenary of the death of Luis de Gongora y Argote falls to be observed next year (1927), and Mr Keith and his friends may be advised to perpend, and apply to the Scottish position to-day, what Laurie Magnus, a sufficiently Conservative writer, says of him in his *Dictionary of European Literature*:

Gongora's 'vice' was to play with the words themselves; to introduce strange words; to use forced combinations; somehow, and ultimately, anyhow, to cause surprise by unexpectedness, and thus to attain to a style so obscure, so allusive, so much involved, as to perplex even the learned audience of cultivated linguists to whom his poems were addressed. What of the object of it in the first place? Plainly, no poet of genius would practise Gongorism out of sheer malice; and Gongora's purpose was clearly enough to supple and diversify the resources of the literary language of Spain. It was capable of extension and enlargement; of Grecisms, Latinisms, Italicisms; of borrowings of vocabulary and construction from languages which had proved themselves capable of a more perfect literature than Spain had yet produced. In a sense Meredith was a Gongorist, as Rabelais had been before him; and though all obscurity is not Gongorism, all Gongorism is obscure. Every great writer who is dissatisfied with the powers of the language in which he writes, who finds some words worn by use and others inadequate for emphasis, and who tries to supply such shortcomings by new formations or new combinations, is doing work which will bear future fruit, however much ridicule it may arouse in the present by its more or less violent breach with current usage. A Gongorist is strictly an alturist, though his conscious motives may be mixed. He is risking contemporary misunderstanding, even personal obloquy, for the sake of enriching the inheritance which he administers in his generation. [1]

And that, so far as the Vernacular is concerned, is the course to which Scottish literature is at last – and, happily, without being too late – committed, despite the protestations of its stick-in-the-muds.

II

So much for the Burns Cult!

Is it desirable that there should be a return, especially on the part of the Scottish people, to Scott? Efforts are being made in certain quarters to revive interest in his work, and, in particular, the Waverley Novels. Very diverse writers have recently been claiming that he is greater than Burns, with the implication that Scott and Burns ought to be drastically regraded in popular esteem. It is noteworthy, however, that the writers in question (scarcely one of whom, incidentally, is even a second-ranker either as critic or creator) are all either English or Anglo-Scottish littera-

---

[1] Cf. 'Towards a Synthetic Scots' (13.8.26). – Ed

teurs (meaning by Anglo-Scottish litterateurs writers whose reputations, such as they are, are bound up with the English literary tradition rather than with the quite distinct, if admittedly infinitely inferior, Scots literary tradition). The movement to reinstate Scott in critical esteem and popular regard must therefore be regarded as one designed to conserve and reinforce certain elements in English culture, while taking it for granted that Scotland and England have identical cultural interests. But should this be taken for granted?

English literature to-day may be tending in directions that are undesirable in themselves or, at all events, at variance with its great central traditions; and some such corrective as that which has spontaneously generated this re-appreciation of Scott (or some qualities in Scott) in certain quarters, may be required. To these central traditions of English literature as distinct from Scottish, the bulk of Scott – all but an almost infinitesimal residuum – may, or rather must, be conceded; Burns, on the other hand, belongs mainly to Scots literature. At the moment when, belatedly, tendencies, however tentative to a Scottish Literary Revival, are manifesting themselves, it is peculiarly necessary to ensure that English literary traditions are not recouping themselves by means which are likely to prevent the emergence of the diametrically opposed tendencies upon which the development of distinctively Scottish literature depends. In Scotland itself, at any rate, there should be jealousy to see, since distinctively English forces have so long and so tremendously dominated British literature, that the continued paramountcy of the Southern partner in our most unequal alliance is not any longer ensured by any failure to detect and urge the specific, if contrary, interests of those purely Scottish elements which may have the potentiality of liberating forces capable in the long run of redressing the cultural balance between the two nations.

What factors have been responsible for developing a very great literature in England and a very meagre one in Scotland? Upon the answer to this question depends the question of whether a 'Back to Scott' movement is politic in Scotland to-day. It is noteworthy that Mr Baldwin, Lord Sands, Mr John Buchan, and Sheriff Jameson (all, be it noted, politically at variance with that strongest factor in Scottish politics which is vetoed and denied expression by the overwhelming English Conservative majority at Westminster) who have recently been eulogising Scott – eulogies generally accompanied by a depreciation of distinctively contemporary tendencies in literature – have done so in an almost nakedly reactionary manner, with their eye on certain social and political effects rather than upon cultural goods. They are not advancing any new view of Scott – any special applicability to the present and the future of elements in Scott hitherto overlooked or misprized. On the contrary, they have been praising him anew for the very qualities for which he has always been praised – his 'large sanity', his 'common-sense,' his judicial blend of the educative and the entertaining. The claim that Scott is greater than Burns, advanced by Mrs Virginia Woolf and others, takes its rise from like considerations in the minds of more purely literary and more wholly English people who seek a neo-classical movement.

From the point of view of the Scottish Renaissance Movement, however, these very qualities of Scott's are those which, in unique disproportion in our race, have prevented our developing those imaginative and purely artistic qualities which might have produced a Scots literature proportionate to English, and which, while gaining us a reputation even in our own minds for shrewdness, economy, and industry, have robbed Scotland of the backbone of its population, given us the worst slums in Europe, and filled them with aliens, and handed over vast areas of our country to soap-kings and pickle-manufacturers as sports-grounds – a transformation of Scotland not quite compensated for by a fatuous love of country wholly divorced from realities. The two things go together; and the angle from which all interested in the movement for the revival of Scottish Nationalism will naturally scrutinise Scott to-day is that indicated by Mr Edwin Muir, where he says, 'Scott achieved classical prose, prose with the classical qualities of solidity, force, and measure, only when he wrote in the Scottish dialect; his Scottish dialect is great prose, and his one essay in Scottish imaginative literature, "Wandering Willie's Tale," is a masterpiece of prose, of prose which one must go back to the seventeenth century to parallel.' From the point of view of pure art, Scott's Anglicisation – and those principles which drove him into those methods of composition which gave us the Waverley Novels – represents the greatest loss Scottish literature has sustained in its chequered course; under happier circumstances he might almost have been to it what Shakespeare is to English. Personally, I would gladly scrap the whole of the rest of his output for a dozen such Tales.

It is, at all events, significant to note that the point of view of the Scottish Renaissance Movement in regard to Scott coincides with that of the two great contemporary European critics, Georg Brandes and Croce, and is at complete variance with that of Lord Sands, Sheriff Jameson, and others. Croce and Brandes are the opposite poles of

European criticism – they approach Scott from entirely different directions – but come to identical conclusions, as all real literary critics must.
Political, social, moral, and other extraneous elements have corrupted
the literary criticism of John Buchan, Virginia Woolf and others, competent enough in a very minor degree on subjects where they can discard
such 'blinkers.' No doubt Lord Sands – and perhaps Sheriff Jameson –
think their opinions quite as important, if not more so, than Croce's or
Brandes'. It is useless to discuss the matter.

So far as Scott is concerned, Brandes sums him up by saying that he is
the kind of author whom 'every adult has read, and no grown-up person
can read.' Croce also describes his work as unreadable, but ends with an
appeal for mercy, on the ground that a writer who delighted our parents
and grand-parents 'does not deserve harsh treatment from their children
and grandchildren.' This is an appeal we would be more ready to
respond to if reactionary people in our own country were not always
using him to whip up popular sentiment and prejudice against new
creative tendencies. But neither Croce nor Brandes has anything to say
about Scott as a poet. It never occurred to them that at this time of day
any sane person would consider him as such. That high distinction is left
for Sheriff Jameson.

I need say nothing of the R.L. Stevenson movement, 'run' by such
people as Mr J. Mullo Weir and Miss Rosaline Masson; it is analogous to
the Burns and Scott Cults but feebler and more futile – as are the other
imitative glorifications of poetasters like Tannahill. There is, and can be,
little in any of these 'stunts' beneficial to Scottish arts and affairs.

III

One of the most amusing things that has happened recently in Scotland
was the burning in effigy of Dr Pittendrigh Macgillivray by the Glasgow
art students! Why? What had the splendid gladiator done? He had
ventured to ask if art in Glasgow had suffered a lapse. Even so he
commented on the fashion in which art flourished in Glasgow as against
a region (Edinburgh) where little productive work could be done in a
sterilising atmosphere of social precedence and the bible of 'Who's
Who.' But stood Glasgow where it did in art-life forty years ago; in the
fighting days of the old 'Gluepots' and the young 'Glasgow Green' boys;
the extraordinary and redoubtable warrior, Craibe Angus; and the extra-
militant 'Scottish Art Review' of the first issues? Had it not gone under a
little? Instead of a brilliant coterie of about a dozen firebrands, nearly
every one of whom made his autographic firemark on the Scottish art-

log of his time, they had now, like every other big city in the country, a huge art-school, and, as a result, the illuminated among them must surely admit they had a tiresome plethora of petty picture-makers, many of whom were as clever and slick as they were vacuous.

Dr Macgillivray was, of course, right. The Art Schools are doing in their field just what the Musical Festivals are doing in theirs, and Miss Marjorie Gullan's lachrymose poetry-reading movement (under the patronage of English poetasters) is doing in a contiguous one, and what the Scottish Folk Dance Society is doing in another (since the old movements are simply an acquired accomplishment, not a spontaneous or natural manifestation of contemporary psychology).

'Art Schools are not, and seem unlikely ever to be,' said Dr Macgillivray in a subsequent communication to *The Glasgow Herald*, 'in effect, what was expected. The education business – School Board and University – all round is little better than a beautifully painted balloon, the pricking of which is about due.'

'It has always been held,' says A.S. Neill,

> that Scotland is far in advance of England in education. The Englishman who refuses to allow a Scot a sense of humour grudgingly admits that Scotland is better educated than England, and according to our present interpretation of education, Scotland certainly is. Scotland's success in Leaving Certificates, University Prelims., M.A. Degrees, is great. Any village cobbler will tell you that 'M.A.'s in Scotland are as common as dugs gaen bare-fut.' Surely we are an instructed nation. But the disturbing question arises – Is an M.A. educated?... Let us be honest and confess that our boasted Scottish Education is only learning. Let us be bold enough to say that our Leavings and M.A. standard is a curse. It is a curse, for it conveys a subtle sense of finality: 'I've graduated; I'm an educated man.' But even from the narrow point of view of learning, an M.A. Degree is a very little thing... I willingly admit that England has a similar standard of education. But the protest against education in the South is stronger than in the North. Experimental schools, so-called, are more popular in England. England is going ahead, while Scotland rests on its Leavings oars. I grant you that the experimental school is usually a timid attempt to patch up the old Ford. It clutches the Dalton Plan to its heart, dimly realising that the Dalton Plan is only a trick to make the old education look attractive. Nevertheless the experimental school has shown many advances – there is no punishment, no

reward; the child is free to be natural, although not to send Mathematics to the Devil; and there is a strong desire to make education fit the child and not make the child fit education. When I was lecturing in a Scots city at Christmas, a doctor friend said to me: 'In this town is a headmaster who beats the children frightfully.' Again and again I have his pupils come to me suffering from neurosis, but I cannot do anything. The law is on his side; he is allowed to punish! I told my friend that in Holland, Germany, and Austria, when teachers asked me if we still had corporal punishment in Scotland, I felt miserable in answering that we had. In these countries a teacher dare not strike a pupil. The pity is, not that there are teachers in Scotland who leather, but that public opinion in Scotland is indifferent to such methods. Education in Scotland is merely a displaced Calvinism. The E.I.S. discusses salaries, but it does not discuss child psychology. The educational paper of Scotland has more interest in Geography than in behaviour. And it may be Calvinism that prevents Scotland from seeing that creation is of more importance than learning; for Calvinism had not much use for art at any time. But modern psychology has shown us that emotion, not intellect, is the driving force in life. A child expresses emotion in making a boat, but not in working out a problem in Euclid. It is in creation that Scottish education fails lamentably. There is about half-an-ounce of creation in the Higher Leavings. True there are woodwork departments where boys learn to mortise, where each lad makes his correct pen-tray, instead of making his boat a kite. Creation must have absolute freedom of choice at all times... So long as Scotland is proud of her education, so long she will remain behind in the things that matter. When she asks herself the question, What is education? and cannot answer it, then will she be on the way to progress. For no one can say what education is. The whole trend of the new movement is to wipe out our adult ideas about what children ought to learn and do. We do not know what a child ought to learn and do. Our education together with European education brought the War. Less boldly one can at least claim that education did not prevent the War. We have failed to clean our civilisation of slums and prostitution and crime and robbery, and when we set out to tell a child how to live and what to learn we are humbugs and fools. We do not know where a child is going, and yet we attempt to guide him. We do not know what is right and what is wrong, and yet we teach children morals. We are all humbugs, and our Leavings and Degrees make us dangerous humbugs, for they make us fancy that we speak with authority. The only possible way in education is to stand by, and allow the child to learn what he likes. Compulsion, in the form of punishment, moral suasion, Leaving Certificates, time-tables, belongs to yesterday. The education of to-morrow will be free. It hurts me to think that England's vision is wider than that of my own country.

And, on top of that, Scots who still boast of the virtues of Scottish education, may well be asked to read William Bolitho's 'Cancer of Empire,' and prove their worth by devising a solution for the appalling problems of the Glasgow backlands (unamenable to any solution within the limits of the existing economic system) depicted there. Not only have we almost unparalleled slum problems in Scotland, greater unemployment than in England, and a continuous drain of emigration which is removing the best of our stock, but our rural problem is an unspeakable scandal. A recent writer on 'Scotland To-day' in the *Observer* (there was a brief spell of unusual interest in Scottish affairs in the London Press about a year ago – as a rule there is none; Irish letters, like Paris letters, flourish, but who ever heard of a Scottish letter?) puts the last in a nutshell:

Suppose that the sporting rights were bought out, lock, stock and barrel, and the Highlands thrown open to the recreation of Scotland and all the world? Suppose that they were thronged with the holiday traffic that fills Switzerland and Norway and swarms over the French Pyrenees? The deer and the grouse would be gone, and their respective slayers, and the rents which they pay, and there would be a big hole in the rate-book. But would no 'rateable values' arise to fill the void? I have never heard that Switzerland was other than a 'business proposition.' The well-equipped Pyrenees are always extending their tourist accommodation, and the prosperity engendered by cheap catering in Norway is equally significant. But it is clear that the eviction by purchase of the sporting interest would leave the way open for a tripartite Highland economy of crofting, forestry, and recreation. The crofts would be greatly enriched by an extension of pasture; afforestation would develop the kind of settlements where the convenience of the pedestrian, the cyclist, and the general tourist would be most easily provided; and the three interests would dovetail into each other as they do in every country where the same conditions exist. And what about the money? A Departmental Committee reported in 1921 that the total assessed rental of the deer forests was £119,543.

Before the War it was £171,438, and it is apt to vary according to the economic weather and the fluctuations of American tastes. To put the matter in the least favourable light, let us call it £200,000. There is no available aggregate for grouse shootings, but it is less, the Committee tells us, than that of the forests. Call it another £200,000. Salmon fishings account for less than £80,000 – a figure I should have rejected as too low, had it not been carefully worked out for me by the best possible authority. The whole thing lies within the compass of an annual sum of half-a-million – scarcely a camel to swallow where modern public finance is confronted with a question of national policy. There I leave the case with only two observations: I have been astonished at the number of responsible people in Scotland who described the sporting interest as a 'curse,' agreed in principle with the policy suggested, and were at first incredulous of the limited cost. And I believe the political and social psychology of Scotland will never be stable till this 'tooth' comes out.

But I would invite Scottish interest in even more far-reaching proposals – those of Major C.H. Douglas, which may well be discerned in retrospect as having been one of the great contributions of re-oriented Scottish genius to world-affairs. His constructive proposals, says A.R. Orage,

concern mainly the only practically important question asked by every consumer – the question of price; and beyond a change in our present price-fixing system, there is in his proposals nothing remotely revolutionary. For the rest, everything would go on as now. There would be no expropriation of anybody, no new taxes, no change of management in industry, no new political party; no change, in fact, in the status or privileges of any of the existing factors of industry. Absolutely nothing would be changed but prices. But what a change would be there! Major Douglas's calm assumption is that from to-morrow morning, as the shops open, the prices of all retail articles could be marked down by at least a half and thereafter progressively reduced, say, every quarter – and not only without bankrupting anybody, but at an increasing profit to everybody without exception. Absolutely nobody need suffer that everybody should be gratified. All that would happen to anybody is that the purchasing power of whatever money they have would be doubled to-morrow, and thereafter continuously increased. Not to put too great a strain upon credulity or suspense, I may explain here that the principle of the proposal is perfectly simple, and it consists of this – that prices ought to fall as our communal powers of production increase.

I do not intend here to detail or discuss Major Douglas's proposals any further; but – while under no more delusion than Orage himself as to the probability of sufficient brain-power developing in Great Britain or elsewhere in the next century to put the Douglas System into operation – I want to record my unqualified pride and joy in the fact that of all the people in the world a Scotsman – one of the race which has been (and remains) most hag-ridden by commercial Calvinism, with its hideous doctrines of the 'need to work,' 'the necessity of drudgery,' and its devices of thrift and the whole tortuous paraphernalia of modern capitalism – should have absolutely 'got to the bottom of economics' and shown the way to the Workless State.

IV

Finally, it may be observed that in the conclusion of his preface to his *Dictionary of European Literature*, Laurie Magnus says:

> It would be interesting to try to discover from this comparative study a clue to the *future* of European literature. It has made its way through so many inhibitions, ecclesiastical and civil, that the problem of the course it will pursue after the last war of liberation from authority is particularly fascinating. Changing values need not be disappearing values, and the real interest of the lives of Abelard, Dante, Reuchlin, Tasso, Rabelais, More, Corneille, Milton, Heine – to name a few among many – does not lie in the stones in their path, but in the path which they carved through the stones. The mind of Europe has found expression, despite obstacles and obscurantism, and its greater freedom in the present century will not be strange to the voices of the past. Possibly, the new renaissance will spring in one of the smaller countries, redeemed or restored in recent years.

Oswald Spengler hazards a similar speculation. May it not be in Scotland that the next great Culture will arise? There can, at all events, be no doubt that if an adequate group of the younger Scottish authors and artists who are now manifesting themselves got together and determined to take up the distinctive threads of Scottish culture where the Union severed them – to undo the work of the eighteenth century, and, to a large extent, of the reformation – and to develop their arts and affairs in accordance with Scottish psychology without reference to England – the resolution of the diverse inhibitions which have so long and so completely restricted Scottish genius (a resolution they could hardly fail to accomplish in adequate measure if they made it, and no other, their conscious objective) would disclose a more important world-destiny for Scotland than even to keep on supplying England with its materialistic brains – a destiny more in keeping with the world-estimate of the Scottish genius than the actual condition of affairs from which that is derived.

III 'Books to Read'
(from Contemporary Scottish Studies, 1926)
by Hugh MacDiarmid (C.M. Grieve)

The following books – by no means a complete list – are suggested as affording a basis for an understanding of the past and present position of Scottish arts and affairs in their relation to each other, or for the further study of some of the special issues touched upon in the foregoing chapters. Titles already mentioned in the text have, however, not been repeated in this list.

ART

Scottish Painters, a Critical Study, by Walter Armstrong (London, 1888).

History of Art in Scotland: Its Origin and Progress, by Robert Brydall (Blackwood, 1889).

Modern Scottish Portrait Painters, with an Introductory Essay by Percy Bate (Edinburgh, 1910).

BIBLIOGRAPHY AND PRINTING

Annals of Scottish Printing from the Introduction of the Art in 1507 to the Beginnings of the Seventeenth Century, by Robert Dickson and John Philip Edmond (Cambridge, 1890).

A List of Books Printed in Scotland before 1706, including those printed furth of the Realm for Scottish Booksellers, by Harry G. Aldis (Printed for Edinburgh Bibliographical Society, 1904).

Edinburgh Bibliographical Society Publications (Bibliographies of Mary Queen of Scots, the Darien Scheme, Aberdeen Universities, Solemn League and Covenant, Burns, Holyrood and Rae Presses, etc.).

A Bibliograhy of Middle Scots Poets, by Wm. Geddie, M.A. (Scottish History Society, 1912).

Records of Glasgow Bibliographical Society.

A Catalogue of the Publications of Scottish Historical and Kindred Clubs and Societies, and of the volumes relative to Scottish History, issued by H.M. Stationery Office, 1780-1908, by Professor Charles Sanford Terry (Maclehose, 1909).

Bibliotheca Scotica (Messrs John Smith & Co., Glasgow, 1926).

Typographia Scoto-Gadelica (1567-1917), by Donald Maclean (Edinburgh, 1915).

LANGUAGE AND LITERATURE

Scottish Chap-Book Literature, by William Harvey (Paisley, 1903).

The Devotional Literature of Scotland, by Rev. Dr Adam Philip (London).

Records of Early Drama in Scotland, by Anna J. Mill (St Andrews University – now being printed).

The Story of the Scots Stage, by Robb Lawson (Paisley, 1917).

Scottish Literature, by Professor G. Gregory Smith (Macmillan, 1919).

Specimens of Middle Scots with Historical Introduction and Glossarial Notes, by Professor Gregory Smith (Blackwood, 1902).

Scottish Men of Letters in the Eighteenth Century, by Henry Grey Graham (Black, 1908).

Manual of Modern Scots, with Glossary by Wm. Grant and Dixon Scott (Cambridge Press, 1921).

'For Puir Auld Scotland's Sake' (Literary Essays), by 'Hugh Halliburton' (1887).

In Scottish Fields (Literary Essays), by 'Hugh Halliburton' (1890).

Scottish Vernacular Literature, by T.F. Henderson (1898).

The Literature of the Highlands, by Magnus Maclean (Blackie, 1925).

A Literary History of Scotland, by Professor J.H. Millar (Unwin, 1903).

Scottish Prose of the Seventeenth and Eighteenth Centuries, by Professor J.H. Millar (Unwin, 1912).

The Dialect of Robert Burns as spoken in Central Ayrshire, by Sir James Wilson, K.C.S.I. (Oxford Press, 1923).

An Etymological Glossary of the Shetland and Orkney Dialect, by Thomas Edmonston (Edinburgh, 1866).

Old Shetland Dialect and Placenames of Shetland, by Dr Jakob Jakobsen (Lerwick, 1926).

An Etymological Dictionary of the Scottish Language, by John Jamieson, D.D. (1840, and subsequent editions).

Desultory Notes on Jamieson's 'Scottish Dictionary', by J.B. Montgomerie-Fleming (Glasgow, 1910).

A Dictionary of Lowland Scots, by Charles Mackay, LL.D. (Ballantyne Press, 1888).

A Scottish Dialect Dictionary, by Rev. Alex. Warrack, M.A. with Introduction and Dialect Map, by William Grant, M.A. (Chambers, 1911).

The Scottish Tongue, by W.A. Craigie, John Bulloch, Peter Giles, and J.M. Bulloch, with Foreword by Wm. Will (Cassell, 1924).

Lowland Scotch as Spoken in the Lower Strathearn District of Perthshire, with Dictionary, by Sir James Wilson (Oxford Press, 1915).

Roxburghshire Word Book, by George Watson (Oxford Press, 1924).

The Royal Stuarts in their Connection with Art and Letters, by W.G. Blaikie Murdoch (Edinburgh, 1908).

Three Centuries of Scottish Literature (from the Reformation to Scott), by Hugh Walker, 2 Vols. (Macmillan, 1893).

Studies in Prefixes and Suffixes in Middle Scottish, by Elizabeth Westergaard (Oxford Press, 1924).

EDUCATION

History of the Burgh Schools of Scotland, by James Grant (Collins, 1876).

Scottish Education, School and University, from Early Times to 1908, with an addendum 1908-1913, by J. Kerr (Cambridge Press, 1913).

A History of Secondary Education in Scotland to the Act of 1908, by John Strong (1909).

MUSIC

Musical Scotland, a Dictionary of Scottish Musicians from 1400 onwards, with a Bibliography of Musical Publications connected with Scotland from 1611, by David Baptie (Paisley, 1894).

The Highland Bagpipe: Its History, Literature and Music, with Bibliography, etc., by W.L. Manson (Paisley, 1901).

PHILOSOPHY

Scottish Philosophy in its National Development, by Professor Henry Laurie (Maclehose, 1902).

HISTORY, POLITICS AND ECONOMICS

A History of the Working Classes in Scotland, by Thomas Johnston, M.P. (Forward Publishing Co., Ltd.).

The Scottish Staple at Veere, by John Davidson and Alexander Gray (Longmans, 1909).

Commercial Relations of England and Scotland, 1603-1707, by T. Keith

(Cambridge Press, 1910).

The Industries of the Clyde Valley During the War, by W.R. Scott and J. Cunnison (Oxford Press, 1924).

Spanish Influence in Scottish History, by Professor John Elder (Maclehose, 1920).

Our Noble Families, by Thomas Johnston, M.P. (Forward Publishing Co., Ltd.).

Highland Reconstruction: A Survey of the Problems, by H.F. Campbell (Glasgow, 1920).

The Industries of Scotland, by David Bremner (Black, 1869).

The Constitutional History of Scotland, to the Reformation, by James and James A.R. Mackinnon (Longmans, 1924).

The History of Civilisation in Scotland, by John Mackintosh, 4 Vols. (Paisley, 1892-96).

The Intellectual Development of Scotland, by Hector Macpherson (Hodder & Stoughton, 1911).

An Outline of the Relations between England and Scotland (500-1707), by Professor R.S. Rait (Blackie, 1901).

The Parliaments of Scotland, by Professor R.S. Rait (Maclehose, 1924).

An Essay on the Economic Effects of the Reformation, by G. O'Brien (1923).

The Scottish Parliament Before the Union of the Crowns, by Professor R.S. Rait (Blackie, 1901).

Thoughts on the Union between England and Scotland, by Professors A.V. Dicey and R.S. Rait (Macmillan, 1920).

The Union of England and Scotland; A Study in International History, by James Mackinnon (Longmans, 1896).

The Early History of the Scottish Union Question, by G.W.T. Omond (Edinburgh, 1897).

The Union of 1709, by various writers, with Introduction by Professor Hume Brown (Glasgow, 1907).

Rural Scotland During the War, by D.T. Jones, Joseph F. Duncan, H.M. Conacher and W.R. Scott (Humphrey Milford, 1926).

THEOLOGY

Theology in Scotland (Reviewed by a Heretic), by Alexander Webster (Lindsey Press, 1915).

Puritanism in the Scottish Church, by W.S. Provand (1923).

Religion Since the Reformation, by L. Pullan (1923).

Celtic Mythology and Religion, by A. MacBain (1917).

IV 'Scottish Studies after 50 Years'
(from The Scottish Educational Journal, 3 October 1975) by
Hugh MacDiarmid (C.M. Grieve)

[This essay was the first in a series entitled 'Writers on Education'. It was followed by essays by George Mackay Brown (17 October); Iain Crichton Smith (31 October); George MacDonald Fraser (14 November); Forbes MacGregor (28 November) and Donald Campbell (12 December).]

Fifty years ago in a series of articles in *The Scottish Educational Journal* I put the cat among the pigeons to a remarkable extent. One of the outcomes of these 'Contemporary Scottish Studies' was a great outpouring of letters to the editor. I wish these could now be published in book form, with suitable annotations.

Scotticisims like the 'This England' in the *New Statesman* would be completely excelled. Most of these letters were from members of the teaching profession in Scotland and they showed conclusively an incredibly low level of literary appreciation, and in particular general ignorance and indifference to Scottish literature and to the problems of our native languages, Scots and Gaelic.

So there was no reason to be surprised a year or two later when the Scottish Education Department issued a report suggesting and sanctioning a relaxation of the 'standard English' monopoly in our educational system and the use of Scots and/or local dialects where desirable.

Alas, it was found that these recommendations could not be implemented because almost all the members of the teaching profession knew nothing of Scots and were incapable of dealing with it either in a spoken or written form. It could be added that it seemed from the correspondence that most of the letter-writers were strongly opposed to any modification of the hegemony of English in our class-rooms.

Yet there could be no denying the truth the late Dr Edwin Muir expressed when he wrote: 'Since English became the literary language of Scotland there has been no Scots imaginative writer who has attained greatness in the first or even second rank through the medium of English.' Acquiescence in the existing state of affairs therefore meant permanent inferiority for the over-Anglicised Scottish people.

But paradoxically that was not the conclusion Dr Muir drew. On the contrary he proceeded to advocate a still more complete abandonment of Scots in favour of English. Yet he had himself said in one of his letters:

It seems a pity that Scotland should always be kept back by England, and I hope the Scottish Republic comes about; it would make Scotland worth living in. He (*i.e.* the present writer) thinks that if Scotland were a nation we would have Scottish literature, art, music, culture, and everything that other nations seem to have and we haven't. I think that would probably be likely.

Elsewhere Dr Muir attacked any attempt to reconstitute independent Scottish literary traditions on the basis of our native languages. He (and most of the *SEJ* correspondents) evidently thought he was on a safe wicket. The last thirty to forty years have proved the opposite.

Millions of people all over the world have felt themselves rootless and in an effort to re-root themselves have sought (and are seeking today) to revert to their ancient traditions, revive their native languages even when these had become more or less obsolete and had never been media of any indigenous literature.

In short it has been realised all over the world that literature is not a monopoly of the Big Five but rather that the future of creative writing lay more probably with the little nations rather than with the World Powers.

It was my prophetic or at least premature declarations along these lines that evoked the bitter opposition of the conventionally minded readers, least of all, could they be expected at that time to realise that for the best part of the previous century leading British writers had been unanimous in expressing concern at the increasing unfitness of English for creative purposes and that it was becoming the general view in concerned quarters at home and abroad that the extended acceptance of English as a *lingua franca* throughout the world had been accompanied by an impoverishment at the very heart of the language.

Still less could the majority of so-called educated people in Scotland imagine for a moment that it could come to pass (and this was the confident prediction underlying 'Contemporary Scottish Studies' that

> like far galaxies bending over the horizon of invisibility, the bulk of English poetry, from Caxton's *Ovid* to *Sweeney among the Nightingales*, is now modulating from active presence into the inertness of scholarly conservation.

Based, as it firmly is, on a deep many-branched anatomy of classical and scriptural reference, expressed in a syntax and vocabulary of heightened tenor, the unbroken arc of English poetry, of reciprocal discourse that relates Chaucer and Spenser to Tennyson and to Eliot, is fading rapidly from the reach of natural reading. A central pulse in awareness, in the language, is becoming archival.

Yet that 'unbroken arc' (manifestly beyond recovery now) is still the substance of the teaching of literature in our Scottish schools and colleges. The consequence is but for rare exceptions a general minimal literacy in our whole Scottish population.

It is useless so far as such people are concerned to hold that the Scottish Renaissance Movement has 'given Scottish poetry a place in the European scene. It has reinstated Scots as a serious literary language'.

There has been a great outpouring of books on Scottish subjects of all kinds, which has gone a very long way to fill the gap the preceding two centuries of over-Anglicisation had created in our national political, literary and social documentation.

The truth of this is more and more copiously realised in many countries. European universities proliferate in PhD theses on contemporary Scottish literature. Colloquies on the subject are held in Canadian and American universities. The best periodical of studies in Scottish literature is published in North Carolina. In Scotland itself there are the activities of the Lallans Society, and of the Universities Association for Scottish Literature.

There has in short been a great deal of activity, but what in the end has it really amounted to? What proportion of the new Scottish authors has won any international regard? Who among them can claim to have produced work that can meet, and indeed calls for, judgment on the same level as that applied to the most significant products today of the pens of leading writers in the different departments of literature in other European countries?

Questions such as these are bound to evoke bitter controversy just as fifty years ago my *SEJ* articles did. Has there been any general improvement? Have we really emerged from the kailyaird or the kirk vestry? It is very questionable, but yet think of the names of the best of those Scottish writers too young to be discussed in 'Contemporary Scottish Studies (1925-26)' viz. 'James Bridie', Lewis Grassic Gibbon (Leslie Mitchell), Neil M Gunn, A.S. Neill, Sydney Goodsir Smith, Moray Maclaren, Helen B. Cruickshank, 'Fionn MacColla' (T.D. MacDonald).

Surely the body of work published by these writers is worthy of serious consideration. But how far does it go *in toto* to bridge that gulf indicated by the fact that the greatest English poets of the past half century have been two Americans, an Irishman, and a Welshman. Not one English poet amongst them! Nor one Scottish poet either.

And the same thing is true in other fields of culture. The greatest dramatists of the period were also an Irishman and a Welshman. How does James Bridie stand in comparison to G.B. Shaw and Sean O'Casey? Can it be said (and I think it is precisely of whom this can be said) as it was said by Mr Andrew Cruickshank of our late Duncan MacRae:

> My feeling now is that MacRae was the first example in Scotland of how Scottish actors might differ from English actors. (Even Stanislavsky confessed that his company could not act the symbolic plays of Ibsen because they were Slavs.) MacRae gave a hint in his acting to Scottish playwrights to go back to our contradictory roots in which we have our being, and provide that ambiguity which is the note of the modern as it breaks away from the classical. And while the world politically proceeds painfully to a unity, culturally it must seek diversity. Even in these islands, Scotsmen should have no doubt as to the tune they must play in this consort. MacRae has set it. The theatre and acting may be ephemeral, but MacRae was so surely within the roots of our country that so long as it survives he will be remembered and reflected in our style.

Can the like be said of any Scottish novelist, playwright, poet or other writer working today? I doubt it. Yet it is just such a person – or persons – we need, and it is futile to talk about a real revival of an indigenous Scottish literature unless we get them, just as it is futile to talk about our great Scottish educational system unless we can rewrite that claim with the fact that our people go through their school years and emerge only mini-mally literate; and in the same way we have to recognise that the football hooligans, and train wreckers and the hordes of young delinquents of all kinds are in fact the product of our schools and that 'by their fruits shall they be judged'.

V 'Introduction'
(from Contemporary Scottish Studies, 1976)
by Hugh MacDiarmid (C.M. Grieve)

I regard it as an honour (and not only an honour totally unexpected, but a sign of the times) that *The Scottish Educational Journal* should have decided to publish as part of its centenary celebrations this edition of my

Contemporary Scottish Studies, which consists of a series of articles published in the *Journal* fifty years ago. And not only so, but the correspondence these articles evoked. These letters are vitally important because they throw a flood of light on the attitude to Scottish literature and our native languages (Scots and Gaelic) and the desperate provincialisation which made so large a part of our reading public hang on to what for lack of anything better they regarded as typically Scottish – 'a poor thing but our own.'

The late Mr T.S. Eliot said that Burns was 'a decadent representative of a great alien tradition', meaning alien to English literature. Now it was precisely to set going a process towards recovering that 'alien tradition' in full that these articles were written, and to seek to carry that tradition to new levels of expression in accordance with the requirements of our vastly changed circumstances today – and (presumably) tomorrow, in accordance, that is to say, with the needs of a period of acceleration of change unprecedented in all history. These articles were the means in addition to my own Scots poetry whereby I sought to further that aim and were in truth an attempt to carry out a revaluation of modern Scottish literature, and, indeed, culture generally, as in the leaflet issued by the *Journal* announcing the series it was said that it would 'discuss in all the work of new fewer than three hundred men and women of Scotland in Literature, Music, Art, Drama, Education and other branches of cultural activity.' Most of the people I wrote about have since died, and the greater part of their work, only a moiety of which was ever really alive, is dead too. I had to made do with the available material. Matters have improved immensely in the interval. The dead include Lewis Grassic Gibbon, Neil M. Gunn, Douglas Young, Sydney Goodsir Smith, A.S. Neill, Edwin Muir, George Blake, Mrs Violet Jacob, Charles Murray, William Soutar, William Jeffrey, James Bridie, John Buchan, Moray Maclaren, Eric Linklater, T.D. MacDonald (Fionn MacColla) and others. *Festschriften* have been published in honour of several of them and five or six of them have had autobiographies published. In short, the Scottish Renaissance Movement initiated in the early twenties, has passed into history. I had hoped that once the bugle sounded it would be in Scotland as it had been in Ireland with its Irish Literary Revival and that the reawakened national genius would throw up in the course of a single generation an unparalleled host of exceptional personalities. Varied as were the men and women who in fact contributed to that development the number of any real significance remained disconcertingly small. What is important here, however, is that all of them have been adequately documented. That was not the case when I wrote these articles. It was difficult to gather the necessary information. But there has been a marked improvement in the quality of critical assessment of Scottish writers, *festschriften* have been published in honour of quite a few of the dead (*festschriften* containing essays by various hands and including some of the best literary criticism Scotland has had). Not only so, but there has been a shift in the type of Scot deemed worthy of appraisal – this was emphasised recently by the fact that though his name and work was virtually unknown to most of the population the importance of John Maclean was signalised by the publication of several biographies and other writings about him, and the foundation of a John Maclean Society to republish his writings and carry on his work. Two other Scottish Marxists have had a similar measure of renewed attention – Professor John Millar who in some respects anticipated Marxist doctrines, and Professor John Anderson who close on half a century ago left Edinburgh to become Challis Professor of Philosophy in the University of Sydney – an occasion which has just been marked by a set of commemorative lectures. I feel that in many respects Anderson was a man after my own heart, especially in his statement that 'the measure of freedom in any community is the extent of its opposition of the ruling order, of criticism of ruling ideals; and belief in established freedom, or in state – guaranteed "benefits" is a mark of the abandonment of liberty.' As I showed in my *Scottish Eccentrics*, Scotland has throughout the centuries thrown up an astonishing number of men who shared and promulgated that opinion.

While it is a welcome sign of the vitality of the Renaissance Movement that emphasis should now be placed so emphatically on men like these – Professor Patrick Geddes is another of whom a great deal has been written in the last year or two – it cannot be claimed that the main objective of the Movement has been reached, viz. the emergence of distinctively Scottish genius. The upper echelon is much better than in the previous ten generations, but the aim called for a better answer to the question Muhammad Ali put in his autobiography *The Greatest* when, apropos his visit to Burns Cottage, he was prompted to write:

> I'd heard of a man named Burns – supposed to be a poet;
> But if he was, how come I didn't know it?
> They told me his work was very, very neat.
> So I replied: 'But who did he ever beat?'

Nor does the revival of interest in John Buchan, exemplified in several books and many newspaper and periodical essays, dispose of the point made by a recent American writer who wrote in his diary: 'The summer holidays. August nineteen thirty. Father in flapping flannels, banging his copy of the *Morning Post* against his leg. He used to take the *Mail* till he happened to read an article by that toadying Scot, Buchan.' 'But for the bold experiment of Fascism', said that novelist and former Lord High Commissioner of the General Assembly of the Church of Scotland, 'the decade has not been fruitful in constructive statesmanship.'

There are in fact many instances that show there is still a lamentable hangover of the kailyaird tradition. Even Professor Edwin Morgan in his *Essays* (Carcanet Press, 1974) says of my own work:

There's an enormous gap of ordinary human experience which MacDiarmid's poetry scarcely represents at all. Hardly ever, in any poem, do you get a sense of a man who is committed emotionally to something other than ideas, words, or landscapes. The beautiful and terrible bonds that are not geological but between individual persons, bonds of love or friendship, of desire, misery, doubt, or forgiveness – these are strikingly absent. This is the greatest lack in MacDiarmid's poetry – though he would hardly agree. He must be the most unexistential poet ever to have written. The deficiency would cripple any writer who had less to fall back on, in himself and in books, than MacDiarmid has always had. I said he wouldn't agree with me, because this deficiency goes hand in hand with a polemic. He would regard it as an essential part of his historical mission as a Scottish poet to undo the over-reliance on human feelings and human situations in Burns and his Victorian successors. As he remarks disgustedly in the Foreword to *The Kind of Poetry I Want*: 'Almost all modern Scottish poetry gives off a great sense of warmth and offering, like a dog when it loves you.' Well, this is fair enough in the sense that we don't want a wet poetry. But a poetry of human feeling is not necessarily wet, and one would suspect that an inadequacy as well as a polemic lay behind this rejection of warmth.

It is only fair to point out that while Professor Morgan – for whom deservedly a personal Chair was created at Glasgow University – is perhaps the best literary critic in Scotland today and certainly one of the best poets and a brilliant translator from Russian and other languages, others like Lady Antonia Fraser in her anthology of Scottish Love Lyrics, and Kathleen Raine think otherwise, and personally I believe Professor David Daiches is nearer the mark when he calls my work 'transhuman'.

However that may be, there are still too many who hanker after the old fashion. George Bruce, for example, 'is also concerned with something of the traditional and communal nature. It is concerned, too, with its opposite: the developing isolation of the individual in communities on which speciously collective interests, like the Miss United Kingdom Competition, are imposed from outside, to the detriment and alienation of the individual. Mr Bruce's concern is with art which fails to recognise the value of environmental stimulus and art which takes community into account. Assuming the latter, he contends that one of the most grievous sins an individual can commit is the rejection of acceptable, traditional norms.'

The Poet Laureate, Mr John Betjeman, has recently said that versifying used to be regarded as natural and something almost anybody can do. That is still the case, unfortunately, but it not only in itself hardly ever produces anything worth while but it debases the currency and all too often sets itself in opposition to elitist work and claims superiority on the ground that it pleases a far larger public. This misconception of poetry – the apparently ineradicable general 'preference for the inferior' – Mr Betjeman attributes largely to 'Eng. Lit.'

There are few, if any, of the of the positions I take up in these essays that I have since abandoned or modified. Mr Moray MacLaren said to me 'of course he has hostile, sometimes bitterly hostile, critics among the mandarins as well as the Philistines.' That is still the case – but almost entirely now among the Philistines. T.S. Eliot said that it was 'highly desirable that there should be a flourishing literature in Scots for the sake of English Literature,' and he went further and said that in addition to the influence I was having on Scottish literature I would 'have an influence on English literature too.' I have not had it all my own way, of course, as the late Professor Douglas Young pointed out from being a rebel I had become to many of the younger generation an Establishment they had to fight against. Their names are legion, but few, if any, of them have learned the great lesson that 'banality is not enough' or that 'nostalgia isn't what it used to be' and are content to appeal to a reading public and the endless stream of poetasters who cater for it, since his declaration that he was an unlettered ploughman led countless people to imagine that if such a one could write poetry so could they. So we had (and still have) a vast proliferation of butcher poets, policemen poets, tailor poets and so on, none of whom ever write a poem worth the name at all but are undeterred by that since they are writing for their own kind, and deem that enough. Because that attitude has been so general in Scotland for the past two centuries, inevitably my insistence in these articles on the Poundian precept 'Make it new!' has been seldom welcome or pursued. It is indeed very difficult to define authenticity. I am reminded of a broadcaster the other day who, having gone to Skye and attended local *ceilidhs*, felt that there was something false or artificial about many of the singers and reciters, but was delighted by a little old lady who was, he felt, the genuine article. On talking with her, however, he found that she 'came up from Oxford almost every year. It is such a change.' That reminds me of a Shetland laird's wife who said to me, 'Ah, Mr Grieve, I do so love pipe music – but tell me what is (or should it be are) *piobaireachd*!'

I advocated the resumption of the use of Scots as a medium, not only for occasional poems but for the whole range of literary purpose, but for the past thirty years I have written practically nothing in Scots but almost entirely in English. How does this accord with my contention that English is virtually useless today as a medium for creative literature? It surprises a sequence of critics who go into the matter closely to find that the inconsistency is more apparent than real and that practically every extreme position expressed in my writings was adumbrated in my first book away back in 1923 and that I have adhered since in all my work to what I advocated then. So I make no apologies for failing to carry the young with me – the young who write pop songs or even those who fancy they are reviving folk poetry.

If I were asked to name the most important Scottish writers of today or the past few decades I would probably say Ian Fleming and his brother Peter, R.D. Laing, Kenneth Galbraith, the late J.B.S. Haldane. But I would demur if the name of Muriel Spark or Alistair Maclean were suggested. These are not matters for discussion in a preface, however. Whatever differences of detail there may be it is undoubtedly the case that the past forty years have seen a great development of the various departments in Scottish literature, and particularly in Gaelic and Scots, both of which were supposed to be on the way out when in fact they were on the way in. It is a fact that even in the essays in this book I did not overlook anyone of consequence, and did spot several likely talents since developed far beyond what I could have reasonably expected at the time – the late Neil Gunn, for example, and Lewis Grassic Gibbon, and Fionn MacColla [*sic*]. Unavoidably, of course, I was too generous to others who soon afterwards 'fell by the way.' On the whole, however, in my unlikely role of prophet, I see on rereading these essays, that I was quite improbably successful. As for the correspondents, they were for the most part unconscious victims of the super-imposition of English literature to the exclusion of Scots or Gaelic in our schools and colleges, and it gives me no little pleasure today to think of how they would feel if they could come back today and see this book, or attend the classes in Scottish literature now available in all our universities and many of our senior schools, or ponder the phenomenon of the development of societies like the Lallans Society or the Association for Scottish Literary Studies.

As I said in an article in the *Journal* in October 1975, one of the main aims of my *Contemporary Scottish Studies* has now been realised – the recognition that anything that purports to be a contribution to Scottish literature must be judged by the standards applied to literature in all other civilised countries, and that no allowances whatever can be made for the preferences of Auchenshuggle, or what smacks of the legacy of Sir Harry Lauder or William McGonagall.

I made it clear in these essays that I have no use, or respect for the kind of 'education' that is devoted to technological subjects or equipping students to become engineers, etc., and that I wanted a return to the *status quo ante* of the Scottish universities as delineated in Dr George Davie's *The Democratic Intellect* – that is to say, a reversal to the rightly styled Scottish Educational System as opposed to the English and the consequences of the imposition of English standards on Scottish education. I have nothing to withdraw in that connection. I have referred to the successful prophesying in some of these essays. Unlikely as it may seem at the moment, who will venture to assert that I prophesy in vain in this connection? A reversal of anti-intellectualism now prevalent, and a return to respect, if not reverence, for 'education for its own sake' is what underlies all I have written here – or will write – and who will may consider it an instance of the 'optimism' of a Communist. But, in my 84th year, I can quite complacently reflect that 'who lives will see.' And in prefacing this reissue of my articles I admit no inconsiderable confidence.

Biggar 1976   Hugh MacDiarmid

Index of Names